Problems of Idealism

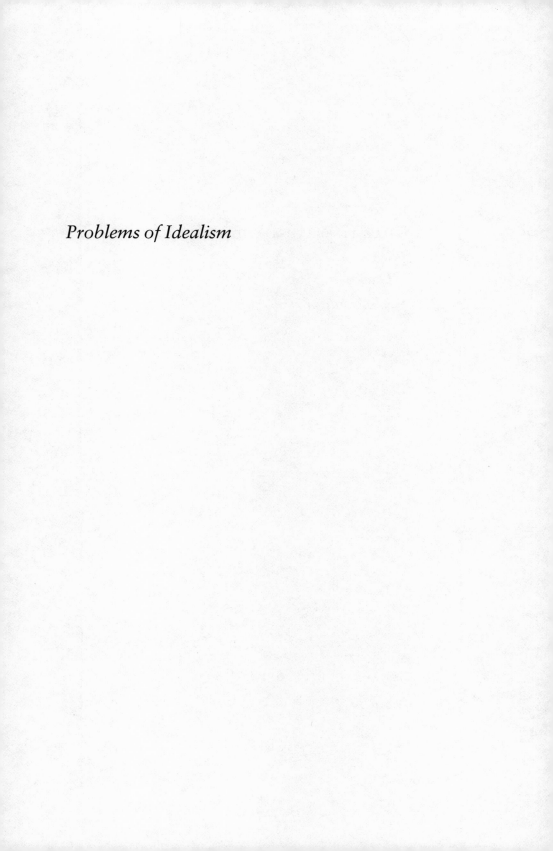

RUSSIAN LITERATURE AND THOUGHT

Gary Saul Morson
Series Editor

Translated, Edited, and Introduced by
RANDALL A. POOLE
Foreword by
CARYL EMERSON

Problems of Idealism

ESSAYS IN RUSSIAN SOCIAL PHILOSOPHY

Yale University Press
New Haven &
London

Published with assistance from the Louis Stern Memorial Fund.

Printed in the United States of America.

Library of Congress Cataloging-in-Publication Data
Problemy idealizma. English
  Problems of idealism : essays in Russian social philosophy / translated, edited, and introduced by Randall A. Poole ; foreword by Caryl Emerson.
    p.   cm. — (Russian literature and thought)
  Includes bibliographical references and index.
  ISBN 0-300-09567-8 (alk. paper)

  1. Idealism. I. Poole, Randall Allen, 1964–   II. Title. III. Series.

B823 .P7413   2003
197–dc21   2002034883
A catalogue record for this book is available from the British Library.

10 9 8 7 6 5 4 3 2 1

Contents

PROBLEMS OF IDEALISM

Foreword

CARYL EMERSON

In March 1993, with the world still bewildered at the collapse of Communism, an international conference was held in Moscow to discuss the recuperable past and future prospects of Russian philosophy. Four of the papers (two by Americans, two by Russians) were later published as a forum in the professional journal *Voprosy filosofii* (*Questions of Philosophy*).[1] The Russian entries addressed the "Eternal Values of Russian Culture" and "Russian Philosophy and Religious Consciousness"; the two Western academics, while acknowledging the depth and aesthetic productivity of those quests, were more sober and pointedly secular. James Scanlan had provocatively entitled his talk "Does Russia Need Russian Philosophy?" — and concluded that an exceptionalist or *uniquely* Russian philosophy for the post-communist era was most definitely not needed. The organicist-collectivist bias in Russian philosophy (which in any event was not uniquely Russian, but part of the general nineteenth-century Romantic critique of modernization), made more intense by the native Russian tendency toward legal nihilism, now required a serious overhaul. The world of Russian philosophy was larger than "Lenin's Marxism" versus "Berdiaev's Russian Idea" (64).

As a first step toward filling in that world, Scanlan recommends that attention be paid to those complex, nuanced thinkers who had been suppressed or distorted beyond recognition during the era of "competing maximalisms," a group including Russian students of the French *philosophes*, natural-law theorists, Russian neo-Leibnizians, and "those Russian liberal legal philosophers of the late nineteenth and early twentieth centuries" (65). Andrzej Walicki concurred. He even ventured to remark that much of what he heard at the Moscow conference would not be considered philosophy at all in university departments devoted to that discipline in the United States, where more mundanely theoretical, not grandly "historiosophical," questions are considered suitable for research. Outside of Russia, Walicki observed, Russian philosophy is read largely by historians, political scientists, literary critics, and Slavists (69). To be sure, there is much of great interest and richness in this tradition, but its tendency to focus on Russian historical and spiritual experience must be resisted if professional philosophers are to listen.

The Russians, naturally, disagreed. Russian thinkers had long prided themselves on bringing abstract analysis down to earth and speaking beyond a professional audience. In giving such advice, Scanlan and Walicki were themselves acting like *politologi,* "political scientists," their eyes pragmatically focused on what was useful, necessary, and perhaps most of all safer for Russia's future development. Yet all parties in this impressively frank exchange surely sensed the larger import of the issues raised. Since 1990, Russian bookstores had been featuring reprint editions of the famous 1909 anthology *Vekhi* (*Landmarks*), directed against the follies and philosophical deficiencies of the Russian radical intelligentsia, as well as its 1918 successor volume *Iz glubiny* (*De profundis,* or *Out of the Depths*), a mournful postmortem by some of Russia's greatest philosophers on that country's then-current Revolution. Both those anthologies are angry, eloquent, topical, and accessible to a concerned lay public. The first caused one of the mightiest scandals in the history of Russian thought; the second would have caused another, had it not been suppressed by the Bolsheviks. Much less in evidence during the reprint festivals of the early 1990s was the more academic volume that preceded them both, compiled by the same core group of thinkers but at a different phase in their intellectual evolution (and in Russia's political evolution): *Problemy idealizma* (1902). When Randall Poole, Walicki's student, decided to prepare a scholarly English-language edition of this extraordinary volume, it was with two goals in mind. First, he wished to restore this difficult, brilliant, unjustly neglected collection of essays to its rightful place in the history of Russian philosophy. And second, as if in response to Scanlan's and Walicki's summons at the Moscow conference, he wished to reinvigorate one part of the rich Russian tradition that "competing maximalisms" had squeezed out, namely: the power of idealism (as understood by these thinkers, trained in European philosophy but working within Russian culture) to advance and celebrate liberal values.

Poole's detailed introduction provides the necessary historical, institutional, and intellectual background to their argument. This foreword aims only to orient readers in the most general way to what was at stake, pointing out some representative concerns of the anthology and its overall strategy. In passing, I will suggest how some of its more provocative positions resemble critiques mounted by Russian thinkers whose ideas are more familiar in the West: Dostoevsky, Tolstoy, Bakhtin. Several of the contributors to *Problems of Idealism* were, or were soon to become, accomplished literary critics.[2] All were deeply engaged in the Russian reform movement. None, however, confused the tasks of philosophy with literary-cultural criticism or political activism. It was precisely because they were so alert to the political crises of their time, and also to the temptations of the creative imagination, that they had become such fastidious close readers of the dominant ideological systems of the day, insisting that the autonomy of each moral part was essential to the integrity of the whole. They knew that when individual thinkers are turned into "schools of thought," the potential for a minor carelessness or inconsistency to be fixed into a slogan escalates alarmingly. Their opening question, therefore, is a procedural one. How much disciplined philosophical rigor would be required to profess with integrity the sorts of doctrine that Russian radical activists professed? And they conclude: a very great deal. In their opinion, this work had often been slighted. Thus the usual tactic of the philosophers in this volume — a method that Poole elsewhere calls "immanent critique" — is to take a currently influential theorist or body of thought, grant it (as an opening courtesy) maximum legitimacy, analyze it carefully, and then show how the system in question refutes itself from within.[3]

Patience here was not only a matter of intellectual courtesy, however. The most famous of these thinkers (Struve, Bulgakov, Berdiaev, Frank) had gone through a positivist-Marxist phase of their own. In working their way through "legal Marxism" to idealism, they did not reject wholesale what earlier doctrines had allowed them to see, especially as regards the polemics surrounding Russian populism and "subjective sociology." Rather than move from one fervent ideal to another fervent ideal (the common route of utopian thinkers, for whom the end of a belief system so often comes as a shock and a collapse, a God that Failed), these philosophers are more likely to express their gratitude for any coherence they can find, and make ever more modest claims about what can be fully known. Among their most pressing tasks is the recovery of the ideal from its utopian and supra-personal transpositions. If this agenda seems counterintuitive for a group of thinkers investigating questions of idealism, it is because this group had its own rigorous and (for our time as well as their own) original ideas about the proper functioning of an ideal.

Russia 1902 and the Neo-Idealist Critique

Problems of Idealism appeared at a pivotal time. The debacle of 1905 had not yet happened, but Russian social thought had matured significantly since the naïve, radical generation of the 1860s, disappointed as it was with the Great Reforms. Terrorism was again on the rise, and the zemstvo movement was less and less satisfied with "small deeds" alone. Fin-de-siècle Russia was an autocratic empire, in certain ways more entrenched than ever: just past the most rapacious phase of its capitalist revolution, it had barely recovered from a disastrous famine that was widely blamed on government policies. In 1895, the new Tsar Nicholas II had made known his categorical refusal to consider even the most tentative steps toward consultative representation. Pobedonostsev and other high-ranking court apologists relied on the innate religiosity, forbearance, and communal instincts of the Russian folk (a misty myth, but one much beloved) to preserve the status quo. In the realm of art, the Symbolist movement had begun to offer a powerful alternative to both the massive Realist novels of the 1860s–1880s and the modest, more contemplative twilight-era writings of Anton Chekhov. Philosophically, however, the most vocal political opposition remained positivist and materialist.

In this polarization, certain prejudices — or perhaps merely reflexes of the mind — had formed around certain terms. Positivism was associated with progress, with empirical science, with Realism in psychology and literature, and thus with the courage to see the world concretely, "as it really exists." Idealism, on the other hand, was felt to be pie-in-the-sky, dreamy, abstract, passive, a mystical realm, and thereby reactionary. It was the burden of *Problems of Idealism* to challenge this dichotomy, and at the same time to enlist the Kantian concept of "ought" (*Sollen*) in a truer account of the experience of living by ideas — or, in the special sense these philosophers will impart to the phrase, living by the ideal. They were fully aware that positivists were in fact more prone than others to build dreamy utopias, and that materialists often smuggled in nonmaterial values to make their systems more compelling. But they did not wish to descend to hurling potshots in a journalistic war. Nor, for that matter, did they intend to duplicate the brilliant belletristic exposé of positivism, both psychological and historical, that had been mounted by Fëdor Dostoevsky forty years earlier in his *Notes from Underground*. As professional philosophers, they were after first principles, and as such they were obliged to build up an affirmative position, not merely laugh down a defective one. What is more, in the spirit of Lev Tolstoy's moral tracts of the 1890s, they wished to rehabilitate the concept of the ideal wholly "on this side," from within a concrete world of mortal behaviors and attitudes, a world that even empiricists might accept. Prior to doing so, they had to define what an ideal could and could not do, and cleanse it of confusing attributes falsely adhering to it. So: What were these confusions?

First: an ideal — just because it is spatially or temporally distant — is not for that reason abstracting, homogenizing, or depersonalizing. As we shall see, these philosophers are all committed personalists, who regard the individual consciousness (or "personhood," *lichnost'*) as the central value of philosophy, its most precious capital. They took their inspiration from Kant's "subjective idealism," with its insistence on the human being as an end in itself and not a means, rather than from those more monistic, objective idealisms (such as Hegel's) which aimed to restore lost unity in a future Absolute. It is their eagerness to argue on behalf of the dignity of the person in the palpable here-and-now, and moreover in a Russia divided between authoritarian mystics and radical materialists, that wins for them the role of defender of liberal values. In their variant of philosophical pluralism, there are potentially as many ideals as there are persons. And thus the originary responsible relationship to be worked out is not among ideals — ideals do not need to arrange themselves in some attractive or coherently integrated design in the sky — but between an individual person and the ideal posited by that person as a guide.

Second: an ideal need not be a fixed or permanent value. The content of an ideal can change. All that is fixed is the status of the ideal within a given person's purview. While the mandate of my ideal might be utterly, inescapably vivid for me, "the absolutism of the moral law," as Novgorodtsev remarks in his defense of natural law, "relates to its form and basis, not to its content" (see Chapter 8). Berdiaev, too, argues that "no hardened empirical content can pretend to the title of absolute morality" because personhood is most real when it is restless; "the absolute moral norm is always only a call forward, a beacon" (see Chapter 4). Kistiakovskii, in his analysis of Russian subjective sociology, concurs: "We call an ideal that which does not exist in a ready and complete form, but appears only as a task in which we believe and toward which we consider it our duty to strive" (see Chapter 9).

Third: living by ideals is not, in the denigrating sense of the word, "idealistic." Quite the contrary. Absolute ideals — unlike the worldly utopia of the positivists — are not positive because one expects to arrive at them and live comfortably in them (several contributors to this volume, Novgorodtsev and Kistiakovskii especially, will have harsh things to say about such expectations).

I posit an ideal because I want to be oriented by it and move toward it, in a world that otherwise offers me little by way of security, reasonableness, or reward. Idealism is completely alien to those sorts of naïveté that counsel us to await a change in environment that will then bring about (for the most part automatically) a change in the self. Such mechanical solutions are castles in the air. In contrast, living by ideals is supremely realistic, since coherence or justice is at no point expected from the outside world or imposed upon it. External events, "what happens to us," can never be counted on to cohere for our benefit—that is not the way the world is made—but each individual can choose to be answerable for a coherent set of *responses* to events, which is what the ideal facilitates. In other words, positing ideals makes wholeness possible in my life.

Again and again, these philosophers demonstrate their superb grasp of the balance in the human subject between material necessity and spiritual freedom. In his spectacular lead essay, Sergei Bulgakov insists that human beings "must have an integral idea of the world." To seek such an idea is a fundamental need, like seeking air and nourishment, and is thus almost a human right. In like spirit does Semën Frank defend, as a moral and *realistic* pursuit, Nietzsche's "Liebe zum Fernsten" (love of the distant), for this type of love responds to drives toward integration and harmony natural to our organism (see Chapter 5). Frank adds that love for humanity as a whole is probably *not* such an instinct (drawing on that "exquisite psychologist Lev Tolstoy," who presented just such an idea to the Moscow Psychological Society in March 1887). Altruistic systems that presume the existence of such love in us are singularly unrealistic. But to turn the idea of generalized love into a distant ideal and resolve to work consciously toward it: this task might indeed satisfy, in certain persons, deeply rooted appetites and needs.

In this economy, it is simply not enough to be governed by "interests." At the end of his luminously gracious essay on the role Marx and Engels allot to ideas in history, Evgenii Trubetskoi submits that social and material interests are undeniably real, but that "interest alone neither creates consciousness of truth nor frees human thought from error" (see Chapter 2). What, after all, are our interests? They are illusory, often arbitrary, and once satisfied are taken for granted and then fade away. One could say that interests share with two other human aspirations, pleasure and happiness, the peculiarity of not being directly addressable or targetable; they are better realized as by-products, that is, as benefits reaped during our pursuit of something else. (In his essay for this volume, Berdiaev will argue along these lines against hedonism in ethics.) When seeking a good and just life, therefore, it is utopian to rely exclusively upon a sense of one's interests. Only the ideal, which in principle can never be satisfied, is reliable. We cannot achieve it, but we are optimally liable to feel ourselves whole while striving toward it.

Idealism, then, need not be abstract, impersonal, homogenizing, impractical, or unrealistic as a guide to individual moral behavior. But *Problems of Idealism* had a more "professional" message to deliver, which in the view of its authors could clarify much that had plagued Russian sociopolitical thought. Here Randall Poole's early work on Mikhail Bakhtin and the Russian response to European rationalism provides a useful framework.[4] Poole directs our attention to a well-known passage at the beginning of chapter 3 of *Problems of Dostoevsky's Poetics*, where Bakhtin provides an exposé of the "ideological monologism" that had conquered modern European thought with its promise of a "unity of existence and of consciousness."[5] In such a world, persons cannot be fully valid (or even fully visible and audible) participants; everything of value strives to unite under a singular concept, and radical difference is registered simply as error. Poole observes that in positing dialogism as a corrective to this state of affairs, Bakhtin drew on one of the West's most seminal thinkers, Kant. From its earliest contacts with modern Europe, Russian thought had been highly susceptible to monologic rationalism (the positivism that the Russian idealists were analyzing in 1902 being only the most recent instance). This susceptibility can be variously explained, Poole notes, but the crucial factor was the weakness of the Russian church relative to the state and the resulting militant, intemperate nature of secularization in imperial Russia. Bakhtin's response to the enticement of monologism was much like that of the authors of *Problems of Idealism*: while not denying it, devise a remedy for it out of Russia's own resources. Such a remedy might well begin, for example, by emphasizing those insights of Russian Orthodox personalism (the irreducibility of the self) that are compatible with Kantian ethics, with the notion of moral duty ("ought") as an autonomous and nonderived value, and with epistemological modesty (or, in Poole's later expansion of this point, with "apophatic" modes of thought).[6] Out of such philosophical debates, Bakhtin fashioned his own theologically inflected aesthetics, as earlier, *Problems of Idealism* had advanced its positive agenda, liberalism—to which we now return.

Delimitation, Autonomy, Coexistence, Tolerance

The authors here vary widely in their expertise and technical display of it. But in their corrective to the social thought of their time they are united around one point: that moral philosophy must be, first of all, a defense of individual consciousness. These philosophers perceived nineteenth-century positivism, materialism, and historicism — especially in their Russian redaction — as major threats to this prime site of human value. But they develop their case in a remarkably formal way, "structurally," as it were, preferring on the whole *not* to consider lapses in a given thinker's logic a blot on personal integrity but rather the result of miscalculations at a more impersonal level, a failure of that thinker's professional discipline to guide and restrict the speculation (and the law-building) that goes on within its borders. What strikes one in this book (in Pëtr Struve's essay particularly (Chapter 3), but by no means only there) is its overall sweet-temperedness, its generosity to individual thinkers and lack of ad hominem attack. These pages abound with appreciations, even to movements that have proved to be far more culprit than friend. Consider, for example, what Evgenii Trubetskoi writes of Marxist economics: "In this whole theory there is a large share of truth" — and this after a critical but compassionate exposition of that doctrine, as if to assure the reader that whatever deficiencies might be found, social thinkers of earnestness and breadth always serve knowledge. In part, of course, this open-mindedness can be traced to the fact that several of these Russian idealists themselves once professed the very ideologies they now find wanting. But more important is their conviction — not routinely associated with idealism — that it is not evil intent, not a will to power or the desire to mystify our opponents, that does us in as much as it is bad methodology, misclassification, trying to do what cannot be done from where we stand, denying quests and needs (in this case the metaphysical need) that cannot for long be denied. Struve's fury, such as it is, is directed against falsely defined fields, not against human beings. Since we inherit categories of thought, and since we are mentally wired to seek integral knowledge and wholeness, the temptation is great to simplify a domain and do all our thinking within it. But real needs that have been expunged or defined out of a field can only give rise to flawed and dangerous theories.

In addition to such principled courtesy to their opponents, these authors have another strategy: it is, they say, already over. Positive science no longer reigns supreme. The second half of the past century was indeed a heady time, Bulgakov admits in his lead essay; empiricism became "the religion of humanity." "But of course, such a situation could not last forever." For all its passionate energy, it could not sustain itself coherently from within. "Marxism was strong not in its scientific, but in its utopian elements," he concludes, "not in its science, but in its faith." The resurrection of metaphysics will nevertheless be arduous. It cannot hide away in the safe realms of culture; it will have to take real social problems seriously. Sergei Askol'dov devotes his entire contribution to the question of "Philosophy and Life"; and a shadow theme engaged by all these authors is the parallel between the harmony — aesthetic and spiritual — that we have a right to seek in our personal lives and the social harmony we can reasonably expect from the outside world (see Chapter 6). On the most general level, then, what must happen in social philosophy so that balance, vigor, and clear-sightedness can be restored?

First, the world must be confirmed as a place where autonomous spheres have a right to coexist. Each sphere resolves problems within its own area of competence. There is no reason to believe that these competencies will ever be wholly compatible with one another, or that a particular competence will increase or decrease with time. The positivism of Comte and the historical materialism of Marx, in which stages displace one another in linear sequence, allow us to organize past (and future) events in a satisfying way and speculate on many things, but at considerable cost; as Novgorodtsev puts the matter, "philosophy must restore its own rights and show history its limits." Or to recall Bakhtin's echo of this demand in *Problems of Dostoevsky's Poetics,* the world that successfully resists monologic rationalism is a world where delimited, autonomous entities gain their legitimacy not through accidents of genesis but through coexistence and interaction (28). Delimitation is not an insult to a field, not a restriction, but an enablement. As Kistiakovskii notes, an exclusive empiricism might be appropriate in the natural sciences, but when "this type of thinking was made the basis of the whole philosophical system of positivism, then soon thereafter not only all its poverty, but also its enormous harm to the further development of science, had to be revealed."

In short, the contributors to *Problems of Idealism* did not perceive themselves as anti-science. They believed they were working on its behalf, because the authority and scientific validity of a position increase when the tasks for which it answers are made more precise. What is more, in their opinion the human sciences are not designed to come together; they are valuable precisely in their heterogeneity. In his essay on "What the History of Philosophy Teaches," Sergei Trubetskoi insists that "the differences and contradictions of separate philosophies testify to the truthfulness of the *philosophy* itself in them, to its authenticity and veracity" (see Chapter 7). Eliminating borders between separate disciplines is not harmony, but fraud. As Novgorodtsev remarks of historicism, a theory invites its own demise when it "takes on tasks beyond its strengths."

The necessity of autonomous, interacting spheres in human culture is matched by an analogous call for interaction between body and spirit. The main authors of *Problems of Idealism* are deeply indebted to Vladimir Solov'ëv, although they secularize his teachings in varying degree; for each, spirit and matter are irreducible to each other, interpenetrate each other, and both deserve our reverence. Finally, in the sphere of ethics, each of these philosophers begins on a Kantian foundation and insists that what "ought to be" in our lives cannot be derived from what *is*. Or to cast this truth in a form that brings it into direct confrontation with positivist-Marxian thought: what ought to be is not "reflected" from what is, but all the same is absolutely real.

Evgenii Trubetskoi addresses directly this notion of "ideas as reflections or 'reflexes' of economic relations"—a doctrine that is, he observes, "very widespread among Marx's followers." He has two big problems with it. First, it makes no sense, even as a metaphor. One half of the picture is missing. "In general," he observes, "any reflection is invariably the result of the joint action of at least two causes—the reflected object, and the medium which reflects it." In the Marxist model, the human psyche as active receiving medium receives no scientific grounding. How can "productive relations" be considered the singular origin of any human activity, when production itself depends on ideas? Second, the reflection theory makes no allowance for evaluation, which (especially in legal structures) sits at the normative center of any relevant "relation." Struve carries this critique further, in his inquiry into the very nature of creativity. The world, he admits, is largely present to us as a "given." We can never explain the world "from the point of view of causation; the larger part always was and remains pure 'givens,' that is, genuine and supreme mysteries." But against these unrecuperable everyday mysteries, locked in matter and present to us in their immutable outer aspect, are the equally everyday miracles of creative being, which emanate from the psyche. They too are not reducible to any perceptible cause, but unlike the mysteries of the outer world, they are penetrable, malleable, and free. Struve intimates that such surprising new realities can be urged out of the present if an ideal, a "what ought to be," exists on the horizon for the creator; but in no way can these realities be predetermined by, or reduced to mere reflections of, "what is." At the beginning of the twenty-first century, in the wake of so much excellent insight into the creative process (in the Russian field, one thinks especially of Gary Saul Morson's work on Dostoevsky and Bakhtin) and amid the ruins of so much Marxist practice, these ideas may no longer have the cutting edge of discovery.[7] But one hundred years ago, in 1902, they must have been an inspiration. It was not necessary or possible for science to solve everything. It was, however, both necessary and possible for each individual to accomplish some concrete thing. Or as Sergei Bulgakov puts the matter at the end of his essay: "A person, within the limits of the understanding of reality that he has succeeded in achieving (an understanding in which science plays not the last role), selects from the boundless sea of evil precisely what can and ought to be eradicated just then by his own particular efforts; he selects that upon which he should concentrate his struggle at that given moment" (see Chapter 1).

It is part of the pathos of this centennial edition that Pëtr Struve, the most politically astute mind of the group, appeared to believe that the history of social philosophy would self-correct. Badly or inconsistently constructed fields would simply fall apart, because surely the makers of history could not be satisfied with mere slogans or illogical heaps of words. As his essay indicates, he was gladdened that critical work had appeared from within Marxist thought, and that the "subjective sociology" of Russian populists like Nikolai Mikhailovskii now appeared ripe for auto-critique. Struve put a great deal of hope in "the new people of the metaphysical need." But the overall critical assessment that these philosophers leveled against the positivists' theory of progress could only come back to haunt their own hopes. For in fact, they understood well that no guarantees obtained in this matter of creative miracles overcoming, one evil at a time, the mysterious givens of the world.

At the end of November 1901, Sergei Bulgakov delivered a lecture in Kiev on Ivan Karamazov as a philosophical type. He noted that the sort of "sickness of conscience" driving the second Karamazov brother insane was a "native Russian sickness." Why was this so? "In its very essence," Bulgakov explained, "the ideal is a concept that does not correspond to reality, it repudiates reality. But the degree of this non-correspondence can differ widely. In Russia, this non-correspondence is measured by a difference of several centuries; and thus, while our intelligentsia is in step with the most advanced European thought, in other respects our reality lags behind Europe by several hundred years. Which is why nowhere else in Europe does life so insult one at every step, so torment and cripple one, as in Russia."[8]

What followed was the twentieth century. These essays — so ably translated and edited for this centennial edition — remain radiant testimony to ideals that even the most savage reality could not put permanently to rest.

Notes

1. "Vzgliad na russkuiu filosofiiu," in *Voprosy filosofii* 1 (1994): 54–72. The Russian representatives in this forum are M. N. Gromov and N. K. Gavriushin; the Americans are James P. Scanlan and Andrzej Walicki (a Pole, of course, but then based in the United States). Page references henceforth included parenthetically in the text.

2. Berdiaev wrote an acclaimed study of Dostoevsky in 1934; Frank, a series of studies on Pushkin, and, between 1908 and 1933, five essays on Tolstoy. Askol'dov and Bulgakov also wrote incidental essays on Dostoevsky.

3. See Randall A. Poole, "Utopianism, Idealism, Liberalism: Russian Confrontations with Vladimir Solov'ëv," in *Modern Greek Studies Yearbook: Mediterranean, Slavic, and Eastern Orthodox Studies* (University of Minnesota), vols. 16–17 (2000–2001), pp. 43–87.

4. Randall A. Poole, "Epistemology, Ethics, and Self in Bakhtin's *Problems of Dosto-*

evsky's Poetics: A Russian Response to Rationalism," paper delivered at the Fifth International Bakhtin Conference at the University of Manchester, England, July 1991.

5. Mikhail Bakhtin, *Problems of Dostoevsky's Poetics* [1963], ed. and trans. Caryl Emerson (Minneapolis: University of Minnesota Press, 1984), 79–81.

6. On the latter, see Randall A. Poole, "The Apophatic Bakhtin," in Susan M. Felch and Paul J. Contino, eds., *Bakhtin and Religion: A Feeling for Faith* (Evanston, Ill.: Northwestern University Press, 2001): 151–175. The Felch-Contino volume also contains a translation and annotation of Lev Pumpiansky's notes of Bakhtin's lectures on Kant, delivered in the mid-1920s (193–237). For a recent treatment of Bakhtin's assimilation of Kant with emphasis on the reality of the Other as noumenal, not phenomenal, for both thinkers, see Greg Nielsen, "The Norms of Answerability: Bakhtin and the Fourth Postulate," in Michael Mayerfield Bell and Michael Gardiner, eds., *Bakhtin and the Human Sciences* (London: Sage Publications, 1998), 214–230.

7. For a powerful synthesis, see Gary Saul Morson, *Narrative and Freedom: The Shadows of Time* (New Haven: Yale University Press, 1994), esp. 23–30.

8. Lecture delivered in Kiev, 21 November 1901, published in the journal *Voprosy filosofii i psikhologii* 13:1, kn. 61 (1902), pp. 826–863. Repr. in *F. M. Dostoevskii: 1881–1981* (London: Overseas Publications Interchange Limited, 1981), 84–108, quotations at 107.

Acknowledgments

It is a pleasure to express my gratitude to all those who enabled me to complete this project. Gary Saul Morson proposed that I undertake it and supported its publication in his Russian Literature and Thought series at Yale University Press. I was gratified that Jonathan Brent, editorial director at the press, also took an interest in the volume. My greatest debt, in this project and much else, is to Caryl Emerson for her unflagging encouragement and boundless willingness (and ability) to help, not least during the summer of 2001, when she took six weeks from her own schedule to go through the entire manuscript, make all manner of improvements, and write the foreword. At the beginning of the project, my colleague and friend Anatol Shmelev at the Hoover Institution helped me revise draft translations of several essays. At its end, George L. Kline, American dean of the study of Russian philosophy, was characteristically very generous in providing invaluable detailed commentary on the manuscript. It was also my good fortune to have Nancy Moore Brochin as my editor at Yale University Press.

I was privileged to pursue doctoral studies in Russian intellectual history with Professor Andrzej Walicki at the University of Notre Dame; my intellectual obligation to him is evident in these pages. I am grateful for his continued support, including assistance with certain aspects of this project. I am likewise obliged to Gary M. Hamburg for his time and attention in graduate school and in the years since (and especially for his very helpful reading of an earlier version of the introduction to the present volume). Jaroslaw Dobrzanski was also one of my teachers at Notre Dame. Richard Wortman, Richard Pipes, Terence Emmons, Bernice Glatzer Rosenthal, and Marc Raeff read the editor's introduction in one version or another and made valuable suggestions. I am fortunate to share the rich intellectual community of a number of wonderful scholars in Russian culture and thought, including Paul Valliere, Richard F. Gustafson, James P. Scanlan, Philip J. Swoboda, Laurie Manchester, Catherine Evtuhov, David M. McDonald, and Brian Horowitz. All are contributors in their own way to this volume. Stephen H. Blackwell invited me to the University of Tennessee to lecture and present a seminar, and helped with a point of translation. Special thanks to Michael David-Fox, Yanni Kotsonis, Eric Lohr, and Dirk Moses, friends and colleagues, for their warm support. In Russia, I remain grateful to Leonid V. Poliakov, Nellie V. Motroshilova, Albert V. Sobolev, and Oleg S. Pugachev. At Boston University, I have benefited from discussions with colleagues in the International History Institute, including Jay P. Corrin, William R. Keylor, Michael Kort, Cathal J. Nolan, William Tilchin, and Henry Burke Wend. Finally, personal thanks to my parents, grandparents, and Don, Cathy, Jen, Dan, and John.

This volume is part of a project on philosophical liberalism in the Moscow Psychological Society that has been generously supported by research fellowships from the Social Science Research Council (SSRC), the Remarque Institute at New York University, the Institute for Advanced Study in Princeton, the Hoover Institution at Stanford University, the Harriman Institute at Columbia University, the Kennan Institute for Advanced Russian Studies (where Jeannie Sklar and Karen Aguilera provided helpful research assistance), the International Research and Exchanges Board (IREX), the Fulbright-Hays Doctoral Dissertation Research Abroad Program (U.S. Department of Education), and the University of Notre Dame. For this institutional support, I am very grateful.

Note on the Text and Translation

The original Russian edition of *Problems of Idealism* runs to 521 pages.* This translation abridges the text by a little less than twenty percent. I have deleted the most from Kistiakovskii's essay; by the author's own admission it appeared in a "somewhat unfinished form" and was done in haste. His thesis is an important one, but does not require the nearly one hundred pages he devoted to it. Most of what I have left out consists of his long restatements, with abundant use of quotations, of certain fairly straightforward ideas by N. K. Mikhailovskii and V. P. Vorontsov. Similarly, Lappo-Danilevskii's article is a long, painstaking, and important critique of Comte; I have abbreviated it somewhat, with minimal loss of content. To a lesser extent I have also abridged Frank's essay, mainly by cutting some of his extended quotations from Nietzsche. The essays by Ol'denburg and Zhukovskii are the "least classic" in the volume and have also been shortened, but with no real loss of content. The other contributions are included in their entirety or with very slight abridgments. The essays are translated from their original version in *Problems of Idealism,* not from subsequent reprints (with changes) by their respective authors.

Spaced ellipses indicate my deletions: in brackets [. . .] for one or more full paragraphs, including in some cases several pages, without brackets . . . for less than a paragraph, even if that amounts to a long passage. Unspaced ellipses ... are from the original. In places, I have "silently" (without ellipses) eliminated wordiness, repetition, and metadiscourse that have no bearing on meaning. More generally, this translation strives to be literal with regard to meaning, but not always with regard to expression, and I have not refrained from attempting to make the English text more direct and economical than the Russian original.

For quotations in the text, source references have been supplied where needed. Also, I have avoided "back-translating" quotations from the Russian. Instead, I have either used existing English translations or retranslated from the original (French or German), generally indicating this as "editor's translation." The one somewhat problematic essay in this respect is Lappo-Danilevskii's, whose translations into Russian are often unusually loose and interpretive. Where possible, I have retranslated from the original sources, but in some cases Lappo-Danilevskii's quotations appear to be paraphrases or combinations of elements from separate passages.

Full citations have been provided for bibliographical references that are incomplete in the Russian text, but I have used brackets only for more signifi-cant additions, in order to avoid further cluttering the text. Non-Russian names have, of course, been restored from Russian transliteration to their original form, and where appropriate have been given in full rather than by initials. Names are identified in the notes or, for those that occur in more than one essay, in the Glossary of Names, except for merely bibliographical refer-ences and a few well-known figures. Notes supplied by me are designated "Ed." Russian terms in brackets are given in the nominative, not in declension (except for whole phrases). Finally, contributor biographies appear at the back of the book.

The Russian term *lichnost'* can mean personality, person, individual, indi-viduality, or self. In this period the term was acquiring greater philosophical specificity and increasingly could refer to the concept of "person," as this book attests. In general, I have used "person" or "personhood" where the emphasis was on the absolute worth and dignity that make human beings (although not necessarily only human beings) persons or, in Kant's terminology, "ends-in-themselves." (Of course, "person" can also mean "human being" (*chelovek*) in a more generic sense, without any particular philosophical implications. Where necessary I have provided the relevant Russian term in brackets.) For the contributors to this book, "personhood" entailed some type of idealist commitment in philosophy, since categories such as absolute worth and dig-nity were not empirical ones and yet were intrinsic to moral consciousness.

This reflected a philosophical development of the idea of lichnost' compared to its earlier use among, for example, Aleksandr Herzen and, after him, the Russian "subjective sociologists" (P. L. Lavrov, N. K. Mikhailovskii, N. I. Kareev), for all of whom its meaning was closer to "individual," "individuality," or "personality." These Russian populist thinkers stressed that the individual was an active moral agent capable of introducing his or her own values and ideals into history (Lavrov), or of striving to harmoniously and integrally develop all sides of his or her personality (Mikhailovskii). It was through the fuller theoretical elaboration of these ideas, as well as through other philosophical and theological sources (such as classical German idealism and Orthodox religious thought), that the contributors to *Problems of Idealism* invested lichnost' with the meaning "personhood."

Another central concept in these pages is the distinction between "is" and "ought," or between "what is" and "what ought to be" (in German, between *das Sein* and *das Sollen*). As a logical principle, its meaning is that propositions about "what ought to be" cannot be derived deductively (analytically) from major premises limited to "what is." This separation is often summed up as the rule, no "ought" from "is." The classic formulation of the logical fallacy of deriving "ought" from "is" belongs to David Hume in *A Treatise of Human Nature* (Book III, part 1, section 1). More generally, the distinction has often been used to capture the irreducibility of our ideals and values to the empirical world, an irreducibility that, for some philosophers, holds implications that go well beyond analytic logic. In the *Critique of Pure Reason* and the *Critique of Practical Reason,* Kant defines "ought" as the form of the categorical imperative (regardless of content), in contrast to "is" as the form of a theoretical proposition. He thought moral consciousness of "ought" implied metaphysical conclusions ("postulates") about freedom, immortality, and God.

In Russian, the distinction is between *bytie* or *sushchee* ("is" or "what is") and *dolzhenstvovanie* or *dolzhnoe* ("ought" or "what ought to be"). I have generally enclosed the English terms in quotation marks, regardless of whether the Russian terms have them in the 1902 text. In each part of the distinction, either Russian term can be used synonymously for "is" or "what is" and "ought" or "what ought to be," respectively. Dolzhenstvovanie is, however, somewhat more abstract, suggesting "ought" or "oughtness," compared to the more concrete "what ought to be" for dolzhnoe. As for bytie and sushchee: in common usage, bytie means "being" or "existence," but can be translated as "is" or "what is" to make the distinction from "ought" or "what ought to be." Sushchee (which suggests more "what is") is less common and tends to imply essentiality. In certain philosophical contexts, such as in the works of Vladimir Solov'ëv and Sergei Trubetskoi, it has a more metaphysical or ontological meaning, to convey, for example, the sense of wonder that anything is ("something rather than nothing") and to suggest, from that, the idea of necessary being or God. At these metaphysical heights, the distinction between "is"/ "what is" and "ought"/"what ought to be" loses the validity it has in the empirical world, and here some of the contributors to *Problems of Idealism* speculated about a higher metaphysical synthesis of "is" and "ought." In this they were continuing the perennial Russian search for "*pravda*" as a higher unity of the truth of "what is" (theoretical truth or verity, "*istina*") and the truth of "what ought to be" (practical truth as "justice").

Problemy idealizma: Sbornik statei, ed. P. I. Novgorodtsev (Moscow: Moskovskoe Psikhologicheskoe Obshchestvo [Moscow Psychological Society], [1902]). A new Russian edition appeared as the present English edition went to press: *Problemy idealizma: Sbornik statei*, ed. M. A. Kolerov (Moscow: Tri Kvadrata, 2002), with lengthy introductory essays by N. S. Plotnikov and M. A. Kolerov. The Kolerov edition usefully compares the essays by Bulgakov, Struve, Berdiaev, Frank, and Kistiakovskii to their subsequent reprints and lists the changes; otherwise it is generally not annotated. Kolerov's introductory essay has also been published in somewhat different forms in his books, *Ne mir, no mech: Russkaia religiozno-filosofskaia pechat' ot "Problem idealizma" do "Vekh", 1902–1909* (St. Petersburg: Aleteiia, 1996) and *Sbornik "Problemy idealizma" (1902): Istoriia i kontekst* (Moscow: Tri Kvadrata, 2002). In the editor's introduction to the present edition, I draw on Kolerov's seminal 1993 essay "Arkhivnaia istoriia sbornika 'Problemy idealizma' (1902)" (for full citation, see p. 61, note 45).

Editor's Introduction: Philosophy and Politics in the Russian Liberation Movement

The Moscow Psychological Society and Its Symposium, *Problems of Idealism*

RANDALL A. POOLE

The appearance in late 1902 of *Problems of Idealism* was a philosophical watershed in the Russian Silver Age, as the remarkable cultural renaissance at the end of the nineteenth and beginning of the twentieth centuries has come to be known.[1] The Russian critic Ivanov-Razumnik, in his classic *History of Russian Social Thought,* described the publication of the volume, a collection of twelve essays by some of Russia's most important philosophers and philosophical thinkers, as an "event" in the history of Russian thought.[2] This assessment has endured.[3] *Problems of Idealism* was published by the Moscow Psychological Society, a learned society founded at Moscow University in 1885. By the end of its activity in 1922, the Psychological Society had attracted most of the country's outstanding philosophers and had made the major contribution to the growth of Russian philosophy.[4] In pursuit of its goal of the free, autonomous development of philosophy in Russia, the society advanced a powerful neo-idealist critique of positivism, an outlook that had been remarkably pervasive in Russia since the middle of the nineteenth century and that sought to eliminate speculative philosophy as "unscientific." For leading philosophers in the society, neo-idealism offered compelling theoretical support not only for the autonomy of philosophy against reductive positivism, but also for rule-of-law liberalism and constitutional reform. *Problems of Idealism,* edited by Pavel I. Novgorodtsev, one of the society's most prominent social philosophers, helped publicize the connection between neo-idealism (in theoretical philosophy and ethics) and liberalism (in social philosophy). This connection consisted, first of all, in the neo-idealist concept of the irreducibility of the self to naturalistic explanation, on the one hand, and in the special claims liberalism makes for the absolute value and dignity of the person, on the other.

Problems of Idealism was followed by two better known symposia exploring the differences between philosophical and ideological thought, *Vekhi* (*Landmarks* or *Signposts*, 1909) and *Iz glubiny* (*Out of the Depths*, 1918). Four writers (the most famous) contributed to all three collections: N. A. Berdiaev, S. N. Bulgakov, S. L. Frank, and P. B. Struve. S. A. Askol'dov and Novgorodtsev wrote for both the first and third volumes, while B. A. Kistiakovskii contributed to the first and second. Pëtr Struve had a major organizational role in all three projects. *Vekhi* is a scathing critique of the radical Russian intelligentsia and its positivist ideology, which the volume's contributors blame for the failure of Russian liberalism in the aftermath of the 1905 Revolution. It generated one of the most famous controversies in all of Russian intellectual history and has been the subject of extensive analysis and commentary, most recently in post-Soviet Russia where the volume has been widely reprinted. It has also been translated twice into English.[5] *Out of the Depths* assesses the role of the radical intelligentsia in the revolutionary events of 1917, as *Landmarks* did for the 1905 period. It, too, has recently been reprinted in Russia and is available in English translation.[6] *Problems of Idealism,* by contrast, has not been translated until the present edition and has not received the attention it merits, not only as the first in the set but more importantly as a crucial source that occupies its own place in the Religious-Philosophical Renaissance of the Russian Silver Age.

Problems of Idealism develops the theoretical foundations of liberalism more consistently than its two successor volumes, which concentrate on relentless critique of the radical intelligentsia. In some ways it is a more substantial and less tendentious text, and thus more relevant to the post-Soviet search for a national liberal tradition in pre-revolutionary Russian thought. The collection demonstrates one of the paradoxes of Russian liberalism — that its frail social foundations made its intellectual defense all the more imperative. This theoretical need was less urgent elsewhere in Europe, in countries where liberalism was more deeply rooted and better realized in practice. As a result, the philosophical premises of liberalism can be seen with greater clarity through the idealism of the "Russian prism" (to borrow Joseph Frank's metaphor).[7] These premises are of wide-ranging interest, involving problems of perennial importance to human identity: freedom, moral responsibility, and the nature of the self. The powerful formulation *Problems of Idealism* gives to these and related problems makes it a classic of Russian thought. The symposium informs the work of its great predecessors, from Herzen and Dostoevsky to B. N. Chicherin and Vladimir S. Solov'ëv, and anticipates its successors, from Bakhtin to Solzhenitsyn.[8] It forms part of a liberal tradition that, if not characteristically Russian, is nonetheless authentically Russian in its defense of the absolute value and dignity of personhood.

The Moscow Psychological Society and Russian Liberalism

The Moscow Psychological Society, the sponsor of *Problems of Idealism*, distinguished itself as the philosophical center of the revolt against positivism in the Russian Silver Age. The Psychological Society was founded by sixteen Moscow University professors headed by M. M. Troitskii (1835–1899), an empiricist psychologist whose specialization accounts for the society's name. The founders, most of whom were, ironically, inclined toward positivism, took little role in the society after its initial establishment. Rather, its direction was taken over by a group of idealist philosophers led by Nikolai Ia. Grot (1852–1899),[9] who became chairman in 1888. Among Grot's main colleagues were Solov'ëv, Sergei N. Trubetskoi, and Lev M. Lopatin. A. A. Kizevetter, in his classic memoirs, describes how in Moscow University circles at the time "all the talented young people occupied with philosophy stood in opposition to Troitskii and immersed themselves at once in metaphysical problems. At the head of these young people were Lopatin, Sergei Trubetskoi and — the most brilliant diamond of this philosophical generation — Vladimir Solov'ëv." They embraced Grot, "in all respects well-suited to this tight and friendly philosophical company. It was this company that captured the Psychological Society, transforming it into a philosophical society in the broad sense of the word."[10] By the 1890s the society had about 200 members, a number that remained fairly constant throughout its existence. In 1889 it began publication of Russia's first regular, specialized journal in philosophy, *Voprosy filosofii i psikhologii* (*Questions of Philosophy and Psychology*). Published five times a year until 1918, the journal was invaluable in promoting the growth of philosophy in Russia. Grot characterized the journal's prevailing direction as idealist or, "in respect to method, metaphysical."[11] In 1910, when the Psychological Society celebrated its twenty-fifth anniversary, one of its officers could evaluate it as a "profoundly significant fact in the life of Russian society, where in general philosophical questions could only relatively very recently become the object of free and, to the extent possible, objective discussion."[12]

While the Silver Age as a whole can be seen as a broad revolt against positivism, in which respect Russia was an integral part of the European fin-de-siècle,[13] neo-idealist philosophy in the Psychological Society was distinctive in the theoretical depth of its critique. In ethics, epistemology, ontology, and social philosophy, neo-idealism emerged as a response to the dominant posi-tivist background, the main characteristics of which were *reductionism,* which dismisses as a meaningless proposition (i.e., neither analytic nor empirical) the possibility of being beyond the positively given data of sense experience; *scien-tism,* the claim, consistent with the positivist reduction of being to natural phenomena, that the natural sciences cover everything; and *utopianism,* or faith in human perfectibility through (in this case) application of natural scien-tific methods to man and society.[14] In its popular naturalistic and scientistic forms, positivism asserted that philosophy had no special methodology and thus no legitimate right to exist as its own type of scientific (*nauchnyi* or *wissenschaftlich*) discipline. Empirical sciences were the only sciences; philos-ophy could serve, at best, as a field that systematized empirical research. The measure of reality was empirical experience: positively given, external sense data. Against these reductionist claims, the Psychological Society sought to defend the autonomy of philosophy by arguing that the positivist criterion of reality was far from exhaustive, and that what it did not exhaust constituted the special domain of philosophy. This domain was human consciousness itself, to the extent it could be shown to be irreducible to empirical experience (the positivist sphere). Neo-idealism thus took shape as a type of philosophy of consciousness.

The effort to base the autonomy of philosophy on the irreducibility of con-sciousness had direct implications for the core value of liberalism, the human person. Russian neo-idealism substantiated the foundational liberal princi-ple of personhood (*lichnost'*), the idea that human beings bear an absolute value and dignity because they are persons or, in Kant's terminology, ends-in-themselves. From the Kantian idea of autonomy, Psychological Society idealists typically came to the ontological conclusion that the self was not free-floating, anchored in neither this world nor another, but metaphysically grounded. For them, Kant's *transcendental* idealism entailed a *transcendent* ontological real-ity.[15] In its main representatives, Russian neo-idealism thus took the form of a modernized, theoretically explicit theism, in which the value of the person was rooted in transcendent being (personalism). Psychological Society philoso-phers drew here on the "concrete" or personalistic traditions of Orthodox theology (and of theism more generally), in which it is the "image and likeness" of God in man that constitutes personhood.[16] This was a project to raise liberalism to an ontological level, in sharp contrast to empirical-positivist conceptions of liberalism (John Stuart Mill in England, Pavel Miliukov in

Russia). An important link in this development was Solov'ëv's concept of Godmanhood (*bogochelovechestvo*), which refers to humanity's divine potential and vocation, the ideal of its transformation in and union with God. The self-realization of each individual human person is at the same time a step toward the divinization of the cosmos.[17]

By the turn of the twentieth century, the Psychological Society was clearly the theory center behind Russian liberalism. Six of its most prominent philosophers were main theorists of Russian liberalism: Chicherin, Solov'ëv, S. N. Trubetskoi, E. N. Trubetskoi, Novgorodtsev, and S. A. Kotliarevskii.[18] *Questions of Philosophy and Psychology* regularly published essays and studies in liberal political philosophy, including some now classic works of Russian liberalism.[19] While advancing the theoretical development of Russian liberalism, the Psychological Society also played an integral part in the intellectual, political, and social history of the Russian Liberation Movement. Under way from the very beginning of the century, the Liberation Movement was a broad-based public opinion campaign designed to bring the autocratic regime to recognize the need for constitutional reform. It culminated in the Revolution of 1905.[20] Solov'ëv died on the eve of the movement, and Chicherin was too old to take an active part in it,[21] but their legacy inspired the four neo-idealist professors from the Psychological Society who did have leading roles in the campaign for constitutional reform: the two Trubetskois, Novgorodtsev, and Kotliarevskii. V. I. Vernadskii, the well-known Russian geologist and another major figure in the Liberation Movement, was also a member of the society. His philosophic interests offered valuable support from within the natural sciences for the neo-idealist program. These scholars were very much aware of their influence, as professors, in shaping public opinion, and were thus natural participants in the constitutional reform movement. The Psychological Society was an important focus in their common intellectual and institutional background.

Four philosophical thinkers well known for their evolution from Marxism to idealism — Struve, Bulgakov, Berdiaev, and Frank — were also involved, to one extent or another, in the work of the Psychological Society, and all became members, sooner or later. Another prominent liberal theorist associated with the Society was B. A. Kistiakovskii. All five were active in the Liberation Movement. This is especially true of Struve, who, together with Novgorodtsev, organized the society's important programmatic symposium, *Problems of Idealism.* The volume, which publicized the connection between neo-idealism and liberalism that the society had advanced for fifteen years, was its main institutional contribution to the campaign for constitutional reform. The symposium was conceived as a theoretical statement of Russian liberalism in the first stages of the Liberation Movement, when the liberation-ists (*osvobozhdentsy*) saw in the zemstvo institutions of local self-government (established in 1864) the most promising social support for liberalism. In this way it constitutes the theoretical counterpart to the first issues of Struve's famous émigré newspaper, *Osvobozhdenie* (*Liberation*), which began pub-lication earlier the same year (1902).[22] Both were concurrent projects orga-nized by zemstvo constitutionalists (typically landed gentry) and their allies outside the zemstvo, whose cooperation launched the Liberation Movement. The Moscow Psychological Society, one of the learned societies promoting the growth of civil society in late imperial Russia,[23] is itself a paradigmatic exam-ple of the vital importance, in both the intellectual and social history of Rus-sian liberalism during this period, of the interconnections and cooperation between zemstvo activists (*zemtsy*) and "new liberals" from the professions and intelligentsia.[24]

Problems of Idealism: *Conception and History*

ZEMSTVO CONSTITUTIONALISTS AND NEW LIBERALS

Turn-of-the-century Russian liberalism was represented by two basic groups: constitutionalists from the zemstvo institutions and "new liberals" from the free professions and certain ideological currents within the intelli-gentsia, such as "legal Marxism," "economism," and "legal populism" (con-nected with the short-lived People's Rights party). Between traditional zemstvo and the new Russian liberalism, university professors like Novgorodtsev had a special role as intermediaries. The intransigence of the autocracy convinced leaders from both groups to join forces in a public opinion campaign that, they hoped, would persuade the regime to enter the path of constitutional reform.[25] Initially this effort, although orchestrated by both zemstvo constitutionalists and their allies from the professions and intelligentsia circles, hoped to draw primarily on the zemstvos. The goal was to raise zemstvo political conscious-ness well beyond the relatively few already committed liberals, who numbered not more than 300 district- and provincial-level deputies at the turn of the century (by Pirumova's count).[26] Later, the concept of public opinion ex-panded to include the "democratic intelligentsia," and for its allegiance the liberationists entered into competition with openly revolutionary parties. The most important instrument of this public opinion campaign, whether in its early identification with the zemstvo or subsequent leftward shift, was Struve's journal, *Osvobozhdenie*. *Problems of Idealism,* as noted above, took shape as a philosophical defense of liberalism during the zemstvo phase of the Liberation Movement. The planning and collective authorship of the volume also clearly reveal, as I will try to show, the social composition of the constitutional reform movement: zemstvo constitutionalists, liberals from the professions, and certain groups from the intelligentsia (in this case, the "legal Marxists").

Struve, the most prominent of the new liberals, had long recognized the oppositional potential of the zemstvo. The earliest demonstration of his interest in rallying the zemtsy to the cause of constitutional reform was an "Open Letter to Nicholas II" he wrote in response to the tsar's infamous speech of 17 January 1895 in which the new emperor dismissed as "senseless dreams" even quite modest zemstvo hopes for some form of consultative representation. "In this manner," according to Richard Pipes, "Struve established connections with the constitutional wing of the zemstvo movement, whose principal theoretician he was to become after being ejected from the ranks of Social Democracy."[27] The effect of the "senseless dreams" speech was all the stronger because the great famine of 1891–1892, and the official incompetence it disclosed, were still fresh in everyone's mind.[28] Olga N. Trubetskaia called the famine a turning point in the life of her brother, Sergei Trubetskoi, who worked on behalf of famine relief in Riazan'.[29] "First-hand acquaintance with the Russian countryside," Martha Bohachevsky-Chomiak writes in her study of Trubetskoi, "completed his break with the quasi-Slavophilism of the Moscow tradition and led to the forceful development of liberal political convictions."[30] Evgenii Trubetskoi, like his brother Sergei a contributor to *Problems of Idealism*, describes in his memoirs how the famine and Nicholas II's speech affected the "Lopatin Circle," which formed around Lev Lopatin's father, Mikhail Nikolaevich (1823–1900), a prominent Moscow jurist. The dinners Mikhail Nikolaevich hosted every Wednesday were attended by some of Moscow's leading intellectual figures, including the Psychological Society philosophers (Solov'ëv, Grot, Lopatin, the Trubetskois, and also N. A. Ivantsov, similarly interested in metaphysics).[31] Trubetskoi characterized the circle as "moderately liberal" in its political outlook. The circle became animated during the famine, "which provoked terrible discontent with the government and gave a strong push to constitutional dreams." Such political excitement returned during the first hopeful months of the new reign, until the tsar's speech, which immediately depressed the mood in the circle.[32]

Nicholas II's rebuke to the zemtsy, amplified by Struve's "Open Letter," prompted the revival of zemstvo efforts to confer regularly on a national level. These efforts bore temporary fruit in the zemstvo conference held at Nizhnii Novgorod in August 1896, and more permanent results in the "Beseda circle" of zemstvo opposition. Founded in 1899, Beseda was the first organized group of the emerging Liberation Movement.[33] Three of its members were from the

Psychological Society: S. N. Trubetskoi, E. N. Trubetskoi, and Kotliarevskii.[34] Through them, Novgorodtsev was also closely connected to the circle. Beseda's initial goal was the development of public opinion in the zemstvo institutions, to help defend local self-government and rural interests against bureaucratic infringement and Minister of Finance Sergei Witte's industrialization drive. The threat to the zemstvo was made very real by Witte's confidential (but nonetheless widely discussed) memorandum, written in 1898 and first published (with a long introduction) by Struve in 1901, who gave it the title *Samoderzhavie i zemstvo (Autocracy and the Zemstvo)*.[35] Struve's efforts further "consolidated his authority in leading zemstvo circles," Shakhovskoi recounts.[36]

Witte's memorandum argued that since the zemstvo was by its nature pro-constitutional and therefore incompatible with autocracy, the tsar should abolish the former if he wished to preserve the latter.[37] D. N. Shipov, a Beseda member and perhaps one of the circle's founders, wrote that upon reading the paper in November 1899, "I experienced a feeling of deep indignation."[38] Trubetskaia records that its circulation in late 1899 "powerfully radicalized" the educated public.[39] In 1900–1901, several Beseda members were involved in the preparation of petitions to the tsar to articulate zemstvo responses to the Witte memorandum.[40] This activity, together with Beseda's consideration in early 1902–when its agenda had shifted from zemstvo to national political concerns — of a report by N. N. Lvov "on the causes of Russia's present unsettled state and on measures for improving it," clarified the differentiation of Beseda members into two political orientations: the neo-Slavophiles, headed by Shipov, who sought principally to curb bureaucratic arbitrariness and ensure respect for civil liberties: and the constitutionalists, among whom were the three Psychological Society philosophers.[41]

The Beseda Circle and the Psychological Society shared a commitment to advancing Russian liberalism through publication of scholarly works. The Beseda book program began in 1902, the same year that *Osvobozhdenie* started publication and that *Problems of Idealism* appeared. It produced seven collections of articles, several in two-volume sets and in more than one edition.[42] Kotliarevskii contributed to a volume on the constitutional state.[43] Most Beseda books were devoted, however, to concrete problems of rural economy and local self-government, not to the theoretical development of liberalism. For this, Russian constitutionalists had other outlets, including the Psychological Society's *Questions of Philosophy and Psychology* and *Problems of Idealism*. In addition to the purely intellectual side of the circle's book series, Emmons singles out another dimension: "Beseda's publishing enterprise provided an important institutional setting for contacts between zemstvo political leaders and the 'intelligentsia' (the journalists and academics without gentry or zemstvo ties),"[44] contacts that were also furthered by the Psychological Society.

In early March 1901 Struve, within a few months of preparing his edition of the Witte memorandum, was arrested for involvement in a student demonstration on Kazan Square in St. Petersburg. He chose Tver, the traditional stronghold of zemstvo constitutionalism, as his place of exile. There he occupied himself with two projects: *Osvobozhdenie* and *Problemy idealizma*.[45] They were concurrent initiatives not only for Struve, but also for Novgorodtsev, D. E. Zhukovskii, and, to a lesser extent, Vernadskii and Kotliarevskii.

Plans for *Osvobozdenie* had been under way between Struve and his various zemstvo contacts (especially I. I. Petrunkevich) since 1900, and were finalized in Tver.[46] After Struve went abroad in December 1901 to set up shop for the émigré journal (it began publication in Stuttgart, 18 June/1 July 1902), a special conference convened in Moscow (February or March 1902) to deliberate its program, funding, and method of distribution. Among those present were Vernadskii, Novgorodtsev, Zhukovskii, and possibly Kotliarevskii.[47] In May 1902 Kotliarevskii was part of a zemstvo delegation that visited Struve in Stuttgart.[48] Although Beseda did not adopt *Osvobozhdenie* as its official organ, its programmatic articles were discussed at a meeting in May 1902.[49] Throughout this period — at the same time *Problems of Idealism* was taking shape — the osvobozhdentsy followed a policy conceived "primarily in order to pursue the task of mobilizing the zemstvo institutions in support of constitutional reform and the application of pressure on the government from that quarter."[50] What Emmons characterizes as *Osvobozhdenie*'s "zemstvo campaign" lasted until late 1902; an exchange between Struve and Pavel Miliukov in the seventeenth issue (16 February/1 March 1902) marked its end, and the beginning of the "intelligentsia campaign."

Novgorodtsev worked most closely with Struve in planning *Problems of Idealism*. At the end of September 1901 Struve sent him his first conception of the philosophical symposium (see below). In October they consulted in person in Tver, after which Novgorodtsev assumed most of the organizational and editorial responsibility, especially after Struve left Russia in early December. Struve solicited Zhukovskii's involvement in the *Problemy* project simultaneously with Novgorodtsev's; it was, in fact, through Zhukovskii that Novgorodtsev first learned of the idea. Zhukovskii, a wealthy zemets, financed both *Problems of Idealism* as well as the start-up of *Osvobozhdenie*.[51] He also contributed one of the essays to the volume, and later became a member of the Psychological Society itself (in 1914).[52]

Two other zemtsy involved in planning *Osvobozhdenie* were also associated with the *Problemy* project: Kotliarevskii and Vernadskii, both close colleagues of Novgorodtsev. Kotliarevskii (1873–1939) and Novgorodtsev became members of the Psychological Society within a few weeks of each other, in February 1898.[53] This is the first indication of the great deal they had in common. Both were social and legal philosophers at Moscow University, shared very similar conceptions of neo-idealism and its implications for social theory, and had parallel parts in the Liberation Movement. Kotliarevskii, a provincial zemstvo deputy from Saratov, had the distinction of defending four dissertations at Moscow University, the first two in the Historical-Philological Faculty,[54] the second two in the Juridical Faculty.[55] During these years he lectured in history as a *Privatdozent*. With his second doctorate in 1909, he became professor of public law at Moscow University. Kotliarevskii did not contribute to *Problems of Idealism*, but he did write an important review essay defending it against what he describes as the "false realism" of the positivists, who responded to *Problems of Idealism* with their own collective effort, *Ocherki realisticheskogo mirovozzreniia* (*Essays in the Realist Worldview*).[56] His essay formulated with eloquence and precision certain main ideas of neo-idealism, particularly the "contraband" critique of positivism (see below).

Vernadskii (1863–1945) and Novgorodtsev first met in Paris in 1890. Their close association was a source of Vernadskii's philosophical interests.[57] Through the example of his life and work, Vernadskii showed that the true spirit of scientific inquiry had nothing in common with reductive positivism or scientism. He was a Tambov zemstvo deputy (district and provincial levels) and professor of mineralogy at Moscow University from 1898 to 1911, making him another *professor-zemets*. Vernadskii, "moved by his general sympathy for the *Sbornik*," as Novgorodtsev put it, wanted to contribute to *Problems of Idealism*,[58] but instead chose to publish in the Psychological Society's journal that year a major essay, "On the Scientific Worldview," which argued, just like the symposium, for the relative autonomy of distinct spheres of human consciousness and experience — empirical or natural scientific on the one hand, moral or idealist on the other — and against their conflation in positivism.[59] Vernadskii was also part of the Psychological Society's examination of Kant's legacy, delivering one of the three papers at its jubilee Kant meeting held in December 1904.[60] He had a close colleague not only in Novgorodtsev but also in Sergei Trubetskoi,[61] who nominated him for Psychological Society membership, to which he was elected in December 1901.[62]

Two of the zemstvo constitutionalists involved in the *Problems of Idealism* project, Vernadskii and S. F. Ol'denburg, connect it to the "Bratstvo Priiutino," a circle of socially conscious, civic-minded students united by their belief in the transforming power of modern knowledge, who gathered around Sergei

Ol'denburg and his brother Fëdor at St. Petersburg University in early 1880s.[63] The Brotherhood, which remained intact long after its members finished at the university, constituted an important part of the generational and intellectual experience of the leadership of the future Constitutional-Democratic (Kadet) party.[64] Several of the *Priiutintsy* were close to Lev Tolstoy and were inspired by some of his ideas. They adopted his techniques, for example, in organizing famine relief in Vernadskii's Tambov province in 1891–1892.[65] "But in contrast to Tolstoy," G. V. Vernadskii stresses in his account of his father's circle, "the majority of the members of the Brotherhood considered science one of the highest manifestations of the human spirit, recognizing the value of modern culture in general, and also the necessity of courts and the state."[66] Although the Priiutintsy did use populism to justify their devotion to *nauka* (science), their ideal of service to the *narod* (people) did not degenerate into a reductive utilitarianism. Science, in the broad sense of higher learning, preserved its autonomy.

In 1916 Vernadskii described the intellectual outlook of the Priiutino Brotherhood: "In the beginning of the 1880s, along with purely socialist moods, there existed other tendencies, close to the latter but not included within their boundaries. The purely socialist tendency was permeated by a feeling of social morality, close in its philosophical ideals to scientific positivism, linked with a negative attitude to religion, art, and especially to political life." The non-socialist tendencies, by contrast, "did not share the same attitude toward religion, art, philosophy, political life, or science which was part of the socialist mood of youth at that time. Many intellectuals considered it difficult to reconcile socialism with other sides of the human spirit that were dear to them — with a feeling for their nation or the state, and even more so with their belief in the freedom of the personality."[67] The Priiutintsy were among the non-socialist intellectuals. The defense of the autonomy of religion, philosophy, and "other sides of the human spirit" against scientistic positivism would be one of the central themes in *Problems of Idealism*.[68]

The zemstvo constitutionalists were one of the two major liberationist groups represented in *Problems of Idealism;* the other was the intelligentsia "new liberals," among whom the "legal Marxists" were the most theoretically articulate, even before their four most famous representatives became idealists.[69] Marxism, in its conception of the historical necessity for Russia to pass through a prolonged stage of capitalism and "bourgeois" freedoms during which the country would be fully Europeanized, was already compatible on a practical level with liberalism. The potential for cooperation with more traditional representatives of Russian liberalism widened as the legal Marxists abandoned positivism for idealism and came to see liberal values as ends, not merely means. Already in April 1900 Vernadskii noted the "curious progress of the Marxists" Struve, Bulgakov, and others, who "are now coming close to the democrats and liberals."[70] In pinning his first hopes for the Liberation Movement on the zemstvo milieu, Struve needed to convince zemstvo liberals that they had nothing to fear from legal Marxism because it had evolved into a consistent and powerful philosophical defense of liberal values. The contributions by the former Marxists to *Problems of Idealism,* once they became involved in the project, helped serve this end.

The Psychological Society helped provide the intellectual resources the Marxists needed as they made their way past positivism,[71] for the simple reason that the society had long spearheaded the philosophical critique of positivism and included Russia's leading idealist philosophers. In fact, the intellectual trajectory from positivism to idealism had been followed before the legal Marxists by several society philosophers themselves, including Solov'ëv, Grot, and the Trubetskoi brothers. In a review of Grot's posthumous collection of articles spanning his positivist and idealist periods, *Filosofiia i ee obshchie zadachi* (*Philosophy and Its General Tasks,* 1904), E. V. Spektorskii drew the parallel between it and both *Problemy idealizma* and Bulgakov's collection, *Ot marksizma k idealizmu* (*From Marxism to Idealism,* 1903).[72] Far more important than Grot as a source of inspiration was Vladimir Solov'ëv, the society's most visible philosopher. Bulgakov included in his autobiographical set of essays an article devoted to Solov'ëv, to mark his part in the intellectual evolution the volume traces.[73] Bulgakov himself became a member of the Psychological Society in November 1897.[74] A year before, *Voprosy filosofii i psikhologii* published part of a developmental polemic between Struve and Bulgakov, a harbinger.[75] By 1902 Bulgakov had completed his transition to idealism.[76] At a meeting of the society in February, he delivered a paper, "Osnovnye problemy teorii progressa" ("Basic Problems of the Theory of Progress"),[77] which became his contribution to *Problems of Idealism.*

The Psychological Society also helped turn Berdiaev and Frank toward philosophical idealism, although they did not become members until later (1909 and 1914, respectively). As a student, Frank attended public sessions of the society, and later recalled that the society's special commemoration in 1896 of the 300th anniversary of Descartes's birth was "for me the first stimulus to the study of philosophy."[78] At this time he was also inspired by Novgorodtsev's lectures in the Law Faculty at Moscow University.[79] Berdiaev began to contribute regularly to *Voprosy filosofii* in 1902. His major programmatic article of 1904, "On the New Russian Idealism," names several of the Psychological Society's outstanding philosophers — Chicherin, Solov'ëv, A. A. Kozlov, Lopatin, and S. N. Trubetskoi — as sources of the idealist *Weltan-*

schauungen he and his former Marxist colleagues had come to embrace.[80] They could look to the Psychological Society not only for theoretical philosophy, but also for the reconstruction of liberal social philosophy on idealist principles, a project that, as Andrzej Walicki has shown in detail, engaged Chicherin, Solov'ëv, and Novgorodtsev in particular.[81]

As it turned out, the collective authorship of *Problems of Idealism* reflected the social history of the leadership of the Liberation Movement remarkably well. The zemstvo constitutionalists were represented by S. N. Trubetskoi, E. N. Trubetskoi, S. F. Ol'denburg, and Zhukovskii. The other two zemtsy associated with the *Problemy* project were Vernadskii and Kotliarevskii. The new liberals were represented by the four former Marxists (Struve, Berdiaev, Bulgakov, and Frank), all contributors. Close to them in background and outlook was Kistiakovskii, another contributor. Novgorodtsev, editor of the volume, was the professor-intermediary between the two groups. Most of these figures (including Vernadskii and Kotliarevskii) took part in the important liberationist conference held abroad at Schaffhausen, Switzerland, in July 1903.[82] Organized by Zhukovskii, the conference planned both the Union of Liberation (formally established in St. Petersburg in January 1904) and the Union of Zemstvo Constitutionalists (formally established in Moscow in November 1903). Most members of the *Problemy* project continued to exercise significant political influence in the Liberation Movement after their meeting at Schaffhausen (for details, see the biographical notes on the contributors at the end of this book).[83]

P. B. STRUVE, P. I. NOVGORODTSEV, AND NEO-IDEALISM

Among the former Marxists, Struve's new philosophical ideas were the closest to neo-idealism as developed by such Psychological Society philosophers as Lopatin, the Trubetskois, Novgorodtsev, and Kotliarevskii — even though he would not become a member of the society unti 1912.[84] Struve was the first of the Marxists to make the transition from positivism to idealism, a process completed by autumn 1900, in the long introduction he wrote to Berdiaev's book *Subjectivism and Individualism in Social Philosophy: A Critical Study of N. K. Mikhailovskii.* His formulations there already have much in common with neo-idealism in the Psychological Society, which was distinctive (1) in its broadly theistic or ontological direction (in contrast to the purely epistemological, phenomenalist, and axiological currents common in neo-Kantianism), and (2) in its conviction that the fullness or plenitude of being (the absolute) is transcendent and cannot be realized in space and time, that is, in the natural and historical world. The common point of departure for many idealist currents in Russia, including those represented in *Problems of*

Idealism, was ethical idealism: the claim that the irreducibility of ethical ideals to empirical reality gave the individual a certain autonomy relative to the natural and social environment. From autonomy, Psychological Society neo-idealists drew ontological conclusions about the self, to the effect that person-hood was metaphysical in nature. Lopatin's moral philosophy, for example, has been characterized as follows: "This conviction in the ontological signifi-cance of ethics flows like a red thread through all of Lopatin's statements on ethical questions."[85] Lopatin and his colleagues stressed the ontological im-plications not only of morality, but also of the unity of consciousness as the transcendental condition of experience.[86] For them, these ontological implica-tions also entailed a belief in the *transcendence* of absolute being. This convic-tion helped make neo-idealism in the Psychological Society resistant to the utopianization (the "immanentization" of the absolute) that was not uncom-mon for other idealist currents in the Russian Silver Age, including those that Berdiaev and to some extent Bulgakov represented soon after the appearance of *Problems of Idealism.*

In his introduction (written in September—October 1900) to Berdiaev's book, Struve was most concerned with the problem of objectivity in ethics. Positivists seek to derive morality, like everything else, from empirical criteria. The solutions they propose (such as eudaemonism) strike him as inadequate because they deny the presence of duty, on which moral autonomy rests. Positivism must reject the authenticity of duty, or consciousness of moral obligation, because to do otherwise would violate positivist rules for what is real. Positivist prohibitions notwithstanding, moral experience persists. Scien-tific ethics wishes away this central aspect of human identity. "To reject the moral problem means in essence to defy the immediate consciousness of every person," as Struve puts it.[87] But if morality cannot be justified empirically, in what does its objectivity consist? If our sense of moral obligation is not reduc-ible to naturalistic explanation, how is it authentic or real? What does the reality of duty as such entail? In a famous passage, Struve writes: "The com-pulsive presence in every normal human consciousness of the moral problem is beyond doubt, as is the impossibility of an empirical solution to it. Acknowl-edging the impossibility of such a solution, we at once recognize the objectivity of ethics as a problem, and, accordingly, come to the metaphysical postulate of a moral world-order, independent of subjective consciousness."[88]

For Struve, the irreducibility of moral consciousness to empirical experi-ence, the autonomy of "ought" relative to "is," postulates a higher level of being than natural existence, a trans-phenomenal or supernatural ontological reality that grounds the objectivity of values. Conscience is, in short, the voice of God. Either duty is a naturalistically explicable psychological illusion, or it is real, and thus capable of determining the will in violation of natural causation. "Freedom is the capacity to act, without being determined by anything external, foreign, or other; it is independence from the uninterrupted causal chain, and only substance possesses this capacity."[89] In this way, from duty and free will, Struve infers the substantiality of the person, a main tenet of ontological neo-idealism in the Psychological Society. Lopatin had formulated it in nearly identical terms, in the second volume of his *Positive Tasks of Philosophy*.[90] Lopatin was influenced, in turn, by Rudolf Hermann Lotze, whose defense of personal substantiality Struve now considers "metaphysically incontrovertible."[91]

Novgorodtsev took notice of Struve's evolution toward neo-idealism. In the autumn of 1901, in the midst of his work with Struve on *Problems of Idealism*, Novgorodtsev published one of his own studies, *Kant and Hegel in Their Theories of Law and the State*. There he praised Struve's essay:

> It is impossible not to welcome this return to the traditions of idealist philosophy. The author expresses one of the most profound needs of our time, abandoning the narrow limits of positivism all the more when he speaks about the necessity of "metaphysics as a theory of the transcendent, i.e., of that which is not given in experience and cannot be revealed by it." For us it is especially interesting to note that Mr. Struve comes to this requirement on the ground of a strict demarcation of the limits of science and a clear posing of the moral problem.[92]

Clearly, if similarity in philosophical views was any indication, there were solid grounds for cooperation between Struve and the Psychological Society.

No doubt of this was left when, on the basis of the neo-idealist philosophy he had just advanced in his introduction to Berdiaev's book, "Struve constructed a theory of liberalism, outlined most fully in a marvelous essay called 'What Is True Nationalism?' "[93] The essay Professor Pipes celebrates appeared (pseudonymously) in the Psychological Society's journal in the autumn of 1901,[94] at the same time as Novgorodtsev's book on Kant and Hegel and at the height of preparations for *Osvobozhdenie* and *Problems of Idealism*. For Struve, liberalism is the defense of the absolute value of the person, or of personhood. For him, this value is absolute by virtue of the metaphysical nature of the self as substance. From this it follows that individual self-determination ought to be the moral foundation of every social and political order.[95] This principle of the autonomy of the individual gained increasing acceptance in political theory, Struve observes, after Kant made it the cornerstone of ethics.[96] The guarantee of individual rights is a necessary condition of the fullest realization of personhood. "The idea and practice of such rights, in our view, reveal all the deep philosophical meaning and all the enormous practical significance of the remarkable doctrine of natural law, lying at the basis of all *true liberalism.*" Natural law is absolute, "rooted in the ethical concept of the person and its self-realization, and serving as the measure of all positive law."[97] True nationalism and true liberalism are, for Struve, identical concepts: "In historical development the absolute, formal principle of ethics has become clear to us — freedom, or the autonomy of the person. . . . Liberalism in its pure form, i.e., as the recognition of the inalienable rights of the person . . . is also the only form of true nationalism."[98]

By 1901 the philosophical similarities between Struve and Novgorodtsev were quite striking. Parts of Novgorodtsev's book on Kant and Hegel were first published in *Voprosy filosofii i psikhologii.* One essay, "Kant's Theory of Law and the State," appeared in the issue immediately preceding Struve's "What Is True Nationalism?"[99] Novgorodtsev's essay summarized the main thrust of his book, the philosophical substantiation of the revival of natural law in Russia. For Novgorodtsev, a specifically Kantian neo-idealism offered the best defense of the autonomy of natural law against positivist and historicist reductionism. This autonomy resided in moral consciousness, in Kantian practical reason: respect for natural law was a moral obligation or categorical imperative. The source of positive law was the state; the source of natural law was moral consciousness, given a priori. The force behind positive law was the police; the force behind natural law was duty. Natural law provided a normative framework for the evaluation of existing positive law; it served as an ideal toward which the real ought to constantly strive.[100] In this, natural law was inherently progressive, a conclusion Novgorodtsev stressed.[101] The idea of natural law with changing content, made popular by Rudolf Stammler, was a direct consequence of Kant's ethical formalism: "As an expression of infinite moral aspirations, this idea is not satisfied by any given content or claim to perfection, but constantly strives toward the higher and better." The essence of natural law was its critical spirit. "It is a challenge to improvement and reform in the name of moral ends."[102] In this way, for both Novgorodtsev and Struve, natural law was the nexus between ethical idealism and Russian liberalism.

In *Kant and Hegel in Their Theories of Law and the State,* Novgorodtsev does not explicitly draw the ontological conclusion that the person as a bearer of natural rights is substantial, as Struve does in his writings at this time. In his introduction to Berdiaev's book, for example, Struve states that the principle of the equality of persons as ends-in-themselves rests ultimately on the substantiality of the human spirit.[103] Novgorodtsev's relative silence on metaphysical questions prompted a call for clarification from one of his Psychological Society colleagues, Evgenii Trubetskoi. In a review of Novgorodtsev's book, Trubetskoi suggested that "in his relation to metaphysics a wavering is sensed between fear and attraction. Apparently the issue here is a point of view still not fully formed and in the process of development."[104] Novgorodtsev took up the challenge. In responding to another review of his book, by Leon Petrażycki, Novgorodtsev wrote that "affirmation of the contingency [*uslovnost'*] of empirical knowledge means for me also the admission of free, creative, uncaused being."[105]

Novgorodtsev was the most consistent and profound Kantian philosopher in the Psychological Society, and unlike Lopatin, the Trubetskois, and Kotliarevskii, he did not hesitate to acknowledge his debt to Kant. Moreover, he found no incompatibility in principle between the German philosopher and the ontological direction characteristic of Russian philosophical and religious thought. This enables the Russian historian of philosophy A. V. Sobolev to write, "for Novgorodtsev the person is the ontological center, the spindle of light rays with the help of which it is alone possible to illuminate problems of being and knowledge."[106] True, Novgorodtsev's debt to Kantian theory of knowledge and ethics is most evident in his earlier work, while the influence of Russian Orthodox thought becomes explicit later, in the midst of revolution, civil war, and emigration. Yet, according to his student I. A. Il'in (1883–1954), "Pavel Ivanovich did not 'become' in his last years a religious man, he always was one. The wise depths of Russian Orthodoxy, revealed to him in years of strife and suffering, imparted not the first, but a new and, I believe, final form of his religiosity."[107] The inevitable consequence of his synthesis of Kant and Russian ontologism was a conviction in the *transcendence* of the fullness of being. He concisely formulated this liberal principle, which had always guided his thought, in one of his last essays, "The Essence of Russian Orthodox Consciousness," where he wrote, "The Kingdom of God cannot be constructed within the order of earthly activity, but nonetheless all earthly life must be infused with the thought of this anticipated Kingdom."[108] The Russian theologian G. V. Florovskii, who greatly admired Novgorodtsev, suggests that he proceeds here not only from Orthodox consciousness, but also from Kantian philosophy of history.[109] This synthesis of Kantianism and Russian religious philosophy was also highly characteristic of Struve's thought after 1900.

Another indication of Struve's intellectual proximity to neo-idealism was his new understanding of Solov'ëv, the most visible member of the Psychological Society. Struve dedicated his essay on "true nationalism" to Solov'ëv, reversing his earlier positivist contempt for Russia's greatest religious philosopher. Struve's hostility is obvious in a shrill article he published on Solov'ëv in 1897, "A Philosophy of the Ideal Good or an Apologia of Real Evil?" When

Struve reprinted this review in his collection *Na raznye temy* (*On Various Themes*) in 1902, he removed the passages that now seemed "unjust," and was forced to explain, "at that time I still stood on the ground of critical positivism, but now I profess metaphysical idealism and, therefore, have become much closer to Solov'ëv than before."[110] In 1900 he published a generally laudatory obituary of Solov'ëv, in which he claimed that the philosopher's greatness rests not so much on his speculative and theoretical works as on his series of publicistic articles devoted to the critique of Slavophile nationalistic isolation of Russia from European culture.[111] First published between 1883 and 1891, these articles were later collected in two volumes under the title, *The National Question in Russia.*[112] By dedicating his 1901 *Voprosy filosofii* essay to Solov'ëv, Struve hoped to associate his own conception of "true nationalism" with the ideas Solov'ëv developed in *The National Question.*[113]

At the beginning of 1901, Novgorodtsev published an essay that directly addressed Solov'ëv's contributions to the intellectual defense of Russian liberalism. The issue of *Voprosy filosofii* in which it appeared was dedicated to Solov'ëv, who had died on 31 July 1900. Novgorodtsev's article "The Idea of Law in Vl. S. Solov'ëv's Philosophy" argued that the idea of law was precious to Solov'ëv and lay at the basis of his moral and social philosophy. "The role of law in human life appeared to him first of all in the light of its higher ideal meaning. To serve the ends of moral progress, to help the moral principle take hold among people—here was the higher task of law that Solov'ëv emphasized."[114] Solov'ëv's defense of law, against Slavophile and Tolstoian efforts to denigrate it, could help overcome the contemporary crisis in legal consciousness that Novgorodtsev diagnosed and inspire the neo-idealist development of Russian liberalism. *Opravdanie dobra* (*Justification of the Good,* 1897), Solov'ëv's famous treatise on ethics, had done jurisprudence a great service in vindicating respect for and trust in the idea of law.[115] Like Struve, Novgorodtsev extolled Solov'ëv's censure, in *The National Question in Russia,* of national egoism and its Slavophile roots, as well as his refutation of the "most fantastic of Slavophile fantasies," that for the Russian people political rights are neither important nor needed.[116] In contrast to the Slavophiles, Solov'ëv's positive ideal, for the foreseeable future, was the *Rechtsstaat,* or law-governed state (*pravovoe gosudarstvo*), his hopes for the ultimate triumph of theocracy notwithstanding.[117] Solov'ëv, Novgorodtsev stressed, was a progressive, liberal westernizer.

FREEDOM OF CONSCIENCE

Solov'ëv was, no doubt, one of the main influences under which Struve arrived at his initial conception of *Problems of Idealism:* a symposium defending freedom of conscience.[118] In Tver Struve took note of a speech delivered in

September 1901 by Mikhail A. Stakhovich (1861–1923), marshall of the nobility of Orel province, a Beseda member, and close acquaintance of Lev
Tolstoy. Stakhovich, addressing a conference in Orel on missionary work,
spoke of the need for the church to defend freedom of conscience against
intrusion by the state — in sharp contrast to Tolstoy's excommunication by the
Holy Synod the preceding February. Struve wrote Stakhovich thanking him
for his "splendid and courageous speech," which he learned of through the
newspapers. Struve's letter was intended for circulation among the zemtsy, to
further prepare the ground for cooperation in working toward a liberal Russia: "You have again demonstrated by this that you belong to people who
understand that high social status obliges one not to flatter [the authorities],
but to speak the truth. With joy I welcome in you a talented spokesman of the
best intentions of the Russian nobility." Struve then sent to Novgorodtsev in
Moscow a plan for a collection of thirteen articles devoted to freedom of
conscience and its importance in idealist philosophy, liberalism, and philosophy of law. The authors he suggested included himself, Novgorodtsev, S. N.
Trubetskoi, E. N. Trubetskoi, K. K. Arsen'ev, M. A. Reisner, V. M. Hessen,
R. Iu. Vipper, S. F. Ol'denburg, and even Adolph von Harnack, the famous
German historian of Christian dogma.[119] The former Marxists (except Struve
himself) were conspicuous by their absence at this stage of the project.

Struve's enthusiastic response to Stakhovich makes clear that *Problems of
Idealism* was designed, among other things, to raise the level of political consciousness in the zemstvo milieu. Stakhovich was a prominent representative
of the "neo-Slavophile" current in the zemstvo movement. In his Orel speech
he appealed not only to the heritage of the Slavophiles (A. S. Khomiakov, Iu. F.
Samarin, I. V. Kireevskii), but also to the memory of Solov'ëv.[120] This might
seem an untenable combination in view of Solov'ëv's criticism of Slavophilism
in *The National Question in Russia*. Solov'ëv's attack, however, was directed
primarily (although by no means exclusively) at the nationalistic and Panslav-
ist interpretation of Slavophilism among its epigones, while the classic Slavophiles (followed in this respect by Ivan Aksakov) championed freedom of
conscience and expression, as did Solov'ëv. The label "neo-Slavophile" or
"Slavophile" did not imply that the zemtsy to whom it was applied were
nationalists or Panslavists, only that they were distinguished by their respect
for religion from the constitutionalists in the zemstvo movement, most of
whom were rather positivistic in their general outlook.[121] The Stakhovich
speech convinced Struve that in freedom of conscience he had an excellent
platform by which he could hope to bring to the side of constitutional reform
conservative zemstvo elements (such as those represented in the letter "from
zemstvo deputies" that he printed in the second number of *Osvobozhdenie*).

Struve apparently thought that the religious outlook of the "Slavophile" zemtsy, once tapped and made theoretically explicit, might become a major source of Russian liberalism. His approach was not merely tactical: he recognized that freedom of conscience had been very important in the development of liberalism in Europe and America and thought it was crucial to Russian liberalism. He dwelled on this conclusion in his article "What Is True Nationalism?" There he traces the idea of the inalienable rights of man to the sixteenth and seventeenth centuries, in the proliferation of sects following the Reformation and the consequent growth of religious toleration, freedom of conscience, and separation of church and state. Struve points in particular to the English Independents and Roger Williams, who for the first time established a government — in Providence, Rhode Island (1636) — on the general principle of toleration and freedom of conscience. Struve informs us of his source: Novgorodtsev, who in his course "The History of the Philosophy of Law" gives an "extraordinarily clear and elegant exposition of this important moment in the development of man's legal consciousness."[122]

Struve went on to explain in "What Is True Nationalism?" that his historical survey revealed the inaccuracy of the doctrine, "very popular in Russian society," that liberalism arose in defense of the political and material interests of the bourgeoisie (of course, Struve had contributed more than anyone to the popularity of this doctrine, Marxism). Instead, liberalism grew from the demands of religious consciousness. "The first word of liberalism was freedom of conscience. And this ought to be well known and firmly remembered in any country where liberalism has not yet said one word."[123] In its ideal origins and aspirations, liberalism transcends class. With this, Struve may well have hoped to convince the zemtsy that he had overcome the "progressive class" point of view of his Marxist past. Even his association with the Psychological Society, home to a number of zemstvo liberals, benefited him in this respect.

In defending freedom of conscience as a basic premise of liberalism Struve proceeded from intellectual conviction, but in enlisting the late Slavophile Aksakov in support of his views — as he did at some length in "What Is True Nationalism?" — he seems to have acted mostly out of political expediency in order to woo "Slavophile" zemtsy, among whom Aksakov enjoyed popularity. Aksakov was no liberal,[124] but he could be selectively appropriated for liberalism. This was done not only by Struve but also by S. N. Trubetskoi and Novgorodtsev. Sergei Trubetskoi lauded Aksakov's defense of freedom of conscience and the need for church autonomy, speaking in the same breath of Aksakov and Solov'ëv as the best among Russian publicists, "who exposed with such force the sores on our state church with its anti-canonical administration and absence of independent spiritual power and ecclesiastical freedom."[125] Novgorodtsev, in a long two-part article, "The State and Law," published in *Voprosy filosofii* in 1904, enlisted Aksakov for the critique of legal positivism. Novgorodtsev quotes Aksakov's words that, according to formal jurisprudence, "there is nothing in the world except the dead mechanism of the state; that everything is and should be accomplished in the name of and through the means of state power, no matter what form it takes, if only it bears the stamp of external legality; and that, finally, life itself, and consequently the life of the spirit, is one of the branches or functions of the state organism."[126] Walicki, who also quotes these lines, writes that Novgorodtsev "obviously hoped in this way to influence the right wing of the zemstvo liberals."[127] Novgorodtsev was pursuing the same end Struve had three years earlier in his "true nationalism" article, which quoted these exact words (with much else) from Aksakov. Novgorodtsev chose not to mention, as did Struve, that Aksakov's remarks were written against Chicherin's 1861 inaugural lecture at Moscow University, where Chicherin had been appointed to the chair in public law. Aksakov saw in Chicherin an extreme *gosudarstvennik*, not an uncommon perception after the inaugural lecture.[128] Interestingly enough, Struve contrasts Chicherin's étatist, Hegelian approach to law in the 1860s to his later autonomization of law on the basis of a natural-rights liberalism, best explicated in his *Filosofiia prava* (*Philosophy of Law*, 1900). "A significant change," Struve exclaims, "the result of the triumph of idealistic metaphysics over sociological and juridical positivism!"[129]

It is very likely that Struve came to (or was at least reinforced in) his appreciation of the importance of freedom of conscience under the influence of Solov'ëv and the Psychological Society. Chicherin, Sergei and Evgenii Trubetskoi, Novgorodstev, Kotliarevskii, and the Moscow University historian Vladimir I. Ger'e (Guerrier), also a prominent member of the Psychological Society,[130] had long advanced separation of church and state and freedom of conscience as axioms of liberalism. In his programmatic statement of the principles of Russian liberalism, written in 1855, Chicherin identified freedom of conscience as "the first and most sacred right of a citizen."[131] His later works remained resolute in their defense of this right. Notable in this respect is his book *Nauka i religiia* (*Science and Religion*, 1879), which extends the principle of freedom of conscience to the broader concept of the necessary autonomy of the various distinct spheres of human need, experience, and aspiration: not only church and state, or religion and politics, but also economy, science, philosophy, and art, for example.[132] This understanding of autonomy was further developed by Novgorodtsev in particular and became one of the main themes in *Problems of Idealism*.

Sergei Trubetskoi was another ardent champion of freedom of conscience. In his remarkable analysis of Russian state and society, "On the Threshold," written in February 1904, he observes despairingly how, in the course of Russian history, "the Orthodox Church becomes the church of bureaucratic caesaropapism." Russian liberalism rested on reversing this historical trend. As Trubetskoi proclaimed, "an independent church and freedom of conscience — here are the demands which any law-governed state and, first of all, any state calling itself Christian, must meet."[133] Kotliarevskii, an astute student of religion and society, was also convinced that liberalism grew from the demands of religious consciousness and that a liberal civic culture had its foundations in free spiritual life. Like Struve and Novgorodtsev, he pointed to the example of American religious history, with its principle of expanding toleration and "recognized diverse forms and symbols under which is felt a unity of content."[134]

The defense of freedom of conscience by the Psychological Society professors was a response not only to the illiberal effects of the state-dominated church in Russia, but also to the utopianism of their colleague, Solov'ëv.[135] In the middle period of his creativity (i.e., from the early 1880s to the early 1890s), Solov'ëv was preoccupied with a grant project for the unification of Eastern and Western Christianity in a world theocracy under the spiritual authority of the pope and the imperial authority of the Russian tsar, all in preparation for the advent of the Kingdom of God on earth. In this utopia of "free theocracy," Solov'ëv's Psychological Society colleagues could see the mirror image of the subordination of church to state characteristic of modern Russian history. They came to a clear appreciation that theocracy and the "state church" in Russia (as the Trubetskois referred to it) were illiberal in the same way: both infringed the necessary autonomy of church and state. As Evgenii Trubetskoi later put it, Solov'ëv's theocratic project would have violated the "most precious of all freedoms — freedom of conscience."[136] In explication of the parallel the Psychological Society contributed to a considerable literature on church history and church-state relations.[137]

From the early 1880s, Solov'ëv himself sharply criticized the subordination of church to state in Russian history[138] and religious intolerance within the Russian Empire.[139] Facing the weakness of the Russian church, he placed his theocratic hopes on Roman Catholicism. His plan for a world theocracy evoked very little sympathy among contemporaries.[140] Therefore, Solov'ëv admirers welcomed this abandonment, beginning in the early 1890s, of "free theocracy" as anything other than a remote ideal, "stripped of its millenarian features and reduced to something like a Kantian 'regulative idea' in ethics," as Walicki characterizes the transformation.[141] Solov'ëv began to dismantle his utopian project under the impact of the great famine, which left no doubt of the gap between Russian reality and the theocratic ideal.[142] In conversations

with friends at the time, "he openly spoke of his disappointment in the contemporary state order and of the necessity for representative, constitutional
institutions," Evgenii Trubetskoi recalls. "In these circumstances Solov'ëv very
soon faced the necessity of choosing between theocracy and constitution."[143]
He expressed his disillusionment in a major public lecture, "On the Reasons
for the Collapse of the Medieval Worldview," delivered before the Psychological Society on 19 October 1891.[144] The speech became a cause célèbre because
the ultra-conservative newspaper *Moskovskie vedomosti* made a scandal of
it.[145] The lecture could be seen as an important step forward: if ten years
earlier Solov'ëv had highlighted the baneful effects of state domination of the
church, now he seemed to come closer to recognizing that theocracy was the
flip side of the coin. What mattered was the principle of separation of church
and state, the defense of the autonomous rights of the sacred and secular
realms that medieval theocracy and the "state church" in Russia alike denied
(true, the lecture was less a clear defense of this principle itself than a valuation
of secular work from the perspective of Christian progress). The example of
Solov'ëv's dramatic intellectual evolution reinforced his Psychological Society
colleagues in their conviction that freedom of conscience was a fundamental
premise of liberalism.

Although Solov'ëv appears never to have abandoned the theocratic ideal
altogether,[146] further talk of its possible realization took a distant second place
to the immediate task at hand—real progress. This was the message behind
"On the Reasons for the Collapse of the Medieval Worldview": the medieval
worldview was not progressive, the modern one is.[147] Modernity is progressive
in its recognition of the autonomy and value of secular activity. In this it is truer
to the spirit of Christianity than medievalism, with its "monstrous doctrine"
that the only path to salvation is faith in church dogma.[148] Godmanhood, the
realization of humanity's divine vocation, cannot be achieved without the
active participation of man. "For it is clear," Solov'ëv writes, "that the spiritual
rebirth of humanity cannot take place apart from humanity itself. It cannot be
only an external fact; it is a *deed* with which we are charged, a *task* which we
must solve."[149] Unbelievers who work contribute to Christian progress no less
than believers, sometimes much more so, as modern times show. If Christians
in name only ("nominal Christians") betray the spirit of Christ, then why
should it be denied that people who work, although not necessarily in Christ's
name, nonetheless serve his purposes?[150] Solov'ëv's new emphasis on modernity, progress, and secular work was a necessary first step toward reversing the
long-held association of idealism with obscurantism in social philosophy, an
association only reinforced, after all, by the enthusiasm Russia's most visible idealist philosopher had shown for theocracy. The de-utopianization of

Solov'ëv's thought cleared the way for the Psychological Society to take up a forthright idealist defense of liberalism.

Solov'ëv's lecture heralded a new conception of liberal progress. The paper itself, while widely known, was not published until ten years later, in the same issue of *Voprosy filosofii* as Novgorodtsev's article (discussed above) on Solov'ëv's significance for Russian liberalism. Novgorodtsev interpreted the central idea of the lecture as an original and bold combination of the Christian ideal with westernizing progress. Liberal Westernizers had always stressed the value of energetic cultural work and external social forms as conditions for the free development of persons. Now Solov'ëv added the new philosophic foundation of a theistically inspired idealism.[151] This revision of the traditional (and often vague) view that positivism was the natural ally of liberalism, in favor of an idealist substantiation, set the agenda of the Psychological Society in social philosophy and was clearly reflected in *Problems of Idealism*.

The culmination of the secularization (valuing the autonomy of the secular sphere) and de-utopianization (relegating theocracy to a remote or even transcendent ideal) of Solov'ëv's thought came with the appearance in 1897 of *Justification of the Good*. The treatise produced a great impression on Russian society, requiring a second edition in 1899, raising interest in idealist philosophy and creating a favorable climate for the reception of *Problems of Idealism*. Nowhere in *Justification of the Good* does Solov'ëv invoke "free theocracy." Walicki formulates very well the significance of the volume in this respect:

> Solov'ëv now proclaimed the need for a formal separation of church and state, expressing his hostility to state-promoted religious intolerance in Russia. The cause of religious and moral progress, consisting in the Christianization of political and social life, was thereby radically divorced from the ideal of binding together the spiritual power of the church with the coercive power of the state. On the contrary: the realization of the idea of Godmanhood in history was made dependent on man's maturity, on his full moral autonomy, incompatible with any form of tutelage in the spiritual sphere.[152]

Solov'ëv had made the autonomy of the sacred and secular a central part of his liberal philosophy of progress. Clearly, *Problems of Idealism* was, from its first conception as a defense of freedom of conscience, integrally related to the top priorities of the Psychological Society.

We have seen that Struve knew Novgorodtsev's published lectures on the history of the philosophy of law. In his introduction to them, Novgorodtsev contrasts the modern concept of the Rechtsstaat to medieval theocracy.[153] The secular ideal of the Rechtsstaat is the principle of equality before the law, shown by Kant's philosophical justification to be absolute. "As in the middle ages the ultimate dream of church philosophy was the unification of all peoples under the moral authority of the church, so now in the philosophy of Kant the highest goal of history is the unification of all humanity under the rule of one law equal for all."[154] In this, Novgorodtsev expresses a certain sense of misgiving. Neither the sacred nor the secular can, if taken in isolation from the other, satisfy the full range of the demands of human nature. In an interesting twist to Solov'ëv's lecture on the collapse of the medieval worldview, Novgorodtsev writes that the modern secular state cannot successfully resist the Christian spirit that infuses modern moral consciousness. He quotes Solov'ëv's words that, "the unbelieving engines of modern progress have acted in the interests of true Christianity," and that, "social progress in recent centuries has been accomplished in the spirit of the love of man and justice, that is, in the spirit of Christ."[155] There must be a correlation of the two ideals, sacred and secular, although Novgorodtsev is quite tentative about how this might be achieved. However, his ideas unmistakably point to the insight, which he would develop in much of his later work, that without delimitation of, and equilibrium between, the spheres of church and state, the principles each represent are either compromised and diluted by cross intrusion and usurpation, or are hypostatized as one sphere looks on itself as absolute in trying to exclude the other.[156] Progress miscarries in utopianism. Freedom of conscience concisely formulated the principle of respect for the autonomy of the parts that enables the balanced and integrated development of the whole (in reference to both self and society), and that prevents utopian derailment. This principle was not limited to the archetypes of church and state, but extended to the various distinct spheres of human experience and consciousness (such as religion, politics, science, and philosophy). These spheres are legitimate in their own domain; one cannot be substituted for any of the others; they are relatively autonomous parts of a whole in which each has its own place. This was a guiding principle of neo-idealist social philosophy, forcefully advanced in the final version of *Problems of Idealism*.

PROGRESSIVE IDEALISM

The connection that Solov'ëv had come to stress, and that Novgorodtsev amplified further, between autonomy and liberal progress was the key link between *Problems of Idealism*'s initial focus, as Struve conceived it, on freedom of conscience and the broader approach the symposium took in its published version. There, freedom of conscience was subsumed under the more general thesis that idealism offered a far better defense of liberal progress than positivism could. Although the expansion of the project's scope had its accidental moments as the list of contributors came to include Struve's former

Marxist colleagues,[157] there was clear logic in it as well. Positivism was in its own way a denial of freedom of conscience in its claim that what is positively given in sense data is the only measure of reality and in its tendency to discount other aspects of human experience and consciousness. Struve's expression for official ideology — "state positivism" — captured the similarity.[158] The initial tight focus on freedom of conscience sought to tap the amorphous religious outlook of the "Slavophile" zemtsy. The final version still fit Struve's original premise that the religiosity of the conservative zemtsy was potentially constitutional, but in addition the broader approach could hope to convince zemstvo liberals more generally, most of whom probably subscribed to a "soft" positivism, that neo-idealism was a better articulation of their liberal convictions. The original policy of the osvobozhdentsy to pin their hopes on the zemstvo milieu was based on a judgment that that environment offered the most reliable basis for Russian liberalism by virtue of social background and civic experience. *Problems of Idealism,* by theoretically substantiating the liberal values that (it was assumed) the zemsty held by life experience, might inspire them to more resolute action in working for a liberal Russia. Struve and Novgorodtsev wanted the best of both worlds for Russian liberalism: zemstvo civic background and neo-idealist theoretical backing.

One of the Moscow Psychological Society's contributions to Russian social thought — a contribution *Problems of Idealism* publicized — was to help reverse the traditional association of positivism with liberalism and of idealist and religious philosophy with reaction. The neo-idealist program in the first stages of the Liberation Movement, in seeking to put the social strengths of zemstvo liberalism on new theoretical foundations, adds another element to the distinction between the old and new Russian liberalism. New liberalism can thus refer not only to the emergence of social support beyond the zemstvo, for example, within the urban intelligentsia (in the broad sense), but also to the replacement of positivism by *neo*-idealism as the theoretical justification of liberalism. Often the social and theoretical dimensions did not coincide: Miliukov and E. D. Kuskova, for example, were new liberals by social background but old liberals theoretically, in their positivism. From the opposite end of the political spectrum, Chicherin, the grand old man of zemstvo liberalism, was rather a new liberal in the theoretical sense.[159] The Psychological Society was home to other traditional zemstvo liberals who were new philosophical idealists, including the brothers Trubetskoi, Kotliarevskii, and (in some respects) Vernadskii.[160] In the case of the four former Marxists, the new social and theoretical sources of liberalism did coincide, as they did for Novgorodtsev.

Problems of Idealism took up no mean task in challenging the received opinion that idealism was intellectually and politically retrograde. Idealism was perceived as dangerous to science, enlightenment, and social progress, while positivism was thought to be their natural champion, or at least that is how most *intelligenty,* who set the standards for progressive opinion, represented things. Against the charge that idealism was adverse to the spirit of scientific inquiry and a mask for political and intellectual obscurantism, the philosophers could (and did) invoke the authority of Vernadskii, who wrote in his 1902 companion article to *Problems of Idealism:* "Today, in an epoch of the extraordinary flowering of scientific thought, the close and deep connection of science with other currents in the spiritual life of humanity is not infrequently forgotten. . . . Sometimes it is heard that . . . the creative and vital role of philosophy for humanity has ended and in the future must be replaced by science. But such an opinion . . . can hardly withstand the test of science itself."[161] *Problems of Idealism* stressed throughout that idealism was intrinsically progressive. Iu. Aikhenval'd, in a fine contemporary review, thought this was the volume's main message. He wrote that the majority of the Russian reading public is accustomed to think

> that those freedom-loving aspirations, the attractive and bright imprint of which lies on nearly every page of our collection, have their only and necessary basis in a completely different worldview—the positivistic-mechanical. The acknowledged heralds and champions of free citizenship [*grazhdanstvennost'*] turn out to be advocates of ethical-religious views that are ordinarily professed by representatives of a rather different social camp. And in this respect *Problems of Idealism* can provide a great educational service in dispelling the dominant prejudice among us that the spiritualist worldview is incompatible with the cherished precepts of social liberalism.[162]

The public reception of neo-idealism was a paramount concern for its representatives active in the Liberation Movement, the very purpose of which was to bring public opinion to bear against the autocracy. They feared that positivist intelligenty might caricature idealism as a reactionary doctrine. This concern may well have been heightened by the Liberation Movement's initial reliance on the zemstvo milieu, since the democratic intelligentsia saw zemstvo liberalism as a defense of gentry interests, inimical to genuine progress for the narod. What is certain is that neo-idealists went to even greater lengths to stress their progressive social views because the former Marxists in the group were seen by the left as traitors. "The idealism of our days would hardly have brought against itself such polemics," Novgorodtsev wrote in 1904, "if among its proponents were not persons who had left Marxism."[163] This helps account for the publicity surrounding the appearance of *Problems of Idealism.*

Aikhenval'd saw it the same way. The volume attracted the attention it did not so much because of its philosophical ideas, which had long been advanced by the Psychological Society, as because of the previous reputations of some of its contributors, "who until now were known for their work in other fields of theory and practice and who were most often attached to active Marxism — these very names concentrate around themselves a new and broad contingent of readers."[164]

At a meeting of the Psychological Society on 11 May 1902,[165] Novgorodtsev proposed that *Problems of Idealism* be published in its series, "Editions of the Psychological Society." The proposal was accepted. As a condition of publication, Lopatin provided a one-paragraph opening statement to the volume, indicating that it expressed the views of only one group of society members, but deserved the support of the society as a whole in view of its outstanding interest. Novgorodtsev, promoting the symposium two days before its actual appearance, delivered a public lecture, "On the Question of the Revival of Natural Law," before a well-attended meeting of the society.[166] The lecture summarized his own *Problemy* essay and directed attention to what he thought was the main service of the collection, the neo-idealist defense of liberalism. The volume saw light of day on 16 November 1902 in a solid printing of 3,000 copies, and was sold out in a year.[167] "*Problems of Idealism* was a challenging, self-confident manifesto of the neo-idealist revival in Russian thought," Waliciki writes,[168] a revival Psychological Society philosophers had advanced for more than a decade and that they would continue to champion as offering a powerful theory of the main principles of liberalism: personhood, autonomy, law, and progress.

Problems of Idealism: *Key Ideas*

ETHICAL IDEALISM AND THE IRREDUCIBILITY OF THE SELF

Ethical idealism, the claim that ethical ideals do not derive from the empirical world, that "what ought to be" is not reducible to "what is," was the common point of departure for the contributors to *Problems of Idealism*. From this initial premise, Russian idealism pursued different directions and took on diverse forms. This process of differentiation is already evident in *Problems of Idealism,* but for the moment it was held in check by the common idealist defense of liberalism and critique of positivism. Later, some currents represented in the 1902 symposium diverged from the neo-idealist defense of liberalism (Berdiaev and to some extent Bulgakov), while others did not pursue that defense to its ontological depths, as did the Psychological Society professors.

Problems of Idealism strove to convey the importance, not only for the critique of positivism but for human self-understanding, of the distinctiveness of moral experience. The contributors pointed to the glaring contradiction between the positivist criterion of reality — empirical experience — and the persistent human predilection for moral evaluation of it. They were struck by the very presence of a category such as "what ought to be" when the empirical world speaks to us only of "what is," of positive data and facts, not of ideals and standards. The positivist conception of reality discounts these ideals, central to human identity. Russian idealists differed over their origin, but agreed it was not empirical. The recognition of moral obligation (duty) was already something startling; the freedom to act on it was nothing short of miraculous. The capacity of the categorical imperative to determine the will, the capacity to act as one ought, in opposition to impulse, upheld the autonomy of the self against reduction to naturalistic explanation. In all this, the contributors to the symposium drew heavily on Kant's moral philosophy, even where they did not accept his system as a whole. An important intermediary between Kant and *Problems of Idealism* was Solov'ëv's major treatise on ethics, *Justification of the Good.*[169]

Ethical idealism, in short, took the distinctiveness of moral experience as refutation of the positivist conception of reality and as testimony to the irreducibility of the self to the empirical world. This gave the person a special dignity, the defense of which was liberalism. As Novgorodtsev affirmed in 1904,

> Contemporary idealist philosophy can well indicate that in its practical ideals it continuously emphasizes and advances the principle of the person, its absolute dignity, its natural and inalienable rights. For all the various shades dividing even idealists themselves, it is that point in relation to which they are in full agreement. But in the end do not all living and progressive movements of Russian thought meet on this point?[170]

Russian idealists of all shades did concur on the dignity of the self, but not all thought that meant substantiality.[171] Among the *Problemy* authors known for their contributions to Russian philosophy,[172] Frank did not at this point, and Kistiakovskii never would, draw ontological conclusions from the irreducibility of the self to empirical experience.[173] The rest did.

Ethical idealism marked the culmination of an important stage in the intellectual evolution of the four former Marxists. Henceforth Struve's general philosophical outlook changed little, while Berdiaev, Bulgakov, and Frank continued to work toward their later philosophical and theological conceptions. But the Kantian-inspired recovery of ethical ideals that the Marxists

undertook already in their revisionist period received its highest expression on
the pages of *Problems of Idealism.* "Scientific socialism" was no doubt the
most reductive form of positivism in Russia, as expounded by G. V. Plekhanov.
The "necessitarian" Marxism of the Second International that Plekhanov embraced was based in large part on the interpretation of Hegel that Engels
advanced in his *Anti-Dühring.*[174] To this, Plekhanov added his own great
admiration of Hegel's fatalistic side. A certain similarity does suggest itself
between Hegelian identity, the idea that in *Sittlichkeit,* "there is no gap between what ought to be and what is, between *Sollen* and *Sein,*" as Charles
Taylor puts it,[175] and the deterministic contention of orthodox Marxism that
historical necessity, operating on its own without inspired human agency, will
bring about the Golden Age.[176] The association of Hegel with "scientific socialism" helps explain why, in both Germany and Russia, revisionist attempts
to invigorate Marxism with ethical ideals sought to recover the Kantian distinction between *das Sein* and *das Sollen.*[177] In this way the legal Marxists
contributed to the critique of positivism, to the autonomization of ideals and
values, even before their revisionism precipitated their full conversion "from
Marxism to idealism," as Bulgakov immortalized the whole development.[178]

For the Marxists, ethical idealism thus began with a recovery of the ideals
that "scientific socialism" castigated as "utopian" in the socialist tendencies it
opposed (in Russia, populism). In Struve, this critical rehabilitation of utopianism, as he put it,[179] remained critical (as it did for Frank), but in Berdiaev
and Bulgakov the process derailed soon after the appearance of *Problems of
Idealism.* They quickly embraced post-Kantian, absolute forms of idealism
that conflated the absolute and the relative, the ideal and the real.[180] Both
tended to revert to, or had not overcome in the first place, the utopian vision of
the total revolutionary transformation of society (the "leap to the kingdom of
freedom") that characterized orthodox Marxism ("scientific socialism," its
own protestations notwithstanding, was, of course, far more utopian than
socialists who took matters into their own hands and worked toward the
gradual realization of socialism through reform). Their new utopianism was
explicitly millenarian and chiliastic, while Marxist utopianism can be seen as a
secular transposition of eschatological impulses under the guise of science.
Bulgakov and Berdiaev themselves labeled such positivist conflations of science with religious and metaphysical hopes as "contraband,"[181] apparently
not realizing that the logic of their criticism required that the ideal of salvation
be strictly that, a transcendent ideal.[182] By contrast, the "core" Psychological
Society neo-idealists were critical of utopianism as such, stressing its incompatibility with transcendence.

Struve's contribution to *Problems of Idealism,* "Toward Characterization of

Our Philosophical Development," is an overview and self-evaluation of his evolution from Marxism to idealism. He presents the results of that evolution in a succinct statement of what he calls the basic error of positivism.[183] Man conceives all that is conceivable in two basic forms, "what is" and "what ought to be." Causation and necessity completely govern the realm of "what is." In it there is no room for freedom or creativity. "The present is entirely determined by the past, and the future by the present (and thus by the past). In this way, everything is determined or predetermined" (78/147). Scientific understanding reduces one thing to another, as its cause, and examines the mode of this causal dependence. "What is" and "what ought to be" are completely incomparable categories, not reducible to each other. "Meanwhile the basic idea and also the basic error of positivism consists in subordinating 'what ought to be' ('ought') to 'what is' ('is') and in deriving the first from the second." This is the monstrous idea of *scientific* ethics. It is rooted in idolatry before the principle of causation. "It forgets that in experience or science we discover the causation and mode of being, but that being itself [*samoe bytie*], as such, always remains for us unknown and unexplained" (79/148). It is "being itself" that makes possible duty and the freedom to act on it, or ethical idealism.

Struve's argument can be clarified by Kant's distinction between the phenomenal and noumenal. The category "what is" is the phenomenal world; "being itself, as such" is the noumenal. Therefore, the basic error of positivism is the reduction of "what ought to be" to the phenomenal world. This reduction is uncritical because positivists identify the phenomenal and noumenal, that is, they make unconscious metaphysical claims through unjustified extrapolation from empirical knowledge. Struve insists that philosophy be critical, that it not make dogmatic metaphysical claims by confusing the phenomenal and the noumenal. Noumenal being is inaccessible to scientific method (it cannot be known as phenomena are), although its presence is felt in the depths of moral consciousness. "Philosophical reflection, by its own critical approach to belief in causation, cannot but support immediate consciousness of the special nature of moral 'ought,' presupposing free or creative activity," Struve writes. From this we acquire the right to metaphysics. "Yes, metaphysics," but, Struve adds, critical, Kantian metaphysics (81–82/150). Conforming the will to duty is an autonomous act; it breaks the chain of phenomenal necessity and thus constitutes a leap of being to the noumenal level. This, Struve says in so many words, gives us the right to metaphysics, although a critical metaphysics that, while grasping the presence of noumenal reality, recognizes its unknowability.

The critical caution with which Struve approached the metaphysical conclusions he drew from the nature of moral experience is one of the ways he compared to the Psychological Society neo-idealists. Berdiaev is not so critically cautious, as is clear, for example, in the boldness of his declaration of allegiance to metaphysical idealism and spiritualism, "to which I have now finally arrived."[184] Despite the differences, which would soon become pronounced, his *Problemy* essay is an eloquent statement of ethics as the common point of departure in the idealist revival. In this, Berdiaev relies on Kant's establishment of "what ought to be" as an autonomous category, given to consciousness a priori, independent of empirical knowledge. Ethics is an autonomous discipline: it has no need of empirical science, since its principles are available before experience. Otherwise we would merely perceive the world, instead of also evaluating it. "Moral evaluation of 'what is' from the point of view of 'what ought to be' is inherent to every consciousness" (94/163).

In opposition to the Kantian dualism of "what is" and "what ought to be," positivists deny that consciousness has two separate, parallel sides. In place of violently distorting positivist reductionism, Berdiaev calls for the rehabilitation of both sides of human consciousness into an integral whole. Positivist interpretations of human behavior and motivation, such as hedonism and utilitarianism, reduce everything to an empirical criterion such as pleasure or happiness; they fail to treat morality as an autonomous force in human conduct. Ethics is its own thing, not something else, like pleasure or happiness. "Happiness itself is subject to *moral* judgment, which determines the quality of happiness, recognizing it as worthy or unworthy of our moral nature" (100/167). One ought to strive not for happiness but for moral perfection (or to deserve happiness, in Kant's words). Nothing in the empirical world approximates our a priori notion of perfection, which thus cannot be phenomenal in origin but must arise from a connection to noumenal grounds. The moral law is a link to transcendence. "It is a beacon, shining to us from infinity. . . . It is the voice of God inside man, it is given for 'this world' but it is 'not of this world' " (104/170).

Self-perfection is, for Berdiaev, the basic idea of ethics. Drawing on Wilhelm Windelband, he develops a distinction between the empirical and ideal or normal self: "*Morality is first of all the internal relation of a human being to himself, the search for and realization of his spiritual 'I,' the triumph of 'normative' consciousness in 'empirical' consciousness*" (106/171). Recognizing one's spiritual self makes possible, in turn, normative relations toward other people, based on recognition of them as persons. The higher self is affirmed in the exercise of freedom, that is, in the fulfillment of moral duty. In fact, "to be a 'person,' to be a free human being, means to be conscious of one's moral-rational nature and to distinguish one's 'normal,' ideal 'I' from the chaos of a contingent empirical cluster of facts; in itself this empirical chaos is not yet a 'person,' and the category of freedom is inapplicable to it" (133/188). Since morality consists in the internal relationship of a person to himself, Berdiaev rejects the ethical primacy of "thou" or "other." Egoism versus altruism is a false opposition; the ideal self stands above these hypostatized poles. "The relation of one human being to another is ethically derivative from the relation of a human being to himself. . . . Higher moral consciousness demands that every human being relate to every other human being not as to 'thou' . . . but as to 'I' " (111/174). This is Berdiaev's interpretation of the Kantian notion of man as an end, never merely a means, and of the equality of persons as ends-in-themselves.

For Berdiaev, the moral problem takes on a tragic character. The absolute ideal of moral perfection can never be realized in experience. The empirical self cannot fully coincide with its ideal side in historical reality. The result is an eternal challenge to infinite improvement as well as an invitation to speculation about a metaphysical resolution of the impasse. The inevitability of metaphysics has led Berdiaev to now embrace the substantiality of the spirit (spiritualism), as Struve had in the introduction he wrote to his book on Mikhailovskii. Berdiaev differentiates his own approach from Kant's, whose method is to postulate immortality and the existence of God from morality. Berdiaev thinks this is too timid, declaring, "I reject Kantian skepticism and more than the Kantians believe in the possibility of constructing metaphysics by various paths" (107n./194, n. 34). The various paths he suggests are tentative. He refers to the triumphant march of the world spirit in Hegelian metaphysics and philosophy of history, which he contends have never been refuted, although at this point he also informs us that "in certain respects I am, incidentally, closer to Fichte than to Hegel" (113–114n./194, n. 37). He often compares his views to Struve's on one question or another, assuring us that they are in basic agreement on everything, except that "my metaphysics has a somewhat different shade than the metaphysics of Leibniz and Lotze, with which Struve, apparently, especially sympathizes" (132n./197, n. 65). That examples such as these are contrivances was pointed out (with annoyance) by Aikhenval'd in his review (to which I return below).

Some of the contributors to *Problems of Idealism*, Berdiaev and Frank in particular, found that they could appropriate Nietzsche to promote their conceptions of ethical idealism.[185] Frank's essay is devoted entirely to the German thinker. It attempts to defend the autonomy of certain moral principles by developing Nietzsche's contrast between "love of one's neighbor" and "love of the distant." The first is based on the elementary feeling or instinct of compassion and the utilitarian desire for people's happiness, while the second is based on respect for "abstract moral goods" that possess internal value. Nietzsche also referred to "love of the distant" as "love of things and phantoms," where "phantoms" stand for such principles as truth, justice, beauty, honor and other "objective ideals possessing absolute and autonomous [*avtonomnyi*] moral value."[186] These ideals are autonomous because their value cannot be accounted for by extrinsic criteria such as the happiness of oneself or one's neighbor, or because, in other words, their value is self-inherent and independent of their consequences. Frank uses the term "ethical idealism" for this Nietzschean critique of positivist utilitarianism and defense of autonomy, so conceived, but this is the only sense in which Frank's position is "idealist." For him, the autonomy of "distant" moral ideals does not entail any conclusions about the irreducibility of the self. In fact, at the end of his essay, Frank writes, "this idealism remains in Nietzsche *realistic*: no matter how far the 'distant' lies from regular life and its interests, it does not fall beyond the limits of earthly, empirical life" (178/233).[187] Berdiaev agrees, but gives a different evaluation: "Nietzsche is a dreamer whose idealistic soul is poisoned by naturalism. He splendidly understands the failure of all positivist theories of morality, but he himself nonetheless remains on the ground of naturalistic positivism" (124/182).

In trying to face the problem of the origins of autonomous moral ideals, Frank falls back on positivism and utilitarianism. "There is no doubt," he writes, "that *genetically* the whole aggregate of moral feelings and principles — including 'love of phantoms' — grew from the needs of social welfare" (167/217). "Love of one's neighbor" and "love of the distant" are only different types of moral "feeling"; somehow the second type becomes autonomous after arising naturally. Most Russian neo-idealists found this type of "idealism" untenable. Frank's essay is interesting insofar as it points in the direction of the more sophisticated formulations of neo-Kantian value theory and a strictly axiological idealism (to which Kistiakovskii, for example, aspired). It is also revealing of what the ontological neo-idealists thought were the weaknesses of the purely axiological approach, such as the tendency to revert to naturalism. This tendency is quite evident in Frank's essay, as in his usage of the terms "feeling," "instinct," and "impulse," as well as in the bizarre language of "phantoms."[188] It can be argued that Frank was striving for the most earnest possible defense of autonomy, one that would avoid any ontological backing of moral ideals. Two years later, in his important essay "On Critical Idealism," he freed himself of naturalistic vestiges, maintaining that consciousness was absolute and its own explanation.[189] But this type of radical autonomy was in the end no less untenable for the ontologists, who argued that the autonomy of moral ideals was ultimately grounded in a transcendent level of being. Frank himself would later become one of the most distinguished representatives of the ontological direction in Russian idealism.

"CONTRABAND" AND THE SEARCH FOR AN INTEGRAL WORLDVIEW

In a way that reflects its beginnings as a defense of freedom of conscience, *Problems of Idealism* insists throughout on the strict delimitation of separate spheres of human experience and consciousness. It was the common concern of the contributors that morality, religion, philosophy, and positive science each be given its own autonomous space and that no one of them usurp the legitimate rights of the others. The conflation of these relatively distinct spheres, or the hypostatization of one at the expense of another, results in various forms of utopianism, from scientism to chiliasm and millenarianism. Russian neo-idealists used the term (or, when not the term, the concept) "contraband" to describe the intellectual distortion and muddling that result when elements from one area of thought (ethical or metaphysical) are smuggled into another (empirical or natural scientific). Lopatin appears to have introduced the concept in the first volume of his influential *Positive Tasks of Philosophy* (1886). He wrote there that the inevitability of metaphysical suppositions needs to be acknowledged and justified. "Why not call things by their names?" Otherwise, metaphysical ideas can figure in thought only as contraband, distorting it on an unconscious level and preventing clear and precise intellectual discourse. "Is it desirable to perpetuate such contraband of reason? . . . Every case of lack of consciousness in the scholarly sphere leads only to confusion of concepts, ambiguity, and lies."[190]

Bulgakov's essay, "Basic Problems of the Theory of Progress," opens *Problems of Idealism* with the "contraband" critique of positivism. For Bulgakov, the quest for an integral, whole worldview is inherent to humanity. Such integrity requires free expression of each of the individual elements in our intellectual and spiritual nature. "Man cannot be satisfied by exact science alone, to which positivism hoped to limit him; metaphysical and religious needs are ineradicable and have never been removed from the life of man. Precise knowledge, metaphysics, and religion must exist in a certain harmonious relation, the establishment of which always constitutes the task of philosophy."[191] Positivists deny metaphysics the right to exist, yet they cannot help asking metaphysical questions: they merely fail to do so squarely and honestly. Metaphysics thus enters into their inquiries on an unconscious level, leading to distortion and conflation. This is clear, Bulgakov shows, in sociological theories of progress based on the idea of human perfectibility (on this idea, see also A. S. Lappo-Danilevskii's essay in this volume). Such theories are, he explains, secular transpositions of religious faith (eschatology in particular) under the guise of science. The result is the "religion of progress," a strange admixture of religious themes (faith in salvation) with scientific pretension. Bulgakov identifies these transpositions as a major source of utopianism (thus anticipating subsequent western scholarship in intellectual history). The solutions positivists devise to the problem of progress are fraudulent because they use contraband, introducing under the banner of positive science elements foreign to it (17/96).

> Such conflation puts positive science in an ambiguous position and, together with that, crudely violates the rights of metaphysics and religious faith. Therefore, what is necessary first of all is careful differentiation of the various elements and problems that are conflated in the theory of progress. It is necessary to return to Caesar what is Caesar's, and to God what is God's. The correct formulation of the theory of progress must . . . delimit and, within the proper sphere, restore in their own rights science, metaphysics, and religion. (32/107).

This was a classic formulation of one of the most important principles in the neo-idealist development of Russian liberalism.

Bulgakov was not, however, very consistent in his defense of this principle. For he also proposes that the problem of progress should be approached from a "metaphysics of history." In this mood Bulgakov maintains that (1) a theory of progress presupposes that history has meaning, (2) philosophy of history constitutes a theodicy, and (3) history is a revelation of higher reason, which is simultaneously transcendent to and immanent in history (32/107). These positions are problematic from a consistently neo-idealist point of view (such as Novgorodtsev's), according to which history as a whole cannot be an object of analysis since we are participants in it and therefore lack an Archimedean perspective on it (in this sense history as a whole is noumenal and inaccessible to reason).

Bulgakov is explicit that he has gone well beyond Kantian idealism: "I know that for many Kantians, the concurrence of transcendence and immanence seems to be an epistemological contradiction. . . . Together with Hegel, Schelling, Solov'ëv, and others, I do not see a contradiction here" (32n./122, n. 33). As a result, he can claim that the meaning of history is straightforward: history is the revelation and fulfillment of a creative and rational plan, of cosmic, providential meaning, in which the cunning of absolute reason is triumphant. In the end, however, Bulgakov expresses reservations about his idea for a metaphysics of history, as if anticipating the objections of critical philosophy. He grants that absolute reason in history is epistemologically inaccessible to us; our link to it is conscience, the moral law. "From this point of view, progress is not a law of historical development, but a moral task . . . not 'is,' but absolute 'ought'" (37/111). In this, Bulgakov returns to the safer ground of his contraband critique of positivist conceptions of historical progress. Progress should not be ascribed to history as a natural law, nor should it be awaited as divine dispensation. Rather, it is something we must take responsibility for.

Several contributors to *Problems of Idealism* (Struve, Novgorodtsev, and Kistiakovskii) saw a clear case of contraband in Russian "subjective sociology," advanced by the prominent populist thinkers Pëtr Lavrov and Nikolai Mikhailovskii. The subjective sociologists argued that man and society could not be studied with the methods of natural science alone, since human beings have the capacity to act according to values and ideals (such as justice). The putative advantage of the "subjective method" was that it recognized these values and approached social evolution as an interaction between objective factors and subjective aspirations. Progress, in particular, was not a necessary historical law but a category of historical interpretation (which varied according to subjective criteria about what was progressive) and, most importantly, a moral task to be accomplished by "critically thinking individuals" (Lavrov). In the prevailing climate of "objectivist" positivism, subjective sociology played an important role in rehabilitating human will and purposiveness as real influences in the historical process. It also tended, however, to undermine the pursuit of objective knowledge in the social sciences by suggesting that the investigator could not escape his or her own subjective value judgments and preferences (and, indeed, should not try to escape them). Historical and sociological knowledge could never be "value-free." By the same token, subjective sociology fostered the notion that values were "merely subjective" and deprived of any "objective" validity (including an objectivity that might be of an order different from that in natural science).

Struve's essay reveals the importance the "contraband" critique of subjective sociology had in the development of neo-idealism. Mikhailovskii sought to integrate the categories of "what is" and "what ought to be" in one worldview. According to Struve, he failed at the task because he approached it primarily as a positivist, when it falls instead to the metaphysician. "In the figure of the philosophizing Mikhailovskii there were two *personae* who neither recognized themselves nor delineated between themselves, and who therefore only interfered with each other. In him positive science was unconsciously distorted by metaphysics, while metaphysical thought was burdened, bound, and made barren by its subordination to 'positive science'" (84/151). Despite this judgment, Struve felt a certain sympathy for the subjective sociologists, because in them ideal demands, although not fully articulate, were at least not completely silenced. This was a necessary element in the revolt against positivism, one Struve expressed in his call for the critical rehabilitation of the utopianism for which Marxism berated populism. But there was another necessary element in the revolt, and this time, Struve contends, Marxism made the positive contribution. In his account, the Marxist polemic against subjective sociology singled out the illegitimate intrusion of ethical problems into what the Marxists saw as their own sphere — objective, scientific sociology. Struve explains that in this debate Miliukov, whom he calls one of the most visible Russian positivists, took the side of the Marxists, "of course because he clearly saw in Marxism a reaction of the positive-scientific spirit against an alien 'ethical' element intruding into science" (84/152). Struve's argument is that subjective sociology and Marxism each made a positive contribution to the revolt against positivism. In the first case it was the rehabilitation of ethical ideals and consequent erosion of the view that positive science could answer all human aspirations, and in the second case it was criticism of the conflation of distinct areas of thought (the contraband critique). The Marxist charge that populism was utopian captured both contributions, although in different ways.

The problem is that Marxism did not highlight the need for the mutual autonomy of positive science and ethics; it simply denied the existence of ethics altogether. In this, it was much more a case of contraband than was subjective sociology. Struve himself recognizes how strained his argument is that even orthodox Marxism made a positive contribution to the critique of positivism.[192] But it is interesting that he now sees the conflation of separate spheres of human experience as so characteristic of positivism that he tries to interpret his own Marxist past as preparing the way for the defense of their autonomy. In his self-evaluation, "P. G." acknowledges the role of subjective sociology, but still he wants to stress that of Marxism: "Mikhailovskii's idea about 'what ought to be,' as a category independent of 'what is' in experience and therefore having autonomous value," is recognized by the former Marxists.

> But it is also these writers who have stressed that posing this question within the limits of positive science and in its terms is illegitimate and does not make sense, that doing so is an *uncritical conflation of metaphysics with empirical knowledge, or with positive science.* Thus it is not true that the philosophical direction of such metaphysicians-idealists as Struve shares nothing in common with Mikhailovskii, but it is still less true that this current, which came out of Marxism, has capitulated before "subjective sociology." (85/152–153, emphasis Struve's).

In this effort to depict his own recent intellectual development as a certain synthesis of subjective sociology and Marxism, Struve might have done better to cast the Marxist contribution in terms of "objectivity" rather than autonomy. As we have seen, Struve squarely faced the problem of objectivity in ethics, but it was a different type of objectivity than that which the Marxists presumed to command. It was an objectivity that sought to provide a firmer basis for the ethical ideals subjective sociology helped recover from positivist reductionism. It was an objectivity that, for Struve, came to rest ultimately in metaphysics.

Bogdan Kistiakovskii, in his contribution to *Problems of Idealism,* also develops the contraband critique of subjective sociology and addresses the problem of objectivity in ethics, although for him this problem does not require a metaphysical solution. His criticism of subjective sociology is important; no less a social theorist than Max Weber commended it.[193] Kistiakovskii shows how the subjective sociologists, within the confines of their positivist worldview, formulated the concept of an ideal not in terms of "ought," but in terms of "possibility." Instead of what "ought to be," they use the category of what is "possible" or "impossible." Mikhailovskii, for example, speaks of something as "impossible" when he should rather say that it is not what "ought to be." This is a clear example of how "contraband" results in the muddling of concepts. The subjective sociologists failed, in short, to understand that the criterion of an ideal is not "possibility," but "ought," which we recognize in conscience. "We strive for the realization of our ideals not because they are possible," Kistiakovskii concludes, "but because our conscious duty imperatively demands it of us and everyone around us."[194] Consciousness of duty does not, however, entail metaphysics. The category of "ought" is its own type of objectivity or necessity, which Kistiakovskii defines as "transcendental-normative." This was the basis for what he later formulated as "scientific-philosophical idealism,"[195] in contrast to the more common metaphysical direction in Russian neo-idealism.

Novgorodtsev pursued the contraband critique in much of his work. In *Problems of Idealism,* he strenuously objects to the attempts of Russian subjective sociology to include ethics within its sphere in the hope of redressing exclusive objectivism. The mistake of the subjective sociologists

> was that instead of strict delimitation of the ethical element from the scientific, they permitted their compounding. From this came the unsuccessful concept of *subjective* sociology and the idea of the "subjective method," surprising in its philosophical untenability. It is understandable that as a whole this construction had to evoke protests both from the side of positive science and the side of moral philosophy, for the correct correlation of these two spheres is their complete delimitation. Morality shows its distinctiveness precisely in that it judges independently of the necessity disclosed by science; it has its own necessity.[196]

This evaluation of subjective sociology has much in common with Struve's and Kistiakovskii's; Novgorodtsev points out that the mistake he outlines has already been subjected to irrefutable critique.

Novgorodtsev presents a clear and concise statement of the contraband approach to positivism in one of his companion articles to *Problems of Idealism*, "The Significance of Philosophy,"[197] written in 1903 as an introduction to a course on the history of German idealism that he delivered at the Higher Women's Courses and Moscow University. Disillusionment with Comtean positivism was one of the first indications of today's idealist revival, Novgorodtsev observes. Comte had enjoyed great popularity in Russia, but his ideas have become increasingly outmoded with the realization that science cannot take the place of religion and metaphysics. Novgorodtsev stresses the careful delimitation of science and the autonomization of philosophy from positivist reductionism (paradigmatic in Comte's hypertrophy of science). The integral worldview emerging from this process will accommodate not only scientific interests, "but also the so-called metaphysical requirements and mystical needs, all the dreams and hopes that comprise the deepest foundation of our spirit."[198] In the ongoing collapse of positivism, Novgorodtsev sees a return to Kant, whose system of transcendental idealism makes possible the noumenal world by limiting science to the phenomenal.

Economic materialism, even more influential in Russia than Comtean positivism, has shared its same fate, Novgorodtsev proclaims. The enthusiasm for orthodox Marxism has already spent itself. Its decline — in terms of intellectual influence, Novgorodtsev is right to describe it this way — is further evidence of heightened consciousness toward the ideal. This is clear first of all in the intellectual evolution of the former "legal Marxists." Novgorodtsev has no quarrel with the historical observation that economic factors have a definite and continuous effect on historical phenomena, writing that "in this modest aspect economic materialism exists even now." But the reductionist premise, which is the gist of the doctrine, that economic materialism is the "universal explanation of all thought, life and history,"[199] exposed its patent inadequacy as a philosophical system, "and in the end all the main and most talented representatives of the school went off in other directions, to seek satisfaction first in Kant and Fichte, then in the works of Russian philosophical thought, especially in Vladimir Solov'ëv."[200]

Novgorodtsev's conclusion, then, is that idealism has arisen from disaffection with the reductionist doctrines of "scientific philosophy," Comtean positivism and economic materialism first of all. In this Novgorodtsev no doubt wants to point back to the influence of *Problems of Idealism*: A. S. Lappo-Danilevskii's essay, which is a significant contribution to the history of positivist thought, shows the large extent to which Comte relied on concepts (such as purposiveness) that were inconsistent with his theory of knowledge,[201] while E. N. Trubetskoi's powerful immanent critique of Marxism argues that economic factors cannot be the only ones fundamentally at work in human affairs, for the simple but compelling reason that people are ashamed of their selfish interests and try to mask and justify them with various ethical, religious, and legal ideas. Disillusionment with these doctrines was inevitable: the ideal aspirations inherent to human consciousness resist reduction to the empirical. With the return to idealism, "clear consciousness has emerged that these doctrines *take for themselves more than they can give*," as Novgorodtsev puts it.[202] This formulation captures very well the force behind the contraband critique. First, it indicates that reductive positivism, despite itself, cannot eradicate or ignore the idealist impulse, which is not only moral but more generally metaphysical. Second, although positivist doctrines fail to block the idealist impulse, in trying they must promise to somehow make good on it — this is what they "take for themselves." But here they are utopian and constitute a form of contraband that abuses the authority of the natural sciences to predict the historical realization of ideal hopes. Following up on this pattern, Novgorodtsev writes, "the first problem over which the narrow formulations of the positivists and economists fell apart was the moral problem,"[203] because it encapsulates all our ideal aspirations that cannot long be resisted. "And with this once more arises the whole set of so-called metaphysical questions, which might temporarily be held in contempt, but to which human thought constantly turns anew, as soon as it comes to consciousness of its deepest foundations and ambitions."[204]

In 1904 leading Russian positivists responded to *Problems of Idealism* with a collection of their own, *Essays in the Realist Worldview*.[205] Kotliarevskii's review of this volume, "On True and False Realism," further develops the contraband critique.[206] First, Kotliarevskii finds that he must help the realist-positivists define their own basic concepts, which they have left unclear. Therefore, he proposes that realism is the claim that all knowledge is empirical; nothing is known a priori. From this epistemological premise most realists (like S. A. Suvorov) make the ontological claim that nothing nonempirical exists. Realism is, in short, the reduction of being to phenomena (naturalism). Metaphysics is an empty, illusory world.[207] Realists have, however, put themselves in the difficult position of needing to explain how ethical and metaphysical ideals arise in the first place and exert such hold on us if what is positively given in empirical experience exhausts the possibilities of being. Ultimately, they must dismiss such ideals as naturalistically explicable psychological illusions, again the unreal world of metaphysics. This explanation cannot satisfy

even the realist-positivists themselves; the presence and force of ideals remain, although at a repressed, subconscious level. And with this, Kotliarevskii
writes, "banished metaphysics, renounced religion, take their revenge, burst-
ing lavishly into the realm of real science and greatly obscuring its pure realism. . . . Most dangerous of all, this metaphysics looms unconsciously, so to
speak, passing under a foreign flag,"[208] or as contraband. The "false realism"
of scientistic monism is thus inherently unstable. The proper relationship between the distinct spheres of human experience and inquiry is not mutual
usurpation (Kotliarevskii's term) but mutual delimitation, making possible the
integrity of "true realism."[209]

NATURAL LAW AND PROGRESS

The revival of natural law, its elevation to an ethical ideal that could
serve as a measure of and spur toward liberal progress, can be treated as an
outstanding example of the neo-idealist autonomization of philosophy from
positivist reductionism. This is Novgorodtsev's approach in his *Problems of
Idealism* essay, "Ethical Idealism in the Philosophy of Law: On the Question
of the Revival of Natural Law." The specific form of positivist domination in
jurisprudence was historicism, a nineteenth-century reaction to Enlightenment conceptions of natural law, which historicists characterized as abstract,
overly speculative, rationalistic, and utopian. The turn-of-the-century revival
of natural law after the dominance of historicism typifies a pattern in the
history of ideas. Novgorodtsev describes how a given intellectual current,
suppressed for a time, experiences a revival when an opposing intellectual
current has exaggerated its own claims to such an extent that its one-sidedness
becomes obvious. The cycle then recurs. Both currents offer their own genuine insights and valuable perspectives.[210] In his first book, *The Historical
School of Jurists: Its Origin and Fate,* Novgorodtsev strove for a balanced
approach to the relative merits of both historicism and natural law.[211] His
Problemy essay concentrates rather on the philosophical justification for the
urgency of the revival of natural law.

To historicist methodology, which properly examines the historical and
sociological context, Novgorodtsev contrasts philosophy, which (he states
baldly) focuses on the autonomous person. Historicism ought not to be concerned with values and absolute ideals, since these are properties of persons,
not their environment. In his concern with relativism in values, Novgorodtsev
makes some categorical assertions: "The concept of personhood and the absolute principles connected with it are foreign and inaccessible to historical method." This is rather the domain of "special philosophical analysis."
"Philosophy must restore its own rights and show history its limits" (240–

241/277). It would be difficult to find more forceful statements among Russian idealists of the need for the autonomization of philosophy from the dominance of historicism and positivism. The special philosophical methods for the study of the concept of personhood constitute ethical idealism, of which the revival of natural law was an integral part.

Natural law meets the requirement of the idealistic and progressive side of human nature to look forward to the realization of our present aspirations and hopes. In an allusion to the urgency of constitutional reform in Russia, Novgorodtsev wrote, "this need [to turn to the future] is especially striking in epochs of crises and turning-points, when past forms of life clearly expose their decrepitude, when society is seized by an impatient desire for new structures" (250/283–284). But idealistic and progressive aspirations are a constant feature of human motivation. Novgorodtsev's appreciation of them was a main underpinning of his philosophy of progress and theory of natural law: "Human thought has this quality of living not only in the present, but also in the future, of bringing to the future its ideals and aspirations, and in this sense natural-law constructions are an integral property of our spirit and testimony to its higher calling" (250–251/284). Idealism designates not only theoretical philosophy but also the progressive, idealistic, and even utopian strivings in human nature. The progressive ideas of the future are often first conceived in the dreams and bold projects of utopians and visionaries. "The creativity of life is broader than limited human experience, and therefore it constantly happens that utopian theory is more far-sighted than sober practice" (263/292). In this, Novgorodtsev shared the common concern of the new Russian idealists to refute associations of idealism and reaction. In the inexhaustibility of the utopian impulse he saw further evidence that consciousness is not limited to the empirical, phenomenal world but is connected to absolute, noumenal reality. At the same time, he insisted that utopian ideals be made ideals in the strict (transcendent) sense. Attempts to fully realize them in history defeat the genuinely progressive spirit.

Novgorodtsev distinguishes between two interpretations of natural law: idealist, and the claim that it is given by nature as an eternal, unchanging norm common to all cultures. Historicists typically define natural law according to the second interpretation. In contrast to this are Rudolf Stammler's concept of "natural law with changing content" and V. M. Hessen's "evolutionary natural law." Since the variability of legal ideals is accepted by all modern advocates of natural law, the historicist characterization is a strawman. But if even natural law evolves, "where then is the break with the historical outlook?" (254/286). The distinctiveness of the philosophical approach to natural law consists in the idealist opposition between the categories *das Sein* and *das*

Sollen. In looking to the future, we think not of what *will be,* but of what *ought to be.* We envisage a future that unfolds not by historical inevitability, but by our moral evaluation of the present and the course of action deemed necessary to improve it.

According to Novgorodtsev, the task of natural law is to order ideal paths of progressive development. Natural law seeks criteria for moral evaluation of history in the service of a better future. Therefore, it cannot draw its principles from history itself. "To the question of what ought to be, knowledge of what has been and what is cannot give an answer. Here it is necessary to turn to the a priori indications of moral consciousness." This makes the theory of natural law autonomous, "sharply distinguishing it from the purely historical question of the development of law," which can describe its past but cannot prescribe its future (255/286–287). Historicism must recognize that natural law, as a special problem of moral philosophy, does not fall within its proper domain, because historical necessity excludes the very possibility of evaluation and criticism of law. By historical methodology, critique of historical events is no more justified than critique of processes of nature. History exceeds its bounds in making moral conjectures — this is philosophy's area of competence. The same applies to sociology. Novgorodtsev does, however, somewhat soften his attack in granting that historical and sociological study of law and morality is fully justified, as long as it is recognized that this approach does not exhaust their very essence. But on the basis of the familiar reduction of "what ought to be" to "what is," positivists are prone to make illegitimate knowledge claims. "Thus does fully legitimate sociological analysis turn into a highly pretentious construction, claiming to explain 'the ultimate foundations of law and society'" (270/297). Together with historical and sociological research, philosophical approaches are needed, "not in the least supplanted by the sociological method nor any less important" (273/299).

Novgorodtsev's own philosophical inquiry into morality and natural law was deeply indebted to Kant and culminated in a well-developed philosophy of progress. Neo-idealism is inherently progressive and open-ended: for true idealism, the ideal (in epistemology, ethics, and legal and social philosophy) is a transcendent, absolute goal that can never be mistaken for any of its relative approximations. The absolute quality of the ideal relates only to its form, not its content. In this, Novgorodtsev follows Stammler's concept of natural law with changing content, which he celebrates as the direct conclusion of ethical idealism. The overriding concern is to prevent the absolutization of the content, mistaking it (which is temporary and historical) for the ideal itself. The absolute, ideal form is given a priori to consciousness, "but the content of this form must be sought, and therefore moral life presents itself as constant cre-

ativity" (287/309).[212] Progress is the constant pull toward the ideal. Since the
philosophy of progress is firmly grounded in the absolute (the ideal form), it is
also a thoroughgoing critical philosophy. Positivism and relativism are neither
progressive nor critical, since they deny the absolute. They have no standard of
criticism and nothing toward which to strive. As is often the case, Novgorodtsev's is a Kantian formulation: "the categorical imperative is the form of and
call to searching. This form must be fulfilled, and the call must lead to a
definite result. But this absolute form can never be filled by an adequate content, and the moral call can never be satisfied by an achieved result." The often
bemoaned "merely formal" character of Kantian ethics and philosophy of law
does not strike him as a problem. Rather, "the formal moral principle is the
recognition of the idea of eternal development and improvement" (288/309).

The incompatibility of Novgorodtsev's philosophy of progress with conservatism is obvious, but he also drew out its resistance to utopianism: the ideal
advances as the content catches up. "But this must lead not to an utter denial
of the achieved stage or to doubts in the possibility of progress, but to improvement of the present and to a search for the higher" (289/309). The
distinction between the ideal and the historically real ought not to be despised,
for it is clear consciousness of the ideal that spurs continuous real movement
toward it. Progressive approximation of the ideal is the only way to be worthy
of it. Such idealizing progress is the "justification of the good" (Solov'ëv).
Utopianism collapses all this. Another aspect of the critical side of Novgorodtsev's attitude to utopianism was his conception of philosophy as an exacting
and rigorous discipline having nothing to do with ideology or utopia. The time
has passed when philosophers could take to flights of fantasy (295/314). This
in no way excluded Novgorodtsev's own search for a higher metaphysical
synthesis of "is" and "ought."

Novgorodtsev always remained true to the neo-idealist defense of progressive, rule-of-law liberalism, giving it further profound development in his
future works. Berdiaev, by contrast, soon drew quite illiberal conclusions from
idealism. But for the moment, in *Problems of Idealism,* he too supported the
neo-idealist defense of liberalism. At this stage, his fervent individualism had
not yet become anarchism. He has a liberal appreciation of the importance of
society in the development of personhood. The person has ethical primacy
over society ("ethical individualism"). "But the moral law is embodied in
the life of humanity through social progress; the human person develops
and works out its own individuality through diverse interaction with the social sphere, in social-psychic intercourse with people" (116–117/178). The
goal and justification of social progress is the full development of the person.
The rule of law ensures that the end (the person) is not compromised by the

necessary means (society). "The external relations of people must be regulated and formalized. . . . Legal and political progress is nothing other than the realization and guaranteeing of the absolute *natural rights* of man [*estestvennoe pravo cheloveka*]" (117/178). Here Berdiaev explicitly follows Novgorodtsev and Struve in proclaiming natural law an integral part of the idealist revival in Russia. Like them, he revises the Enlightenment view of natural law by equating the concept of "natural" with that of "normal," or that which corresponds to the ideal norm. "The historical variability and relativity of law cannot be an argument against 'natural law,' because 'natural law' is 'what ought to be,' and not 'what is'; it is a 'norm' that ought to be realized in the historical development of law" (117n./195, n.45). Likewise with the Enlightenment notion of popular sovereignty: it is the person who is sovereign; nothing is higher than its intrinsic value and rights (118/179).

Berdiaev put particular stress on the progressive social and political implications of idealism. "The idealist spirit is a spirit of freedom, a spirit of light, which calls forward, to the struggle for the right of humanity to infinitely improve itself" (119/179). Like Struve, he points to Solov'ëv's *The National Question in Russia* as a classic example of the idealist critique of reactionary nationalism in Russia. Berdiaev encouraged the growth of civil society in late imperial Russia, noting that the struggle for rights has historically been most effective when waged not by individuals but by civic associations and social groups. The formation of such groups (*gruppirovka*) opens up wide prospects for the human spirit to create a better, freer future. In this connection he again highlights the importance of natural law: "The new idealist direction, to which I proudly attach myself, draws the necessity of the liberation struggle for 'natural law' from the spiritual hunger of the intelligentsia [*intelligentnyi*] soul" (135/189).

With this reference to the "intelligentsia soul" Berdiaev signals his disdain for bourgeois culture. He fits well within Ivanov-Razumnik's interpretation of the history of Russian social thought as a struggle for universal intelligentsia ideals against bourgeois *meshchanstvo* (philistinism). He had little sympathy for bourgeois economic liberalism; his liberalism was not "ideological" (in the Marxist sense of class interests) but a rarefied doctrine of the supraclass intelligentsia. Berdiaev defends liberalism only "in its ideal essence," and looks to socialism for new methods of realizing the eternal liberal principles of personhood, natural rights, freedom, and equality. The tendency toward socialeconomic collectivism is a useful and even necessary means, although ethical and spiritual collectivism is a terrible evil. For Berdiaev, liberalism represents the immediate interests of the proletariat more than those of the bourgeoisie: "In concrete historical circumstances the struggle for the 'natural rights' of man takes the form of a struggle for the oppressed and exploited. In contemporary society, for example, it takes the form of a struggle for the rights of the working masses" (118/179). In general, Berdiaev continued to follow the Marxist point of view on the social and economic development of Russia.

THE AUTONOMY OF PHILOSOPHY AND VALUE OF ITS HISTORY

Neo-idealism was not only a theory of liberalism; it was, first of all, a defense of the autonomy of philosophy against reductive positivism. In this, *Problems of Idealism* was clearly the product of its institutional sponsor, for the Psychological Society had promoted the free development of Russian philosophy for fifteen years. Novgorodtsev, in his foreword to the symposium, declares that "the directions that sought to eradicate philosophy, or else supplant it with constructions based exclusively on the data of experience, have lost their leading significance" (vii/81). The decline of positivism and return to the "authentic sources of philosophical knowledge" reflected the recognition, which at any rate was becoming more widespread, that moral ideals cannot be derived from empirical experience. *Problems of Idealism* dwells on the importance of ethics in the overall rehabilitation of philosophy because it is here that the inaccessibility of philosophy's subject matter to positivist approaches is most clear. In its domain of the ideal, ethics is not, however, a peculiar philosophical discipline but a typical one; it exemplifies the epistemic autonomy of philosophy as a whole.

We have seen that Novgorodtsev treats the revival of natural law as a case study of the neo-idealist autonomization of philosophy. His *Problemy* article draws on his 1901 book, *Kant and Hegel in Their Theories of Law and the State,* the methodological introduction to which he also published as a separate article in *Voprosy filosofii.* The essay, "On the Historical and Philosophical Study of Ideas," is a straightforward statement of the autonomy of philosophy.[213] Novgorodtsev identifies three types of positivist reductionism: historical, psychological, and sociological. None of these explain thought; an autonomous and creative intellectual core remains that cannot be accounted for by the set of factors each approach respectively privileges. Novgorodtsev does not, of course, deny that these approaches inform the study of ideas; he warns only against the reduction of ideas to the contexts within which they are articulated and develop. The history of philosophy, for example, helps us to appreciate that, as S. N. Trubetskoi put it, "genius is not explained without historical conditions . . . but its whole peculiarity consists precisely in the fact that it is not explained by them alone."[214] In addition to the contextual methodologies, Novgorodtsev recommends the analysis of ideas on their own terms, or by what he calls the philosophical method.

In answering a review of his book on Kant and Hegel, Novgorodtsev counters the view that the history of philosophy is of historical interest only, an archive of outdated theories. It is rather a living and progressive unveiling of truth.[215] In this Kant has special importance; he need not necessarily be the culmination of the contemporary development of idealism in Russia, but he ought to serve as the point of departure and reference. Of Kantian philosophy, Novgorodtsev writes,

> We are convinced that some of its foundations — in theory of knowledge and in moral philosophy — must remain the secure property of thought; but together with this what we consider necessary is the broadest study of the historical past of philosophy and the most active relation to the tasks opening before its future. "Back to Kant!" means first of all, "back to serious philosophical education!" This education was missing in the recent epoch of enthusiasm for positivism, and it is necessary now to revive it.[216]

The deepening of philosophic consciousness in Russia requires systematic study of the history of philosophy, not necessarily originality, and certainly not originality for its own sake. Novgorodtsev again quotes Sergei Trubetskoi, this time from his *Problems of Idealism* essay, "What the History of Philosophy Teaches": "Philosophy seeks truth, not originality. *Independence* in philosophical work is determined not by subjective arbitrariness, not by absence of proper education or positive knowledge, but by depth, sincerity, integrity of philosophical interest, and breadth of conception."[217]

Prince Sergei Trubetskoi was one of the Psychological Society's most respected members. His contribution to *Problems of Idealism* is an eloquent defense of philosophy. For Trubetskoi, the very possibility of philosophy rests on the ideal or transcendental nature of consciousness. Positivists denigrate philosophy as "merely speculative" when its claims cannot be verified by empirical knowledge. Yet this is Trubetskoi's very point: it is startling that speculative ideals should arise in the first place, when sense experience conveys only empirical data and contingent facts. Even the category of "contingency" presupposes that of "necessity," a metaphysical idea and a priori condition of the awareness of contingency. Philosophy, "no matter how we define it, strives toward a universal, *integral worldview;* speculation seeks a final system of knowledge, explanation of the origin and final cause of our existence."[218] Every worldview, positivist no less than openly metaphysical, involves integral understanding, the quest for unity, system, and necessity. The Kantian question Trubetskoi poses is not whether understanding can proceed from pure experience excised of all speculative elements (it cannot), but whether such a priori elements are critically analyzed or remain unconscious metaphysical assumptions. The idea of pure experience is itself a speculative abstraction; like all systematic thought, it transcends experience in seeking to understand it.

The very capacity for philosophy is, in this way, the ground of its autonomy. Its ideals cannot be derived from empirical experience alone. The speculative ideals of philosophy persist, against positivist injunctions, because they seek to complete in an ever higher unity the synthesizing work of reason that makes experience possible in the first place. In this, Trubetskoi is heavily indebted to Kant's *Critique of Pure Reason.* Consciousness transcends experience by enabling it a priori. Or, as Trubetskoi writes, "our reason is an innate metaphysician, and it cannot limit itself to phenomena alone" (222/263).[219] But if speculative philosophy is inevitable, why can it not reach its goal? The answer, it is clear, consists in the nature of the ideal as such. "*Consciousness of the ideal* is given to man, and in this consciousness is the force that gives flight to his thought, lifting it high into the air. But this same consciousness indicates to him all the difference between the ideal and what he possesses in reality. As long as he sees this distinction, he will not lose consciousness of the ideal and will continue to strive toward it" (225/265). This was the principle behind the neo-idealist philosophy of progress. It also explains why "philosophy, in the precise sense of the word, is not 'wisdom' . . . but rather 'love of wisdom' " (225/265). The history of philosophy teaches, in short, that it is consciousness of the ideal that makes us capable of philosophy at all.

The autonomy of philosophy and value of its history are the framework within which Iu. Aikhenval'd reviewed *Problems of Idealism,* and the point of view from which he took to task those contributors whom he calls "recent or new guests in the home of abstract thought."[220] Aikhenval'd contends that the volume does not entirely succeed on its own terms: if the authors intended to base their "civic worldview" (liberalism) on philosophical idealism, "then the speculative significance of this attempt turns out to be rather slight and the predominating role in the book falls to the lot of social, not philosophical, elements" (335). This is because several contributors dwell on Russian publicistic writers rather than the philosophers to whom they could have turned more often for theoretical substantiation of liberalism. Struve, for example, writes about the publicist Mikhailovskii under the title, "our philosophical development." The former Marxists even include themselves in the history of Russian philosophy. "They quote, encourage, and praise each other" (338). Berdiaev is a particular example of the distasteful tendency to evaluate one's own philosophical significance (this irritates Aikhenval'd). Reading the symposium, Aikhenval'd has the impression he is in the presence of dilettantes. "It is as though writers, once professing economic materialism, have unexpectedly learned of the existence of moral philosophy, of the *Critique of Practical*

Reason, of Fichte. And having learned of these fine things, they, of course, witnessed completely new horizons and had to impart them to their readers" (338).

Aikhenval'd prefers scholarship to confession of personal philosophies. He suggests that Lappo-Danilevskii's article may well be the best in the collection, and also thinks well of the contributions by E. N. Trubetskoi, S. N. Trubetskoi, and Novgorodtsev. Sergei Trubetskoi's essay is a "profound justification of philosophy and valuation of its theoretical and practical significance" (343). Novgorodtsev's article is "an exhaustive analysis within the reach of only a jurist" (353). By contrast, the articles by the former Marxists are, for the most part, lacking in solid and convincing argumentation. The attempts by Berdiaev, Frank, and Zhukovskii to bridge Kant and Nietzsche are highly dubious; instead Aikhenval'd commends Askol'dov for seeing that Nietzsche's ethics was based on the idea of beauty. Berdiaev promises to pass "from epistemological premises to further examination of the ethical problem," but keeps turning to other problems, such as his relations with Struve and their previous publications. Bulgakov on the second page of his article says that reason is unable to give integral knowledge, but one page later talks about metaphysics (and later metaphysics of history). S. F. Ol'denburg is wrong to celebrate Renan's skepticism as a solution to dogmatism; the proper solution is the critical search for objective truth, not indifference toward it. In light of all this, Aikhenval'd can only conclude that, *"Problems of Idealism* victoriously struggles with utilitarian ethics and gains the upper hand over the 'subjective method' of Russian sociology. But . . . victory over them is easy. *Problems of Idealism* shows well that service to progressive civic ideals and a spiritualist worldview are fully compatible. But no one familiar with the history of philosophy ever doubted it" (356).

Aikhenval'd's criticism may have a certain validity from a purely philosophical standpoint, but this does not diminish the importance of the volume in Russian intellectual history. Part of what makes intellectual history fascinating is the unique and powerful formulation of ideas at certain historical moments, when they acquire a special clarity and urgency. Idealist philosophy within the social and political context of the Russian Liberation Movement was such a moment. From this perspective, even the essays by the former Marxists have an importance Aikhenval'd slights, apart from their developmental interest in view of the later philosophical and theological achievements of these thinkers (which Aikhenval'd did not, of course, foresee). True, Frank's essay is perhaps mostly developmental,[221] and Berdiaev's already bears the style that would long irritate some professional philosophers (while engaging most other readers), but Struve's is a nice résumé of an important juncture in Russian thought, and Bulgakov's essay is widely recognized as a classic. More generally, it may well be, as Aikhenval'd contends, that the history of philosophy leaves no doubt of the compatibility of idealism and liberalism, but the main task of *Problems of Idealism* (as Aikhenval'd himself recognized) was to convey that to a broader audience in the interests of constitutional reform, in a country where (as elsewhere in Europe) it was hardly the common assumption.

Continuations and Differentiations

Problems of Idealism and its successor volumes, *Vekhi* (*Landmarks*, 1909) and *Iz glubiny* (*Out of the Depths*, 1918), spanned sixteen years of intellectual development among their common contributors, as well as three revolutions. Thus it is not surprising that there are significant differences among the three collections, but there are also impressive continuities. On the whole, *Problems of Idealism* is a more constructive work than its successors: its positive task was to advance neo-idealism as a theory of liberalism, although this required, as we have seen, refutation of the common view that positivism was the natural philosophical basis of progress. The successor volumes concentrated rather on the negative task of criticizing the psychology of the Russian intelligentsia and its "mystique of revolution." In this, however, the *Vekhi* group could, and did, draw heavily on the *Problemy* critique of positivism.[222]

For example, Berdiaev's *Vekhi* essay, "Philosophical Verity and Intelligentsia Truth," proceeds from the neo-idealist defense of the autonomy of philosophy in arguing that the intelligentsia conception of "truth" (*pravda*) did not respect philosophical "truth" or "verity" (*istina*). Before the intelligentsia can come to "a synthesis which will satisfy its valuable demand for an organic union of theory and practice, of 'just truth' and 'true justice,'" it needs to recognize truth as a value in itself.[223] Berdiaev laments the continuing politicization and ideologization of philosophy at the hands of the positivist intelligentsia (his example is A. A. Bogdanov). He recommends Lopatin, chair of the Psychological Society, as a true representative of philosophy, although Bogdanov would no doubt always be preferred, since "Lopatin's philosophy demands serious intellectual effort, and no programmatic [or partisan] slogans follow from it."[224] The contraband critique, which underlies Mikhail Gershenzon's description of positivism as the "general constitutional derangement of consciousness,"[225] also reappears in *Vekhi* (Bulgakov and Frank, in particular) and in *Iz glubiny* (Novgorodtsev and others). It informs some of Struve's important writings in this period as well,[226] and many of Novgorodtsev's. Another continuity is the idea that the relative autonomy of the parts is necessary for the integrity of the whole (either self or society) — freedom of conscience in its broader sense. It underlies part of the sharp criticism of intelligentsia maximalism and nihilism, and is also evident in the related concern, expressed in some of the *Vekhi* and *Iz glubiny* essays (i.e., the ones that are most consistently liberal), for the development of legal consciousness, civil society, and free cultural creativity.

One of the main criticisms *Vekhi* and *Iz glubiny* level against the radical intelligentsia is that its attitudes were not propitious for the development of personhood.[227] In this, *Problems of Idealism* and the Psychological Society exercised perhaps their strongest influence on the *Vekhi* group as a whole: neo-idealist personalism. But while recognition of personal autonomy and dignity is a necessary foundation of liberalism,[228] it is not a sufficient one. Liberalism also requires a normative sense of the rule of law, which safeguards the scope of negative liberty necessary for self-realization by setting limits to the exercise of state power, and the power of one person over another.[229] In other words, liberalism requires not only an abstract recognition of personhood, but also citizenship, conceived as respect for and willingness to defend each other's civil rights, or as the basis of civil society (probably a condition, in turn, of the fullest development of personhood). Legal consciousness was the subject of Kistiakovskii's classic *Vekhi* essay, "In Defense of Law," but some members of the *Vekhi* group combined personalism with disregard for the idea of law and civil society, for the relative autonomy of spheres such as church and state, and, in general, for the necessary distinction between the absolute and relative (in metaphysics and philosophy of history as well as social philosophy).[230] For this reason, it is risky to say that the group as a whole criticized the intelligentsia from a consistently liberal perspective.[231] Meanwhile, some scholars, notably Leonard Schapiro,[232] have tried to situate *Vekhi* squarely within the philosophical tradition of Russian liberalism, comparing it to one of the best representatives of that tradition, Chicherin. *Vekhi* can be placed within the tradition (if not perfectly), as long as it is kept in mind that Chicherin, the other Psychological Society neo-idealists, and *Problems of Idealism* laid the tradition itself. Among the contributors to *Vekhi* and *Iz glubiny*, I would identify the following as most consistently liberal: Struve,[233] Frank, Kistiakovskii, Novgorodtsev, and Kotliarevskii.[234]

The great divide that separates *Problems of Idealism* from its successor volumes is the Revolution of 1905, the hopes before it and the bitter disappointments after it. *Problems of Idealism* was conceived and its contributions were written, as indicated above, when the founding fathers of the Liberation Movement hoped to rely on the zemstvo milieu in persuading the autocracy to introduce constitutional reform. This initial approach was soon abandoned in

favor of "no enemies on the left," a policy endorsed at the July 1903 Schaffhausen conference that preceded the formation of the Union of Liberation.
Present at Schaffhausen were most members of the *Problemy* project. They
seem to have accepted the idea of a united front between liberals and radicals,
convinced by the intransigence of the autocracy that only working in concert
with all disaffected groups in Russian society, regardless of their level of civic
consciousness, could force the tsarist regime to give in. Kistiakovskii was one
of those who participated in the Schaffhausen meeting. But he took exception
to the policy of radicalization, warning against facilitating the replacement, in
his words, of the Romanov autocracy with a Leninist autocracy.[235]

Although the neo-idealist critique of positivism was implicitly critical of the
outlook of most Russian intelligenty, this was not given the sharp edge in
Problems of Idealism that it acquired with *Vekhi*. Such discretion proved
fortuitous, once the Liberation Movement shifted leftward and began solicit-
ing the support of the "democratic intelligentsia." The progressive character of
neo-idealism, which its representatives had been so concerned to stress, could
now be given a different spin, as if to convince the positivist radicals that the
idealists in the Union of Liberation posed no threat to the united-front strategy. This was apparently Novgorodtsev's intent when he seemed to write with
regret in 1904:

> In the oppressive atmosphere of our social life, theoretical disagreements that
> divide people who are otherwise apparently close in their social ideals and
> that, generally speaking, are a necessary condition of the free development of
> thought, nonetheless take on the character of tragic clashes, providing mate-
> rial for whole social dramas, in which one side inevitably turns out to be in the
> position of representing an evil force, while the other considers itself to be the
> defender of the true good.[236]

What matters is that everyone is progressive. This was the implication when
Novgorodtsev went on to say, in words I have already quoted, that for all the
theoretical differences among even idealists themselves, the practical principle
on which they are in full agreement is the absolute dignity of the person. "But
in the end do not all living and progressive movements of Russian thought
meet on this point?"[237]

Thus, in the interests of the united front, the idealist critique of the intelligentsia remained muted. This is not necessarily to say that the neo-idealists, or
liberals more generally, in the Liberation Movement violated their own principles. It may well be that only something very much like the united front that
the liberationists forged could have brought Nicholas II to grant a constitution. After all, their strategy worked. The issue seems to reside more in

whether, as Richard Pipes writes, "once unleashed, Bakunin's 'evil passions' might not subside, even after the country had been given its freedom."[238] In any event, the perception after 1905 among the idealists who formed the *Vekhi* group was that the radical intelligentsia caused the miscarriage of Russian liberalism by blocking constructive work with what might otherwise have become a real Duma monarchy. Given this perception (right or, more probably, wrong),[239] the idealist focus shifted from liberal theory in *Problems of Idealism* to relentless critique of the intelligentsia in *Vekhi*. And as idealism had been commended for its inherent progressive aspirations and therefore as the best philosophical foundation of liberalism, now the positivist intelligentsia was condemned for its rigid — indeed, conservative — mentality and inability to adjust to constitutional life, civic responsibility, and the demands of freedom.

Neo-idealists and other liberals in the Liberation Movement faced dismal prospects over the longer term. For while it did prove possible to unite society for the immediate political goal of forcing the autocracy to capitulate, this expedient (and short-term) unity was very far from the type of civil society on which the fate of a liberal Russia ultimately depended. The autocracy had for too long prevented the development of citizenship and a commitment to the rule of law among all but a small section of the population, and it continued to do so after 1905.[240] The result was that when the old regime collapsed in 1917, Russian civil society was too thin and fragile to long sustain itself before the workers, soldiers, and peasants, each concerned with their own particular interests rather than with the defense of universal civil rights.[241] This was the situation that enabled the Bolsheviks to come to power. The clarify and force of the neo-idealist defense of Russian liberalism were not enough in a country where the autocracy had deprived liberalism of the necessary social support. The tragic irony was that the same frail social basis of Russian liberalism that contributed to its strength in theory (by making its intellectual defense all the more necessary) also prevented it from being realized in practice.

Notes

1. Good surveys include James H. Billington, *The Icon and the Axe: An Interpretive History of Russian Culture* (New York: Vintage Books, 1970), pp. 464–518; Gleb Struve, "The Cultural Renaissance," in *Russia under the Last Tsar*, ed. Theofanis George Stavrou (Minneapolis: University of Minnesota Press, 1969), pp. 179–201; Georges Florovsky, "On the Eve," in *Ways of Russian Theology* (Part Two), trans. Robert L. Nichols (Belmont, Mass.: Büchervertriebsanstalt/Notable and Academic Books, 1987); Christopher Read, *Religion, Revolution and the Russian Intelligentsia: The Vekhi Debate and Its*

Intellectual Background (London: Macmillan, 1979); and N. M. Zernov, *The Russian Religious Renaissance of the Twentieth Century* (New York: Harper and Row, 1963). For particular currents and developments, see George L. Kline, *Religious and Anti-Religious Thought in Russia* (Chicago: University of Chicago Press, 1968); James P. Scanlan, "The New Religious Consciousness: Merezhkovsky and Berdiaev," *Canadian Slavic Studies* 4: 1 (1970), pp. 17–35; Bernice Glatzer Rosenthal, *D. S. Merezhkovsky and the Silver Age: The Development of a Revolutionary Mentality* (The Hague: Nijhoff, 1975); Rosenthal, ed., *Nietzsche in Russia* (Princeton: Princeton University Press, 1986); James West, *Russian Symbolism: A Study of Vyacheslav Ivanov and the Russian Symbolist Aesthetic* (London: Methuen, 1970); John Bowlt, *The Silver Age: Russian Art of the Early Twentieth Century and the "World of Art" Group* (Newtonville, Mass.: Oriental Research Partners, 1979); Irina Paperno and Joan Grossman, eds., *Creating Life: The Aesthetic Utopia of Russian Modernism* (Stanford: Stanford University Press, 1994); Jutta Scherrer, *Die Petersburger religiös-philosophischen Vereinigungen. Die Entwicklung des religiösen Selbstverständnisses ihrer Intelligencija-Mitglieder (1901–1907)* (Berlin: Otto Harrassowitz, 1973); Andrzej Walicki, *Legal Philosophies of Russian Liberalism* (Oxford: Oxford University Press, 1987); George F. Putnam, *Russian Alternatives to Marxism. Christian Socialism and Idealistic Liberalism in Twentieth-Century Russia* (Knoxville: University of Tennessee Press, 1977); Richard Pipes, *Struve: Liberal on the Left, 1870–1905* (Cambridge: Harvard University Press, 1970); Pipes, *Struve: Liberal on the Right, 1905–1944* (Cambridge: Harvard University Press, 1980); Catherine Evtuhov, *The Cross and the Sickle: Sergei Bulgakov and the Fate of Russian Religious Philosophy* (Ithaca: Cornell University Press, 1997); Judith Deutsch Kornblatt and Richard F. Gustafson, eds., *Russian Religious Thought* (Madison: University of Wisconsin Press, 1996); Paul Valliere, *Modern Russian Theology. Bukharev, Soloviev, Bulgakov: Orthodox Theology in a New Key* (Grand Rapids, Mich.: Eerdmans, 2000); Maria Carlson, *"No Religion Higher than Truth": A History of the Theosophical Movement in Russia, 1875–1922* (Princeton: Princeton University Press, 1993); and V. A. Kuvakin, *Religioznaia filosofiia v Rossii nachalo XX veka* (Moscow: Mysl', 1980). Vladimir Solov'ëv exercised vast influence on the period. Studies of him include A. F. Losev, *Vladimir Solov'ëv i ego vremia* (Moscow: Progress, 1990); Dimitri Strémooukhoff, *Vladimir Soloviev and His Messianic Work*, trans. Elizabeth Meyendorff (Belmont, Mass: Nordland, 1979); and Konstantin Mochul'skii, *Vladimir Solov'ëv. Zhizn' i uchenie* (Paris: YMCA Press, 1951).

2. R. V. Ivanov-Razumnik, *Istoriia russkoi obshchestvennoi mysli*, II, 2d edition (St. Petersburg, 1908), p. 453. His discussion of the volume concentrates on the essays by Berdiaev and Novgorodtsev, pp. 468–481.

3. Echoing Ivanov-Razumnik, Leszek Kolakowski writes that, "*Problems of Idealism* was an important event in Russian cultural history." See his *Main Currents of Marxism*, trans. P. S. Falla, vol. 2, *The Golden Age* (Oxford: Oxford University Press, 1978), p. 422. Bernice Glatzer Rosenthal calls it a "foundational work" in her article "Russian Religious-Philosophical Renaissance," *Routledge Encyclopedia of Philosophy*, vol. 8 (London: Routledge, 1998), p. 426. Christopher Read discusses the symposium under the appropriate rubric "philosophical liberalism" in his *Religion, Revolution and the Russian Intelligentsia, 1900–1912*, pp. 15–17, 20–21. Also see the introduction to *A*

Revolution of the Spirit: Crisis of Value in Russia, 1890–1924, ed. Bernice Glatzer Rosenthal and Martha Bohachevsky-Chomiak, trans. Marian Schwartz (New York: Fordham University Press, 1990), pp. 20–22; Jutta Scherrer, *Die Petersburger religiös-philosophischen Vereinigungen,* pp. 86–98; Andrzej Walicki, *Legal Philosophies of Russian Liberalism,* pp. 307–310; Leonard Schapiro, "The Vekhi Group and the Mystique of Revolution," in his *Russian Studies,* ed. Ellen Dahrendorf (New York: Viking, 1987), pp. 69–71; and Aileen M. Kelly, "Which Signposts?" in her *Toward Another Shore: Russian Thinkers between Necessity and Chance* (New Haven: Yale University Press, 1998), pp. 160–164.

4. On the Psychological Society, see Martha Bohachevsky-Chomiak, *Sergei N. Trubetskoi: An Intellectual Among the Intelligentsia in Prerevolutionary Russia* (Belmont, Mass.: Nordland, 1976), pp. 63–80; Bohachevsky-Chomiak, "Filosofiia, religiia i obshchestvennost' v Rossii v kontse 19-go i nachale 20-go vv," *Russkaia religiozno-filosofskaia mysl' XX veka,* ed. Nikolai P. Poltoratsky (Pittsburgh: University of Pittsburgh, 1975), pp. 54–67; introduction to *A Revolution of the Spirit: Crisis of Value in Russia, 1890–1924,* ed. Bernice Glatzer Rosenthal and Martha Bohachevsky-Chomiak, pp. 16–22; and Randall A. Poole, *The Moscow Psychological Society and the Neo-Idealist Development of Russian Liberalism, 1885–1922* (Ph.D. dissertation, University of Notre Dame, 1996). The most important source on the society is its journal, *Voprosy filosofii i psikhologii (Questions of Philosophy and Psychology,* 1889–1918) — hereafter designated "VFP" — most issues of which summarize society meetings and business. There is a book of translations from the journal: *Readings in Russian Philosophical Thought,* ed. Louis J. Shein (The Hague: Mouton, 1968). For two brief contemporary histories of the society, see A. S. Belkin, "Obzor deiatel'nosti Moskovskogo Psikhologicheskogo Obshchestva za pervoe desiatiletie (1885–1895)," VFP 6: 2, kn. 27 (1895), pp. 251–258; and N. D. Vinogradov, "Kratkii istoricheskii ocherk deiatel'nosti Moskovskogo Psikhologicheskogo Obshchestva za 25 let," VFP 21: 3, kn. 103 (1910), pp. 249–262. Also see Ia. K. Kolubovskii, "Iz literaturnykh vospominanii," *Istoricheskii vestnik* (April 1914), pp. 134–149.

5. *Vekhi. Landmarks: A Collection of Articles about the Russian Intelligentsia,* trans. and ed. Marshall S. Shatz and Judith E. Zimmerman (Armonk, N.Y.: M. E. Sharpe, 1994); and *Landmarks: A Collection of Essays on the Russian Intelligentsia, 1909,* trans. Marian Schwartz, ed. Boris Shragin and Albert Todd (New York: Katz Howard, 1977).

6. *Out of the Depths (De Profundis): A Collection of Articles on the Russian Revolution,* trans. and ed. William F. Woehrlin, foreword by Bernice Glatzer Rosenthal (Irvine, Calif.: Charles Schlacks, 1986). For analysis also see Jane Burbank, *Intelligentsia and Revolution: Russian Views of Bolshevism, 1917–1922* (Oxford: Oxford University Press, 1986), pp. 190–199.

7. Joseph Frank, *Through the Russian Prism: Essays on Literature and Culture* (Princeton: Princeton University Press, 1990).

8. In 1974 the exiled Aleksandr Solzhenitsyn and several intellectuals still in Russia published a collection of essays entitled *Iz-pod glyb (From Under the Rubble),* which was modeled on *Out of the Depths* (whose title it echoes) and *Vekhi.* It, too, can be seen as a (remote) successor volume to *Problems of Idealism.* A. Solzhenitsyn et al., *From Under the Rubble,* trans. A. M. Brock et al. (Boston: Little, Brown, 1975).

9. An important source on him and the Psychological Society is *Nikolai Iakovle-vich Grot v ocherkakh, vospominaniiakh i pis'makh tovarishchei i uchenikov, druzei i pochitatelei* (St. Petersburg, 1911).

10. A. A. Kizevetter, *Na rubezhe dvukh stoletii. Vospominaniia, 1881–1914* (Prague, 1929; reprinted Newtonville, Mass.: Oriental Research Partners, 1974), p. 85.

11. N. Ia. Grot, "Eshche o zadachakh zhurnala," VFP 2: 2, kn. 6 (1891), p. i. According to Ivanov-Razumnik, *Istoriia russkoi obshchestvennoi mysli*, II, the journal "played a large role in the history of the revival of philosophical thought in Russia. Perhaps it received its special importance because it was not the organ of a particular philosophical group but was, on the contrary, nonpartisan in the philosophical sense. True, the directors of this journal and the large part of its continuous contributors quite definitely adhered to 'idealism' in one respect or another; but at the same time the pages of the journal were always open to the most 'realistic' doctrines and to lively exchange of opinions among opposing philosophical views. . . . Readers thus had before them a kind of 'parliament of philosophical opinions' " (p. 452).

12. N. D. Vinogradov, "Kratkii istoricheskii ocherk deiatel'nosti Moskovskogo Psikhologicheskogo Obshchestva za 25 let," VFP 21: 3, kn. 103 (1910), pp. 261–262.

13. For a classic account of the "revolt against positivism," see H. Stuart Hughes, *Consciousness and Society: The Reorientation of European Social Thought, 1890–1930,* revised edition (New York: Vintage, 1977).

14. Leszek Kolakowski, *The Alienation of Reason: A History of Positivist Thought,* trans. Norbert Guterman (Garden City, N.Y.: Doubleday, 1968).

15. Randall A. Poole, "The Neo-Idealist Reception of Kant in the Moscow Psychological Society," *Journal of the History of Ideas* 60, no. 2 (April 1999), pp. 319–343.

16. Greek patristic thought gives particular attention to the theological foundations of the idea of personhood, the mystical culmination of which is *theosis,* transcendent salvation in immortality and deification, "becoming" or union with God. See Vladimir Lossky, *On the Image and Likeness* (Crestwood, N.Y.: St. Vladimir's Seminary Press, 1974); Lossky, *The Mystical Theology of the Eastern Church* (Crestwood, N.Y.: St. Vladimir's Seminary Press, 1976); Timothy Ware, *The Orthodox Church,* new edition (London: Penguin Books, 1993), pp. 218–221, 231–238; John Meyendorff, *Byzantine Theology: Historical Trends and Doctrinal Themes* (New York: Fordham University Press, 1979), pp. 2–3, 32–33, 37–39, 77–78, 163–165, 225–226; Jaroslav Pelikan, *The Emergence of the Catholic Tradition (100–600)* (Chicago: University of Chicago Press, 1971), pp. 155, 344–345; Pelikan, *The Spirit of Eastern Christendom (600–1700)* (Chicago: University of Chicago Press, 1974), pp. 10–16, 30–36, 254–270; and Lars Thunberg, *Microcosm and Mediator: The Theological Anthropology of Maximus the Confessor,* 2d edition (Chicago: Open Court, 1995). *Russian Religious Thought,* ed. Judith Deutsch Kornblatt and Richard F. Gustafson (Madison: University of Wisconsin Press, 1996), demonstrates the influence of the Orthodox doctrine of *theosis* on late nineteenth- and early-twentieth-century Russian religious philosophy.

17. Vladimir Solovyov, *Lectures on Divine Humanity,* trans. Boris Jakim (Hudson, N.Y.: Lindisferne Press, 1995). These seminal lectures were delivered in St. Petersburg, 1878–1881. Godmanhood, which can also be translated "divine humanity" or the "humanity of God," is the main subject of Paul Valliere's new study, *Modern Russian*

Theology. Bukharev, Soloviev, Bulgakov. Also see Richard F. Gustafson's important essay, "Soloviev's Doctrine of Salvation," in *Russian Religious Thought,* ed. Kornblatt and Gustafson, pp. 31–48.

18. Andrzej Walicki, *Legal Philosophies of Russian Liberalism,* gives detailed consideration to Chicherin, Solov'ëv, and Novgorodtsev. Moreover, B. A. Kistiakovskii, to whom Walicki also devotes a chapter of his study, was associated with the Psychological Society (a formal member from 1910) and published in its journal and symposium, *Problems of Idealism.* On Kistiakovskii, see also Susan Heuman, *Kistiakovsky: The Struggle for National and Constitutional Rights in the Last Years of Tsarism* (Cambridge: Harvard Ukrainian Research Institute, 1998). Chicherin is the subject of a major study by G. M. Hamburg, the first volume of which is *Boris Chicherin and Early Russian Liberalism, 1828–1866* (Stanford, Calif.: Stanford University Press, 1992). Also see *Liberty, Equality, and the Market: Essays by B. N. Chicherin,* ed. and trans. G. M. Hamburg (New Haven: Yale University Press, 1998). Judith E. Zimmerman, "Russian Liberal Theory, 1900–1917," *Canadian-American Slavic Studies* 14: 1 (Spring 1980), pp. 1–20, is a good, concise presentation of the ideas of these philosophers.

19. A prominent example is Chicherin's *Filosofiia prava* (*Philosophy of Law,* 1898–1899).

20. On the Liberation Movement, see Abraham Ascher, *The Revolution of 1905: Russia in Disarray* (Stanford, Calif.: Stanford University Press, 1988); Terence Emmons, "The Beseda Circle, 1899–1905," *Slavic Review* 32: 3 (September 1973); Emmons, *The Formation of Political Parties and the First National Elections in Russia* (Cambridge: Harvard University Press, 1983); Emmons, "Russia's Banquet Campaign," *California Slavic Studies,* vol. X (1977); George Fischer, *Russian Liberalism: From Gentry to Intelligentsia* (Cambridge: Harvard University Press, 1958); Shmuel Galai, *The Liberation Movement in Russia, 1900–1905* (Cambridge: Cambridge University Press, 1973); V. V. Leontovich, *Istoriia liberalizma v Rossii, 1762–1914* (Paris: YMCA Press, 1980); Pipes, *Struve: Liberal on the Left;* N. M. Pirumova, *Zemskoe liberal'noe dvizhenie: Sotsial'nye korni i evoliutsiia do nachala XX v.* (Moscow: Nauka, 1977); and K. F. Shatsillo, *Russkii liberalizm nakanune revoliutsii 1905–1907 gg.* (Moscow: Nauka, 1985).

21. Chicherin died on 3 February 1904, just after the outbreak of the Russo-Japanese War. His last works, *Filosofiia prava* (Moscow, 1900) and *Rossiia nakanune dvadtsatogo stoletiia* (Berlin, 1900), were powerful intellectual spurs to the Russian Liberation Movement, especially in its initial phase, when the constitutionalists hoped to rely mostly on the zemstvo milieu for social support.

22. In March 1903, on the very pages of *Osvobozhdenie,* Struve specified the connection between *Problems of Idealism* and the Liberation Movement. He wrote that *Problems of Idealism* represented the strengthening and broadening of the union between philosophical idealism and liberalism ("practical-political idealism") established by the brilliant publicistic writings of Vladimir Solov'ëv. The task of the Russian Liberation Movement, Struve concluded, was to base its own "self-consciousness and dignity" on the ideas and principles that idealism showed to be irrefutable. P. B. Struve, "O chem dumaet odna kniga?" *Osvobozhdenie,* I, no. 18 (2/15 March 1903), pp. 311–312. Also see Catherine Evtuhov, *The Cross and the Sickle: Sergei Bulgakov and the Fate of Russian Religious Philosophy,* p. 88.

23. A learned society of philosophers and social theorists had special significance in Russia, where, as mentioned in the text, the weak social foundations of liberalism made its intellectual defense all the more important. This historical peculiarity helps explain why, "as Russian liberalism broadened from its gentry base, professors were among the earliest and most prominent adherents from the professions," according to George Fischer in his pioneering study, *Russian Liberalism: From Gentry to Intelligentsia*, p. 53. In the face of government infringement of university autonomy, especially after the University Statute of 1884, professors turned increasingly to learned societies. A. D. Stepanskii, "Liberal'naia intelligentsiia v obshchestvennom dvizhenii Rossii na rubezhe XIX–XX vv.," *Istoricheskie zapiski* 109 (1983), p. 68, describes their significance: "The most influential and authoritative organizations of the Russian intelligentsia [in the broad sense] were the learned societies. . . . The leading role in these societies was played by the professoriate, in which the cultural intelligentsia saw their natural leader (and not only in scientific questions). Learned societies made an enormous contribution to the country's culture." Valuable studies on the professions, learned societies, and civil society in late imperial Russia include Richard S. Wortman, *The Development of a Russian Legal Consciousness* (Chicago: University of Chicago Press, 1976); *Between Tsar and People: Educated Society and the Quest for Public Identity in Late Imperial Russia*, ed. Edith W. Clowes, Samuel D. Kassow, and James L. West (Princeton: Princeton University Press, 1991); Harley D. Balzer, ed., *Russia's Missing Middle Class: The Professions in Russian History* (Armonk, N.Y.: M. E. Sharpe, 1996); Laura Engelstein, *The Keys to Happiness: Sex and the Search for Modernity in Fin-de-Siècle Russia* (Princeton: Princeton University press, 1992); Nancy M. Frieden, *Russian Physicians in an Era of Reform and Revolution, 1856–1905* (Princeton: Princeton University Press, 1981); Samuel D. Kassow, *Students, Professors, and the State in Tsarist Russia* (Berkeley: University of California Press, 1989); James C. McClelland, *Autocrats and Academics: Education, Culture, and Society in Tsarist Russia* (Chicago: University of Chicago Press, 1979); Charles E. Timberlake, "Higher Learning, the State, and the Professions in Russia," *The Transformation of Higher Learning, 1860–1930*, ed. Konrad H. Jarausch (Chicago: University of Chicago Press, 1983); and David Wartenweiler, *Civil Society and Academic Debate in Russia, 1905–1914* (Oxford: Oxford University Press, 1999).

24. Emmons, *The Formation of Political Parties*, pp. 21–72, esp. p. 64, emphasizes this aspect of the history of the constitutional reform movement in Russia. Liberal professionals themselves often had a zemstvo background. A highly visible example of this combination was the *"professor-zemets."* The Psychological Society was home to several such figures, including B. N. Chicherin, S. N. Trubetskoi, E. N. Trubetskoi, S. A. Kotliarevskii, and V. I. Vernadskii. The zemstvo service records and other data on these five men can be found in the appendix, "Zemskie glasnye (gubernskie i uezdnye), uchastvuiushchie v zemskom liberal'nom dvizhenii kontsa XIX-nachala XX veka," to Pirumova, *Zemskoe liberal'noe dvizhenie*, pp. 232–283, and, for the last three, in the appendix, "Party Alignments of Zemstvo Activists in 1905 and 1906," to Emmons, *The Formation of Political Parties*.

25. The convergence of interests between traditional zemstvo constitutionalists and the "new liberals" has been an influential paradigm in the historiography ever since George Fischer's 1958 study, *Russian Liberalism: From Gentry to Intelligentsia* (see esp.

pp. 85–116). Gregory L. Freeze, "A National Liberation Movement and the Shift in Russian Liberalism, 1902–1903," *Slavic Review* 28: 1 (1969), pp. 81–91, clarified the picture by stressing that the leadership itself of the Liberation Movement did not shift "from gentry to intelligentsia," since from the beginning it took the form of an alliance of *zemtsy, intelligenty,* and representatives of the learned professions (especially jurists and professors). The shift consisted in their reappraisal of the dynamics and available social support for the Liberation Movement, from initial reliance on the zemstvo milieu to a policy of "no enemies on the left." This paradigm is employed extensively in Shatsillo, *Russkii liberalizm.*

26. N. M. Pirumova, *Zemskoe liberal'noe dvizhenie,* p. 91; in the appendix she identifies 241 oppositional or liberal zemstvo deputies (a much broader category than the constitutionalists). For comparison, the Zemstvo Statute of 12 June 1890 assigned the number of zemstvo deputies at the district level to 10,236 and at the provincial level to 1,618, as reported in Kermit E. McKenzie, "Zemstvo Organization and Role within the Administrative Structure," *The Zemstvo in Russia: An Experiment in Local Self-Government,* ed. Terence Emmons and Wayne S. Vucinich (Cambridge: Cambridge University Press, 1982), p. 44.

27. Pipes, *Struve: Liberal on the Left,* pp. 153–156.

28. Kizevetter, *Na rubezhe dvukh stoletii,* p. 195, makes this connection.

29. O. N. Trubetskaia, *Kniaz' S. N. Trubetskoi. Vospominaniia sestry* (New York: Chekhov, 1953), pp. 19, 177–178.

30. Martha Bohachevsky-Chomiak, *Sergei N. Trubetskoi: An Intellectual Among the Intelligentsia in Prerevolutionary Russia,* p. 105.

31. E. N. Trubetskoi, *Vospominaniia* (Sofia, 1921; reprinted Newtonville, Mass.: Oriental Research Partners, 1976), pp. 179–183. In addition to the philosophers, the regular guests were Mikhail Nikolaevich's colleagues from the judicial profession; Moscow University professors, including the historians V. I. Ger'e, V. O. Kliuchevskii, and M. S. Korelin; V. A. Gol'tsev, editor of *Russkaia mysl';* S. A. Iur'ev, a well-known Russian *litterateur* from the generation of the 1840s; V. P. Preobrazhenskii, an editor of *Voprosy filosofii i psikhologii;* and L. I. Polivanov, a respected pedagogue, gymnasium director, and specialist in Russian language and literature. All were members of the Psychological Society. Also see N. P. Korelina, "Za piat'desiat let (Vospominaniia o L. M. Lopatine)," *Voprosy filosofii,* no. 11 (1993), pp. 115–121. Nadezhda Petrovna Korelina was married to M. S. Korelin (1855–1899), a historian of Italian humanism and active member of the Psychological Society. After her husband's death, she became secretary of *Voprosy filosofii i psikhologii* in January 1900 and served it the remaining eighteen years of its existence. She was Lopatin's valuable colleague and an important factor in the continued success of the journal.

32. E. N. Trubetskoi, *Vospominaniia,* pp. 179–183.

33. Emmons, "The Beseda Circle," pp. 461–490.

34. Emmons, "The Beseda Circle," pp. 489–490, for membership. Five members of the circle were professors (p. 467); three of them were the Psychological Society philosophers. Sergei Trubetskoi was one of only two Beseda members without formal ties to zemstvo or gentry institutions (the other was V. A. Maklakov).

35. Pipes, *Struve: Liberal on the Left,* pp. 269, 274–275.

36. D. I. Shakhovskoi, "Soiuz Osvobozhdeniia," *Zarnitsy,* 1909, no. 2 (Part II), p. 85. Prince Dmitrii Shakhovskoi (1861–1939) was a Beseda member and one of the most prominent figures in the Liberation Movement.

37. Shmuel Galai, *The Liberation Movement in Russia, 1900–1905,* pp. 47–51.

38. D. N. Shipov, *Vospominaniia i dumy o perezhitom* (Moscow, 1918), p. 128. Further consideration, however, led Shipov to the judgment that Witte's purpose in arguing that autocracy and local self-government were incompatible was, in fact, to demonstrate the inevitability of a constitution (pp. 129–130). Shipov was a strong defender of zemstvo autonomy, but his neo-Slavophile social philosophy rejected the need for a constitution. Therefore, his second reading of Witte's memo distressed him as much as the first. A. A. Kizevetter, *Na rubezhe dvukh stoletii,* similarly suggests that it is too easy to see Witte as simply an apologist for autocracy: "Is not someone who demonstrates that on behalf of preserving the autocracy it is necessary to destroy any public independence — in essence a disowner of autocracy" (p. 331).

39. Trubetskaia, *Kniaz' S. N. Trubetskoi,* p. 34. Trubetskoi himself refers obliquely (but transparently enough) to the Witte document in a penetrating analysis of Russian state and society, written just after the outbreak of the Russo-Japanese War: "In the course of a quarter century they have tried to convince us that autocracy is incompatible with zemstvo self-government, with freedom of conscience and the press, with freedom of association, with inviolability of the person, with a universal [*vsesoslovnyi*] civic order, with an independent and open court, with university autonomy. Not only the opponents of autocracy, but still more its appointed guardians have unanimously demonstrated this. And it has been indisputably and incontrovertibly proved not by arguments, not by pamphlets or ministerial memoranda and official documents, but by the facts themselves." S. N. Trubetskoi, "Na rubezhe," *Sobranie sochinenii Kn. Sergeia Nikolaevicha Trubetskogo,* I, *Publitsisticheskie stat'i* (Moscow, 1907), pp. 459–460.

40. Emmons, *The Formation of Political Parties,* p. 90; and E. D. Chermenskii, "Zemsko-liberal'noe dvizhenie nakanune revoliutsii 1905–1907 gg.," *Istoriia SSSR* 9: 5 (1965), p. 44. Beseda was corporately independent of these efforts: Emmons, "The Beseda Circle," pp. 464–465 (note 10).

41. See Emmons, "The Beseda Circle," pp. 473–474, on the Lvov report and the two political orientations.

42. Ibid., pp. 482–485.

43. I. V. Gessen, A. I. Kaminka, and the editors of *Pravo,* eds., *Konstitutsionnoe gosudarstvo: Sbornik statei,* (St. Petersburg, 1905), as cited by Emmons, "The Beseda Circle," p. 483 (note 69).

44. Emmons, "The Beseda Circle," p. 486. Chermenskii, "Zemsko-liberal'noe dvizhenie nakanune revoliutsii 1905–1907 gg.," p. 50, also makes this important point, as does D. I. Shakhovskoi, "Soiuz Osvobozhdeniia," pp. 104–105.

45. M. A. Kudrinskii, "Arkhivnaia istoriia sbornika 'Problemy idealizma' (1902)," *Voprosy filosofii,* no. 4 (1993), pp. 157–165, presents invaluable research on the history of the *Problems of Idealism* project. The author of the article is not "Kudrinskii," but M. A. Kolerov.

46. Shatsillo, *Russkii liberalizm,* pp. 65–66; Galai, *The Liberation Movement in Russia,* p. 116.

47. Shatsillo, *Russkii liberalizm,* pp. 73–74; Kizevetter, *Na rubezhe dvukh stoletti,* pp. 336–337; Galai, *The Liberation Movement in Russia,* p. 116. G. V. Vernadskii, "Bratstvo Priiutino," *Novyi zhurnal* 28: kn. 96 (1969), pp. 164–165, states that between 1900 and 1902 "several" such conferences took place in Moscow, usually at Vernadskii's apartment.

48. Shatsillo, *Russkii liberalizm* p. 76.

49. Shakhovskoi, "Soiuz Osvobozhdeniia," p. 104; Emmons, "The Beseda Circle," p. 475.

50. Emmons, *The Formation of Political Parties,* p. 24.

51. See M. A. Kudrinskii [Kolerov], "Arkhivnaia istoriia sbornika 'Problemy idealizma' (1902)," pp. 158–160, for the details in this paragraph. Bernice Glatzer Rosenthal and Bohachevsky-Chomiak, in their introduction to *A Revolution of the Spirit,* p. 21, also identify Zhukovskii as the financier of *Problemy idealizma.*

52. "Moskovskoe Psikhologichekoe Obshchestvo," VFP 25: 3, kn. 123 (1914), p. 353. On Zhukovskii, see Pipes, *Struve: Liberal on the Left,* pp. 311–312.

53. "Psikhologicheskoe Obshchestvo," VFP 9: 2, kn. 42 (1898), pp. 164–165.

54. *Frantsiskanskii orden i rimskaia kuriia v XIII i XIV vv. (The Franciscan Order and the Roman Curia in the Thirteenth and Fourteenth Centuries,* 1901), for the *magister,* and *Lamenne i noveishii katolitsizm (Lamennais and Recent Catholicism,* 1904), for the doctorate.

55. *Konstitutsionnoe pravo. Opyt politiko-morfologicheskogo obzora (Constitutional Law: An Attempt at a Political-Morphological Survey,* 1907), and *Pravovoe gosudarstvo i vneshniaia politika (The Law-Governed State and Foreign Policy,* 1909).

56. *Ocherki realisticheskogo mirovozzreniia: Sb. statei po filosofii, obshchestvennoi nauke i zhizni* (St. Petersburg, 1904) was the most significant positivist response to the idealist revival. It included articles by V. A. Bazarov, A. A. Bogdanov, A. V. Lunacharskii, and S. A. Suvorov. On the polemic, see A. A. Ermichev, " 'Problemy idealizma' i 'Ocherki realisticheskogo mirovozzreniia' — polemika o sotsial'nom ideale," *Filosofiia i osvoboditel'noe dvizhenie v Rossii,* eds. A. A. Ermichev, S. N. Savel'ev (Leningrad, 1989), pp. 167–184.

57. Kendall E. Bailes, *Science and Russian Culture in an Age of Revolutions: V. I. Vernadsky and His Scientific School, 1863–1945* (Bloomington: Indiana University Press, 1990), pp. 49–50.

58. Kudrinskii [Kolerov], "Arkhivnaia istoriia sbornika 'Problemy idealizma' (1902)," p. 161.

59. V. I. Vernadskii, "O nauchnom mirovozzrenii," VFP 13: 5, kn. 65 (1902), pp. 1409–1465. On 20 August 1902 Vernadskii wrote to his wife: "I am now working out one of the first introductory lectures to my course [on the history of physical-chemical and geological sciences], which perhaps I will publish separately in 'Voprosy filosofii.' The lecture is about the relation of science to philosophy (and in part religion) in the development of thought (. . .). These old ideas, arising in me long ago, have become especially clear these days thanks to conversations with Pavel Ivanovich [Novgorodtsev] (with whom I do not completely agree)." Quoted by Kudrinskii [Kolerov], p. 161 (ellipses his).

60. "Moskovskoe Psikhologicheskoe Obshchestvo," VFP 16: 1, kn. 76 (1905), pp. 145–147. Vernadskii's paper, "Kant i estestvoznanie XVIII stoletiia," appears in the

same issue, pp. 36–70. Also see V. I. Shubin, "Kant i Vernadskii," in *Kant i filosofiia v Rossii,* eds. Z. A. Kamenskii and V. A. Zhuchkov (Moscow: Nauka, 1994), pp. 212–226.

61. Bailes, *Science and Russian Culture,* p. 34.

62. "Moskovskoe Psikhologicheskoe Obshchestvo," VFP 13: 1, kn. 61 (1902), pp. 633–634.

63. Emmons, *The Formation of Political Parties,* p. 65, identifies S. F. Ol'denburg as a zemets. G. V. Vernadskii, "Bratstvo Priiutino," *Novyi zhurnal* 28: kn. 96 (1969), p. 156, identifies him as a deputy to the St. Petersburg City Duma. F. F. Ol'denburg studied Greek language and philosophy at the university, where he wrote his senior (*kandidatskii*) thesis on Plato. He then directed a school in Tver. See G. V. Vernadskii, "Bratstvo Priiutino," *Novyi zhurnal* 27: kn. 93 (1968), pp. 152–153. I. M. Grevs, another *Priiutinets,* considered Fëdor the spiritual center of the group (ibid, p. 161).

64. Emmons, *The Formation of Political Parties,* pp. 66–67, stresses this in his account of the Priiutino Brotherhood.

65. G. V. Vernadskii, "Bratstvo Priiutino," *Novyi zhurnal* 28: kn. 95 (1969), p. 205; Bailes, *Science and Russian Culture,* pp. 61–63.

66. G. V. Vernadskii, "Bratstvo Priiutino," *Novyi zhurnal* 27: kn. 93 (1968), p. 147. Bailes, *Science and Russian Culture,* p. 28, quotes the nearly identical words of Vladimir Ivanovich himself. D. I. Shakhovskoi was closest to Tolstoy among the Priiutintsy (Emmons, *The Formation of Political Parties,* p. 66). Yet, before his death in the Soviet Union in 1939, he pursued interests in a philosopher whom Tolstoy would likely have found inimical: Pëtr Chaadaev. The most significant result of Shakhovskoi's research into Chaadaev, his great uncle, was his discovery in 1935 of five unknown "Philosophical Letters," which Shakhovskoi published in the journal *Literaturnoe nasledstvo* that year. During this time Shakhovskoi prepared two editions of Chaadaev's works, neither of which saw light of day. P. Ia. Chaadaev, *Polnoe sobranie sochinenii i izbrannye pis'ma,* I, ed. Z. A. Kamenskii (Moscow: Nauka, 1991), pp. 680–681.

67. Quoted by Bailes, *Science and Russian Culture,* p. 28.

68. I wish to acknowledge here G. M. Hamburg's valuable suggestions about possible connections between the Bratstvo Priiutino and the *Problems of Idealism* project.

69. The conversion of the "legal Marxists" to idealism has long been considered a milestone in Silver Age intellectual history, and is one of its best known chapters. In addition to Richard Pipes's classic two-volume study of Struve, see Richard Kindersley, *The First Russian Revisionists. A Study of 'Legal Marxism' in Russia* (Oxford: Oxford University Press, 1962), and Arthur P. Mendel, *Dilemmas of Progress in Tsarist Russia: Legal Marxism and Legal Populism* (Cambridge: Harvard University Press, 1961). Hereafter, I follow Kindersley's suggestion: inverted commas properly enclose "legal Marxism," but it would be tedious to persist with them.

70. Quoted by Shatsillo, *Russkii liberalizm,* p. 60.

71. As Rosenthal and Bohachevsky-Chomiak write in their introduction to *A Revolution of the Spirit* (p. 20): "The philosophers were their first, and natural, allies in the process. A concrete result of that collaboration was . . . the symposium *Problemy idealizma.*"

72. Spektorskii's review is reprinted in *Nikolai Iakovlevich Grot v ocherkakh, vospominaniiakh i pis'makh tovarishchei i uchenikov, druzei i pochitatelei* (St. Peters-

burg, 1911), pp. 374–386; here, p. 374. Evgenii V. Spektorskii (1873–1951) was professor (from 1913) and later rector at Kiev University, president of the Philosophical Society there, and an active émigré scholar after the Revolution in the theory of the social sciences, philosophy of law, and philosophy of religion.

73. S. N. Bulgakov, "Chto daet sovremennomu soznaniiu filosofiia Vladimira Solov'ëva?" in *Ot marksizma k idealizmu: Sbornik statei, 1896–1903* (St. Petersburg, 1903), pp. 195–262. This essay was first published in VFP 14: 1–2, kn. 66–67 (1903).

74. "Psikhologicheskoe Obshchestvo," VFP 8: 5, kn. 40 (1897), p. 815.

75. S. N. Bulgakov, "O zakonomernosti sotsial'nykh iavlenii," VFP 7: 5, kn. 35 (1896), pp. 575–611. Struve's response was "Svoboda i istoricheskaia neobkhodimost'," VFP 8: 1, kn. 36 (1897), pp. 120–139. Arthur P. Mendel, *Dilemmas of Progress in Tsarist Russia,* p. 167, writes that in Struve's article, "Legal Marxism took its first hesitant step . . . toward neo-Kantian idealism." Bulgakov at the time was still committed to positivism and Marxism. On this debate, see also Richard Pipes, *Struve: Liberal on the Left,* pp. 184–189.

76. For Bulgakov's development from Marxism to idealism, see the fine studies by Evtuhov, *The Cross and the Sickle,* pp. 28–65, and Paul Valliere, *Modern Russian Theology,* pp. 227–251.

77. "Moskovskoe Psikhologicheskoe Obshchestvo," VFP 13: 3, kn. 63 (1902), p. 862.

78. Quoted by Philip J. Swoboda in his study, *The Philosophical Thought of S. L. Frank, 1902–1915: A Study of the Metaphysical Impulse in Early Twentieth-Century Russia* (Ph.D. dissertation, Columbia University, 1992), p. 138. Also see Philip Boobbyer, *S. L. Frank: The Life and Work of a Russian Philosopher, 1877–1950* (Athens: Ohio University Press, 1995), p. 23.

79. Swoboda, *Philosophical Thought of S. L. Frank,* pp. 134–135.

80. N. A. Berdiaev, "O novom russkom idealizme," VFP 15: 5, kn. 75 (1904), pp. 683–724, esp. pp. 695–696.

81. Walicki, *Legal Philosophies of Russian Liberalism,* treats Chicherin under the rubric of the "old liberal" philosophy of law and Solov'ëv and Novgorodtsev as representatives of new liberalism, a contrast that involves differences not so much between philosophical foundations (all three were idealists) as between their own social backgrounds (zemstvo in Chicherin's case and urban professional in the other two) and in the social content of their respective liberal philosophies (classical liberal versus the new right to a dignified existence). This distinction helps explain why Solov'ëv and Novgorodtsev were more popular among the former Marxists than Chicherin was. Chicherin, a Hegelian, cannot be called a neo-idealist without qualification. Yet, his *Philosophy of Law* "appeared not as the work of an epigone but, rather, as a milestone on the new road," Walicki writes. "It was indeed such a revival of the old philosophical idealism, which took account of new trends in philosophy and the theory of law, and could therefore be treated as representing a neo-idealist current in legal philosophy" (p. 161).

82. The Trubetskois and Ol'denburg were not present at the Schaffhausen conference. See Shatsillo, *Russkii liberalizm,* p. 158, for Schaffhausen attendance. Pipes, in *Struve: Liberal on the Left,* makes the connection between the *Problemy* authors and Schaffhausen. Referring to the four former legal Marxists, he writes, "In the winter of 1902–

1903 members of this group published an important symposium, *Problems of Idealism,* in which they attempted to provide a generalized metaphysical and religious foundation for liberal politics" (p. 334). The other two contributors to *Problemy,* A. S. Lappo-Danilevskii and S. A. Askol'dov, had no significant role in the Liberation Movement, insofar as I know.

83. Since Kotliarevskii and Vernadskii were not contributors, I will briefly note here their political activity during this period, which has parallels with Novgorodtsev's. Kotliarevskii was co-opted with Novgorodtsev onto the Council of the Union of Liberation immediately after its constituent congress. Both served in "Group A" of the Moscow branch of the Union of Liberation, as did Vernadskii. Group A, which consisted primarily of zemtsy and professors, was the union's theory and policy planning center. In his important role in Group A's work on a draft constitution for the Russian Empire, Kotliarevskii was nearly alone in insisting on women's suffrage. He and Vernadskii were founders and Central Committee members of the Kadet party, and Kotliarevskii was a deputy to the First State Duma. See Shatsillo, *Russkii liberalizm,* pp. 158, 204, 259–260; Emmons, "The Beseda Circle," p. 469; and Shakhovskoi, "Soiuz Osvobozhdeniia," pp. 122–123.

84. "Moskovskoe Psikhologicheskoe Obshchestvo," VFP 23: 2, kn. 112 (1912), p. 357.

85. S. A. Levitskii, *Ocherki po istorii russkoi filosofskoi i obshchestvennoi mysli,* II (Frankfurt/Main: Posev, 1981), p. 18. L. M. Lopatin, "Teoreticheskie osnovy soznatel'noi nravstvennoi zhizni," VFP 2: 1, kn. 5 (1890), pp. 34–83, is an excellent statement of his moral philosophy; the last part of the essay, "The idea of the immortality of the soul," is a defense of the soul's substantiality (irreducible ontological reality).

86. For example, see S. N. Trubetskoi, "O prirode chelovecheskogo soznaniia" (1889–1891), and "Osnovaniia idealizma" (1896), reprinted in *Sobranie sochinenii Kn. Sergeia Nikolaevicha Trubetskogo,* II, *Filosofskie stat'i* (Moscow, 1908), pp. 1–110, 161–284; L. M. Lopatin, "Uchenie Kanta o poznanii" (1905), reprinted in his *Filosofskie kharakteristiki i rechi* (Moscow, 1911), pp. 56–69; and Evgenii Trubetskoi, *Metafizicheskie predpolozheniia poznaniia. Opyt preodoleniia Kanta i kantianstva* (Moscow, 1917).

87. Pëtr Struve, "Predislovie," to Nikolai Berdiaev, *Sub"ektivizm i individualizm v obshchestvennoi filosofii: Kriticheskii etiud o N. K. Mikhailovskom* (St. Petersburg, 1901), pp. liv–lv.

88. Ibid., p. liv. Pipes, *Struve: Liberal on the Left,* pp. 293–307, provides a fine reconstruction of Struve's philosophy of liberalism.

89. Struve, "Predislovie," p. xxxii. Richard Kindersley, *The First Russian Revisionists,* pp. 118–122, analyzes Struve's argument from duty and free will to the substantiality of the self, or the entailment of ontology from ethics.

90. L. M. Lopatin, *Polozhitel'nye zadachi filosofii. Chast' vtoraia: Zakon prichinnoi sviazi, kak osnova umozritel'nogo znaniia deistvitel'nosti* (Moscow, 1891), esp. pp. 213–224.

91. Struve, "Predislovie," p. xxxiii.

92. P. I. Novgorodtsev, *Kant i Gegel' v ikh ucheniiakh o prave i gosudarstve. Dva*

tipicheskikh postroeniia v oblasti filosofii prava (Moscow, 1901), pp. 98–99 (note). The words he quotes from Struve (he does not give the citation) can be found in Struve, "Predislovie," p. xxxv. Novgorodtsev's preface is dated 9 October 1901.

93. Pipes, *Struve: Liberal on the Left,* pp. 300–301.

94. P. Borisov [Struve], "V chem zhe istinnyi natsionalizm?" VFP 12: 4, kn. 59 (1901), pp. 493–528; reprinted in his collection of articles, *Na raznye temy* (St. Petersburg, 1902), pp. 526–555.

95. P. Borisov [Struve], "V chem zhe istinnyi natsionalizm?" pp. 503, 511.

96. Ibid., pp. 504, 520.

97. Ibid., p. 507 (emphasis Struve's).

98. Ibid., p. 512.

99. P. I. Novgorodtsev, "Uchenie Kanta o prave i gosudarstve," VFP 12: 3, kn. 58 (1901), pp. 315–361.

100. Novgorodtsev, *Kant i Gegel' v ikh ucheniiakh o prave i gosudarstve,* pp. 146–147. In the journal article, "Uchenie Kanta o prave i gosudarstve," see the corresponding section on natural law, pp. 350–361. Walicki devotes a chapter of his *Legal Philosophies* to "Pavel Novgorodtsev: Neo-Idealism and the Revival of Natural Law," pp. 291–341; on Novgorodtsev's *Kant i Gegel' v ikh ucheniiakh o prave i gosudarstve,* see pp. 304–306.

101. Novgorodtsev, *Kant i Gegel' v ikh ucheniiakh o prave i gosudarstve,* pp. 148–149.

102. Ibid., pp. 150.

103. Struve, "Predislovie," p. lxviii. Also see his essay, "K voprosu o morali," from October 1901, reprinted in *Na raznye temy,* pp. 508–521, esp. p. 520.

104. E. N. Trubetskoi, "Novoe issledovanie o filosofii prava Kanta i Gegelia," VFP 13: 1, kn. 61 (1902), p. 602.

105. P. I. Novgorodtsev, "K voprosu o sovremennykh filosofskikh iskaniiakh. (Otvet L. I. Petrazhitskomu)," VFP 14: 1, kn. 66 (1903), p. 138.

106. A. V. Sobolev, "Pavel Ivanovich Novgorodtsev," introductory essay to his edition of P. I. Novgorodtsev, *Ob obshchestvennom ideale* (Moscow: Pressa, 1991; *Voprosy filosofii* series), p. 5.

107. Quoted by Dimitrii Levitskii, "P. I. Novgorodtsev," *Russkaia religiozno-filosofskaia mysl' XX veka,* ed. Nikolai P. Poltoratsky (Pittsburgh, PA.: University of Pittsburgh, 1975), p. 304.

108. P. I. Novgorodtsev, "Sushchestvo russkogo pravoslavnogo soznaniia," *Pravoslavie i kul'tura. Sbornik religiozno-filosofskikh statei,* ed. V. V. Zen'kovskii (Berlin, 1923), p. 22. A translation of this essay can be found in *A Revolution of the Spirit,* eds. Bernice Glatzer Rosenthal and Martha Bohachevsky-Chomiak.

109. G. V. Florovskii, "Pamiati P. I. Novgorodtseva," *Novyi mir,* no. 12, December 1991, p. 218, reprinted from *Rossiia i Slavianstvo* (Paris), 27 April 1929. Walicki, *Legal Philosophies of Russian Liberalism,* pp. 340–341, also stresses the continuity in Novgorodtsev's thought.

110. Struve, "Filosofiia ideal'nogo dobra ili apologiia real'nogo zla?" *Na raznye temy,* pp. 187–197; quotation at p. 187. Pipes, *Struve: Liberal on the Left,* p. 294, and Kindersley, *The First Russian Revisionists,* p. 145, also point to Struve's about-face on Solov'ëv.

111. Struve, "Pamiati Vladimira Solov'ëva," *Na raznye temy,* pp. 198–202, esp. pp. 200–202.

112. *Natsional'nyi vopros v Rossii. Vypusk pervyi* (St. Petersburg, 1888) and *Natsional'nyi vopros v Rossii. Vypusk vtoroi* (St. Petersburg, 1891). Also, S. M. Solov'ëv and E. L. Radlov, eds., *Sobranie sochinenii Vladimira Sergeevicha Solov'ëva,* 2d edition (St. Petersburg, 1911–1914), vol. 5, pp. 3–401. For a recent analysis of these and related writings of Solov'ëv, see Greg Gaut, "Can a Christian Be a Nationalist? Vladimir Solov'ëv's Critique of Nationalism," *Slavic Review* 57, no. 1 (Spring 1998), pp. 77–94.

113. This did not prevent him, however, from attempting to appropriate for Russian liberalism Ivan Aksakov's defense of freedom of conscience ("V chem zhe istinnyi natsionalizm?" pp. 513–519). See the section below, "Freedom of Conscience."

114. P. I. Novgorodtsev, "Ideia prava v filosofii Vl. S. Solov'ëva," VFP 12: 1, kn. 56 (1901), p. 114.

115. Ibid., pp. 125–126.

116. Ibid., p. 119.

117. Ibid., p. 120.

118. The following details and quotations in this paragraph are from Kudrinskii [Kolerov], "Arkhivnaia istoriia sbornika 'Problemy idealizma' (1902)," pp. 157–158.

119. Kudrinskii [Kolerov], p. 158, provides the initial table of contents. Most of the proposed contributors were zemtsy and/or professors. Kudrinskii [Kolerov], p. 159, reports that through K. K. Arsen'ev (whom Pipes, *Struve: Liberal on the Left,* p. 341, calls "the idol of Struve's youth"), Struve became acquainted with the "Bratstvo Priiutino," one of his connections, in turn, to Novgorodtsev. According to Emmons, *The Formation of Political Parties,* p. 65, from the late 1880s Arsen'ev organized regular "evenings" and colloquia in St. Petersburg between zemtsy and nonzemstvo professionals and intellectuals that were attended by, for example, Struve and S. A. Kotliarevskii.

120. Kudrinskii [Kolerov], p. 157.

121. D. N. Shipov, the head of the neo-Slavophile direction, himself rejected the label and did not think that Orthodoxy was superior to other Christian faiths. See Emmons, *The Formation of Political Parties,* p. 407, nt. 20; and Leonard Schapiro, *Rationalism and Nationalism in Russian Nineteenth-Century Political Thought* (New Haven: Yale University Press, 1967), p. 148.

122. P. Borisov [Struve], "V chem zhe istinnyi natsionalizm?" pp. 505–506. Struve does not provide a specific citation for Novgorodtsev. In the fourth edition of his excellent *Lektsii po istorii filosofii prava: Ucheniia novogo vremeni, XVI–XIX vv.* (Moscow, 1918), Novgorodtsev's consideration of Williams (on which it is clear Struve entirely bases his account) is on pp. 65–68. Both Novgorodtsev and Struve refer to a series of articles by M. M. Kovalevskii, "Rodonachal'niki angliiskogo radikalizma," *Russkaia mysl'* (January–March 1892).

123. P. Borisov [Struve], "V chem zhe istinnyi natsionalizm?" pp. 508–509.

124. Andrzej Walicki, *The Slavophile Controversy: History of a Conservative Utopia in Nineteenth-Century Russian Thought,* trans. Hilda Andrews-Rusiecka (Oxford: Oxford University Press, 1975), striving for fairness, identifies the arguments that could be made on Aksakov's behalf, including his defense of freedom of conscience and speech. "All these facts do not, however, affect the over-all diagnosis that Ivan Aksakov

represents a glaring example of the evolution of Slavophilism towards chauvinistic nationalism and extreme social and political reaction," which included anti-Semitism (p. 501).

125. S. N. Trubetskoi, "Na rubezhe," *Sobranie sochinenii Kn. Sergeia Nikolaevicha Trubetskogo*, I, p. 477.

126. P. I. Novgorodtsev, "Gosudarstvo i pravo," VFP 15: 4, kn. 74 (1904), p. 405. Novgorodtsev does not quite finish the quotation. I have translated it from the fuller version in P. Borisov [Struve], "V chem zhe istinnyi natsionalizm?" p. 514.

127. Walicki, *Legal Philosophies of Russian Liberalism*, p. 312. Walicki provides a full analysis of Novgorodtsev's essay (pp. 312–318).

128. G. M. Hamburg, *Boris Chicherin and Early Russian Liberalism*, pp. 225–233, provides a full account of Chicherin's lecture and its reception. According to Hamburg, "by expressing only the conservative dimension of conservative liberalism, the inaugural lecture opened Chicherin to the charge that he had abandoned liberalism altogether, that he was nothing but a reactionary anti-revolutionist and, worst of all, a blind worshiper of the state" (p. 228). Hamburg also considers Aksakov's criticism of Chicherin (pp. 230–231), which appeared in the periodical *Den'* (11 November 1861).

129. P. Borisov [Struve], "V chem zhe istinnyi natsionalizm?" p. 513 (note). Walicki, *Legal Philosophies of Russian Liberalism*, p. 137, notes that Struve was wrong in describing Chicherin's earlier views as positivistic.

130. Ger'e (1837–1919) was an active member of the society from its earliest years, and was elected to honorary membership in January 1899, "in commemoration of Vladimir Ivanovich's outstanding services, well-known to everyone, before Russian philosophical thought." See "Moskovskoe Psikhologicheskoe Obshchestvo," VFP 10: 1, kn. 46 (1899), pp. 68–69, 78. Following the defense of his doctoral dissertation, *Leibnits i ego vek* (St. Petersburg, 1868), he became professor of European history at Moscow University. His works focused on the history of political thought, philosophy of history, and historiography. He devoted three of his later books to church history and the idea of the "Kingdom of God" in medieval historical and political thought: *Blazhennyi Avgustin* (Moscow, 1910), *Zapadnoe monashestvo i papstvo* (Moscow, 1913), and *Rastsvet zapadnoi teokratii* (Moscow, 1916). His important book, *Filosofiia istorii ot Avgustina do Gegelia* (Moscow, 1915), includes a chapter on theocratic ideas of human history. Ger'e also wrote *Frantsisk [St. Francis of Assisi], apostol nishchety i liubvi* (Moscow, 1908). His work in church history stressed that theocracy can be no less transcendent an ideal than the Kingdom of God itself, not a practical goal of politics. Western Christianity, in the final analysis, recognized this. "The papacy," Ger'e wrote in a review, "even in the epoch of its greatest triumph, did not reject in principle the independence of political power and civil law." See his "K voprosu o sushchnosti teokratii," VFP 10: 3, kn. 48 (1899), p. 311.

131. "Contemporary Tasks of Russian Life," in *Liberty, Equality, and the Market: Essays by B. N. Chicherin*, ed. and trans. G. M. Hamburg (New Haven: Yale University Press, 1998), p. 134.

132. See Paul Valliere, "Theological Liberalism and Church Reform in Imperial Russia," in *Church, Nation and State in Russia and Ukraine*, ed. Geoffrey A. Hosking (London: Macmillan, 1991), pp. 108–130 (on Chicherin, pp. 119–124). Valliere writes that theological liberalism "affirms two axioms with respect to religious life: freedom of conscience, and the relative autonomy of the secular spheres of life" (p. 108). This con-

cept of autonomy was central to the neo-idealist development of liberalism in the Psychological Society.

133. S. N. Trubetskoi, "Na rubezhe," *Sobranie sochinenii Kn. Sergeia Nikolaevicha Trubetskogo,* I, pp. 477–478. Also see his unfinished article, "O sovremennom polozhenii russkoi tserkvi," pp. 438–446.

134. S. A. Kotliarevskii, "Predposylki demokratii," VFP 16: 2, kn. 77 (1905), p. 126. Kotliarevskii's first essay in *Voprosy filosofii* was "Religiia v amerikanskom obshchestve," VFP 15: 1, kn. 71 (1904), pp. 1–33, a review of Henry Bargy, *La religion dans la société aux États-Unis* (Paris, 1902). Kotliarevskii was very interested in William James as a religious thinker. See Randall A. Poole, "William James in the Moscow Psychological Society: Pragmatism, Pluralism, Personalism," in *William James and Russian Culture,* ed. Joan Delaney Grossman and Ruth S. Rischin (Lanham, Md.: Rowman and Littlefield, 2003), pp. 131–158.

135. See Randall A. Poole, "Utopianism, Idealism, Liberalism: Russian Confrontations with Vladimir Solov'ëv," *Modern Greek Studies Yearbook: Mediterranean, Slavic, and Eastern Orthodox Studies* (University of Minnesota), vols. 16–17 (2000–2001), pp. 43–87.

136. E. N. Trubetskoi, *Mirosozertsanie Vl. S. Solov'ëva,* I (Moscow, 1913), p. 177. Trubetskoi's classic two-volume study takes as its overall framework the critique of Solov'ëv's utopianism.

137. E. N. Trubetskoi wrote two substantial volumes on the idea of theocracy in medieval Europe: *Religiozno-obshchestvennyi ideal zapadnogo khristianstva v V veke: Mirosozertsanie bl. Avgustina* (Moscow, 1892); and *Religiozno-obshchestvennyi ideal zapadnogo khristianstva v XI veke: Ideia bozheskogo tsarstva v tvoreniiakh Grigoriia VII-go i ego publitsistov—sovremennikov* (Kiev, 1897). Novgorodtsev's debut on the pages of *Voprosy filosofii* took the form of a review, co-authored with V. I. Ger'e, of the second volume: "K voprosu o sushchnosti teokratii," VFP 10: 3, kn. 48 (1899), pp. 304–311. Also see Gere's works cited above. Novgorodtsev's major study, *Ob obshchestvennom ideale* (Moscow, 1917), claims that every utopia "in essence reproduces the idea of medieval theocracy about the salvation of people through a society of the faithful" (pp. 17–18). S. A. Kotliarevskii also wrote a great deal on religious history, including his first two dissertations (cited above). The great historian V. O. Kliuchevskii, another member of the Psychological Society (although not an idealist in his philosophical views), authored a series of articles entitled, "Zapadnoe vliianie v Rossii XVII v. (Istoriko-psikhologicheskii ocherk)," VFP 8: 1, 3–4, kn. 36, 38–39 (1897), in which he argued that the impact of western ideas in Russia was so great because the Russian church failed to provide a strong source of indigenous intellectual traditions. Kliuchevskii pointed in particular to the debilitating effects of the seventeenth-century Schism, which increased the church's dependence on the state and led to a precipitous decline in its influence on educated society. Deprived of religious *vospitanie,* Russians turned to ideology as a surrogate for spiritual satisfaction the Russian church could not provide. Kliuchevskii's student Pavel Miliukov, also a (nominal) member of the Psychological Society, pursued essentially the same argument in his *Ocherki po istorii russkoi kul'tury* (*Studies of Russian Culture*), which first appeared in 1896. See Melissa Kirschke Stockdale, *Paul Miliukov and the Quest for a Liberal Russia* (Ithaca, N.Y.: Cornell University Press, 1996), pp. 70–71.

138. See Solov'ëv's series of articles published from 1881 to 1883 in Ivan Aksakov's

Rus': "O dukhovnoi vlasti v Rossii," "O tserkvi i raskole," and "Velikii spor i khristianskaia politika." They have recently been collected in V. S. Solov'ëv, *Sochineniia v dvukh tomakh*, I, *Filosofskaia publitsistika* (Moscow: Pravda, 1989; the *Voprosy filosofii* series). For summary and analysis, see E. N. Trubetskoi, *Mirosozertsanie Vl. S. Solov'ëva*, I, pp. 437–448; Losev, *Vladimir Solov'ëv i ego vremia*, pp. 342–347; Mochul'skii, *Vladimir Solov'ëv*, pp. 134–144; and Strémooukhoff, *Vladimir Soloviev and His Messianic Work*, pp. 141–46, 187–188.

139. Especially important in this respect is Solov'ëv's *Evreistvo i khristianskii vopros* (*Jewry and the Christian Question*, 1884): *Sobranie sochinenii Vladimira Sergeevicha Solov'ëva*, vol. 4, pp. 135–185.

140. According to Losev, "Of all of Solov'ëv's ideas, none was so far removed from contemporary Russian public opinion [*obshchestvennost'*]. Everyone considered this Solov'ëvian theocracy something queer" (p. 629).

141. Walicki, *Legal Philosophies of Russian Liberalism*, p. 191.

142. Solov'ëv was involved in organizing famine relief. He was among the thirty prominent citizens who met at the Moscow apartment of I. I. Petrunkevich for this purpose at the end of September or beginning of October 1891. The meeting was convened by V. I. Vernadskii, his wife Natasha Egorovna, A. A. Kornilov, and D. I. Shakhovskoi, all members of the Bratstvo Priiutino. See G. V. Vernadskii, "Bratstvo Priiutino," *Novyi Zhurnal* 28: kn. 95 (1969), p. 204; also, more generally, S. M. Solov'ëv, *Zhizn' i tvorcheskaia evoliutsiia Vladimira Solov'ëva* (Brussels: Foyer Oriental Chretien, 1977), p. 298. For Solov'ëv's articles on the famine, "Narodnaia beda i obshchestvennaia pomoshch'," and "Nash grekh i nasha obiazannost'," see V. S. Solov'ëv, *Sochineniia v dvukh tomakh*, II (Moscow: Pravda, 1989; *Voprosy filosofii* series), pp. 370–386.

143. E. N. Trubetskoi, *Mirosozertsanie Vl. S. Solov'ëva*, II, pp. 7, 10. Trubetskoi devotes this entire chapter of his study to arguing that Solov'ëv's disappointment in Russian state and society spurred the collapse, or at any rate marked de-utopianization, of his theocratic project (pp. 3–38).

144. The lecture was an event: 80 members of the society and about 300 guests were present. "Psikhologicheskoe Obshchestvo," VFP, kn. 10 (Nov. 1891), p. 91. The censors banned publication of the lecture, together with two articles on the famine (by N. Ia. Grot and L. N. Tolstoi) that were scheduled to appear in the same issue of *Voprosy filosofii*. The lecture was later published in the 1901 issue dedicated to Solov'ëv's memory: "O prichinakh upadka srednevekovogo mirosozertsaniia," VFP 12: 1, kn. 56 (1901), pp. 138–152.

145. A few of Solov'ëv's comments, such as his suggestion that a few hardworking atheists contribute more to Christian progress than many believers, were infelicitous with respect to the possible reception in officially connected circles. Ia. K. Kolubovskii, "Iz literaturnykh vospominanii," *Istoricheskii vestnik*, tom cxxxvi (April 1914), pp. 139–143, provides an eyewitness account of the lecture and the ensuing controversy. Solov'ëv's lecture, the debate on it in the Psychological Society, and two of Solov'ëv's letters to *Moskovskie vedomosti* are included in V. S. Solov'ëv, *Sochineniia v dvukh tomakh*, II, pp. 344–369; the editors of this volume reconstruct the history of the affair (pp. 689–692). On it also see Losev, *Vladimir Solov'ëv i ego vremia*, pp. 481–490, and Mochul'skii, *Vladimir Solov'ëv*, pp. 193–196.

146. I believe Losev is correct in maintaining this, as he does throughout *Vladimir Solov'ëv i ego vremia*. Evgenii Trubetskoi, by contrast, argues for the utter collapse of the theocratic ideal in the 1890s.

147. Dimitri Strémooukhoff, *Vladimir Soloviev and His Messianic Work*, pp. 247–250, appraises the 1891 Psychological Society lecture as particularly revealing of Solov'ëv's new outlook: "The new elements in this attitude are a more active alliance with the liberals, . . . positive criticism of the Church, and finally a new theory in which the manifestation of the Kingdom of God is taking place through progress" (p. 250).

148. Vl. S. Solov'ëv, "O prichinakh upadka srednevekovogo mirosozertsaniia," *Sochineniia v dvukh tomakh*, II, p. 351.

149. Ibid., p. 345 (emphasis Solov'ëv's).

150. Ibid., pp. 354–355.

151. P. I. Novgorodtsev, "Ideia prava v filosofii Vl. S. Solov'ëv," VFP 12: 1, kn. 56 (1901), pp. 121–122.

152. Walicki, *Legal Philosophies of Russian Liberalism*, pp. 194–195.

153. Novgorodtsev, *Lektsii po istorii filosofii prava*, p. 3.

154. Ibid., p. 5.

155. Ibid., p. 6. Novgorodtsev does not specify that he is quoting from Solov'ëv's "O prichinakh upadka srednevekovogo mirosozertsaniia," no doubt because it was still banned at the time he was writing. The quotations can be found in V. S. Solov'ëv, *Sochineniia v dvukh tomakh*, II, pp. 354–355.

156. Novgorodtsev, *Lektsii po istorii filosofii prava*, pp. 4–6.

157. According to Kudrinskii [Kolerov], "Arkhivnaia istoriia sbornika 'Problemy idealizma' (1902)," pp. 159–163, Struve soon discovered in the first, "narrowly political" conception of the project much broader perspectives that offered him and the other former Marxists the opportunity to defend their intellectual evolution. With that he expanded the focus from freedom of conscience to the "defense of idealism." Berdiaev and Bulgakov at once wrote Struve of their eagerness to contribute to the project. Novgorodtsev invited the participation of A. S. Lappo-Danilevskii, who had connections to the Priiutintsy, and S. A. Askol'dov (perhaps on the recommendation of E. N. Trubetskoi). He also wanted L. O. Petrażycki, expecting from him a "very valuable" article. Struve objected rather strongly to Petrażycki's candidacy, after which it was apparently dropped. Novgorodtsev expressed reservations about the participation of M. I. Tugan-Baranovskii and S. L. Frank, both proposed by Struve, fearing they might compromise the clear idealist direction he (Novgorodtsev) intended for the *sbornik*. Tugan-Baranovskii declined to contribute. The article Frank wrote for *Problemy*, on Nietzsche, confirmed Novgorodtsev's misgivings. As a student, B. A. Kistiakovskii had been close to Marxism; after his final break with it in 1899 he impressed Novgorodtsev (thus, either Struve or Novgorodtsev could have involved him).

158. "P. G." [Struve], "K kharakteristike nashego filosofskoga razvitiia," *Problemy idealizma*, ed. P. I. Novgorodtsev (Moscow: Moskovskoe Psikhologicheskoe Obshchestvo, 1902), p. 86. In the present edition, p. 153.

159. See note 81 above.

160. Vernadskii cannot be described as a neo-idealist; his philosophical views were eclectic. Bailes, in his *Science and Russian Culture in an Age of Revolutions*, writes that

the evidence suggests "that there were both rationalist and mystical sides to his nature, although rationalism usually predominated. The nature of his philosophical outlook in this respect is not altogether clear, but one fact is certain: Vernadsky . . . had great respect for the religious side of mankind's nature (even as a stimulus to science) and worked well with religious figures who shared his own ideals for a more progressive and democratic Russia" (p. 34).

161. V. I. Vernadskii, "O nauchnom mirovozzrenii," VFP 13: 5, kn. 65 (1902), p. 1432.

162. Iu. Aikhenval'd's review appears under "Obzor knig," VFP 14: 2, kn. 67 (1903), pp. 333–356; quotation at p. 334. Ivanov-Razumnik, *Istoriia russkoi obshchestvennoi mysli,* II, similarly writes, "Idealism demonstrated that it is possible to combine demo-cratism with a metaphysical and even religious philosophical basis" (p. 467).

163. P. I. Novgorodtsev, "O filosofskom dvizhenii nashikh dnei," *Novyi put',* no. 10 (1904), p. 61.

164. Iu. Aikhenval'd, "Obzor knig," p. 333.

165. "Moskovskoe Psikhologicheskoe Obshchestvo," VFP 14: 1, kn. 66 (1903), pp. 156–157.

166. Ibid.

167. Kudrinskii [Kolerov], "Arkhivnaia istoriia sbornika 'Problemy idealizma' (1902)," pp. 163–164.

168. Walicki, *Legal Philosophies,* p. 352.

169. For the Kantian "autonomy of the good" in Solov'ëv's tract, see Sergius Hessen's major essay, "Bor'ba utopii i avtonomii dobra v mirovozzrenii F. Dostoevskogo i Vl. Solov'ëva," *Sovremennye zapiski* (Paris), nos. 45–46 (1931), especially no. 46, pp. 340–342. More recently, V. V. Lazarev, "Kategoricheskii imperativ I. Kanta i etika V. So-lov'ëva," *Kant i filosofiia v Rossii,* ed. Z. A. Kamenskii and V. A. Zhuchkov (Moscow: Nauka, 1994), pp. 42–80, has drawn attention to Solov'ëv's rehabilitation of Kant's clear distinction between "is" and "ought," a distinction Hegel's monism collapsed in asserting that "what ought to be" already is. At the same time, Lazarev dwells on what he sees as Solov'ëv's main criticisms of Kant, including the argument that an act done by inclina-tion, and not by duty alone, is not necessarily deprived of ethical value. The criterion is not motive, but the internal moral quality of the act. There is no necessary incompatibility between inclination and duty; I can, in fact, desire to do what I know by duty I would be obligated to do, even were I not so inclined. Solov'ëv's line of criticism has certain merits (in regard, for example, to holy beings who, presumably, never experience a contradic-tion between duty and inclination, and yet are no less the good for it), but it glosses over Kant's main point: freedom consists in the capacity to determine the will by duty, in opposition to natural inclination, in instances of such opposition.

170. P. I. Novgorodtsev, "O filosofskom dvizhenii nashikh dnei," p. 66. Not all "living and progressive movements" could defend the dignity of the self as consistently as neo-idealism, which was precisely the thrust behind the idealist rejection of positivists' claims to be the best philosophical representatives of liberalism. However, the politic Novgorod-tsev passes over this in silence now, in the interests of the Union of Liberation's united-front strategy (see the section that ends this chapter, entitled "Continuities and Differ-entiations").

171. Solov'ëv himself came to reject the idea of personal substantiality, in three late essays on epistemology, first published in *Voprosy filosofii* (1897–1899) and later collected under the title *Theoretical Philosophy*. There he criticizes Descartes's *cogito ergo sum* on the grounds that the substantiality of the subject is not revealed in, and cannot be inferred from, consciousness. See V. S. Solov'ëv, *Sochineniia v dvukh tomakh*, I (Moscow: Mysl'', 1990), pp. 758–797, esp. p. 776. Lopatin responded to Solov'ëv's *Theoretical Philosophy* in a paper he read before the Psychological Society in October 1899, "Vopros o real'nom edinstve soznaniia" ("The Question of the Real Unity of Consciousness"), VFP 10: 5, kn. 50 (1899). According to Lopatin (p. 870), "it is difficult to imagine a more decisive expression of a purely phenomenalist [*fenomenisticheskii*] view of spiritual life" than Solov'ëv's essay "Pervoe nachalo teoreticheskoi filosofii" ("The First Principle of Theoretical Philosophy"), the first in the set. E. N. Trubetskoi, in his *Mirosozertsanie Vl. S. Solov'ëva*, II, pp. 247–259, offers a more benign interpretation of Solov'ëv's denial of personal substantiality. Solov'ëv ascribed substantiality to God alone, who (according to Christian dogma) has the power of creation ex nihilo. Souls that were in the strict sense substantial could not be created, since they would have always existed, nor would they be capable of self-improvement, since they would already be perfect. These reasons explain why, according to Trubetskoi, "for Solov'ëv in the last period of his creativity *God was the only substance in the real sense of the word*," and why the self was not substantial but rather a hypostasis [*ipostas'* or *podstavka*] for God (pp. 247–248, 251). Or, in Walicki's suggestive formulation, "only after death is man finally substantiated in eternal ideality; substantiality, therefore, is the ultimate destiny and not an innate property of the human soul." Andrzej Walicki, *A History of Russian Thought from the Enlightenment to Marxism*, trans. Hilda Andrews-Rusiecka (Stanford: Stanford University Press, 1979), p. 389. Significantly, E. N. Trubetskoi places Solov'ëv's conception of personal progress toward substantiality within the overall de-utopianization of his thought in this period. Self-perfection must be a process and transcendent goal, not a presumed state by virtue of a premature substantiality. Seen in this perspective, Solov'ëv did not advance a radical de-ontologization of the self, only a delay in its ontological self-realization.

172. That would exclude A. S. Lappo-Danilevskii, S. F. Ol'denburg, and D. E. Zhukovskii, although Lappo-Danilevskii did significant work in the theory and methodology of history.

173. In fact, Frank does not even claim that the self is irreducible (see below).

174. On "necessitarian" Marxism, see Andrzej Walicki, *Marxism and the Leap to the Kingdom of Freedom* (Stanford, Calif.: Stanford University Press, 1995), pp. 111–268.

175. Charles Taylor, *Hegel* (Cambridge: Cambridge University Press, 1975), p. 376.

176. S. L. Frank, "O kriticheskom idealizme," *Mir Bozhii* 13: 12 (December 1904), p. 252, compares Hegelianism and Marxism in their "complete ethical indifferentism." In both, "the idea of what ought to be [*dolzhnoe*] has no significance in itself."

177. It is interesting to observe that in countries where the positivist background was more empirical than rationalistic, less reductive, and granted more room to the individual, the neo-idealist revival drew more on Hegel: Great Britain (T. H. Green, E. Caird, F. H. Bradley, B. Bosanquet, R. G. Collingwood), Italy (B. Croce, G. Gentile), and America (W. T. Harris and the St. Louis Hegelians; J. Royce, J. E. Creighton and the Cornell School of objective idealism; W. E. Hocking). France, by contrast, seems to fit the German

and Russian pattern. The historical determinism and scientistic sociology (or socio-logism) of Comte's positivism easily compares to "scientific socialism," while the best-known French neo-idealist Charles Renouvier thought of himself as a Kantian and called his own philosophy "neo-criticism."

178. S. N. Bulgakov, *Ot marksizma k idealizmu: Sbornik statei, 1896–1903* (St. Petersburg, 1903).

179. The relevant quotation can be found in Arthur P. Mendel, *Dilemmas of Progress in Tsarist Russia*, p. 188.

180. S. L. Frank, "O kriticheskom idealizme," clearly suggests the return to utopian-ism in Berdiaev and Bulgakov as they embraced absolute idealism: "The proximity of Marxism to Hegelianism or, more precisely, the identity of their basic view on the relation between 'what is' and 'what ought to be,' is useful to recall just now, when some former Marxists, having recognized the philosophical inadequacy of Marx's doctrine, are, as a result of their metaphysical roving, turning into true students of Hegel" (p. 252).

181. S. N. Bulgakov develops the concept of contraband in his *Problemy* essay. N. A. Berdiaev uses it in his article "O novom russkom idealizme," VFP 15: 5, kn. 75 (1904), p. 700.

182. Aileen M. Kelly, "Which Signposts?" in her *Toward Another Shore: Russian Thinkers Between Necessity and Chance* (New Haven: Yale University Press, 1998), pp. 155–200, contrasts the utopianism of both Berdiaev and Bulgakov to Struve and Frank. Catherine Evtuhov, *The Cross and the Sickle: Sergei Bulgakov and the Fate of Russian Religious Philosophy*, advances a very different interpretation that emphasizes Bulgakov's liberalism and anti-utopianism, particularly with regard to the "sophic econ-omy" (see esp. pp. 182, 185, 249). Certainly Berdiaev's utopianism is the more obvious.

183. "P. G." [Struve], "K kharakteristike nashego filosofskogo razvitiia," *Pro-blemy idealizma*, pp. 72–90; here, p. 78. In the present edition, see p. 147. Subsequent page references cited parenthetically in text, first to the Russian edition, then to the English.

184. N. A. Berdiaev, "Eticheskaia problema v svete filosofskogo idealizma," *Problemy idealizma*, pp. 91–136; quotation at p. 95 (note). In the present edition, see p. 192, n. 15. Subsequent page references (to Russian/English) cited parenthetically in text.

185. On the Russian reception of Nietzsche in this period, see Bernice Glatzer Rosen-thal, ed., *Nietzsche in Russia* (Princeton: Princeton University Press, 1986).

186. S. L. Frank, "Fr. Nitsshe i etika 'liubvi k dal'nemu,'" *Problemy idealizma*, pp. 137–195; quotation at p. 184. In the present edition, p. 228. Subsequent page refer-ences (to Russian/English) cited parenthetically in text.

187. It is revealing that Frank dropped several paragraphs (including the one contain-ing this sentence) from the conclusion of his essay when it was reprinted in his collection, *Filosofiia i zhizn'* (St. Petersburg, 1910), no doubt finding them incompatible with the more consistently idealist position he had by then adopted.

188. "Bizarre" is Swoboda's apt characterization in his *The Philosophical Thought of S. L. Frank*, p. 257. Swoboda provides a full analysis of Frank's essay (pp. 250–291). Also see Boobbyer, *S. L. Frank*, pp. 23–28.

189. S. L. Frank, "O kriticheskom idealizme," *Mir Bozhii* 13: 12 (December 1904), pp. 224–264. On the self (*lichnost'*), Frank writes, "Not only can it not be subordinated

to any empirical end, not only must it always be seen in empirical life *as an end in itself, and not a means,* as this was put by Kant's ethics, but it can just as little be made the servant of any transcendent principle or force surpassing it. The self can have neither an empirical nor a metaphysical owner. If human reason has the need to recognize as sacred the whole of life and its bearer, then we once more recall that this whole, from the point of view of critical idealism, is *consciousness,* and its bearer, the *transcendental self"* (p. 261). Soon Frank began to move, however, toward the metaphysical position expounded in his major treatise, *Predmet znaniia (The Object of Knowledge,* 1915), that absolute being is the ground of consciousness.

190. L. M. Lopatin, *Polozhitel'nye zadachi filosofii. Chast' pervaia: Oblast' umo-zritel'nykh voprosov,* 2d edition (Moscow, 1911; 1st edition, 1886), p. 434.

191. S. N. Bulgakov, "Osnovnye problemy teorii progressa," *Problemy idealizma,* pp. 1–47; quotation at p. 6. In the present edition, p. 89. Subsequent page references (to Russian/English) cited parenthetically in text.

192. He writes that Russian Marxism represented a case of the basic error of positivism, the monstrous idea of scientific ethics, the reduction of "what ought to be" to "what is." "P. G." recalls that, "at the time Struve lacked the philosophic clarity that, as a matter of principle, does not admit such subordination" (85/152).

193. Kistiakovskii's essay influenced Weber's own understanding of the concept of "possibility" in social analysis. See Alexander Vucinich, *Social Thought in Tsarist Russia: The Quest for a General Science of Society, 1861–1917* (Chicago: University of Chicago Press, 1976), pp. 136–137. On Kistiakovskii, see Vucinich, pp. 125–152; Walicki, *Legal Philosophies,* pp. 342–403; and Susan Heuman, *Kistiakovsky: The Struggle for National and Constitutional Rights in the Last Years of Tsarism* (Cambridge: Harvard Ukrainian Research Institute, 1998).

194. B. A. Kistiakovskii, "Russkaia sotsiologicheskaia shkola i kategoriia vozmozhnosti pri reshenii sotsial'no-eticheskikh problem," *Problemy idealizma,* p. 393. Present edition, p. 352.

195. B. A. Kistiakovskii, "V zashchitu nauchno-filosofskogo idealizma," VFP 18: 1, kn. 86 (1907), pp. 57–109. Kistiakovskii followed the value-theory of the Baden school of neo-Kantianism, where the modality of values is not being but validity. In this connection, Herbert Schnädelbach, *Philosophy in Germany 1831–1933,* trans. Eric Matthews (Cambridge: Cambridge University Press, 1984), pp. 162–163, 180–185, refers to the "ontological dilemma" of the neo-Kantian posing of the value-problem without a ground of being for the good, a free-floating axiology.

196. P. I. Novgorodtsev, "Nravstvennyi idealizm v filosofii prava (K voprosu o vozrozhdenii estestvennogo prava)," *Problemy idealizma,* p. 265. Present edition, p. 294.

197. P. I. Novgorodtsev, "Znachenie filosofii," *Nauchnoe slovo,* kn. 4 (1903), pp. 108–115.

198. Ibid., p. 112.

199. Ibid.

200. Ibid., p. 113.

201. On Lappo-Danilevskii, see Alexander Vucinich, *Social Thought in Tsarist Russia,* pp. 110–124. In connection with the importance freedom of conscience had in the conception of *Problems of Idealism,* it is interesting that Comte found the dogma a "revolting

monstrosity." See F. A. Hayek, *The Counter-Revolution of Science: Studies on the Abuse of Reason* (Glencoe, Ill.: Free Press, 1952), pp. 253, 257.

202. Novgorodtsev, "Znachenie filosofii," p. 113 (emphasis Novgorodtsev's).

203. Ibid.

204. Ibid., p. 114.

205. See note 56, above.

206. Kotliarevskii delivered his paper before the Psychological Society in October 1904: "Moskovskoe Psikhologicheskoe Obshchestvo," VFP 16: 1, kn. 76 (1905), p. 144. Three contributors to *Ocherki realisticheskogo mirovozzreniia* attended the meeting as guests: S. A. Suvorov, A. A. Bogdanov, and V. M. Friche. The review appeared in the next issue of *Voprosy filosofii*: "Ob istinnom i mnimom realizme," VFP 15: 5, kn. 75 (1904), pp. 624–644.

207. S. A. Kotliarevskii, "Ob istinnom i mnimom realizme," pp. 625–626, 631.

208. Ibid., p. 627.

209. Ibid., pp. 642–643.

210. P. I. Novgorodtsev, "Nravstvennyi idealizm v filosofii prava. (K voprosu o vozrozhdenii estestvennogo prava)," *Problemy idealizma*, pp. 236–296; here, at p. 237. Present edition, p. 275. Subsequent page references (Russian/English) cited parenthetically in text.

211. P. I. Novgorodtsev, *Istoricheskaia shkola iuristov: ee proiskhozhdenie i sud'ba* (Moscow, 1896).

212. Bulgakov also voiced this notion of absolute form and changing content: "Every age, every epoch has some historical task of its own, determined by the objective course of things. Thus, although the moral law is absolute, and its imperatives have significance *sub specie aeterni*, still its content is always given by history," *Problems of idealism* (40/113).

213. P. I. Novgorodtsev, *Kant i Gegel' v ikh ucheniiakh o prave i gosudarstve*, pp. 3–28; "Ob istoricheskom i filosofskom izuchenii idei," VFP 11: 4, kn. 54 (1900), pp. 658–685. Walicki, *Legal Philosophies*, pp. 299–300, summarizes the introduction.

214. Quoted by Novgorodtsev, "Ob istoricheskom i filosofskom izuchenii idei," p. 666, from Trubetskoi's book, *Uchenie o Logose v ego istorii*.

215. P. I. Novgorodtsev, "K voprosu o sovremennykh filosofskikh iskaniiakh. (Otvet L. I. Petrazhitskomu)," VFP 14: 1, kn. 66 (1903), p. 122.

216. Ibid., p. 124.

217. Ibid., p. 125, from S. N. Trubetskoi, "Chemu uchit' istoriia filosofii," *Problemy idealizma*, p. 229. Present edition, p. 268.

218. S. N. Trubetskoi, "Chemu uchit' istoriia filosofii," *Problemy idealizma*, pp. 216–235; quotation at pp. 217–218 (emphasis Trubetskoi's). Present edition, p. 259. Subsequent page references (Russian/English) cited parenthetically in text.

219. The phrase "the human mind is an innate metaphysician" is Lopatin's: *Polozhitel'nye zadachi filosofii: Chast' pervaia*, p. 433.

220. Iu. Aikhenval'd, "Problemy idealizma," in "Obzor knig," VFP 14: 2, kn. 67 (1903), p. 333. Subsequent page references cited parenthetically in text. Iulii I. Aikhenval'd (1872–1928), an important literary critic and historian, was a secretary of the Psychological Society and a member of the editorial board of *Voprosy filosofii*.

221. It is interesting to contrast Frank's celebration here of Nietzsche's "love of the

distant" to his very different evaluation of it seven years later in his *Vekhi* essay: *Vekhi. Landmarks: A Collection of Articles about the Russian Intelligentsia,* trans. and ed. Marshall S. Shatz and Judith E. Zimmerman (Armonk, N.Y.: M. E. Sharpe, 1994), pp. 140–141.

222. I will use the term "*Vekhi* group" to designate the authors of both *Vekhi* and *Iz glubiny,* who were united by a general idealist critique of the intelligentsia, although not all were consistently liberal in this critique.

223. Shatz and Zimmerman, trans. and eds., *Vekhi. Landmarks,* p. 15. "Just truth" and "true justice" are free but suggestive translations of truth-verity (*pravda-istina*) and truth-justice (*pravda-spravedlivost*), i.e., *pravda* in its dual meaning of truth and justice. On this, see Struve's essay (Chapter 3) of this book, note 28, as well as Kistiakovskii's essay (Chapter 9).

224. Ibid., p. 7.

225. Ibid., p. 59.

226. Pipes, *Struve: Liberal on the Right,* pp. 99–101.

227. See, for example, the essays by Bulgakov and Struve in *Vekhi,* pp. 33–34, 36–37, 119–120, 124–127.

228. To repeat, personal autonomy and dignity do not necessarily mean ontological substantiality ("spiritualism" in the philosophical sense), but they did for most Russian idealists.

229. The importance Russian liberals attached to dismantling the "interconnected structures of domestic patriarchy, *soslovie* society, and arbitrary autocratic and state power (*proizvol*)" has been masterfully demonstrated by William G. Wagner, *Marriage, Property, and Law in Late Imperial Russia* (Oxford: Oxford University Press, 1994) and Wagner, "Family Law, the Rule of Law, and Liberalism in Late Imperial Russia," *Jahrbücher für Geschichte Osteuropas* 43: 4 (1995), pp. 519–535, quotation at p. 521.

230. Berdiaev is the best example of this. In his essay "O novom russkom idealizme" VFP 15: 5, kn. 75 (1904), pp. 683–724, he still employs neo-idealism in the defense of liberalism, including a liberal interpretation of natural law and affirmation that Christian eschatology should not be interpreted as salvation in history (pp. 717–721). Subsequently, however, his idealism developed in directions incompatible with liberalism. This evolution has been reconstructed by Andrzej Walicki, "Russian Liberalism and the Religio-Philosophic Renaissance in Russia," paper for the 1991 National Convention of the American Association for the Advancement of Slavic Studies. Walicki shows that Berdiaev fused a redefined notion of natural law with his eclectic ideas of stateless theocracy or theocratic-mystical anarchism. Since this order would function by divine rule of law alone, without any state organization or institutionalized forms of power (ecclesiastical or secular), it would be a theonomy rather than a theocracy in the strict sense, "theonomic anarchism." Whatever Berdiaev's new ideas might entail, they had very little to do with liberalism. Rather, his new religious consciousness was a utopianization of the idealism he had embraced in *Problems of Idealism.*

231. Aileen M. Kelly thus writes about "Which Signposts?" in her *Toward Another Shore,* pp. 155–200. She argues that Berdiaev, Bulgakov, and Gershenzon (three of the seven *Vekhi* authors) adhered to an illiberal, Slavophile-inspired religious and national messianism. The case of Bulgakov is, however, more complicated: see Catherine Evtuhov,

The Cross and the Sickle; Paul Valliere, "Sophiology as the Dialogue of Orthodoxy with Modern Civilization," in *Russian Religious Thought,* pp. 176–192; and Valliere, *Modern Russian Theology,* pp. 227–278.

232. Leonard Schapiro, "The Vekhi Group and the Mystique of Revolution," in *Russian Studies,* p. 90.

233. With the notable exception of his increasing Russian nationalism, which became a matter of dispute between him and Kistiakovskii, Kotliarevskii, and E. N. Trubetskoi.

234. This can also be said of A. S. Izgoev, whose essay in *Iz glubiny,* "Socialism, Culture and Bolshevism," is very incisive, but he stands somewhat apart from the others because he was not much interested in idealist theory. I. A. Pokrovskii also wrote an interesting liberal critique in *Iz glubiny* of the intelligentsia and revolution.

235. Shatsillo, *Russkii liberalizm,* provides the quotation at p. 153.

236. P. I. Novgorodtsev, "O filosofskom dvizhenii nashikh dnei," *Novyi put',* no. 10 (1904), p. 61.

237. Ibid., p. 66.

238. Pipes, *Struve: Liberal on the Left,* p. 326.

239. By 1909 *obshchestvo* (liberal educated society) seems to have been reintegrating a significant part of the once alienated intelligentsia so deplored by *Vekhi.* See Edith W. Clowes, Samuel D. Kassow, and James L. West, eds., *Between Tsar and People: Educated Society and the Quest for Public Identity in Late Imperial Russia* (Princeton: Princeton University Press, 1991).

240. The inability or unwillingness of Russian monarchs to conceive the state as a public sphere rather than as their own private domain was especially pronounced under Alexander III and Nicholas II. See Richard S. Wortman, *Scenarios of Power: Myth and Ceremony in Russian Monarchy,* vol. 2 (Princeton, N.J.: Princeton University Press, 2000). According to Wortman, "The Russian state never assumed an existence independent from the person of the monarch. . . . The notion of the state as an impersonal institution, operating according to laws of its own, remained an ideal of enlightened officials through the early twentieth century, but it could not take hold in the highly literal and personalized symbolic world of Russian monarchy" (p. 7).

241. S. A. Smith, "Workers and Civil Rights in Tsarist Russia, 1899–1917," in *Civil Rights in Imperial Russia,* ed. Olga Crisp and Linda Edmondson (Oxford: Oxford University Press, 1989), pp. 157–169.

From the Moscow Psychological Society

Publishing the present volume of essays, the Moscow Psychological Society takes special pleasure in adding this serious collective work to its series of editions. The expression of the views of only one group of its members, those who belong to the idealist direction, this work was bound, however, to meet the support of the whole Psychological Society, in view of the outstanding interest it represents. Following in its editions the principle of impartiality with regard to different philosophical currents, the Society in this way expresses its faith in the undoubted triumph of truth, which in and of itself carries the force of its own confirmation, and of its abiding significance and supremacy.

CHAIR OF THE MOSCOW PSYCHOLOGICAL SOCIETY
L. M. LOPATIN

Foreword to the Russian Edition

P. I. NOVGORODTSEV

Today there can be no doubt that the negative relation to philosophy, only recently so widespread in Russian society, has been replaced by lively interest in its problems. The directions that sought to eradicate philosophy, or else supplant it with constructions based exclusively on the data of experience, have lost their leading significance. Needs that can never disappear have again awoken, and as before thought seeks satisfaction in the authentic sources of philosophic knowledge.

This awakening of philosophic interest gave rise to the idea, among several people participating in the new movement, to respond to these new searchings with a collection of essays devoted to certain basic philosophical problems. The initiators of the present work defined the realization of their task in connection with the general conditions of the contemporary development of philosophy. Taking a critical approach to the recent past of Russian thought, associated with the dominance of positivism, they looked to its future in anticipation of new perspectives, not contained in the program of "positive philosophy." They were led by the conviction that the contemporary critical movement is called not only to affirm science on solid and truly positive foundations, but also to defend the necessary diversity of the needs and tasks of the human spirit, for which science is only one sphere of manifestation.

This conviction among the persons who conceived the present collection presented so broad a basis for mutual work that this work was in fact met by other critical efforts, which had as their exclusive goal the reexamination, from the point of view of pure science, of some of the constructs of positivism. Such critical efforts, while not predetermining our new constructions, but only paving the way for them, fully corresponded, however, to the general plan of our proposed work. But for the initiators of the collection, in the name of whom the author of this foreword speaks, this critical task was only the first step. The basic problem that in our day is spurring the revival of idealist philosophy is first of all the moral problem. Accordingly, it seemed important for us to direct special attention to the clarification of ethical questions, admitting here the widest possible scope of views.

The contemporary turn to philosophy is the fruit not only of theoretical curiosity: not only the abstract interests of thought, but first of all the complex questions of life and the profound needs of moral consciousness are advancing the problem of "what ought to be" [*dolzhnoe*], of the moral ideal. We are convinced that the directions that do not want to know anything except empirical principles are incapable of resolving this important and, for us, precious question. We seek absolute precepts and principles — in precisely this lies the essence of moral searchings — and we are answered with the indication that everything in the world is relative and conditional. From the moral problem emerges a series of other problems, profound and important and in the tightest way connected with the active life of the spirit, and we are told that these are all questions for which there is no place in philosophy, which has clearly defined its own limits.

The inescapable importance of these questions is too obvious for doubts not to have arisen about the grounds of the system that rejects them. Now the view is being more and more upheld that this system, while claiming to be truly scientific, is not only narrow within its own perspectives, but also dogmatic and deprived of firm foundations and critical caution. In this respect the direction that is succeeding positivism proceeds from stricter starting principles in its scientific goals. The new direction, in replacing the dogmatic approach to questions of knowledge with epistemological criticism, persistently advances the question of rigorous verification of scientific means and categories. But while directing positive science to its proper limits, it also recognizes, together with science, other spheres and removes the superstitious prejudices that impede going freely and directly to meet the great questions of the spirit.

Idealist philosophy is not a novelty for the Russian public. In the epoch of the highest development of positivism, Vladimir Sergeevich Solov'ëv came out assuredly and boldly against it, and B. N. Chicherin also raised his authoritative voice against it. Readers of our collection will find among its contributors names who point to the living link between this philosophical tradition and the direction that is now taking up the defense of idealist principles. The peculiarity of this new direction is that while it expresses a certain eternal need of the spirit, it also is arising in connection with a profound process of life, with a general aspiration toward moral renewal. New forms of [social and political] life now no longer represent the simple demand of expediency, but the categorical imperative of morality, which gives primary importance to the principle of the absolute significance of personhood [*lichnost'*].

This is how we understand the origins of the contemporary idealist movement. It is first of all and primarily an expression of the progressive principles of moral consciousness. Positivist constructions have not sustained and cannot sustain the examination of mature thought: they have turned out to be inadequate in the face of the complex and ineradicable problems of moral consciousness, philosophical searching, and living creativity. The light of philosophical idealism is necessary to satisfy these new challenges.

The task of this collection is to pose some of the problems that are being revealed to the contemporary philosophical movement. Of course, their further clarification will still require complex and concentrated work.

October 1902

Basic Problems of the Theory of Progress

S. N. BULGAKOV

Was zu wünschen ist, ihr unten fühlt'es:
Was zu geben sei, die wissen's droben.
Gross beginnet, ihr Titanen! Aber leiten
Zu dem ewig Guten, ewig Schönen
Ist der Götter Werk: die lasst gewähren.[1]
–Goethe

I.

According to the so-called law of three stages (*loi des trois états*) established by Auguste Comte,[2] humanity progresses in its development from the theological to the metaphysical understanding of the world, and from the metaphysical to the positive or scientific. Nowadays Comte's philosophy has already lost credit, but even so his imaginary law is apparently a basic philosophical conviction in broad circles of our society. Yet this law represents a crude misunderstanding, because neither the spirit's religious need and the sphere of ideas and feelings corresponding to it, nor the metaphysical requirements of reason and the speculation answering them, are in any way annihilated or even diminished by positive science, magnificently developing alongside them. Religion, metaphysical thought, and positive knowledge answer basic spiritual needs of man, and their development can lead only to mutual clarification, never to annihilation. These needs are universal, for all people, in all times, and constitute the spiritual principle in human nature, in contrast to animal nature. Only the methods of satisfying these needs change; the methods evolve in history, but not the needs themselves.

Most understandable and indisputable is the universal need for positive scientific knowledge of the laws of the external world. Having its original source in the material requirements of man, in the struggle for existence, positive science in its further development sets for itself the purely theoretical goal of determining necessity [*zakonomernost'*] in the world of phenomena. Today we observe the unparalleled development of the exact sciences, to which no end is in sight. However, no matter how well-developed, positive science will always remain limited by its object — it studies only fragments of a reality that widens constantly before the eyes of the scientist. The problem of full and complete knowledge in the world of experience is in general insoluble and incorrectly posed. It is likewise deceptive and mendacious, like trying to reach the horizon that constantly recedes into infinite space. The development of positive science is itself infinite, but this infinity is at once its strength and weakness: a strength in that there is not and cannot be a specified limit to science in its forward movement, a weakness in that this infinity of movement hinges precisely on the inability of reason to solve once and for all its task — providing integral knowledge. We have here an example of what Hegel called bad, imperfect infinity (*schlechte Unendlichkeit,* or, strictly speaking, *Endlosigkeit*),[3] in contrast to the infinity synonymous with perfection. The first can be illustrated geometrically by a line continuing indefinitely into space, the second — by a circle. Since, arguing purely mathematically, all finite quantities lose significance in comparison with infinity, no matter how much their absolute values differ, it is possible to say that positive science is no closer now to the task of giving integral knowledge than it was centuries ago or will be centuries from now.

But man must have an integral idea of the world. We cannot agree to wait patiently for the fulfillment of this need until science, sometime in the future, provides enough material; and we must also obtain answers to questions that fall completely outside the field of vision of positive science and of which it cannot even be aware. Man is not capable of suppressing in himself these questions, of creating the appearance that they do not exist, of practically ignoring them, as is in essence proposed by positivism and various shades of agnosticism, including neo-Kantianism, especially its positivist strand. Infinitely more important for man, as a rational being, than any specialized scientific theory is the solution to questions about our world as a whole, about its substance, about whether it has some meaning or rational end, about whether our life and deeds have any value, about the nature of good and evil, and so on and so forth. In short, we ask and cannot but ask not only *how,* but also *what, why, and for what.* Positive science has no answer to these questions; more precisely, it does not pose and cannot solve them. Their solution lies in the sphere of metaphysical thought, defending its rights alongside positive science. The sphere of competence of metaphysics is greater than that of positive science, both because metaphysics settles more important questions than those of empirical knowledge, and because it, employing speculation, answers questions that are beyond empirical science. Metaphysics and science are, of course, united by an indissoluble tie; the results of positive science provide the material on which metaphysical thought works, and so metaphysics is also subject to the law of development. But this is not the place to analyze these complex correlations.

A number of philosophical schools (positivism, materialism, neo-Kantianism, and some others) do, however, deny the rights of metaphysics to exist. Does this not contradict the above assertion about the universality and necessity of metaphysical thought? Not at all, for in essence all these schools reject not metaphysics, but only certain results and methods of metaphysical thought. But they cannot thus abolish metaphysical questions, as the development of science abolished questions about goblins and poltergeists, about the elixir of life or alchemical manufacture of gold, and so forth.

On the contrary, all these schools, even while denying metaphysics, have their own answers to its questions. If I ask about the existence of God, the essence of things (*Ding an sich*) [thing-in-itself], or about freedom of will, and then negatively answer these questions, in no sense am I annihilating metaphysics; rather I am recognizing it in acknowledging the legitimacy and necessity of posing these questions that do not fall within the limits of positive knowledge. Differing answers to metaphysical questions divide representatives of various philosophical schools, but this does not nullify the general fact that all philosophers are metaphysicians by the very nature of human thought.

In our atheistic era the claim that religion answers as basic a need of the human spirit as do science and metaphysics can arouse the greatest misunderstandings. Destroying or temporarily abolishing one or another form of religious faith, people often think they have destroyed or abolished religion itself. To humanity's credit, this opinion is completely unjustified. Religious feeling remains, despite change of religions. Indeed, it would be myopically naïve to think that a person, losing faith in God at the age of twenty, and consequently changing his philosophic views, also loses his religious feeling —

and on returning to faith, recovers this feeling anew. There are no nonreligious people, only people pious or profane, righteous or sinful. Atheists also have their religion, although, of course, their creed is different from that of theists. Auguste Comte can serve as an example: following the destruction of Christianity and metaphysics, he considered it necessary to found a religion of humanity, which would have as its object "la grande conception de l'Humanité, qui vient éliminer irrévocablement celle de Dieu."[4] Are people today not speaking of the religion of humanity, of the religion of socialism? Is Eduard von Hartmann not advancing, before our very eyes, his own religion of the unconscious, in sharpest contradiction to all deistic religions and to Christianity in particular? And is Nietzsche's cult of the superman not its own type of religious cult? This usage is not at all a simple play on words, but rather contains a profound meaning, indicating that a religious feeling or attitude, as a formal principle, can be combined with diverse content, and that in a certain sense the ancient wisdom of Aqiva ben Yosef is true: "It is not *in what*, but *how*, we believe that adorns man."[5]

What we apprehend [*poznat'*] in metaphysics as the higher meaning and higher principle of the world becomes, as an object of religious adoration, a sacred thing of the heart. We shall not, of course, endeavor to give here a definition of religion that would grasp every side of religious life in all its concrete complexity. It is important at this point only to delimit religion from related spheres of the spirit's activity. Religion is an active passing beyond the limits of the self, a living feeling of the connection the finite and limited self has with what is infinite and higher, an expansion of our feeling for infinity in the aspiration toward an inaccessible perfection. Only religion establishes the link between the human mind and heart, between our thoughts and deeds. The person who would live without any religion, at the personal responsibility and reckoning of his own tiny self, would be a repulsive monstrosity. And contrariwise, religion defines the whole life of the truly religious person, from the momentous to the trivial, so that nothing would appear indifferent in the religious respect.

The basic claims of religion are at the same time the ultimate conclusions of metaphysics, conclusions that are thus justified before reason. But religion, as such, is not satisfied by these products of the reflection of discursive thought. It has its own method of immediately and intuitively receiving the truths it needs. And this method of intuitive knowledge (if only the word "knowledge" is applicable here, inextricably connected as it is with discursive thought and, consequently, with proof and demonstrability) is called *faith*. Faith is a mode of knowledge without proof, "the substance of things hoped for, the evidence of things not seen," in the splendid characterization of the apostle Paul.[6] The indisputability or incontestability of claims that are, as objects of proof, replete with all the doubt and precariousness intrinsic to our knowledge, constitutes the distinctive feature of all religious truths (regardless of whether we are concerned with theistic or atheistic religions), and it is precisely the immediate obviousness of these truths that makes possible the living connection here between human thought and will.[7]

As a result of these peculiarities, the sphere accessible to faith is wider than the sphere accessible to discursive thought. It is possible to believe even in that which not only is indemonstrable, but cannot be made fully comprehensible to reason, and this sphere is the special domain of faith. Examining the matter exclusively from the formal side, we must therefore say that the knowledge (no matter how little appropriate, to repeat, this word is here) faith gives is richer and broader than that which empirical science and metaphysics give: if metaphysics breaks the limits of empirical knowledge, then faith nullifies the limits of the intelligible. (The question of the mutual relation of faith and speculation belongs to the most important and interesting questions of metaphysics. We recall here the theories of Jacobi, Fichte in his second period, and others, in particular Vladimir Solov'ëv's profound theory of knowledge.[8])

Thus, man cannot be satisfied by exact science alone, to which positivism hoped to limit him; metaphysical and religious needs are ineradicable and have never been removed from the life of man. Precise knowledge, metaphysics, and religion must exist in a certain harmonious relation, the establishment of which always constitutes the task of philosophy. It will be interesting to look now at how this matter is handled by positivists (understanding this term in the broad sense, that is, all currents of thought that reject metaphysics and the autonomous rights of religious faith).

II.

The mechanistic understanding of the world is thought to best correspond to the state of modern thought and knowledge. According to this view, mechanical causation governs the world. The world, having begun who knows when and how, or perhaps having always existed, develops according to the law of causation, which encompasses dead as well as living matter, physical as well as psychic life. In this lifeless movement, deprived of any creative idea or rational meaning, there is no living principle, only a certain state of matter. There is no truth or error — both are equally necessary effects of equally necessary causes — no good or evil, only states of matter corresponding to them. One of the most bold and consistent representatives of this outlook, Baron d'Holbach, speaks thus of the fatal necessity (*fatalité*) that rules the world: "Fatal necessity is the eternal, immutable, necessary order established in nature, or the indispensable connection of causes and their effects. According to this order, heavy bodies fall, light bodies rise; like substances mutually attract each other; unlike ones repel each other; people live together in society, affect each other, become good or evil, naturally make each other happy or unhappy, and necessarily love or hate each other, according to the manner in which they act upon each other. From this it can be seen that the same necessity that governs the movements of the physical world also governs those of the moral world, where consequently everything is subject to fatal necessity."[9]

This view, seeing the whole solution to the mystery of being in mechanical causation and thus raising such causation to the level of an absolute cosmic principle (in opposition to Kant's view, which sees in it a simple condition of empirical knowledge), is entirely metaphysical, although it belongs to those philosophical schools that reject metaphysics on principle (agnostics, positivists, materialists). Indeed, the universal significance this view ascribes to the law of causation not only has not been, but cannot be, demonstrated from experience, which always pertains to fragments of being and which is, by its very conception, incomplete and cannot be complete. The mechanistic understanding of the world is, moreover, one of the most contradictory and unsatisfactory metaphysical systems, for it leaves without explanation a whole series of facts of consciousness, and without answer a whole series of persistent questions. There is no more dreary and deadening outlook than that for which the world and our life are the effect of pure chance, absolutely deprived of inner meaning. Before the chilling terror of this outlook even the most pessimistic systems pale, because they nonetheless free the world from pure chance, although they abandon it to the hands of an evil force rather than a good one.

Not surprisingly, the basic efforts of self-conscious philosophic thought, beginning with Socrates, have been directed toward finding a higher principle and meaning behind being, beyond the law of causation and its transitory dominance. All the great philosophic systems of the nineteenth century, proceeding from Kant, converge in recognition of teleology alongside causation. Fichte views the world as a kingdom of moral ends, forming in their totality a moral world-order; Schelling regards it, above that, as a work of art (*Kunstwerk*); and Hegel sees in it the development of absolute reason. Recognition of the supreme principle of teleology characterizes the metaphysical views of Lotze. Finally, Wundt and Eduard von Hartmann also meet here. That's not to mention our Russian philosopher Vladimir Solov'ëv, who proposed God's love and goodness [*blagost'*] as the absolute principle of the world.

But it is curious that the mechanistic philosophy turns out to be incapable of supporting the consistent development of its principles to their conclusion, but ends up by also trying to bring teleology within its borders, acknowledging the ultimate triumph of reason over irrational causation, as is done in philosophical systems proceeding from just the opposite principle. This flight from its own philosophical principles is expressed in tacit or open recognition of the fact that at a certain stage in world development this very same causation creates human reason, which then begins to arrange the world in accordance with its own rational purposes. The victory of reason over the irrational principle takes place not at once, but gradually, with the collective reason of people united in society increasingly conquering lifeless nature and learning to use it for their own ends. Thus, dead mechanism gradually gives way to rational purposiveness, its complete antithesis. You have recognized already that I am speaking of the *theory of progress,* which constitutes an indispensable part of all doctrines of the contemporary mechanistic understanding of the world.

If, following Leibniz, we call the unveiling of a higher reason or higher purposiveness in the world a *theodicy,* then it can be said that for the mechanistic understanding of the world, the theory of progress is a theodicy, without which man obviously cannot manage. Together with the concept of evolution — aimless and meaningless development — the concept of progress arises, teleological evolution in which causation and the gradual revelation of the goal of this evolution converge until their complete identification, quite like in the above metaphysical systems. Thus, both doctrines — mechanistic evolution and progress — however much they differ in their conclusions, are united by a necessary inner connection, if not logical, then psychological.

Therefore, the theory of progress is for present-day humanity something much more than any ordinary scientific theory, no matter how important a role the latter plays in science. For humanity today, the significance of the theory of progress is that it is called to replace lost metaphysics and religion, or, more precisely, it takes the form of both. In it we have, perhaps, the only example in history where a scientific theory (or a theory imagining itself to be scientific) has played such a role. We discuss and ponder the future fates of humanity with such fervor not from Platonic interest, but from our own personal interest as real people; for upon these future fates depends the fatal question, unique in its significance, of the meaning of our own life, of the purpose of existence. In Athens at the time of the apostle Paul, amid the temples of a multitude of gods in whom people had long since ceased to believe, towered an altar devoted to the "unknown god."[10] In this is expressed the inextinguishable search for God on the part of a humanity that has lost its former faith. And our theory of progress, our religion of humanity, is an altar to the "unknown God."...

What gives the theory of progress its unique philosophic interest and distinguishes it from other religious-philosophic doctrines is that — according to the basic idea of the metaphysical doctrine that created the theory of progress in the first place — this philosophy, which is also a religion, is constructed exclusively by means of positive knowledge. It is thus a philosophy that not only does not cross into the sphere of the supra-empirical or transcendent, but on principle censures and rejects such a passage, a philosophy that not only does not have recourse to the usual mode of religious knowledge (recourse, that is, to faith), but consciously rejects all the rights and significance of faith. In the theory of progress, positive science wants to absorb metaphysics and religious faith, or, more precisely, it wants to be a trinity of science, metaphysics, and religious teaching. A bold idea, deserving, in any event, close philosophical examination! And for contemporary philosophizing reason there cannot be an object more worthy of consideration, in view of the importance this theory has for humanity today.

And so we shall try to determine in what measure positive science is capable of making metaphysics and faith unnecessary and of providing a truly *scientific* (i.e., empirical) metaphysics and religion (such a combination of concepts is a *contradictio in adjecto,* but it does not belong to us, but to the philosophical doctrine under scrutiny).

III.

Every religion has its own *Jenseits* [beyond] — a belief in that time and place where its hopes will be fulfilled, where religious longing will be assuaged, where the religious ideal will be realized. The theory of progress also has such a Jenseits in its notions of the future fortunes of humanity — free, proud, and happy. But, rejecting faith and supra-empirical knowledge, it wants to inspire confidence in the certain advent of this future kingdom through science; it wants to scientifically foresee and predict it, as an astronomer predicts a lunar eclipse or other astronomical phenomena that he can precisely calculate several centuries ahead. Such insight into the future is also ascribed to the science of social development, sociology, which thus takes on a completely exceptional significance among other sciences, becoming the theology, as it were, of a new religion. This explains the extraordinary development of social science in the nineteenth century, and the extraordinary, completely exceptional interest in this science, which today has as sovereign a role in public opinion as theology had in the Middle Ages or as classical literature had in the epoch of humanism. One sociological doctrine has shown the greatest faith in its own strengths and has aroused the most enthusiasm. It constitutes to this day the creed of many millions of people: the doctrine of Marx and Engels, the theory of scientific socialism. This doctrine has sought to scientifically demonstrate the inevitability of the advent of the socialist mode of production, the ideal of present-day humanity. To the extent this doctrine pertains to the future, it represents a very typical and most vivid example of scientific theodicy (in the sense described above).

Faith in the reliability of social predictions has been so strongly undermined in recent times that to attack such predictions with excessive zeal would mean, to a certain extent, knocking at an open door. At the same time, a proper demonstration of the claim that social science, by its own cognitive nature, is incapable of prediction would require a full epistemological analysis. Here it is enough to limit ourselves to a few basic points.[11]

First of all, what does it mean to predict the future? It means to *precisely* determine the advent of future events, at a definite point in space and time (as astronomy makes predictions). Any other predictions are simply common-places, which in social science are sometimes called, for the sake of propriety, a "tendency" of development, after the Latin word.[12] Thus, if someone informs me that the tendency of my development consists in the fact that I will some-day die, I would hardly consider this a prediction in which I would expect to find a designation of the time and place of my death. Prediction in this latter sense fully concurs with prophecy, as understood in Old Testament history, or with soothsaying and fortune-telling. Is social science capable of prophecy or, what is the same, prediction?

There are two methods of studying reality: in one case, attention is directed toward the *general;* in the other, toward the *particular.* According to Rickert (developing here the ideas of Windelband), in one case we have natural scien-tific knowledge, science relying on general concepts, while in the other case we have history, which has as its task the most precise possible determination of reality in its individual particularities. In application to social science, we distinguish history in the strict sense from sociology, the science of the laws of the coexistence and development of social phenomena. Regarding the ability of history as such to make predictions, there cannot be, and indeed has not been, any talk. All hopes in this respect have been placed on sociology. In sociology we have a system of concepts that are abstracted from a definite historical reality and that seek to make this reality *comprehensible,* that is, expressible in a coherent system of logical concepts, the various correlations of which are sociological laws. In this way all individual events, that is, events in space and time, are canceled in abstract concepts; sociology in this sense has nothing to do with events that can be predicted. It is necessary, moreover, to note the following peculiarity of the formation of concepts in sociology, in

contrast to certain branches of natural science. The general concepts of natural science are obtained by identifying, through abstraction, a certain sum of
the properties of an object. But these properties themselves stand for an independent reality. Science can therefore use its conclusions for practical goals, as
long as it gives these conclusions some practical accounting. Within these
bounds, natural science does become capable of prediction. Sociological concepts, by contrast, do not represent such an identification of what is general
and recurrent in all individual cases. Rather, they are obtained by merging a
number of different but interrelated events into a concept that takes on, to a
certain degree, the significance of a symbol, or conventional sign, of this class
of phenomena (for example, the feudal order, capitalist production, freedom
of trade, and so forth). The first method of formation of concepts can be
likened to mechanical separation, the second to chemical combination, for in
this [latter] case the elements-events lose their independent existence and are
combined into a new synthesis, distinct from each of these elements.

From the character of sociological concepts it follows, in my view, that they
depend entirely on the concrete historical material from which they are abstracted. As this material changes, so do the concepts. They can exist in count-
less numbers, as a result of the diversity of material arising from the inexhaustible creativity of history, and also as a result of the different special aims
pursued by the investigator in each individual case. Sociological concepts are
therefore distinguished, so to speak, by their passive, derivative character; they
represent only a more or less accurate, logical mirror of reality. Their value as
an instrument of knowledge can thus in no way be compared with natural-
scientific concepts. Historical concepts do not in any way increase our knowledge, only our *understanding* of relations among events. From this it is evident
that sociology is not at all capable of expanding our historical horizon or
revealing the future, since history, on which sociology is directly dependent, is
incapable of this.

Be that as it may, the capability of social science (at one time enjoying all the
rights of juridical presumption) for prediction has never been adequately demonstrated, neither theoretically nor practically, so that in any case the *onus
probandi* [burden of proof] falls on the proponents of this view. In general I
believe that knowledge of the future would bring not happiness, but grief for
man, for it would make life and especially the future uninteresting and unap-
pealing, whereas now the imagination is free to fill in the future as it sees fit.
Hardly any of us would feel happy if our future, up to and including the day of
our death, were revealed in every detail. On the contrary, I think it would be
hard to imagine greater unhappiness. Omniscience is not our lot.

However, to avoid misunderstanding, I should add here that humanity will
never cease to think of tomorrow or to bring, to its ideas of tomorrow, a

social-scientific understanding of today's and yesterday's reality. In just the same way, no one can manage without forming, on the basis of common sense and scientific experience, a certain judgment not only of the present, but of the immediate future toward which each of us is working. If this too is called prediction, then making predictions about the future is a right and obligation of every conscious person. But it must not be forgotten that prediction in this sense has nothing in common with precise scientific prognosis, but amounts to its own type of impressionism, not so much a scientific as an artistic synthesis, having subjective persuasiveness but objectively indemonstrable with full clarity.[13] Reality provides here, of course, a number of transitions from more or less sober scientific conclusions to wild fantasy.

In this a large role is usually played by judgments *according to analogy,* the logical value of which should be perfectly clear in advance by means of logic itself (an example of a judgment by analogy can be found in one of the most popular claims of Marxism, namely, that an economically more advanced country reveals to another, less developed country a picture of its future development).

But let us fully acknowledge the legitimacy of the scientific theory of progress. Let us acknowledge that scientific prediction is in general possible and that the scientific predictions made up to now — in particular, predictions of the inevitably necessary advent of the future socialist order — are scientifically incontrovertible. Let us thus grant the theory of progress all the likeness to science to which it pretends. But is this theory capable of satisfying those who seek in it a firm sanctuary, the basis of faith, hope, and love?

The boldest theories of progress do not go further in their predictions than the visible historical future, and the historical gaze does not extend far. Suppose that we know the fortunes of humanity in, say, the twentieth century, but even with that we will still know nothing at all about what awaits humanity in the twenty-first, twenty-second, or twenty-third century, and so on. The scientific theory of progress is like a dim candle that someone has lit at the very beginning of a dark, unending corridor. The candle faintly lights the nooks a few feet around it, but all remaining space is shrouded in deep darkness. It is beyond the power of positive science to reveal the future fortunes of humanity; it leaves us in *absolute uncertainty* about them. The gratifying assurance that in the end everything good and rational triumphs and stands invincible has no grounds in the mechanistic understanding of the world: after all, everything here is pure contingency, so why does the same contingency that extolls reason today, not ruin it tomorrow, and which makes knowledge and truth expedient today, not make ignorance and error as expedient tomorrow? Does history not know the collapse and ruin of whole civilizations? Or does it testify to regular and uninterrupted progress? Let us forget about a cosmic cataclysm or the freezing of the earth and universal death as the ultimate finale to the history of humanity—the perspective of pure contingency, full of impenetrable gloom and obscurity, is itself enough to freeze the blood. And it is impossible to object to this with the usual indications that future humanity will cope better than us with its needs, for the issue here is not about future humanity, but about us, about our ideas of its fortunes. Such an answer will hardly satisfy anyone. No, all that honest positive science has to say here is: *ignoramus* and *ignorabimus*.[14] It is not within its power to solve the hidden meaning of history and its final goal.

But, of course, the human spirit can never be content with this answer. To stop at it means to turn one's back on the most basic questions of conscious life, after which there is no longer anything to ask about.[15] And humanity in the best of its representatives has never turned its back on the question of the final calling and destinies of the human race, but has always answered it one way or another. The positivists answer it as well. They not only answer it, but have founded a religion on their idea of the future fortunes of humanity, a religion that ignites in people the most sacred feelings, that calls for exploit and struggle, and that sets hearts today on fire.

Where did this conviction in and, as it were, firm knowledge of humanity's future fortunes come from, since positive science is not in the position to impart it? It arises from the same source generally as all religious truths, or what is religiously taken for truth. Its source is *religious faith,* but a faith that has crept in clandestinely, as contraband, without regal grandeur, but that has nonetheless secured regal dominion where it was assumed only science was called to rule.

Thus, the attempt to construct a scientific religion did not succeed: faith powerfully proclaimed its rights where science had sought to dominate, and science failed to live up to the expectations that had been placed on it. But was it not mistaken and utopian to even dream of basing religion, concerned with the infinite and eternal, on the concrete and always limited foundation which is all that positive science provides! One of two things is possible: either science will preserve only its name, but will in fact cease to be science, or it will not be able to become a religion. What has happened is the first.

Now let us turn to further examination of the religion of progress.

IV.

The subject of unlimited progress turns out to be Humanity. It fully plays the role of the divine in the religion of progress—this is so not only in the idea of the founders of this religion, Comte and, I would say, Feuerbach (who is especially significant for us in his immediate influence on Marx and Engels), but by the very essence of the matter. Why is it precisely humanity that is deified, why is this impersonal subject endowed with divine attributes, first of all eternity or, at least, immortality, as well as perfection and absoluteness (for only with these qualities is a religious attitude possible)?

In this, man is led by a normal and irrepressible religious need. It is intolerable to see the highest and ultimate end of being in this fleeting and chance existence. But, according to the philosophy of positivism, the supreme and absolute meaning of life, a meaning refuting the limitedness and conditional character of life, cannot be sought in the sphere of the transcendent or in the sphere of religious faith. It must be found in the world of empirical, sensible being. Human thought once more faces an insoluble task, the illusory resolution of which can be obtained only at the cost of internal contradictions and self-delusion.

A human being is mortal, humanity is immortal. A human being is limited, humanity has the potential for unlimited development. Living for others, a human being defeats the sting of death and merges with eternity. A vivid expression of this idea is given by Guyau (*L'Irréligion de l'avenir*) in his marvelously elevated reflection on immortality:

> It [Stoicism] was right when it recommended insensibility to one's own death. A man needs no other consolation than to feel that he has lived a complete life, that he has done his work, and that mankind is not the worse, nay, is perhaps the better for his having existed; and that whatever he has loved will survive, that the best of his dreams will somewhere be realized, that the impersonal element in his consciousness, the portion of the immortal patrimony of the human race, which has been entrusted to him and constitutes what is best in him, will endure and increase, and be passed on, without loss, to succeeding generations; that his own death is of no more importance, no more breaks the eternal continuity of things, than the shivering of a small mirror does. To gain a complete consciousness of the continuity of life is to estimate death at its proper value, which is perhaps that of the disappearance of a kind of living illusion. Once more, in the name of reason, which is capable of understanding death, and of accepting it as it accepts whatsoever else is intelligible — be not a coward (*pas être lâche*)![16]

I would be hard pressed to find a more successful and lofty expression of the view under consideration than that given by the French philosopher. And all the same a sad refrain resounds in him with captivating sincerity: *pas être lâche,* not to be a coward before this terror of extinction.

To characterize still more clearly the theory in question, I will cite here Fichte's contrasting view — the fruit of exalted thought and a no less elevated mood, but nourished by other, much more gratifying ideas (see *Bestimmung des Gelehrten*). Of the infinite tasks of moral life, Fichte says:

> Yes! and this is the loftiest thought of all: Once I assume this lofty task I will never complete it. Therefore, just as surely as it is my vocation to assume this task, I can never cease *to act* and thus I can never cease *to be*. That which is called "death" cannot interrupt my work; for my work must be completed, and it can never be completed in any amount of time. Consequently, my existence has no temporal limits: I am eternal. When I assumed this great task I laid hold of eternity at the same time. I lift my head boldly to the threatening stony heights, to the roaring cataract, and to the crashing clouds in their fire-red sea. "I am eternal!" I shout to them, "I defy your power! Rain everything down upon me! You earth, and you, heaven, mingle all of your elements in wild tumult. Foam and roar, and in savage combat pulverize the last dust mote of that body which I call my own. Along with its own unyielding project, my will shall hover boldly and indifferently above the wreckage of the universe. For I have seized my vocation, and it is more permanent than you. It is eternal, and so too am I."[17]

Thus we have two faiths, one of which can be called faith in what is dead, the other in living immortality. But who is immortal and absolute in the first of these faiths, if a human being is mortal and relative? We already know the answer: humanity with its capacity for infinite development. But just what is this *humanity*, and do its properties distinguish it from a *human being*? No, it is in no way distinguished from a human being; it is simply a large, indeterminate number of people, with all the properties of people and as little endowed with new qualities in its nature as a heap of stones or grain in comparison with each individual stone or seed. What positivism calls humanity is an indeterminate repetition, in indeterminate space and time, of each of us with all our weakness and limitation. If our life has absolute meaning, value, and purpose, then so does humanity; but if the life of every human being, taken individually, represents meaninglessness and absolute contingency, then humanity's fortunes are likewise meaningless. Not believing in the absolute meaning of the life of a person [*lichnost'*] but hoping to find it in the life of a whole collection of others like us, we, like frightened children, hide behind each other. We seek to pass off a logical abstraction as a supreme being, thus lapsing into a logical fetishism, which is no better than simple idolatry, for it ascribes qualities of the living God to a dead object created by us.

Its supposed capacity for infinite development lends to the concept of humanity the semblance of the absolute. But this infinity is only illusory or apparent — bad infinity, according to Hegel's terminology, already familiar to us. It is based simply on the fact that the development of humanity in time, at least in accordance with a given state of knowledge, cannot be assigned an end, but not at all on the fact that there cannot in principle be an end. In order to grasp the difference, it is enough to compare this bad infinity, or, it would be better to say, this indeterminateness, this indeterminate duration, with Fichte's idea of infinity, which flows from the absolute character of the goal that the infinite movement serves.[18] But humanity, according to the positivist view, has no absolute goal of development that could sanction this infinity and turn it, so to speak, from passive to active, from contingency and indeterminateness to rational necessity.

Nor is progress unlimited from the qualitative side. There are, of course, no limits to the achievements of the human mind and conscience [*sovest'*], to the extent they are expressed in objective results, or in cultural goods of generally any type. But these objective accomplishments of all humanity constitute, at any given moment and for any given generation, only a starting point, from which it is necessary to go forward, for a given level of culture is inherited not as an achievement, the fruit of struggle and striving, but as a finished result. Progress itself consists not in these objective results — it need only be suggested that humanity has already accomplished enough and has stopped in its development, to understand that this could mean only death and complete decay — but in unflagging movement forward. And the only real carriers of this movement are people (and not "humanity") who are incapable of being satisfied and of taking their relative existence for the absolute, people like us. From this side as well, the idea of humanity as the absolute turns out to be an illusion.

Thus, the attempt to present humanity as the absolute leads to a vicious circle: we try to give meaning to our existence through others, and others through us; the whole argument hangs in the air.

Religious faith in humanity is therefore an irrational, blind faith. This faith, in comparison with faith that has at its basis metaphysical truths justified before reason, has no such rational foundation and is its own kind of superstition. Positivism, having aspired only to positive knowledge and so having rejected both metaphysics and religious faith on principle, ends in superstition. Faith in humanity — this sacred and cherished faith — is reduced by positive philosophy to the level of simple fancy and superstition.

V.

In what precisely is the infinite progress of humanity expressed? To this question various answers have been and are given. The simplest and most widespread is that the goal of progress is the greatest possible growth of happiness for the greatest possible number of people. The point of view of eudaemonism, social as well as individual, is ethically the most crude and is incapable of answering the needs of any consciousness that is even slightly developed. It is based, incidentally, on the supposition that a eudaemonistic scale can be found and that the general quantity of pleasure and displeasure in the world can be precisely determined; in the final tally, the plus signs should exceed the minus signs, all the time increasing at the expense of the minus signs until the complete disappearance of the latter. Social eudaemonism approximates in this case the teaching of Eduard von Hartmann, who also considers it possible to calculate the final balance of the world's joy and sorrow, but who comes to completely opposing conclusions. His eudaemonistic pessimism, which is combined in an original way with evolutionary optimism, finds its ultimate affirmation in his metaphysics, in his theory of the unconscious as the absolute substance of the world, and of the purely contingent origin of the world, as if by a mistake of the absolute.[19] (But it is necessary to give Hartmann his due, for in ethics he is a fierce enemy of all eudaemonistic tendencies.) The mere fact that in different cases this world balance sheet comes up differently, now with a plus, now with a minus, testifies to the dubiousness of such arithmetic. The difficulty of striking a precise balance is explained by the impossibility of finding a unit for measuring joy and sorrow, for in each of these states we have something individual, defined not quantitatively but qualitatively, so that a scale of measurement by time or number is inapplicable here. Are we even able to say of ourselves which sensations, pleasant or unpleasant, we had more of in the course not only of a life, but even of a day or a year? Besides that, according to Solov'ëv's apt remark (in *Justification of the Good*), this balance is not an object of immediate perception; every pleasure or displeasure is perceived separately, and their algebraic sum is only a theoretical total.[20] Thus, it is impossible to clearly determine whether or not some kind of eudaemonistic progress exists in history, all the more so in that together with new sources of enjoyment humanity receives new sources of suffering, new diseases and anxieties. The pursuit of universal happiness as the goal of history is an impossible undertaking, for this goal is completely elusive and indeterminable.

The developed moral consciousness condemns social eudaemonism (in essence Epicureanism) because of the baseness of its underlying principle. Happiness is a natural aspiration of man, but the only happiness that is moral is that which is incidental to, not an intended concomitant of, moral activity and service to the good. Obviously, happiness cannot be posed as a goal in itself, by the mere fact that it does not represent anything independent. But if an equal sign were to be put between the good and pleasure, then there is no fall, no monstrous vice, no animalistic egoism, no drowning of all spiritual needs in sensuality, that could not be sanctified by this principle. The ideal from this point of view would be the conversion of humanity into an animal state. Such a doctrine is completely incapable of valuing the whole necessity and elevating significance of suffering, the interpreter of which in our literature is Dostoevsky. The predicate of absolute blessedness [*vseblazhennost'*] is conceivable only in relation to God, the most perfect possible being [*vsesovershennei-shee sushchestvo*]; for man, however, moral life without struggle and suffering is impossible. Therefore, if moral life constitutes man's true calling on earth, suffering will always remain unavoidable. Suffering is morally necessary for man. "The cross" — this is the symbol of suffering and sanctification.

Striving to ease or eliminate the suffering of other people is one of the basic forms of moral life and of active love, and compassion one of the basic virtues (Schopenhauer wanted to see in it even the only virtue).[21] Thus it can appear that eliminating suffering, as such, is the true, main goal of moral activity. But the incorrectness of this judgment becomes clear as soon as we turn attention to the fact that not every suffering deserves our sympathy, not that which is rooted in the immoral strivings of a given person, and not that which does not injure but morally elevates man. We would not want to allay the suffering of a usurer who is deprived of the possibility of taking an exorbitant percent, and we would consider it madness to wish to relieve Faust's sufferings in the same way as Mephistopheles, who delivered him from them on Walpurgis Night. From this it is clear that compassion itself stands under the control of a higher moral principle, and that what is morally good must be valued higher than suffering, our own as well as that of others. The struggle with human suffering thus loses its character as a basic moral goal, and takes on subordinate significance.

A distinctive type of eudaemonism penetrates the main outlook of contemporary political economy, according to which the growth of needs and, consequently, of pleasures from their satisfaction, amounts to the basic principle of economic development. In the eyes of economic science, the growth of sensuous needs and their satisfaction equals culture and cultural development [*kul'turnost'*]. Sombart, one of the most resolute economists in this sense, once directly called this growth of needs "*Menschenwerden*" [becoming human].[22] This is a wholly pagan and also immoral point of view that, not distinguishing the needs of the spirit from those of the body, deifies the growth of needs as such. Both economic life and the economic science reflecting it are subject to moral evaluation, and only this can guard against lapsing into crude paganism. Growth of material needs and their satisfaction is not immoral only to the extent it liberates the spirit and spiritualizes man, not to the extent it, strengthening the sphere of sensuousness, abets the spirit's downfall and the victory of the flesh. In a certain measure this growth of needs, or economic progress, constitutes a necessary precedent to spiritual development and sometimes to the awakening of personhood [lichnost'] (this characterizes, in my view, the current moment in the economic development of Russia). But the growth of moral and sensuous needs can lag behind and become detached from each other. In such a case the refinement of sensuousness, not rousing but depressing the activity of the spirit, constitutes a peculiar moral disease, a moral squalor arising not from poverty, but from wealth. This two-sided nature of economic progress is forgotten by economists when they, carried away by their own special point of view, identify it with one that has universal significance for man and culture. The cultural barbarism produced by contemporary economic life is no better, indeed worse, than primitive barbarism, precisely because of the refinement of the needs of modern man. Ethical materialism or spiritual bourgeoisness [*burzhuaznost'*] is an undeniable and apparently worsening disease of contemporary European society; this same bourgeoisness once ruined Roman civilization. This bourgeoisness is ethically sanctioned by pagan science, declaring bodily pleasure an independent and undeniable good. Without denying the completely irrefutable fact that the growth and moral development of personhood are to a certain degree inextricably connected with material progress, we cannot but acknowledge the healthy ascetic kernel in L. N. Tolstoy's teaching, despite its excesses and obvious exaggerations. In any case it is much more moral and higher than those current doctrines that see culture in frock coats and top hats.

A wholly bourgeois and thus hedonistic character distinguishes one current theory, coming from the camp of those who consider themselves the greatest enemies, and the greatest enemies on principle, of the bourgeoisie. We have in mind the celebrated theory of class interests and the class struggle, class egoism and class solidarity, if the class struggle is treated not as a contingent historical means for the achievement of a higher ethical goal, but as a fully independent ethical principle. Class struggle appears as a form of defending one's rights to participation in life's goods. In the distribution of these goods there are the deprived and the deprivers (the bourgeois haves and have-nots, as Herzen put it), but from the ethical point of view both warring parties are equal, insofar as they are guided not by ethical or religious enthusiasm, but by purely egoistic aims. It is obvious that a new bourgeoisie can be raised on naked class interest, but a great historical movement cannot be founded on it. Of course, the greatest movement of recent times was never entirely founded, and could not have been founded, on this principle of class struggle, but was always higher than it. In any event, it can be said that the degree of triumph of this principle is inversely proportional to the ethical height of the movement, and that the complete triumph of the principle would be capable of lowering the movement to complete bourgeoisness.

The eudaemonistic ideal of progress, as a scale for evaluation of historical development, leads to conclusions directly contrary to morality. For, from this point of view, the sufferings of some generations form a bridge to the happiness of others; for some reason, some generations must suffer for others to be happy, some must by their sufferings "be the manure for future harmony," in Ivan Karamazov's expression.[23] But why must Ivan sacrifice himself for the future happiness of Peter, and why does Ivan, as a human individual, not possess, from this point of view, the same rights to happiness as the future Peter? Would not Ivan's wish to exchange roles with the future Peter, to make his own lot happiness and Peter's lot suffering, be completely logical and consistent with the eudaemonistic theory? Like the theory of progress, is not the theory *après nous le déluge,* that is, complete egoism, also demonstrable from eudaemonistic principles?![24]

On the other hand, what ethical value is there in this future happiness, bought by the sweat and blood of others? Can anything justify such a price for progress and this happiness? Our descendants turn out to be vampires, living off our blood. Building one's happiness on the unhappiness of others is in any case immoral, and the view justifying such a manner of action, even if it relates to a future generation, is also immoral. Any suffering is an absolute evil from the eudaemonistic point of view, and future happiness cannot and must not be bought by this absolute evil. A world constructed in such a manner and on such principles would not be worth living in by any self-respecting person. It would be left for him to "most respectfully return his ticket." It is against just such a world that Ivan Karamazov "rebels."

VI.

In truth, it must be recognized that although all versions of the theory of progress have some tint of eudaemonism, in none of them is eudaemonism followed through consistently and exhaustively. Thus, together with happiness, the perfectibility [*usovershenstvovanie*] of humanity is also posed as a goal of progress. "Positivism," Comte says, "holds universal perfectibility (*perfectionnement*) to be the constant goal of our whole existence, personal as well as social, first in our external condition, but also and more especially in our internal nature."[25] Limitless perfectibility forms the content of progress for Condorcet as well, in his youthfully enthusiastic, *Esquisse d'un tableau historique des progrès de l'esprit humain.*

Without doubt, this ideal is much more elevated than the preceding one [eudaemonism], but the attempt at its substantiation from the point of view of positivism leads to still greater difficulties. To speak of perfectibility, as the approximation or aspiration toward some ideal of perfection, it is necessary to have this ideal in advance. And this is doubly true because perfectibility is conceived as infinite, which means no given stage of development can enjoy perfection, which in turn means the concept of perfection cannot be arrived at inductively from experience. Thus on the one hand this ideal does not fit into the limits of relative experience, in other words, it is absolute; yet on the other hand this absolute ideal, since its development and realization do not fit into experience, can obviously only be of an extra-experiential or supra-experiential origin. Here as well the worn path of experience necessarily takes us to the difficult and rocky road of speculation. Positivism once more borrows, beyond all expectations, from metaphysics, again demonstrating the impossibility of solving the most basic questions of life and the spirit within the parameters of empirical knowledge.

What has been said must be emphasized still more when we turn to the last and most elevated formula of progress, according to which it consists in the creation of conditions for the free development of personhood [lichnost']. This formula, together with the doctrine of the class struggle and in general with a more or less eudaemonistic understanding of progress, constitutes the esoteric wisdom of Marx, which he owes to his acquaintance with Hegel's philosophy. This formula thus represents a direct borrowing from metaphysics, but it is done in the same superficial, mechanical way in which Hegel's philosophy is generally "turned right side up" in Marx.[26] From a living formula — the doctrine of the development of the spirit toward freedom, or self-consciousness — a formula that stood in connection with a whole Weltanschauung and that grew organically from it, a dead scheme was obtained that destroyed its philosophical meaning. It is difficult to have a high opinion of this whole philosophical operation (proper elucidation of which would require a broad excursus into Hegel's philosophy), but only through such an operation did there result the doctrine of the leap from the kingdom of necessity to the kingdom of freedom,[27] the doctrine of "*Vorgeschichte*" [prehistory], only after which will *Geschichte* [history] begin.[28]

The free development of the person as the ideal of social evolution is the basic and common theme of all classical German philosophy; it is expressed with the greatest force and clarify in Fichte. We propose that this ideal should now have the significance of a moral axiom. It is only an expression in different words of the basic idea behind Kant's ethics — the autonomy of moral life and the self-legislation of the will in the choice of good or evil.[29] At the present time the will is not self-legislating, in the sense that any coercion —

political, economic, or social — that is brought to bear on a person aims to add its transient and deadening influence and to impose its alien and despotic will where only a self-legislating will ought to reign and freely choose between good and evil. The liberation of the person therefore creates the conditions of autonomous moral life. This ethical axiom adds an axiomatic indisputability to — and puts beyond any doubt the legitimacy of and obliging force behind — the current aspirations toward political and economic democracy. It gives them an ethical sanction, thus raising them from a simple struggle for existence to the level of fulfilling the moral law.

The reader will understand that this is an idea of a supra-empirical, metaphysical character (which is why metaphysics gives a higher sanction to the present social movement). It is necessary to have an unshakable conviction in what Fichte called the "vocation of man,"[30] a definite idea of his moral nature, in order to advance an itself purely negative demand such as the free development of the person. The metaphysical content of this negative demand is what gives it a positive character. Deprived of this content, it, like all negatively defined concepts, is empty and unconscious.

Marxism takes the formula of the free development of the person without, of course, any metaphysical content. Here the person is not a bearer of absolute tasks, endowed with a definite moral nature and capabilities, but entirely a product of historical development, changing with this development. The concept of the person, strictly speaking, is completely missing here, reduced only to the purely formal unity of the self. But in such a case, what can the formula "free development of the person" mean? Once more, positive science knocks at the door of metaphysics. ...

There remains, finally, an area that speaks most strongly of all to the impotence and inadequacy of the positivist theory of progress, to its inability to solve the most basic problems of a Weltanschauung. According to the basic idea of the theory of progress (regardless of its content), the future, arriving with natural necessity and subject to the law of causation, is at the same time the ideal of action, that is, an "ought," a moral demand directed toward the will. Here we come up against the basic antithesis of consciousness, the opposition between "is" [*bytie*] and "ought" [*dolzhenstvovanie*], and it does not take many words to show that empirical science cannot cope with this antithesis.

First of all, it is obvious that "ought" can in no way be substantiated from "is." How can it follow from the fact that a given event will actually ensue, that I ought to strive toward it as "what ought to be" [*dolzhnoe*]? From the course of my past deeds, all of which have completely equal significance from the point of view of the reign of the law of causation that is common to them, why do I classify some as moral — as consistent with the law of "ought" — and others as immoral, as inconsistent with it, whereupon my conscience torments me, although I cannot alter or annihilate them [the offending deeds]? All the refinements of positivists to present morality as a fact of natural development (and thereby to undermine its sanctity, equating it with all other natural needs, such as hunger, sexual reproduction, and so forth) relate only to particular forms and expressions of morality, but they presuppose the fact itself of the existence of morality, without which such investigations would themselves be impossible. (So it is with atheists, who, proving God's nonexistence with even greater fanfare, thus reveal all the more obviously what role this problem plays in their consciousness and the extent to which God is present there, even as an object of negation.) "Ought" is of supra-empirical origin, and because it penetrates our life, it can be said that human life consists of a constant combination of the empirical and supra-empirical, of the material and spiritual principle.

The problem of "ought" is only a general designation for a whole set of problems, and before all of them the positivist theory of progress remains silent.

"Ought" is directed toward the will. It necessarily supposes the possibility of moral wanting [*khotenie*], the possibility of choice, and consequently it is inconceivable without free will. At the same time, all acts are motivated, that is, subject to the law of causation. Philosophy is faced with reconciling this possibility of the combination of free will and determinism. Determinism must respectfully step aside in order to make way for the moral deed, but it must also constantly sustain a closed order of causation, for any break in causation annihilates experience. Directed toward the future, free will sees only "ought," but experience sees only causes and effects.[31] Is there some connection between causation and "ought" and between the principles of necessity and freedom corresponding to them, and which of them is primary? These are the questions that are necessarily raised by the antithesis we are examining, and that can be answered only through a metaphysical synthesis. And in fact all these questions have always been the central questions of metaphysics; in particular, the question of freedom and necessity is the basic problem in the philosophy of Kant, Fichte, Schelling, and Hegel.

This problem is posed with full clarity only by those who have shown, once and for all, the relativity of empirical knowledge and the conditional rights of science, but also the possibility of transcendent, intelligible freedom alongside the necessity governing in the world of experience. Schopenhauer rightly considered this distinction to be one of the greatest achievements of the human mind and Kant's immortal service to philosophy. But Kant dualistically juxtaposed empirical necessity and intelligible freedom, and therefore all the efforts of post-Kantian philosophy were directed toward overcoming this dualism and showing the final triumph of freedom. Such is the theme and basic content of the philosophy of Fichte, Schelling, and Hegel.

We have thus reviewed all the basic problems of the theory of progress and have come to the general conclusion that they exceed the power of positive science. Either they are plainly not resolved by it, or they lead to unavoidable internal contradictions, or they are resolved with the help of contraband, that is, by introducing under the flag of positive science elements that are foreign to it. Such conflation puts positive science in an ambiguous position and, together with that, crudely violates the rights of metaphysics and religious faith. Therefore, what is necessary first of all is careful differentiation of the various elements and problems that are conflated in the theory of progress. It is necessary to return to Caesar what is Caesar's, and to God what is God's.[32] The correct formulation of the theory of progress must show by which means it resolves the problems it raises; it must show to which more general problems these solutions necessarily lead; and, consequently, it must delimit and, within the proper sphere, restore in their own rights science, metaphysics, and religion.

The exposition below will be devoted to an attempt at making this delimitation and giving an appropriate formulation of the problems of the theory of progress.

VII.

The first and basic task the theory of progress sets for itself is to show that history has meaning, that the historical process is not only evolution, but also progress. The theory of progress argues, consequently, for a final identity between causal necessity [*zakonomernost'*] and rational purposiveness, in which sense it is, as we have already said, a theodicy. Its goal is thus the discovery of a higher reason that is simultaneously transcendent to and immanent in history, the discovery of the plan of history, its goal, movement toward this goal, and the forms of this movement.[33]

We have already seen that this task is beyond positive science and is in general insoluble by the means of experience. But the task itself is posed entirely correctly and is inevitable for the philosophizing mind, which searches for constant, immutable being in the stream of fleeting events and which refuses to see in history only dead causation. This task is supra-empirical, metaphysical, and can be answered by the speculative discipline that until now has carried the name of the philosophy of history, but which might more correctly and precisely be called the *metaphysics of history*.

The metaphysics of history does not, of course, have an autonomous, independent character, but is only a part or division of a general metaphysical system, an application of general metaphysical principles to the historical life of humanity. Therefore, the general metaphysical views of one or another philosopher determine the content of the metaphysics of history, which will be one thing for Hegel, another for Schopenhauer, another for St. Augustine, and still another for Vladimir Solov'ëv. The classic and dazzling example of the metaphysics of history is Hegel's historical philosophy (of course, this is not at all to say that it can satisfy the requirements of modern scientific consciousness).

The metaphysics of history is the discovery of the absolute in the relative; it strives to see how the eternal radiance of the absolute is reflected within the limited framework of space and time. In terms of content, what is essential for the metaphysics of history is not only how the absolute is understood, but also how broadly the limits of space and time are understood, that is, how extensively and profoundly historical research in space and time is understood. This affirms the indissoluble link between the metaphysics of history and the positive content of history. Metaphysics must not only not ignore the positive progress of historical science, it must constantly take it into account, expanding in this way its tasks of interpreting the meaning of this historical material. Naturally, a metaphysics of history that ignores or contradicts the data of historical science is a bad metaphysics of history. Anyone who wishes to create a metaphysics of history must be in the same measure both a philosopher and a historian.

We have already said that the problems of the metaphysics of history are ineradicable from our consciousness, and there is no need to think that they could ever have been completely removed. Only the content of the answers given to the basic questions of the metaphysics of history has changed, so that some schools (such as positivism and materialism) have rejected the meaning of history, regarding mechanical causation as the absolute principle, while others have sought absolute reason in history.

What does it mean to find the meaning of history? It means, first of all, to show that history is the unveiling and fulfillment of one creative and rational plan, that the historical process expresses a universal, providential idea. Therefore, everything that ever was and will be in history is necessary for the disclosure of this plan, for the ends of reason. In this sense Hegel's prophetic words take on their full significance: "all that is real is rational, and all that is rational is real."[34] But this position, which in Hegel is the final result of a system born of genius and the ultimate product of the enormous labor contained in this system, also constitutes the basic theme of the metaphysics of history and the basic problem this metaphysics must solve. It is a problem of theodicy in the true sense of the word, and the metaphysics of history is necessarily a theodicy, as Hegel himself understood.

This is the greatest and most important problem not only of the metaphysics of history, but also of all moral philosophy. Here must be given a "justification of the good" (as the late Solov'ëv formulated this very problem), which must also be a justification of evil, of evil in nature, in man, and in history. Philosophy must show the internal impotence of evil, its illusoriness, and its — terrible to say — ultimate rationality.

Philosophy must honestly confront this question in all its scope, not faint-heartedly evading or diminishing its difficulty, but dauntlessly looking hope and despair in the eye. And the philosophy that will bear this struggle bravely and travel this thorny and agonizing path of doubts, losing nothing of its previous conviction in the rationality of existence and in the triumph of truth, is worthy of its name and can be the teacher of people. But how many are there who, pusillanimously giving in before this mystery, cowardly rush to fill in the cracks of their Weltanschauung with cheap optimism and to somehow shun the mystery! Heinrich Heine's well-known epigram about the professor, patching the holes in the universe with the rags of his nightgown and with his cap, applies to them. But happy, oh, thrice happy is the person who has managed, honestly and piously, to suffer through to this gratifying conviction, for there can be nothing more joyous in the world.

If we acknowledge that history is the revelation of the absolute, we thereby also recognize that chance and the dead necessity [zakonomernost'] of causation do not reign in history, that here there is only the necessity of the development of the absolute. The causal necessity of history has significance only as an auxiliary means for the ends of the absolute. And if the absolute is a synonym for freedom, then the metaphysics of history is the revelation of the principle of freedom in history, its victory over mechanical causation.

At the same time we also recognize that there is in history a living and rational force, going beyond our intentions and guiding them. And our intentions and deeds turn out to be a means for the ends of the absolute. Hegel in his distinctive language called this the cunning of reason (*List der Vernunft*). "Reason is as *cunning* as it is *mighty*. Its cunning generally consists in the mediating activity which, while it lets objects act upon one another according to their own nature, and wear each other out, executes only *its* purpose without itself mingling in the process. In this sense we can say that, with regard to the world and its process, divine Providence behaves with absolute cunning. God lets men, who have their particular passions and interests, do as they please, and what results is the accomplishment of *his* intentions, which are something other than those whom he employs were directly concerned about."[35]

Positive science also knows the cunning of history. An individual cannot be judged by what he thinks about himself, says Marx (in the well-known preface to *Zur Kritik der politischen Ökonomie*); for this, it is necessary to ask the economic base.[36] This idea of the cunning of the economic base, or in general of dead historical necessity, is capable of killing any energy or moral enthusiasm, for it leaves in complete obscurity and gives over to the will of pure contingency the final outcome of our personal intentions. True, we are expected to struggle against this necessity, mastering and controlling it, but it still has not been (and never will be) mastered in a way that would give fully reliable direction to individual action. With this, our acts turn into a moral lottery: inspired with good intentions, I risk serving evil in the end, while the servants of evil prove to be the benefactors of humanity.

We already know that the theory of progress tries to mend this tear by introducing a positivist theodicy. But, first, where is the guarantee that, in consequence of the cunning of history, incomprehensible to us, the epoch of progress we are now experiencing is not leading us directly to its very opposite? Second, progress is limited in time and space; we acknowledge only some events and epochs as progressive. From all historical reality, we cull only a little, rejecting all the rest. The formula of the theory of progress, contrary to Hegel, is therefore: not everything actual is rational, that is, many historical epochs and events are irrational. Such a view, carrying the traces of contingency and arbitrariness, constitutes the complete opposite of the one we are examining. Before the face of the absolute there is no past, present, or future, no selected epochs; all history serves to reveal the absolute. As Hegel says, "it is the whole unfolding that constitutes its content and its interest. ... Everything which, taken by itself, appears to be restricted gets its value by belonging to the whole, and being a moment of the Idea" (*Moment der Idee*).[37]

In this way, all history is the manifestation of the absolute, all of it is the living garment of God, about which the spirit of the earth speaks in Faust: "So schaff ich am sausenden Webstuhl der Zeit / Und wirke der Gottheit lebendiges Kleid."[38]

However, no matter how convinced we are that history represents the revelation of absolute reason, and no matter how conscientiously we strive to understand this reason, our inquiries will always remain incomplete, and this reason will remain more or less concealed from our weak eyes. To know the reason behind all that exists, to understand equally "every blade of grass in the field and every star in the sky"[39] is accessible only to God's omniscience. For us, the individual events of our own life as well as of history will forever remain irrational, and it falls on us to contend in our actions with this irrational reality, presenting as it does a struggle of good and evil. Thus, if we cannot make the ends of the absolute directly our own, what can guide us in our actions? But the absolute constantly guides us in life, constantly gives us direction, and chastises us for disobedience and mistakes. Every day, every hour, we hear its authoritative voice, categorical, stern, and implacable. It is conscience, the moral law, the categorical imperative, the absolute character of which Kant established beyond any doubt. The moral law commands us to want the good, always and everywhere, for the sake of the good itself. The absolute law of the good must also be the law of our life.

This law, in application to historical development, commands us to want the good in history and to further its realization by our own efforts; it commands us, in other words, to want *progress*. From this point of view, progress is not a law of historical development, but a moral task (as Professor Siebeck correctly indicates in his superb speech, *Über die Lehre vom genetischen Fortschritte der Menscheit*), not "is," but absolute "ought."[40] The finite and relative cannot contain the absolute, therefore progress is infinite.

Does recognition that progress is a binding moral task require certainty that this progress is being realized with mechanical necessity? Does it require, in other words, raising the curtain of the future, rushing to scientific prophecies? No, no crutches are needed for the moral law. The absolute character of its dictates, wanting the good for the sake of the good, does not depend on any contingent conditions of the realization of the good in history. From the eudaemonistic perspective, it makes a big difference, of course, whether this struggle is heavy or light, whether it ends in victory or defeat, whether it requires heroic effort and courage or makes do with modest everyday work, but this changes nothing about the absolute character of the moral imperative, once it is recognized as such before one's own conscience — it can be violated, but not changed. Suppose for a minute that we have the most precise prediction of the next decade, and on the basis of this prediction all our finest aspirations are doomed to failure. Does it follow from this that they cease to be binding? In no way. You can, for you ought to — such is the moral law. This is a terrible formula, and few are the heroes who will retreat before nothing and go to their death for what they consider their duty. But for those who do not have the strength to follow the moral imperative, the pain of conscience attests to the fact that here this imperative is violated, and a sin is committed.

The positivist theory of progress flatters our weakness; it is a eudaemonistic concoction, which promises the external support of the natural course of things to that which does not find adequate support internally. In this, the positivist theory of progress represents its own type of eschatology, invoked to inspire warriors and sustain religious faith in the final triumph of the good. But another type of eschatology is needed before man can find in it real support for his moral activity. This requires a conviction that our ethical deeds and intentions have more than ephemeral significance, that they matter to the absolute and are necessary for its cunning. What is needed is a conviction in the existence of an objective moral world-order, a kingdom of moral ends, in which our modest life will find its own place. This lofty idea (ethical pantheism, in Windelband's apt expression) found its most complete development in J. G. Ficthe's theory. For Fichte, "that there is a moral world order, that in this order a definite position has been assigned to every rational individual and that his work counts, that the destiny of every person (unless it is the consequence of his own conduct) is derived from this plan, that without this plan no hair drops from a head, nor a sparrow from a roof, that every good deed succeeds while every evil one fails and that everything must go well for those who love only the good — all this is not doubtful at all but the most certain thing in the world and the basis of all certainty,"[41] and so on. In a certain sense, in Fichte's system the existence of other people, of the external world, even of God, all derives from the necessity of this idea of the moral world-order; the world exists only insofar as it is — or in order for it to be — an arena for moral activity. (It is not difficult to see in this the further development of Kant's theory of the primacy of practical reason and his moral proof of the existence of God.)

This is the true theory of progress — is any other needed! Yet it is obvious that the proof of this type of theory cannot be done empirically, but lies wholly in metaphysics.

The moral law, notwithstanding the absolute character of its dictates, is realized only through concrete goals, in concrete life. This sets a new task for moral life — to fill the empty form of absolute "ought" with concrete relative content, to find a bridge from the absolute to the relative. Here positive science enters into its own rights. It is the arsenal from which the moral will selects its arms. Science must serve the ends of the moral will (this does not, of course, exclude the possibility that knowledge itself, as such, can be a moral end). In particular, the social sciences, investigating different forms of social being in the past and present, are in our time specially called, as it were, to realistically orient good and evil and to illuminate them in social life. As with everything relative, reason travels a precarious path here: ideas of good and evil in concrete life are disputable and mistakes are possible; only the very concept of good and evil that unites everyone is beyond dispute. A person, within the limits of the understanding of reality that he has succeeded in achieving (an understanding in which science plays not the last role), selects from the boundless sea of evil precisely what can and ought to be eradicated just then by his own particular efforts; he selects that upon which he should concentrate his struggle at that given moment. In this, man cannot manage, of course, without determining the likelihood of one or another course of things, without glancing into the future, without making predictions. From the totality of all these data and ideas arises consciousness of what is called the historical task. Every age, every epoch has some historical task of its own, determined by the objective course of things. Thus, although the moral law is absolute, and its imperatives have significance *sub specie aeternitatis* [from the perspective of eternity], still its content is always given by history. To be a child of your time, to answer its calls in everything, to understand all its tasks and take the lead in struggling for their resolution — such are the obligations that the moral law imposes. Without such content this law is a clanging cymbal,[42] which will rouse not a great deed [*podvig*], only hypocrisy and deceit.

Pitiful is the person who in our time is incapable of seeing the radiance of the absolute moral ideal in the hearts of people devoting themselves to helping the proletariat in its struggle for human dignity, in the hearts of people capable of living and dying for the cause of freedom, and pitiful is the person who will not see this radiance in the dull and prosaic paragraphs of factory legislation or in the charter of a labor union, and so forth. Fichte's rigorous ethics wants to subject all life, down to the most trifling details, to the control of the moral law. Perhaps such an elevated understanding of ethics is too much for the average person to carry out in life, but it is beyond doubt that there is nothing morally indifferent wherever the human will acts, and this pertains not only to acts, but to human institutions (law, first of all), which after all represent only a certain series of acts, repeated until established as a rule. Therefore, the emancipation of the peasants, the introduction of land captains,[43] the limitation of zemstvo revenues,[44] the municipal reform,[45] and the censorship and university statutes[46] are all subject to moral evaluation. Everything is either good or evil.

Positive historical science, and sociology as well (understanding the first as concrete history, and the second as a system of abstract concepts), are relevant, of course, to the determination and causal explanation of reality. But if the individual events of life are subject to our evaluation, then we can also evaluate historical events and select as an object of research an event of special interest and value to us. Of course, with this the selection of scientific material will be entirely relative and determined by the particular goals of the research, and for the same reason the number of scientific disciplines might be unlimited. But, in any event, we have here, in historical science, a combination of the category of "ought," or evaluation, with the category of historical being ("is"). Generalizing such historical values into the concept of culture, Rickert (in his *Kulturwissenschaft und Naturwissenschaft*) proposes to distinguish the sciences that have as their goal the study of the development of culture — sciences of culture — from those that do not set themselves such goals, or the natural sciences.[47] The group of the sciences of culture have enormous practical significance, since they most further the discernment of good and evil in a complex reality and indicate the most fruitful methods of struggling with evil; these sciences develop together with the increasing complexity of social life. Positive science thus has a very definite and, moreover, enormous significance; at the present time science is, one might say, the sine qua [non] of a moral act. But at the same time it certainly does not have the defining and leading role the positivist theory of progress ascribes to it; on the contrary, it is only a means, an instrument of a higher moral end, standing apart from and independent of it.

We already know that, together with knowledge, faith has autonomous rights. Only it can put beyond doubt what is doubtful as an object of human knowledge, as all such objects are; only it can warm cold theoretical knowledge with the heart's ardor and can provide a basis for conduct, external as well as internal, a basis not only for deeds, but for feelings. Faith establishes a religious context for truths that are the product of empirical as well as of supra-empirical knowledge, and extends the sphere of the indisputable beyond science. In this sense it is possible to believe, for example, in one's calling, mission, or task; it is possible to believe in the imminent realization of certain goals, although science says nothing about this. Without faith it is impossible to take a religious approach to any teaching, no matter how inspired it is.

Religion — no matter what kind — penetrates by its very idea the whole active life of every conscious human being. All the moral aims that a human being sets for himself must also be the prescriptions of his religion. This idea is expressed by Kant, in *Die Religion innerhalb der Grenzen der blossen Vernunft,* which defines religion as follows: "religion is (subjectively regarded) the recognition of all duties as divine commands."[48] In life every human being must therefore solve an arduous task: to combine the absolute with the relative, to direct one's activity in a way that meets the demands of one's religion, to be imbued with the consciousness that precisely these deeds and duties are the ones that our God wants from us. Solving this question of practical religion, the celebrated question of "what is to be done" is extraordinarily difficult and gives free range to limitless and interminable doubts. Only faith can put an end to them and morally stand a human being on his feet and affirm him. Without it, a human being cannot take a step forward in the most basic questions of life.

Faith is a completely independent aptitude of the spirit, which is far from evenly disbursed among people. There is a talent or genius for faith, as there is philosophic or scientific genius. If Hegel is correct in saying that nothing in history is accomplished without great passion, then his words are correct precisely in the sense that nothing great is accomplished without passionate faith in oneself and in one's feat. It is this that has led martyrs to the stake, rack, and dungeon, to exile and to death, all for an idea. But as knowledge always supposes ignorance and is in essence a passage from ignorance to knowledge, so faith supposes doubt and struggle with unbelief, and in this consists the life of faith. The classic formula of this sense of the psychology of faith is expressed in the words of the gospel story: I believe, Lord, help my unbelief![49] It is impossible to believe in something obvious, for example, that two times two is four — here there is no place for faith, which always pertains to that which admits doubt. Therefore, we are denied firm support from the outside, the power of faith must be found in oneself; faith itself is a moral task. No matter what form it has taken, faith in the good has never been depleted in humanity, but there are epochs of history marked by either a decline or rise in faith. No development of knowledge or flowering of material culture can make up for a decline in faith; it is possible to allow that humanity will be deprived of its science, of its civilization, as it lived without them over the course of centuries. But a complete loss of faith in the good would mean moral death, from which no forces of science or contrivances of civilization would save us.

VIII.

I will permit myself in conclusion to express a few remarks about the tasks of philosophy today. Hegel rightly indicated that "every individual is a child of his time; so philosophy too is its own time apprehended in thoughts (*ist ihre Zeit in Gedanken erfasst*)," and that "the task of philosophy is to comprehend what is."[50] Which peculiarities of our time does philosophy need to take into consideration?

Everyone is familiar with the basic features of the history of philosophical thought in the nineteenth century. In the first part of the century philosophy experienced an almost unprecedented flowering, when in the course of less than half a century Germany produced four philosophical geniuses: Kant, Fichte, Schelling, Hegel. The pinnacle of philosophical speculation was achieved in Hegel, whose philosophy ruled, albeit briefly, in all the most important branches of thought. Then followed the collapse of metaphysics. Hegel's prophetic words, in the preface to his *Logic*, were justified: "If science were to join with common sense" — which Hegel always viewed with contemptuous irony — "in order to bring ruin to metaphysics, a strange spectacle apparently could result: a cultured people might be seen without metaphysics, like a temple once richly adorned but without what is most sacred (*ohne Allerheiligstes*)."[51] What Hegel considered an improbable possibility became a reality soon after his death, and for more than half a century this "strange spectacle" could be seen. The thrust of scholarly thought at this time went to positive science, as humanity was intoxicated with the successes of natural science and technology.

The higher needs of the spirit were satisfied, as we already know, by the positivist theory of progress and the religion of humanity.

But, of course, such a situation could not last forever. The limited competence of natural science and in general of positive science, which had already abandoned the audacity of renouncing metaphysics, became more and more clear. Philosophical thought then began to raise its head. It is interesting that philosophy was so stunned by the blossoming of the positive sciences and had so lost its living philosophical tradition that it developed in a roundabout way, taking as its starting point not Hegel, but Kant, and then not the authentic, historical Kant, but only the Kant of the *Critique of Pure Reason,* which does not have a primary role in the general system of Kant's philosophical views, but rather only a propaedeutic significance, so to speak. Therefore, the epistemological problem became the central one of modern philosophy; the special contribution of recent philosophical thought consists in working out the theory of knowledge. But thought could not, of course, stand still on the theory of knowledge, and had to turn sooner or later to knowledge itself; in other words, having recognized the authentic Kant, it had to pass to his successors. In this way the philosophical tradition will be revived. Contemporary philosophy, despite the opinion of the neo-Kantians, must not be only the development of "critical" philosophy, but must rather give a creative synthesis of all the latest philosophical systems, or at least take them into account. Moreover, any contemporary philosophical system must not only know its whole spiritual inheritance, it must also consider the achievements of that time when this inheritance was in a position *hereditas jacens,*[52] without a successor. It must bring in and rework all the finite conclusions of contemporary positive science. Philosophy has never been posed with so difficult a task as now, but our time is full of philosophical presentiments and our young century will, I believe, show an unprecedented efflorescence of metaphysics. Among recent philosophical systems, these formally specified demands are best satisfied by the systems of Eduard von Hartmann and V. S. Solov'ëv; in my view, Solov'ëv's philosophy is so far the last word in world philosophical thought, its highest synthesis.

But philosophy must stand at the heights of its time in another sense as well: it must embrace not only the science, but also the life of its time; it must understand the needs of the times and answer them one way or another. Not one great philosopher has turned his back on reality and its tasks. Classical German philosophy provided the ideal of the philosopher-citizen in the person of Fichte. The pulse of Hegel's mighty thought still beats in Marxism. And contemporary philosophy must face the great social struggle of our days, and be its exponent and interpreter. It must not withdraw from life to the study, the sin of present-day German philosophy — the representatives of which unfortunately show, in their social views, the influence of their bourgeois sympathies. As a result, between philosophy and life a strange misunderstanding has formed, in which consciousness has been lost of the extent to which life is necessary for philosophy, and philosophy for life. Yet philosophy is necessary for life now more than ever, because of certain peculiarities of the historical moment we are experiencing.

Everyone knows what crisis the workers' movement is presently enduring, a movement that takes Marx's doctrine as its faith. This crisis is not economic or political in character — on the contrary, its very possibility rests on the movement's growing power — but rather moral or, I would even say, religious in character. We already know that Marxism represents the most vivid version of the theory or religion of progress; it inspired its followers with faith in the immediate and inevitable [*zakonomernyi*] arrival of a different, perfect social order, the end of *Vorgeschichte* and the beginning of *Geschichte*. In this way, Marxism was strong not in its scientific, but in its utopian elements, not in its science, but in its faith. But this faith, improperly directed, had to dissipate or at least weaken with the growth of the movement. Its place has been taken by more and more practical tasks, which have overshadowed the ultimate goals. The former social-political utopianism has been replaced by social-political realism, connected only by chance with the name of Bernstein. The present development is thus distinguished by a two-sided nature: on the one hand, the practical achievements of the working class [*soslovie*] are increasing, but on the other hand this very success kills the previous, religiously inspired beliefs. Into the sanctuary's shade this success brings the prosaic light of day. The decline of idealism (in this case, as expressed in social utopianism) threatens to lower the movement to utter spiritual bourgeoisness, to deprive it of its soul, despite all the practical victories. I thus fully understand those who are filled with indignation at this Philistine-sacrilegious work. But at the same time I consider this work inevitable and historically necessary, and in vain do the fanatical adherents of the old view want to resist this work, like sectarians. It is impossible to resurrect a faith that has been undermined. But it is possible and necessary to create a new faith and to find a new source of moral enthusiasm. And this source should be seen in the elevating philosophy of idealism, in the eternal radiance of the absolute, in being religiously imbued by its dictates. Only this philosophy will return to humanity the living God it has lost and for which the soul today longs and is restless, and only this philosophy will help humanity recover from the utter godlessness, from the devotion to the flesh rather than to God's truth, that like a cancer more and more afflict and putrefy present-day European society. The issue is not to give up or lower one or another of the practical demands of the current social movement, but to restore moral force and religious enthusiasm to it, to raise it — *aufheben* in the Hegelian sense[53] — to the height of a moral task.[54]

The current social struggle is for us not merely a confrontation of hostile interests, but the realization and development of a moral idea. And our participation in it will be motivated not by egoistic class interest, but by religious duty, by an absolute order of the moral law, by a dictate of God.

Humanity will then restore the lost harmony of the various spheres of the spirit's activity, and religion will occupy the central place proper to it, becoming the basis of the thought and action of people. When the Teacher of love was asked, what is the main content of the law, He expressed it in two commandments. The first commandment was about love for God, and the second, derivative commandment was about love for one's neighbor.[55] He thereby indicated the correct, normal correlation between the religious and social interest; while not diminishing the latter in its significance, He nonetheless gave it second place. Present-day humanity has lost this correct relationship, and the contemporary doctrine recognizes only the second commandment, having subordinated or replaced the first. We have seen what logical contradictions this doctrine suffers and how little it can satisfy the serious adept. It has been the lot of this doctrine to thus negatively affirm the truth, having shown the whole impossibility of its negation. And in this consists the positive significance of the theory of progress, for the full revelation of truth requires not only its affirmation and positive development, but also its successive negation.

Notes

1. "You, the nether folk, can feel what's wished for, / Those above you know what should be given. / Grandly, Titans, you begin; but guidance / To eternal good, eternal beauty / Is the work of gods; let them conduct it." (The final words of Eos, from Goethe's *Pandora*, translated by Michael Hamburger.) Johann Wolfgang von Goethe, *Verse Plays and Epic*, ed. Cyrus Hamlin and Frank Ryder, trans. Michael Hamburger, Hunter Hannum, and David Luke, *Goethe's Collected Works*, vol. 8 (New York: Suhrkamp, 1987), p. 246. Ed.

2. On Comte's "law of the three stages," see Lappo-Danilevskii's essay in this book (Chapter 10). Ed.

3. "This *infinity* is *spurious* or *negative* infinity, since it is nothing but the negation of the finite, but the finite arises again in the same way, so that it is no more sublated than not. In other words, this infinity expresses only the requirement that the finite *ought* to be sublated." G. W. F. Hegel, *The Encyclopaedia Logic (with the Zusätze): Part I of the*

Encyclopaedia of Philosophical Sciences with the Zusätze, trans. T. F. Geraets, W. A. Suchting, and H. S. Harris (Indianapolis: Hackett, 1991), p. 149 (§ 94). This work is sometimes referred to as the "Lesser Logic" (three editions, 1817, 1827, 1830), to distinguish it from the *Wissenschaft der Logik (Science of Logic)* of 1812–1816, sometimes called the "Greater Logic," to which Bulgakov also refers below. Ed.

4. "The great idea of Humanity, which will irrevocably eliminate the idea of God." Auguste Comte, *Système de politique positive,* vol. I (Paris, 1851), p. 329 [page citation corrected].

5. Aqiva ben Yosef (ca. 50–ca. 135), early rabbinic commentator of Palestine who died during the Bar Kokhba Revolt, which his religious authority helped inspire. Perhaps the most eminent of all rabbis, he is famous for his exegetical techniques and his influence on the Mishnah, Tosefta, and later Jewish intellectual traditions. He is also associated with Merkabah (Chariot) mysticism, revived in the twelfth and thirteenth centuries by Kabbalah mystics. Ed.

6. Hebrews 11:1. Bulgakov's version is "upovaemykh izveshchenie, veshchei oblichenie nevidimykh." Ed.

7. The distinctive and in practice extraordinarily important intermediary level between faith and knowledge is *conviction,* as it is called. Conviction is subjectively the most valuable part of our ideas. At the same time, it is possible to be convinced only of what is not logically indisputable, but is upheld in greater or lesser degree by faith. It is impossible to be convinced, for example, that $2 \times 2 = 4$, or that today is such and such a date.

8. Friedrich Heinrich Jacobi (1743–1819), German philosopher whose "philosophy of feeling and faith" maintains that reality is immediately "given" to us and taken on faith, since cognition and analysis cannot establish the existence of the thing-in-itself. On Fichte, see the Glossary of Names. Vladimir Solov'ëv, in his *Kritika otvlechennykh nachal (Critique of Abstract Principles,* 1880), argued that faith is the foundation of all knowledge, borrowing from the Slavophile Aleksei Khomiakov's epistemology. Ed.

9. Paul-Henri Thiry, Baron d'Holbach, *Système de la nature, ou des lois du monde physique et du monde moral,* vol. I (Paris, 1770), p. 221 [editor's translation].

10. Acts 17:23. Ed.

11. The present work was already written when Heinrich Rickert's pathbreaking investigation appeared: *Die Grenzen der naturwissenschaftlichen Begriffsbildung: Eine logische Einleitung in die historischen Wissenschaften.* Zweite Hälfte (Tübingen und Leipzig, 1902). The thesis of the impossibility of establishing historical laws and predictions is shown here with perfect incontrovertibility, so that any further demonstration is in essence completely unnecessary. . . . (Incidentally, I do not at all share Rickert's general epistemological views.) . . .

12. The word "tendency," although it is among those expressions that are frequently used (or misused), does not at all represent a well-defined term. It is most often used in reference not to the future, but to the present, in which case it designates simply a generalization from the study of separate facts. For example, if on the basis of analysis of statistical data we conclude that the tendency of contemporary development consists in the concentration of production, this is simply the most general formula expressing and summarizing the meaning of development thus far. But if deprived of such factual content

and only mentally extended from the present to the future, this tendency at once becomes a commonplace, a mind game lacking any serious significance.

13. In the concluding chapter of my book, *Kapitalizm i zemledelie* (*Capitalism and Agriculture*, St. Petersburg, 1900), I spoke in the language of social skepticism, and in various places there I did not refrain from making judgments about development in the immediate future (mainly about the tasks of social policy), insofar as I could form a view of this. I did not consider it necessary to explain and specify how these judgments, which bear the character of personal conviction, differ from precise prognosis of all social development, the possibility of which I reject on principle. To my surprise, this alleged contradiction became the *locus minoris resistentiae* [place of least resistance], as it were, for objections to my book.

14. "We do not know, we shall never know," the phrase with which the German physiologist Emil DuBois-Reymond (1818–1896) concluded his celebrated lecture, "Über die Grenzen des Naturerkennens" ("On the Limits of the Knowledge of Nature"), originally delivered in 1872 and widely reprinted thereafter. His tract, *Die sieben Welträtsel* (*The Seven Riddles of the Universe*, 1880), was also famous. Ed.

15. Concluding my book, *Capitalism and Agriculture*, with a conviction of *ignorabimus* in the field of positive science, I, of course, did not at all suggest that the whole matter ended with positive science and this *ignorabimus*. The impossibility and even insufferability of this point of view, as an exhaustive doctrine, were clear to me even then, but I did not consider it possible to treat with the required facility the necessary foundations of our *Weltanschauung* beyond positive science.

16. Jean-Marie Guyau, *L'Irréligion de l'avenir: Étude sociologique* (Paris, 1887), as translated in *The Non-Religion of the Future: A Sociological Study* (New York: Schocken Books, 1962), p. 535. Translation slightly revised. Ed.

17. Johann Gottlieb Fichte, *Einige Vorlesungen über die Bestimmung des Gelehrten* (*Some Lectures on the Scholar's Vocation*, 1794), as translated by Daniel Breazeale, *Fichte: Early Philosophical Writings* (Ithaca, N.Y.: Cornell University Press, 1988), pp. 168–169. Ed.

18. In this case the idea of the infinity of humanity's development corresponds to the idea of the infinity of the world's existence (cosmological [*fizicheskie*] antinomies). Examined formally and logically, this idea, as Kant showed in his theory, ends in an antinomy; that is, both the thesis and antithesis turn out to be equally demonstrable. Thus eternity, which positivism can ascribe to humanity and its development, is inconceivable, and the problem becomes insoluble by means of formal logic alone. Infinity or eternity can be conceived not as infinite existence in time, but only as the annihilation of time, as victory over it.

19. See Hartmann, *Begründung des Pessimismus* (Berlin, 1880). Ed.

20. Vladimir Solov'ëv, *Opravdanie dobra: Nravstvennaia filosofiia* (*Justification of the Good: Moral Philosophy*, St. Petersburg, 1897, 2d. edition 1899), chapter 6, section 4. Ed.

21. Bulgakov likely has in mind Schopenhauer's essay "Über das Fundament der Moral" ("On the Basis of Morality," 1840). Ed.

22. Werner Sombart (1863–1941), German economist and sociologist, author of *Sozialismus und soziale Bewegung im 19. Jahrhundert* (1896) and *Der moderne Kapitalismus* (1902). Ed.

23. Fëdor Dostoevsky, *The Brothers Karamazov,* Book V, ch. 4, "Rebellion." Ed.

24. "After us, the deluge." Phrase attributed to Louis XV of France or to his mistress, the Marquise de Pompadour. Ed.

25. Comte, *Système de politique positive,* vol. I, p. 106 [editor's translation].

26. In *Ludwig Feuerbach and the End of Classical German Philosophy* (1886), Engels wrote that with the materialist understanding of history, Hegelian dialectic was stood on its head, "or, rather, turned off its head, on which it was standing, and placed upon its feet." See *Basic Writings on Politics and Philosophy: Karl Marx and Friedrich Engels,* ed. Lewis S. Feuer (Garden City, N.Y.: Anchor Books, 1959), p. 226. Earlier, in 1873, in the afterword to the second German edition of *Capital,* Marx wrote, "The mystification which dialectic suffers in Hegel's hands by no means prevents him from being the first to present its general form of working in a comprehensive and conscious manner. With him it is standing on its head. It must be turned right side up again." See the editor's introduction to *The Marx-Engels Reader,* ed. Robert C. Tucker, 2d edition (New York: Norton, 1978), pp. xx–xxi. Ed.

27. The phrase "from the kingdom of necessity to the kingdom of freedom" belongs to Friedrich Engels. See his *Anti-Dühring: Herr Eugen Dühring's Revolution in Science* (Moscow, 1978), p. 344. Ed.

28. Our positivists reproach Marx for preserving certain traces of Hegelian metaphysics, while Engels and the orthodox Marxists see in this, on the contrary, a virtue: in their opinion, Marx retains all the advantages of Hegelian philosophy, the dialectical method, for example. We ourselves cannot but express regret that the link between Hegelian philosophy and Marx's teaching is distinguished by a superficial, mechanical character (right up to the unnecessary imitation of Hegelian terminology), and does not represent the fruit of an organic working through and further development of this philosophy.

29. In the *Critique of Practical Reason,* § 8, Kant distinguishes between a negative and positive sense of the autonomy of the will: the first is independence from material causes, the second is self-determination or self-legislation. Ed.

30. *Die Bestimmung des Menschen* (1800). Ed.

31. A few years ago this question — about the freedom and necessity of human acts — was the subject of a polemic (on the pages of *Voprosy filosofii i psikhologii* and *Novoe slovo*) between myself and P. B. Struve, in connection with the well-known conception of Stammler. This argument was not concluded at the time; indeed, it could hardly have been concluded, because both of us, like Stammler, took the neo-Kantian point of view, and yet this question is resolvable only within the sphere of metaphysics. I now see that the relative truth of my point of view consisted in my defense of the reign of causation in the world of experience, while the constructions of Struve and Stammler sought to combine freedom and necessity in the sphere of science, of empirical knowledge. Therefore, my point of view, if it did not resolve, at least it did not distort the problem by formulating it incorrectly in an attempt to introduce, with various reductions and simplifications, the metaphysical principle of freedom into the sphere of experience. Since Struve's philosophical views have changed essentially since then, I do not think he would now support his epistemological construction. [On this debate, see Richard Pipes, *Struve: Liberal on the Left, 1870–1905* (Cambridge: Harvard University Press, 1970), pp. 184–189.]

32. Matthew 22:21. Ed.

33. "God cannot be only the God of geometry and physics; He must also be the God of history." (V. Solov'ëv, "Poniatie o Boge," *Voprosy filosofii i psikhologii* 8: 3, kn. 38 (1897), p. 409.) I know that for many Kantians, the concurrence of transcendence and immanence seems to be an epistemological contradiction (see, for example, Rickert's consideration of the philosophy of history in the work cited above). Together with Hegel, Schelling, Solov'ëv, and others, I do not see a contradiction here.

34. Or, "what is rational is actual and what is actual is rational." G. W. F. Hegel, *Philosophy of Right,* trans. T. M. Knox (Oxford: Oxford University Press, 1942), Preface, p. 10. Ed.

35. Hegel, *The Encyclopaedia Logic,* p. 284 (§ 209). Ed.

36. "Just as our opinion of an individual is not based on what he thinks of himself, so can we not judge of such a period of transformation [an epoch of social revolution] by its own consciousness; on the contrary, this consciousness must be explained rather from the contradictions of material life, from the existing conflict between the social productive forces and the relations of production." Karl Marx, Preface to *A Contribution to the Critique of Political Economy* (1859), in *The Marx-Engels Reader,* ed. Robert C. Tucker, 2d edition (New York: Norton, 1978), p. 5. Ed.

37. Hegel, *The Encyclopaedia Logic,* p. 304 (§ 237). Ed.

38. "I work at the whirring loom of time/And fashion the living garment of God." Johann Wolfgang von Goethe, *Faust,* Parts I and II, ed. and trans. Stuart Atkins, *Goethe's Collected Works,* vol. 2 (Cambridge, Mass.: Suhrkamp/Insel Publishers Boston, 1984), p. 16 (lines 508–509). Ed.

39. From Aleksei K. Tolstoi's poem "Ioann Damaskin" (1858). Ed.

40. Hermann Siebeck (1842–1921), *On the Theory of the Genetic Progress of Humanity* (1892). Ed.

41. "Über den Grund unsers Glaubens an eine göttliche Weltregierung" ("On the Foundation of Our Belief in a Divine Government of the Universe," 1798), as translated by Paul Edwards in Patrick L. Gardiner, ed., *Nineteenth-Century Philosophy* (New York: Free Press, 1969), p. 26. Bulgakov's version is slightly abridged. Ed.

42. "If I speak in the tongues of mortals and of angels, but do not have love, I am a noisy gong or a clanging cymbal." 1 Corinthians 13:1. Ed.

43. The reign of Alexander III (1881–1894) is known as "the age of counterreform" to stress its hostility to the liberal spirit of the Great Reforms introduced under Alexander II (1855–1881). The Great Reforms included the abolition of serfdom (1861), establishment of the zemstvo institutions of limited local self-government (1864), and major improvements to the judiciary (1864). Despite the overall success of the judicial reforms, one defect was the retention of the special *volost* (township) courts, which continued the judicial isolation of the peasants. At the same time, the introduction of justices of the peace, elected by district (*uezd*) zemstvos, represented a step toward equality before the law in that this office exercised jurisdiction over the entire population, including peasants, for minor offenses. On 12 July 1889, in the first of the major counterreforms, this popular office was abolished in most of Russia. In rural areas, justices of the peace were replaced by the new land captains (*zemskie nachal'niki*), members of the nobility appointed by the governor or minister of interior. In Hugh Seton-Watson's evaluation, this measure was "designed to maintain the peasants in a condition of tutelage, and to

make it more difficult for them to acquire the practice in self-government so necessary to the process of transforming former serfs into citizens of a modern state." Hugh Seton-Watson, *The Russian Empire, 1801–1917* (Oxford: Oxford University Press, 1967), p. 469. Ed.

44. Beginning in 1866, restrictions were placed on the ability of zemstvos to levy taxes and on how these taxes could be spent. A regulation of 1900 fixed annual increases in zemstvo revenues to three percent. Ed.

45. In 1870 a municipal reform reorganized city government along the lines of the zemstvo administration, providing for elected city councils (dumas). An act of June 1892 restricted the franchise by sharply raising property qualifications. Ed.

46. The University Statute of June 1863 considerably increased university autonomy. A new statute of August 1884 reversed these gains, stipulating that university rectors, deans, and professors were to be appointed by the minister of education rather than elected by the university councils. A similar pattern applied to censorship: a law of April 1865 reduced use of preventive or preliminary censorship, which was largely replaced by the milder punitive censorship, but regulations of August 1882 imposed preliminary censorship on newspapers and journals that had previously received three official warnings. Ed.

47. Rickert, *Cultural Science and Natural Science* (Tübingen, 1899). Ed.

48. Immanuel Kant, *Religion within the Limits of Reason Alone,* trans. Theodore M. Greene and Hoyt H. Hudson (New York: Harper Torchbooks, 1960), p. 142. Ed.

49. Mark 9:24. Ed.

50. Hegel, *Philosophy of Right,* trans. T. M. Know, Preface, p. 11. Ed.

51. Bulgakov changes the tense of this quotation. Cf. Miller: With "philosophy [*Wissenschaft*] and ordinary common sense thus cooperating to bring about the downfall of metaphysics, there was seen the strange spectacle of a cultured nation without metaphysics — like a temple richly ornamented in other respects but without a holy of holies." G. W. F. Hegel, *Science of Logic,* trans. A. V. Miller (Atlantic Highlands, N.J.: Humanities Press International, 1969), p. 25. This work is sometimes called the "Greater Logic." Ed.

52. Literally, "lying (inactive) inheritance," an inheritance not taken up by the heir. Ed.

53. To transcend or supersede. For Hegel, dialectical movement — from thesis, through antithesis, to synthesis — achieves a higher level not through simple rejection of the lower, but through transcendence of it. The synthesis, through negation or antithesis, restores the thesis at a higher level. (Although Hegel did not actually use these three terms in this way, they do capture what he meant by *Aufhebung*.) Ed.

54. I will note here, as an interesting symptom of the moral turning point now being reached in Western European society, [Gert] Carring's book, *Das Gewissen im Lichte der Geschichte sozialistischer und christlicher Weltanschauung* (Berlin, Bern, 1901). This small book, characterized by a large swell of moral and religious feeling, advances the following position: "The socialist and Christian worldviews are not oppositions. One and the same person can hold both at the same time, can live under both, can be both a Christian and a socialist." [Translated from the German, which Bulgakov quotes.]

55. Mark 12:28–31. Ed.

2

Toward Characterization of the Theory of Marx and Engels on the Significance of Ideas in History

E. N. TRUBETSKOI

I.

The present essay has a more modest goal than giving a detailed analysis of the materialist understanding of history as a whole. Rather, its task is to subject to critical evaluation certain claims of Marx and Engels about the significance of ideas in history. Very much in this direction has been done by contemporary criticism: especially in recent years there have been many valuable works that have pointed to the precariousness of the basic positions of historical materialism, to the incompleteness of its constructions, and to its internal contradictions. And nonetheless the question cannot be considered exhausted: on the one hand, the very enthusiasm for the struggle against today's most popular form of historicism [*istorizm*] has involved several critics in exaggeration and imprecision, which must be corrected; on the other hand, no matter how well founded the critical work of scholars such as Barth,[1] Stammler, Masaryk,[2] Bernstein, Woltmann, and others, it nonetheless contains certain gaps, which must be filled.

The main difficulty with which the critic must somehow cope is the vagueness of the basic positions of historical materialism. The well-known critic of Marxism, Professor Stammler, agrees with one of today's most visible Marxists, Kautsky,[3] that historical materialism is not a fully formed *Weltanschauung*: in his 1899 brochure,[4] containing an apologia for Marx against

Bernstein, Kautsky directly declares that the theory of historical materialism is even today still in the beginning stage of its development. The more difficult it is to identify an idea, the more difficult it is to critique it, of course. Evaluation of any theory must be preceded by its clarification, yet any critic who tries to express Marx's thought more clearly than Marx himself at once risks accusations of deliberate distortion or of having misunderstood Marxism. To avoid these reproaches, it is necessary to expound the views of Marx and Engels as much as possible in their own words, noting everything that is unclear.

For the question that interests us, Marx's celebrated preface to his *A Contribution to the Critique of Political Economy* (1859) has exceptionally important significance.[5] What does this text offer toward characterizing the significance of ideas in history? Current criticism has rightly noted a number of ambiguities in it; I need only summarize what others have said before.

From Marx's point of view, the role of the prime mover of history is played by "material productive forces," under which "mode of production" is, apparently, to be understood. Marx directly says that, "the mode of production of material life conditions the social, political and intellectual life process in general." Conditions in what sense, however? Is the "mode of production" the only primary cause of social development, or is it rather only *one of the causes,* acting together with other causes and conditions? At the beginning of the text under consideration Marx says that the "sum total of productive relations," or, what is the same, the "economic structure of society," *corresponds* to a definite stage in the development of "material productive forces." From his further exposition it turns out, however, that there cannot be such a correspondence: at a certain moment in their historical development, productive relations turn "from forms of development of the productive forces into their fetters." The very possibility of a struggle of productive forces against one or another social order demonstrates that the existence of the latter is not conditioned by these forces alone. But recognizing any other causes of social development that could not *in the final instance* be reduced to "material productive forces" would be incompatible with the very essence of the materialist understanding of history.

In exactly the same way, it is unclear how Marx conceives the relation between the economic structure of society, on the one hand, and "forms of social consciousness," or ideas, on the other. As an answer to this question we find in Marx's text not philosophic definition, but simple architectural comparison: productive relations in their totality constitute the "economic structure of society," "the real foundation, on which rises a legal and political superstructure"; to this superstructure, in turn, "correspond definite forms of social consciousness." Obviously we have here an explanation that explains absolutely nothing. In this architecture, the base does not explain the super-structure that rises above it. The base is not the cause of the superstructure: in order to explain how and why one or another superstructure has risen over a given base, it is necessary to seek some other cause. In the case at hand we have, moreover, a superstructure with a rather strange property: it possesses the capability to outlive its base over a more or less extended period of time: "with the change of the economic base," says Marx, "the entire immense superstructure of legal and political institutions, to which correspond definite forms of social consciousness, *sooner or later* collapses." The words italicized by me, "sooner or later," indicate that the superstructure does not at once collapse with the destruction of the base. Further, what does it mean that "definite forms of social consciousness correspond" to the legal and political superstructure? Is there a simple parallel here between certain institutions and ideas, or rather a causal link?

"It is not the consciousness of men," we read further, "that determines their being, but, on the contrary, their social being that determines their conscious-ness." It is obvious that Marx's thought does not gain in precision from this explanation either: for once more the question arises, is the development of people's consciousness determined only by social being, only by productive forces and relations, or in addition to these economic factors and together with them are there other causes, other conditions, determining the develop-ment of our consciousness? Finally, it remains unclear whether these economic factors should be understood as *productive causes* or only as *necessary condi-tions* of the growth of social consciousness. Marx leaves this question without an answer, yet its resolution, one way or another, would have enormous signif-icance for the theory under consideration. For anyone it is clear that soil does not serve as the productive cause of the growth of vegetation, for, on its own, without seeds, soil cannot produce any plants: it is necessary to seek the productive cause of the growth of vegetation in the seeds themselves. Such is the difference between the productive cause and the conditions of the growth of social consciousness. Therefore, it would be extraordinarily important to know whether Marx sees in productive forces and relations only the ground on which, with the assistance of other causes, certain forms of social con-sciousness develop, or whether from his point of view the economic factor is in itself an adequate basis for explanation of the growth of social consciousness, as its productive cause.

Thus nearly every word of the celebrated text of *A Contribution to the Critique of Political Economy* evokes a number of questions and perplexities. In only one respect does this text leave no place for doubt: from Marx's point of view, people's consciousness and will are not factors in the development of the economic structure of society; the productive relations into which people enter do not depend on their consciousness and will. On the contrary, the process of the development of human consciousness and will exists in a certain dependence on productive forces and relations, but in what consists this dependence, Marx, as we have said, does not precisely state.

The formulation of historical materialism that we have set forth was given by Marx in 1859. Before and after this time both he and Engels advanced these same ideas; later they somewhat adjusted and supplemented their original point of view, but nonetheless essential ambiguities and gaps remained in their theory. In the *Communist Manifesto* (1848), under the main factors behind the development of the social order, modes of exchange and modes of communication figure alongside modes of production. In his essay *The Eighteenth Brumaire of Louis Bonaparte* (1852), Marx speaks of a "superstructure of distinct and peculiarly formed sentiments, illusions, modes of thought and views of life," which rises "upon the different forms of property, upon the social conditions of existence."[6] In the first volume of *Capital* (1867), Marx stresses the significance of instruments of production as "indicators of the social relations of people";[7] the technology of work, he says here, reveals the nature of "living relations and the intellectual notions corresponding to them."[8] In the third volume of *Capital,* Marx, as before, sees in relations of production the "basis of the whole social structure," but he also recognizes that this economic base of social development can variously manifest itself in reality, depending on a number of concrete circumstances, such as the conditions of external nature, race relations, and external historical influences. As a whole, in all Marx's works the "material conditions of existence" play the role of the prime movers of the historical process; everywhere the dependence of ideas on economic relations is indicated, but nowhere do we find an exact determination of the nature of this dependence.

The same must be said of the works of Engels. In his polemical tract, *Anti-Dühring* (1878), he says: "the final causes of all social changes and political revolutions are to be sought, not in men's brains, not in men's better insight into eternal truth and justice, *but in changes in the modes of production and exchange* [Trubetskoi's italics]. They are to be sought not in the *philosophy,* but in the *economics* of each particular epoch."[9] In the same work, among the final causes explaining the political order and dominant views of any given epoch, Engels also includes the modes of communication among people.[10] To this his book *The Origin of the Family, Private Property, and the State* (1884) adds the "reproduction of human life," that is, sexual propagation. Finally, in an 1894 letter, Engels ascribes the technology of production, distribution of goods, race, and geographical location to the economic causes determining the course of history.[11] Perhaps most interesting of all for our theme is the passage from the biography Engels compiled of Marx, where he evaluates the significance of Marx's revolution in the understanding of world history. All previous understanding of history, we read here, proceeded from the notion that changes in human ideas are the ultimate grounds of historical changes, and that of all historical changes, political ones are the most important, governing the whole historical process. Marx, on the contrary, showed that ideas are not the prime movers of the historical process, that changes in human views, precisely like political transformations, depend on the process of class struggle, which is the very essence of history. With exact knowledge of the economic state of any given society, all historical phenomena and, in particular, all the intellectual notions and ideas of any given epoch can be explained in the simplest manner, "from the living conditions of the economy and the social and political relations conditioned by the latter." Marx first made obvious the fact, until then ignored by historians, "that mankind must first of all eat, drink, have shelter and clothing," and consequently must work, "before it can pursue politics, science, art, religion, etc."[12] The economic explanation of the genesis of ideas, as is obvious from this, seems simple and exhaustive to Engels. Let us see if it is really so.

II.

On the question of the relation of ideas to the economic structure of human society, a typical vacillation between two different characterizations is apparent in Marx, as in Engels. On the one hand, as we have seen, "forms of social consciousness" are for them the "superstructure" or part of the superstructure over the economic base; on the other hand, they see in ideas a *reflection* of economic relations, a cloak or mask of economic interests. These expressions are met especially often in *Ludwig Feuerbach and the End of Classical German Philosophy* (1886) and in other works by Engels. The same idea is, incidentally, advanced in the *Communist Manifesto* of Marx and Engels. Already in the preface to a "Contribution to the Critique of Hegel's 'Philosophy of Right' " (1844), Marx describes religion as a celestial reflection of terrestrial relations, in particular of the earthly sufferings of humanity: "thus the criticism of heaven turns into the criticism of the earth, the *criticism of religion* into the *criticism of right,* and the *criticism of theology* into the *criticism of politics.*"[13] In the first volume of *Capital* he speaks of Christianity as a reflection of commodity production: for Marx, religion is generally a reflection (*religiöser Wiederschein*) of the economic order; the religious ideas of the bourgeoisie amount to commodity-worship [*tovaropoklonstvo*]; and the legal relations of bourgeois society, the form of which is contract, "reflect" economic relations.

It is not difficult to be convinced that we have here not only differing characterizations, but incompatible ones: in no case is the "superstructure" the "reflection" of its base, and obviously it cannot serve as a "mask" of it. In Marx and Engels, scientific explanation of the relation of ideas to economy is replaced by comparisons and images that contradict each other.

Characterization of ideas as reflections or "reflexes" of economic relations is very widespread among Marx's followers, and therefore should be given our full attention. First of all, it is perfectly plain that such words as "reflection" and "reflex" are extremely imprecise expressions, explaining nothing. In general, any reflection is invariably the result of the joint action of at least two causes — the reflected object, and the medium that reflects it. For example, my reflection in a mirror depends not only on the characteristics of my appearance, but also on the characteristics of the mirror itself. My reflection in a smooth, polished mirror will reproduce my features quite accurately, but a reflection in a curved mirror or round samovar either will not be anything like the original or will have the semblance of a caricature.

Therefore, if we say together with Marx and Engels that political, legal, moral, and religious ideas are reflections or "reflexes" of economic relations, interests, and needs, we still have not given any satisfactory explanation of the properties of these ideas. First, is the reflection similar to the original in every individual case, is there a likeness between the economic interests and the ideas that, according to Marx and Engels, serve as their reflections? From the examples given by both writers, it is clear that there can be no talk of any similarity. Let us take even political ideas. It is well known that Engels in his book on Feuerbach calls the state a "reflex of the economic needs and production of the ruling class."[14] It is obvious that here we have a reflection that presents not the slightest likeness to the reflected object; Engels, calling the state a "reflex," evidently wanted to say that the state serves as an instrument for the oppression of the lower classes by the ruling class, that it serves as an expedient agency for the latter's interests, but not at all that it has some *likeness* to these interests. Or we can take other examples. If in one or another of their works Marx and Engels depict the ideas of the French Revolution as a reflection of the interests of the bourgeoisie, or the Christian religion as a reflection of capitalist production, does this mean that in their eyes exploitation of the "have-nots" by the "haves" presents some *likeness* to the religion of love and all-forgiveness or to the ideas of freedom, equality, and brotherhood? Obviously, the issue here is not about likeness, but about the ideas of the French Revolution owing their existence to the bourgeois interests that they conceal and justify, and about the Christian religion drawing its living force from the conditions of capitalist production, to which it supposedly gives its religious sanction.

In short, there is not the slightest semblance between the economic phenomena that, according to Marx and Engels, serve as the real basis of history, and the intellectual [*ideinyi*] reflection of these phenomena in the human mind or in the institutions created by people. How is this to be explained? Clearly, by the fact that the properties of any reflection depend not only on the characteristics of the reflected object, but also on those of the reflecting medium. In order to explain how economic relations are reflected in people's minds, it is necessary to take into account not only economic relations, but also the human mind, in general the whole human psyche, which reworks, in conformity with the laws of logic and psychology, all the diverse material of the impressions derived from the economic sphere. Here the economic explanation of history finds its limits: it is clear that by economic causes alone we will not explain any idea — religious, moral, or political — not even those ideas that justify or sanction economic interests. In order to understand anything about the origin and development of ideas, it is necessary to look closely at the characteristics of the human psyche, that is, to introduce into history a factor reducible to neither productive forces nor economic relations.

The expression "reflex" is, in essence, not at all apt for depicting the relation of ideas to economic relations, and therefore Engels often and readily resorts to other expressions, referring, for example, to ideas as a cloak or mask of economic interests, as we have already seen. Thus, in his book on Dühring, he says that during the English Revolution Calvinism served as a "cloak" [*kostium*] for the interests of the bourgeoisie; he also states there that Christianity in the last stage of its development serves as "ideological dressing" for the aims of nothing but the ruling classes.[15] In his article "On the History of Early Christianity" (1894–95), he calls religion a "mask of economic interests."[16]

Here the inadequacy of the economic explanation of history is still more conspicuous, if that is possible. There is no need for me to get involved in analyzing the strange idea that any religion, as such, is only a mask of economic interests, although for its refutation the most superficial acquaintance with the history of religions is sufficient. I would rather acknowledge the share of truth in Engels's words. Ruling classes do, in fact, love to conceal their interests behind ideological motives of one kind or another, and in particular are eager to resort to the sanction of positive religion. Thus, for example, American planters justified slavery by saying that in virtue of the order established by God, Whites, as the higher race, should rule over Negroes, as the lower boorish race. Russian serf-owners adduced analogous arguments in justification of the power of the father-master over the children-serfs granted him by God. In general, conservative parties up to and including the conservatives of our own day love to present the state and social order advantageous for them as the order established by God himself.

The same striving to find support in religion for their class interests is evident not only among the ruling classes, but also among the hapless ones. Thus, in Luther's days German peasants, rising against their lords, declared that they did not wish to be the property of masters, for all people — from shepherd to king — are redeemed by the blood of the Savior, and therefore no one ought to be a slave to anyone. Among our simple people, the opinion can sometimes be heard that the church does not pray for the rich or nobles, but only for "Orthodox peasants." But if religion has been advanced at various times as a banner for concealing party interests, it is not to blame in this, least of all Christianity, which proclaims the salvation of all people and thus stands by its very essence above any class or party. Rather, the guilty in this are the people who wrongly involve Providence in their worldly interests and, not rarely, in their everyday filth. Be that as it may, the fact of conscious or unconscious hypocrisy, personal as well as class, remains a fact, only this fact speaks not for but against Engels.

In this hypocrisy there are obviously two sides: the first is party interest, the second is the pious mask covering up this interest. In many cases, if not in a majority of them, there is no similarity nor even anything in common between these two elements: what can, for example, slavery, exploitation of the "have-nots," and piety have in common? Nothing, and if we say that piety serves as a mask for selfish interests, we thus only affirm that these interests are essentially alien to piety, that this mask radically differs from *what it masks*.

What explains this mask, where did it come from, and how did it originate? Are we to explain hypocrisy as a conscious justification, or as unconscious motives of some kind, urges of which people are not clearly aware? In any event, to explain this phenomenon we will need to introduce a psychic factor irreducible to interests, a psychic activity of the human soul by virtue of which material interest is clothed in an intellectual shell alien to it. It is thus clear that economic interests alone will explain neither sincere piety nor even false, interested piety. By itself economic interest is not able to explain any idea: proceeding from interest, we can in some instances understand the *need* for ideas of one type or another, but on its own such need is likewise unable to produce the idea corresponding to it, as hunger is unable to produce bread.

If we look carefully at the very fact of class hypocrisy, it turns out to be instructive on other grounds as well. *This hypocrisy is an involuntary tribute, as it were, which interests are compelled to pay to ideas.* The fact that people are ashamed of their selfish interests, try to hide them in every way and to mask them with ethical and religious considerations, shows that interest is not the only force ruling human society: if class interests must be somehow reconciled with the religious, moral, and legal views prevailing in society, if such interests must seek justification and support in these views, then this shows that above class interests is another force, distinct from and higher than them — the force of the idea.

III.

On exactly this question of the significance of ideas in history, critics of Marxism note a certain evolution in the views of Marx and even more so of Engels. In the last years of their life, Marx and Engels, as has been said, somewhat changed their original point of view and came to recognize that besides purely economic causes, other noneconomic principles influence historical development. For example, Marx, in the third volume of *Capital,* teaches that the political force of the state, originally determined by economic relations, can itself in turn affect economic relations. Engels, in an 1890 letter, directly acknowledges that earlier he and Marx had somewhat exaggerated the significance of the economic factor in history. The production and reproduction of real life, he says here, is the decisive moment in the final instance, but it is not the *only* one determining the course of history. In addition, various elements of the political and legal superstructure over the economic base, forms of state organization, forms of law, and, finally, all possible mental reflections of the class struggle (i.e., political theories and juridical, philosophical, and religious views) influence the course of historical development.[17] In a word, apart from economic factors, Engels recognizes the significance of intellectual factors in history.

It seems to me, however, that critics who see Engels's words as tantamount to a departure from the basic principles of historical materialism somewhat exaggerate the significance of the change in him. In fact, the ideas expressed by Engels in the last years of his life represent rather an addendum to, not a departure from, Marx's original point of view.[18] Although Engels does speak about ideas as causes of historical development, all the same he does not take them for primary causes. As before, he treats ideas as mental *reflections* of the class (that is, economic) struggle, and describes political and legal institutions as the "superstructure" over the economic base; finally, production remains for him the "ultimately determining element in history."[19] In short, Engels's thought comes down to saying that the only *primary* factor in history — that which *in the last instance* determines its direction — is an economic factor, *production.* All other causes influencing the course of historical development—juridical and political institutions, as well as ideas—are not primary but *derivative* causes dependent on the action of economic principles. These intellectual causes are either elements of the superstructure over the economic base or mental reflections of the economic struggle.

In Engels's letters from the 1890s Marx's point of view appears in a significantly improved form, but even in this form it does not withstand criticism.[20] Its weakness comes to light as soon as we consider the essence of production, the factor Marx considers the basic cause of historical development. Describing human work in the first volume of *Capital,* Marx says the following:

> We presuppose labor in a form that stamps it as exclusively human. A spider conducts operations that resemble those of a weaver, and a bee puts to shame many an architect in the construction of her cells. But what distinguishes the worst architect from the best of bees is this, that the architect raises his structure in imagination before he erects it in reality. At the end of every labour process, we get a result that already existed in the imagination of the labourer at its commencement. He not only effects a change of form in the material on which he works, but he also realises a purpose of his own that gives the law to his modus operandi, and to which he must subordinate his will. And this subordination is no mere monetary act. Besides the exertion of the bodily organs, the process demands that, during the whole operation, the workman's will be steadily in consonance with his purpose. This means close attention. The less he is attracted by the nature of the work, and the mode in which it is carried on, and the less, therefore, he enjoys it as something which gives play to his bodily and mental powers, the more close his attention is forced to be.[21]

It would be hard to find a more devastating objection to Marx's philosophy of history than this characterization of work given by Marx himself. According to this philosophy of history, the "whole spiritual process" experienced by society is conditioned by production: the conscious ideas of man are in no case the prime movers of historical development, for their content and development depend on productive relations. Yet from the text quoted above it turns out that in general any work and, consequently, *any production, depends on ideas:* before getting down to work, a person has already accomplished it in his head. This means that an idea, as the conscious goal of production, *precedes* production itself. Production is the embodiment of the idea in matter. But if so, production, as a phenomenon conditioned by ideas, can no longer be the *primary* factor in historical development.

Exactly the same needs to be said about generally all economic factors of historical development: the state of technology and the means of distribution respond, first, to the *conscious goals* of production and distribution for the sake of which man invents tools of one kind or another, and, second, to inventions in the field of mechanics. The creative activity of the human mind and the purposive will precede and condition the economic phenomenon in this case as well; in general, all economy is the manifestation of man's conscious, goal-oriented activity. Of course, the economy depends not only on the activity of consciousness and the will, but also on a number of external conditions independent of the human individual, conditions of the natural and social environment in which he realizes his economic goals. But in any case, since the economy is a complex result of the interaction of conscious human activity with the surrounding environment, it cannot be treated as a factor determining, in *the final instance,* the course of historical development. Engels, as we have seen, reproached the old materialism not because it saw in ideas the movers of social development, but because it ascribed to them the role of *prime movers* and had not tried to reduce ideas to their motive causes. An analogous reproach can be made to Engels himself. His mistake is not that he saw in economic phenomena an important factor of historical development, but that he did not consider it necessary to reduce these phenomena to their primary causes.

At the present time no one will deny the important role of economic causes in history. The indisputable service of Marx and his followers is that they underscored and brought out the significance of these causes. In the final instance, however, the course of history is determined not by economic factors, but by a number of primary givens [*dannye*] that condition the economy as well as generally all manifestations of social life: by the circumstances of the external environment in which human life unfolds, by the characteristics of the human psyche (individual and social), and, finally, by that empyrean sphere of *what ought to be* [*dolzhnoe*], the kingdom of ends that, rising *above man,* gives direction to his consciousness and activity.

IV.

The shortcomings of the Marxist theory of the significance of ideas in history are revealed as clearly as possible in all that Marx and Engels say about the origin of legal ideas and institutions. Here the wavering, typical of historical materialism, between two opposing characterizations is again evident: law is understood sometimes as a direct *reflection* of economic factors, sometimes as the *superstructure* over the economic base.

There is no lack of attempts by Marx and Engels to explain juridical institutions as immediate reflections of economic phenomena. We have already seen that in the preface to *A Contribution to the Critique of Political Economy,* Marx says that property relations are the "legal expression for relations of production." In the first volume of *Capital* he declares that a contract is a relation of human wills that reflects economic relations. In both Marx and Engels law is often described as an expression of the economic dominance of one class or another. In his book *The Poverty of Philosophy: An Answer to Proudhon's "Philosophy of Poverty"* (1847), Marx gives the most general expression of the idea that "legislation, whether political or civil, never does more than proclaim, express in words, the will of economic relations."[22]

Critics of Marx have repeatedly indicated that this method of explanation is not applicable to entire vast areas of legislation, such as to laws defining the position of various religious sects in the state or to those relating to national education. And in fact it is difficult to specify what economic phenomena are reflected, for example, in Russian laws prohibiting the conversion of Orthodox believers to other faiths or forbidding prayer meetings of certain dissenting sects.[23] Nor is one likely to find an economic materialist who would be prepared to maintain, for example, that Count Tolstoi introduced to Russia the classical gymnasium with two ancient languages because it was "the will of economic relations,"[24] or that changed economic conditions later forced him to replace ancient languages with the study of native history and drafting. Not all national and state needs subject to legislative decision are economic needs. But even if these needs were economic *at their original source,* could it be thought that legislation always precisely reflected the needs and interests it was called to satisfy?

If laws actually did give literal expression to only the will of economic relations, then between laws and the economic needs that gave rise to them there could be no discrepancy or even contradiction: *in legislation there would be no mistakes.* If in legislation there is much that is arbitrary and fantastic, much that contradicts the very same economic and other needs the legislator wanted to address, then this is because needs in general and economic needs in particular are not at all the only cause shaping legislation. Another cause is the *intellectual activity* of the legislator, who in turn experiences the influence of the intellectual activity of all society or some of its layers, the influence of scientific theories, and the influence of intellectual factors in general. A legal norm, issued by a legislator, is always an expression of the *evaluation* he makes of social needs. This evaluation can be mistaken, which is why legal norms not rarely lead to results diametrically opposed to the goals originally intended. Laws protecting industry or agriculture in a particular country more often than not turn out to be disastrous for precisely these industrial and agricultural interests. Can it be said of such laws that they give literal expression to the will of economic relations? Would it not be more accurate to say that they express the *legislator's mistaken evaluation of economic needs?*

We have seen that Engels, especially in the last years of his work, did not deny the influence of intellectual causes on legislation. But can these intellectual causes not be reduced to economic ones, even if only *"in the final instance?"* The very possibility of mistakes by the legislator proves the opposite: it turns out that the pressure of economic causes on legislation and thus on the intellectual activity expressed in it is far from insurmountable.

The untenability of Marxist theory is perhaps even more conspicuous in the passages of the works of Marx and Engels where law is depicted as the *superstructure* over the economic base. Among the relevant texts, Engels's brochure, *Ludwig Feuerbach and the End of Classical German Philosophy,* presents particular interest. His course of thought is in general the following. The state appears as the immediate reflection or "reflex" of economic needs. For the preservation of common interests against external and internal attacks, society creates a special organ — state power. But as soon as this state power is created, it becomes independent of society as a whole, an independence that increases the more state power becomes an organ of one social class, whose dominance over other classes is the state's very goal. The struggle of the oppressed classes against the ruling class necessarily becomes a political struggle, that is, a struggle directed first of all against the political dominance of the ruling class. In this, consciousness of the link between the political struggle and its economic underpinning dims and may finally be lost. The state, once it has become an independent force relative to society, creates a further ideology, where consciousness of the link between law and economic facts is first lost, and lost for good, among professional politicians, theorists of public law, and jurists of civil law. Since in every separate case, economic facts, in order to receive legislative sanction, must take the form of juridical motives, and since for this the whole system of law currently in force must, of course, be taken into account, jurists behave as if juridical form were everything and economic facts were nothing. Public and civil law are treated as autonomous spheres, developing independently of economic facts.

It cannot be said that Engels's thought is expressed clearly. Apparently, he wants to say that law is not a direct, but an *indirect* result of economic facts. In the process of law-formation, jurists and legislators play the role of the mediating link between legal norms and the economic facts giving rise to them in the *final instance*. It is not difficult to notice that the economic explanation of law is not sustained here. If the consciousness of jurists and legislators can *dim and distort* economic facts, then obviously these facts cannot explain consciousness as its primary cause. Consciousness plays the role of an independent cause, a factor of law-formation that is *irreducible to economy*. Here again it turns out that the human psyche (in this case of jurists and legislators) is not merely a passive medium in which economic relations are reflected, but a *creative principle* that reworks impressions taken from the external world.

No matter from what side we approach legal norms, it constantly turns out that "*in the final instance*" economic facts are not at all the only cause behind their formation. As we have already seen, Marx, in his preface to *A Contribution to the Critique of Political Economy,* acknowledges that the "legal superstructure" can outlive its economic base: the process of change in law does not always immediately follow change in the corresponding economic relations. Obviously, economic causes cannot explain such a delay in the development of law: this delay demonstrates that in certain cases the effect of economic causes, which were to have modified the law, is paralyzed by other causes of a non-economic nature. What are these other causes? *Historical tradition* clearly plays a most important role here; this is another cause of a purely psychic nature, a phenomenon of social psychology. If legal institutions can survive by force of tradition, despite the economic causes working to destroy them, then this again proves that in addition to economic causes there is a psychic factor, irreducible to economy, conditioning the existence and development of law.

Finally, the untenability of an exclusively economic explanation of law is shown by the fact that all human economy, as such, depends on law. Human economy supposes, first, a conscious goal of production that man actualizes in the external world, and, second, the *cooperation* of many people working for the realization of this goal. It is clear that the conscious cooperation of people would be impossible without a certain limitation on the spheres of freedom and activity of each of the participants in production: cooperation inevitably presupposes some set of property laws, as well as the right of some persons to the services of others. Without law no productive and, consequently, no economic relations in general would be possible among people. As Stammler has quite correctly observed, productive relations are nothing other than "precisely defined legal relations, legally regulated relations among people."[25] From this it is clear that law, taken as a whole, can be understood neither as a *reflection* of economic relations nor as a *superstructure* over the economic base.

V.

Any attempt at an exclusively economic explanation of the history of law inevitably entails the rejection of natural law as an independent force in legal development. We have already seen that according to Engels, "the final causes of all social changes and political revolutions are to be sought, not in men's brains, not in men's better insight into eternal truth and justice, but in changes in the modes of production and exchange. They are to be sought not in the *philosophy*, but in the *economics* of each particular epoch." Here the ideas of truth and justice obviously mean *law as it ought to be* in contrast to positive law, in other words, the same thing as is ordinarily understood by natural law. Engels does not deny the influence of ideas of natural law on the course of historical development, but he does not acknowledge their significance as prime movers or "final causes" of social transformations, because from the Marxist point of view legal ideals are themselves effects of economic causes, direct or indirect reflections of economic relations.

Thus, from this point of view, the ideas of freedom and equality that inspired the French revolutionaries should not be counted among the final causes of the French Revolution, for these concepts are themselves rooted in the conditions and needs of commodity production. Capitalist production supposes the *freedom* of the capitalist (to buy the worker's labor) and the freedom of the worker (to sell his labor-power on the market); at the same time the worker, selling his labor, and the capitalist, buying it, proceed in this transaction as persons juridically equal in rights. Consequently, both freedom and equality appear as needs of capitalist production. In the first volume of *Capital*, Marx says among other things that the sphere of circulation or of commodity exchange, within which the sale and purchase of labor-power take place,

> is in fact a very Eden of the innate rights of man. There alone rule Freedom, Equality, Property and Bentham. Freedom, because both buyer and seller of a commodity, say of labour-power, are constrained only by their own free will. They contract as free agents, and the agreement they come to, is but the form in which they give legal expression to their common will. Equality, because each enters into relations with the other, as with a simple owner of commodities, and they exchange equivalent for equivalent. Property, because each disposes only of what is his own. And Bentham, because each looks only to himself. The only force that brings them together and puts them in relation with each other, is the selfishness, the gain and the private interests of each. Each looks to himself only, and no one troubles himself about the rest, and just because they do so, do they all, in accordance with the preestablished harmony of things, or under the auspices of an all-shrewd providence, work together to their mutual advantage, for the common weal and in the interest of all.[26]

The ideas of freedom and equality, as is evident from this, are rooted in economic relations and interests, first of all in the class interests of the "buyers of labor-power," that is, the bourgeoisie. Juridical freedom and equality in modern society do not exclude economic dependence and factual inequality; juridical equality of rights coexists with the class dominance of the bourgeoisie and the slavery of the proletariat. The contemporary social order, resting on the basis of class inequality, contradicts the interests of the worker — thus the socialist ideal of the proletariat, the demand for the annihilation of classes and private ownership of the means of production. From the Marxist point of view, both the natural-law ideal of the eighteenth century and the present-day socialist ideal represent nothing more than reflections of economic relations and interests. In these economic facts, and not in their intellectual casing, the final causes are to be sought of social and political transformations such as the French Revolution and that revolution of the future which will replace the bourgeois social order with a socialist one.

In this whole theory there is a large share of truth. It is impossible to deny that economic facts play a primary role in social revolutions, or that people are generally inclined to sympathize with precisely the legal and political principles that most correspond to their interests. It is another question *whether only* economic interests should be treated as independent causes of social revolutions, whether they alone determine the legal and political ideals of people.

Only the last part of this question need concern us here, since Marx and his followers deny the influence neither of intellectual factors nor, consequently, of ideas of natural law on social development. In the preceding account we have had repeated occasion to be convinced of the untenability of attempts to explain ideas by economic causes alone. Now we need to be convinced that legal ideals are no exception in this respect, that in them human consciousness manifests itself as a *creative* principle, that in them there is something irreducible to economic data and inexplicable by such data alone.

Legal ideals cannot be only reflections of existing economic relations, for the very reason that any ideal expresses something that *ought to be* [*dolzhenstvuiushchee sushchestvovat'*]. "Ought" [*dolzhenstvovanie*] always exceeds reality: it often radically contradicts what has been historically formed and is never fully covered by it. When French writers in the epoch preceding the Great Revolution proclaimed the principle of universal freedom and equality, their ideal contained something that was not in surrounding reality. The law of the future for which they worked was completely unlike the legal and economic relations that existed at the time and that were determined not by the principle of universal equality in civil rights, but by the diametrically opposed feudal-aristocratic principle. If it is said that this ideal was already in the prerevolutionary epoch an expression of the *real aspirations* (i.e., needs and interests) of the French bourgeoisie, still it is not difficult to demonstrate that in general no ideal is identical with the needs and interests it is invoked to satisfy, that it contains something they do not.

This is proved first of all by the fact that individual persons, social classes, and even entire peoples do not always correctly understand their interests. A legal or social ideal can include an arbitrary or fantastic element: it might, of course, be an expression of real interests, but it might also be the result of a mistaken understanding of social needs. The very proponents of the materialist understanding of history, beginning with Marx, unanimously attest to the rich element of illusion in the legal ideals of their predecessors. One of the favorite themes of Marx and Engels is that all the liberal and socialist ideals of the preceding epoch were dreamy and utopian, in contrast to the ideal of scientific socialism, advanced for the first time by Marx. Obviously, utopias and illusions do not correspond to real interests, economic and otherwise, and therefore cannot be explained by them alone.

Let us suppose, on the other hand, that a legal ideal is constructed on the exact data of science and bears not the slightest hint of utopia. Again it is clear that interest alone neither creates consciousness of truth nor frees human thought from error. A legal ideal, scientific or utopian, true or false, always results from a complex intellectual process; whether this process leads in the final result to a scientific discovery or a utopian dream does not depend on interests. The human mind, whether it makes a scientific discovery or falls into error, is in any event one of the prime movers in history, an independent factor irreducible to economic or other causes.

Notes

1. Paul Barth (1858–1922), author of *Die Geschichtsphilosophie Hegels und der Hegelianer, bis auf Marx und Hartmann* (Leipzig, 1890). Ed.

2. Tomáš Garrigue Masaryk (1850–1937), Czech statesman and philosopher, first president of Czechoslovakia (1918–1935). Trubetskoi likely has in mind Masaryk's work *Die philosophischen und soziologischen Grundlagen des Marxismus* (1899), a translation of the Czech original (1898). Ed.

3. Karl Kautsky (1854–1938), the most important theorist of orthodox Marxism after Marx and Engels, and its main defender in the Second International (1889–1914). Founder and editor (1883–1917) of *Die neue Zeit,* the official organ of the German Social Democratic party and the most influential Marxist journal of its day. Ed.

4. Kautsky, *Bernstein und das sozialdemokratische Programm.* Ed.

5. This text can be considered common knowledge, but for the convenience of readers unfamiliar with Marx, I will quote its most important part. "In the social production of their life, men enter into definite relations that are indispensable and independent of their will, relations of production which correspond to a definite stage of development of their material productive forces. The sum total of these relations of production constitutes the economic structure of society, the real foundation, on which rises a legal and political superstructure and to which correspond definite forms of social consciousness.

The mode of production of material life conditions the social, political and intellectual life process in general. It is not the consciousness of men that determines their being, but, on the contrary, their social being that determines their consciousness. At a certain stage of their development, the material productive forces of society come in conflict with the existing relations of production, or — what is but a legal expression for the same thing — with the property relations within which they have been at work hitherto. From forms of development of the productive forces these relations turn into their fetters. Then begins an epoch of social revolution. With the change of the economic foundation the entire immense superstructure is more or less rapidly transformed." [Karl Marx, Preface to *A Contribution to the Critique of Political Economy,* in *The Marx-Engels Reader,* ed. Robert C. Tucker, 2d edition (New York: Norton, 1978), pp. 4–5. This English version and Trubetskoi's Russian translation correspond very closely, except for the last sentence, which Trubetskoi renders as follows: "Then ensues an epoch of social revolution: with the change of the economic foundation the entire immense superstructure of legal and political institutions, to which correspond definite social forms of consciousness, sooner or later collapses." The phrase, "sooner or later," to which Trubetskoi returns below, is consistent with the German original. In his quotations, Trubetskoi usually cites the title of the quoted work, but without page references. I have provided the references and dates, and have used existing English translations for his quotations.]

6. Karl Marx, *The Eighteenth Brumaire of Louis Bonaparte* (New York: International Publishers, 1963), p. 47. Ed.

7. "Instruments of labour . . . are also indicators of the social conditions under which that labour is carried on." Karl Marx, *Capital,* vol. I, trans. Samuel Moore and Edward Aveling (Moscow: Progress Publishers, 1954), pp. 175–176. Ed.

8. "Technology discloses man's mode of dealing with Nature, the process of production by which he sustains his life, and thereby also lays bare the mode of formation of his social relations, and of the mental conceptions that flow from them." Ibid., p. 352, note 2. Ed.

9. Friedrich Engels, *Socialism: Utopian and Scientific,* in *The Marx-Engels Reader,* p. 701. Ed.

10. Ibid., p. 711. Ed.

11. "Engels to Heinz Starkenburg," in Karl Marx and Friedrich Engels, *Basic Writings on Politics and Philosophy,* ed. Lewis S. Feuer (Garden City, N.Y.: Anchor Books, 1959), pp. 410–412 (here, p. 410). Ed.

12. Friedrich Engels, "Speech at the Graveside of Karl Marx," in *The Marx-Engels Reader,* p. 681. Ed.

13. Karl Marx, "Toward the Critique of Hegel's Philosophy of Right," in *Basic Writings on Politics and Philosophy,* p. 263 (Marx's italics). Ed.

14. The state "is on the whole only a reflection, in concentrated form, of the economic needs of the class controlling production." Friedrich Engels, *Ludwig Feuerbach and the End of Classical German Philosophy,* in *Basic Writings on Politics and Philosophy,* p. 235. Ed.

15. These appear to be paraphrases rather than direct quotations. Ed.

16. Friedrich Engels, "On the History of Early Christianity," in *Basic Writings on Politics and Philosophy,* pp. 169–170. Ed.

17. The letter, to Joseph Bloch, is included in *The Marx-Engels Reader,* pp. 760–765 (here, p. 760). Ed.

18. Already in his book on Feuerbach, Engels acknowledges the influence of intellectual motives (*ideelle Triebkräfte*) on historical development. The mistake of the old materialism, in his opinion, was not that it admitted these motives, but that it treated them as final causes, not attempting to reduce ideas to their driving forces. ["What driving forces in turn stand behind these motives? What are the historical causes which transform themselves into these motives in the brains of the actors?" Engels asks. "The old materialism never put this question to itself. Its conception of history, insofar as it has one at all, is therefore essentially pragmatic; it judges everything according to the motives of the action. . . . Hence it follows . . . that in the realm of history the old materialism becomes untrue to itself because it takes the ideal driving forces which operate there as ultimate causes, instead of investigating what is behind them." Friedrich Engels, *Ludwig Feuerbach and the End of Classical German Philosophy,* in *Basic Writings on Politics and Philosophy,* p. 231.]

19. Engels to Joseph Bloch (1980), *The Marx-Engels Reader,* p. 760. Ed.

20. These "Letters on Historical Materialism" are available in *Basic Writings on Politics and Philosophy,* pp. 395–412, and in *The Marx-Engels Reader,* pp. 760–768. Ed.

21. Karl Marx, *Capital,* vol. I, in *The Marx-Engels Reader,* pp. 344–345. Ed.

22. Karl Marx, *The Poverty of Philosophy* (New York: International Publishers, 1963), p. 83. Ed.

23. Trubetskoi is likely referring to the Stundists and Dukhobors. The Stundists, whose name comes from the eighteenth-century German evangelical communities (*Stunde*), were found in southern Ukraine. They left the Orthodox Church in 1870 and were successful in making converts among the peasants. Konstantin P. Pobedonostsev (1827–1907), chief procurator of the Holy Synod of the Russian Orthodox Church from 1880 to 1905, regarded the Stundists as an "especially dangerous" sect and in 1894 prohibited their prayer meetings. The Dukhobors, who settled in the Caucasus in the 1840s, came into conflict with the authorities as a result of their refusal to bear arms. They were cruelly persecuted until their emigration in 1898 and 1899, first to Cyprus and then to Canada. Ed.

24. Dmitrii A. Tolstoi (1823–1889), widely detested by civic-minded Russians for his reactionary views, became minister of education on 14 April 1866. A law of 30 June 1871 greatly increased the required hours for the study of Greek and Latin in Russian gymnasiums. The aim was to limit the time available for study of subjects that might have subversive implications. Ed.

25. [*Wirtschaft und Recht nach der materialistischen Geschichtsauffassung* (Leipzig, 1896), p. 254. Trubetskoi's quotation is a paraphrase.] Of course, this is true only in the case of the productive relations among *people,* for only conscious relations can be legal ones: in animal societies productive relations are determined not by legal norms, but by instinct. Therefore, Stammler's idea that *generally all* social relations depend on law, that law relates to economy as form to matter, is obviously mistaken.

26. Karl Marx, *Capital,* vol. I, in *The Marx-Engels Reader,* pp. 343. Ed.

3

Toward Characterization of Our Philosophical Development
(Apropos of S. P. Ranskii's book, *The Sociology of N. K. Mikhailovskii*)

P. G. [P. B. STRUVE]

We have before us a new book devoted to N. K. Mikhailovskii, by S. P. Ranskii.[1] It will not be superfluous in our literature, despite the existence of Krasnosel'skii's brochure and Berdiaev's book.[2] The burden of Berdiaev's work consists not in exposition or even in critique of Mikhailovskii's theories, but in opposing a different *Weltanschauung* to them.[3] By contrast, Ranskii, although he offers a critique of Mikhailovskii's views—a critique at the basis of which obviously lies the critic's own more or less definite, positive point of view—undoubtedly saw his main task in a precise and complete as possible account of Mikhailovskii's ideas. It can be said that he has carried out this task very satisfactorily, having given a clear and precise reproduction of the foundations of the sociology of the influential Russian journalist. With full justification is the epigraph, "*sine ira et studio,*"[4] placed on this book. It is impartially written, yet Mikhailovskii emerges lifelike and whole, with all the essential and vivid traits of his literary individuality, instead of the pale and often vague rendition that we find in Krasnosel'skii's brochure, which is silent about many things and does not emphasize still others.[5] With some satisfaction it can be stated, on the basis of S. P. Ranskii's book, that a firm and fully objective point of view on certain aspects of Mikhailovskii's sociological doctrine is beginning to form and take hold, a point of view that is obviously destined to replace, on the one hand, the naive adulation of people who see in

the teaching of the publisher of *Russkoe bogatstvo*[6] an anticipation of practically every achievement of contemporary philosophical and sociological
thought,[7] and, on the other hand, the indiscriminate denial of his significance
in the development of our social-philosophical thought. Thus Ranskii establishes, completely independently of Berdiaev and Struve,[8] that Mikhailovskii
not only did not refute or reject the "organic" theory of society, but surren-
dered to the power of this theory *much more fully and deeply* than Spencer
and the other "organicists" (pp. 37–39, 104).[9] This irrefutable (and so un-
refuted) conclusion — outlined already in 1887 by M. M. Filippov,[10] as several
of Ranskii's references clarify, and then stated clearly enough in 1895 by
Beltov[11] — can be considered, after the explanations given by Berdiaev-Struve
and Ranskii, the solid and permanent possession of scholarly criticism of
Mikhailovskii's sociological doctrine. It throws clear light on the objective
value of the central parts of Mikhailovskii's sociological doctrine and turns
into naught the views (which have become nearly a tradition) of his admirers
that he "refuted" Spencer and thus accomplished a revolution in sociology.

In just the same way — and Ranskii's arguments, free from any polemical
fervor, can also serve as proof of this — a negative evaluation is beginning to
take hold of the subjective method as a poorly thought-out and illicit intrusion
of the *ethical* point of view into the theoretical study of what was, is, and will
be according to the law of causation. The most recent attempt at interpretation of the subjective method — an attempt Mikhailovskii was forced to make
in answer to Berdiaev and Struve's criticism — amounts to the *self-destruction*
of this method, as Struve showed in the May 1901 issue of *Mir Bozhii*.[12] To
demonstrate that the matter seems so not only to this one opponent of Mikhailovskii, it is possible to refer to the remarks of F. V. Sofronov in his
intriguing, well-thought-out article, "The Mechanics of Social Ideals."[13] "In
the February issue of *Russkoe bogatstvo* for the current year,"[14] Sofronov
remarks, "Mikhailovskii says that by his 'subjective method [he] is not thinking of subordinating intellectual conscience to ethical conscience,' but is only
elucidating this ethical conscience and, in the interests of knowledge itself,
'regulating' the influence of an inevitable social-psychological fact — the pressure of ethical elements on the course of research. But to regulate such influence in the interests of knowledge means excluding it, to the extent possible —
and *this would be the self-destruction of the subjective method*."[15] Sofronov
continues: "This is not, of course, what Mikhailovskii wants, and so for him
'regulation' acquires a peculiar meaning — not the exclusion but the introduction of the ethical element, only under conscious control. Unfortunately, this is
precisely the subordination of intellectual conscience to the ethical," or just
what Mikhailovskii tries to defend himself against. As a result, Mikhailovskii,

as Sofronov correctly stresses, cannot escape the alternatives: to either abolish the "subjective method" or affirm it.

It seems to us that sooner or later it will be recognized and enter into general consciousness that the significance of Mikhailovskii's literary activity, spanning many years, should be sought not in the sphere of positive science or even in publicism, but in that sphere of spiritual creativity — at first glance indefinite, but in essence clearly outlined — which is called *philosophy* and which has the task of elaborating an integral Weltanschauung. Despite the remarkable acuteness of his mind and his very considerable erudition, the scientific significance of what Mikhailovskii has written is quite small, simply because his intellectual makeup is characterized by an absence of the purely theoretical interest that is the most important motive behind any scientific work.

As a result, Mikhailovskii's works cannot leave a large mark on positive science. His criticism of Spencer's sociology, his theory of progress, and his theory of the struggle for individuality are the same "organic" view of society, only taken to an extreme and obviously tendentious expression; his subjective method is a misunderstanding that the esteemed writer had to renounce. The brilliant journalist devoted empirical research most of all but also truly original thought to clarifying the question of "imitation," or the problem of "heroes and the crowd" (to use Mikhailovskii's own favorite expressions).[16] But this is the basic conclusion to which Mikhailovskii arrived and which amounts to the identification (or at least approximation) of the phenomena of social imitation or the herd instinct with individual-psychic automatism or hypnotism — a slight and meager result compared to the work and wit involved. One enigmatic phenomenon is explained by another, still more enigmatic.

Mikhailovskii is often called a publicist. This word usually encompasses almost everything that cannot be brought under the concept of either scientific writing or belles-lettres. In this sense Mikhailovskii is, of course, a publicist. But it would be better to avoid such careless usage altogether. By publicist we mean a writer who not only does not avoid but, on the contrary, aims to give and introduce into the consciousness of readers clear and precise formulations of the immediate social-political tasks of the day. A publicist is first of all and mainly a politician. His sphere consists of the questions of public law and social relations, in their application to the real, concrete interests and needs of the present historical moment. Publicism, so understood, has essentially very little place, externally as well as internally, in N. K. Mikhailovskii's literary activity. In the 1870s Mikhailovskii provided a very expressive and broad formula of his social policy: "Legislative strengthening of the commune [*obshchina*]." But he did not develop, as would a true publicist, all the social-political content contained in this much-encompassing formula. In the 1880s

Mikhailovskii brilliantly defended in several articles certain practical demands of liberalism,[17] but when the "new ideas" of the beginning of the 1880s came to a ruinous end,[18] he fell silent as a publicist. This circumstance cannot, however, be explained only by the change in the whole course of our political life; it cannot be derived entirely from the onset of reaction. No less role was played here by reasons internal to Mikhailovskii himself, first of all the absence of an intense and enduring interest in the concrete and immediate problems of law and economy that form the content of "politics," an interest that constitutes the driving force and characteristic trait of any publicistic activity.

We are not reproaching the esteemed editor-publisher of *Russkoe bogatstvo* for the absence of this publicistic interest. We are only stating an indisputable fact — that in Mikhailovskii's numerous articles there is very little publicism in the precise and, if you wish, generic sense of the word — and giving this fact a certain psychological interpretation. We humbly ask that what has been said not be understood in a crude sense. To be a publicist, it was not necessary for Mikhailovskii to analyze in his articles the customs-tariff or even the position of zemstvo institutions.[19] But a publicist in contemporary Russia cannot ignore protectionism or local self-government as practical problems, as problems of politics, but rather must touch upon and illuminate them from a point of view based on principles. Populist publicism of the 1870s could not, however, but suffer from two of its main, tightly interconnected sins: economism and utopianism. The tasks of economic policy were considered basic, while at the same time these tasks received utopian formulation. As a result, the publicism of the most radical Russian trend of the 1870s could not but bear a certain narrowness, connected with utopianism, in the sense of fanciful dreams. In its most cherished demands it was far from practicality. In the 1880s populist publicism became more practical, but not more idealistic; on the contrary, it was even further removed from idealism. It is not surprising, therefore, that idealistic needs and cravings took their main refuge not in publicism, but in the sphere of that pseudo-scientific sociology in which the savage and hermaphrodite, as types of development, were extolled over the cultured person and distinctly gendered individual.[20] The main spokesman for these idealistic cravings was N. K. Mikhailovskii, with his sharply expressed philosophical interest in the construction of an integral Weltanschauung. Not having become a philosopher-publicist, he became a philosopher-sociologist. But we have already said that N. K. Mikhailovskii's sociology cannot be ascribed any particular scientific significance. It is possible to grant that he may enter the history of sociology as a follower (not devoid of originality) of the "organic" theory of society and as a precursor of Tarde.[21]

Whatever this may be in the history of science, it is absolutely nothing in the history of Russian philosophizing or in the construction of an integral world-view. In other words, were Mikhailovskii only a research sociologist, he would occupy in the history of Russian philosophical thought approximately the same place as his like-minded colleagues in sociology who lack a philosophical grasp of things, philosophical energy, and breadth of thought.

Thus, not the sociologist, but the philosopher Mikhailovskii constitutes the major figure. Why and in what sense? To explain this it is necessary to turn our attention to the state of the development of world and Russian philosophical thought and to the issue Mikhailovskii raised. The 1850s and 1860s signify the collapse of the philosophical systems of the German idealists and an extreme enthusiasm for the ideas of *positive* science, as distinct from and in opposition to metaphysics. The repudiation of metaphysical problems, of their solution and even their posing, was an act not simply of ascetic abstention, but of militant rejection. True, the repudiated metaphysics, in the form of materialism, intruded as though from the back porch into philosophical and scientific thought.

Both materialistic metaphysics, imagining itself to be science, and militant positivism, imagining itself to be philosophy, have at their basis a number of dogmatic presuppositions. We will try to give a succinct but precise formulation of what we consider the *basic error of positivism*. Man conceives everything conceivable in two basic forms or, more correctly, with two symbols: as "what is" ("is") [*sushchee (bytie)*] and as "what ought to be" ("ought") [*dolzhnoe (dolzhenstvovanie)*]. "What is" or "is" — material or physical, psychic or spiritual — is what is, was, and will be according to the law of causation. "Is" does not contain in itself freedom or creativity. These concepts are foreign to "is." The present is entirely determined by the past, and the future by the present (and thus by the past). In this way, everything is determined or predetermined. The whole world of "what is" is necessary: it could not and cannot be other than it was, is, and will be, according to the immutable law of its being. The necessity [*zakonomernost' ili neobkhodimost'*] of what is flows from the necessity [*zakonomernost'*] of what was, and the necessity of what will be depends on the necessity of what is. Reflecting on this necessity, we see that it consists of two moments: first, the necessary and total reduction of any particular being [or existent] to another, as its cause, and, second, the mode of this dependence. Thus, it is not the being [or existence] of something, as such, that is necessary, but rather the causal dependence of this existence on some other being [or existent] and the mode of this dependence. Everything conceivable,[22] or "what is," is understood scientifically to the extent we reduce one being [or existent] to another, as its cause, and examine the mode of this causal dependence. In other words, we can scientifically understand only *why and how* something exists.[23]

When a person conceives or experiences something as "what ought to be," with the symbol of "ought," his relation to the content of this "ought" is completely different from his relation to the content of "is." These relations are incomparable and irreducible to each other. From the fact that something is conceived by me as "what ought to be," it does not follow that it necessarily will be. And in just the same way, from the fact that something is, or necessarily will be by the laws of nature, in no way does it follow that it is "what ought to be" according to the moral law apprehended by me.

Meanwhile the basic idea and also the basic error of positivism consists in subordinating "what ought to be" ("ought") to "what is" ("is") and in deriving the first from the second.

On this subordination rests the monstrous idea of *scientific* ethics, not in the sense of psychology or psychological explanation of morality, but in the sense of normative or prescriptive theory of "what ought to be." What is can substantiate what ought to be! The subordination of "ought" to "is," the derivation of the first from the second, is rooted in an uncritical approach to — we would say in idolatry before — the principle of causation. It forgets that in experience or science we discover the causation and mode of being, but that being itself [*samoe bytie*], as such, always remains for us unknown and unexplained. We always defer, but never complete, explanation of the fact that something exists. This fact, which goes by the name of the unknowability of "final" causes, was pointed out long ago and has since become a commonplace. But, as is well known, commonplaces enjoy the *privilegium odiosum* [odious privilege] of not being thought out. They are not thought out in a negative-critical sense; that is, they are taken on faith without adequate foundations. But they are perhaps still more often not thought out in a positive-critical sense; that is, their content remains to a significant degree undisclosed. It seems to me that the commonplace about the unknowability of final causes is rarely thought out in the positive-critical direction, and that the core of this contention, the unknowability of being as such, remains unclear.

In empirical knowledge or positive science we tacitly suppose that the facts called final causes are situated at some infinite distance from us, not only from the point of view of our knowledge, but as real being; in other words, we suppose that the so-called "final" causes were at one time decreed, but that now everything occurs according to the "law" of causation. Meanwhile, the unknowability of being as such designates precisely the impossibility of rejecting uncaused being. Critical philosophy has shown the impossibility, from the point of view of experience, of either proving or refuting the existence of God. Logical necessity suggests to me that this criticism ought to be extended. The formula of such an expanded criticism would declare: uncaused being cannot in general be rejected. It is inexplicable in terms of experience and, in this sense, unknowable, but to reject it would mean rejecting what is least in doubt, namely, the very fact of the existence [bytie] of the world. The world is, first of all, a "given" for us. As a whole, the world is a product of our synthesis of a multitude of "givens." Only an insignificant part of them is treated and explained from the point of view of causation; the larger part always was and remains pure "givens," that is, genuine and supreme mysteries. And what is most important, the world cannot be for us anything except given, since, in reducing it to causes "final" for experience, we would only come face to face with a mystery that was for us absolutely "given." At the same time we would not have, just as we do not have now, any guarantee that such mysteries — "final" causes or uncaused being — were not constantly arising before us, but were only hidden from us. To be sure, we do not want our arguments to be understood as a fanciful invitation to belief in so-called miracles. But, on the other hand, they must not be understood in a completely abstract sense, remote from the tasks of science and the problems of life.

Apart from *belief* in causation — a belief that is the guiding principle in empirical knowledge (but only that) — there is no basis to deny uncaused being, as such. Uncaused being is, of course, a mystery, but so in the final account is any being [or existent] taken in itself. Nor is there, apart from *belief* in causation, any basis to deny *creative* being. True, from the point of view of causation, any being [or existent] is entirely reducible to another, and so forth and so on. But only unconditional belief in causation or the most thoroughgoing religious fatalism forbids a *break* in this chain, that is, forbids admitting creative being, which is creative of other being from itself and only from itself.[24]

Belief in causation excludes any thought of uncaused or creative being. But can this be an incontestable and universally binding belief? This is the question critical doubt raises. Critical reflection, it seems to us, does not permit rejection of either uncaused or creative being, and therefore there is no philosophical compulsion to reduce "what ought to be" to the causally determined. On the contrary, philosophical reflection, by its critical approach to belief in causation, cannot but support immediate consciousness of the special nature of moral "ought," presupposing free or creative agency. Causation, of course, unconditionally requires reduction of one phenomenon to another, according to an invariable law. Causal explanation not only does not admit the freedom and autonomy of the creative activity of the spirit, but, on the contrary, completely dismisses them as illusory ideas, out of place and justified by nothing, muddled lapses of the human mind, which otherwise proceeds from one cause to another. We are not talking about what determinists of one type or another think, since they can be illogical, but about what the idea itself of determinism maintains and cannot but maintain. This idea, as the application of causal explanation to the human spirit, demands the reduction of what is individual, free and creative to what is general (social), necessary, and dependent.

But what philosophical right do we have to assert that spirit, in the form of personhood [*lichnost'*] bringing about "what ought to be," cannot be autonomous in its activity, a spontaneous principle, creative from itself. This is metaphysics, we are told. Yes, metaphysics, but a metaphysics to which the spirit is drawn both by immediate consciousness of its own creative function and by critical reflection.[25]

Boundless enthusiasm for the ideas of an all-embracing and all-deciding *positive science* seized Russian thinking society at the end of the 1850s and beginning of the 1860s, and this enthusiasm avidly assimilated the doctrines of positivism and materialism worked out in the West. This assimilation did an enormous service for the cause of Russian culture, representing, like the western Enlightenment of the eighteenth century, a liberation of the mind from subordination to dead and deadening metaphysical dogma and plain nonsense. But, clearing certain paths, positivism and materialism laid others. Uncritical positivism and materialism are both equally dogmatic constructions, promising much more than they can deliver. These doctrines, entirely guided by the category of causation as the highest principle of explanation, reduce "ought" and freedom to this category, that is, they annul — fully consistently from their point of view — these basic concepts of morality as autonomous concepts. Positivism becomes dogmatic to the extent that in its image positive science shows the pretension of using its definitions to exhaust the whole fullness of the life of the spirit and to give a balanced and integral worldview. From the point of view of causation this is impossible, and not for nothing did Comte, in his subjective phase, break the iron ring of positivism that he himself forged and enter into the sphere of true metaphysics, with its religious character. "Working out the system of positive philosophy on the basis of his 'objective method,'" Vladimir Solov'ëv says,

> Comte considered it the final, supreme expression of humanity's spiritual development; but upon the completion of his work he recognized its inadequacy and felt that this mental construct did not give even its founder the right to be considered a true philosopher, since it represented only one side of man as he really is and only one side of the truth accessible to him. Comte recognized this side of being, newly revealed to him, as even more important and

primary. ... In any case, the positive religion and politics were not the direct result or application of the positive philosophy, but a completely new construction, on a new foundation (the "subjective method") and with a different task (moral-practical). Here the idea of humanity turns out to be a kind of conduit or connection: the positive philosophy leads to this idea, while the religion and politics follow from it. But the idea itself, in the sense in which it appears in the last volume of the *Cours de philosophie positive,* no longer corresponds to the objective method and, instead of a positive-scientific character, it undoubtedly has a *metaphysical* one. The *one [edinyi]* humanity of which Comte speaks here does not exist as a fact of external experience and cannot be reduced to such a fact; the concept of such a humanity could not be achieved by science, as Comte understood it, and since he did not claim a pretension to divine revelation, his idea can only be recognized as purely speculative or metaphysical. Thus, in his own intellectual development Comte submitted to the law of three stages, but in reverse order: he began with the positive-scientific worldview and, through means of the metaphysical principle of humanity, came to the religious and plainly theological stage.[26]

Mikhailovskii, accepting Comte's subjective method, also transgressed the borders of positivism.[27] In his demand for a system of truth [*pravda*] that combined truth-verity [*pravda-istina*] with truth-justice [*pravda-spravedlivost'*],[28] he formulated the philosophical problem, inaccessible to positive science, of an integral view uniting "what is" and "what ought to be" in one construction. This problem belongs by its essence to metaphysics. Mikhailovskii's mistake, which condemned him to almost complete philosophical barrenness, was that he expressed a metaphysical problem in the concepts of positive science and thought of resolving it by means of positive science. Sociology, even "subjective" sociology, could not, of course, answer the grand metaphysical challenge presented to it. In the figure of the philosophizing Mikhailovskii there were two *personae* who neither recognized themselves nor delineated between themselves, and who therefore only interfered with each other. In him positive science was unconsciously distorted by metaphysics, while metaphysical thought was burdened, bound, and made barren by its subordination to "positive science."

Be that as it may, in the history of Russian philosophical thought Mikhailovskii shares a place with P. L. Lavrov as a brilliant spokesman of the first dim, almost unconscious reaction of an ineradicable "metaphysical need" against positivism, a reaction that came, moreover, from the depths of positivism itself. Only such a characterization of Mikhailovskii's philosophizing throws light on the philosophical meaning and significance of Marxism's dispute with "subjective sociology." This dispute, examined from the side of its philosophical content, was a completely natural, pertinent, and very timely reaction on the part of positive scientific thought against an illicit intrusion of metaphysical-ethical problems into its sphere, problems that appeared under the flag of subjective sociology. Defending themselves against this reaction, Mikhailovskii and his followers very much enervated their point of view, with the result indicated above, that the subjective method degenerated to the point of self-destruction. Its valuable metaphysical core could not, however, be lost.

It is characteristic, on the other hand, that one of the most visible Russian positivists, P. N. Miliukov,[29] from the very beginning sided philosophically with the Marxists in their controversy with the subjectivists, of course because he clearly saw in Marxism a reaction of the positive-scientific spirit against an alien "ethical" element intruding into science. But no matter how legitimate this reaction, it went too far in both its metaphysical form (N. Beltov [Plekhanov], *On the Question of the Development of the Monistic View of History*) and positive-critical form (Struve, *Critical Notes on the Question of the Economic Development of Russia*).[30] In saying this, we do not have in mind the exaggerations and one-sidedness of so-called economic materialism, which has no fundamental philosophical significance and which positive science and specialized methodology should simply jettison. The issue is rather that in its positive-critical formulation, Russian Marxism, as a philosophical construct, initially fell into the basic error of positivism indicated above, subordinating "ought," as such, to "is" and submerging freedom into necessity; that is, it turned out to be an uncritical and dogmatic view. Struve fell into dogmatism, adapting the views of Riehl and Simmel to the substantiation of "economic materialism."[31] In itself this adaptation was conceived correctly. But Riehl's critical realism and Simmel's social psychologism were interpreted incorrectly in the sense of a fundamental philosophical subordination of "ought" to "is." At the time Struve lacked the philosophic clarity that, as a matter of principle, does not admit such subordination. But Beltov [Plekhanov], in his dual capacity as materialist and Hegelian, and approaching the theory of knowledge with sovereign disdain and slighting it as scholasticism, was in general foreign to any critical reflection and therefore could neither relate critically to the basic error of positivism nor even pose the problem itself in its pure form.

Now the position of things has changed. Critical work began in "Marxism" itself, certain results of which can already be seen. Mikhailovskii's idea about "what ought to be," as a category independent of "what is" in experience and therefore having autonomous value, is acknowledged by those Marxists-writers who, from critical positivism, have come or passed to metaphysics. But it is also these writers who have stressed that posing this question within the limits of positive science and in its terms is illegitimate and does not make sense, that doing so is an *uncritical conflation of metaphysics with empirical knowledge, or with positive science.* Thus it is not true that the philosophical direction of such metaphysicians-idealists as Struve shares nothing in common with Mikhailovskii, but it is still less true that this current, which came out of Marxism, has capitulated before "subjective sociology." It is interesting to clarify and establish, of course, not who has beat whom (let such questions occupy the fanatic "disciples" of Marx and Mikhailovskii, or newspaper feuilletonists), but how Russian philosophical thought — in its various representatives — has progressed and what it has arrived at, how the lines of its development have *diverged and converged.* Looking closely at the shape the latest metaphysical idealism has taken, we see in it an attempt to pose in pure metaphysical form the problem of the correlation between "what is" and "what ought to be," between historical reality and the eternal ideal, a problem speciously simplified and solved, but in essence violently effaced, by positivism. The new direction has hardly gone further than a critical prolegomena (Berdiaev-Struve's book) and has given only a few hints at positive constructions. Before it a broad field of metaphysical creativity is opening up. But here one does not find mere empty space.

The movement of Russian philosophical thought since 1870 has not been exhausted by positivism, and first place in it does not belong to positivism. True, Russian positivism searched for solutions in the objective Comte, then in the subjective Comte; it drew new inspiration from Kant and neo-Kantianism, then from Marx's social materialism; it reconciled Marx's theory with Kant, Riehl, Simmel, Avenarius, even with Mikhailovskii, then opposed Marxism, as alone offering salvation, to all other constructions. But all along Russian metaphysics created the brilliant ontology and ethics of Vladimir Solov'ëv, original in their substantiation and formulation of ancient religious, metaphysical, and moral ideas; the harmonious system of Chicherin; the panpsychism of Kozlov and his students,[32] rich in its possible conclusions; and the "concrete idealism" of Prince S. N. Trubetskoi. The new people of the metaphysical need,[33] who have left and even are still only leaving positivism, must try to grasp and take into consideration all these constructions. Russian metaphysics, in the person of Vladimir Solov'ëv, also performed an outstanding public deed in giving for the first time an *idealist* critique of Slavophilism and Katkovism,[34] and in thus establishing that philosophical idealism and state positivism are irreconcilable in spirit. This is an enormous service, often praised, but still inadequately appreciated in its philosophical sense.

With Marxism, which begot metaphysics from its very depths, Russian positivism came full circle in its development. V. A. Miliutin's Comteanism;[35] the (natural scientific) materialism of Herzen, Chernyshevskii[36] and Pisarev;[37] the sociological subjectivism of Lavrov and Mikhailovskii; Beltov's [Plekhanov's] dialectical Marxism; and Struve's positive-critical Marxism, strongly colored by Kantianism and neo-Kantianism—here are the different expressions of Russian positivism, stages that have different content and therefore different value, but that are identical at their philosophical core. Russian Comteanism and Russian (natural scientific) materialism are the least original and, in the works of their philosophical representatives, hardly complicated by any valuable positive-scientific content (this is characteristic in the highest degree). Nor did they present a clearly expressed publicistic program. Chernyshevskii's main (and enormous) significance for his time was rooted in the fact that he was a materialist and socialist who cast his theoretical and practical Weltanschauung in formulas more seductively clear and resolute than any until or since then. But what is distinctively his in his political economy has no positive-scientific worth; he did not provide a clear publicistic program because socialism as such could not give such a program, either then or now. Chernyshevskii's role is analogous to Mikhailovskii's. He was the philosopher of his generation, but not a scholar; he wrote several brilliant publicistic essays, but was not a publicist. Russian sociological subjectivism is an attempt—original to a significant degree, despite its attachment to Comte—to satisfy the metaphysical need within the bounds of positivism. The philosophical intent in this attempt or, more precisely, the fruitful philosophical bewilderment it expressed, is valuable. P. L. Lavrov and N. K. Mikhailovskii, it seems to me, were never the "dominant influences" on their generation that N. G. Chernyshevskii was on his, but as philosophers and scholars they are significantly above their more influential predecessor, the force of whose influence stemmed from what constituted the weakness of his philosophizing and scholarly efforts. I have in mind Chernyshevskii's dogmatic cast of mind and his simple point of view.

Marxism, tightly attached to Marx not only as a social reformer but also as a scholar, suddenly found itself as if heir to a great positive-scientific estate, which it strived in every way to utilize and increase. The contributions of Russian Marxism in the positive-scientific field are, to our view, very significant. Let us mention one, for example. The Marxists have repeatedly reproached their opponents for being bourgeois [burzhuaznost'], and have received the same reproach in return. These reproaches, as such, will not concern us here; let them pass entirely into oblivion. We would like to point out, however, that reproaching the Marxists for being bourgeois hints at a very great *service* of Russian Marxism: it has given (is it even possible to still doubt this?!) a scientific explanation of the historical necessity of capitalism in Russia. Such an explanation encompasses a contingent historical justification of capitalism as well. In this way Russian Marxism fulfilled the task that everywhere, in other countries, fell to the lot of "liberal" political economy, which took the form, moreover, of an official science. Meanwhile Russian Marxism "justified" capitalism in its direct polemics not only with populism, but with almost all official science. This work required significant theoretical courage, which—as often tends to be forgotten—always has great moral value. Together with its outstanding positive-scientific content, Marxism provided a new, clear, and practical publicistic program. We said above that N. K. Mikhailovskii was not a publicist. For him, relying in part on his own sociological ideas, publicism was the affair of the true "populists" grouped, incidentally, around *Otechestvennye zapiski*.[38] Against this publicism, which in the end turned out to be unacceptable to Mikhailovskii himself, the Russian Marxists directed their own publicism, no less well-composed and deliberate.

The Achilles heel of Russian Marxism was its philosophy. Marx was hardly the critical philosopher—bearing an inner affinity to Kant, Fichte, Schelling, and Hegel—that Woltmann imagines him to be. This was rather a dogmatic materialist who came out of Feuerbach's school but, attached to eighteenth-century French materialism, was more dogged than Feuerbach. In this respect Marx is a direct continuer of the French socialists and communists, who proceeded philosophically, like him, from materialism and sensualism. The philosophically fruitful bewilderment contained in subjective sociology is completely alien to consistent or orthodox Marxism, as expressed, in our literature, by Beltov's [Plekhanov's] book. For this form of Marxism, the metaphysical need remains as if *beyond the threshold of consciousness* and is unconsciously satisfied by naive dogmatic materialism. Beltov's Marxism, in its philosophical content, is therefore a return to Chernyshevskii, that is, to the most simple philosophical point of view in Russian positivism.

The approach of Struve's positive-critical Marxism in his *Critical Notes* to the basic error of positivism, or to the metaphysical problem of the relation of "what ought to be" to "what is" (in experience), is completely different: in it there is not a shade of naïveté. The problem is sharply formulated, and the Gordian knot is cut: "what ought to be" is violently and dogmatically—with the help of social psychology—reduced to "what is" in experience. If the basic error of positivism arouses a vague uncritical protest among the subjectivists, if it constitutes the unconscious presupposition of philosophizing among the dogmatists-materialists, then in Struve's form of Marxism it is openly proclaimed, with full consciousness that an integral worldview cannot be satisfied simply with critical restraint on this point, but must offer a perfectly definite solution. Only a very attentive and keen reader could have detected even then, concealed behind Struve's sharp conclusions, an inner uncertainty about the correctness of his solution, an uncertainty that tormented the author, but that he suppressed and did not face. The uncritical coerciveness of this solution ought to have been revealed, however.

Having reexamined his solution, Struve renounced it and, finding neither critical restraint nor psychological subjectivism possible, openly passed to metaphysics, that is, having broken with positivism, in the *philosophical* sense Struve ceased to be a Marxist. His foreword to Berdiaev's book marked the turning point. Berdiaev reveals in his book a still dualistic approach to metaphysics, while Struve now resolutely devotes himself to metaphysics. The metaphysical bewilderment of the "subjectivists," which vainly sought satisfaction in positivism, finds its outcome in metaphysics itself.

The scientific-positive results of Marxism and the valuable achievements of its publicistic program are not affected by the metaphysical turn. But it is impossible to conceal from oneself the fact that this turn carries not only the possibility but also the necessity of further reconsideration of *all* sides of this, the youngest of the philosophical worldviews to have emerged among us. Its representatives, who have experienced and brought about the transition to metaphysics, are not, as we have already shown, carving out a completely new channel of thought. They will, however, bring to the idealist course of Russian thought a new current, new thoughts and attitudes. They are not arriving with empty hands or, more correctly, with empty souls. Their convictions are the fruit of a struggle that, arising on a broad arena of literature, was at the same time a deep process. This was a struggle not only with opponents, but also with itself, a struggle capable of producing firm convictions and yet of giving them a special tone of tolerance, a tone testifying not to languor or indifference of the spirit, but to a living and joyous faith in the force of truth and strength of the good.

Notes

1. S. P. Ranskii, *Sotsiologiia N. K. Mikhailovskogo* (St. Petersburg, 1901).

2. [A. I.] Krasnosel'skii, *Mirovozzrenie gumanista nashego vremeni* (*The Worldview of a Humanist of Our Times*, St. Petersburg, 1900). N. A. Berdiaev, *Sub"ektivizm i individualizm v obshchestvennoi filosofii: Kriticheskii etiud o N. K. Mikhailovskom. S predisloviem Pëtra Struve* (*Subjectivism and Individualism in Social Philosophy: A Critical Study of N. K. Mikhailovskii.* With a foreword by Pëtr Struve. St. Petersburg, 1901).

3. This is even more true of Struve's foreword to Berdiaev's book. [The book and Struve's foreword were an important milestone in the development Bulgakov characterized as, "from Marxism to idealism." In his book Berdiaev's approach was still positivist

(albeit of a critical type) in its Kantian revision of Marxism, but Struve had passed to idealism, the first of the "legal Marxists" to make the transition.]

4. "Without indignation or partisanship." From Tacitus, *The Annals of Imperial Rome,* Book 1, ch. 1. Ed.

5. The most valuable or, more correctly, the only valuable thing about Krasnosel'skii's booklet is that the notes make a start at a much needed *subject index* to Mikhailovskii's works.

6. *Russkoe bogatstvo (Russian Wealth)* was a "thick" journal published in St. Petersburg from 1876 to 1918. Mikhailovskii was chief editor from 1892 to his death in 1904. During this period it was the leading organ of "legal populism." Ed.

7. Chernov provides an example of such ... excessiveness, so to speak, in his recent articles in *Russkoe bogatstvo.* [Viktor M. Chernov (1873–1952), leader and theoretician of the populist Party of Socialist Revolutionaries (SRs) founded in 1901, minister of agriculture under the Provisional Government, elected chairman of the ill-fated Constituent Assembly in January 1918. Struve is referring to Chernov's long essay, "Sub"ektivnyi metod v sotsiologii i ego filosofskie predposylki," serialized in *Russkoe bogatstvo* (1901), nos. 7, 8, 10, 11, and 12.]

8. Ranskii's book, as he indicates in the preface, was written before Berdiaev and Struve's book.

9. The organic theory of society compares society to an organism that evolves, like the rest of the organic world, through a process of increasing heterogeneity, complexity, and division of labor. Mikhailovskii thought this entailed regression for the individual human being, who as a specialized monofunctional organ of the social organism would be deprived of all-around versatility, wholeness, and independence. Social evolution or progress was thus incompatible with individual growth and Mikhailovskii's ideal of the integral personality. Struve's point is that Mikhailovskii accepted the premises of the organic theory of society and that it was a powerful negative frame of reference for him. See Andrzej Walicki, *A History of Russian Thought from the Enlightenment to Marxism,* trans. Hilda Andrews-Rusiecka (Stanford, Calif.: Stanford University Press, 1979), pp. 252–253, 262. Ed.

10. Mikhail Mikhailovich Filippov (1858–1903), philosopher, writer, and literary critic. His philosophical outlook was marked by faith in science, human progress, and the influence of Comte and Marx. Author of *Filosofiia deistvitel'nosti,* 2 vols. (St. Petersburg, 1895–1897). Struve is referring to Filippov's essay "Literaturnaia deiatel'nost' N. Mikhailovskogo: Kriticheskii etiud M. M. Filippova," *Russkoe bogatstvo* (1887), no. II, section III. Ed.

11. *K voprosu o razvitii monisticheskogo vzgliada na istoriiu (On the Question of the Development of the Monistic View of History,* St. Petersburg, 1895), pp. 61–67. ["Beltov" was a pseudonym of Georgii V. Plekhanov (1856–1918), known as the "father of Russian Marxism."]

12. "Na raznye temy," *Mir Bozhii,* X, no. 6 (June 1901), part 2, pp. 12–27. Reprinted as "Protiv ortodoksal'noi neterpimosti — Pro domo sua," in Pëtr Struve, *Na raznye temy (1893–1901 gg.). Sbornik statei* (St. Petersburg, 1902), pp. 291–308, here pp. 297–299. Ed.

13. F. Sofronov, "Mekhanika obshchestvennykh idealov," *Voprosy filosofii i psikhologii* 12: 4, kn. 59 (1901), pp. 301–341, quotation at pp. 310–311, nt. 3. Ed.

14. *Russkoe bogatstvo,* February 1901, pp. 310–311.

15. Struve's italics.

16. "Geroi i tolpa," an essay by Mikhailovskii (1882). Ed.

17. For example, in an 1884 article published in *Listok Narodnoi Voli,* Mikhailovskii called on the government to give "a legal place to free representatives of the country." In 1889 he contributed to *Samoupravlenie (Self-Government)*, a journal published in Geneva since 1887 and devoted to the proposition that socialists should engage in legal agitation for political rights such as popular representation. His 1892 pamphlet, *Svobodnoe slovo (The Free Word)*, appealed for a "convocation of elected representatives of the land." In the summer of the following year Mikhailovskii helped draft the manifesto of the People's Rights party. See James H. Billington, *Mikhailovsky and Russian Populism* (Oxford: Oxford University Press, 1958), 145–146, 154–155, 158. Ed.

18. In November 1879 and January 1880 Mikhailovskii published his "Political Letters of a Socialist" in the organ of the "People's Will," a populist revolutionary organization formed in October 1879 and dedicated to the terroristic overthrow of the tsarist regime. In his "Letters" Mikhailovskii endorsed the new "political" approach over the traditional populist emphasis on social and economic goals. But his advocacy of political struggle did not necessarily include terrorism; instead, he supported an alliance with the liberals to secure a representative government that would better enable socialists to work for the social and economic improvement of the life of the *narod.* Facing the revolutionary movement, the emperor moved toward important reforms, including limited participation of elected representatives in government (which Struve may have in mind under "new ideas," together with the populist shift to "political" measures). On 1 March 1881 Alexander II was killed by the "People's Will," reaction followed under Alexander III, most populists retreated to "small deeds," and Mikhailovskii's interest in political-constitutional struggle waned (although he still worked to keep the broader goals of populism in view). Ed.

19. Ministers of Finance Ivan A. Vyshnegradskii (1887–1892) and Sergei Iu. Witte (1892–1903) promoted the development of heavy industry in Russia through imposing high import tariffs. In 1891 import duties were so high that Russia was the most protectionist country in the world. The zemstvo institutions were organs of local self-government established in European Russia in 1864. Their work was obstructed by the repressive policies and "counterreforms" of Alexander III. By an act of 1890, peasant representation in the zemstvo assemblies was reduced, gentry representation was increased, and bureaucratic interference (by provincial governors and the minister of the interior) was extended over the entire field of zemstvo activities. Ed.

20. Mikhailovskii believed that in tribal societies people enjoy simple but full lives, because at this early stage of social evolution, the "integral personality" has not yet been destroyed by division of labor and social differentiation. He also believed the hermaphrodite was an ideal personality type in its unity, wholeness, and self-sufficiency. Ed.

21. Gabriel Tarde (1843–1904), prominent French sociologist and social psychologist, whose theory of imitation was anticipated to some extent by Mikhailovskii. Ed.

22. We say "conceivable," in the sense of what we conceive or contain in consciousness.

23. Struve writes "why" here [*pochemu*], but he must mean "in what way." Ed.

24. In the debates over freedom of will, positivist thought has always stood for absolute causation or necessity, and religious fatalism for God's omnipotent will, in the sense of predestination. The parallel between positivist determinism and religious fatalism (Luther and Calvin, for example), is not by chance: both these forms of determinism are based on uncritical faith.

25. The reader familiar with the history of philosophy will recognize in the above arguments only a special form of certain basic positions of Kant's moral metaphysics.

26. Vladimir Solov'ëv, "Kont (Auguste Comte)," *Entsiklopedicheskii slovar'*, eds. K. K. Arsen'ev and F. F. Petrushevskii [vol. 16 (St. Petersburg: F. A. Brockhaus and I. A. Efron, 1895), pp. 130–131].

27. See Ranskii's perfectly correct observations about this, pp. 124–125.

28. Russian has two main words for "truth": *istina* and *pravda*. *Istina* means truth in the theoretical, objective sense, truth as "verity." It derives from "is." *Pravda* is the more general term for "truth." It derives from "right," "just," or "true-to"; it is "practical" in the Kantian sense and can include the idea of justice (*spravedlivost'*). Mikhailovskii held that *pravda* was a higher unity of *istina* and *spravedlivost'*. Also see Kistiakovskii's essay, Chapter 9 in this volume. Ed.

29. Pavel N. Miliukov (1859–1943), major Russian historian, the leading figure in the Constitutional Democratic (Kadet) party, and foreign minister in the Provisional Government. As Struve suggests, he was very impressed with Plekhanov's *Monistic View of History* and its criticism of Mikhailovskii. Intellectually he remained a positivist all his life. In 1901–1902, while Struve was planning *Problems of Idealism,* both men were involved in establishing *Osvobozhdenie (Liberation)*, the journal of the Liberation Movement. Ed.

30. *On the Question of the Development of the Monistic View of History* is Plekhanov's exposition of dialectical and historical materialism. It advances a necessitarian conception of historical development, arguing for the inevitability of Russia's capitalist development, against populist "subjective sociology." Struve's *Critical Notes (Kriticheskie zametki k voprosu ob ekonomicheskom razvitii Rossii,* St. Petersburg, 1894), published a few months before Plekhanov's work, also argued for the inevitability of capitalism but stressed its importance for cultural development, and anticipates some of the main ideas of Eduard Bernstein's revisionism. Ed.

31. Struve interpreted Alois Riehl and Georg Simmel to mean that all ethical and metaphysical elements should be excluded from social science, that is, that the "subjective method" should be rejected, with the result, however, that the very category of "ought" was eliminated. For their influence on Struve, see Richard Pipes, *Struve: Liberal on the Left, 1870–1905* (Cambridge: Harvard University Press, 1970), pp. 54–59, 106–107. Ed.

32. Aleksei A. Kozlov (1831–1901), Russian Leibnizian personalist philosopher, was a professor at Kiev University. In 1885 he founded the first (short-lived) philosophical journal in Russia, *Filosofskii trekhmesiachnik (Philosophical Quarterly)*. Panpsychism is a spiritualistic metaphysics that regards all being as psychic or conscious, at least potentially. Kozlov also characterized his system as "pluralistic monism," pluralistic because it is a personalistic metaphysics of individual spiritual substances or agents, monistic because these substances share in the same ontological reality (spirit) and find their unity in

God. Russian philosophers who worked in the same direction as Kozlov include his son, Sergei Askol'dov, who contributed to this volume (Chapter 6), and Lev Lopatin. Ed.

33. The term "new people" is from Nikolai Chernyshevskii's celebrated novel, *What Is to Be Done? From Stories about the New People* (1863). It refers to his heroes, the Russian radicals of the 1860s who represented a new morality and were dedicated to the transformation of Russian society on rationalist and materialist principles. Ed.

34. Mikhail N. Katkov (1818–1887), conservative publicist, editor of the newspaper *Moskovskie vedomosti* and the literary journal *Russkii vestnik*. A liberal and Anglophile earlier in his career, he became a nationalist and reactionary ideologist after the Polish uprising of 1863 and exercised considerable influence on Alexander III. By "Slavophilism" Struve is referring mostly to the chauvinistic nationalism of its epigones such as Ivan S. Aksakov (1823–1886), in whose journal *Rus'* Solov'ëv ceased to publish in 1883. Solov'ëv then leveled his critique in a series of articles (1883–1891) published in the liberal journal *Vestnik Evropy (European Messenger)* and collected in his *Natsional'nyi vopros v Rossii (The National Question in Russia): Sobranie sochinenii Vladimira Sergeevicha Solov'ëva*, ed. S. M. Solov'ëv and E. L. Radlov, 2d edition (St. Petersburg, 1911–1914), vol. 5, pp. 3–401. Ed.

35. Vladimir A. Miliutin (1826–1855), prominent economist and social thinker, lecturer in law at Moscow University. In 1847 he published his long study, "The Proletariat and Pauperism in England and France," in *Otechestvennye zapiski (Annals of the Fatherland)*. At that time he was one of the "Petrashevtsy," a circle of intellectuals interested in socialist ideas, led by Mikhail Butashevich-Petrashevskii. Miliutin was one of the first popularizers of Comte's ideas in Russia. His two brothers, Nikolai and Dmitrii, were liberal officials instrumental in preparing the Great Reforms of Alexander II. Ed.

36. Nikolai G. Chernyshevskii (1828–1889), radical publicist, literary critic, and hero of the radical intelligentsia. As a main representative of Russian utilitarianism, he wrote for and helped edit the influential "thick" journal *Sovremennik (The Contemporary)* from 1853 until his arrest in 1862; while in prison he wrote his famous political novel, *What Is to Be Done?* (1863). His main philosophical work is "The Anthropological Principle in Philosophy" (1860), a defense of Feuerbachian materialism. In another essay, "A Critique of Philosophical Prejudices against Communal Ownership of Land" (1858), Chernyshevskii argued, like Herzen, that the peasant commune might enable Russia to bypass capitalism. Ed.

37. Dmitrii I. Pisarev (1840–1868), radical publicist and critic of the 1860s who perhaps best embodied nihilism, the naturalistic outlook of the "thinking realist" extolled by Bazarov in Turgenev's novel *Fathers and Sons*. His essay "The Abolition of Aesthetics" (1865) sums up his attitude toward art. Ed.

38. Long one of Russia's most influential "thick" journals, *Annals of the Fatherland* became the leading journal of the populists in the 1870s. Mikhailovskii was one of its critics and editors from 1868 to 1884, when it was closed by the government. Ed.

4

The Ethical Problem in the Light of Philosophical Idealism

N. A. BERDIAEV

Zwei Dinge erfüllen das Gemüt mit immer neuer und zunehmender Bewunderung und Ehrfurcht, je öfter und anhaltender sich das Nachdenken damit beschäft.gt: Der bestirnte Himmel über mir, und das moralische Gesetz in mir.

Kant, Kritik der praktischen Vernunft[1]

Der Mensch und überhaupt jedes vernünftige Wesen, existirt als Zweck an sich selbst, nicht bloß als Mittel zum beliebigen Gebrauche für diesen oder jenen Willen, sondern muß in allen seinen, sowohl auf sich selbst, als auch auf andere vernünftige Wesen gerichteten Handlungen jederzeit als Zweck betrachtet werden.

Kant, Grundlegung zur Metaphysik der Sitten[2]

Ich gehe durch dies Volk und halte die Augen offen: sie sind kleiner geworden und werden immer kleiner: — das aber macht ihre Lehre von Glück und Tugend.[3]

Zu viel schonend, zu viel nachgebend: so its euer Erdreich! Aber daß ein Baum groß werde, dazu will er um harte Felsen harte Wurzeln schlagen![4]

Ach, daß ihr mein Wort verstündet: "tut immerhin, was ihr wollt, — aber seid erst solche, die wollen können!"[5]

Neitzsche, Also sprach Zarathustra

Ich lehre euch den Übermenschen. *Der Mensch its etwas, das überwunden werden soll. Was habt ihr getan, ihn zu überwinden?*

Nietzsche, Also sprach Zarathustra[6]

I.

The aim of my article is to attempt to pose the ethical problem on the ground of philosophic idealism. I would like to do this in broad but, to the extent possible, sure strokes. Our theme is congenial to every conscious person, especially now, when ethical questions are again being raised with tormenting urgency and when the idealistic wave that has rushed upon us demands the elucidation of all current social problems from the point of view of the eternal ethical problem. The formulation of a philosophical ethics, as the highest court of human aspirations and acts, is perhaps the most important task of contemporary thought, and here every mind philosophizing over the problems of life must do its own share. I am not speaking of small-minded practical morality, which can hardly be deduced philosophically and which leaves the deadly mark of banality on the philosopher's work; I am speaking of the philosophical posing of the basic problems of moral life.[7] Ethics is not a sociological or psychological science, tracing the laws of "what is" [*sushchee*]; it is a philosophical discipline, establishing the norms of "what ought to be" [*dolzhnoe*].[8] "In practical philosophy," Kant says, "we are not concerned with accepting reasons for what *happens,* but with accepting laws of what *ought to happen,* even if it never does happen."[9]

Ethics begins with the opposition between *what is* and *what ought to be,* and is possible only as a result of this opposition. Rejection of "what ought to be," as an autonomous category independent of empirical being [*empiricheskoe sushchee*] and not deducible from it, leads to the abolition not only of ethics, but of the moral problem itself. Ethics in the only true sense of the word is not scientific research on existing morality, on morals and moral notions: the moral problem with which ethics is concerned lies beyond everyday, conditional, conventional morality, beyond empirical good and evil with their stamp of "what is."

The ethical problem must be examined first of all from its epistemological side, and here we need to recognize the *formal* irremovability of the category of "what ought to be" (of the content of this category nothing has yet been said). The efforts of positivists and immoralists to eliminate the idea of "what ought to be" and adhere exclusively to "what is" are very naive, and sometimes even comic. The denier of "what ought to be" betrays himself at every step and falls into the most monstrous contradiction with his own anti-ethical assertions. A protest against one or another manifestation of "what is," a protest that is necessarily an evaluation of this "what is," all too often slips from the lips of the "immoralist"; an appeal to what is not yet in reality, to the better and higher from his point of view, is all too often heard from him. Man ought to reevaluate all moral values, man ought to defend his "I"[10] against every infringement, man ought to rise above the shameful feeling of pity, man ought to be strong and powerful, man ought to be "superman." So speaks the Nietzschean, who has the naiveté to consider himself an "immoralist," thinking he stands "beyond good and evil" and has finally buried the idea of "what ought to be," associated by him with antipathetic slave morality. In reality our "immoralist" stands only beyond historical good and evil, beyond the historical morality of one or another epoch, and into the eternal idea of "what ought to be" he tries to infuse a new moral content. All Nietzsche is a passionate, bitter protest against reality, against "what is," a protest in the name of an ideal, in the name of "what ought to be." I will return to Nietzsche and we will see that his proclamation of the "superman" is a proclamation of absolute duty.[11]

Too often in history present reality, with its moral tastes and demands, is taken for "what ought to be," and a revolt against it for a violation of duty. This gives rise to a mass of psychological illusions, reinforced in false theoretical ideas. There is an utter failure to understand that the pure idea of "what ought to be" is a revolutionary idea, a symbol of revolt against reality in the name of an ideal, against existing morality in the name of a higher one, against evil in the name of good. I am now taking the category of "what ought to be" in its formal, epistemological purity; later I will examine it from other sides. Kant did more than anyone to affirm once and for all the autonomy of the category of "what ought to be," as a principle given *a priori* to our consciousness; he thus made ethics independent of scientific knowledge.[12] This is his immortal service, and in this philosophical ethics must always adhere to him. Moral evaluation of "what is" from the point of view of "what ought to be" is inherent to every consciousness: every dispute about good and evil, every change among the different systems of morality, occurs within this eternal ethical function; here it is impossible to stand "beyond." Thus, following Kant, we recognize, already from the epistemological point of view, the autonomy of the ethical category of "what ought to be," or the necessity of the ethical perspective on life and the world, which sharply differs from the scientific-cognitive perspective: the moral problem, the problem of "what ought to be," cannot be derived from "what is," from empirical being. Ethics, or philosophical theory about "what ought to be," is autonomous and does not depend on science, on knowledge of "what is."[13]

Before passing from epistemological premises to further examination of the ethical problem, I want to make several clarifications about the part on ethics in my book *Subjectivism and Individualism in Social Philosophy*, because it seems I gave cause for certain misunderstandings.[14] I also want to more precisely define my relation to P. B. Struve's point of view, developed in his foreword to my book. From my account it will be clear that I have fairly significant episte-mological disagreements with Struve, but almost no ethical disagreements.[15]

"For the theory of knowledge," Struve says, "there is no sharper opposition than between 'is' [*bytie*] and 'ought' [*dolzhenstvovanie*], between 'what is true' [*istinnoe*] and 'what ought to be' [*dolzhnoe*]."[16] The indisputable truth in these words is intertwined with a misunderstanding. For me as well there is no sharper opposition, from the point of view of the theory of knowledge, than between "is" and "ought," but this is not an objection against teleological criticism.[17] Teleological criticism transcendentally (not empirically) unites truth [*istina*] and the good in the general concept of the normal, that is, of "what ought to be," but it does not also seek to unite "is" and "ought," which can be brought to unity only on the ground of metaphysics, a ground teleologi-cal critics [*krititsisty*] like Windelband do not reach.[18] I completely fail to understand why Struve considers it possible to replace the opposition between "is and ought" with that between "what is true and what ought to be." The concept of "is" cannot be identified with the concept of "what is true"; such an identification would be based on a confusion of consciousness with knowl-edge:[19] from the point of view of the theory of knowledge, "what is true" is "what ought to be," but not "what is," even though "what ought to be" cognitively is not at all identical with "what ought to be" morally, but only parallels it. I agree with Struve that the theory of knowledge is first of all an analytic-descriptive discipline, but surely he himself recognizes that at a fur-ther stage it encounters the teleological problem. When we introduce the con-cept of truth into the theory of knowledge, as the goal of knowledge, we raise the teleological problem. Truth is a value that *ought* to be realized in our knowledge, but that might not be realized. The basic, internal characteristic of truth is its *Geltung* [validity], and in this it coincides with the good. The transcendental unification of truth and the good in the concept of a universally binding norm ("what ought to be") occupies a middle position between the complete empirical distinction between truth and the good and their complete metaphysical identity. This, I want to again stress, does nothing to bridge the impassable gulf, within the limits of empirical reality and science, between

"what is" and "what ought to be." Kant firmly established the dualism between ethics and science, and I share this dualistic point of view no less than
Struve. Like other teleological critics, I compare the ideal universally binding
force of the moral good not to the natural necessity [*prinuditel'nost'*] of experience, in which "what is" is given, but rather to the equally ideal universally
binding force of truth.

All the arguments of the positivists-evolutionists against the absolute idea of
"what ought to be," independent of experience, usually miss the point because
they make the moral law, inherent to the subject, an object of scientific knowledge by placing it in the world of experience, where everything is relative.
Since we first contrast the absolute moral law (as "what ought to be") to the
entire empirical world (as "what is"), it is very easy to show that in "what is,"
as the object of empirical knowledge, there is no absolute "ought." But only by
a crude mistake can this be considered an argument against Kant and his
followers in moral philosophy. From the point of view of scientific knowledge,
which relies on experience, the positivist-evolutionist can only show that
"what ought to be" (the moral law) does not exist, that "what ought to be" is
not "what is." But it was not necessary to show this, for we know it perfectly
well and take it as the starting point of our ethical constructions. Positivists do
not want to understand that human consciousness has two different, parallel
sides: a cognitive-theoretical side, directed to the natural necessity [*zakonomernost'*] of experience ("what is"); and a moral-ethical side, directed to the
normative necessity or lawfulness of the good ("what ought to be").[20] Positivism (-empiricism) employs the scientific-cognitive function of consciousness
when it is inappropriate, and believes too naively in experience, in its exclusiveness and ultimateness, forgetting that experience is a product of our
consciousness and even only one side of it. This expresses the limitedness of
positivism, a certain blindness connected with dogmatic self-satisfaction. Besides "what is," which science knows in experience, there is still all infinity, in
which much can be discerned, only not from the point of view of scientific
knowledge. In order not to remain blind, it is necessary to pass to another side
of consciousness, in a certain sense the most important side. Kant's supreme
and immortal service is that he shattered once and for all the narrow dogmatism that believes only in the sensible world and that takes upon itself the audacity to prove that the ideas of God, freedom, and immortality are empty and
illusory. But to demand scientific-logical demonstrability for ethical claims is
to fail to understand the essence of the ethical problem. Such claims have their
own specifically ethical demonstrability; they draw their value not from the
cognitive activity of consciousness, but from its purely moral activity. The

moral law, "what ought to be," rests on unshakable foundations in the infinity that opens beyond positive empirical knowledge. This is the object of ethics. In this way the epistemology of critical idealism opens wide the doors to the free moral creativity of the human spirit.

II.

Before passing from the epistemological premises of ethics to further examination of the moral problem, I want to make several critical remarks about hedonism.[21] Hedonism in ethics is completely untenable and has already been adequately refuted by all contemporary philosophy and science, but, because of a misunderstanding explicable only by a narrow philosophical and, in general, spiritual culture, it nonetheless continues to be the most widespread point of view: it is the average man's current view on morality.[22] The removal once and for all of all the sophisms of hedonism has not only philosophical-ethical, but also social-cultural significance.

Man always strives toward pleasure — here is the psychology of hedonism. Man always ought to strive to the greatest pleasure — here is the ethical imperative of hedonism. First of all, hedonism does not withstand even the easy trial of psychological criticism. Psychology definitely teaches that we strive not toward pleasure — that would be a completely empty aspiration — but toward various objects having a certain content. If I go to a concert to hear music, then the object of my desire is not pleasure, but music; pleasure is only the consequence. If I work on scholarly research, then the object of my desire is knowledge, not pleasure. Human life is made of desires and aspirations directed toward any number of objects; the realization of these desires and aspirations is a discharge of the energy inherent to the human soul. An organic link exists between what we want, and what we are by our nature. In our life we therefore realize not pleasure and happiness, but our own nature and energy, even if this is achieved through suffering. Suffering is often preferred to pleasure; it is fused with the very essence of human individuality. When a human being tries to solve some complex problem of knowledge or struggles for the realization of social justice, his psychic life must be concentrated on these objects, for precisely they are his goals. Were he to be preoccupied with pleasure, considering it his conscious goal, he would never solve problems of knowledge or realize justice. With this we are finally convinced that hedonism is psychologically *non sens* and contradicts the basic facts of psychic life. Even John Stuart Mill says that to be happy, it does not follow that one should especially trouble over happiness.[23] I would say much more: happiness is a wonderful thing and man constantly dreams of it, but psychologically it is impossible to make happiness the goal of life or the object of one's wishes and to consciously direct one's activity to its realization. We find our highest happiness in the realization of something *valuable* from the point of view of our conscious nature, such as the realization of the good in our will, truth in our knowledge, or beauty in our feelings; these values are also goals, the realization of which constitutes spiritual life. The whole content of psychic life disappears when pleasure and happiness are the only goals in the field of consciousness. The quality of happiness is entirely determined by the quality of the objects of desire, that is, by one's spiritual nature. Here we encounter an insurmountable difficulty for the hedonistic theory of morality.

Pleasures are quantitatively incommensurable and, adding them up, we cannot at all say in what consists the greatest happiness. The pleasure from good roast beef or champagne cannot be compared with the pleasure from a philosophical book or a work of art; it cannot even be asked what gives the greater *quantity* of pleasure. In a word, we must recognize that pleasures — the result of the realization of desires — are *qualitatively* different, and that this quality depends on the objects of desire, on the quality of our wants. Happiness is a still less definite concept than pleasure, and the question of the quality of happiness cannot be reduced to its quantity. If happiness is separated from the whole content of human consciousness, which imparts to it a qualitative coloring, then a completely empty concept is obtained, from which nothing can be drawn. But hedonistic ethics recognizes no *qualitative* criteria; it evaluates everything according to the *quantity* of pleasure. Here we face an obvious absurdity. Hedonism must recognize not only its own psychological untenability, for pleasure is not the goal of life, but also its own ethical untenability, for no moral imperatives can be derived by relying on pleasure. Pleasure is evaluated not by its quantity — quantitatively it is incommensurable and incomparable — but by its quality, which is determined by quite different, in fact ethical criteria.

We know perfectly well that pleasure is a plus, and suffering a minus; we also know that happiness is man's dream, but all this has very little relation to ethics. Pleasure can be hideous and immoral, happiness can be shameful, while suffering can be morally valuable and heroic. The end that ethics seeks is not the empirical happiness of people, but their *ideal moral perfection*. Therefore, in opposition to hedonists of all shades, I acknowledge the following necessary psychological premise of ethics: morality is an autonomous *quality* of the human soul, it cannot be derived from such nonethical concepts as pleasure or happiness. Happiness itself is subject to *moral* judgment, which determines the quality of happiness, recognizing it as worthy or unworthy of our moral nature.

Let me say a few words about a type of hedonism that can be called social, altruistic utilitarianism. This is considered the most progressive direction in ethics, practically the highest form of moral consciousness. The dogmas of social utilitarianism have turned into a deadening cliché and hinder any profound penetration into the very heart of the moral problem. In essence the moral problem is quite eliminated here, for the question of *value* is replaced by the question of *utility*.

The general good, the great happiness of the greatest number of people — here is the ethical criterion advanced by social, altruistic utilitarianism. As a whole this direction is subject to the critique of hedonism in general, but it possesses its own specific shortcomings as well. If it is impossible to construct ethics on individual happiness, then universal happiness is already a completely fictitious concept. How is it possible to pass from a human being's individual happiness to the general happiness of humanity; in the name of what can a human being be subordinated to the general good and be seen as a means? Why does altruistic utilitarianism put the happiness of another human being higher than my own happiness; if happiness is all the same the ultimate criterion, why do my deeds qualify as moral only when I serve another's happiness? There is no answer to these questions, only a vicious circle. It is possible to show how a historical human being serves the general good, and consequently it is possible to carry out a *genetic* justification of social utilitarianism. But I am not asking about this, I am asking about an *ethical* justification. For ethics it is important to show why some principle is "what ought to be," not why it turns out to be necessary. There is no ethical justification for passing from the happiness of one human being to the happiness of another or to the happiness of all. Serving my own pleasure or happiness does not have any *moral* value, but neither does serving the pleasure or happiness of Peter and Ivan or even of all the Peters and Ivans in the world, because my pleasure and happiness and Ivan's pleasure and happiness are completely equal in value and fall outside the sphere of ethics in exactly the same way, having nothing in common with the *moral* ends of life. Adding up such ethical zeroes as the pleasure and happiness of X or Y, no ethical quantity can be obtained. Egoistic hedonism contains fewer internal contradictions than altruistic hedonism; it at least fairly unambiguously destroys the moral problem and exposes the immoral nature of all hedonism. And if it is shameful to dedicate one's life to one's own greatest pleasure, then it is no less shameful to turn oneself into the instrument of another's greatest pleasure.

It will be seen below how much hedonism and utilitarianism, individual as well as social, sharply contradict the basic idea of ethics — the idea of *personhood* [*lichnost'*] and its development toward perfection. These are in essence deeply reactionary doctrines, and it is only through a misunderstanding and failure to think things through that progressive people support them. Satisfaction and well-being, in which hedonism and utilitarianism see the only end of life and morality, do not include higher development, for otherwise such development would need to be put above contentment and happiness, and this would contradict the basic principle of hedonism. That which seems to hedonism as the ultimate end is in fact only a temporary moment of equilibrium, a current personal or historical system of accommodation, which is constantly upset by further development toward higher and higher forms of life. Progress, or movement toward the supreme goal, takes place through great dissatisfaction and suffering, which have enormous moral value, completely unlike contentment and well-being.[24]

The evolutionary direction in ethics tries to introduce certain amendments to hedonism and utilitarianism, and brings to ethics the idea of the development of life.[25] But, unfortunately, evolutionism passes by the moral problem; it gives no answer to the question of the morally *valuable,* of *"what ought to be,"* and in the end does not rise above hedonism. The difference is only that evolutionism speaks not about utility or the greatest pleasure, but about the greatest fitness, that is, once more about something that has nothing to do with ethics. A specific and grave sin is inherent to evolutionism in particular: worship before the God of necessity instead of the God of freedom. Evolutionary theory often successfully explains the historical development of morals, of moral notions and tastes,[26] but morality itself slips away from it; the moral law is outside its narrow cognitive horizon. I have already spoken about this from the point of view of epistemology. Evolutionism can only indicate *how* morality (some eternal value, absolute "ought") is revealed in the process of social development, but it has no right to derive morality from nonmorality, from the absence of morality; it must presuppose morality as something given before any evolution and as only unfolding in it, not arising from it. Evolutionism has as little place in philosophical ethics as in the theory of knowledge; it is appropriate only in psychological and sociological research, and all evolutionary arguments against absolute morality are strikingly uncritical. Marxism, as a philosophical understanding of the world, shares all the sins of evolutionism and especially testifies to the necessity of ethical idealism.[27]

There is no longer any need to break lances proving the idea that all of "what is" develops, but from this indisputable truth not one argument can be drawn against the absolute moral law, which we conceive as the category of "what ought to be," not "what is." From evolutionism only one true conclusion can be made: the absolute moral law, the ethical norms of "what ought to be," are only gradually realized in the life of humanity, that is, through social development they become part of "what is," of empirical reality. Ethical norms themselves can be as little evolutionized as logical laws; morality is immutable, and only the degree of approximation to it changes. The absoluteness and eternity of the moral law we see not in the fact that it is always and everywhere present in empirical being, not in the immutability of existing morality, but in its immutable value as "what ought to be," in the fact that this value does not depend on empirical reality, that the moral law is the autonomous lawgiver of our consciousness and that positive [*prinuditel'nyi*] experience does not have force over the moral good, valuable in itself.

No hardened empirical content can pretend to the title of absolute morality; the absolute moral norm is always only a call forward, ever forward—it is a beacon, shining to us from infinity. The moral law is an immediate revelation of the absolute, it is the voice of God inside man, it is given for "this world" but it is "not of this world."[28] If evolutionism with its limitedness has no significance for ethics, the teleological idea of progress has great significance for it. We recognize the principle of the maximum of life, its highest development, but for us this principle does not have a biological meaning, as it does for the evolutionists, but an ethical meaning.

III.

Kant gave us much more than only a formal, epistemological substantiation of ethics. The whole content of ethics can be constructed relying only on Kant. Kant recognized the absolute value of a human being [*chelovek*]: a human being is an end in itself, who from the moral point of view cannot be treated as a means; all people, moreover, are morally equal in value.[29] This is the eternal, absolute moral law, and the basic condition of any realization of the moral good; the whole fluid content of morality can be deduced only from it, and can be justified only by it.[30] All my further exposition will be an attempt to disclose and substantiate the ethical principle of the human person [*lichnost'*], as an end in itself and an absolute value.

The fundamental idea of ethics is the idea of the *person,* the only bearer of the moral law. What is personhood from the point of view of ethics; what is the relation of the ethical idea of personhood to the empirical person, with all its diverse concrete content, in which the blend of beauty and ugliness, high and low, sparkles? Here, it seems to me, the tight link of ethics with metaphysics, and ultimately with religion, is illuminated. Within the limits of experience, with which positive science is concerned, the ethical idea of personhood slips away. We cannot take the empirical person as an absolute value, for in empirical reality a human being too often fails to be a *human being,* a human being whom we consider an end in itself and who must be sacred. This sharp contradiction between the empirical person and the ideal person makes the moral problem a tragic problem. There is great — in truth, tragic — moral suffering in the impossibility for us, within the limits of empirical relations, of honoring the human being in Judas the betrayer, of honoring the absolute value in him, of seeing a brother in him, an end in itself equal to us in spirit. This takes us to the very depths of the moral problem. *The moral problem is first of all the problem of the relation between the empirical "I" and the ideal, spiritual, "normal" "I."*[31] Kant proceeded from the dualism of the "sensible" and "moral-rational" nature of man and saw in this dualism the whole *raison d'être* of the moral problem. He recognized moral value only in that which flows from respect for the moral law, not from sensible inclinations and instincts, which in themselves are neither moral nor immoral. From this Kant drew certain false rigoristic conclusions, directed against the life of feeling and the instinctive inclinations of human nature, but true and profound is his idea that morality is a distinctive human quality, independent of sensible life, that it is the conformity of the will (practical reason) to its own laws [*zakonomernost' voli*].[32]

Thus, we come to the conclusion that *morality is first of all the internal relation of a human being to himself, the search for and realization of his spiritual "I," the triumph of "normative" consciousness in "empirical" consciousness.* In usual language this is called the *development of personhood* in a human being. Morality, as the relation of one human being to another, is the unconditional recognition in every human being of his spiritual "I" and the unconditional respect for his rights. It is also what in everyday language is called *humanness:* to be humane means to recognize and respect in every human being a brother in spirit, to consider his spiritual nature the same end in itself as one's own spiritual nature, and to promote its development on the ground of a universally human spiritual culture.

From such a formulation of the question it is clear that the moral problem is first of all an individualistic problem and that it becomes a social problem only in its further conclusions. But ethical individualism will be suspended in the air if it is left on the ground of experience. The empirical person, as such, cannot lead to ethical individualism, but throws us into the arms of hedonism and immoralism. In short, the idea of personhood and the moral problem (the subject of which is the person) are comprehensible only on the ground of spiritualism.[33] Kant, with perfect consistency, also postulated spiritualism.[34] A human being possesses absolute value because he is an eternal spirit, and people are equal in value because they are of one and the same spiritual substance. Spiritual individuality possesses absolute, inalienable rights, the value of which cannot be calculated; there is nothing higher than this individuality except its own highest development. What is morally valuable in a human being is determined not by the approval or condemnation of other people, not by the good of society, not by the external world in general, but by accordance with one's own internal moral nature, by the relation to one's own God. Only such an approach removes the degrading and opprobrious view of morality that sees in it some external measure against man, something imposed on him from without, something almost hostile to him. Usually it is not understood that Kant himself — the very same Kant who put the idea of duty at the basis of his moral philosophy — identified morality with internal freedom, that it is not Kant's ethics that is inimical to personhood and its freedom, but rather utilitarian and evolutionary ethics, which resort to purely external criteria, which evaluate the sacred rights of the person from the point of view of social utility and fitness, and which see the moral ideal in a disciplined herd animal. The moral law is the autonomous lawmaker in man's moral-rational nature; it is not forced on him from without, but constitutes the very essence of his spiritual individuality. To fulfill the moral law does not mean to limit one's "I" in the name of "not-I," but to affirm one's true "I." Moral conscience is responsibility before oneself, before one's own spiritual "I."

IV.

The basic, governing idea of ethics is thus the idea of the "I," from which all morality must be derived. Here we encounter the question of the relation between "I" and "thou" and must untangle a number of sophisms connected with this central question of ethics. The majority of moral systems recognizes the ethical primacy of "thou" over "I," the primacy of "other" over "one's own"; in the moral philosophy of the nineteenth century this was called "altruism," and it sought to replace the true spiritual essence of human life. Friedrich Nietzsche's protest against the denigration of the "I," a denigration done ostensibly from moral considerations, needs to be recognized as one of his outstanding contributions.[35] Only this affirmation of the primacy of "I" over "thou" is not, from our point of view, "immoralism," but rather the greatest triumph of genuine morality.

The concepts of "I" and "thou" are relative, they can be transposed at will: if A is "I," then B in relation to it will be "thou" or "other"; but B is also an "I" and for it A is "thou." Ethics takes a detached view of A as of B, so for ethics there exists no comparative difference between "I" and "thou." For ethics A and B are equally "I's," one is no less a human person than the other, and these "I's" are equal in value. "Thou" is a completely negative concept; in the "other" it is possible to find something positive only if it is seen as an "I." Common altruism in its utilitarian version always avows the moral supremacy of "thou" and all "thou's," combined in the concept of "not-I" over "I"; in this way it annihilates the "I," the only bearer of the moral principle, and so leads to an absurdity. This means throwing out the baby with the bathwater, destroying morality out of moral fervor. Adding up all the limitations and denials of "I's" done in the name of "others," it is impossible to obtain in the total an affirmation or development of these "I's." We come up against a morally empty place, to some universal depersonalization and extinction of the spirit, for only the developed "I" is a bearer of the spiritual principle. I would especially stress that in ethics we must recognize not only the primacy of the "I" (of the person, spiritual individuality), but must even recognize this "I" as the only element of ethics. Then the ancient question of the relation between "egoism" and "altruism" takes on new light.

This opposition between "egoism" and "altruism" is in essence extraordinarily vulgar, and ought not to have any place in philosophic ethics. The stamp of moral disapprobation lies on the word "egoism," the stamp of moral approval on the word "altruism." Why? Philologically, "egoism" comes from the word "I," and "altruism" from the word "other." If we recall the distinction made above, basic for ethics, between the empirical "I" and the spiritual "I," between our sensible and moral-rational nature, then all misunderstanding disappears. Our real "I" — the "I" that has absolute value, the "I" that we must affirm and realize and for whose rights we must struggle — is the spiritual, ideal "I," our moral-rational nature. To be an *ego*-ist in this sense means to be a moral human being, to be a *person*. But in ordinary life egoism is understood mainly as following one's lower inclinations, as slavery to empirical nature, and ethics condemns this egoism as the defeat of the truly human, spiritual "I" in its struggle with the contingent empirical "I." Defending one's own human personhood does not mean defending its whole diverse empirical content; it is a stark fact that in this empirical content there is much that radically contradicts the very idea of personhood, much that is hideous and revolting, and all this is foreign to our "I" and comes from outside. There takes place in man a tormenting process of the emancipation of the "I" from lower slavish motives; this is a working-out of personhood, a moral development by which higher spiritual energy is attained. Now let us see what "altruism" offers with such a formulation of the question.

Eudaemonists frequently defend altruism, saying that it is necessary to put the happiness of another human being higher than one's own, and even to sacrifice one's own happiness in the name of another's. This whole argument is deprived of any ethical meaning whatsoever. Every "I" has the same right to happiness as every "thou"; no one has the advantage here, but at the same time both the happiness of the "I" and that of the "other" are equally nonethical concepts, as was demonstrated above. If "altruism" demands that one's spiritual "I" be sacrificed in the name of the happiness of the "other," then this demand is positively immoral, because my spiritual "I" has absolute moral value, while the happiness of the "other" is sometimes an excellent thing, but it has no moral value. If altruism, however, demands that one sacrifice the lower instincts of his empirical nature in the name of the spiritual, moral-rational nature of another human being, that one not infringe on the inalienable rights of another's spiritual nature, that one facilitate another's spiritual development through common work in the creation of human culture, then all this is demanded first of all by one's own spiritual "I." Since this moment enters into the struggle for one's own moral personhood, the word "altruism" does not apply here. A human being must sometimes sacrifice his life to save his spiritual "I"; here sacrifice and death are likewise ways of moral self-realization and are justified only as such. In general *personhood* (the "I," spiritual individuality), with its inalienable rights, stands above "altruism" and "egoism." This common opposition has only one true meaning: ascertainment of the different *qualities* in personhood or, as it is usually put, discrimination between higher and lower needs, between what morally elevates a human being and what debases him.

It has already long been time to eliminate this ethical fiction of "thou" and "others," which only hinders the correct posing and solution of the ethical problem. The relation of one human being to another is ethically derivative from the relation of a human being to himself. Obligations must be derived from rights: only a right is positive, an obligation is nothing other than the demand for a right to be recognized. A human being is obliged not only to respect a right, but also to further its realization. To recognize and respect in the "other" a human being, to relate to him *humanely,* means to see in him an "I," a value like one's own "I." To be *humane* means to be a human being, to develop the spiritual person in oneself, in the same way that not to be *humane,* not to recognize in every "I" an unconditional value, means to be an animal, to still not have reached the state we call human personhood. And higher moral consciousness demands that every human being relate to every other human being not as to "thou" — out of compassion for whom he must sacrifice his "I," or sacrifice it accommodating the demand of "others" — but as to "I," to the same end in itself, as he himself. Higher humanity demands an equality of relations, of which there is still nothing in pedestrian "altruism." Unconditional respect for the human person, for its autonomy, for its right to self-determination — here is the basic feature of the ethical point of view we are developing. The spiritual individuality of the human being — in the name of which a whole living struggle is being waged, by which a whole social movement is justified, and to which all the progressive aspirations of humanity are gravitating — is an individuality that for positivism in general and hedonism and social utilitarianism in particular simply does not exist, but is rather sacrificed (in the sphere of theoretical thought) to the social good, to historical adaptation, and so forth. The moral liberation of the human person demands recognition of the following truth, an elementary one to our view: the moral problem is not a problem of the herd as, unfortunately, not only reactionaries but many progressives are inclined to think; it is solved neither by the state, nor by the social process, nor by the judgment of people; it is an internal, individual problem of the human "I" as it strives toward ideal perfection.

V.

We have come to the conclusion that the moral good is the affirmation of the "I," self-realization. This leads to the idea of the "normal" development of the person. Not every affirmation and development of one's own person is a moral good, only that which leads to perfection, to the ideal spiritual state. From the ethical point of view the realization of one's "I" and the attainment of ideal perfection are identical concepts. But the tragedy of the moral problem is that the absolute ideal of moral perfection cannot be concretely expressed in terms of experience and can never be fully realized empirically. Our whole moral life, the whole moral development of the individual human being as well as all humanity, presupposes such an absolute ideal, without which life would be deprived of any meaning. The tortuous *search* for the supreme moral good, a search that constitutes the most valuable content of the life of humanity, presupposes that there is such a good, that it is not a phantom, and that man *must* draw closer to it. The idea of *moral development* is inconceivable without the idea of a supreme *end,* which must be realized through this development.

We can formulate the absolute condition of the realization of the moral good: it is the recognition of the unconditional value and right to self-determination of the human person, recognition of it as an end in itself (not a means), together with recognition of the equal value of people. From this flows the principles of humanity and justice, for which we strive to find ever more perfect expression in historical development. But the absolutely valuable content, the highest good with which the life of a human being (recognized as an end in itself) ought to be filled, cannot be indicated in empirical reality; it is never "what is," but is rather an eternal challenge to infinite development, to the highest spiritual energy, disappearing beyond the limits of any given human horizon. Every attempt to more precisely define the absolute good, the good that ought to be the content of the life of a human being as an end in itself, inevitably takes us beyond the limits of the world of experience. The idea of the realization of the "I" through achievement of the ideal spiritual state is fixed in eternity and infinity, where boundless perspectives open up before us. The human person, unique and individual, always gravitates in its striving for perfection to one and the same point, to the Supreme Good, in which all *values* are united. Infinite power and might, infinite knowledge, everlasting beauty and harmony—all enter into the realization and development of the "I." We must conceive the final step on this long path, on which the empirical world is only a small lump, as the joining of the individual "I" with the universal "I," or, in more common terminology, as the merging of the human with the Divine. In this, the Divine is conceived not as something foreign or external to the human "I," not as something to which this "I" must be subordinated, but as its own ideal of ultimate perfection.

Metaphysics, to which ethics inevitably leads, unites the individual spiritual "I" and the universal spiritual "I" in the concept of the Supreme Good.[36] On all these claims, which can be developed only in a metaphysical treatise, teleological criticism casts its own unique light. The supra-individual consciousness appears as the subject or bearer of universally obligatory norms—logical, ethical, and aesthetic. Therefore, moral development, which is accomplished in the human person, for it and through it, is the triumph of "normative" consciousness in empirical consciousness, the triumphant march of the universal "I" or, in the terminology of ontology, of the world spirit.[37] The starting point of view on ethics can only be individualistic. The moral problem is the problem of individualism, the problem of *personhood,* but it is necessary to overcome individualism metaphysically and arrive at universalism or, more correctly, to combine individualism and universalism harmoniously in one worldview. I consider it possible to at once profess a consistent ethical individualism and a no less consistent ethical universalism. About this important question we shall now speak.

VI.

In his foreword to my aforementioned book, Struve opposed his ethical individualism to my ethical universalism. Here, I think, there can be no opposition. Individualism and universalism revolve in different planes, answering different sides of the ethical problem and supplementing each other. I can with every right say that Struve is a universalist in my sense and that I am an individualist in his sense; our ethical disagreements are only apparent and lie exclusively in the sphere of epistemology.[38] The extent to which I share Struve's ethical individualism is sufficiently clear from my entire exposition. But now let us see why individualism inevitably crosses over to universalism.

We have seen that the basic idea of ethics is the idea of "personhood," the idea of the "I," which must be realized and the sanctity of which must be recognized. But recognizing the ideal, "normative" character of this "I" and the universally binding force of the moral law inherent to it, we overcome both ethical empiricism and solipsism.[39] From the ethical point of view, personhood — the "I," individuality — is everything, but only because we conceive a universal spiritual content in it. A human being is sacred and inviolable not in his contingent empirical content, but as a bearer of a higher spiritual principle. In the "individual," in the human person, we esteem the "universal," that is, one spiritual nature, multifariously and individually manifesting itself in the empirical world. A human being honors his God in another human being. Ethical individualism without universalism is deprived of its *raison d'être;* it turns fatally into empiricism and so enters into contradiction with the very idea of individuality and morality. It can be said directly that a person's moral level is a function of the degree of his penetration by universal life and interests. A human being realizes his spiritual "I" only by leaving the narrow sphere of individual experiences (in the special sense of the word) and entering the broad arena of world life. He finds his "individuality" by developing the "universal" in himself. Struve also recognizes ethical universalism, postulating a "moral world-order." To recognize a "moral world-order" means to recognize that the world has moral meaning, that individual life is found in an indissoluble moral link with universal life, with the world-order.

Such a harmonious combination of individualism and universalism leads to the following resolution of the ethical problem. The moral contradiction between "what ought to be" and "what is," between the human "I," striving toward ideal perfection, and empirical reality, is resolved by two paths, which in the end converge: by the path of *individual development* and the path of *universal development.* The individual thirst for perfection, for realization of the spiritual "I," is satisfied by infinite individual development, which is secured in spiritual immortality, and by infinite universal development or the progress of culture.[40] By these two paths a human being proceeds to the Supreme Good. The free spirit raises a banner of protest against the surrounding world, against the empirical reality that oppresses it. It strives to put the stamp of its primordial freedom on the external world and to create its own culture, using the necessary material means for ideal goals. Progress from the philosophic and ethical point of view is first of all the liberation of the human "I" from external paths.⁴¹ Kant gives almost no indications about how the moral law can and must be realized in human life.⁴² In this respect the philosophy of Fichte and Hegel was a big step forward, for it advanced the question about the realization of the moral good in history. Posing this question leads to the philosophy of progress, which was just barely hinted at in Kant. In this way the individual moral problem turns into the social problem.

VII.

Society, social development, is a necessary instrument of the moral development of the human person. The person has ethical (not sociological) primacy over society; evaluation of society is always conducted by the person, by virtue of the autonomous moral law inherent to him, a law not derived from society. Every social form requires justification from the point of view of ethical individualism. But the moral law is embodied in the life of humanity through social progress; the human person develops and works out its own individuality through diverse interaction with the social sphere, in social-psychic intercourse with people.⁴³ To be capable of unfolding in the empirical history of humanity, spiritual culture (the bearer of which is the person) needs a material, social basis. Therefore we demand economic development and welcome more perfect forms of production. After that, to guarantee the natural rights of the person [*estestvennoe pravo lichnosti*],⁴⁴ the external relations of people must be regulated and formalized, that is, freedom and equality — demanded and sanctioned by the internal moral autonomy of every human person — must be realized in the state and legal order. Legal and political progress is nothing other than the realization and guaranteeing of the absolute *natural rights* of man,⁴⁵ which need no historical sanction, because these rights are the immediate expression of the moral law, given before any experience. All economic progress, constituting from the sociological point of view a *conditio sine qua non* of any culture, always remains, from the ethical point of view, only a means for the triumph of the natural rights of the person. Therefore, the social side of the moral problem is rooted first of all in the demands of "natural law." Every new form of public life [*obshchestvennost'*], that is, every new form of production with the social organization corresponding to it, must be evaluated and justified as a *means* for the realization of an ideal *end* — the natural rights of the person, freedom and equality, these basic moments in the realization of natural law.⁴⁶

But natural rights themselves are not subject to any valuation, whether from the point of view of public benefit, public well-being, public adaptability, and so forth, for they already represent an absolute value. It would be impossible, for example, to strip a human being of his right to freedom of conscience because the majority found it useful to do so. The person in his "natural" rights [*estestvennye prava*] is sovereign; only under the pressure of brute force could he waive these rights. Ethically, nothing can justify violation of the natural rights of man, for there is no end in the world, in the name of which the sacred strivings of the human spirit could be infringed upon or in the name of which the principle of the human person as an end in itself could be betrayed. We reject the ethical-legal principle of "popular sovereignty" and oppose it to the principle of *inalienable* personal rights. From this flows a moral imperative: struggle for the natural rights of man, do not permit violation of them. To fight for one's natural rights is a matter of honor for every human being, and it is a matter of conscience to relate likewise to the natural rights of other people. In concrete historical circumstances the struggle for the "natural rights" of man takes the form of a struggle for the oppressed and exploited. In contemporary society, for example, it takes the form of a struggle for the rights of the working masses.

The struggle for "sociality" [*sotsial'nost'*], or for a form of social cooperation, is ethically always subordinate to the struggle for "humanness," or to the struggle for man, and is sanctioned by it; even so, those who, out of higher humanitarian considerations, come to profess social-political indifferentism cannot be condemned forcefully enough. Such indifference can result only from not having thought things through. Philosophical and ethical idealism must inspire and ennoble the social-political struggle and instill in it a living spirit, but in no way can it lead to a passive relation to the surrounding world or to patient contemplation of violence and outrage over man and his spiritual nature. I will return to the question of the relation between morality and freedom, and will try to show all the sophistry behind the claim that internal freedom does not require external freedom. I would brand with shame those who blatantly and brazenly permit themselves a shocking contradiction: avowal of the unconditional value of the human spirit, on the one hand, and justification of oppression, exploitation, and violation of the elementary rights of man, on the other. The idealist spirit is a spirit of freedom, a spirit of light, which calls forward, to the struggle for the right of humanity to infinitely improve itself. Only the complete eclipse of thought can explain how the most radical idea of absolute "ought," understood spiritualistically, could be associated with the strengthening of the most outrageous and reactionary forms of "what is." Absolute "ought" can be fixed to no set form of empirical being; "what ought to be," about which the spiritualist speaks if he is worthy of the name, is a call to eternal struggle with the existing in the name of ever higher forms of life. It is an idea that never permits one to be content with anything.

VIII.

The moral problem cannot be written about now without saying something about Friedrich Nietzsche, as I am especially impelled to do by the point of view I tried to develop above. With time, Nietzsche, the "immoralist" and denier of morality, will be counted among the outstanding moralists, among the heralds of a new, positive, free morality. His suffering image stands on the border of two epochs and combines in itself the most dogged contradictions. Nietzsche is first of all an idealist: his is a deeply religious soul, and the longing for a lost God runs like a red thread through everything he wrote. "Do we hear nothing as yet," cries the madman in *The Gay Science*, "nothing as yet of the noise of the gravediggers who are burying the God? Do we smell nothing as yet of the divine decomposition? Gods, too, decompose. God is dead. God remains dead. And we have killed him. How shall we comfort ourselves, the murderers of all murderers? What was holiest and mightiest of all that the world has yet owned has bled to death under our knives."[47] Nietzsche approaches the moral problem with a morbid passion and an astuteness not often met among "moralists." The agonizing search for the absolute, for the highest good, and all the bitterness of spiritual losses, took in Nietzsche the form of an impassioned protest against historical morality, against the morals of altruism, social utilitarianism, hedonism, and evolutionism, a protest in the name of the sovereign "I." The "last man,"[48] the same one who has invented happiness, forgot about this "I" in his historical morality. To Nietzsche all contemporary prevailing morality seems cowardly, slavish, a herd morality, a purely negative, police morality, for at its basis lies constraint and limitation of the "I." Nietzsche's critical work has everlasting value and constitutes his immortal service. His protest against petty bourgeois morals — against ethical theories that seek higher moral sanction not in the "I" but in public opinion and well-being, in adaptation to the environment, and so forth — clears the ground for a more correct and profound posing of the moral problem, forgotten by the "last man," in his pursuit of petty virtues and petty well-being. . . . [Berdiaev quotes at length from Zarathustra's discourse, "On Virtue that Makes Small."[49]]

Nietzsche strives toward a *positive* morality: not toward negation and curtailment of the "I," toward guarding against pickpockets, toward limiting appetites, but toward affirmation and realization of the "I."[50] It does not follow, speaking figuratively, that one should pilfer others' handkerchiefs — this is a truth not worth arguing, and in essence Nietzsche himself accepts all this external, limiting morality. But it would be degrading for man to see in this the essence of the moral problem, which lies much deeper and only begins when the morality of the external drill, the police-hygienic morality for making life tidy, is already coming to an end, having done its work. Nietzsche sensed these depths of the moral problem and was outraged by theories that see in morality an external measure against the human "I" on the part of "others," "society," or "public opinion," all in the interests of general well-being. But Nietzsche himself did not cope well with the moral problem and muddled it.

What does morality reject, what does it restrict? It rejects every infringement of the "I," it restricts every manifestation of disrespect for the rights of the "I." But what does it affirm? It affirms the "I," its right to self-determination and infinite development, its craving for strength and perfection. There are thus many points of contact between us and Nietzsche. For us morality is an internal and positive problem, not external and negative. Morality is not a measure against hunger and cold that loses all meaning with the elimination of evil; on the contrary, it is a positive value that grows parallel with the negation of evil, *ad infinitum.*

All that Nietzsche says about the altruistic morals of pity and compassion contains a terribly profound psychological and ethical truth. None of this morality overcomes the opposition between slave and master,[51] weak and strong, and therefore it cannot be the morality of the future. I think it is a disgrace to human dignity to construct morals on the revolt of slaves, of the weak and suffering, who bring with themselves the demand for limitation and curtailment of the "I," who infringe upon the very essence of life and the spirit. "Woe to all who love," Zarathustra says, "without having a height that is above their pity!"[52] And in fact to relate to a human being only with pity and compassion means to see in him not a human being equal in value to oneself, but a weak and sorry slave; it means, finally, to be oneself a slave to his sufferings and weaknesses. There is a higher morality, which will correspond to a higher level of human development. It is based on the revolt of human strength, not weakness; it demands not pity for the slave, but respect for the human being, relating to him as to "I." It demands the affirmation and realization of every "I" and, consequently, not the extinguishing of life, but the raising of it to a higher spiritual state. Only such a morality corresponds to a high consciousness of human dignity and befits that part of contemporary humanity that is leading the great liberation movement.

The moral law demands, first of all, that a human being never be a slave, even if it is slavery to another's suffering and weakness and to one's own pity for him, that a human being never smother his own spirit or renounce his rights to a powerful life and limitless development and improvement, even if it is a renunciation in the name of the well-being of other people or all society.

The human "I" must not bow its proud head before anything except its own ideal of perfection, its own God, before which it is alone responsible. The human "I" stands above the judgment of other people, above the judgment of society and even of all being, for the only judge is the moral law that constitutes the true essence of the "I" and that is freely acknowledged by it. The demonic protest of the person against external morality, against public opinion and even against the whole external world, seems "immoral" to many, to too many, but from our point of view it is a profoundly moral revolt of the autonomous moral law — a law opening up infinite perspectives to man — against the feeble efforts of any given objective reality to turn a human being into a means or instrument. It is a revolt of the strong in spirit, in the name of spiritual strength, and therefore it possesses internal moral justification, against which the whole surrounding world is morally impotent. In Nietzsche's "immoral" demonism there are elements of that higher morality that ordinary, established morality typically condemns.

Man not only has the right to, but even must, become "superman," for the "superman" is the path from man to God. "*I teach you the superman*," Zarathustra says to the crowd gathered around him. "Man is something that shall be overcome. What have you done to overcome him?"

"All beings so far have created something beyond themselves; and do you want to be the ebb of this great flood and even go back to the beasts rather than overcome man? What is the ape to man? A laughingstock or a painful embarrassment. And man shall be just that for the superman: a laughingstock or a painful embarrassment."

"Behold, I teach you the superman. The superman is the meaning of the earth. Let your will say: the superman *shall be* the meaning of the earth!"[53]

But further Nietzsche enters onto a false path.

The idea of the "superman" is a religious-metaphysical idea. Zarathustra is a religious preacher and idealist, but Nietzsche is thrown off track by a biological understanding of the "superman"; to his lofty ideal clings earthly filth, the filth of man's exploitation of man. Nietzsche is a dreamer whose idealistic soul is poisoned by naturalism.[54] He splendidly understands the failure of all positivist theories of morality, but he himself nonetheless remains on the ground of naturalistic positivism. He could not understand that the affirmation and realization of the "I," its craving for infinite power and perfection, can be conceived neither biologically, in the forms of a Darwinian struggle for existence and selection, nor at all empirically, that here it is necessary to postulate a supra-empirical ideal world. An animal relation between the "superman" and man would be only a slavish imitation of natural necessity and would take us from the heights of ethics to the lowest parts of zoology.[55] At the heights of ethics, an aristocracy of the spirit (of the superman) can be imagined only in the image of a spiritual leader of people; this will not be physical, economic, or political coercion, but the rule of spiritual perfection in knowledge and beauty. Carlyle with his "cult of heroes,"[56] despite his antiquated tendencies, was in this respect more farsighted than Nietzsche.

The "I" on behalf of which Nietzsche undertook a titanic struggle, the "I" that might well turn out to be the most ordinary, empirical fact in all its grotesqueness, does not exist within the narrow bounds of the positivist-biological understanding of life. On this path we can meet the commonplace, everyday egoism of the average bourgeois, but not the ideal self-realization about which Nietzsche dreams in his proclamation of "individualism." In some of his positive constructions, which bear the stamp of "immorality" and cruelty, Nietzsche errs in the direction of naturalistic evolutionism and even hedonism, against which he himself so often protests. If the "I" is seen as a chance empirical bundle of perceptions, if only the sensible nature of man is recognized, then there cannot be any talk of ethical individualism, and we risk getting trapped by the crudest hedonism and will again have to construct morality not internally, but externally, subordinating personhood to the external criteria of "utility," "fitness," and so forth. But in such a case what is that "I" which rises in revolt in Nietzsche and gives such a brilliant critique of all petty bourgeois morality and all positivist theories of morality? Everything in Nietzsche that is valuable and excellent, everything that his name adorns in everlasting glory, is based on one supposition, necessary for any ethics, the supposition of an ideal "I," of spiritual "individuality." And with this, "immoralism" is philosophically eliminated as a colossal misunderstanding, and Nietzsche can extend his hand to his enemy — Kant. They both struggled for the moral autonomy of the human person, for its sacred right to self-determination. Kant provides the philosophical foundations for ethical individualism, for recognition of a human being as an end in itself and unconditional value, while Nietzsche overcomes the petty bourgeois elements of Kantian practical morality and prepares the free morality of the future, the morality of a strong human individuality.

If we take the antithesis of Nietzsche's morality — Christian morality — we will find in it the same ideal essence. The central idea that Christianity brought to the development of humanity's moral self-consciousness is the idea of the absolute value of the human being, as the image and likeness of God, and of the moral equality of people before God. Together with this, Christianity understood the moral problem as an *internal* problem, the problem of the relation of the human spirit to God. This was an enormous step forward compared to the moral consciousness of the ancient world, which did not recognize the absolute value of the human being, subordinating person to state and demanding external sanction for morality. Today's idea of personhood is incomparably better developed than the incomplete idea of two thousand years ago, but it is still Christian spiritualism that gives the eternal sanction to the ethical individualism to which we are striving, and which is also dear to the "immoralist" Nietzsche. Christianity, as an ideal (not historical) dogma, never descends to a police understanding of morality, and its respect for the dignity of the human being and his internal freedom (which constitutes the everlasting moral essence of Christianity) cannot be taken away from it by today's hypocrites, who have the audacity to conceal their spiritual barrenness with spiritualistic words stripped of any valuable content. Christian avowal of internal goodness and gentleness, in the name of the ideal perfection of the human being who is drawing closer to God, and all the beauty and charm of this internal morality, are comprehensible to neither official statists nor social utilitarians, with their crude external criteria. Unfortunately, for reasons beyond my control, it is not possible for me to discuss this question in all its fullness.[57]

IX.

I have already said that practical ethics usually bears the stamp of banality, offensive to any thinker. The only way to raise ethics above triviality and banality is to relate the moral problem to the basic problems of metaphysics, as I have tried to do. The "accursed questions" that torment an Ivan Karamazov correspond more to the heights and depths of the moral problem than do all the injunctions and prohibitions of petty everyday morals, in their desire to train people to live together.[58] A Leonardo da Vinci or Goethe is labeled immoral by every moral mediocrity, proud of their trivial, "useful" virtues, but who among these judges is in the position to measure the depths of the spirit of a "superman" such as Goethe or Leonardo da Vinci? We say that one of the basic tasks of morality is the struggle against philistinism [*meshchanstvo*] and quasi-intellectual triviality, the struggle for the spiritual aristocratization of the human soul. But this is possible only through the creation of a radiant individuality capable of defending its human form, in all its uniqueness, from every attempt to erase or level it. Philistinism and moral pettiness still make themselves too well known in the life of progressive humanity, and ethical idealism must make a point of struggling against this evil.[59] Here philosophical ethics declares war against everyday traditional morals, in which philosophy must too often see the enemy of human individuality and consequently of true morality. The human "I," at the basis of which lies one and the same spiritual essence in all people, takes on flesh and blood in life; it must be unique and have its own colors; in a word, it must be an *individuality*. A human being is a "creature of diversity" [*raznostnoe sushchestvo*] and must not tolerate leveling or attempts to be drilled from one pattern, to be made a "choir member," or to be turned into an example useful for the herd, no matter what "public benefits" these infringements might protect. There is no single impersonal way of realizing the moral good; the ways are diverse and individual. In the social respect, equality, which rests on the equal moral worth of people, cannot and must not go further than equality of rights and elimination of classes (as a condition of the actual realization of equality of rights), and in the psychological respect it cannot and must not go further than an affinity in the basic spiritual traits that make everyone human. I think that a spiritual aristocracy is possible in a democratic society, although this aristocracy will have nothing in common with social-political oppression. The first spurs to further progress must belong precisely to this aristocracy, rising above any class or group morality; without it, the kingdom of stagnation and the herd would ensue. A great moral imperative declares that a human being must always be himself, which means being true not only to one's spiritual "I," but to the "individual" path by which it is realized. A person has a sacred right to freely follow his "calling," which cannot be thrust on him by any collective empirical entity.

> Go along your free path;
> Whither your free mind calls you,
> Protecting the fruits of your cherished thoughts,
> Asking no rewards for your noble exploit.[60]

The greatest moral transgression is to disown one's "I" [*obezlichenie*], the betrayal of one's "I" under the pressure of external force.[61]

But "duty," we are told, what has happened to the "duty" that constitutes the basis of morality? I have already said that duty, "what ought to be," is first of all a formal idea, epistemologically opposed to "what is," to "is." Now we can turn to the content of duty. The moral duty of a human being is self-realization, the development of one's spiritual "I" to ideal perfection; to follow duty and to follow one's moral-rational nature are identical concepts. Only petty bourgeois morality understands duty as something external to man, imposed from outside and hostile to him. Consciousness of duty or, what is the same, the moral law, is consciousness of one's true "I," one's lofty human destiny. To maim one's "I," one's human individuality in the name of duty — these are words that do not make any sense to us. We profess the morals of absolute duty, a duty fulfilling the higher spiritual good, but the word "duty" does not have any unpleasant historical association for us. An opposition between "duty" and the "I" is absurd from the ethical point of view, for "duty" is the lawmaker of the "I."

It is the man of strict duty, we often hear, who never gives in to his inclinations, who constantly struggles with and restrains himself, who always acts as duty dictates, not as he himself wants. Here is the everyday psychological notion of duty. Philosophical ethics must rise above this conventional understanding of duty. It can even sharply chide such a "man of duty," confirm the absence in him of any developed self-consciousness, and indeed recognize the duty he fulfills as immoral, even inhuman, if it suppresses his human "I" in the name of traditional external prescripts.[62] "Humanness," or the realization of the "human being" in oneself and respect for the "human being" in another, is our supreme duty, and the extent of its realization is the first measure of someone's moral level. In man a struggle is always going on between good and evil, between the higher and the lower, between the spiritual "I" and the chaotic content of empirical consciousness, in which there are so many strange inhuman and inhumane admixtures. In this way "personhood" is worked out and moral development takes place. But the morally great and excellent human being is not the one who creates good by gnashing his teeth, limiting and curtailing his human individuality, but the one who, in creating good, is joyously aware of self-realization, of the affirmation of the "I."

Kant still upheld the traditional view that human nature is sinful and corrupt. He therefore arrived at a number of false ethical positions, which fundamentally deny the *Dionysian* principle of life. He was right only in that he considered the moral law to be a law of the will, not of feeling. I take the point of view of the metaphysical denial of evil, not seeing in it anything positive and considering it only an empirical appearance, the inadequate realization of the good. For me human nature is neither sinful nor corrupt; its evil is empirical-negative and in a state of "abnormality," that is, in inadequate correspondence with the "ideal norm."[63] We would like to liberate the life of feeling, immediate life. Sensuous nature is not in itself evil, but ethically neutral; it becomes evil only when it impedes the development of *personhood,* when it obscures higher self-consciousness and self-realization. To say more: the purely instinctual play of forces in man has enormous aesthetic value and is not condemned by ethics, but is merely outside ethics. Instincts are in themselves neither moral nor immoral, but a human being without them would have no flesh or blood and would not live within the bounds of experience. The human "I" develops through the heightening of life and therefore the old adage "live life to the fullest," never loses its meaning. There is in us a wild thirst for life, for life intense and fervent, strong and potent, for life even with its evil, if not with its good. This is an extraordinarily valuable thirst; it is better to be intoxicated with it than for it to be missing altogether. It is the God Dionysus making himself felt, the same one to whom Nietzsche raised such a fine monument in all his works, and he powerfully calls out to life and its growth. The moral task consists not in the limitation of this craving, but in its unification with the affirmation and development of the spiritual "I." Without this moral self-consciousness, "a mountain becomes a molehill," and the Dionysian craving for life will be satisfied exclusively by an indulgence in which it is impossible to find anything greater. We bow down before the beauty of all powerful living impulses, we affirm life endlessly and in all its scope, but for life to be really strong, sweeping, and infinite, it must be filled with *valuable* content, within it *spirituality* must grow, and within it must be realized the ideal godman-like "I" [*bogo-chelovecheskoe "ia"*].

X.

Now we turn to perhaps the most important question, the relation of the moral problem to freedom. Kant constructed his whole ethics on the postulate of freedom. For him the moral problem is first of all the problem of freedom; it presupposes the dualism of the kingdom of freedom and the kingdom of nature (necessity).[64] The moral law by its origin and nature belongs to the kingdom of freedom, not to the kingdom of necessity; it demands the autonomy of the human person. Only free fulfillment of the moral law elevates man, for freedom is the moral nature of the human "I." All arguments from the arsenal of the kingdom of necessity against the kingdom of freedom are equally naive and untenable. They are based on the undemonstrated and indemonstrable supposition that the scientific-cognitive point of view on necessity is the only and ultimate point of view, that experience, which is the child of only one side of our consciousness, is the only and ultimate instantiation. We know perfectly well that within the bounds of experience determinism cannot be breached, that here there cannot be a greater or lesser degree of necessity, but we are not opposing freedom to determinism in the sense of mutual exclusion, but rather recognize a parallelism between the world of freedom and the world of necessity.

Freedom is the self-determination of the person; everything that accords with the "I" and flows from its internal essence bears the stamp of freedom. Freedom is not a negative concept or only the absence of constraint, as bourgeois thinkers contend; freedom is a positive concept, a synonym for all the internal spiritual creativity of the human person. But to be free does not mean to be determined by the empirical "I," with its contingent content derived from experience; freedom is the self-determination of the spiritual "I." From Kant's point of view a human being is free when he is determined not by his sensible, but by his moral-rational nature. And I think an equal sign can be put between internal moral freedom and the spiritual "I" that we have made the basis of ethics.[65] From the epistemological point of view freedom is the determination of the person by "normative consciousness" (ethical norms) in opposition to determination by contingent empirical motives.[66] And this takes us to the identity of freedom and morality. The triumph of the moral good is the triumph of "normative" consciousness, of the spiritual "I," that is, the triumph of freedom. If morality is nothing other than self-realization, then it is liberation. Individual and universal moral development is the triumph of the kingdom of freedom in the kingdom of necessity, that is, the growth of the self-determination of the human person, when all human creativity is subordinated to the spiritual "I." Now we can evaluate the true worth of the widespread contention that "ethical norms" or the "absolute moral law" infringe upon human freedom. The demand of the absolute moral law is a demand of absolute freedom for the human "I." Fulfillment of the moral law as coercion over the "I" is a *contradictio in adjecto,* for such a fulfillment is always autonomous. But some will say, perhaps, that from this the empirical person suffers, that the issue at hand is its freedom. Unfortunately, the concept of the empirical person is not only indefinite but even quite inconceivable; there are no paths from it to the kingdom of freedom. To be a "person," to be a free human being, means to be conscious of one's moral-rational nature and to distinguish one's "normal," ideal "I" from the chaos of a contingent empirical cluster of facts; in itself this empirical chaos is not yet a "person," and the category of freedom is inapplicable to it. To bow down before an empirical fact is idolatry before the altar of necessity, not divine service before the altar of freedom.

Just what is the relation of internal freedom[67] to external freedom, of moral freedom to social freedom? I have already said that the moral problem inevitably turns into the social problem, because the human person can develop and be filled with diverse content only in society, in psychic interaction with other people, in the process of creating a common culture. Can the internal self-determination, moral freedom, and recognition of the absolute value of the person be reconciled with external oppression, with exploitation by other people and by whole groups, with violation of human dignity by public institutions? Can people and groups who have finally recognized their own human dignity and the inalienable "natural" rights of personhood tolerate violence and denial of rights [*bespravie*]? To these questions there can be only one answer; any equivocation would be disgraceful. What intellectual justifications can be adduced in defense of the point of view of reactionaries and obscurantists, of the high priests of crude violence, what can diminish their terrible guilt before the human spirit or allay their just requital? Here there can be historical explanation of social evil, but not moral justification of it.

Ethics clearly and definitely demands realization of the "natural rights" of the human person and permits no compromise in this respect; it thus also demands guarantee of the rights of the citizen. Together with this, ethics unconditionally condemns class antagonism as the most important obstacle to human development. From the ethical point of view all efforts are justified that are directed toward winning that minimum of rights by which an existence worthy of man is alone possible. From the ethical point of view it is shameful for a human being not to defend those rights that are a necessary condition of ideal self-realization. If it turned out, from the point of view of natural necessity, that violence, injustice, and human oppression had to increase and that freedom were an unrealizable dream, even so the imperatives of ethics would remain in full force and evil would be no less appalling, only humanity would have to fall in the struggle with it. But the assertions of the reactionaries also crumble from the point of view of necessity.

In society, people struggle through association and group formation [*gruppirovka*]. In history we do not actually encounter the struggle of individual people, but rather of social groups. Contemporary social group formation opens up broad prospects; necessity provides the conditions by which the human spirit can and must create a better, freer future. Creation of the future is always painted for us not only in the color of natural necessity, but also in the color of our moral freedom. Now we can, it seems, boldly say that not only truth [*pravda*] but also strength are on our side.[68]

Reactionaries are used to a materialist basis and justification for liberationist aspirations, but the challenge of idealism will be much stronger and telling. Idealism exposes the utter spiritual poverty of every reactionary ideology: the Christian preaches wild violence over people, the spiritualist drags off every manifestation of the spirit to the police station.[69] Spiritualism, recognizing the absolute value of the human spirit, cannot be combined with justification of external and often directly physical violence over the spirit, nor can it appear in official garb and profess the ugly lie that the free spirit ought to be perfectly aware of itself in an enslaved society. The new idealist direction, to which I proudly attach myself, draws the necessity of the liberation struggle for "natural law" from the spiritual hunger of the intelligentsia [*intelligentnyi*] soul.[70]

We have not adequately valued or even adequately understood the deep significance of Lev Tolstoy's critique of the existing order, made from the point of view of Christian idealism. After Tolstoy it is already impossible to relate to many things as indifferently as before; the voice of conscience more urgently demands that life be understood morally, that shocking moral contradictions, which take on a criminal character among the representatives of force, be removed.⁷¹

I close my article with the following conclusion, which seems basic to me: one must be a *human being* and cannot give up one's right to the *image and likeness of God* for any worldly goods, for one's own happiness and contentment or even those of all humanity, for tranquility and the approval of people, or for power and success in life. And one must demand the recognition and guarantee of the human right to self-determination and development of all one's spiritual potentialities. But for this it is first necessary to affirm on unshakable foundations the basic condition of respect for man and spirit — freedom.

Notes

1. "Two things fill the mind with ever new and increasing wonder and awe, the oftener and more steadily we reflect on them: the starry heavens above me and the moral law within me." Immanuel Kant, *Critique of Practical Reason* [1788], trans. Lewis White Beck (New York: Macmillan, 1993). Conclusion, p. 169. Ed.

2. "Now I say that man, and in general every rational being, exists as an end in himself, not merely as a means for arbitrary use by this or that will: he must in all his actions, whether they are directed to himself or to other rational beings, always be viewed at the same time as an end." Immanual Kant, *Groundwork of the Metaphysic of Morals* [1785], trans. H. J. Paton (New York: Harper Torchbooks, 1964), p. 95. Ed.

3. "I walk among this people and I keep my eyes open: they have become smaller, and they are becoming smaller and smaller; *but this is due to their doctrine of happiness and virtue.*" Friedrich Nietzsche, *Thus Spoke Zarathustra* [1883–1885], "On Virtue that Makes Small," in *The Portable Nietzsche*, ed. and trans. Walter Kaufmann (New York: Viking Penguin, 1954), p. 281. Subsequent references to *Thus Spoke Zarathustra* are to this edition. Ed.

4. "Too considerate, too yielding is your soil. But that a tree may become *great*, it must strike hard roots around hard rocks." Nietzsche, *Thus Spoke Zarathustra*, "On Virtue that Makes Small," p. 283. Ed.

5. "Alas, that you would understand my word: 'Do whatever you will, but first be such as *are able to will*.'" Nietzsche, *Thus Spoke Zarathustra*, "On Virtue that Makes Small," p. 284. Ed.

6. "*I teach you the overman* [or superman]. Man is something that shall be overcome. What have you done to overcome him?" Nietzsche, *Thus Spoke Zarathustra*, "Zarathustra's Prologue," p. 124. Ed.

7. In the philosophical literature I would not be able to point to one practical ethics that would not offend the dignity of philosophy or the philosopher. When one passes, for

example, from the theoretical part of Wilhelm Wundt's *Ethik* (Stuttgart, 1886) to its practical morality, a certain unpleasant sensation is experienced. The same can be said of the ethics of Spencer, Paulsen, Høffding, and many others. Everyday petty bourgeois [*meshchanskii*] morality adheres only artificially to higher philosophical principles. [Friedrich Paulsen (1846–1908), German philosopher and educational theorist, inclined toward idealism; his ethics was a type of anti-hedonistic utilitarianism, oriented teleologically toward the objective perfection of the ends of the life. Harald Høffding (1843–1931), Danish philosopher and historian of philosophy, distinguished by a broad and learned liberal humanism; in ethics he followed British utilitarianism.]

8. This in no way, of course, excludes psychological or sociological research into the development of morality.

9. Kant, *Grundlegung zur Metaphysik der Sitten* [*Groundwork of the Metaphysic of Morals,* trans. H. J. Paton, p. 94]. See Wilhelm Windelband's excellent book, *Präludien: Aufsätze und Reden zur Einleitung in die Philosophie* (Freiburg and Tübingen, 1884), chiefly the essays "Normen und Naturgesetze," "Kritische oder genetische Methode?" and "Vom Prinzip der Moral." Also see George Simmel, *Einleitung in die Moralwissenschaft: Eine Kritik der ethischen Grundbegriffe,* 2 vols. (Berlin, 1892–1893).

10. Here and below (see especially sections III ff.), I have translated "ia" as "I" to reflect Berdiaev's emphasis on one's perspective on oneself (only I have an "I" from my perspective, there is an "I" only for myself), on self-referentiality and self-value, and on the ethical importance he attaches to recognizing that others are also "I" from their own perspective and ought to be valued as "I." Berdiaev's sense of "ia" as "I" is stronger than the more detached "ia" as "self." This is one of the points on which I am especially indebted to Caryl Emerson's reading of the text. Ed.

11. See Lev Shestov's original and very sincerely written book, *Dobro v uchenii gr. Tolstogo i F. Nitsshe* (*The Good in the Teaching of Count Tolstoi and F. Nietzsche,* St. Petersburg, 1900). Shestov speaks with repugnance about duty, about Kant's moral philosophy, about any moral prescription, but all this is entirely a misunderstanding, based on insufficiently thought out philosophical principles. In essence Shestov yearns for the "good"; not for nothing does he conclude his book with the words, "it is necessary to seek God." [Lev Shestov (Schwarzman) (1866–1938), Russian irrationalist religious philosopher. He drew a sharp antithesis between faith and reason, claiming that religious belief has no need for rational justification and can rest on divine revelation. His last work, *Athens and Jerusalem* (1938), thus contrasts the faith of Jerusalem to the rationalism of Athens. The work Berdiaev refers to is available in English as Lev Shestov, *Dostoevsky, Tolstoy, and Nietzsche,* trans. B. Martin and S. Roberts (Athens: Ohio University Press, 1969), which also includes Shestov's essay *Dostoevskii i Nitsshe: Filosofiia tragedii* (*Dostoevsky and Nietzsche: Philosophy of Tragedy,* St. Petersburg, 1903).]

12. See the excellent consideration of Kant's moral philosophy in Pavel I. Novgorodtsev's recent book, *Kant i Gegel' v ikh ucheniiakh o prave i gosudarstve* (*Kant and Hegel in Their Theories of Law and the State,* Moscow, 1901).

13. To avoid misunderstanding, I should add that I am opposing ethics only to positive science. As regards metaphysics, it unites ethics and science in a higher supra-empirical knowledge.

14. N. A. Berdiaev, *Sub"ektivizm i individualizm v obshchestvennoi filosofii: Kritiche-skii etiud o N. K. Mikhailovskom.* S predisloviem Pëtra Struve (*Subjectivism and Individualism in Social Philosophy: A Critical Study of N. K. Mikhailoskii.* With a foreword by Peter Struve. St. Petersburg, 1901). Ed.

15. It ought to be mentioned that since the time of the appearance of my book, I have advanced far in the direction at which I only then hinted. I now approach philosophical positivism and orthodox Marxism even more critically. I recognize that my book reflected the shortcomings of a transitional state of mind from positivism to metaphysical idealism and spiritualism, to which I have now finally arrived. Struve himself noted this in his rich "foreword." I still intend to return, in a special article, to the question of the relation of my epistemological and metaphysical point of view to Struve's. Regarding the majority of my other critics, they little inspire response, because of their absence of philosophical education and quite obvious inability to formulate problems philosophically. Our task is to replace the *feuilleton* approach to the most important social problems with philosophical consideration of them.

16. Berdiaev, *Sub"ektivizm i individualizm v obshchestvennoi filosofii,* p. xlviii. Ed.

17. "Teleological criticism" is a term Struve uses often in his foreword to Berdiaev's book. It refers to neo-Kantian theory of value, according to which the main task of philosophy is to establish the transcendental validity (*Geltung*) of values or norms and to distinguish on that basis between the factual and the normative. Ed.

18. See Windelband, *Präludien,* "Normen und Naturgesetze." Within the spirit of teleological criticism, Windelband gives the most classic and elegant interpretation of Kantianism. See also Bogdan A. Kistiakovskii's fine article "Kategorii neobkhodimosti i spravedlivosti pri issledovanii sotsial'nykh iavlenii" (The Categories of Necessity and Justice in Studying Social Phenomena), *Zhizn'* (May and June 1900) [reprinted in his *Sotsial'nye nauki i pravo: Ocherki po metodologii sotsial'nykh nauk i obshchei teorii prava* (Moscow, 1916), pp. 120–188]. It explains perfectly well the parallel between what is meant by "universally binding" in logic and in ethics.

19. In the Russian literature, see Sergei A. Askol'dov's book, *Osnovnye problemy teorii poznaniia i ontologii (Basic Problems of the Theory of Knowledge and Ontology,* Moscow, 1900), chapter 1, "Consciousness and Knowledge."

20. Metaphysics unites "what is" and "what ought to be" in absolute ideal being, in a single [*edinyi*] cosmic consciousness.

21. I am using the very broad term "hedonism," but I also have in mind all its branches, for example, eudaemonism, utilitarianism, and so forth.

22. For criticism of hedonism, see Simmel, *Einleitung in die Moralwissenschaft,* vol. 1, pp. 293–467; Wundt, *Etika. Issledovanie faktov i zakonov nravstvennoi zhizni* (St. Petersburg, 1887–1888), pp. 432–449; Jean-Marie Guyau, *La morale anglaise contemporaine: morale de l'utilité et de l'évolution,* 3d edition (Paris, 1895). An excellent critique of hedonism can also be found in John Stuart Mackenzie (1860–1935), *A Manual of Ethics,* 3d edition (London, 1899) [Berdiaev refers to a Russian translation of Mackenzie, pp. 78–103].

23. This deeply sincere and upright thinker frequently revealed the internal contradiction of his point of view; the narrow positivist-utilitarian outlook on life did not satisfy him. See his interesting and instructive *Autobiography* (London, 1873).

24. I cannot fail to take note of Pëtr Lavrov's articles on morality, in which he reveals a very precise understanding, for his time, of the whole vulgarity and reactionary character of hedonistic and utilitarian doctrines. But his idealistic theory of the person could not be based and developed on the ground of positivism. In the Russian literature, see the critical remarks in P. Nezhdanov's book, *Nravstvennost'* (Moscow, 1898). Nezhdanov correctly understands that morality is the quality that elevates man. [Berdiaev is referring to Lavrov's essays, "Ocherk teorii lichnosti" (Outline of a Theory of Individuality), published in *Otechestvennye zapiski,* nos. 11–12 (1859), and reissued in 1860 as a separate brochure under the title *Ocherki voprosov prakticheskoi filosofii;* and to "Tri besedy o sovremennom znachenii filosofii" (Three Debates about the Contemporary Significance of Philosophy), *Otechestvennye zapiski,* no. 1 (1861). Both essays are available in P. L. Lavrov, *Filosofiia i sotsiologiia. Izbrannye proizvedeniia v dvukh tomakh,* vol. 1 (Moscow, 1965), pp. 339–461, 509–573).]

25. See Herbert Spencer, *The Principles of Ethics,* vol. 1 (London, 1879), pp. 56–58. The universal ethical evolutionism of Wundt and Paulsen is, in our view, mistaken from the epistemological point of view.

26. In this respect the Marxist understanding of history, which needs to be recognized as the highest form of sociological evolutionism, has very much to offer.

27. The new critical direction singles out the healthy and living elements of Marxism and combines them with philosophical and ethical idealism.

28. "You are of this world, I am not of this world." John 8:23. Ed.

29. See Immanuel Kant, *Grundlegung zur Metaphysik der Sitten* [herausgegeben und erläutert von J. H. von Kirchmann (Berlin, 1870)], pp. 52–54; and *Kritik der praktischen Vernunft* [herausgegeben und erläutert von J. H. von Kirchmann, 3rd edition (Heielberg, 1882)], p. 158. [*Groundwork of the Metaphysic of Morals,* trans. H. J. Paton (New York: Harper Torchbooks, 1964), pp. 95–96. *Critique of Practical Reason,* trans. Lewis White Beck (New York: Macmillan, 1993), p. 138.]

30. "This principle of humanity, and in general of every rational agent, *as an end in itself* (a principle which is the supreme limiting condition of every man's freedom of action) is not borrowed from experience; firstly, because it is universal, applying as it does to all rational beings as such, and no experience is adequate to determine universality; secondly, because in it humanity is conceived, not as an end of man (subjectively) — that is, as an object which, as a matter of fact, happens to be made an end — but as an objective end — one which, be our ends what they may, must, as a law, constitute the supreme limiting condition of all subjective ends and so must spring from pure reason. That is to say, the ground for every enactment of practical law lies *objectively in the rule* and in the form of universality which (according to our first principle) makes the rule capable of being a law (and indeed a law of nature); *subjectively,* however, it lies in the *end;* but (according to our second principle) the subject of all ends is to be found in every rational being as an end in himself. From this there now follows our third practical principle for the will — as the supreme condition of the will's conformity with universal practical reason — namely, the Idea *of the will of every rational being as a will which makes universal law.*" Kant, *Groundwork of the Metaphysic of Morals,* trans. H. J. Paton, p. 98. [Berdiaev quotes this in German from the Kirchmann edition cited above, pp. 55–56.]

31. I use the word "normal" here in a sense corresponding to "norm." All empirical

reality (the kingdom of nature) in the strict philosophical sense is *not normal;* only the ideal world of "what ought to be" is normal.

32. See Kant, *Grundlegung zur Metaphysik der Sitten* [Kirchmann edition], p. 7. [*Groundwork of the Metaphysic of Morals,* trans. H. J. Paton, pp. 58–59.]

33. Struve emphasizes especially clearly the necessity of an individual spiritual substance for the ethical idea of personhood. I might have certain metaphysical disagreements with him, but within ethics I also recognize the substantiality of the soul.

34. Kant's mistake was that he considered the position of spiritualism too hopeless from the point of view of philosophical knowledge and constructed his metaphysics exclusively by the method of moral postulates. I reject Kantian skepticism and more than the Kantians believe in the possibility of constructing metaphysics by various paths.

35. "You flee to your neighbor from yourselves and would like to make a virtue out of that: but I see through your 'selflessness,' " Zarathustra says. "The *you* is older than the *I;* the *you* has been pronounced holy, but not yet the *I:* so man crowds toward his neighbor." *Thus Spoke Zarathustra,* "On Love of the Neighbor," p. 172. [Berdiaev quotes this in German, from vol. VI of *Nietzsches Werke* (Leipzig, 1899–1905), p. 88.]

36. I would characterize my metaphysical point of view as a combination of *spiritualistic individualism* with *ethical pantheism.*

37. Such, in general, is the metaphysics of Hegel, and his philosophy of history in particular, which have in essence never been refuted. See Kuno Fischer, *Hegels Leben, Werke und Lehre* [vol. VIII of his *Geschichte der neuern Philosophie* (Heidelberg, 1901)]. In certain respects I am, incidentally, closer to Fichte than to Hegel.

38. Incidentally, Struve himself recognizes this. I would especially emphasize this, because I feel it could give cause for misunderstanding. Thus, for example, P. Novgorodtsev accuses me of inclining toward the complete elimination of individualism. See his book *Kant i Gegel',* p. 225.

39. In my view, solipsism, in the theory of knowledge and in ethics, is on the decline, as is empiricism. Ethical solipsism is founded on the apparent impossibility of passing beyond the limits of individual consciousness, but individual consciousness, as an empirical fact, still gives no grounds for the idea of personhood, of individuality, which can be conceived only spiritualistically, as a bearer of the absolute spiritual principle.

40. In Struve the idea of progress, which possesses primary significance for ethics and metaphysics, is left in the background. He says almost nothing about it. To my view this is the major flaw in his deeply interesting and valuable "foreword."

41. The scientific-sociological point of view investigates social development quite diferently, disclosing the laws of "what occurs" [*proiskhodiashchee*].

42. Novgorodtsev notes this in his book (cited above) and, proceeding from this gap in Kant's philosophy, draws a highly instructive parallel with Hegel's philosophy.

43. Sociology treats individuality as the result of the intersection of different social circles. This scientific truth in no way contradicts the ethical-metaphysical theory of personhood.

44. Here and below, I have substituted "natural rights" for this usage of "natural law" or "natural right." Ed.

45. With the revival and more profound interpretation of Kant's philosophy, the arguments of the historical school of law and the evolutionists against the theory of "natural

law" have completely collapsed. The expression "natural law" might arouse misunder-standing, because it bears the stamp of the obsolete worldview of the eighteenth century with its faith in a "natural" order of things, to which belongs the call to "nature" of Jean-Jacques Rousseau and many others. For us the concept of "natural" is identical with "normal," that is, corresponding to an ideal norm. The historical variability and relativity of law cannot be an argument against "natural law," because "natural law" is "what ought to be," and not "what is"; it is a "norm" that ought to be realized in the historical development of law. See Novgorodtsev, *Kant i Gegel'*, pp. 146–156. See also Rudolf Stammler, *Wirtschaft und Recht nach der materialistischen Geschichtsauffassung* (Halle, 1896), "Das Recht des Rechtes." Professor Leon Petrażycki leans toward natural law in his *Ocherki po filosofii prava* (1900), although he fumbles when it comes to philosophy. Also see Boris Chicherin, *Filosofiia prava* (1900).

46. It is necessary to approach socialism in this way as well. Liberalism, in its ideal essence, poses the following goals: the development of personhood, realization of natural rights, freedom and equality. Socialism only opens up new ways for the more consistent implementation of these eternal principles. The tendency toward social-economic collec-tivism has been designated an advantageous and even necessary means, but ethical and spiritual collectivism in general has nothing to do with this and in itself is a terrible evil.

47. [Friedrich Nietzsche, *The Gay Science,* section 125, "The madman," trans. Walter Kaufmann (New York: Vintage Books, 1974), p. 181.] See *Nietzsches Werke,* vol. V, p. 163. I am quoting from M. Nevedomskii's [M. P. Miklashevskii's] translation, the best of the existing translations of Nietzsche. See Likhtenberzhe, *Filosofiia Nitsshe* [1901] [Nevedomskii's translation of Henri Lichtenberger, *La philosophie de Nietzsche* (Paris, 1898).]

48. See *Nietzsches Werke,* vol. VI, pp. 19–20. [*Thus Spoke Zarathustra,* "Zarathu-stra's Prologue," pp. 129–130.]

49. See Nietzsche, *Thus Spoke Zarathustra,* pp. 279–284.

50. M. Nevedomskii [M. P. Miklashevskii] has very astutely noted this in his "Instead of a Preface" to his translation of Lichtenberger's book. Nevedomskii has original and interesting ideas. It can even be said that his is one of the best essays in the extensive literature on Nietzsche. But like Shestov, Nevedomskii leaves much to be desired in respect to philosophy. His approach to Kant's moral philosophy is a clear example of superficial thinking in philosophy.

51. I am not using the words "slave" and "master" in a social sense. Nietzsche himself never takes the social point of view.

52. *Nietzsches Werke,* vol. VI, p. 130. [*Thus Spoke Zarathustra,* "On the Pitying," p. 202.]

53. *Nietzsches Werke,* vol. VI, p. 13. [*Thus Spoke Zarathustra,* "Zarathustra's Prologue," pp. 124–125. Translation slightly revised ("superman" for Kaufmann's "overman").]

54. In the greatest of his creations, *Zarathustra,* Nietzsche returns to the idealistic spirit he displayed in *The Birth of Tragedy,* but he must pay cruelly for all the sins of nineteenth-century thought.

55. Struve has noted this very well in his "foreword" to my book. In general, Struve's critical observations about Nietzsche are very discerning.

56. Thomas Carlyle (1795–1881), Scottish essayist and historian. Author of *On Heroes, Hero-Worship, and the Heroic in History* (1841). Ed.

57. Our point of view is a synthesis of the ideas of the "Godman" and the "mangod." [The "Godman" is Christ, while the "mangod" is the man who tries to prove that he is his own absolute, or god, through the unrestrained, individualistic exercise of free will. The idea of the "mangod" is associated with Max Stirner (1806–1856), especially his call to rebellion and crime as the supreme assertion of the ego. Dostoevsky gave powerful literary expression to the theme of the mangod; see Andrzej Walicki, "The Devious Paths of the Man-God," in his *A History of Russian Thought from the Enlightenment to Marxism,* trans. Hilda Andrews-Rusiecka (Stanford, Calif.: Stanford University Press, 1979), pp. 315–320.]

58. See Fëdor Dostoevsky, *The Brothers Karamazov,* Book 5, chap. 3. Ed.

59. This can be said of the working class as well. To its progressive social-political aspirations it is still necessary to introduce an ideal moral content, which cannot, of course, have a "class" character.

60. A. S. Pushkin, "Poetu" ("To the Poet," 1830). *Pushkin: Selected Verse,* with an introduction and prose translations by John Fennell (Baltimore: Penguin, 1964), pp. 59–60. Ed.

61. It is sufficiently clear that in relation to society and all collective entities, I maintain the point of view of ethical nominalism.

62. In this respect the image of Brand in Ibsen is extraordinarily interesting and characteristic. [Henrik Ibsen (1928–1906), Norwegian dramatist and poet. Berdiaev's reference is to Ibsen's early verse play, *Brand* (1866).]

63. We establish the premises for such a metaphysical doctrine of good and evil, which considers good to be positive and evil to be negative, already in epistemology. Only the category of "what ought to be," i.e., of the good, is autonomous and positive; evil is merely the inadequate realization of "what ought to be" in "what is." We find such a metaphysical denial of evil in the philosophical theories of Fichte and Hegel. Only in this way can the existence of evil be reconciled metaphysically with the idea of God. This is the most "accursed" of all "accursed questions," the question of a "moral world-order," which Dostoevsky posed with such genius through Ivan Karamazov. Ivan asks Alësha: "imagine that you yourself are building the edifice of human destiny with the object of making people happy in the finale, of giving them peace and rest at last, but for that you must inevitably and unavoidably torture just one tiny creature, that same child who was beating her chest with her little fist, and raise your edifice on the foundation of her unrequited tears—would you agree to be the architect on such conditions? Tell me the truth." And Ivan Karamazov returns to God the admission ticket to a higher harmony based on the unredeemed tear of one tiny infant. It is not God he does not accept, but God's world. But the world does not need to be morally accepted, for the world is *"what is"* (the kingdom of necessity); rather God needs to be accepted, for God is *"what ought to be"* (the kingdom of freedom). Our task is to realize God in the world, since we conceive God not as the culprit of the world, but as its ideal. [Fyodor Dostoevsky, *The Brothers Karamazov,* trans. Richard Pevear and Larissa Volokhonsky (New York: Vintage Classics, 1991), Book V, ch. 4, "Rebellion," p. 245.]

64. See Kant, *Grundlegung zur Metaphysik der Sitten* [Kirchmann edition], pp. 74–77. [*Groundwork of the Metaphysic of Morals,* trans. H. J. Paton, p. 114–116.]

65. Struve identifies freedom with substance, because he conceives the "I" as substantial. In essence I completely agree with him, although I come to this truth by a somewhat different path, and my metaphysics has a somewhat different shade than the metaphysics of Leibniz and [Rudolf Hermann] Lotze, with which Struve, apparently, especially sympathizes. To repeat once more, all these differences are immaterial and cannot infringe upon our unanimity in the basics.

66. See Windleband, *Präludien,* p. 239.

67. I avoid the expression "freedom of will" in view of the unfavorable associations connected with it. I have nothing against being considered an adherent of "freedom of will," but would resolutely object were I to be counted among the indeterminists or were an understanding of freedom as empirical indeterminacy ascribed to me.

68. In this respect it is impossible not to recognize the enormous services of Marxism, the realistic side of which we must accept. On the question of the social-economic development of Russia I in general continue to take the Marxist point of view, although my practical program is somewhat broader than the Marxist one.

69. Vladimir Solov'ëv's *Natsional'nyi vopros v Rossii* (*The National Question in Russia*) is a classic example of the idealist critique of such reactionaries-nationalists, but Solov'ëv did not think spiritualism through to the end or draw all the necessary conclusions from it. [*Natsional'nyi vopros v Rossii. Vypusk pervyi* (St. Petersburg, 1888) and *Natsional'nyi vopros v Rossii. Vypusk vtoroi* (St. Petersburg, 1891).]

70. Struve hinted at this idea in his article "Vysshaia tsena zhizni" (Life's Highest Value). Beginning with this unfinished article, the conscious idealist direction has become increasingly evident in progressive Russian literature. [Berdiaev is referring to Struve's essay, "O nashem vremeni. 1. Vysshaia tsennost' zhizni," *Severnyi Kur'er* (16 Jan. 1990), p. 2. Reprinted in *Issledovaniia po istorii russkoi mysli." Ezhegodnik 2000* (Moscow, 2000), pp. 42–46.]

71. "Tolstoianism," with all its negative sides, has already long lost any significance in the life of the Russian intelligentsia, so Tolstoy's positive services can now be objectively evaluated.

5

Friedrich Nietzsche and the Ethics of "Love of the Distant"

(Dedicated to P. B. S.)

S. L. FRANK

Die Zukunft und das Fernste sei dir
die Ursache deines Heute ...
Meine Brüder, zur Nächstenliebe rate
ich euch nicht: ich rate euch zur
Fernstenliebe.

Nietzsche, Also sprach Zarathustra.[1]

I.

Nah hab' den Nächsten ich nicht gerne:
Fort mit ihm in die Höh' und Ferne!
Wie würd' er sonst zu meinem Sterne?

Nietzsche, Fröhliche Wissenschaft.[2]

The modern science of morals leads to the conviction that the totality of the moral feelings people experience and the moral principles they recognize cannot be reduced to one supreme axiom from which all of them would derive, like conclusions from a logical premise. There exists no single moral postulate from which it would be possible to develop a logical system of ethics encompassing, without exception, all the judgments that bring phenomena under the categories of "good" and "evil." The complex and intricate pattern of the moral world cannot be unraveled by finding the end of *one* of its threads, for this pattern is formed from *many* interweaving and mutually intersecting threads.[3] The task of the science of morals can consist only in separating these threads from each other and in showing how they intertwine in the living fabric of moral life. The entirety of moral ideas and feelings can thus be reduced only to a number of basic principles that are independent of each other, each of which serves as the inner basis of a whole mass of moral phenomena and provides the principle behind a particular, closed *system of morality*. But these principles do not themselves depend on, and therefore do not substantiate, each other. On the contrary, each of them, as a moral axiom, comes into conflict with all the rest and carries on a struggle with them for absolute supremacy in the kingdom of morals. "Behold how each of your virtues," Friedrich Nietzsche says in his descriptive language, "covets what is highest: each wants your whole spirit that it might become *her* herald; each wants your whole strength in wrath, hatred, and love. Each virtue is jealous of the others."[4]

The outcome of this struggle can be either a full or partial displacement by one principle of all the others, or a distribution of power among them according to the particular competencies of each of them (thus, for example, entirely different and contradictory moral principles not uncommonly prevail in public and personal life, because what is considered good in the first is seen as bad in the second, and vice versa); even the absence of any outcome is possible, an eternal struggle of moral feelings in the soul of man, its own type of "*Bürgerkrieg in Permanenz*" [permanent civil war]. *Psychologically,* the correlation of the strengths of the separate principles, and the outcome of the struggle among them, depend on people's natural inclinations, on the conditions of their life, on their personal disposition and the disposition of society and the times. *Morally,* the outcome of this struggle can be *decreed* only by firmly recognizing one of the competing principles as the supreme axiom of moral life and by rejecting, just as firmly, all the rest; but such an outcome cannot be *substantiated,* because the very recognition of one principle as the *supreme* moral instance removes the possibility of searching for further, higher grounds. The basis of a higher moral law, like any law, is not its own lawfulness [*pravomernost'*], but the actual strength of the feelings making up and supporting it.

Among the collisions occurring on this ground, special interest belongs to the clash of two ethical systems founded on two powerful moral principles, which Nietzsche successfully contrasts as "love of one's neighbor" and "love of the distant." It is hardly necessary to refute the opinion that "love of the distant" is a feeling invented by Nietzsche, the fruit of his anguished fantasy or indeed even of his anguished moral constitution. In fact "love of the distant" is a feeling as familiar to people and as old as "love of one's neighbor." This, we hope, will be sufficiently clear from all that follows. But here we need to dwell on the preliminary clarification of the meaning of these concepts.

The concept of "love of the distant," with which we shall mainly be concerned, does not have a strictly defined scope: it corresponds to the opposing concept of "love of one's neighbor" and to a certain extent depends on the meaning ascribed to the latter. In order to give as complete an idea as possible of "love of the distant" and its significance in Nietzsche's ethical system, we shall trace its content, starting from its broadest conceivable scope and then gradually delimiting it, in this way defining the concept of "love of the distant" more and more precisely.

In its broadcast sense, the concept of "love of the distant" is characterized by opposition to "love of one's neighbor," in the specific meaning of the latter concept, which does not coincide with its general meaning, but which does have much in common with it and forms, so to speak, its root. "Love of one's neighbor," in its [specific] sense with which we are now concerned, is understood as the totality of sympathetic feelings experienced in relation to the people closest to us (*"neighbors"*), feelings founded on the elementary instinct of compassion, on the keen reproduction in one's soul of the psychic life of these "neighbors." If these feelings also carry over to a wider circle of people — "neighbors" in the broad, metaphorical sense of the word — it is only by analogy to the sensations felt in relation to "neighbors" in the narrow, literal sense of the word. The ethics of "love of one's neighbor" is thus a moral system founded on the instinct of compassion.[5] The concept of "love of the distant" does not have so definite a meaning. It can mean any love not coinciding with "love of one's neighbor." We can describe it as a feeling experienced in relation to everything "distant" or remote from us, either spatially, temporally, or morally/psychologically, and therefore acting not immediately, not through the affect of compassion, but through the mediation of more abstract moral impulses. In this broad sense, "love of the distant" will include love for goods and interests more remote than "neighbors," as well as love for "distant" people: our fellow-citizens, descendants, humanity. Finally, love of everything abstract will fit in here — truth, the good, justice — in short, love of everything that is called an "ideal," or, as Nietzsche expressed it, "love of things and phantoms." All these aspects of "love of the distant" have in common the fact that they are not based on the immediate instinct of compassion or, at least, are not exhausted by it; this sharply separates every "love of the distant" from "love of one's neighbor." True, in Nietzsche, as we shall see below, love of the distant has its own more narrow and definite meaning; but to a certain degree the formal character of this feeling, in its antithesis (which most interests us) to the feeling of love of one's neighbor, is independent of the content of the object itself of this feeling, of the meaning attached to the concept of the "distant." Therefore, our characterization of both feelings is adequate for preliminary analysis of their mutual relations.

Corresponding to the breadth of the concept of "love of the distant," the antithesis between this feeling and the feeling of "love of one's neighbor" can take on the most diverse forms. The root of this antithesis can be observed in the shades of maternal love. Love for a child, in the desire to satisfy all its wishes and spare it any suffering, can be contrasted, as "love of one's neighbor," to maternal "love of the distant," love directed toward providing remote goods for that child, even at the cost of much present suffering and privation. The same antithesis is revealed more sharply in a nurse's treatment of a patient, compared to a doctor's (an example given by Nietzsche himself): a nurse's gentle, compassionate love, in its desire to ease the patient's present suffering and state of mind, is a typical case of "love of one's neighbor," while the severe love of the doctor, directed toward the future good and remote interests of the patient . . . is a type of "love of the distant." And this antithesis manifests itself still more sharply in the abundant tragedies, large and small, past and present, that arise on the ground of the collision between public interests and private affections: the content of all these tragedies is exhausted by the struggle between "love of one's neighbor" — the feeling of compassion and intimacy for people nearby — and "love of the distant," for a favorite issue or party, for one's native country or for humanity. But even within the sphere of public interests the same antithesis recurs in the most diverse forms: everyone knows, for example, the opposition between two types of patriotism, where one type is love, so to speak, for one's country "here and now," and the other type is love for its future, in the "distance." Chaadaev,[6] already in his day, pointed to this antithesis, contrasting the "patriotism of a Samoed"[7] to the "Englishman's patriotism."[8] Finally, at the highest stage of development of moral feelings, a confrontation between public interests and abstract moral motives is possible (for example, if love of a party or one's country comes into conflict with love of justice, truth, and so forth). Here we find, once more, the antithesis between love of one's neighbor and love of the distant, in its most abstract and characteristic form.

No one, of course, will deny that the principle of "love of one's neighbor" (in its specific sense) has long served, serves, and can serve as the basis of a whole moral system. The basic axiom of this system was most sharply expressed in Dostoevsky's famous idea that all human progress is not worth one tear from a child. It is possible to understand and respect such a system, and indeed to share it. But it cannot be denied that "love of the distant" can also serve as the basic axiom for an extensive, self-contained moral system. And more than one mother would object to Dostoevsky that not only the progress of humanity, but even the physical and spiritual welfare of this one child is more dear to her than many of its tears. ...

One of Friedrich Nietzsche's brilliant services is the discovery and conscious evaluation of this antithesis between love of one's neighbor and love of the distant, an antithesis as old as the world, but never formulated openly and clearly. Both these moral principles come to a sharp and often irreconcilable clash, and this clash ought not to be ignored or denied. Rather, it is necessary to recognize this openly, face it directly, and resolutely take the side of one or another of the competing principles — such is the severe but salutary idea Nietzsche brings to ethics. Nietzsche himself is a convinced and enthusiastic apostle of "love of the distant." But he is not only its advocate: he is the creator of an entire grandiose moral system, based on this moral feeling. All his moral teaching, as expressed in its most mature form in Zarathustra's discourses,[9] can be understood and evaluated as a gospel of "love of the distant." Many of Nietzsche's boldest moral maxims, which at first glance are striking to the ordinary moral consciousness in their paradoxical quality, and which have frequently caused suspicion of a morally perverse character in their author, acquire a profound veracity and mighty moral force when seen as links in an ethical system of love of the distant. The profundity of Nietzsche's spiritual nature and the diverse content of his ideas have made it possible to approach him from various sides, to understand and value him from very different points of view. If Riehl[10] sees in him a "philosopher of culture," if Simmel[11] considers him the father of an ethics of "nobility," they have surely grasped the most basic and striking features of his spiritual makeup. But neither defini-tion — not to mention many other less successful ones — completely covers Nietzsche's moral physiognomy or infringes the legitimacy of completely dif-ferent characterizations of it, based on its other features, which are just as basic and striking. While consciously avoiding any claim to exhaustive signifi-cance, our understanding of Nietzsche's teaching as an ethical system of "love of the distant" does, we suggest, contain the key to elucidating essential moral ideas in Nietzsche (the most valuable ones, in our personal view).[12]

Let us turn to the moral demands that issue from the ethics of "love of the distant." We hope to be forgiven for the abundant quotes with which we will be compelled to illustrate Nietzsche's thought.[13] The poetic power of Nietz-sche's language requires literalness in conveying his ideas.

From the very beginning we encounter one idea, paradoxical in appearance, but profoundly true: in opposition to "love of one's neighbor," the source of love of the distant is a feeling that is unethical from the point of view of ordinary morality: alienation from the "neighboring," a complete break with the surrounding milieu and its life. "Neighbors," living according to the interests of the day and accustomed to the settled structure of their existence, do not understand and fear one who has fallen in love with the distant. When Zarathustra first descended to people in order to proclaim his teaching to them, the hermit meeting him warned: "Our steps sound too lonely through the streets. And what if at night, in their beds, they hear a man walk by long before the sun has risen—they probably ask themselves, Where is the thief going?"[14] But the lover of the "distant" repays his neighbors with the same: his love for the distant forces him to hate and despise everything neighboring, the real, present-day life of the people surrounding him, with all its everyday petty virtues and interests. Nietzsche's attacks on the hypocrisy and banality of contemporary life are too well-known and numerous to cite them here. We cannot, however, deny ourselves the pleasure of quoting one of his most successful characterizations of the various types of contemporary hypocritical virtue. Before us passes an entire collection of types of modern virtuous people. "There are those for whom virtue is the spasm under the scourge," and "there are others who are like cheap clocks that must be wound: they tick and they want the tick-tock to be called virtue." "And then again there are such as sit in their swamp and speak thus out of the reeds: 'Virtue—that is sitting still in a swamp. We bite no one and avoid those who want to bite; and in all things we hold the opinion that is given to us.'" "And then again there are such as love gestures and think that virtue is some kind of gesture. Their knees always adore, and their hands are hymns to virtue, but their heart knows nothing about it." Finally—and here there is something in Zarathustra's proud words that strikes quite close to home—"there are such as consider it virtue to say, 'Virtue is necessary'; but at bottom they believe only that the police is necessary."[15]

One who loves the distant has nothing in common with the life of such virtuous people, in whom it is not difficult to notice a copy of our "Tashkenters" and of people from a "milieu of moderation and correctness" (Zarathustra sums up their virtue with the words: *cowardice* and *mediocrity*).[16] Love of the distant, the striving to embody this "distant" in life, has as its indispensable condition a break with the neighboring. The ethics of love of the distant, in view of the fact that any "distant" requires time for its realization and "approach" to real life, and that it can happen only in the future, is an ethics of *progress*. In this sense Nietzsche's moral *Weltanschauung* is a typical Weltanschauung of a *progressive,* of course not in the political, but in the formal-sociological meaning of the term. Any such striving toward progress is founded on a rejection of the present position of things and on complete moral alienation from it. In a wonderful artistic contrast of the relation to the "country of my *fathers*" and the "country of my *children*," Nietzsche portrays the moral position someone takes to his country, if he has accepted the principle of the ethics of "love of the distant."

"Strange and a mockery to me are the men of today to whom my heart recently drew me; and I am driven out of fatherlands and motherlands. Thus I now love only my *children's land,* yet undiscovered, in the farthest sea: for this I bid my sails search and search."

"In my children I want to make up for being the child of my fathers — and to all the future, for *this* today."[17]

In Zarathustra's eyes, people today are material only for the future, stones for the great edifice being built. "I walk among men," he says, "as among the fragments of the future — that future which I envisage. And this is all my creating and striving, that I create and carry together into One what is fragment and riddle and dreadful accident."[18] "The now and the past on earth — alas, my friends, that is what I find most unendurable; and I should not know how to live if I were not also a seer of that which must come."[19]

Thus, love of future, distant humanity is inseparably linked with hatred and contempt for contemporary, neighboring humanity; love and contempt are two sides of one and the same feeling. "What does he know of love," Zarathustra exclaimed, "who did not have to despise precisely what he loved!"[20] In his very first oration to the people Zarathustra taught them "great contempt," as the source of the moral renewal of humanity: "What is the greatest experience you can have? It is the hour of the great contempt. The hour in which your happiness, too, arouses your disgust, and even your reason and your virtue," when in all this you see only "poverty and filth and wretched contentment."[21]

But contempt for surrounding life and its current, everyday interests, for its "happiness and reason and virtue," must be only the first stage in the spiritual development of the lover of the "distant," the purification of his soul for the complete triumph in it of this love. Woe to the one who stops at contempt! Nietzsche-Zarathustra, himself once penetrated by the ideas of pessimism and feeling his spiritual closeness to the profound moral impulses at the basis of this doctrine, indignantly attacks the metaphysicians-pessimists, the *Hinterwelter* as he calls them, people who only see the "world *from behind.*"[22] "They encounter a sick man or an old man or a corpse, and immediately they say, 'Life is refuted.' But only they themselves are refuted, and their eyes, which see only this one face of existence."[23] And despite his cry of protest against pessimism, for which the "world itself is a filthy monster," and which ends with the sad recognition, "oh my brothers, there is much wisdom in this, that there is much filth in the world,"[24] still he found an exit from the heavy chains of this doctrine: "Was it my nausea itself which created wings for me and water-divining powers?"[25] The creative will, the aspiration to change the present and bring the "future and distant" closer to it—here is what loathing for the present day must lead to. "To will liberates, for to will is to create: thus I teach. And you shall learn solely in order to create."[26] "Creation—that is the great redemption from suffering, and life's growing light."[27]

Love of the distant is therefore a *creative* love; alienation from the "neighboring" and closeness to the "distant" make it necessary to strive to embody the "distant" in life, transforming the latter in a direction that brings it closer to the "distant." In this as well we observe the highly characteristic difference between "love of one's neighbor" and "love of the distant." The first (like any love) also can and ought to be an *active* love; but this activity, which amounts to a manifestation of the instinct of compassion, is deprived of the element of *creativity*, the unflinching and systematic destruction of the old and the creation of the new, that distinguishes "love of the distant." Not worrying about the principles and makeup of life, "love of one's neighbor" (in its specific sense) is concerned to immediately eliminate or ease every current manifestation of evil, while "love of the distant," by contrast, sets for itself the goal of purposefully changing the very principles of life, *creative* work in the name of a definite "distant." This contrast comes out still more sharply in examining the attitudes toward nearby people that express the active manifestations of both of these moral feelings. The activity of love of one's neighbor is expressed first of all in a peaceful, friendly, kind approach to all people; the creative activity of love of the distant necessarily takes the form of *struggle* with people. From the point of view of the first, the moral ideal is peace, gentleness, the desire to yield to one's neighbor and to suppress one's own wishes for the sake of his; from the point of view of the second, such submissiveness and compliance deserve the strongest moral condemnation because, Zarathustra says, "it is those farther away who must pay for your love of your neighbor."[28] Love of the distant demands persistence in carrying out *one's* aspirations in the face of all obstacles; its ideal is an energetic, uncompromising *struggle* with surrounding "neighbors," in the name of clearing the path for the triumph of the "distant." Such is the meaning of Zarathustra's famous discourse, "On War and Warriors."

"To you I do not recommend work but struggle. To you I do not recommend peace but victory. Let your work be a struggle. Let your peace be a victory!"

"War and courage have accomplished more great things than love of the neighbor. Not your pity but your courage has so far saved the unfortunate."[29]

A creative struggle, creativity in the form of struggle, such is the work, such is the life of someone who loves the "distant." Zarathustra's inspired orations draw in great detail the spiritual makeup of his hero, a creator of and fighter for the "distant." In this respect Zarathustra's moral teaching is an ethical code of the life of this hero, the first written gospel for people given to creativity and struggle.

[. . .] [Using ample quotations, Frank extols two psychological characteristics Nietzsche-Zarathustra recommends as necessary for champions of love of the distant: strength and firmness of character, and courage.]

These two basic traits, in their higher development and clash with the contemporary forces that run counter to the triumph of the "distant," are the sources of the "tragic beauty" of the life of the lover of the "distant": they simultaneously abet his ruin and give him the strength to calmly meet it. One who lives for the "distant," one for whom, in Nietzsche's expression, "love of life shall be love of your highest hope,"[30] is one who seeks out danger and knows that for the future he must perish in the present. The exhortation to voluntary death, the view that the best and even the only valuable type of life consists in sacrificing it for the good of the "distant," also constitutes one of the basic notes prevailing in Nietzsche's Weltanschauung. Among all the distortions to which both shortsighted followers and opponents have equally subjected his teaching — distortions from which, as from a pile of garbage, Nietzsche's ideas need to be cleaned by anyone who sets to reading his works for the first time, having only read and heard about the trends of "Nietzscheanism" — the crudest distortion and, from the moral point of view, the gravest sin seems to us to be the disregard of Nietzsche's doctrine of the moral imperative of self-sacrifice. Not rarely is it heard that the gist of Nietzsche's teaching consists in the appeal to boundless and unrestrained license of the passions, unhindered by moral considerations; in this there are too few who recall his severe admonishment: *you ought not to seek pleasures!* Nietzsche's heroes are not brazen hosts at the feast of life but, on the contrary, those who by their very nature do not know how, cannot, and do not want to settle into contemporary life. "And verily," Zarathustra exclaims, "I love you for not knowing how to live today, you higher men! For thus *you* live best."[31] Ruin, he teaches, is the lot of all that rises above the current level, all that in the present is a representative of the future.

[. . .] [Frank quotes Zarathustra at length on the virtue of self-sacrifice.]

The doctrine of voluntary ruin resounds with powerful, triumphant chords in Zarathustra's discourse, "On Free Death." If it is said that the measure of the height of a moral Weltanschauung is the strength it gives man to meet death boldly and fearlessly, then Nietzsche's Weltanschauung is second to none in this respect. It is doubtful if anyone has spoken about death more forcefully and joyously than Zarathustra in his apotheosis of "free death."

[. . .] [Frank quotes the discourse at length.]

Thus, firmness in the achievement of the intended goal, in the creation of the "distant"; courage in struggle; and a peaceful and even joyous attitude toward one's death, flowing from consciousness of its necessity for the triumph of the "distant"—here are the basic traits of the moral character demanded by the ethics of love of the distant. Reared in the spirit of pessimism, Nietzsche from the very beginning set for himself the ideal of *"tragic beauty."* The original motif of his ethical worldview was the conviction that, in view of the impossibility of true happiness in the world, the only worthy and excellent thing on earth is to proudly and consciously face the tragedy of life. The further development of Nietzsche's worldview added to this conviction only one feature, but one essential and valuable in the highest degree: "tragic beauty" ceased to be fruitless in his eyes. It is, for Nietzsche-Zarathustra, no longer an end in itself; the end of life is creativity in the name of love of the distant, and death is only a means for realizing this end. Death is not only an *Untergang* [a going-down], but also an *Übergang* [a going-over]: tragic beauty became *creative*. In such form, the original and basic motif of Nietzsche's ethics is harmoniously worked into an ethical system of "love of the distant."

The ethics of "love of one's neighbor" turns in its development into an ethics of compassion, resignation, and, finally, passive martyrdom. The ethics of "love of the distant," as we have seen, becomes an ethics of *active heroism*.

Despite the heterogeneity of these two moral systems, the demands of the ethics of "love of the distant" possess an indisputable and self-evident moral worth. The disparity between these demands and those of the ethics of "love of one's neighbor" obviously does not prevent general recognition and profession of the former, nor does it cast doubt on their moral significance. Such tacit recognition of the demands of the ethics of "love of the distant," amid the manifest avowal of the opposing principles, derives in part because this disparity is very subtle and not rarely slips from the view of a superficial observer of moral life, and in part because it relates only to the psychological correlates of one or the other ethics and not to their very principles. Let us now focus on the aspects of this antithesis that take on the character of an open and decisive struggle. We have in mind certain attacks of Nietzsche on moral principles that are ordinarily ascribed absolute and unshakable value, and in relation to which Nietzsche makes his celebrated attempt at a "transvaluation of all values."

On this theme very much has been said but, to the extent I am aware, it has not been examined from the point of view of the confrontation between "love of the distant" and "love of one's neighbor." Nietzsche's protest against the idea of *duty* in morality is usually the center of attention. It seems to us, however, that this protest can be correctly appreciated only by a more careful consideration of Nietzsche's moral ideal, and this is impossible, in our view, without a detailed inquiry into the moral antithesis between "love of one's neighbor" and "love of the distant." In Nietzsche the struggle against the idea of duty is — as we shall try to show at a further stage of our analysis — only a reflection of a broader and more fundamental struggle against the ethics of "love of one's neighbor." Let us again try to understand the general meaning of this latter struggle.

Nietzsche's rejection of the moral worth of the feeling of compassion is known to everyone, as is his so-called glorification of cruelty. The time has already passed when it was possible, not having thought through these views of Nietzsche, to be satisfied simply with moral indignation in regard to them. But even now their meaning remains, for many, an incompletely solved riddle. The riddle, in our opinion, can be solved only by establishing the link between these ideas of Nietzsche and his general ethical system of "love of the distant." The opinion exists that Nietzsche advocates, so to speak, "villainy for the sake of villainy," cruelty solely for the sake of the beauty and force intrinsic to it. Nothing could be less true. It is true that Nietzsche, at times castigating the weakness and decrepitude of people today, is prepared to prefer even people with a criminal, and so stronger, will. "Not your sin but your thrift cries to heaven; your meanness even in your sin cries to heaven," he exclaims.[32] But such a thought, fully understandable, of course, and amounting, so to speak, only to a psychological overtone of respect for strength of will and wealth in life's energy, does not warrant including Nietzsche among the proponents of cruelty *an und für sich* [in and for itself]. No one, of course, will suspect Heine of a particular passion for villainy, yet he, prompted by the same feeling as Nietzsche, exclaimed his view of Philistine society much more forcefully than Nietzsche:

> O daß ich große Laster säh, —
> Verbrechen, blutig, kolossal,
> Nur diese satte Tugend nicht
> Und zahlungsfähige Moral![33]

Together with Nietzsche's protests against "meanness in sin," we find in him an equally resolute protest against criminal and antisocial impulses. "Cursed I call all who have only one choice: to become evil beasts or evil tamers of beasts; among such men I would not build my home."[34] The true meaning of Nietzsche's moral condemnation of compassion and justification of cruelty can be explained, to repeat, only in connection with the ethics of "love of the distant."

"Thus my great love of the farthest demands it: *do not spare your neighbor!*"[35] in this exclamation lies, I believe, the explanation of all Nietzsche's views that are relevant here:[36] compassion, in his opinion, is inappropriate and cruelty is necessary where and to the extent that love of the distant demands it. The latter, as we have seen, is necessarily connected with struggle, that is, with the striving to destroy the "neighboring" in the interests of the "distant." But the struggle and striving for destruction are always founded on feelings directly opposed to the moral impulses of "love of one's neighbor." A soft, yielding, compassionate struggle is a moral *contradictio in adjecto;* the more *fierce* and *uncompromising* the struggle, the better it is. All the worst instincts of man — hatred, anger, cruelty, recalcitrance, love of revenge — are ennobled and sanctified, if the impulse behind them is "love of the distant"; more precisely, the egoistic, immoral nature of all these feelings is just what is characteristic of them, but when this nature is replaced by the moral inducement of love of the distant, these feelings are transformed into their very opposite. When human passions are based on moral impulses, anger becomes indignation, thirst for revenge becomes a striving for the restoration of defiled justice, hatred becomes intolerance of evil, and cruelty becomes the severity of a man of conviction. "You commended your highest goal to the heart of these passions," Zarathustra says, "then they became your virtues and passions you enjoyed."[37] This is a truth as ancient as the world and man, but never clearly formulated. Recall the "*sacred vengeance*" about which Kochubei speaks in Pushkin, as the last "treasure" left for him;[38] recall Nekrasov's "muse of *vengeance*";[39] recall the spiteful mood penetrating all the great satirists, from Juvenal[40] and Swift[41] up to and including Saltykov; recall everything that is attractive to us in Bazarov's "passionate, sinful, rebellious heart"[42] — and Nietzsche's thought will be revealed to you in all its moral beauty and sincerity. "The fire of love glows in the names of all the virtues, and the fire of wrath."[43]

Even the doctrine of nonresistance to evil — at first view, the quintessence of the ethics of "love of one's neighbor" — a doctrine that deems illegitimate any active struggle of man against man, cannot deny the legitimacy of the feelings of anger and hatred against evil itself.[44] Moreover, the defender of this doctrine directly, if unconsciously, follows Zarathustra's precept, "do not spare your neighbor," for victory over evil requires the initial ruin of many "neighbors" "nonresistant" to evil, and the proponent of "nonresistance," conscious of the moral height of his cause, quietly leads them to this ruin, just as is done by any other fighter for the "distant." "My suffering and my pity for the suffering — what does it matter?" asks Zarathustra. "Am I concerned with *happiness?* I am concerned with my *work!*"[45] From the point of view of the ethics of love of the distant, a point of view taken by anyone who thinks "of his cause," compassion is not a virtue, but a *weakness;* the thought of a neighbor's suffering must be defeated just as the thought of one's own suffering. "Thus speaks all great love: it overcomes even forgiveness and pity." "Woe to all who love without having a height that is above their pity!"[46] One who does not spare himself is neither obliged, nor even has the right, to spare another. " 'Myself I sacrifice to my love, *and my neighbor as myself'* — thus runs the speech of all creators. But all creators are hard."[47]

Thus does Nietzsche explain the rejection of compassion. The ethics of love of the distant, the ethics of creativity and struggle, cannot be an ethics of compassion. If love of humanity (in the ethics of love of the distant), in its statics, so to speak, is based on its direct opposite — on alienation from people and contempt for them — then in its dynamics, in its quality as *creativity,* love of humanity is also inseparably linked with its antipode, *destruction.* And if love is impossible without hatred and enmity, then it is likewise impossible without cruelty: positive and negative poles of moral life, the cathode and anode of the current of moral feelings, mutually supporting and nourishing each other. "And whoever must be a creator in good and evil, verily, he must first be an annihilator and break values. Thus the highest evil belongs to the highest goodness: but this is creative."[48]

But usually Nietzsche embodies in artistic imagery his teaching on the necessity of severity in the struggle for the "distant":

"O men, in the stone there sleeps an image, the image of my images. Alas, that it must sleep in the hardest, the ugliest stone! Now my hammer rages cruelly against its prison. Pieces of rock rain from the stone: what is that to me?"[49]

At times one is simply astonished how many of Nietzsche's ideas and pronouncements are incorrectly interpreted, to the detriment of his reputation and still more to the detriment of those pursuing his doctrine of moral tasks. Who has not heard about his celebrated, cruel phrase: "What is falling, we should still push"? In this case, however, celebrity has distorted not only the inner meaning of the phrase, but even the phrase itself. Let us listen to Nietzsche himself: "O my brothers, am I cruel? But I say: what is falling, we should still push. Everything today falls and decays: who would check it? But I — I even want to push it."[50] . . . [Frank quotes the rest of this passage.]

The affected opening question, "Am I cruel?"; the turn of speech itself in the celebrated phrase ("*what* is falling," and not "*who*"); and the whole context taken together — all this clearly indicates that the issue here is not about purely personal relations, in which it is supposedly recommended that someone who is falling be pushed, but about the decline of eras, moral structures of life, generations. Nietzsche-Zarathustra teaches that such decline should be accelerated. This behest is as natural, apt, and understandable as possible in the ethics of love of the distant, in the ethics of progress and struggle: Nietzsche's thought expresses only the axiom of any progressive policy, that it is necessary to support and develop everything viable and, in the interests of its success, to hasten the ruin of everything moribund. If in such an image of action there also remains an element of cruelty in relation to what is perishing, then it is a cruelty that is not only necessary, but also *morally valuable*. Progress "asks for sin-offerings," and the one who lives for the "distant" will not want, indeed does not have the right, to act so that "it is those farther away who must pay for your love of your neighbor."[51]

From the same moral considerations derive Nietzsche's sneers at "kindness" and the "kind." Kindness is a complacent, compliant softness of the soul that is compatible neither with struggle, nor with movement forward. Before turning into an innocent child, man, Zarathustra teaches, must pass through still another stage: from a pack camel he must become a strong, fighting lion.[52] One who now professes kindness and innocence rejects movement forward, wants to perpetuate man at the current stage of his development and, for the sake of his own innocence, sacrifices "distant people." For one in whom there is nothing higher than kindness, virtue is only a means toward quiet and sleep. Having heard the sermon of one sage about virtue as a condition of peaceful and quiet sleep, Zarathustra exclaims ironically, "blessed are the sleepy ones: for they shall soon drop off."[53] For Zarathustra himself the ethics of kindness is hateful, as an ethics of *stagnation*: "the noble man wants to create something new and a new virtue. The good [or kind] want the old, and that the old be preserved."[54] But Zarathustra goes still further and affirms that the ideal of kindness is in general unrealizable. Where there is struggle, there is no place for kindness; and because the "kind" must also take part in the struggle, coming out against those who reject their life and virtues and who seek new ones, "the good [or kind] must be *pharisees*":[55] in the name of their peaceful kindness they must *hate* all fighters and creators.[56] . . . [More quotations follow.]

Thus develops the antithesis between the moral systems of "love of one's neighbor" and "love of the distant." The ethics of "love of one's neighbor" unfolds in the ethics of compassion, emotional softness, peacefulness, kindness, and *quietude*. In contrast, Zarathustra gives us "new tablets," developing the ethics of love of the distant and depicting the moral grandeur of the firm and courageous, the rebel and the fighter, of the eternally restless, the ceaseless striver for the reaches of the human spirit. As long as there exists in human life the struggle between the principles of conciliation and indignation — between the desire to preserve the old and the aspiration to create the new, between the longing for peace and the yearning for struggle — the competition in the human soul between these two great moral systems will not cease. ...

II.

Höher als die Liebe zum Nächsten
steht die Liebe zum Fernsten und Künftigen;
höher noch als die Liebe zu Menschen gilt
mir die Liebe zu Sachen und Gespenstern.

Nietzsche, Also sprach Zarathustra[57]

The ethics of "love of the distant," in its antagonism to the ethics of "love of one's neighbor," is peculiar in that it is completely independent of the content of the object itself of love, of the "distant." Regardless of the internal content of the moral ideal, the demands of the ethics of love of the distant remain constant, since only this ideal guides human conduct as an abstract "distant" and puts a human being into relations with other people that may be contrary to relations based on immediate feelings of sympathy and compassion. Therefore, people with the most diverse worldviews, even worldviews completely foreign to Nietzsche's ultimate ideal, can understand and appreciate his ethics of love of the distant. In this way the antagonism between both of the ethical systems with which we have been concerned is only an antagonism of *formal* ethical principles. It is only the difference in the *distance* separating the object of love from its subject, as well as the resulting difference in the paths and means of the active realization of love, that introduces a sharp distinction between the two groups of moral feelings and temperaments, and that gives rise to the radical opposition between the moral evaluations and notions of "good" and "evil" forming these two ethical systems. "Love of the distant" can be love of people no less than can "love of one's neighbor"; and yet there remains an enormous difference between instinctive affinity for the concrete, on hand representatives of the human species who immediately surround us, for our contemporaries and neighbors, and love for people "distant and future," for an abstract, collective entity, "humanity." "Love of the distant" also designates love of one's neighbor, but a neighbor removed to that ideal height where he can become our "star," in Nietzsche's expression.

We see here that the *formal* antithesis between the principles of "love of one's neighbor" and "love of the distant" does not prevent their own unique conciliatory combination, expressed in the fact that "love of one's neighbor" becomes the *content* of the moral ideal, whereas "love of the distant" is the *form of its realization.* The happiness of "neighbors" — the supreme ethical postulate of love of one's neighbor — is itself the "distant" for the sake of which man creates, struggles, and abides by all the aforementioned demands of the ethics of "love of the distant." In this combination we have the essence of the ethical doctrine of *utilitarianism,* in its broadest and most general meaning. Utilitarian morality, seeing its ideal in the "greatest happiness of the greatest number of people,"[58] is undoubtedly based on the feeling of love of one's neighbor, which alone compels us to value the happiness of neighbors. But utilitarian morality will not say, together with Dostoevsky, that the progress of humanity is not worth one tear from a child; on the contrary, if progress leads to an increase in the sum of happiness, then from this point of view it can be bought by many tears and much suffering, if only this moral expense does not exceed the return. In this sense utilitarian morality will regard conflict, absence of compassion, and all the other demands of the ethics of "love of the distant" as legitimate, if their result is the growth of the sum of happiness on earth. The doctrine of utilitarianism thus reconciles the antithesis among moral feelings, laying at the basis of morality simply the principle of economy: the demands of the ethics of love of the distant, demands which counter the happiness of one's neighbor, are, for utilitarianism, only a roundabout way of achieving this happiness, that is, for realizing love of one's neighbor; as expenses of the moral economy, these demands are legitimate to the extent they are justified by the moral return achieved through them.

To this unquestionably highly symmetrical and consistent combination of the two moral principles in the ethics of utilitarianism, Nietzsche opposes his own ethical ideal, and it is precisely in this respect that he is the boldest innovator and destroyer of old "tablets." He rejects love of one's neighbor not only as the basis of the ethics of compassion and conciliation, but also as the supreme instance and ultimate end of even the ethics of love of the distant. Against utilitarian morality, with which all contemporary ethical thought is consciously or unconsciously saturated, Nietzsche declares a decisive war in the name of a new moral ideal, which not only in the means and paths of its attainment, but also in its very content, is, so to speak, the "distant" par excellence, that is, it does not consist in service to one's "neighbor" and his happiness. His struggle with the usual moral worldview proceeds not from the *position* of the object of love, not from its *relation* to the subject, but from its very *content:* the ethical principle of "love of the distant" is characterized here by its opposition to the principle of "love of one's neighbor," understood as *love of people generally.* If in the above epigraph Nietzsche declares that "higher than love of one's neighbor is love of the distant and future," then he clarifies his thought by adding, "still higher than *love of people,* I value *love of things and phantoms.*"[59]

Thus, "love of the distant" is better characterized as "love of things and phantoms." But what should we understand under the latter? What kind of new moral feeling is this, which pretends not only to compete in its ethical significance with love of people, but to stand above it? It has long been customary to divide all human motives that are ascribed positive or negative moral value into two basic feelings: love for oneself and love for surrounding people, *egoism* and *altruism.* The first feeling is recognized as the embodiment of everything morally negative, the second, of everything morally positive. This division is considered the only possible one and completely exhaustive; for ordinary moral consciousness the concepts of altruism and egoism are schemes as solid and all-encompassing as the very categories of good and evil, and indeed mean nearly the same as these categories. Good is altruism and love of people, evil is egoism and "self-love": *tertium non datur* [there is no third possibility]. With such a belief, ordinary moral consciousness relates negatively, of course, to the idea of some unfamiliar third moral feeling — the feeling of "love of things and phantoms," taking it either for a concoction deprived of internal meaning or for a product of some moral perversion.

But the ready-made judgments of everyday consciousness correspond to the truth as little in the case at hand as in the huge majority of cases. We are still speaking about truth not in the moral-practical, but simply in the cognitive-theoretical sense. No matter how we evaluate love of self and love of people, one thing is clear: these feelings *do not exhaust* all our moral motives. There exists a number of impulses, directed neither to one's own good, nor to the good of one's neighbors, but which nonetheless possess indisputable moral value. Let us listen to an intelligent, subtle, and calm investigator of moral facts.

> It must always be emphasized that the contrast between egoism and altruism in no way fully embraces the motivations for our actions. In fact we have an *objective* interest in whether certain events or things are realized or not, and this is so regardless of the consequences for the human subject. It is important to us that a harmony, an order based on ideas, and a significance — which does not have to fit the usual schemes of ethics or aesthetics — prevail in the world. We feel ourselves obliged to cooperate in this without always asking whether it gives pleasure or will be of advantage to any person, that is, whether it is of interest to *oneself* or to *another.* ... In many cases, then, the consciousness of purpose stops short of *objective* reality, and does not borrow its value primarily from its subjective reflexes. ... It is, in any case, a psychological fact. ...[60]

It would be possible to illustrate, with an overwhelming number of examples, such existence of *objective* motives, not falling under the rubric of egoism and altruism. The thinker whose life is directed toward the discovery of truth, apart from any consideration of whether it benefits or is needed by anyone; the artist who strives to perfect an artistic image without thinking about for whom his work is useful or pleasant; the person who avenges defiled justice or honor, achieving this, perhaps, only by his own death and that of his enemy — here are the first, randomly chosen examples, which even as *types* do not, of course, come close to exhausting the whole diversity of motives of this kind. In all these and similar cases people are obviously guided by neither self-love nor love of others: their driving motive is the aspiration to attain a certain *objective* state, apart from any relation to someone's advantage or pleasure. We do not know a more apt or successful designation for this type of aspiration toward *abstract moral goods* that possess internal value than Nietzsche's term, somewhat fantastic at first glance: "love of things and phantoms." Here, the concept of "thing" means that the goal of an act done on such motives is not a human being or subject, but something supra-human or *objective*. The concept of "phantom" describes very precisely the peculiarity of these objects: they are not real, material objects but, from the psychological point of view, fictions, products of subjective mental life, which are, however, ascribed the character of objective, substantial existence. Truth, justice, beauty, harmony, honor — here are some of these "phantoms," love of which has long served and continues to serve as one of the most powerful driving forces of humanity.[61]

Thus, no matter whether "love of things and phantoms" stands, in its moral value, higher or lower than "love of people," the very fact of its existence as a third type of moral feeling, equally removed from both egoism and altruism, cannot — despite the current view — be disputed. But once the problem is resolved theoretically, once there no longer remains any doubt about the presence of a special moral feeling of "love for things and phantoms," then resolution of the moral-practical problem, specifically the question of the *moral value* of this feeling, no longer presents any difficulty, either. In general, *to prove* the moral value of anything is impossible; here there is only one path — appeal to moral feeling. And this moral feeling says forcefully and impressively that love of truth, justice, beauty, honor, and other "phantoms" possesses an indisputable and very high moral value. Whether this value is higher than that of love of people (as Nietzsche affirms or, more correctly, suggests) cannot be demonstrated *logically*. According to the view we are presenting, the contest for supremacy between the two independent moral principles is resolved not by argument, but by the elemental moral force of each of them in the soul of man. There are people, temperaments, societies, and epochs for which the highest moral ideal is the happiness of neighbors, in all the concrete

materiality of such well-being. And there are other people, societies, and epochs for which *abstract moral goods* — *"phantoms"* — become the symbol of
faith, as a religious or moral ideal, a notion of a moral standard, the realization
of justice, or as the defense of truth, freedom, and human dignity. For such
epochs and people the word of Zarathustra resonates: higher than love of
people stands love of things and phantoms!

No matter how each of us decides the question of the comparative value of
"love of people" and "love of phantoms," the critical deepening of our moral
consciousness is, in any event, the service of the Nietzschean "transvaluation
of all values." We have seen that the concept of "love of phantoms" undoubtedly expresses a moral feeling long familiar to humanity and that it, consequently, postulates nothing new in morals. But moral feeling is one thing,
while moral doctrine, like the moral consciousness fostered by it, is another.
Doctrine and consciousness always lag behind feeling, and never completely
correspond to, or precisely and fully express, it. The task of ethics, as a normative discipline, is to establish an accordance between moral *convictions* and
moral *feelings,* to reexamine and deepen moral *consciousness* by juxtaposing
it to innate or unconsciously acquired moral *instincts.* Such is precisely the
service of the Nietzschean "transvaluation of values": elucidation of the moral
conflict between love of one's neighbor and love of the distant, and demonstration of the existence and independent moral value of the feeling of "love of
phantoms," in practice long known, but not consciously evaluated. It is without doubt that this feeling remained in the shadows and failed to pass into the
light of moral consciousness only because of the dominance of the narrow
ethical doctrine of utilitarianism, which took people's happiness to be the only
supreme moral good, and which therefore did not want to see or recognize in
moral feelings anything other than either a desire for the happiness of neighbors (altruism) or its direct antipode (egoism). This is why Nietzsche had to
develop his ethical views in open polemics with the ethics of utilitarianism,
with the "doctrine of happiness and virtue," from which, in his opinion, people "have become smaller, and they are becoming smaller and smaller."[62]

The moral consciousness that is accustomed by the ethics of utilitarianism
and altruism to believe that there cannot be anything morally valuable outside
of love of people and the desire for their happiness will not, it seems, easily
yield to Nietzsche's onslaught against it, that is, to his doctrine of the moral
grandeur of human motivations that are *objective and disinterested* in relation
not only to the "I" but also to every "thou," motivations Nietzsche brings
together under the name "love of phantoms." Against this *ethical idealism,*
utilitarianism contends that "love of phantoms," no matter how dissimilar it
seems to altruism, is nonetheless only an indirect form of expressing love of

people and the desire for their happiness. And in fact it cannot be denied that very often someone who dedicates his life to serving the abstract "phantoms" of truth, justice, spiritual independence, and so forth brings enormous benefit to his fellow citizens and neighbors and so indirectly serves them and their happiness. This gives reason to seek the moral significance of the feeling of "love of phantoms" in its similarity to altruism, both in its basic features and in its objective consequences. Nonetheless, it must be recognized that utilitarianism is entirely wrong in drawing this conclusion, which rests on the utter confusion of two completely different questions in the discipline of ethics, the *moral* problem and the *logical-causal* problem.

There is no doubt that *genetically* the whole aggregate of moral feelings and principles — including "love of phantoms" — grew from the needs of social welfare. It is also highly likely that this link between morality and social welfare is not only genetic, but also *functional*, because any moral feeling or act has, *im großen und ganzen* [all in all], its objective consequence and, as it were, its natural purpose in the promotion of social welfare, that is, in the growth of human happiness and well-being. In this sense, that is, as a *theoretical, sociological hypothesis* establishing the causal and functional link between morality and happiness, utilitarianism has an incontestably serious raison d'être.[63] And yet this link is something completely foreign and irrelevant from the point of view of the *moral* problem. Not the objective consequences of an act or feeling, but its subjective *end* and internal motive determine its moral significance. No matter what the utilitarian results of "love of phantoms," once it becomes indisputable that its subjective motivation is not the desire for increasing people's happiness, but the internal or, so to speak, immanent moral attractiveness of the "phantoms" themselves — and it is just this quality that constitutes the concept of "love of phantoms" in contrast to altruism — then the moral doctrine of utilitarianism is refuted. Perhaps such a contradiction between the genetic and moral point of view on the phenomena of morality, a contradiction that at first glance might seem strange, is itself a highly necessary and useful product of social selection; its obliteration, on which utilitarianism insists, would surely threaten humanity with the most dire consequences. Thus, the successes of science, which have had such enormous practical value, could have been achieved only through the disinterested pursuit of truth apart from any consideration of popular benefit. And how many national calamities could have been averted if contemporary "*Realpolitik*" — this most typical product of state utilitarianism — had been replaced by "*Idealpolitik*," which would have taken into account not only the utilitarian interests of the country, but also even the elementary "phantoms" of justice and uprightness!

Thus, to defend its position utilitarianism must show not that objective, nonaltruistic motivations are generally useful to humanity, but that their utility, in every individual case, is their only moral justification and the sole basis of their moral value. Such a *thema probandum* [test case] does admit one easy, but invalid, escape from the difficulty. Specifically, it is possible to claim that objects of nonaltruistic feelings — "phantoms" — constitute in themselves an invaluable blessing [*blago*] for man (apart from any relation to their further utility), so that love of them is *eo ipso* a desire for human happiness [blago]. "Man lives not by bread alone" — he needs "phantoms" no less than bread; satisfaction of the thirst for truth and justice is as necessary a condition of human happiness as is satisfaction of hunger. The truth of such a contention is self-evident, but only because it is essentially an empty tautology: the concept of well-being [blago], of the condition of happiness, is expanded to include the concept of the moral good [*dobro*] in general, and then it is no longer difficult, of course, to show that any good [dobro] is a blessing [blago]. But such an expansion of the concept of well-being is illegitimate in that it masks the radical distinction between *subjective* and *objective* value, between the good [blago] as a condition of the satisfaction of the subjective wishes of man, and the good [blago] as that which possesses an objective moral significance, completely independent of subjective human views and evaluations. Establishing the *real* link between the phenomena of the good [dobro] and happiness makes sense only on the condition of a sharp *logical* distinction between the good and happiness as *concepts;* it loses all meaning with any attempt to fuse these concepts. There thus remains only the stark, direct, and unambiguous claim of utilitarianism that "love of phantoms" is valuable only to the extent it is love of people and the desire to promote their happiness. But just such a clear posing of the postulate of utilitarianism exposes its complete failure. "Love of phantoms" is characterized, as we have seen, precisely by its *disinterestedness,* by the absence of considerations about its subjective significance, about its benefit (so that even if this benefit is present, it lies beyond the limits of the moral field of vision). Utilitarianism thus faces a dilemma: either to reject categorically the moral value of this feeling [love of phantoms], or to acknowledge just as categorically its own untenability. And in practice utilitarianism actually does relate with hostility to all ideals that cannot answer the direct question: *cui prodest* [whose benefit]? And the dominance of utilitarian principles has significantly contributed to the disregard of such ideals. If utilitarianism ironically points to the principle *"fiat justitia, pereat mundus,"*[64] as the logical conclusion of an *objective,* self-sufficient moral "phantom," then it should not be forgotten that in the struggle with this principle utilitarianism is often forced to rely on the opposite principle: *"fiat utilitas, pereat justitia."*[65]

And if so, then utilitarianism contradicts the clear voice of moral feeling and therefore must itself be rejected.[66]

If the wish to liken "love of phantoms" to altruism, and to seek the source of its moral value in its similarity to service to people and their happiness, must be recognized as untenable, then a comparison to egoism would be just as wrong. Unfortunately, Nietzsche himself is the originator of such a comparison. Possessing more artistic depth and perspicacity than analytic strength of mind, Nietzsche, in his protest against utilitarianism — which sees in altruism the only morally valuable feeling, and in everything contradicting it a moral evil — went to the opposite extreme in likening "love of phantoms" to egoism. This comparison is, however, in essence purely verbal and terminological; even a slightly thoughtful reader will easily understand that the feeling Nietzsche glorifies under the *name* self-love is in its content infinitely far from that. Let us listen to one of Zarathustra's sermons to the "higher men," in which he teaches them "self-love" [or egoism]:

> You creators, you higher men! One is pregnant only with one's own child. Do not let yourselves be gulled and beguiled! Who, after all, is *your* neighbor? And even if you act "for the neighbor" — you still do not create for him.
>
> Unlearn this "for," you creators! Your very virtue wants that you do nothing "for" and "for the sake of" and "because." You shall plug up your ears against these false little words. "For the neighbor" is only the virtue of the little people: there one says "birds of a feather" and "one hand washes the other." They have neither the right nor the strength for *your* egoism. In your egoism, you creators, is the caution and providence of the pregnant. What no one has yet laid eyes on, the fruit: that your whole love shelters and saves and nourishes. Where your whole love is, with your child, there is also your whole virtue. Your work, your will, that is *your* "neighbor": do not let yourselves be gulled with false values![67]

This sermon clearly shows how inadequate the name "self-love" [or egoism] is for the motive described here.[68] The care of the pregnant mother for her unborn child [or fruit] [*plod*], concern for the future child, cannot be called self-love; consequently, what is here equated with love of the unborn child — love of your *work* — resembles egoism as little as the "caution of the pregnant" does. A mother's love for her unborn child, introduced here as an example of the type of motive fitting of "creators," is one of the brilliant images by which Nietzsche, in his artistic genius, is able to reveal his thought better than could tens of pages of abstract analysis. And what, indeed, could be more unselfish or moving than this love of the unborn child? Yet it is not altruism, not love for a living, visible "neighbor," but only love for something coming into being, for what is in the future, for what is being created, love not for a human being, but for the "phantom" of a future human being. And as a mother loves and cares for her future child, so must all "creators," Zarathustra teaches, care for and love the phantoms they strive to embody in life. . . . Given such a meaning of "self-love," it would also be a crude misunderstanding to see in the thought of its necessity for "higher people" and its impermissibility for "little people" a repetition of Raskolnikov's famous unfortunate idea.[69] As a result of the complete difference in the meaning of the concept of "self-love" for "higher" and "little" people, Nietzsche's thought amounts only to saying that altruism must remain the sole moral force for people incapable of creativity in the name of "love of phantoms." At the same time the above passage clearly illuminates the motive that induced Nietzsche to liken "love of phantoms" with egoism: it is his protest against utilitarianism, for which moral justification of an act requires an answer to the question: For what, for whose benefit is it directed? In his struggle with this ethical direction, Nietzsche advances the demand that the moral value of an act be independent of any "for" or "for the sake of," independent, that is, of its consequence for the happiness of neighbors. And it is in just this independence that Nietzsche sees an affinity between such motives and egoism. But if the reason for this comparison of "love of phantoms" with egoism is understandable, the comparison itself, to repeat, remains clearly in error: the egoism of an act is determined precisely by its self-interestedness, by the utility of its consequences for the actor, whereas the moral value of "love of phantoms," in Nietzsche's conception, must be *immanent,* that is, inherent to the feeling itself and fully independent of any of its consequences.

This likening of "love of phantoms" with egoism expresses still another profound and very characteristic feature of Nietzsche's moral Weltanschauung. To clarify this it is necessary to consider Nietzsche's rather well-known — indeed, too well-known — protest against the idea of *duty* in ethics. This protest, in its abstract, theoretical form certainly fails, because the category of duty is not morally, but only *logically* related to the very concept of morality: "moral" is just what we experience and conceive under the category of *duty,* in the form of "*ought*" [*dolzhenstvovanie*]. Therefore, any attempt to separate the concept of duty from morality is always based on a logical misunderstanding, and even if a moralist taught us to refrain from obeying all moral obligations, this very renunciation of obligations would mean a new *obligation,* formally identical with the previous ones. A moral doctrine without the category of duty, without the words "you ought," without the imperative mood, is as much a *contradictio in adjecto* as a scientific theory without the categories of existence [*bytie*] and causation, without the words "is" and "because." The elimination of the category of duty is thus the rejection not of a certain content of morality, but of the formal *idea* of morality. Nietzsche himself realized this and in the last period of his creativity leaned toward the rejection of all morality in general; he even called Zarathustra the "first immoralist." Characteristic enough is the contradiction that this *immoralist* spends his whole life in the *moral instruction* of people, in the establishment of "new tablets."

Notwithstanding the formal, logical connection between the concepts of duty and morality, one must not forget the diversity and richness of moral experiences expressed in the general form: "ought." When a human being finds among his motives one to which he ascribes absolute, objective significance, independent of his wishes and moods, then the need to follow this motive and to let it triumph over all the others is something he experiences in the form of *compulsion, duty, obligation.* This feeling is the most indicative psychological feature of moral motives. But the very character of this compulsion, its force and poignancy, are perceived differently, according to the extent to which all other, subjective motivations counteract the moral motive or, on the contrary, harmonize with and facilitate it. Although moral compulsion, in contrast to the compulsion of law and external power in general, is always internal compulsion, coming from one's own "I" (free from the external side), the burden of compulsion is more tangibly and clearly felt — approximating in its psychological effect external compulsion — when there exists a sharp discord between the moral, commanding "I" and the empirical, submitting "I," than when this discord is not so strong and is softened by an element of harmony. The psychic mechanism itself of moral compulsion likewise differs in both cases: in the first, the purely moral instinct, demanding the triumph of the moral motivation over the immoral, will be coupled with fear of the consequences of moral disobedience — whether the disapprobation of public opinion, a presumed religious-metaphysical punishment, or pangs of conscience — so that moral compulsion will be felt as severe duress by some alien power; but in the second case, easy, free, and disinterested adherence to the path indicated by a compelling inner voice will leave a joyous impression of harmony between an act and the internal nature of the actor. In the distant perspective looms the ideal of the human being for whom moral motives are so closely meshed with the subjective inclinations of his nature that he will no longer need any *prescripts* — just as now people do not need prescripts to eat, drink, or reproduce — and consequently will notice no burden of moral compulsion. Whether or not we realize such an ideal, its moral value is in any case indisputable, as is the fact that the level of a person's moral development is measured not only by the strength of the moral impulses in him, but also by their affinity to his general character and by the relative ease with which they succeed in guiding his conduct. Nietzsche's protest against moral compulsion is only an insistence on the necessity and moral significance of morally integral natures, for which *what ought to be* [*dolzhnoe*] is also *what is desired* [*zhelaemoe*]. He is outraged by a morality based on fear of punishment or expectation of reward; a morality in the form of prescript (foreign to internal inclinations) by a terrible, invisible power; a morality, subordination to which is "the spasm under the scourge." . . . [Frank quotes more of Zarathustra's scorn for this morality.]

From this point of view, which sees moral grandeur in the *coincidence* of moral motives with subjective, personal ones, the ideal of "self-denial" loses its value. Obviously, self-denial is necessary for someone who needs to *renounce himself,* his personal interests and desires, in order to fulfill moral prescripts; self-denial supposes a contradiction between moral and personal motives. Nietzsche indicates another path for the triumph of morality: the *accordance* of moral motives with individual wants, the transformation of the first into the second. Of course, this path supposes a superior level of moral development, completely unattainable for very many people, but it is just this that points to its great loftiness.

"Weary of saying: what makes an act good is that it is unselfish.

"Oh, my friends, that your self be in your deed as the mother is in her child—let that by *your* word concerning virtue!"[70]

Thus, rejection of moral *compulsion* and espousal of "self-love," as the antipode of the morally imperfect ideal of "self-denial," are for Nietzsche only a demand of the type of moral reeducation of humanity that would result in the closest conjunction of individual and moral, subjectively and objectively valuable motives, and in the absence of the feeling of onerous compulsion by the moral law. In what connection does this demand stand to the ethical system of love of the distant (understood as "love of phantoms") and to the special position that "love of phantoms" occupies alongside the moral feelings of egoism and altruism?

In Nietzsche, the struggle against the ethics of altruism and utilitarianism . . . might well be caused, to a significant degree, by the cruel, despotic compulsion, by the dark, violent tyranny of moral motives over egoistic ones that is strikingly characteristic of the moral law in the ethics of altruism and utilitarianism. The reason for this latter circumstance lies, it seems to us, in the following. Factually, it is beyond doubt that love of people, as an innate character trait, as a natural instinct, is hardly at all developed in people. In the overwhelming majority of cases, the sphere of activity of this feeling is limited and, by the very essence of the matter, must be limited to a comparatively small number of people, connected by bonds of love, friendship, and family. Not attempting to substantiate this claim empirically or theoretically, we state this phenomenon simply as a fact known to everyone. For the most authoritative witness to it, we can turn to that exquisite psychologist, Lev Tolstoy. In one of the best and most famous works from his last period,[71] Tolstoy, with his usual lucidity, demonstrates that to love humanity in the real, literal sense of love, to love it as a mother loves her child, or as spouses, brothers, and friends love each other, is completely impossible. To love people in general, merely because they are people, means nothing other than to conduct oneself in relation to them as in relation to intimate, truly loved ones. But such conduct cannot be based on the instinct of love, but rather only on the demand of the moral law, enjoining us to see in all people our brothers. From this, the great thinker and moralist draws the conclusion that love of people requires, for its presence and strength, support in another feeling — in a religious-metaphysical sanction, in the love, inherent to people, for the Being personifying the moral law.[72] Not broaching this conclusion, we cite here only its premise.

The moral prescript of love of people, by virtue of the fact that this feeling, in its abstract form of love of humanity or of all people without exception, has little ground in people's innate instincts, necessarily expresses itself as an exhortation to cruel, uncompromising struggle with egoism. This is why the ethics of altruism is replete with images of people's natural sinfulness, of an eternal struggle between flesh and spirit; why it can hardly accommodate the idea of a harmonious combination of subjective-individual and objective-moral motives or the idea of the possibility of an easy, joyous, and free adherence to the path indicated by the moral law; and why the ethics of altruism is, so to speak, largely an ethics of *duty*, an ethics realized and realizable only by tyrannical suppression of man's rebellious nature, an ethics of asceticism and self-denial. In Nietzsche's words, the ethics of altruism is always a call for the annihilation of *me* to please *you*.

The case is, apparently, somewhat different with the moral feeling that we, following Nietzsche's example, have considered under the name "love of phantoms." In the usual, current codes of morality we will rarely find clear claims for it or stern summonses for obedience to it. And this is because "love of phantoms" lives in a person's soul much more as an instinctive need than as a moral prescript. If written and unwritten law differ, then in ethics, as we have already indicated, it is necessary to distinguish formulated from unformulated morality, ethical doctrine from moral feeling. "Love of phantoms" belongs almost entirely to the latter category. As a result, it turns out in the mass of cases to be a feeling more deeply rooted, more instinctive, and stronger than altruism. Empirically, I believe it can be considered an established fact that a human being spontaneously capable — not through obedience to moral prescript, but through instinctive need — of loving all people without exception, of ailing with all the sufferings of people utterly foreign to him, and of rejoicing over all their joys, is an entirely exceptional phenomenon, in any case encountered much more rarely than someone capable of responding to abstract "phantoms," of being indignant at injustice, falsehood, humiliation, and violence, and of obtaining satisfaction through the instinct of justice, truth, human dignity, and freedom, not at all considering the question, *cui prodest,* or reflecting about whose fate his own moral needs lighten.[73]

In view of this (relative, of course) spontaneity and immediacy of the instinct of "love of phantoms," its likening to egoism, as in Nietzsche, has a deep psychological basis: both feelings resemble each other precisely in their affinity to the human "I," to the natural, as it were physiological inclinations of human nature. I cannot experience love of a Kaffir or a Hottentot, of my enemy or someone antipathetic to me, or even simply of the first person I meet, except by artificially training myself, that is, by suppressing my natural egoistic motives. On the other hand, I can experience, as my immediate, instinctive motive, the desire to uphold justice or righteousness in relation to these same people, that is, love of certain moral "phantoms," a love awakened in me through contact with people. I will experience a violation of truth or justice almost as an injury inflicted against me personally, against my peace of mind and happiness. An analogy with altruistic motives, to the extent they also possess such immediacy, will perhaps better clarify this idea. A mother experiences the most selfless love for her child almost as an egoistic feeling: the person [*lichnost'*] of the child merges with her own person, the child's happiness and welfare become her own happiness and welfare. A mother, Nietzsche says, does not demand a reward for her love; she experiences it not as deprivation, but as joy, as her own egoistic need. The sphere to which such altruistic motives can be applied is, however, extremely narrow. On the other hand, there is no limit to the sphere of relations that "love of phantoms" can encompass, a love that in its force and immediacy sustains comparison with a mother's love for her child. Thus, the instinct of "love of phantoms" is capable, in its psychological effect, of resembling egoism, although theoretically — we again stress this — a moral gulf lies between them, a gulf dividing motives having merely subjective value from those possessing objective moral value. The moral law prescribing concern for the good of one's neighbor will be felt, for the most part, as a command to sacrifice the interests of my "I" to the interests of some "thou"; on the other hand, the moral law commanding love and defense of certain "phantoms" will be perceived as a demand to be concerned about the best, most important and sacred interests of my own "I." In Nietzsche there is a wonderful passage pertaining to the personal relations among people and explaining this difference between love of people and "love of phantoms." "If a friend does you evil, then say: 'I forgive you what you did to me; but that you have done it to *yourself*—how could I forgive that?' "[74] In an offense committed against one's neighbor, not only his interests, but also the interests of the offender himself are thus infringed, to the extent his deed diminishes his own best possession—the "phantom" of justice, nobility, or magnanimity. Such is the meaning of the Nietzschean proximation of "love of phantoms" to egoism.

This concurrence in the feeling of "love of phantoms" of subjective-individual motives with objective-moral ones creates a special category of moral phenomena, perhaps the highest product of moral development—namely, the concept of *moral right* [*moral'noe pravo*]. The concept of moral right is not identical with the current popular concept of it. By the latter is meant simply a certain subjective interest, the pursuit of which is permitted by the norms of morality. Thus, we say that someone has the right to rest after work, that everyone has the right to expect the help of people nearby, or that an honest person has the right to universal respect, and so forth. In all these cases the "moral right" of a person [*nravstvennoe pravo litsa*], like a juridical right in the subjective sense, is only a product or reflection of the corresponding obligation of everyone else. The moral law prescribes respect for honesty, help for people nearby, the provision of rest for workers, and so forth, and this prescript creates a corresponding right for the person [*litso*] on whose behalf it is issued. But by *moral right* [moral'noe pravo] we understand a subjective interest, the subject's defense of which is not only permitted, but positively *prescribed* by the moral law, by virtue of the objective moral value inherent to this interest. The obligation to realize this right thus lies not only on surrounding persons, but also on the very person claiming this interest and bearing this right, because his moral right coincides with his moral obligation. To explain this concept let us again take the example of altruistic feeling, when it assumes the form of both a subjective and moral motive. If external circumstances deprive a mother of the possibility of actively showing her love for her child (if, for example, the child is forcibly taken from her), then her claim to the removal of the obstacles to the realization of her love will be not only morally permissible, but also morally *obligatory,* for any mother not insisting on such a demand ought to be morally condemned. Her right to realize her love for her child is also simultaneously her *obligation;* that is, it is a right morally prescribed to her or, according to our designation, her moral right. But maternal love, to repeat, represents an exception, in its spontaneity and instinctiveness, to that type of moral feeling we call love of people.

The ethics of utilitarianism and altruism, as we have seen, is characterized precisely by a sharp contradiction between personal motives and moral obligations; as a result, the concept of moral right [moral'noe pravo] is, as a general rule, almost unknown to this ethics. Every "I want" and "I demand for myself" is, from the point of view of this ethics, either a sinful thought, which necessarily burdens consciousness with the corresponding moral obligation — "I ought not to want and demand for myself" — or else an ethically irrelevant motive that is a matter of taste or practical benefit. Only an ethics that rests on harmony between egoistic and moral motives can work out the formula of moral right: "I want and demand for myself *and am obliged to demand.*" After all that has been said above, there is no need to demonstrate that it is the moral feeling of "love of phantoms," by virtue of its affinity with subjective interests, that will most often provide the occasion for the emergence of moral rights; the concept of moral right stands at the very center of the ethical system of "love of the distant" (in the sense of "love of phantoms"). If the moral law imposes an obligation to love and defend certain "phantoms" — truth, justice, human dignity, independence — then, given an independent, extra-moral desire for them, it also creates the *moral right* to them. In this way, the moral law itself *prescribes* the defense of certain *rights* — the right to the rule of truth and justice in human relations, to the preservation of human dignity, to the spiritual freedom of man, and so forth. Just such an aspiration to defend the *moral rights of the person* [lichnost'] is what Nietzsche has in mind under the "wholesome, healthy, *blessed selfishness*" that he lauds: "And at that time it also happened — and verily, it happened for the first time — that his word pronounced *selfishness* blessed, the wholesome, healthy selfishness that wells from a powerful soul."[75] . . . [Frank quotes from the rest of this passage.]

The moral rights of the person are the same *sacred and inalienable rights of man* that were once the social-moral catchword of the day, but that now have become "forgotten words," given the dominance of positivist-utilitarian moral views, with their exclusive principle of *"salus populi suprema lex"*[76] and the contradiction they create between social-moral and personal motives. The reader will recall, perhaps, how these ethical views led the Russian intelligentsia, in the seventies of the past century, to the belief in the necessity of renouncing their own human rights in the interests of the good of the popular masses. Apart from the theoretical mistakenness of putting such a contradiction between the material and spiritual good of the people, this belief, notwithstanding the rare moral qualities of its bearers, undoubtedly contained an error of a purely moral type:[77] it was supposed that the spiritual claims of the intelligentsia were not its sacred and inalienable rights, which could not be sacrificed for any ends, but only a matter of its subjective tastes and personal interests. The theoretical mistake has already long been overcome and has passed into the archive of history, but the social-ethical views behind the *moral-practical* error prevail even today. We hear much about self-denial, about giving up personal interests for the good of our neighbors, about heavy moral obligations prescribing that we give everything to others and demand nothing for ourselves, but as before we hear very little about the rights of man, about the interests he is neither obliged *nor even has the right* to sacrifice, about his obligation to remove all obstacles to the realization of these sacred rights, about social-moral work based not on renunciation of one's "I," but on the affirmation and development of the deepest, most sacred, and most human sides of this "I." The motive behind a person's work on behalf of society remains, as before, only the heavy burden of moral obligation, and not "wholesome, healthy, blessed selfishness." "With the names of its happiness it [such selfishness] banishes from its presence whatever is contemptible. From its presence it banishes whatever is cowardly. ... Whatever is servile it spits on, this blessed selfishness."[78] In our view, the ethics of altruism and utilitarianism, the demand to give up one's "I" on behalf of the material well-being of a many-headed "thou," has eclipsed the prescripts of the ethics of "love of phantoms" — the demand to protect and defend moral ideals as the sacred, *personal* possession of every human being. Fulfillment of the moral law, it seems to us, would have a more reliable guarantee, as would social welfare, if morally conscious people thought not only about the interests of *thou*, but also about what is blessed and inviolable in the interests of their own "I" — especially where life so shamelessly flouts these interests. This is why it is well to listen to Zarathustra's words, bold but full of profound meaning: "Higher than love of one's neighbor is love of the distant and future; still higher than love of people, I value love of things and phantoms."

III.

Eure Liebe zum Leben sei Liebe zu
eurer höchsten Hoffnung: und eure höchste
Hoffnung sei der höchste Gedanke des
Lebens.[79]
— Wo ist doch der Blitz, der euch mit
seiner Zunge lecke? Wo ist der Wahnsinn,
mit dem ihr geimpft werden müßtet?
Seht, ich lehre euch den Übermenschen: der
ist dieser Blitz, der ist dieser Wahnsinn![80]

                        Nietzsche, Also sprach Zarathustra

We described above Nietzsche's ethical system as an "ethics of love of the distant." We pointed further to the distinctive logical consistency of this system, in which — in contrast to the ethics of altruism and utilitarianism — the "distant" is not man and his happiness, not the "neighboring," even if temporally, spatially, or psychologically remote, but moral "phantoms," that is, objective ideals possessing absolute and autonomous moral value. But we still have not touched upon one of the central ideas of Nietzschean morality — the image of the superman. In what connection does this image stand to the ethics of love of the distant?

Here there remains just a few things to say.

The "superman" — as the name itself suggests — is a higher being than man. The moral goal of human life consists in promoting the appearance on earth of this higher being.

"*I teach you the superman.* Man is something that shall be overcome."

"What is the ape to man? A laughingstock or a painful embarrassment. And man shall be just that for the superman: a laughingstock or a painful embarrassment."

"Man is a rope, tied between beast and superman."

"What is great in man is that he is a bridge and not an end: what can be loved in man is that he is an *overture* and a *going under.*"[81]

The idea of the superman expresses a belief in the supreme moral value of the cultural perfectibility [*sovershenstvovanie*] of man. This must result, Nietzsche dreams, in the appearance of a type so superior in its intellectual-moral qualities to contemporary man that it will need to be recognized as a special biological form, the "superman," as it were. True, the very image of the superman is fantastic and utopian, *ne plus ultra*, but in Nietzsche it serves, in his own words, only as a "folly that must be fostered in people" to inspire in them — in every individual person, as well as in society as a whole — the strongest desire for moral and intellectual perfectibility, bringing them closer to this image. But in what does the spiritual height of the superman consist?

Nowhere did Nietzsche give a precise answer to this question, nowhere did he more concretely characterize his superman; indeed, this did not fall within his task. The superman is, so to say, a *formal* moral image. It signifies the highest level of the spiritual development of humanity, the fullest extent to which the spiritual buds contained in contemporary man are capable of flowering. The superman is only the personification in a human image of the entire aggregate of abstract, autonomous, and self-sufficient moral ideals, "phantoms," the love of which, as we have seen, Nietzsche strives to make the basic moral stimulus of man. This is why the idea of the superman does not add any essential traits to the ethics of "love of the distant" or "love of phantoms," but rather only gives this ethics an artistic-figurative embodiment. If Nietzsche contrasts "love of phantoms" to love of people and their happiness and if he recognizes "love of phantoms" as the higher moral feeling, then the same views are expressed in the idea of superman: this idea postulates the supreme and autonomous meaning of *cultural progress,* of the moral-intellectual perfectibility of man and society, apart from any relation to the quantity of happiness this progress provides. The accession of the superman is not the triumph of human happiness, the satisfaction of all the personal subjective inclinations and longings of people; it is the triumph of man's spiritual nature, the realization of all his *objectively valuable* claims.

Thus the ethics of love of the distant culminates with a surprisingly strong and bold logical consistency. The supreme moral instance turns out to be something "distant" in the sharpest meaning of the word, something infinitely remote from all the subjective interests of any "neighbors" — namely, the realization of a cultural type, embodying in itself objective moral beauty. Simmel put it well in his study of Nietzsche: the distinctive moral feature of the "superman," a feature that nearly exhausts the whole content of this image, is the moral character of "nobility." But nobility, as Simmel himself showed, is a trait situated on the border between the spheres of ethical and aesthetic evaluation, a trait characterized precisely by the complete absence of everything utilitarian, by utter removal and isolation from everything commonplace, practically useful, and ordinary.[82] Thus, nobility of nature in the broad sense means hardly anything other than an innately high (i.e., exceeding the usual) level of spiritual development in a human being, a level at which all his instinctive, personal, subjective tastes and inclinations are penetrated and inspired by deep natural moral properties. Nobility is a synonym for *exaltedness,* and it is this exaltedness or height above the average level of spiritual development that exhausts the essence of the superman.

Here we encounter once more the autonomy or, if we will be permitted to so express ourselves, the *immanence* of moral value in Nietzsche's ethical system. The moral efforts of people and the cultural progress of humanity are not means to something external and foreign, or even opposed, to them; specifically, they are not means to human *happiness,* to the satisfaction of subjective, *extra-moral* impulses. Rather, the meaning and significance of the good and of perfectibility lie in the good and perfectibility themselves, in the development of our moral nature, in the achievement of ever higher levels of spiritual development. The reader might well recall one of the pessimistic poems of Nadson, which expresses the disappointment that can seize all fighters for an ideal upon the full realization of their aspirations. What will be attained by this realization? The poet answers: "an animal's feast, a stuffed feeling!" and adds bitterly, "a miserable, trite result! No honest fighter will give his crown of thorns for it!"[83] Here the internal contradictoriness of utilitarianism and eudaemonism is clearly expressed: if satiation and well-being are seen not as a necessary step toward further efforts by humanity, not simply as the first, legitimate demand of any hungry person, but as the *ultimate ideal,* then this ultimate ideal, in its moral value, is directly opposed to everything that is morally valuable in the means of its realization. Spiritual purity and elevation, heroism, and the absence of self-seeking motives are, in the ethics of utilitarianism, only like mechanical means, set in motion for the attainment of human well-being, but no longer necessary and cast aside as soon as the goal is achieved. The crown of thorns is replaced by laurels and roses, heroes and fighters are no longer needed — it is the advent of the kingdom of serene happiness and enjoyment.[84]

Such a contradiction is foreign to an ethical system that has as its basis "love of the distant," understood as "love of phantoms," or, what is the same, as "love of the superman." If, as Zarathustra teaches, "love of life shall be love of your highest hope," then this highest hope ought to be not happiness, but *"the highest idea of life."* In this system, every level of human progress has value for humanity only because each level preserves, as the background and source of further progressive movement, the same moral goods by which it was achieved. Heroism and spiritual greatness are spent not on bringing about the kingdom of happy pygmies — the kingdom Zarathustra so cruelly ridiculed in his prophecy "of what is most contemptible, the last man, who has invented happiness"[85] — but on the strengthening and development in man of everything morally great, on the raising of his spiritual height, on the creation of the "superman." Struggle and creativity, according to this ethical system, ought to be dedicated to the *creation of conditions for the free development of all our spiritual capabilities and for the free satisfaction of our spiritual claims.*[86]

The first gracious and thoughtful critic of Nietzsche — Georg Brandes — called Nietzsche's system "aristocratic radicalism,"[87] and Nietzsche himself enthusiastically welcomed this designation as deeply corresponding to the essence of his views. This label would indeed be impeccable, were it not somewhat ambiguous. Nietzsche's "radicalism" — his hatred for what exists and his insatiable urge to "burst tombs, move boundary stones, and roll old tablets, broken, into steep depths"[88] — is not subject to the slightest doubt and makes him congenial and understandable to anyone who has ever and in some respect experienced the same desires. Just as incontestable and characteristic for Nietzsche is the element of "aristocratism" in his teaching. This latter term, however, seems to us rather broad and therefore capable of giving rise to misunderstanding.

"Aristocracy" means *dominion of the nobility* [*gospodstvo znati*]. It is possible to agree that dominion of the nobility makes up the basic content of Nietzsche's social-moral ideal, but only with a clear understanding of the meaning of both concepts ("dominion" and "nobility"). As regards the concept of "dominion," it undoubtedly constitutes, as is well known, one of the points in Nietzsche's worldview most precious to him. He takes *"der Wille zur Macht"* — the will to power — as basic among the vital and necessary human motives, and his "superman" is first of all a powerful man, exercising dominion over the surrounding world. This dominion, however, must not at all be understood as political or in general as juridical. Anyone familiar with Nietzsche's aversion for the state, for this "coldest of all cold monsters,"[89] in Zarathustra's words, knows that this extreme individualist could not dream of a juridical sanction for the dominion to which he called "higher people." Still less is it possible to think of the significance of dominion for Nietzsche as economic, material power [*vlast'*] over people, since all questions of a material order are in general far removed from his thoughts and aspirations. From this it follows that the type of dominion he professes designates simply *spiritual influence,* power acquired over people by the force of outstanding spiritual qualities. In teaching the idea of dominion, Nietzsche sharply distinguishes selfish love of power by petty people from the love of power that "ascends luringly to the pure and lonely and up to self-sufficient heights."[90] Such love of power is not a desire to climb or rise by means of power; on the contrary, it means that "what is high longs downward for power."[91] It is a desire for selfless expansion of the spiritual sphere of their personality, for the type of influence on people of which only the strong in spirit are capable and which is experienced, by those submitting to this influence, not as a burden or suppression of their personality, but as gratuitous participation in the spiritual goods of those exercising influence over them. This love of power is a "gift-giving virtue" (*schenkende Tugend*):

"That the lonely heights should not remain lonely and self-sufficient eternally; that the mountain should descend to the valley and the winds of the height to the low plains — oh, who were to find the right name for such longing? 'Gift-giving virtue' — thus Zarathustra once named the unnameable."[92]

The meaning alone of the concept of "dominion" in Nietzsche's system excludes the idea that "aristocratism" means social power of a select few over the masses. The wholly original sense of Nietzschean aristocratism comes out still more sharply upon examination of the concept of "nobility." It cannot be stressed strongly enough that the "nobility" and the "mob" opposing it are not social-political, but only *moral* categories. The "mob" — it is *"die viel zu vielen"* [the many, far too many], all the "small people, righteous and kind, these simpletons," all who know nothing higher than how "modestly to embrace a small happiness — that they call 'resignation' — and modestly they squint the while for another small happiness."[93] Everyone standing on the rungs of the social ladder, no matter where, falls equally into this category. "Mob above and mob below!" complains one of the "higher people" who has gone to Zarathustra. "What do 'poor' and 'rich' matter today? This difference I have forgotten."[94] This definition of the mob also defines the concept of "nobility." It is not a nobility, says Zarathustra, "that you might buy like shopkeepers and with shopkeepers' gold: for whatever has its price has little value."[95] Nor is it a nobility of the court, or of ancient families, or of "a bulwark for what stands that it might stand more firmly."[96] Zarathustra's "nobility" are chosen people of quite another type:

"O my brothers, I dedicate and direct you to a new nobility."

"Not whence you come shall henceforth constitute your honor, but *whither you are going!* Your will and your foot which has a will to go over and beyond yourselves — that shall constitute your new honor."

"O my brothers, your nobility should not look backward but *ahead!* Exiles shall you be from all father- and forefather-lands! *Your children's land* shall you love: this love shall be your new nobility!"[97]

The "nobility" [*znat'*] is everyone who has outgrown the surrounding milieu, who has severed the tie with the "country of his fathers" and strives toward the "country of his children," who is dedicated to love of the distant and boldly goes forward "to squander a great soul"[98] and spread his influence over people, as a gift. The nobility is the heroes and "higher people," who "like a high soaring eagle gaze below at the crush of gray tiny waves and wills and souls," and strive toward the image of the superman, of whom they are the precursors on earth. If it is thus possible to speak of Nietzsche's aristocratism, it is an aristocratism only in a literal, etymological sense, not in the usual historical one. "Aristocracy," for Nietzsche, is *"dominion of the best,"* and the aristocratic order about which he dreams is a form of life that gives scope for the spiritual development and expansion of personality in all who are rich and strong at heart, for their spiritual influence and dominion over the masses.[99] Perhaps a parallel can be drawn — of course, *mutatis mutandis* [having made the necessary changes] — between the Nietzschean categories of "nobility" and "mob" and the opposition, once popular among us [Russians], between "critically thinking individuals" and the "masses."[100] The Nietzschean "nobility" comes very close to what is meant by "critically thinking individual." Here are Carlylean heroes or, as Nietzsche called them in one place, *Argonauts of the ideal.* Only their moral evaluation in Nietzsche distinguishes them from the significance Russian sociological theory gave them. In the system of utilitarianism (under the banner of which this theory stood), these moral forces driving modernity — the "salt of the earth," in the Gospel expression[101] — are merely an auxiliary means for the achievement of ends (the happiness of the majority) extrinsic by their very nature to these forces; but for Nietzsche the "salt of the earth" is valuable in itself as an index of humanity's intellectual-moral strength, the development of which constitutes the very task of this earthly salt. And it is in his evaluation of the salt of the earth — in his view of it not only as a mechanical, practically useful means for the achievement of human well-being, but as the sole meaning of human existence itself — that Nietzsche's aristocratism consists. His aristocratism is thus only a reflection of his *idealism,* an idealism not, of course, in the broad and vague sense of striving for an ideal, but in the precise and specific sense, in which idealism is contrasted to ethical materialism or utilitarianism. And so it would seem more correct to call Nietzsche's ethical and social-political direction not aristocratic radicalism, but *idealistic radicalism.* A radical break with "what exists" [*sushchestvuiushchee*], together with active work in the name of the "distant," in the name of the triumph of abstract, autonomous moral "phantoms," in the name of the accession on earth of the "superman," as the "highest idea of life," embodying in itself all these "phantoms" — here is the meaning of Nietzschean radicalism, which, to repeat, we cannot call anything other than *idealistic radicalism.*

History has immortalized one classic example of such radicalism: the life and work of the "last of the Roman republicans," Brutus. Nietzsche's attitude to this historical image, expressed in a section of *The Gay Science,* is interesting and highly characteristic of his Weltanschauung, so distorted by hearsay: "I could not say anything more beautiful in praise of Shakespeare *as a human being* than this: he believed in Brutus and did not cast one speck of suspicion upon this type of virtue. It was to him that he devoted his best tragedy — it is still called by the wrong name — to him and to the most awesome quintessence of a lofty morality. Independence of the soul! — that is at stake here. No sacrifice can be too great for that."[102] Supposing that this tragedy reflects some event in the life of its author, Nietzsche adds: "But whatever similarities and secret relationships there may have been: before the whole figure and virtue of Brutus, Shakespeare prostrated himself,"[103] as did, we might add, Nietzsche. The image of Brutus is for Nietzsche the personification of his *idealistic radicalism* — of the heroic struggle for the ideal of independence of the spirit, an ideal that sums up, as it were, respect for all spiritual goods and love for all the sacred rights of the human person [lichnost'].

To our characterization of the ethical and social-political idealism in Nietzsche's system there remains to be added just one more feature, incidental yet highly essential.[104] This idealism remains in Nietzsche *realistic:* no matter how far the "distant" lies from regular life and its interests, it does not fall beyond the limits of earthly, empirical life. Moral "phantoms" and the being embodying them — the superman — remain earthly phantoms, not descended from heaven, but born on earth from the human head and heart. Zarathustra, the "blasphemer," firmly refuses to consecrate his extreme idealism with a metaphysical sanction; this idealism remains earthly not only in its practical application, which consists in fruitful work for the social-moral renewal of humanity, but also in its theoretical significance and substantiation. "I love those," Zarathustra exclaims, "who do not first seek behind the stars for a reason to go under and be a sacrifice, but who sacrifice themselves for the earth, that the earth may some day become the superman's."[105] Taking leave of his pupils, Zarathustra in his farewell speech exhorted them to "remain faithful to the earth":

"Remain faithful to the earth, my brothers, with the power of your virtue. Let your gift-giving love and your knowledge serve the meaning of the earth. Thus I beg and beseech you. Do not let them fly away from earthly things and beat with their wings against eternal walls. Alas, there has always been so much virtue that has flown away. Lead back to the earth the virtue that flew away, as I do — back to the body, back to life, that it may give the earth a meaning, a human meaning."[106]

Although Nietzsche bases all morality on love of abstract "phantoms," he does not forget that these phantoms are only creations of the human spirit; this does not at all lessen their value in his eyes, but only raises the value of their creator — man. "A new pride my ego taught me, and this I teach men: no longer to bury one's head in the sand of heavenly things, but to bear it freely, an earthly head, which creates a meaning for the earth."[107]

This combination of the elements of realism and idealism in Nietzsche's system seems to us highly valuable. Modern philosophical thought, founded by Kant and relying on his synthesis of realistic soberness of mind with bold idealistic impulses of the moral spirit, draws a sharp distinction between critical positivism in the sphere of scientific knowledge and ethical idealism in the sphere of the integral moral consciousness. It must protest equally against the doctrinaire tendency to confine human consciousness, rich with internal experiences, to the sphere of realistic thought, as well as against the careless attempt to hypostatize moral experiences and give them the form of a logical system of precise *knowledge*. In this way it reconciles these two opposed directions of the human spirit, indicating to each its bounds. Nietzsche offered us a model of such reconciliation, and from this point of view his ethical-philosophical system acquires even greater interest today.

In conclusion, we permit ourselves once more to let Zarathustra himself speak for an artistically integral résumé of the general spirit that suffuses the "ethics of love of the distant" we have outlined:

"Go into your loneliness with your love and with your creation, my brother; and only much later will justice limp after you.

"With my tears go into your loneliness, my brother. I love him who wants to create over and beyond himself and thus perishes."[108]

"Indeed, I know your danger. But by my love and hope I beseech you: do not throw away your love and hope."

"Alas, I knew noble men who lost their highest hope. Then they slandered all high hopes. Then they lived impudently in brief pleasures and barely cast their goals beyond the day. Spirit too is lust, so they said. Then the wings of their spirit broke: and now their spirit crawls about and soils what it gnaws. Once they thought of becoming heroes: now they are voluptuaries. The hero is for them an offense and a fright.

But by my love and hope I beseech you: do not throw away the hero in your soul! Hold holy your highest hope!"

"Thus spoke Zarathustra."[109]

Notes

1. "Let the future and the farthest be for you the cause of your today. ... My brothers, love of the neighbor I do not recommend to you: I recommend to you love of the farthest." Friedrich Nietzsche, *Thus Spoke Zarathustra*, "On Love of the Neighbor," in *The Portable Nietzsche*, ed. and trans. Walter Kaufmann (New York: Viking Penguin, 1954), p. 174. Subsequent references to *Thus Spoke Zarathustra* are to this edition. In the text of his essay, Frank quotes Nietzsche in his own (good) Russian translations, but without any references. "P. B. S." in the chapter title refers to Pëtr Struve. Ed.

2. "I do not love my neighbor near, / but wish he were high up and far. / How else could he become my star?" Friedrich Nietzsche, *The Gay Science*, "The Neighbor," trans. Walter Kaufmann (New York: Vintage Books, 1974), p. 53. Subsequent references to *The Gay Science* are to this edition. Ed.

3. See Georg Simmel, *Einleitung in die Moralwissenschaft: Eine Kritik der ethischen Grundbegriffe*, 2 vols. (Berlin, 1892–1893).

4. Nietzsche, *Thus Spoke Zarathustra*, "On Enjoying and Suffering the Passions," p. 149.

5. Precisely in this sense does Schopenhauer say: "Alle Liebe ist Mitleid" [all love is compassion].

6. Pëtr Ia. Chaadaev (1794–1856), Russian philosopher of history. The Russian publication in 1836 of the first of his *Philosophical Letters* (written in French between 1829 and 1831) produced a storm of controversy by its indictment of Russia as a country without history that could offer nothing to humanity. For this view Chaadaev was officially declared insane. In response, he wrote his *Apology of a Madman* (1837). He was a catalyst in the debate between the Slavophiles and Westernizers over Russian national identity. Ed.

7. The Samoed are a people who migrated along the Russian Arctic coast and now live chiefly in the area of the North Urals. Ed.

8. The contrast is made in the second paragraph of Chaadaev's *Apology of a Madman.* Ed.

9. In the present work we are concerned mainly with *Also sprach Zarathustra* [1883–1885], Nietzsche's most brilliant accomplishment and indisputably a work of genius, which in its execution and profundity of content far surpasses everything else Nietzsche wrote. All quotations are from *Zarathustra,* unless otherwise indicated. Incidentally, in view of the inadequacy of Russian translations of Nietzsche, we have exclusively used the German original.

10. Alois Riehl was the author of *Friedrich Nietzsche: Der Künstler und der Denker* (1897). Ed.

11. Georg Simmel was the author of "Friedrich Nietzsche: Eine moralphilosophische Silhouette," *Zeitschrift für Philosophie und Philosophische Kritik,* Neue Folge, Band 107, Heft 2 (1896), pp. 202–215; and later of *Schopenhauer und Nietzsche* (1907). For Simmel's influence on Frank, see Philip J. Swoboda, *The Philosophical Thought of S. L. Frank, 1902–1915: A Study of the Metaphysical Impulse in Early Twentieth-Century Russia* (Ph.D. dissertation, Columbia University, 1992), pp. 268–291. Ed.

12. Perhaps the best way to understand and evaluate Nietzsche is in general not to try to take his teaching as a finished dogma with a precisely determined content, but to seek in him only what answers the inclinations and needs of each particular reader. The poetic cast of Nietzsche's nature, so clearly reflected in his works, and the conviction, inherent to him and fully justifying itself in its application to Nietzsche himself, that, "thoughts are the shadows of our feelings — always darker, emptier, and simpler" (*The Gay Science,* aphorism 179, p. 203), make a dogmatic adoption of his teaching completely impossible. Nietzsche himself came out more than once against a slavish-pedantic approach to his ideas and insisted on their free, spiritually creative acceptance. "You say you believe in Zarathustra? But what does Zarathustra matter? You are my believers — but what do all believers matter? You had not yet sought yourselves: and you found me. Thus do all believers; therefore all faith amounts to so little." *Thus Spoke Zarathustra,* "On the Gift-Giving Virtue," p. 190 [translation slightly revised]. In one quatrain from *The Gay Science,* entitled "Interpretation," Nietzsche expresses with remarkable eloquence and grace his view of the approach he desired toward his own ideas: "Interpreting myself, I read myself back in: / I cannot myself be my own interpreter. / But the one who climbs on his own way / Also carries my image toward a brighter light." These words ought not to be forgotten by any of Nietzsche's "interpreters." *The Gay Science,* p. 49. [Frank gives both the German and his own translation. Kaufmann's translation is too loose; the above is the editor's.]

13. I have deleted some of these where possible. Ed.

14. Nietzsche, *Thus Spoke Zarathustra,* "Zarathustra's Prologue," p. 123.

15. Ibid., "On the Virtuous," pp. 206–207.

16. Ibid., "On Virtue that Makes Small," p. 282. The expression "milieu of moderation and correctness" belongs to Mikhail E. Saltykov-Shchedrin (1826–1889), the greatest satirist of nineteenth-century Russia. See Swoboda, p. 259, and R. V. Ivanov-Razumnik, *Istoriia russkoi obshchestvennoi mysli: Individualizm i meshchanstvo v rus-*

skoi literature i zhizni XIX v., 3d. edition, vol. 2 (St. Petersburg, 1911), pp. 324–325. "Tashkenters" (*tashkenttsy*) is a reference to Saltykov's *Gentlemen of Tashkent* (*Gospoda Tashkenttsy,* 1869–1872), a satire of Russians who went to Central Asia to get rich. Ed.

17. Nietzsche, *Thus Spoke Zarathustra,* "On the Land of Education," p. 233.

18. Ibid., "On Redemption," p. 251.

19. Ibid., "On Redemption," pp. 250–251.

20. Ibid., "On the Way of the Creator," p. 177.

21. Ibid., "Zarathustra's Prologue," p. 125.

22. Ibid., "On Old and New Tablets," p. 316 (translation revised). *Hinterwelter* refers to those who believe in an afterlife; it might be translated as the "afterworldly" or "afterworldsmen." Ed.

23. Ibid., "On the Preachers of Death," p. 157.

24. Ibid., "On Old and New Tablets," pp. 316–317.

25. Ibid., "On the Rabble," p. 210.

26. Ibid., "On Old and New Tablets," p. 318.

27. Ibid., "Upon the Blessed Isles," p. 199.

28. Ibid., "On Love of the Neighbor," p. 173.

29. Ibid., "On War and Warriors," p. 159. Zarathustra so highly values struggle that he thinks it justifies any end. "You say it is the good cause that hallows even war? I say unto you: it is the good war that hallows any cause!" (ibid.) Here we encounter one of Nietzsche's moral "paradoxes," which are usually adduced as evidence of his cruelty and immorality. But as soon as it is recalled that "war" means, as Nietzsche himself expresses it, "war for thought," as soon as the meaning of "love of the distant" is thought through, the paradox disappears, giving way to a profoundly true and noble idea. Does not a "good war," that is, an honest and courageous struggle for one's "distant," for one's convictions and ideals, compel us to treat with respect every ideal of such a warrior, and does not it alone, this "good war," actually sanctify "any cause?"

30. Ibid., "On War and Warriors," p. 160.

31. Ibid., "On the Higher Man," p. 400.

32. Ibid., "Zarathustra's Prologue," p. 126.

33. "Let me see great vices, / Bloody, colossal crimes, / Only not this satiated virtue / And solvent morality!" From Heine's poem, "Anno 1829"; Heinrich Heine (1797–1856) was a German poet and essayist. Ed.

34. Nietzsche, *Thus Spoke Zarathustra,* "On the Spirit of Gravity," p. 307.

35. Ibid., "On Old and New Tablets," p. 311.

36. We are speaking, of course, only of views that are *based on principles* and that can thus be logically linked to a moral system; we are not concerned here with the purely instinctive aversion, not rarely expressed by Nietzsche, for compassion, as an obtrusive and immodest feeling, offensive to every truly noble and profound nature.

37. Nietzsche, *Thus Spoke Zarathustra,* "On Enjoying and Suffering the Passions," p. 148.

38. From Pushkin's romantic historical epic, "Poltava" (1828), second canto, line 211. Ed.

39. Nikolai A. Nekrasov (1821–1878), Russian poet, writer, and publisher. The leading representative of the "realist school" in Russian poetry, his depictions of Russian

peasant life were inspired by both his civic conscience and his sense of artistic integrity. Frank is referring to Nekrasov's late lyric poem, "Muse of Vengeance and Grief" (Muza mesti i pechali). Ed.

40. Decimus Junius Juvenalis (c. 60–140 A.D.), Roman satirist whose poems viciously denounce the vices of imperial Rome. Ed.

41. Jonathan Swift (1667–1745), Anglo-Irish satirist and churchman, author of *Gulliver's Travels*. Ed.

42. Bazarov is the central character in Ivan Turgenev's novel *Fathers and Sons* (1862). He is a nihilist, a radical advocate of scientistic positivism and utilitarianism who pillories art, culture, and liberal values. Ed.

43. Nietzsche, *Thus Spoke Zarathustra*, "On the Thousand and One Goals," p. 172.

44. In Russia at the time, nonresistance to evil was famously championed by Lev Tolstoy, who advanced his views in *What I Believe* (1884) and *The Kingdom of God Is Within You* (1893). Ed.

45. Nietzsche, *Thus Spoke Zarathustra*, "The Sign," p. 439.

46. Ibid., "On the Pitying" [or, On the Compassionate], p. 202.

47. Ibid., "On the Pitying," p. 202.

48. Ibid., "On Self-Overcoming," p. 228.

49. Ibid., "Upon the Blessed Isles," p. 199. This image automatically brings to mind the almost identical image of our poet: "Thus the heavy hammer, / Shattering glass, forges the sword" [tak tiazhkii mlat, drobia steklo, kuet bulat]. [From Pushkin's "Poltava," first canto, line 148.]

50. Ibid., "On Old and New Tablets," p. 321.

51. Ibid., "On Love of the Neighbor," p. 173.

52. Ibid., "On the Three Metamorphoses," pp. 137–140.

53. Ibid., "On the Teachers of Virtue," p. 142.

54. Ibid., "On the Tree on the Mountainside," p. 156.

55. Ibid., "On Old and New Tablets," p. 324.

56. Toward the "kind" Nietzsche, already in his first work, *Untimely Meditations,* appeals with the words of one Goethean hero: "You are annoyed and bitter, and that is fine and good; but if for once you would only get really angry, that would be better still." [Jarno's words to Wilhelm Meister, from Goethe's *Wilhelm Meisters Lehrjahre*, Book 8, ch. 5.] Such "malice," he explains further, will seem evil, "at least to myopic modern eyes, which always see in negation the mark of evil." In reality this malice is man's salvation from philistinism and the condition of any *"heroic life path." Unzeitgemässe Betrachtungen*, vol. 2 (Leipzig, 1900), pp. 43–45. [*Unfashionable Observations*, trans. Richard T. Gray (Stanford, 1995), pp. 203–204.]

57. "Higher than love of the neighbor is love of the farthest and the future; higher yet than love of human beings I esteem the love of things and ghosts." Nietzsche, *Thus Spoke Zarathustra*, "On Love of the Neighbor," p. 173.

58. The principle was formulated by Jeremy Bentham (1748–1832), English social philosopher, legal reformer, and founder of utilitarianism, in his *A Fragment on Government* (1776). Ed.

59. "Liebe zu *Sachen* und *Gespenstern." Sache* — thing, concern; *Gespenst* — literally, *ghost;* we shall translate it as *"phantom"* [*prizrak*], which has a more general meaning and therefore more precisely expresses Nietzsche's thought.

60. Georg Simmel, *Philosophie des Geldes* (Leipzig, 1900), pp. 226–227. [Georg Simmel, *The Philosophy of Money,* trans. Tom Bottomore and David Frisby (London: Routledge, 1978), p. 239.]

61. In "higher than love of people I value love of things and phantoms," by "phantom" (*Gespenst*) Nietzsche seems to mean in particular his own favorite "phantom"—the "superman." We permit ourselves, however, to broaden this concept to mean an *abstract moral good* in general, finding in the term "phantom" an exceptionally successful *Schlagwort* [catchword] for one of the central ideas of Nietzschean ethics.

62. Nietzsche, *Thus Spoke Zarathustra,* "On Virtue that Makes Small," p. 281. The identification of utilitarianism with the ethics of altruism clearly contains a certain imprecision: the ethics of altruism, on the one hand, is broader than utilitarianism, because love of people is not exhausted by the desire for their *happiness* or *benefit;* on the other hand, utilitarianism is broader than the ethics of altruism, because service to people's happiness can be based not only on love of people, but also on other motives. Nonetheless, for our specific task it seems permissible to identify these two—in any event kindred—moral directions, which we have combined according to the common feature of their supreme principles: *service to the interests of neighbors.* This same feature distinguishes both utilitarianism and altruism from the ethics of "love of phantoms," the supreme principle of which is the aspiration toward *abstract, self-sufficient moral ideals, the value of which is independent of their significance for the subjective interests of "neighbors."*

63. The outstanding example of this type of utilitarianism is given by Rudolf von Jhering in his *Zweck im Recht,* and also by Lester Ward in his remarkable sociological works. Nietzsche himself repeatedly expresses the thought that every ethics is, in the last account, the product and function of the instinct of preservation of the species. [On Jhering, see Novgorodtsev's essay (Chapter 8) in this volume. Lester F. Ward (1841–1913) was one of the founders of American sociology; his "anthropoteleological method" recognized the importance of purposiveness in sociological analysis. Ward's *The Psychic Factors of Civilization* and *Outlines of Sociology* appeared in Russian translation in 1897 and 1901, respectively.]

64. Let the world perish, if only justice shall reign. Ed.

65. Let justice perish, if only utility shall reign. Ed.

66. The following remarkable paraphrase of the theme of the superiority of "love of phantoms" over "love of people," contained in the hard-earned words of Chaadaev, must sound like a terrible heresy from the point of view of social utilitarianism: "love of one's country is a very good thing, but there is something still higher: love of truth. ... The road to heaven runs not through love of one's country, but through love of truth" (*Apology of a Madman* [second paragraph]). Compare these words to the fashionable slogan of Englishmen today, "right or wrong—my country!" [English in original], and the relation of a consistent utilitarianism to "love of phantoms" will become clear.

67. Nietzsche, *Thus Spoke Zarathustra,* "On the Higher Man," pp. 402–403 (translation slightly revised).

68. Indeed, how could Zarathustra extol actual self-love, when he is the preacher of selfless love of the distant who indignantly exclaims: "But we shudder at the degenerate sense which says, 'Everything for me.'" *Thus Spoke Zarathustra,* "On the Gift-Giving Virtue," p. 187.

69. Raskolnikov is the hero of Dostoevsky's novel *Crime and Punishment*. He plans and commits the murder of an old pawnbroker, having convinced himself that the deed is justifiable and that he is exempt from ordinary morality. Ed.

70. Nietzsche, *Thus Spoke Zarathustra*, "On the Virtuous," p. 208.

71. *On life* (1887), which was banned from publication in Russia. Tolstoy presented a synopsis of the work before the Moscow Psychological Society in March 1887. Ed.

72. Interestingly, this is the same idea as in Nietzsche, although with a different coloration: higher than love of people stands love of phantoms. It is precisely this idea that forces Tolstoy to demand a change from the "social worldview," as he puts it, to the metaphysical-moral worldview. Compare Nietzsche's thought (identical, almost word for word, to Tolstoy's view) in *Jenseits von Gut und Böse* (*Beyond Good and Evil*), passage 60. By nature these two moralists, the greatest of the nineteenth century, have much in common, despite the complete difference in the content of their teachings.

73. On the clear contradiction between this paragraph and the position Frank just defended, see Swoboda, pp. 287–288. Ed.

74. Nietzsche, *Thus Spoke Zarathustra*, "On the Pitying," p. 202.

75. Ibid., "On the Three Evils," p. 302.

76. The good of the people is the supreme law. Ed.

77. As P. B. Struve has shown; see his foreword to Berdiaev's book, *Sub"ektivizm i individualizm v obshchestvennoi filosofii. Kriticheskii etiud o N. K. Mikhailovskom* (St. Petersburg, 1901), pp. lxxx–lxxxiv. Also see the evaluation there of Nietzsche's ethical system, which in its main outlines approximates ours (pp. lxi–lxxi).

78. Nietzsche, *Thus Spoke Zarathustra*, "On the Three Evils," pp. 302–303.

79. "Your love of life shall be love of your highest hope: and your highest hope shall be the highest idea of life." Nietzsche, *Thus Spoke Zarathustra*, "On War and Warriors," p. 160 (translation slightly revised).

80. "Where is the lightning to lick you with its tongue? Where is the frenzy with which you should be inoculated? Behold, I teach you the overman [or superman]: he is this lightning, he is this frenzy." Nietzsche, *Thus Spoke Zarathustra*, "Zarathustra's Prologue," p. 126.

81. Nietzsche, *Thus Spoke Zarathustra*, "Zarathustra's Prologue," pp. 124–127. Translation slightly revised ("superman" for Kaufmann's "overman").

82. See, in addition to his study of Nietzsche, Simmel's *Philosophie des Geldes*, pp. 407–413.

83. Semën Iakovlevich Nadson (1862–1887), popular "civic" poet. The lines are from his poem "No, I No Longer Believe in Your Ideal" ("Net, ia bol'she ne veruiu v vash ideal," 1883). Ed.

84. Nietzsche discloses this internal contradictoriness of utilitarianism in the following words: "This indicates the fundamental contradiction in the morality that is very prestigious nowadays: the *motives* of this morality stand opposed to its *principle*. What this morality considers its proof is refuted by its criterion of what is moral. In order not to contravene its own morality, the demand, 'You shall renounce yourself and sacrifice yourself,' could be laid down only by those who thus renounced their own advantage. ... But as soon as the neighbor (or society) recommends altruism *for the sake of its utility*, it applies the contradictory principle: 'You shall seek your advantage even at the

expense of everything else' — and thus one preaches, in the same breath, a 'Thou shalt' and 'Thou shalt not.' " *The Gay Science,* section 21, p. 94.

85. Nietzsche, *Thus Spoke Zarathustra,* "Zarathustra's Prologue," pp. 129–130.

86. In *Untimely Meditations,* Nietzsche formulates his ethical ideal, subsequently expressed in the image of the "superman," in the following words: Our duties flow from " … the fundamental idea of *culture,* insofar as it is capable of charging each of us with one single task: *to foster the production of philosophers, artists, and saints within us and around us, and thereby to work toward the perfection of nature.*" *Unzeitgemässe Betrachtungen,* vol. 2, pp. 55–56. [*Unfashionable Observations,* p. 213.]

87. Georg Brandes (1842–1927), Danish literary critic. Ed.

88. Nietzsche, *Thus Spoke Zarathustra,* "The Seven Seals (Or: The Yes and Amen Song)," p. 340. Frank changes the tense of the verbs here; Kaufmann's translation revised accordingly.

89. Ibid., "On the New Idol," p. 160.

90. Ibid., "On the Three Evils," p. 301.

91. Ibid.

92. Ibid., pp. 301–302.

93. Nietzsche, *Thus Spoke Zarathustra,* "On Virtue that Makes Small," pp. 281–282.

94. Ibid., "The Voluntary Beggar," p. 383.

95. Ibid., "On Old and New Tablets," p. 315.

96. Ibid.

97. Ibid., pp. 315–316.

98. Nietzsche, *Thus Spoke Zarathustra,* "On Free Death," p. 184.

99. Nietzsche's comment about the social organization of the *church* is interesting in this respect. He prefers it to the state organization, for the following reasons: "Let us not forget in the end what a church is, as opposed to any 'state.' A church is above all a structure for ruling that secures the highest rank for the more spiritual *human beings* and that *believes* in the power of spirituality to the extent of forbidding itself the use of all the cruder instruments of force; and on this score alone the church is under all circumstances a *nobler* institution than the state." *The Gay Science,* section 358, p. 313. It is necessary to know Nietzsche's general relation to the church in order to understand the extent of his deep respect, revealed by these words, for everything spiritually high and for spiritual rule in contrast to the rule of *force.*

100. The distinction was advanced by the Russian populist thinker and "subjective sociologist" Pëtr Lavrov. See the Glossary of Names. Ed.

101. Matthew 5:13. Ed.

102. *The Gay Science,* section 98, "In praise of Shakespeare," p. 150.

103. Ibid., p. 151.

104. Frank removed this and the next three paragraphs when his essay was reprinted in his collection, *Filosofiia i zhizn'* (St. Petersburg, 1910). Ed.

105. Nietzsche, *Thus Spoke Zarathustra,* "Zarathustra's Prologue," p. 127.

106. Ibid., "On the Gift-Giving Virtue," p. 188.

107. Ibid., "On the Afterwordly," p. 144.

108. Ibid., "On the Way of the Creator," p. 177.

109. Ibid., "On the Tree on the Mountainside," p. 156.

6

Philosophy and Life

S. A. ASKOL'DOV

The characteristic peculiarity of post-Kantian philosophical thought is its own conscious subordination to principles from whose influence philosophy had long considered itself completely free. We have in mind principles of a practical-volitional character, and in particular those forming the categories of duty, the good, beauty, and utility. If in the classic epoch of rationalism the reciprocal relation among thought, will, and action was expressed in the formula, "I think and, in accordance with my thought, want and act," then today's understanding of this reciprocal relation shows a conspicuous inclination to express it in the reverse order, "I want and act and then, in accordance with my desire and action, think." This transfer of the center of gravity from the sphere of theory to the sphere of life practice began with Kant himself. Consciousness of moral duty was for him the highest instance from which the ideas of reason, themselves necessary for the realization of moral duty, received their right to existence: freedom of the will, the existence of God, and the immortality of the soul. It is impossible not to recognize that in this case the cool calm of theoretical thought was not in the least disturbed by interference from a principle foreign to it. In all human history, thought could not have found a more dispassionate guide than Kant's moral law. But it could be predicted a priori that the matter would not remain limited to this, and that with time dispassionate duty would be replaced by more vivid motives from

life. Deprived of its specific authority and weakened in its independence, theoretical thought could not remain on the first point of support offered it, all the
more so in that every life principle had essentially equal rights in claiming it for
its own side.[1] Having begun with subordination to moral duty, theoretical
reason eventually fell under the still greater influence of another life force —
the striving for beauty. The outstanding spokesman of this phase is Nietzsche.

Nietzsche's philosophy is very often called an individualistic morality or a
morality of egoism. But neither of these definitions captures, in our opinion,
the essential peculiarity of his philosophy. In no way is Nietzsche a proponent
of *any* type of individualism or egoism. Not in vain are his ideals so far from
modernity, located as they are in the distant past or hidden in the future. He
did not have to wake the ghosts of Borgia and other coryphaei of human crim-
inality for the sake of mere egoism. The philistine egoism and self-indulgence
of contemporary life could have given him rich material for the construction of
his ethical ideals. Obviously Nietzsche's morality had its foundation not in
egoism, but in some other principle of a completely different order. That
foundation was the idea of beauty. All the positive principles of Nietzsche's
ethics are also the most important principles of his aesthetics and artistic
creativity. Freedom and vivid individuality, force and boldness, nobility and
grace, harmony and artistic unity — here are the demands that equally serve as
criteria of the beautiful and of moral values in Nietzsche's philosophy. For
Nietzsche, to be moral means to be aesthetically excellent. If, from his point of
view, Lady Macbeth or Cesare Borgia are high models of moral dignity, it is
because they also represent high artistic models. It can be stated with complete
certainty that any personality approximating Nietzsche's moral ideals could
be the hero of any artistic work. And if the reverse claim cannot be made, this
only speaks to the extraordinary strictness and refinement of Nietzsche's aesthetic taste.

The standard of beauty in Nietzsche's ethics differs somewhat, of course,
from the same principle in pure aesthetics. But these distinctions seem to us to
be inessential and to derive from differences in the spheres of application of
these principles: real life, on the one hand, and the creativity of art, on the
other. Reality naturally requires evaluation from the point of view of intensity.
Thus, the principle of vital power, absent in traditional aesthetics, is a necessary addition in Nietzsche's moral-aesthetic theory. Subordination of theoretical thought and its ultimate end — truth — to the aesthetic principle in Nietzsche was expressed not only in the content of his philosophy, but also in its
external form. Instead of an extensive and connected system of logical constructions we find terse and fragmentary aphorisms, captivating in their artistic form and completeness. Instead of compelling argumentation — a series of

brilliant theses, striking in their boldness, imagery, and surprising turns of speech. Nietzsche's thought is often completely subservient to artistic whim and transformed into mere hints of something that can perhaps be felt, but not understood.

In subordination to the ideas of moral duty and beauty, philosophical thought fell under the influence of principles albeit foreign to it, but also like it in that they belonged to higher and specific manifestations of the human spirit. At the same time, however, guiding principles of an entirely different order also entered the philosophical arena, principles that were more vague and indefinite, and yet closer to the interests and necessities of life. We have in mind the epistemological theories of the end of the past century, theories that put the demands of economy or the "least expenditure of force," and in the end utility, into the category of basic principles of thought. These theories, connected mainly with the names of Mach, Avenarius, and Simmel, are preparing the ground for the utter annihilation of the very category of truth. Simmel, in fact, essentially arrives at such a result in his article "Über eine Beziehung der Selektionslehre zur Erkenntnisstheorie."[2] The conflation of "truth" with "utility," leading to the insoluble problem of prestabilism,[3] leads Simmel to reduce each of these parallel principles to the other. The hypothesis of selection, which he accepts and introduces into the theory of knowledge, does not decide this question on behalf of the category of truth.

It would be a great injustice to accuse representatives of the views we have just outlined of deliberately distorting truth for the sake of one or another life principle. And we have no doubt that every incontestable claim of scientific knowledge has enjoyed proper recognition from their side. But it would also be mistaken to think that theories incorporating practical life principles into knowledge have had no influence on the content of knowledge itself, philosophical knowledge in particular. If this influence has not taken the form of crude interference in the very process of knowledge, it undoubtedly has been felt in the evaluation of philosophical ideas and constructions, in granting or denying them a certain importance and authority, and generally in bringing them into a certain type of heirarchical dependence. Thus, in the eyes of Kant, Fichte, and their successors only the life force of moral duty could provide unshakable certainty in the ideas of God and a moral world-order, since theoretical thought could not justify such certainty. The same life force, in the form of aesthetic needs, led Nietzsche to abolish the theoretical disciplines of theory of knowledge and metaphysics and to create his aesthetic ethics of life. Finally, the life principles of economy of force and utility give their proponents full certainty in the superiority of the utilitarian ideas of science and philosophy before problematic metaphysical ideas relating to the transcendent world.

We are very far from sharing this tendency of contemporary philosophy. Elevating the importance or truth of an idea according to the needs of immediate life seems to me to be only a variation of that old intellectual vice for which the name is dogmatism. Moreover, evaluating the ideas and constructs of reason from the point of view of one life principle but not another strikes us as necessarily connected with a more or less obvious arbitrariness. Every thinker can argue with equal right, apparently, for the life principle closest to him. The calm and steady nature appeals to consciousness of duty. The philosopher filled with revulsion for vulgar and effete modernity bows before the power of beauty. Thinkers aiming most of all for utilitarian certainty end up subordinating thought to the same principles lying at the basis of steam engines and every type of technical device. They are all right, to the extent they see these strivings for the moral good, beauty, and utility as primary life principles inherent to human nature, naturally coordinating themselves with the activity of reason. But they fall into exaggeration when they think of using these principles to replace or fill the consciousness of truth and aspiration toward its attainment, an aspiration just as primary and irreducible, and one that can never be satisfied or met by something outside truth itself, even if such principles were of infinite dignity and grandeur.

The internal unity of the spiritual forces of the human personality is not rarely put forward as grounds for subordinating cognition to irrational principles. Man's rational spirit, say the proponents of this view, is not a simple sum of thinking, feeling, and willing, but a living unity in which all these activities are mutually determined and connected. Such a living unity should, in their opinion, be put at the center of the theory of knowledge. This frequently met line of argument seems to us deeply mistaken.[4] That our psychic life has at its basis a certain unity and interdependence among all its functions is a thesis that today constitutes a firm psychological truth. But this thesis relates only to the *general* course and development of our psychic life and does not at all exclude the possibility of particular independent functions and specific interdependencies among individual functions. Nor does it exclude the existence in our psyche of some wholly independent principles, regulating the function of various psychological categories. Truth is just such a supreme principle for all our cognitive processes. Within thought in all its forms the supremacy of this principle cannot be replaced by any other. This does not at all contradict the fact that by and large knowledge depends to a significant degree on the interests and needs of life. But life occasions only the *emergence* of cognitive processes, whereas epistemological factors entirely determine their *coherence* and *content*. Life gives rise to truth, but cannot prescribe it to be one thing and not another.

But a question arises: Can the reverse type of dependence be established, can practical principles be subordinate to theoretical thought? This question as well, in our opinion, has to be answered negatively. As in knowledge the aspiration is toward truth, so in acting the ruling principle is aspiration toward the good. This latter aspiration is at root irrational and can only be expressed in concepts, but not determined by them. Thought can help reveal and clarify it, and direct it to the object corresponding to its nature, but is incapable of engendering it or altering its nature, just as it is incapable of changing a sensation of color into sound. Ethics has long tried to discover infallible laws indicating the life path we ought to choose. It has, in other words, sought to indicate the ultimate end to which we ought to strive, and to demonstrate that our responsibility is to this end and not another. Such claims, however, have either had no grounds, or have represented a cleverly disguised *circulus vitiosus*. Obviously, it is possible to indicate and demonstrate only what has existed, exists, or will exist, but to demonstrate what *ought or is obliged to exist* is not within the capability of any theory. Successful resolution of this ethical question could be given, it seems, only if philosophy had the means to demonstrate the concurrence of causal and moral necessity [*prichinnoe dolzhenstvovanie c nravstvennym*], if, in other words, the cosmic process did not leave the possibility of choice, but fatalistically predestined human will to an inevitable result. Ethics would then be reduced to predicting the future. Such a resolution of the question could be obtained, for example, from the materialistic point of view. But with such a formulation of the question, ethics, as a philosophical theory of morality, essentially ceases to exist. Where there is no possibility of choice, there is no morality.

Thus ethics is destined to always wrestle with the theoretically insoluble question: Which possible ultimate end ought to be established as absolutely obligatory? In this question the role of reason consists only in all-round inquiry into the basic directions of human aspiration and action, and in clarification of the final ends reached by following such directions. The choice itself of a particular end must be made not by reason, but by the whole aggregate of the spiritual forces of man, by the unity of the personality, into the composition of which enter feelings, desires, and other irrational principles. At this point the practical principle of life emerges as sovereign arbiter. Therefore, nowhere is theory subjected to such humiliating disregard as in the sphere of morality. The most persuasive arguments about duty and obligation, about their concurrence with the true good, falter under the impact of anonymous blind impulse and feeling. Life and creative literature are rich with vivid examples of such merciless mockery of theory by the practical life principle, of real-life vice over theoretical virtue. The role of theory in moral questions can be compared, in our opinion, to the inscriptions encountered by the fabled Ivan Tsarevich, which declared that he who turns right will lose his horse but save himself, while he who turns left will save his horse but perish in the process.[5] The inscriptions only indicate the paths and their end results, but leave the choice between the paths to the traveller himself. No inscription can convince someone who seeks death to turn right, or someone who wants to save his life to turn left.

But in limiting the significance of theory to the role of an impartial guide among various life paths, we consider this significance to be very great, even essential, at humanity's current level of development. We have no idea of either the world as a whole or the possible stages of human development. We are entirely occupied with our contingent little human world, but are completely unfamiliar with possible paths beyond its limits. In essence all human culture develops instinctively. Its basic motives have, by and large, been strivings to satisfy the diverse needs and whims of body and soul. Everything intellectual and conscious has in the end either served these basic and disparate strivings, or gone along its own road, taking only an indirect and essentially insignificant part in the general movement of culture. If in human history it is possible to trace one goal, more or less uniting the separate manifestations of cultural life, it is the general improvement of the technical side of life. Such a goal cannot, of course, be acknowledged as final, or even as partly justifying the present direction of the development of humanity. Indeed, in the final account the whole technical improvement of life must be considered only a means, not an end. It is very possible that these means are essentially indifferent and capable of equally serving the realization of different ends. But it is also possible that such means are directing humanity to a fully determined result, still far from clear for human consciousness. The thought that human culture carries with it a deviation from the natural norms of life, that it stifles the best instincts of human nature, has already been expressed in different forms, and by very great thinkers. And this thought must be taken into account. Humanity needs to be fully aware where the road it has chosen leads, whether it is still possible to cross to other paths, and what ends might be reached following them. Philosophical thought must be enlisted in the clarification of all these questions, and only after it arrives at a feasible resolution of them can an unswerving course in the progressive movement of human history be consciously charted.

For the development of individual persons as well, it is of enormous significance to identify the final ends to which one or another direction of searching and effort leads. The majority of us wander in life, as if in an unfamiliar forest, following the direction taken by our closest fellow traveller, selecting arid and high places, guided by comfort and pleasantness and hardly thinking about where we will end up, whether our path will be further drawn out, or whether there is a way out from this monotonous forest. And even those who with foresight and concern investigate the cardinal points of the globe and, equipped with scientific knowledge, find north and south, east and west — even they still do not know in the end what is served by knowledge of these directions or which direction is to be followed. Others stubbornly head in the direction of the sun, not suspecting that they are moving in circles and that for all their progressive persistence they are doomed to mark time in one place. The most experienced and wise are sure this pacing in the monotonous forest contains the entire meaning of existence and that the forest is the whole world; suggestions about other places are pure fantasy, diverting us from our immediate task — to make pacing in the forest as comfortable as possible for ourselves and others. And if, from the point of view of these experienced people, the forest does end, that is not to be thought about, since given the shortness of life we could not get there in any case.

Philosophical thought has thus far not been convinced, however, by the arguments of these experienced people and continues to make hypothetical conjectures, revealing for it a somewhat different meaning of life than that which immediate experience indicates. And in this respect its significance has still not been adequately tested or evaluated. We prefer to be guided by accustomed habits than by the not very promising theories of metaphysics and the ethics based on it. However, a considered orientation on life is possible only by means of these theories or by religious perspectives, since only metaphysics and religion discern the final ends of existence and the paths leading to them. The necessary influence of philosophical thought on irrational life principles consists in indicating these paths. In the rights to actually selecting one of these paths, priority undoubtedly belongs, however, to the unconscious feeling for life.

But independently of any subordination of philosophical ideas to the interests and demands of the immediate life of feelings and strivings, clarification of the link between the theoretical and practical principle is of indisputable interest and significance. Philosophy has so far been thoroughly removed from life, and life in turn has always shunned and ignored philosophy. Yet there is every reason to think that a friendly union between them would have to be fruitful for both sides. If the natural coordination of man's psychic needs and abilities is not an exception to all other organic coordinations and, like them, presents a unity of forces directed to the realization of one common goal, then it is obvious that a concurrence of the needs of theory and practice, of the demands of philosophical thought, moral duty, and aesthetic feeling, is only a question of time. In this way, the question of the significance of philosophy for life can be discussed without any detriment to the theoretical principle of truth, but precisely from the point of view of its equal and free *coordination* with the most important principles of life. The norms of this coordination undoubtedly make certain demands on the content of our worldview and corresponding conduct. But these demands relate to the whole of psychic life. Satisfying them, we are not subordinating the theoretical principle to the practical or vice versa; rather we are equally subordinating both these sides of the human spirit to the principle of *harmony* ruling over them. These demands do not say to man, acknowledge such and such ideas as sure and final, or act in such and such a way. They say only, do not permit a disparity between your thoughts and aspirations, be harmonious. Looking at the whole history of philosophical thought from this point of view, we cannot but find certain grounds for the construction of a dialectical triad. The thesis is the self-affirmation of reason, as a fully independent and isolated principle, as in the epoch of rationalism. Kant's critical philosophy provides the principle for the antithesis, consisting in the subordination of reason to life principles. Establishing the synthesis, that is, an equal and harmonious coordination of the theoretical and practical principle, strikes us as a highly important task of the future. This task must be solved by both life itself and theoretical endeavor.

But the question might arise whether there is a need to somehow theoretically ascertain the possible correlations between a philosophical Weltanschauung and life practice. Life, it might be said, itself discloses the norms of the possible correlations between the practical and theoretical principle and it remains for us only to study and follow them. While not denying a certain spontaneous life selection establishing a proper and harmonious correspondence among ideas, feelings, and acts, we nonetheless believe that clarification of this question by philosophical and psychological analysis can hold very great significance.

For every striving and attitude in life, there are corresponding philosophical ideas. Thus, for example, the person living by present and elementary needs alone, occupied exclusively with the "technics" of life, is a representative of theoretical materialism. Even if he himself is not interested in theoretical questions or professes some other worldview, still he cannot fail to be recognized as an unconscious servant of materialistic ideas since, from the point of view of materialism, only his manner of life can be recognized as rational and making sense. From this perspective, only physical-mechanical laws are eternal and absolute, and the triumph and realization of these higher ends of the universe do not require human participation. Therefore it remains for us only to use the chance combinations of these laws to attain our own contingent good. This good can be acquired and maintained only by studying these laws, trying to match them to our needs, and assimilating our own actions to the mechanical course of nature. The natural and harmonious result of such a view must be the turning of all interests to the technical side of life, that is, to the purely mechanical correlation of people to external nature and each other.

On the other hand, all higher manifestations of the human spirit in the sphere of immediate life — aspirations to attain eternal and absolute ideals of a moral or aesthetic character — presuppose a corresponding philosophical worldview that recognizes these ideals as realizable and triumphing in the final stages of cosmic development. Only with such a worldview does it make sense to sacrifice the temporary but indisputable goods of the present day for the sake of goals that can be realized only in the indefinite future. In recent times the opinion can very often be met that sacrifice of personal well-being for the sake of social welfare does not need any metaphysical or religious ideas positing transcendence and the universal triumph of truth and justice. On the contrary, it is said that self-sacrifice is valuable precisely when it occurs without any consideration to some restoration of truth and justice beyond the grave, but exclusively under the influence of benevolence and love for one's neighbors, who will avail themselves in this empirical life, if not now, then with time, of the sacrifice made for them. Such a line of argument is very popular among our soberly thinking intelligentsia. It is very convenient for rejecting, with haughty scorn, any "unscientific idea" of the transcendent, while remaining all along an adherent of customary altruistic morality.

For our part we think that such a line of argument fails in two respects. First, it completely idealizes those acts of self-sacrifice by people living exclusively for empirical reality. To sacrifice oneself for the common good without any view to participation in the universal triumph of justice does not always mean to act from purely altruistic motives. On the contrary, the psychic basis of such deeds can be and most often is highly complex. Such sacrifices can have the character of disguised suicide, or they can be motivated by hidden self-love, pure intellectual enthusiasm, and many other impulses having nothing in common with love of one's neighbor. Second, it is also mistaken to think that confidence in the universal triumph of justice somehow diminishes the moral value of self-sacrifice, or that a sacrifice accompanied by such confidence cannot at the same time be made in the name of the good of others. On the contrary, I think that a Weltanschauung clarifying the general meaning and significance of altruistic motives, indicating their necessity for achieving universal ends, can only nourish and strengthen them. Most high moral deeds are undoubtedly done, as is said, in spiritual innocence, under the influence of spontaneous feelings and impulses, not refined theories. But I cannot agree that such "spiritual innocence" in moral acts is a *necessary* condition of "spiritual purity," but think instead that this latter quality is fully compatible with a religious-philosophical worldview and even presupposes it. The last days of the earthly life of Christ, which ended with the greatest and purest act of self-sacrifice, were also marked, according to the Evangelists, by extraordinarily powerful insight into the distant ages ahead and the future triumph of defiled truth. It was a perfectly harmonious combination of a profound *understanding* of the cosmic struggle of good and evil with great *feelings* of compassion for lost humanity. And in this case a fully conscious approach to the cosmic meaning of the sacrifice only reinforced its moral grandeur.

Apart from fully determined and characteristic forms of morality, every life goal presupposes an idea justifying or substantiating why it should be preferred to others. It is senseless to strive for what is impossible, or for ephemeral goals giving no satisfaction. In order to strive for what is best, eternal, unshakable, and most excellent, it is necessary to know in what it might consist and to have an idea of it. In reality most of us, in striving for our life goals, do not have clear and thought-out philosophical ideas about them, although these ideas are surely presupposed by our strivings and actions as their final, if also indiscernible, end. In this sense all people, even the most removed from intellectual interests, can be recognized as unconscious bearers of philosophical ideas. It can be said about every human being, especially the sharply pronounced and engaged type, that he feels and acts as if pursuing one or another philosophical worldview in life. Thus every person is, regardless of his will, a philosopher and even a metaphysician, since all empirical goals lead ultimately to absolute, metaphysical ends. Disclosing these ends, their philosophical grounds and justification, is a necessary condition for the integral and balanced development of personality. Where there is no distinct end going beyond contingent empirical possibilities, there is no real self-determination, no firm unity of personality: if the conditions or end changes, so does the personality.

Such change of personalities in the same person is brilliantly depicted by Ibsen in his *Peer Gynt*. Peer Gynt is a merry, good-natured fellow; he possesses a rich spiritual nature, he is bold and energetic, and his poetic imagination is inexhaustible. There is also much kindness, humor, and gaiety in him. But he does not want to ponder over life. He creates life, guided exclusively by fits of fantasy and momentary desires. From this comes an infinite number of psychic metamorphoses. At the end of his life Peer Gynt realizes with horror that he was never himself, that he could compare himself to an onion, consisting only of skins that can be easily peeled away. His thoughts, to which he gave no development in his life, remained in his soul like unwound balls of yarn, and these balls torment him: "We are thoughts: / You should have thought us," they say. "We should have soared aloft." Peer Gynt did not have a slogan or password for life, so the withered leaves say to him: "We are the password / You should have given! / Look how your lethargy / Stripped us to skeletons." The tragicomedy of Peer Gynt's life ends in the confrontation with the "but-tonmoulder," by whose assurance Peer Gynt was destined to be a brilliant button on the world's frock coat, but, having lost his "self," he must go instead into the casting-ladle as raw material.[6]

Coordination of the theoretical and practical relation to life takes two directions. If we start from existing life aspirations, we must clarify their ultimate teleological meaning. We must know and theoretically justify that to which we are striving. On the other hand, if we start from theoretically developed perspectives, we must chart the correct life path to the chosen end. There can be no universally binding solution to the question of from what point the coordination of the theoretical and practical principle must be carried out in life. In every individual case the starting point can be either in the sphere of theory or the sphere of practice, depending on the individual and the external conditions of the development of his personality. The practical person, relying on life experience and immediate feeling, might construct a philosophical worldview closer to truth than the theorist proceeding from purely cognitive grounds. The issue is not with what and from where one starts, but that the participation of thought and will in this mutual work be fully equal, that the will not violate the correct course of theoretical thought, and that the honest voice of living feeling not be paralyzed by idle speculation. The correct resolution of this task is without doubt a very difficult matter. If impartial inquiry shows that the aspirations put at the basis of life are essentially unrealizable or in the end contradict each other, the result must be a break with the whole inner spiritual order. Such a break with theoretical convictions can be demanded if they prove contradictory to a feeling for life that has been recognized as absolutely correct and ineradicable. The latter case is fully justifiable from the standpoint of the views expressed above. In supposing that a feeling for life can turn out to be more truthful than a theoretical worldview and can serve as the cause for its radical reworking, we are not at all contradicting the demand for the full autonomy of reason in the matter of theoretical thought. Feeling can demand the correction of theoretical conclusions in the name of the higher principle of general life harmony, since any sharp violation of this principle entails a mistake in one or another of the contradictory elements. And if the conviction of conscience is stronger than the conviction of reason, then the self-justification of reason is to be recognized as an entirely correct solution to this situation.

Such internal contradictions are a very common life occurrence. They end in a compromise, if one of the contradictory elements is an infringement of the rights of the other. But they end also in a great triumph for the unity of personality, if after arduous struggle both opposing sides come to a reconciliation, recognizing their own mistakes and repudiating them in good faith. These last cases represent culminating points in the development of personality, giving occasion to speak about the rebirth of a human being. The majority of people avoid such disturbances to their spiritual equilibrium. These states are usually viewed as unproductive interruptions in a person's development. This opinion seems to us to be deeply mistaken. Any inner discord, excluding, of course, pathological cases, is an occasion for highly important inner work, for the illumination and broadening of one's "self." If these moments are also usually attended by depression, a fall in energy and productivity, and frequently something like the total disappearance of all creative capabilities, all this is redeemed by the spiritual renewal that results from any inner struggle, if only such a struggle does not end with a compromise.

But the question arises, is the realization of a harmonious coordination of thought and feeling, the voices of truth and life temperament, always possible? Was not the great poet right in speaking about "low truths" and "elevated deceit?"[7] We will not debate such a proposition at the present time. Detailed discussion of this question is possible only from the point of view of a definite worldview, in which the world significance of and connection among the great principles of truth, the good, and beauty are fully clarified and defined. We will state only that if the harmony of these principles is not always attainable in the human soul, such harmony must in any event be posed as a goal of human development, for it is one of the conditions of the integrity and stable unity of personality. It is easy to be content preferring an "elevated deceit" to many "low truths," but it is much more fruitful to reveal the kernel of a great truth in an elevated deceit and to expose a concealed lie in a low truth. In many cases this task may be equivalent to a school exercise, but in the basic questions of ethics such disclosure of a masked lie or truth proves to be very difficult and to demand an entire philosophical inquiry. The coordination of life principles is expressed, depending on possible philosophical worldviews, in the influence of the theoretical philosophical disciplines on ethics and in the influence of ethics on life itself. In the general development of philosophy and human culture this influence has rarely had noticeable effect. In individual consciousness, however, it has not infrequently shown itself in the most decisive and unambiguous forms.

For confirmation of this it is enough to recall the steadfast life paths followed by thinkers such as Socrates, Giordano Bruno, Spinoza, and others.[8] If, however, the influence of philosophical ethics on life has had no historical significance, the cause of this is to be seen not only in the general estrangement of all life interests from philosophy, but also in the fact that within philosophical thought itself, firm links have never existed between its theoretical and practical disciplines, between theory of knowledge and metaphysics, on the one hand, and ethics and aesthetics, on the other. Only in rare cases has ethical theory been something like the direct extension and result of the theory of knowledge and metaphysics (as, for example, in Schopenhauer). Most often, even among the greatest thinkers, metaphysics and ethics are utterly independent developments of philosophical thought. The organic link of ethics to metaphysics must, however, be recognized as absolutely obligatory. This link depends on the resolution of ontological problems about existing and possible forms of being and development, a resolution necessary for the construction of ethics. Ethics cannot decide the question of "what ought to be," without first investigating the question of "what is" [*sushchee*] and what is possible. In order to plot the north or south pole as the final goal of a geographical expedition, it is necessary to first know about their existence. Yet ethical theories rarely take account of any type of cosmic geography and are ordinarily occupied with study of immediate contingent goals or else restrict themselves to deduction of purely formal and essentially indefinite basic principles. This, in our opinion, is one of the reasons for the trifling life significance of philosophical ethics compared to the ethical teachings of religion.

In religion ethics is always connected with religious metaphysics (i.e., with religious teaching about God and the world, as "what is" and what is possible). And every believer is perfectly conscious of where and to what the moral demands prescribed by his religion lead. The whole compelling force of religious ethics consists in this clarification of its own ultimate meaning and significance. Moral deeds done on the grounds of such religious metaphysics are not infrequently seen as simply relying on reward beyond the grave. This opinion, in one variant or another, can very often be heard or read among contemporary moralists. For our part, we find in it much more conceited hypocrisy than psychological truth. The search for happiness and the triumph of justice is one of the basic and ineradicable properties of man, and to demand from people its absolute renunciation not only now, but in hopes for the future — is this not asking others to assume a burden beyond one's own strength? Therefore we would consider it possible to direct the following psychological paradox against such overly exalted moralists: the one who does not hope is the one who already possesses. Such moralists usually also forget that religion, in demanding a certain external conduct from a person, also demands that he raise his internal relation to the world to a moral height. Thus, while someone may deceive others by his external behavior, he cannot in the sphere of his internal feeling somehow conceal his soul and deceive his God. And if he, through motives of one type or another, becomes morally elevated in his feelings, strivings, and thoughts, then we can demand nothing more of him. In this respect an openhearted Muhammadan, nourishing in himself a feeling of justice in the hope of being a participant in Muhammad's paradise, is not any lower than the irreligious member of the intelligentsia with his watery altruism, developed as dictated by the demands of public opinion.

As we indicated earlier, the task of philosophy can consist only in discovery of ultimate ends and the directions leading to them. The actual choice among them is determined by the entire aggregate of spiritual forces combined in the unity of personality. This choice is easier, the fewer possible directions theory reveals to us. Philosophy must therefore reduce all the numerous and sinuous life paths to the basic directions of possible change and development.

In conclusion we permit ourselves to briefly outline the basic alternatives that await inquiry, in our opinion, by the ethical theories of the future. At the basis of all these alternatives lies the concept of *personhood,* a concept attracting in recent times special interest, in respect to both theory and life.[9] It is first of all necessary to clarify in what consists the growth and development of personhood, understanding such development in the broadest possible sense, namely as the broadening of life in general. In this respect it is necessary to dwell on studying changes in personhood with respect to the *complexity, intensity,* and *harmony* of its spiritual content.[10] Then the question must be raised: Which of two directions can be accepted into the basis of ethical theory—the direction of the development of personhood in the three respects specified, or the direction of its curtailment and dying away? Apparently, the second direction can be justified only from the point of view of absolute pessimism. For the spirited feeling for life and for optimistic theories, the question is easily decided on behalf of the first direction. But this alternative of the development and strengthening of life leads in turn to a new and more vexing dilemma: Is an independent and unlimited development of personhood possible, unconstrained by any rules of morality, or does the development of personhood include by its very nature some idea of self-limitation and subordination? Nietzsche's whole philosophy is a bold appeal to take the first path presenting itself to the free and absolutely independent development of individual persons.

To Nietzsche's philosophy can be contrasted the theistic worldview, according to which the entire world is one whole, united by a higher unity—the person of God. In this world-whole, the development of individual persons cannot take place in just any way, but only in strict harmony with the development of all other elements in the world-whole and in correspondence with the divine will. From this comes the necessity of conformity with the essence and aspirations of everything living and with the demands of the divine will. The result is a whole system of social obligations and limitations, together with the most important obligation — knowledge of God and the fulfillment of his law.

In the case of theism, there are again two essentially different outcomes. At the basis of world development can be placed the law of justice, according to which every being, even if connected in its existence and development with the whole world, nonetheless represents an utterly isolated entity, responsible exclusively for its own acts and reaping the rewards of its own efforts. But another view is also possible, for which the full separation and isolation [obosoblennost'] of beings is an illusion, and for which the world presents a living unity of interpenetrating essences. In this unity the limits of "yours" and "mine" can fully disappear. Here the law of justice must be supplemented by the law of sympathy, according to which every being must be able to find itself in another. At this point philosophical and Christian ethics can coincide. For this coinciding to be complete, however, another special theory is necessary, explaining the origins of sin and evil in the world and the necessity of their redemption by voluntary suffering.[11] The views that we have sketched about the relation of the human person to the world correspond to the basic attitudes on life: irreligious optimism and pessimism, and the various manifestations of religious feeling. And the more that people, living by these attitudes, come to recognize them as answering a higher truth, the more they are bound to theoretical substantiation of this truth.

Notes

1. "Life principles" is a term Askol'dov frequently uses in this essay. It is a reference to life-philosophy (Lebensphilosophie). Inspired by romanticism and influenced by the cultural presence of the biological sciences and evolutionary theory, life-philosophy came to prominence about 1880. For it, life is the central principle of philosophy and the basic explanatory category of all other phenomena. Life, as lived experience (Erlebnis), is the standard of what is healthy, true, and good; the antithesis between "healthy" and "sick" is itself highly revealing of the outlook of life-philosophy. In this organic conception of reality, biology replaces physics as the queen of the sciences; the world is not mechanism but organism. Life-philosophy emphasized the creative will, the will to life and to power, and deemphasized abstract reason; the result is an irrationalist, anti-intellectual tendency. All values are reduced to the intensification of life, everything is an expression of the experience of life; aestheticism acquires a new status as life and art are one. Thinkers associated with life-philosophy include Friedrich Nietzsche, Georg Simmel, Ludwig Klages, Oswald Spengler, Jean-Marie Guyau, Henri Bergson, and the pragmatists. Ed.

2. ["On the Relation of the Theory of Natural Selection to Theory of Knowledge"], *Archiv für Systematische Philosophie,* 1895.

3. The Leibnizian doctrine of preestablished harmony of body and mind. Ed.

4. Incidentally, adherents of the so-called subjective method in sociology not rarely resort to it.

5. From the Russian folktale "Prince Ivan, the Firebird, and the Gray Wolf," in A. N. Afanas'ev's collection. Ed.

6. Henrik Ibsen, *Peer Gynt: A Dramatic Poem,* trans. Christopher Fry and Johan Fillinger (Oxford: Oxford University Press, 1989), Act V, pp. 145–150. Ed.

7. A. S. Pushkin, "Geroi" ("Hero," 1830), lines 63–64: "A swarm of low truths is dearer to me than a deceit that elevates us." [T'my nizkikh istin mne dorozhe / Nas vozvyshaiushchii obman.] Askol'dov uses the phrase "vozvyshennyi obman," that is, "elevated" rather than "elevates." Ed.

8. Socrates was, of course, convicted of impiety and corruption of youth; he refused to flee and died by drinking hemlock. Bruno (1548–1600), the Italian pantheistic philosopher, was burned at the stake for heresy. Baruch Spinoza (1632–1677), Dutch rationalist metaphysician, was expelled from his synagogue in 1656 for unorthodoxy. Ed.

9. Here at the end of his essay, Askol'dov's use of *lichnost'* tends toward the concept of personhood, but with elements of the more psychological "personality." Ed.

10. For more detailed indications of the significance of these concepts in defining the stages of spiritual development, see my work, *Osnovnye problemy teorii poznaniia i ontologii (Basic Problems of the Theory of Knowledge and Ontology,* St. Petersburg, 1900), pp. 233 ff.

11. Askol'dov had a long-term interest in Dostoevsky. Twenty years later he wrote an essay entitled, "Religiozno-eticheskoe znachenie Dostoevskogo" (Dostoevsky's Religious-Ethical Significance), in *F. M. Dostoevskii: Stat'i i materialy,* I, ed. A. S. Dolinin (Petrograd, 1922). Ed.

7

What the History of Philosophy Teaches

S. N. TRUBETSKOI

I.

Since the time of Socrates, one of the strongest and more obvious objections to the possibility of philosophy has been the universal disagreement among philosophers. Every original philosophical teaching differs from others, diverges from and contradicts them, and is itself fraught with internal contradictions and imperfections. Not one such teaching can satisfy the demands of human reason, because its demands are unconditional.

Time and again means for the reform of philosophy and philosophical activity have been proposed, and time and again they have led to real transformations in the field of thought. But they have not altered the position of philosophy in relation to its ultimate object, to the Truth [*Istina*] it seeks: as before philosophy strives to grasp it, and as before this aspiration is realized in diverse and divergent philosophical theories, which give satisfaction to individual minds but not to human thought as a whole. And it seems philosophy has tried every possible approach to a solution.

Socrates thought that philosophy would enter upon the right path if it renounced speculation "about divine matters," about the nature of things, about the first principles of being [*sushchee*]. To make philosophy trustworthy, we must abandon attempts to know what exceeds our reason, and limit ourselves to knowledge of "human matters," that is, to the moral sphere. But such a remedy did not help: in the sphere of moral philosophy, everything proved to be just as controversial as in the sphere of speculation about the nature of things. Already among the students of Socrates we find the most resolute disagreement over questions about the ends of human conduct, about happiness, the good, virtues, the obligations of a human being relative to his neighbors and society.

The disagreement has not ended, and philosophers can concur neither on general grounds and principles, nor even on the very definitions of right and morality: astronomical phenomena, which Socrates ranked with "divine matters," have long been objects of scientific knowledge, but debate over what right is, over what morality is, continues to the present day.

II.

In order to put an end to fruitless arguments, an even more radical solution has been proposed, equivalent to the renunciation of philosophy itself: unconditional renunciation of speculation on behalf of precise knowledge. Repeated efforts have been made to show that only particular knowledge, obtained through experience, is accessible to human reason, that our reason is reliable only in the sphere of experience or in mathematics and that it loses all ground as soon as it crosses the limits of experience or those of mathematical relations. In fact: we know only what is given to us in space and time, what appears to us, and everything that appears to us is refracted in our conscious, sensing subject;[1] we see everything through the prism of our senses and our understanding,[2] and consequently we cannot know being [sushchee] as it is independent of us and our relative point of view.

Further, in our experience only the particular is given to us; and if we through rational, correct generalization also know certain general laws of the particular phenomena we observe, even so the broadest scientific generalizations give us only *particular* knowledge. But philosophy, no matter how we define it, strives toward a universal, *integral worldview;* speculation seeks a final system of knowledge, explanation of the origin and final cause of our existence. Hence the contention of the impossibility of philosophy in general, and of speculative philosophy in particular: in every philosophical teaching we find only a specific human understanding of the world, bearing the imprint of its time, its environment, and the individual genius who elaborated it. And this human notion is offered in place of the one all-unifying truth [*tselaia vseedinaia istina*], as truth itself!

260 S. N. Trubetskoi

III.

There have been attempts to repudiate philosophy in this sense and to indicate the bounds of human reason, to separate precise knowledge from speculation, "scientific" philosophy from "groundless" metaphysics. But these attempts as well have not led to anything and have proved logically just as unfounded and debatable as the systems against which they have been directed. Not one skeptical doctrine, not one demonstration of the impossibility of metaphysics, has in fact halted the development of metaphysics. Just the reverse: such demonstrations have been a powerful stimulus to speculation, as we see in German philosophy after Kant. On the other hand, attempts to create a "positive" philosophy, limited to the sphere of empirical knowledge alone, have also proved unsuccessful, not only in view of the persistence of the majority of philosophers, who have not wished to abandon speculation, but also in view of the fact that the very limits of positive knowledge remain contentious. The sphere of experience and that of precise knowledge far from coincide. Moral phenomena indisputably fall within our experience, and yet empiricist philosophers, on the basis of the facts of moral experience, construct systems of moral philosophy just as diverse as those of metaphysicians. True, these facts are worked over and experimented on by psychology, but then psychology claims to be an empirical science, investigating psychic phenomena.

And yet, with the exception of a few theses relating more to physiology than to psychology, so much unconscious metaphysics, concealed and crude, is introduced today under the name of psychology! Of course, this could be the result of random mistakes, inconsistency, and inadequate application of empirical methods. But how is it to be explained that among empiricist philosophers, who take experience as the only source of knowledge, fundamental disagreements are not the exception but as common as among philosophers working in the other direction? The reason for this is that the bounds separating experience from what lies beyond it can be difficult to establish. In trying to establish them, we violate them: we could not demarcate our property from someone else's land if we did not know this land was not ours—otherwise there would be nothing for us to demarcate. Our knowledge, we are told, is confined to experience and what we perceive, that is, phenomena. So taught Kant. But he himself posed the critical question: What is experience, and how is it possible? How is an object of experience, a phenomenon, possible, and how is the totality of connected phenomena we call nature possible? These questions take us directly into the sphere of metaphysics, and they cannot be evaded: for experience is not something irrelative or unconditional; it is itself conditioned by the activity of our consciousness and by the influence of the *"not-self"* external to us on our conscious, sensing *"self."* Experience is the relation of the knower to what is being known, where both obviously exist *prior* to such relation. How is this possible? What mediates between the knower and what is being known? Regardless of the answer, it is clear that experience itself *presupposes* the indicated correlation, as well as the reality of the correlating principles. *Experience presupposes something independent of experience and conditioning experience.*

Let us look at the matter from the other side: empiricists assert that we know only phenomena. These phenomena are connected by relations of succession and coexistence, which are subject to certain general rules or laws. But phenomena do not exist in themselves, as neither color nor sound exists without the sight and hearing capable of perceiving them. A phenomenon presupposes, first, something that appears; second, a conscious, sensing being to which this something appears; and third, a relation between them, between self and not-self, subject and object. Phenomena are reducible to relations. But these relations presuppose something conditioning and substantiating them, for we cannot think relations without that which is relating. And if the world of phenomena is an infinitely complex totality of real relations, then it presupposes, first, the totality of all real correlating principles and, second, some general connecting principle as the basis of all relations, substantiating the world of phenomena. But this is a general scheme for a whole metaphysical worldview, no matter how we understand the elements or principles that make possible the world of phenomena. And thus the very concept of *phenomenon* takes us beyond the phenomenal, precisely as the concept of experience takes us beyond experience.

IV.

The basic problem of epistemology (theory of knowledge) — the question of the possibility of knowledge — admits a positive or negative solution, but in both cases any particular outcome is connected with its own type of metaphysics, its own type of general, purely speculative idea about the nature of our reason, about the relation of reason to being [sushchee], and even about the nature of such being itself, about the nature of things. Imagine, for example, a purely negative solution that seemed to irrevocably eliminate any metaphysics. According to this solution, we can know nothing about being, about things as they exist in themselves outside relation to our consciousness, for our cognizing "self" is entirely limited to the subjective states of its consciousness and cannot go beyond them. But from where do we know this? From experience? No, because experience apparently convinces us of the existence of a universe independent of us. Experience, as the conscious relation of our "self" to something "other," as the *perception* of this other, presupposes the reality of this other, a reality preceding experience and independent of our consciousness. Consequently, the hypothesis that our knowledge is subjective, that it is limited to the internal states of the subject and its representations, is the result not of experience, but of speculation about experience or about the nature of consciousness. And any other theory of experience, in pursuing the question of its general conditions and of what substantiates experience, naturally goes beyond experience and inevitably leads to conclusions of a metaphysical character. The hypothesis of the inevitable subjectivity of our knowledge, of the impossibility of knowing things or relations outside our subjective consciousness, is no exception. This theory forces us to take all surrounding, knowable reality as our idea or representation (Schopenhauer's *die Welt als Vorstellung*, "the world as idea or representation") and leads us to phenomenalism or pure *illusionism*. Others, proceeding from the same theory, have acknowledged some unknown "thing-in-itself" (or things-in-themselves) beyond phenomena, without any relation to our reason or to knowable reality, and thus absolutely unknowable. No matter how negative such conclusions may seem, they still have the character of metaphysical claims. Whether we recognize real existence outside our consciousness or deny it, whether we assert that there are only phenomena or else admit — together with phenomena but absolutely distinct from them, "things-in-themselves," even if they are "unknowable" — all these are views that bear direct relation to ontology, to metaphysics, and that in one way or another are connected to a whole worldview.

V.

Thus it is that thinkers who strive to create, as they have since the time of Bacon,[3] an empirical or experiential philosophy cannot succeed in their undertaking or come to an agreed-upon result. And thus it is that the disagreements dividing them in the spheres of theoretical and practical philosophy are the same as those among metaphysicians: various shades of materialism and anti-materialism, idealism and realism, monism and dualism are all encountered here as well, and through the gaps in "empirical" psychology gapes dogmatic metaphysics. This is recognized even by many contemporary proponents of empiricism, who direct all their efforts to purifying it to the fullest extent possible of any metaphysical elements and who aim for the final *sterilization* of empiricism through the critical isolation of "pure" reason. But such a goal is false and illusory, since "pure" experience is a laboratory product, existing only in the mind of theorists. In reality experience is a complex product of the activity of our various cognitive faculties, and in this activity our cognizing reason goes beyond the limits of what is immediately given in sensible intuition, in the subjective states of consciousness — and this is because reason distinguishes its "self" from both these separate states and the real external objects it perceives objectively in their necessary connection with other real objects, also distinct from the "self." Experience is conditioned by the *independent activity* of our reason, which in experience itself transcends the limits of what is immediately *intuited* [*ispytyvaetsia*] by us in our sensations, in the states of our consciousness.

VI.

Our reason is an innate metaphysician, and it cannot limit itself to phenomena alone, just as it cannot think relations without that which is relating, or the conditioned without that which conditions. And it is not a simple unaccountable yearning that forces our reason to search for the absolute and unconditional above everything relative and conditioned, or that forces it to strive to give meaning to all particular knowledge and to understand the general connection within it. For if all our real knowledge is particular and limited, reason itself in its conceptual logical capability, *in potentia,* is not limited: Socrates himself, who so insistently pointed to the limitations of human knowledge, was the first to disclose the *formal logical universality of the concepts of our reason, and consequently of reason itself.* Our concepts are universal in their logical form, since they relate not to the individual, but to the general, to the generic and to formal characteristics, as in such concepts as human being, animal, triangle, and so forth. In experience we encounter particular cases, individual objects and perceptions, yet we know and think by means of concepts, the content of which comprises *general* properties (τα καθολου) [in entirety or totality, generally]. This fact alone has long been a stumbling block for empiricists and sensualists, who have looked for the source of knowledge in our individual sense impressions. They have tried to cancel out this fact by means of the so-called *nominalistic* theory: in reality, they argue, there are no general principles, only individual sensible objects and individual states of consciousness, and therefore our general concepts do not correspond to anything except *words;* concepts are words or names (*nomina*) that we use as artificial signs to designate an indefinite number of similar objects. But, first, it cannot at all be shown from experience that the world consists of individual elements, not united by any general principles, relations, or properties, or that our consciousness consists of individual states: *observation shows just the opposite.* Second, the very capacity for the word presupposes reason, which the wordless lack. The capacity to create general signs (*words*) and to use them for designating similar objects presupposes a capacity for the differentiation, definition, and abstraction of general properties, and in this consists understanding or conceptualization. Third, and finally, the capacity for the word, as a means of communication among minds, demonstrates the objectivity of reason and the objective universality of thought, independent of the limits of subjective consciousness.

Thus, let the actual content of our consciousness, like the content of our separate ideas and concepts, always be limited. But just as our concepts are universal or "catholic" in their logical form, so too our reason in its logical conceptual capacity is universal, that is, it can think everything possible, not limiting itself to the given available content of consciousness. And in its activity it strives to realize this possibility, its possibility, to objectively understand and express the *whole* unconditional truth, all-encompassing and all-substantiating, to know being [sushchee] in its all-unity. Whether we ever realize such an ideal, it is indisputably inherent to human reason. This is demonstrated by the history of reason and by consideration of its nature, and is admitted by those who, like Kant, recognize that the ideal of reason cannot be realized in time. If the nature of our reason places limits on its knowledge, this same nature forces it to strive eternally toward the truth beyond these limits. To disclaim such an aspiration would mean to renounce not a subjective personal dream, but the authentic ideal of reason, organically intrinsic to it by its very nature.

VII.

But if the aspiration to knowledge of unconditional truth is rooted in the very essence of our cognizing spirit, if philosophy is necessary and speculation is inevitable, why can this aspiration not reach its goal, why can philosophy not be one, like truth itself, or one even in the sense in which the unity of scientific knowledge can be recognized? Why does philosophy, in contrast to science, forever split into many contradictory doctrines, and what is the meaning of these contradictions? A powerful, ineradicable attraction draws our reason to an ideal end, but this movement is inevitably halted and broken by an unseen, fatal obstacle — a struggle so artfully depicted by Tyutchev in his poem:

> How like unto a living cloud
> The radiant, sparkling fountain writhes;
> How its damp smoke first blazes up,
> Then burns to powder in the sun.

It rises beam-like to the sky,
It touches the forbidden heights,
And then is fated to fall to earth
Anew in fiery-tinted ashes.

O cascade of mortal thought,
O inexhaustible cascade!
What law beyond our understanding
Impels your striving, then casts you down?
How avidly you dart to heaven!
But a fateful hand, hidden from sight,
Refracting your persistent beam,
Presses down in the spray from heights above.[4]

What does this aspiration to an unattainable end mean, this ideal of Truth, the ideal of the absolute, from which our reason cannot turn but which it can never reach? Such is the fate of human thought. But does thought really, in the highest and most profound of its aspirations, turn out to be unreasonable and condemned to unreasonableness?

VIII.

Consciousness of the ideal is given to man, and in this consciousness is the force that gives flight to his thought, lifting it high into the air. But this same consciousness indicates to him all the difference between the ideal and what he possesses in reality. As long as he sees this distinction, he will not lose consciousness of the ideal and will continue to strive toward it. But where consciousness of the distinction is lost, where people mistake the ideal itself for the reflections of it they find in themselves, in their own thought, there consciousness of the ideal is also lost. Its place is taken by these diverse, deceptive reflections, different in different minds, and what was an *image of truth* becomes a deceptive mirage. Here soaring aspiration, toward the ideal, ceases; for where "mortal thought" imagines itself to be in possession of the ideal, where it identifies itself with the ideal, precisely there is it "pressed down in the spray" from its imagined heights.[5]

Philosophy, in the precise sense of the word, is not "wisdom," that is, ideal perfect knowledge, but rather "love of wisdom." And what is most valuable in philosophy is the philosophy itself—the higher, living, ideal attraction of our knowing spirit to Truth, the yearning to "enter into the reason [or mind, *razum*] of Truth," as Vladimir Solov'ëv expressed it. Such a yearning cannot be fruitless, for it is evoked by the very image of this universal Truth, an image

266 S. N. Trubetskoi

intrinsic to our reason as the ideal guiding its cognitive activity. Let the "cascade of mortal thought" not reach heaven — in its every drop the sun shines, and celestial rays shimmer and play. In every truly philosophical teaching, for all its temporary peculiarities, one or another image of Truth is reflected; and in the many-sided prism of human reason its light is refracted and breaks into many rays. But philosophy is not satisfied by separate rays, it seeks the whole, even where it takes a particular reflection for the whole. And this aspiration to the whole is the living nerve of philosophy, the source of its creativity, of its faith and also its skepticism, its constant doubt and constant critique of everything that has been achieved. Inspired by this aspiration, true philosophy shows us the relative, limited nature of our actual knowledge, and yet also unifies it under the meaning of this very idea of the whole. The force of philosophy is felt in speculative work, through which it creates images of the all-unifying Truth, and it is felt in doubt, in critique, in negation of the lies or half-truths that pose as the whole. This attraction to Truth, constituting the very essence of philosophy, defines its significance in the development not only of human knowledge, but of the human spirit more generally: philosophy, an ideal formative force, is also the greatest liberating force of humanity, removing from it the fetters of spiritual slavery and directing it to the path of true freedom.

IX.

This defines the significance of philosophy, and the purpose of studying it. It is clear that we must study it in its actuality, in its history. We must learn to understand it in its creation and destruction, in all it has done and engendered — in the bold flight of speculation, in the creative synthesis of human knowledge, in analysis of cognitive processes and moral phenomena, in critique, doubt, in negation itself. In such study we will find the answer to that question [about the very possibility of philosophy] raised by the differences and contradictions of individual theories: the differences and contradictions of separate philosophies testify to the truthfulness of the *philosophy* itself in them, to its authenticity and veracity. Studying them, we become convinced that they are not accidental and cannot be reduced to mere peculiarities in the intellectual makeup of individual thinkers, but are rooted in the very nature of human reason, in its relation to the final object of its knowledge. There exist certain general forms of world-understanding, general ideas that pass from century to century, general oppositions that lead to worldwide controversies: idealism and realism, materialism and spiritualism, dualism and monism, empiricism and rationalism, and skepticism, not to name others. All these are categories and basic directions of philosophical reason that have long existed; there are also distinct stages or forms in the development of such directions, and they too have general, classic significance, for example, Cartesianism and Platonism. For all the inadequacy of these separate forms, for all the one-sidedness of these separate directions, they clearly have objective foundations, since through time they have, with certain changes, retained their abiding significance, despite the development of thought and knowledge. Therefore, the task of the scientific study of philosophy is first of all to understand the objective foundations and the internal necessity of these separate forms and directions. For this it is not enough to understand the "grain of Truth" contained in them and, as is said, in every other human mistake: it is necessary to understand the *philosophy* in these philosophies, their actual, living relation to Truth. It is necessary not to consider them from the point of view of one or another theory taken by us to be true, but to strive for the most objective and immanent understanding possible, trying to comprehend how philosophers have seen in them the image of the essential and all-unifying Truth.

X.

Such an approach to the study of philosophy bears the greatest interest for the history of the human spirit, especially, of course, for philosophy itself, as it shows the necessity of an all-encompassing philosophical synthesis, while also critically preparing such a synthesis. In this sense the scientific study of philosophy can be considered one of the foremost philosophical achievements of the past century.

Aristotle's metaphysics, based on systematic study of his predecessors, represents the codification of the ultimate problems of Greek speculation, problems not invented by Aristotle but posed to the entire preceding history of thought. He sought to generalize and rework them, but first of all to understand them objectively. And if he does not give their final solution, he does clarify them objectively, on the basis of careful analysis of earlier doctrines, in all their differences and mutual disagreements. Following Aristotle's example, the first condition of scientific work on metaphysics is thorough, objective study of its actual problems, in their origin and development. In this respect, present-day thought should, of course, be constructed on an incomparably broader foundation, taking into account the new and more complex problems that have been deepened by critical reexamination. If the history of philosophy is a science describing and explaining the concrete emergence and development of philosophical ideas, then elementary metaphysics is an *abstract ideology*, a science providing systematic analysis of the fundamental ideas of Being

[Sushchee], of the basic, most general, and necessary methods of understanding it.[6] The history of philosophy, now as in Aristotle's time, furnishes metaphysics with material for analysis, with the difference that in our day this material is not only infinitely more abundant, but also incomparably better worked out. In the course of its development over the ages, human thought has given, in the great diversity of philosophical teachings, many different expressions to a relatively few basic methods or forms of understanding truth, repeated from century to century. And although specific doctrines and world-views exist in a vast multitude, where their individual differences often have great internal significance, they nonetheless admit a certain classification according to common features: this is because the most general basic concepts of Being, to which correspond general philosophical conceptions, can be reduced to relatively very few ideas that are inherent in the most fundamental relations of our reason to the object of knowledge, *in the objective logic itself of pure reason.*

We can, like Hegel, attempt to construct such logic purely dialectically, through deduction from basic categories or the most general intellectual forms, but such an abstract system will in any case need verification. Therefore, before it is constructed and, indeed, to construct it correctly, we must examine all the different ways human thought has, in the course of its development, defined its relation to Being. We should not invent our own subjective metaphysics, but rather take metaphysics in connection with philosophy, studying the objective metaphysical problems that have been put to human reason and the methods by which it has resolved them.

In this, complaints of "historicism" are not infrequently heard, fears that the originality of individual philosophical thought might suffer from such historical inquiry. But philosophy seeks truth, not originality. *Independence* in philosophical work is determined not by subjective arbitrariness, not by absence of proper education or positive knowledge, but by depth, sincerity, integrity of philosophical interest, and breadth of conception.

XI.

The scientific study of philosophy is closely connected with the general development of historical and philological knowledge, but it was first raised to the level of an independent philosophical discipline by *Hegel.* He was the first thinker to attempt to justify the history of philosophy before the judge of philosophical thought itself and to understand this history as a process of integral and logically consistent development, all the moments of which, in their very differences and contradictions, are rational and necessary in their correlation and as a whole. In his *Logic,*[7] Hegel tries to deduce a priori, from pure thought, the totality of the most general concepts or "categories" by means of which we think and know everything that exists, and in this he argues that all these categories constitute one logically connected whole: we cannot take one of them abstractly, as something absolute and given in itself without relation to others, without it slipping through our hands, having dissolved into internal contradiction and passing into its own negation. When we concentrate on one category, on one abstract determination of being (substance, unity, multiplicity, etc.), affirming it in its abstractness independently of other ideas logically connected to it, then such a determination, by the internal logic of thought, inevitably breaks down and passes into its opposite or antithesis. This latter has the fate of being an intermediary idea that, through negation, passes to a third, higher determination, containing in itself the synthesis of the first determination and its antithesis. Thus, the entire edifice, the whole system of pure concepts constituting Hegel's *Logic,* is constructed from determination to determination, from one abstract category to another. All the history of philosophy is explained from this point of view: human thought as a whole completes this same cycle of development, necessarily passing from one abstract conception to another, just as in the a priori construction of the *System of Logic.* As dialectical transitions from one antithesis to another are necessary and logical in Hegel's system, so are they in human thought as a whole, which cannot limit itself to one particular abstract idea or conception of truth. In the struggle of philosophical doctrines, in their contradictions and succession, there can be discerned a logical, necessary movement, the final goal of which is the *self-consciousness of pure reason:* for Hegel, the expression of such self-consciousness was his own system.

This is not the place to undertake a critical evaluation of the merits and shortcomings of Hegel's doctrine, the past glory of which can only be compared to the almost universal disregard and incomprehension it meets in our own day. Hegel's "panlogism," his theory of the absolute identity of thought and being, his identification of truth itself with the logical thought by which this identification is made, suffers from extreme abstraction. Hegel disclosed perfectly well the false abstraction of all particular determinations or conceptions put forward as absolute, irrelative, or self-sufficient, but his own conception, his all-encompassing "idea of all ideas" or "concept of all concepts," is itself just such an abstraction, and it endured the fate of all abstractions — dialectical decomposition. This general defect of Hegel's teaching was also reflected in his understanding of philosophy in general and in his interpretation of its history, despite the remarkable gift of historical understanding that distinguished the great German thinker.

The history of philosophy is not a process of the dialectical development of abstract thought, nor is it determined by the movement of pure concepts alone; concrete human reason develops in it, in the totality of the cognitive functions of reason and in the creative activity of individual minds. And individual philosophical teachings without doubt represent something incomparably more concrete than the development of any abstract category. If they also give primary or even exclusive development to some particular determination or moment, each of them nonetheless strives, in its own one-sidedness, to an integral understanding of Truth and expresses in its own way a certain conceptual image of it, an *idea of Truth*, a certain *philosophical* relation of reason to it. In studying individual systems or theories we must first of all seek to understand what their creators most valued in them, namely, their philosophy, *their image of Truth*. But this is not enough: the development of philosophical thought is closely tied to the general process of historical cultural development, in which it is not infrequently delayed or diverted by historical conditions. Therefore, individual theories, despite the real and sometimes profound philosophy they contain, are nonetheless *historical* moments in the cognition of Truth and cannot be seen as purely logical moments in the movement of some impersonal idea. On the contrary, they possess individual character and in explaining them the historian is obliged to take into account all the circumstances of their time and place, as well as the personality of their creator, even where such theories acquire general, classic significance, expressing the universal forms of a worldview.

Finally, the close dependence of philosophical thought on the degree of development of scientific knowledge and spiritual culture — of moral and religious consciousness — should be pointed out, in contrast to the abstract, dialectical method of interpreting the history of philosophy. For in its aspiration toward the unification of human knowledge, toward an integral world-understanding, philosophy must somehow take into account science and religion, the results of scientific knowledge and the facts of moral consciousness. Philosophy once encompassed science, and now, when science has emancipated itself from philosophy, no one will deny their close relation and the interaction that will always exist between them. In science itself the evolution of philosophical ideas can be traced, though science has its exact methods of knowing phenomena, distinct from speculation. The influence of philosophical ideas is also powerfully felt in religious teachings, in the sphere of theology. Philosophy does not, however, itself determine the living concrete content of religious consciousness; on the contrary, such consciousness subordinates to itself the philosophical elements of theology. None of this cancels the significance of the purely philosophical investigation of the ideas or concepts lying at the basis of individual systems, in their dialectical and logical development, in their inner correlation. But this requires us to demand the genuinely historical study of philosophy and to not admit any a priori construction of its history.

XII.

It follows that philosophy is to be studied historically, in connection with the general culture; every individual theory must be understood in relation to other theories preceding, contemporaneous to, and following it, in relation to the intellectual and moral currents of the time, in relation to the general worldview of the epoch. But behind such historical inquiry stands fully legitimate philosophical interest, without which historical knowledge itself would be essentially incomplete and unintelligible, incapable of explaining to us the deepest rational foundations of the particular theories and presenting only a miscellaneous succession of various contradictory and odd constructions. To understand the meaning of their differences, to justify philosophy in these very differences, is the task of the scientific and philosophical study of the history of human thought. Therefore, if with the first glance at the history of philosophy, the differences and contradictions among the systems and theories seem to testify against the possibility of philosophy and most immediately against speculative philosophy or metaphysics, it turns out that scientific inquiry, explaining the necessity and rational foundations of such differences, shows us both the necessity and rationality of speculative philosophy, and demonstrates the possibility and necessity of systematic ideology or the science of ideas.

The history of philosophy thus serves as a justification of philosophy. But, apart from theoretical objections, practical objections are not uncommonly brought against philosophy, speculative philosophy in particular — references are made to the uselessness and fruitlessness of speculation, to this dry fig tree of the Gospels,[8] this *virgo Deo consecrata,* a virgin dedicated to God and doomed to eternal barrenness, as Bacon called metaphysics.[9]

Utilitarian objections against pure knowledge can seem crude: such knowledge represents first of all not *utility,* but *value.* But the question of the practical significance of philosophy in the higher and general sense is, nonetheless, an important and legitimate question. Let pure philosophy not represent any immediate utility in respect to external goals: Does this not alone demonstrate that it is valuable in itself, as Aristotle indicated? If it does not serve as a means for applied goals, then does it not set higher and general goals for human reason, placing before reason the ideal of integral knowledge? Let it be an *ideal* science — it is precisely for this very reason that its practical, guiding activity has been so great and felt not only in the sphere of knowledge, in the sphere of all the other real sciences, but also in all those spheres of human activity defined by ideas, principles, and general rational tenets. And here once more is what the history of philosophy teaches.

If simple reasoning convinces us that in today's division and specialization of scientific disciplines, every scholar wishing to intelligently cultivate a particular branch of science must appreciate the place it occupies in the ensemble of human knowledge and the higher end it serves, then the history of philosophy shows us how philosophy has in fact advanced the coherent unification of human knowledge, working out general guiding and methodological principles and placing before human reason the demand for an integral worldview, without which the proper, rational resolution of higher practical and moral tasks is also impossible.

But this is not enough. The work of philosophy has not been limited to only the theoretical sphere. History reveals it as a great and powerful spiritual force, as one of the factors in the world-historical process. And in this way history teaches us that the *ideal* of truth that philosophy serves is a *real* formative force. Greek philosophy created the "Hellenistic culture" [*obrazovannost'*] that became a universal culture; it imparted to this "culture" the store of general ideas that made it universal; and it first formulated the ideal of *humanity,* the ideal of universal human fraternity and *universal human unity,* to which Christianity subsequently gave a religious and a real-mystical basis, and to which Rome tried to give practical realization in a universal state. In this way the "most useless of all sciences" not only revealed to humanity a new world of spiritual values, but created a new world of universal human enlightenment; it awoke the self-consciousness of humanity and promoted its spiritual unification. And it is natural that in philosophy's highest principle, in the principle of Reason, in the principle of the Word, Christianity found the formula to express its own universal ideal. History shows us what philosophy gave to Christian thought, how it served as the school of medieval thought, how it restored and renewed the spiritual forces of European humanity, freeing its thought from the dogmatic paths taken after medieval Christianity deviated from its original pure norms and hardened into ephemeral, half-pagan forms. The great spiritual movement that began with the Reformation has not ceased and will not cease as long as humanity lives and thinks, as long as the ideal of truth stands before it. And we see how the bright and formative force of this ideal, acting through the collective thought of humanity, penetrates ever wider and deeper, illuminating for us the path of exploration and knowledge, and the path of rational moral activity in the sphere of personal and social endeavor.

Notes

1. By "our subject" Trubetskoi means Kant's transcendental self (the transcendental unity of pure apperception). See Immanuel Kant, *Critique of Pure Reason,* trans. Norman Kemp Smith (New York: St. Martin's Press, 1965), pp. 152–155; and Randall A. Poole, "The Neo-Idealist Reception of Kant in the Moscow Psychological Society," *Journal of the History of Ideas* 60, no. 2 (April 1999), pp. 319–343, esp. p. 327. Ed.

2. In Kant's philosophy, the faculties of sensibility (*Sinnlichkeit, chuvstvennost'*) and understanding (*Verstand, rassudok*). Ed.

3. Francis Bacon (1561–1626), English philosopher and statesman who described the inductive method of reasoning and was the forerunner of the British empiricist tradition in philosophy. Ed.

4. Fëdor I. Tyutchev (1803–1873), "Fontan" ("The Fountain," c. 1836), as translated by Jesse Zeldin in *Poems and Political Letters of F. I. Tyutchev* (Knoxville: University of Tennessee Press, 1973), p. 57. I have adjusted the last line from Zeldin's original "gleams in the spray" to the more literal "presses down in the spray," in view of Trubetskoi's subsequent reference to this line (see note 5). Ed.

5. Trubetskoi changes Tyutchev's "svergaet" to "svergaetsia" ("presses down" to "pressed down"). Ed.

6. Ideology, in the proper sense, is the study of ideas, as geology is the study of the earth or zoology is the study of animals. Recently the term "ideology" has come to be abused, especially in Marxist jargon, where it is often used instead of the terms "idea," "ideas," or "series of ideas."

7. This exists in two versions, the two-volume *Wissenschaft der Logik* (*Science of Logic*) of 1812–1816, sometimes called the "Greater Logic," and the first part of the *System der Philosophie,* originally published in 1817 under the title, *Enzyklopädie der philosophischen Wissenschaften im Grundrisse* (*Encyclopaedia of the Philosophical Sciences in Outline*). The second version is thus sometimes called the "Encyclopaedia Logic" or the "Lesser Logic." Ed.

8. Matthew 21:19–21, Mark 11:21. Ed.

9. Francis Bacon, *De dignitate et augmentis scientiarum* (*On the Dignity and Advancement of Learning,* 1623), Book 3, ch. 5; translated in *The Works of Francis Bacon,* ed. James Spedding, Robert Leslie Ellis, and Douglas Denon Heath (London, 1870), vol. IV, p. 365. Ed.

Ethical Idealism in the Philosophy of Law
(On the Question of the Revival of Natural Law)

P. I. NOVGORODTSEV

Even if [the ultimate purpose of law] were always to remain just a pious wish, we still would certainly not be deceiving ourselves by adopting the maxim of working for it with unrelenting perseverance. Indeed, we have a duty to do so, and to assume that the moral law within us might deceive us would give rise to the disgusting wish to dispense with reason altogether and to conceive of ourselves and our principles as thrown in together with all the other species of animals under the same mechanism of Nature.

Kant, Rechtslehre, *"Conclusion."*[1]

I.

When, in 1896, the first pronouncements were made in Russian legal studies about the necessity of the revival of natural law, they were met with mistrust and doubt.[2] It seemed strange and unlikely that an idea, so firmly condemned by the whole movement of thought in the nineteenth century, would ever again be resurrected as a legitimate and necessary concept in the philosophy of law. The very term "natural law" seemed for the modern view to be such an impossible and improper combination of words that this alone was enough to reject not only the term but also the very idea that was once more being advanced under this old designation.

But meanwhile careful study of the most recent literature could already suggest that in this revival of the idea of natural law a certain vital and urgent need was being expressed, I would say even a certain necessary law of scientific development. We have here an example of the common enough fact of the revival of a particular idea, temporarily eclipsed by an opposing direction of thought, but which in essence represents a necessary link in the system of concepts to which it belongs.

The direction that displaced the idea of natural law, but that at the present time itself demands certain limitations, might be designated as historicism [*istorizm*]. The nineteenth century was in general marked by the spread of historicism, and now, when it has come time to talk about the scientific directions of the past century, it is precisely this one that should be recognized as undoubtedly the most vivid and powerful. Everywhere, in all fields of knowledge, the historical method acquired the dominant position. Questions about origin, about genesis, about evolution received primary significance and excluded all others. Not long ago the English jurist Dicey[3] could still joke: "it were far better, as things now stand, to be charged with heresy, or even to be found guilty of petty larceny, than to fall under the suspicion of lacking historical-mindedness, or of questioning the universal validity of the historical method."[4] Application of the historical method perhaps far from everywhere gave the necessary results and was far from always carried out with enough depth, but as a worldview, as a principle, historicism without doubt reached its apogee. At the same time it also reached such a degree of universality in its claims that they were clearly exposed as excessive. This had to evoke a reaction, which itself had to lead, in turn, to a revival of the ideas and methods of thought that had been rejected or forgotten under the influence of the former enthusiasms.

This revival was made all the more necessary by the circumstance that the historical direction, by its original provenance, was not only a scientific doctrine but also a definite attitude. It concealed the moral-practical worldview of an epoch that no longer wanted to believe in the creativity of the person [*lichnost'*], in the power of reason, in the force of legislative initiative, that is, in all those words and slogans that constituted the sacred credo of eighteenth-century Enlightenment philosophy and that gave its works such an elevating, prophetic tone. Representatives of historicism spoke, by contrast, of the internal, imperceptibly acting forces of history, of the natural perfection of its own organic creations, of the necessity for individual persons to bow down before this general course of history and recognize its inevitability and beneficence.

The further development of thought removed from this outlook the drapings of reactionary romanticism and brought the whole complex of historical concepts into the quieter channel of the objective-scientific current. But the new formulations that were then successively introduced into the foundations of the historical method were only corroboration, so to speak, of the original historical view, according to which the general course of events is everything and the individual [lichnost'] is nothing. The previous formula of the organic action of the national spirit was replaced by the more concrete notion of the significance of the milieu and epoch, the milieu was then further divided into classes, and classes into groups. But no matter how the basic concept changed, its essence always remained the same: it was the notion of the individual's tie to a particular environment, which encompassed it and explained its life, aspirations, and ideals. And this notion was solid support for the call, with which the historical outlook first came forward, for the reconciliation of the individual before the general course of events.

I do not want to deny certain exceptions that were made even within the historical view to defend the significance of the person. Still less would it occur to me to diminish out of practical considerations the great scientific contributions of the method. The value of scientific principles cannot, of course, be measured by the practical consequences that follow from them. And if we talk in particular about the historical principle, then unquestionably it has, in its scientific application, given the more brilliant results the more it has preserved the characteristics inherent to it. The historical understanding of phenomena has become deeper and fuller, the more it has been imbued with the goal of examining all phenomena in the process of their necessary [zakonomernyi] development and of bringing them into connection with the whole aggregate of causes conditioning them. The essence of the historical principle indeed consists in nothing other than investigation of all phenomena and all values — to use an expression receiving universal recognition among us as well — from the point of view of their development in the conditions of a given milieu and epoch.

It is not accidental, therefore, that the further development of the historical method has only emphasized and reinforced historicism's initial goal of bringing the person into the sphere of inexorable necessity and binding it inextricably to the surrounding situation. The individual has more and more disappeared, having faded against the background, while the actual object of historical study has more and more become the life of the masses. From the historical point of view, the highest manifestations of the person, like the most basic of its needs, must be equally explained by the general conditions of the surrounding environment. Heroic deeds and the thoughts of a genius, no less than the ordinary business of an ordinary man, must be connected with the invisible but fruitful work of the masses, preparing in their midst the spectacular appearance of geniuses and heroes.

The further elaboration of historical methodology must determine in what measure and in which forms all these goals of historicism can be sanctioned by deeper philosophical analysis. The writings of Simmel, Xenopol,[5] and especially Rickert, who recently completed his remarkable work on the theory of historical knowledge,[6] promise to give us in this respect incomparably more than the rather tiresome arguments of Lamprecht[7] with the neo-Rankians.[8] But it is already clear that in one point the historical method has undoubtedly gone too far and exceeded its competency. I have in mind its relation to values, to those unconditional ideals and aspirations, the bearer of which is man.

It was completely legitimate and necessary for historians to attempt to bring these ideals and aspirations into their own sphere of specialized inquiry and to subject them to analysis from the side of their temporary historical expression in different epochs. But could investigation of the historical form of ideal values lead to a conclusion about their very essence as well? Was it possible to say that the variability of human ideals, as observed in history, characterized their very basis as well, that the absolute values that philosophy had long linked with absolute human personhood were variable and relative by their very nature? It is difficult to understand how so many representatives of historicism could remain innocent of the elementary philosophical differentiation between the temporal development and internal significance of things. But just as with disregard for this differentiation or inadequate attention to it, the oft-repeated view is endlessly maintained that truth, beauty, and the good are transient and relative, like everything in history, and that observation of change in their historical expression serves as adequate proof of their variability. All these values flowing from the absolute nature of the autonomous human person were submerged, like the very concept of the person, in the stream of historical development and put in connection with the material life of the masses.

For thoroughgoing historical examination, this conclusion was completely natural, but this does not mean that it was well-founded. The concept of personhood and the absolute principles connected with it are foreign and inaccessible to historical method. It can approach these principles only from the side, only at the surface. To go further, special philosophical analysis must take over. And if the historical outlook, having forgotten its limits, tries to reject philosophical analysis and the absolute values within its domain, then it is perpetrating an illegitimate exceeding of competency. Philosophy must restore its own rights and show history its limits.

It is not surprising that the first indications of this type were made by writers interested in raising the moral problem. The attempt to make ideal values relative and temporary, conditional in their origin and significance, was especially painful for moral philosophy. Indeed, this meant renouncing what had long been recognized as the foundation of morality. It was easier to accept the relative character of theoretical claims, all the more so that in this sphere it did not occur to anyone to take the point of view of historical relativism to its logical conclusions and show, for example, that all scientific axioms and laws are changeable and relative. But in application to ethical concepts this thought was pursued with particular diligence, to demonstrate that all morality grew from nothing, on the ground of simple egoism and calculation, adapted by the long process of evolution into a rational and expedient means for acquiring common goals. Having grown from egoism, and constantly changing and completely conditional, morality lost the characteristics of absolute "ought" [*dolzhenstvovanie*], inherent to the very nature of man and constituting the internal law of his will. Thus the most precious conviction of moral consciousness — belief in the absolute moral vocation of the person — was undermined at its very basis. Moral philosophy had to rise against these sacrilegious infringements and come to the defense of that foundation without which it is inconceivable.

Just as the philosophy of ethical idealism was coming to the defense of the independent moral principle and of the absolute right of the person to rise above history and pronounce judgment and evaluation of it, profound processes of life were taking place, which foretold the future creation of new forms. Once more the breath of the creative spirit of history was felt. Thought was automatically summoned to reflect on the tasks and calling of the person, through whom the progress of history is accomplished. From the past, thought turned to the future. And as commonly happens, the future that was hoped for, but that remained indefinite and unclear, made people think about the correct posing of ends and means, about the clarification of ideals and aspirations.

Such is the combination of old principles and new tasks by which, it seems to me, the revival of natural law is to be explained, a revival taking place before our very eyes. The idea of natural law appeared as only a partial reflection of a more general worldview and broader moral-practical attitude. Even before the latest jurists began to talk about it, it found a place among the political ideas of progressive parties. In Russia it was assimilated not long ago by writers who treated with the same perspicacity both the current challenges of life and the problems of a general philosophical *Weltanschauung*. But there were also special reasons for the revival of natural law within jurisprudence, which need to be mentioned here as well.

II.

Speaking about these special reasons, I have in mind mainly German legal studies, in which the need for new scientific approaches has recently been repeated with great persistence. It has already been almost ten years[9] since it began to be said that the science of law, while doing some important and even vital work, was not accomplishing all that could and ought to be demanded of it. Reproaches began to be heard about the evasion of certain important and lofty tasks, neglected by contemporary jurisprudence, to the detriment of both the common good and its own reputation. For anyone at all familiar with the development of the legal literature in recent years, there can be no doubt that these reproaches are connected in the closest way with a great event in the sphere of German law. I am speaking about the introduction in Germany of a common civil code that, to satisfy the long-standing wishes of German patriots, had to put an end to the diversity of local laws and the dominance of Roman law.[10] It goes without saying that this major event could not but at once push all thinking jurists into action. Compilation of the new code required colossal legal work, in which the greatest scholars and practitioners in Germany were enlisted and which continued for about twenty years. Such work is always a touchstone of the existing state of the science of law: it reveals how strong current thought is, in what it is strong, and in what it is deficient; it reveals the character of its ideals and goals, its poverty or wealth in this respect. And all this had to be revealed here in the German case as well.

What followed upon the first draft of the code [1888] — the fruit of fourteen years of hard work — was general disappointment. It was said that the draft was distinguished by an absence of living creativity and by slavish imitation of the Roman model; it was called, in view of this, an extraction from the pandects, divided into paragraphs. Thereafter the draft was once more redone and improved [1896]; but in this second edition it continued to elicit complaints about its Roman character and lack of new and bold directions to answer the new requirements of the times. Critics of the project saw the explanation for these shortcomings in the existing methods of jurisprudence, in its excessive devotion to authorities, in its absence of a critical sense. Here I can say in the words of one of these critics who attacked the project, Anton Menger:[11] "For sixty to seventy years, the principle of authority ruled almost absolutely in German jurisprudence, and any criticism of 'what is' [*Bestehend*] was suppressed; after that, what could be expected from the authors of the civil code except a compendium of the pandects arranged into paragraphs? Faith in authority can satisfy the demands of common scientific routine; but for the solution of great scientific tasks, a free critical sense with respect to received opinions and institutions is essential above all."[12]

Menger's voice was not alone. Together with him others spoke out in the same spirit. Their general opinion was that the science of law must become freer in its aspirations, broader in its tasks, more scientific in its methods. Windscheid[13] once called jurisprudence the maidservant of legislation—a maidservant with the crown of power, he added, to console the jurists. Now it is demanded that this servitude be put to an end. A crown on the head of the maidservant, Ofner observes,[14] can only designate what she was or ought to be; chains remain the sign of her actual position. Meanwhile, science must be free; a doctrine that is in servitude betrays the meaning of science. Until jurisprudence quits its false path, as long as it remains only an interpreter of existing legislation, it cannot be scientific, Ofner concludes. It must adopt a broader point of view on social research and take part in the noble task of reforming law.[15] Ofner, no less than Menger, demands that the science of law broaden its horizon and its tasks on behalf of the creation of new legal forms.

It is especially interesting to note that these aspirations have not remained foreign to representatives of the historical school. Thus Neukamp,[16] declaring himself a proponent of the historical direction, at the same time joins the latest jurists who reproach their science for lack of reformist tendencies. Repeating and continuing the thought expressed before him by Jhering,[17] Merkel,[18] Hölder,[19] and Ofner, Neukamp seeks to link the reforming function of jurisprudence to the basic premises of the historical school. Savigny removed the question about the reform of law from jurisprudence, considering this question to arise from the foundations of natural-law philosophy, and in this respect the resulting science remained true to his example.[20] But in this was his mistake, which stood in contradiction with the spirit of his theory. He himself said that the development of law does not know any limits, that it will continue in the future as in the past, according to the same law of internal necessity. But if that is the case, Neukamp observes, jurisprudence must turn its view to the future, as well as to the past. From the history of law, from its internal laws, it must infer paths for its further development, and this task is the real organic part of juridical science.[21] Neglect of this task on the part of jurists shows how far their science is from its essential tasks and from the interests of real life.[22]

But perhaps the most ardent reproaches against jurisprudence have been made not in Germany but in Russia, on the pages of the new law journal, which characteristically has called itself, *The Messenger of Law*.[23] The lead article inaugurating this journal recalled the achievements of the past science of law, when the spirit of natural law prevailed in it, when it lived in union and friendship with philosophy. This past science of law "struggled for freedom, equality, and peace, for justice and fraternity among people and nations. Its mighty word demolished age-old prejudices and superstitions in the law, and cultivated true law and justice, enlightened and humane." Turning then to today's science of law, the Petersburg journal asks: "Whom and what do the theories of current jurisprudence inspire? Where is it leading humanity? It is leading humanity nowhere, for no one listens to or awaits its guidance. Outside its circle, outside it own type of craft guild, apparently no one knows or is interested in knowing what it is occupied with, what themes it discusses or how it resolves them." From further clarifications we learn that here as well the main shortcoming of jurisprudence is seen in the fact that in it the critical spirit and deeper philosophical aspirations have been smothered, that practical interests prevail in it, and that its work has become petty, mechanical, and insular. It is necessary to create a special discipline — legal policy [*politika prava*]. It is necessary to revive the spirit of criticism and ideal aspirations. Then will take place "a return to the precepts of the best, renowned times of the science of law," which will again take up its creative function, adopt firm principles, and once more serve "the eternal ideal of love for man and higher justice."[24]

In due course, behind the bold and eloquent sallies of this unsigned article, the influence was detected of a Russian scholar for whom the German school was just the best occasion to display an original freshness of thought and a free approach to the old authorities. Behind this Russian critic was apparently a writer who, with surprising dialectical force, tried to uncover the gaps in the existing method and who caught the attention of the best German jurists.[25]

I consider it superfluous to multiply the number of quotes from other similar declarations. But I cannot fail to mention here the surprising growth of interest in the idea of natural law, to which V. M. Hessen has pointed in his brilliant article "The Revival of Natural Law."[26] Every year brings us first a new and authoritative censure of the historical school, then an attempt at a new working out of the problem of natural law. The revival of the doctrine, and a critical approach to the past foundations of jurisprudence, can also be noticed in France in recent years. In 1899, Gény,[27] professor at Dijon, published his interesting work *Méthode d'interprétation et sources en droit privé positif,* which represents a protest against traditional jurisprudence.[28] In 1900 Tanon[29] and Deslandres[30] spoke out against the one-sidedness of historicism and sociologism, which exclude ideal constructs.[31] And in the current year, 1902, a new law journal in France has already offered its readers an article by Saleilles,[32] describing the revival of natural law in German and French legal studies.[33] In regard to Germany, here as well we can point to interesting new developments in the literature over the past two years. I am referring in particular to Bülow's brochure,[34] contending that German jurists have studied the history of law too much and have thus been diverted from the living tasks of reality. I would also note L. Savigny's article on the method of natural law,[35] and, finally, the new book by Stammler, who tries, independently of Gény but in the same spirit, to introduce the light of higher principles and generalizations into the elaboration and application of positive law.[36]

The works of Stammler and Gény, like those of Petrażycki preceding them, could not testify better to the fact that the new movement in jurisprudence is not limited to general declarations, but strives to give its principles practical application. It is already impossible to doubt that jurisprudence is on the eve of a new formulation of its tasks and methods. It is hard to expect, of course, that this reform movement will at once embrace the whole juridical world. Success in this respect depends not so much on individual attempts and declarations, as on the general preparedness of jurists to participate in the creative work to which they are called. To be ready for this, the science of law must not only assimilate deeper philosophical aspirations, but beyond that it must be imbued with a living feeling for reality, with an ability to hear the unceasing pulse of life and to answer the great tasks of the times. The creative work of thought in the sphere of legal ideals can never end, although it can remain foreign to professional jurists. The work of jurisprudence can be great and momentous only when it proceeds from ideal principles and is inspired by them, only when it, freely surveying its material, rises above it in the name of higher principles. Without this, what remains is the useful, of course, but purely technical task of adapting legislative material to routine needs.

Returning once more to the statements, cited above, of the need to meet the tasks of jurisprudence by charting the paths of the future development of law, I would note that these statements usually connect their new task with the distinctive striving of natural law in the past. Even Neukamp says that the important question he is raising was long ago worked out by the doctrine of natural law (p. 67). Thus, the authors of these declarations come, directly or indirectly, to recognize the contributions of natural law. If they do not all want to revive its methods, they do all call for the rehabilitation of the problem that was always central for it, that is, the problem of the reform of law. The creative spirit, which blew in German jurisprudence during preparation of the new civil code, automatically had an effect on understanding the tasks of the science. The old limits of the historical school are proving to be narrow; new paths and methods are required. But preparation of the civil code was only a partial cause of this. Among the jurists who came forward most deliberately and firmly with the suggestion of new scientific perspectives, consciousness was felt of certain radical needs of the current epoch, needs that the jurist must face. For these jurists the issue was clearly not about minor technical adjustments, which can be fully made by means of the present state of the science, but about a serious reworking, proceeding from basic principles, of many parts of the law. It was obvious that civil legislation had to enter a new era, and the thought that flashed here and there about the social tasks of private law testified to the fact that jurists had not remained immune to presentiment of the new era. But it was precisely this need for a fundamental reworking of law that suggested the idea of creating a new juridical discipline. For this the technical means of jurisprudence were already inadequate. A much broader system of scientific concepts and means was necessary, in order to go beyond the limits of petty technical matters.

Thus we come to the conclusion that in Germany as well, the revival of natural law is arising from a profound requirement of life that, persistently calling attention to itself, directs thought to new perspectives. If now the idea of natural law is making, in V. M. Hessen's words, "with every year, almost with every day, tremendously rapid successes," then this is because the days of exclusive historicism are numbered. The basic reworking of legal principles, elucidation of the ideals of the future, and the reform of law in light of new guidelines from life all demand special methods of thought and special scientific preparation. The history of law alone, even in the form about which Neukamp speaks, is inadequate here. On the contrary, what is directly needed is a break with the traditions of exclusive historicism and a transition to new points of view. What is needed is precisely a revival of natural law with its a priori method, ideal aspirations, and recognition of the independent significance behind the moral principle and normative consideration. This is the point that must be clarified in more detail.

III.

The revival of natural law that is taking place before our very eyes is linked, as we have seen, with presentiment of new forms from life, which automatically turns thought from the present to the future. This connection of natural-law doctrine with the creation of new legal forms, which explains the spread of the idea in our time, reveals at the same time a constant need that in the past also always led to natural-law constructions. This is the need to consciously go forward to meet the future, as yet undetermined and still within our power, as it were, and to realize in it our ideal strivings and hopes. This need is especially striking in epochs of crises and turning points, when past forms of life clearly expose their decrepitude, when society is seized by an impatient desire for new structures. But in greater or lesser degree the necessity for change and improvement in law is felt constantly, in connection with the constant changes in life. The laws and institutions that in every society are maintained by the state [*vlast'*] and the courts and that constitute its positive law can never be perfected. They can never reconcile the interests of the diverse groups making up society, and still less can they determine, once and for all, a just order of life needing no changes whatsoever over the course of time. Life constantly goes forward and demands new forms. From this stems the constant dissatisfaction with "what is," which has not yet had time to be changed by law; from this also stems the demand for better, ideal, natural law. Human thought has this quality of living not only in the present, but also in the future, of bringing to the future its ideals and aspirations, and in this sense natural-law constructions are an integral property of our spirit and testimony to its higher calling. A society that ceased to create ideal constructions would be a dead society. Such constructions always show a living spirit in society, a movement of moral feeling and consciousness. And they always are connected with law, as that form of social life that determines the external conditions of its existence, conditions having enormous significance for moral development as well. External legal forms are far from indifferent for our moral goals: whether a person in a given situation finds an oppressive lack of freedom, or rather the happy possibility of freely developing his strengths, depends on the quality of these legal forms, on their correspondence to the moral principle. It is from this link of the external social form to the moral strivings of persons that the need inevitably arises to improve law, to bring it ever closer to ideal ends.

In the historical development of natural-law doctrine, this moment of ideal construction was combined with another moment, which thus became linked to the first but was not the same as it. It is often said that ideal demands flow from nature itself; hence the name "natural law." This supposition of the existence of a law deriving from nature was furthered, moreover, by the observation that among the decisions in any body of law there are certain claims that seem to be beyond people's will and prescribed by nature itself. Such, for example, are the norms defining the distinction of people based on age, the division of things into distinct legal categories according to differences in their natural properties, and so forth. This observation prompted the discovery in actually existing law of traces of natural law and the distinction in legal statutes between immutable and natural decisions on the one hand and changeable and arbitrary ones on the other. Thus, the concept of natural law has long had a dual composition: it has rested on the *practical* demand for a more perfect law and on the *theoretical* observation of the natural necessity of certain legal positions. These two elements could support each other, but they could not be reduced to each other: in the first case natural law stands above positive law, while in the second it is only a certain part of positive law. In one case it is seen as an ideal norm, which has not yet been realized in a given body of law and perhaps not in any body of law; in the other case it is seen as a universal fact, inherent to every body of law. Obviously these were different conceptions, far from identical in their philosophical significance. The fact that they have often been confused and improperly identified with each other has not prevented the first — the ideal and normative element — from being advanced with particular vividness, but the confusion and improper identification have often ascribed to it traits resulting in misunderstanding about its very nature.

The notion that natural law is prescribed by nature itself, and that direct evidence for that can be found in the prevalence of certain parts of natural law among all peoples, led to the thought that all of it could be derived from the immutable dictates of nature and that a system of norms could thus be created, suitable for general use as an eternal and true model. This conclusion about natural law, immutable for all times and peoples, was never inseparably linked with the first idea about the possibility and necessity of ideal constructions. It would not be difficult to show, with references to the history of the philosophy of law, that very many philosophers, long before the historical school and the nineteenth century, understood the variability of legal ideals perfectly well. The blanket accusation that all of them imputed absolute and invariable content to the legal ideal is one of those hasty generalizations that, repeated hundreds of times without verification, acquires, as if since antiquity, a claim to truth not belonging to it earlier. The conclusion that some philosophers drew about the immutability of ideal norms was changed into an accusation against all of them, and it was on this misunderstanding that the historical school based its easy victory over natural law.

I would like to stress that a correct understanding of the idea of natural law is possible only if we keep in mind the historical duality of our doctrine and the resulting confusion of concepts. None of today's advocates of the natural-law school is thinking of rehabilitating its past mistakes, and when the latest jurists are reproached for wanting "to resurrect the doctrine of *jus, quod natura omnia animalia docuit*,"[37] then it is easy to respond by referring to the impossibility of answering for another's mistakes. I do not know anyone who would today defend this very shallow philosophy of Ulpian[38] or even the later teaching about a sense of justice innate to man, unchanging in content with the course of time. So familiar a formula now as "natural law with changing content,"[39] first introduced by Stammler, or "evolutionary natural law," recently used by Professor Hessen, adequately speaks to how much contemporary representatives of the school take into account the indisputable fact of the variability of legal ideals. As I will try to show below, in this they not only give the historical view its due, but no less than that comply with the foundations of their own moral-philosophical point of view, as it directly requires.[40]

But it can be asked of us, where then is the break with the historical outlook? Historicism does not in the least reject the necessary appearance of legal ideals, and if it is admitted that they change with time, in connection with the whole course of life, then any affinity with the past school of natural law would seem to be disavowed. Did not Neukamp quite recently show the possibility of putting this very question of new forms of law on the ground of the historical school? And have not other historians and sociologists before and after him posed this same problem, without resorting to any concepts of natural law, completely foreign as such thinkers are to the desire to resurrect a doctrine to which, as it seems to them, there can be no further return?

These questions have led to the most important point of my exposition. The issue here is how precisely to demarcate our philosophical doctrine from the positivist-historicist view. It is necessary to demonstrate that the historical method alone is inadequate to resolve the questions that the natural-law school has posed before and that it poses now, that here we enter a special sphere, autonomous in its methods and tasks and not coinciding at all with the sphere of historical study. For this, our task is first of all to clearly formulate the natural-law problem and then show the approach the historical outlook takes to it.

We have seen that the basic question of natural law is the question about future law. But every time this question has been posed in all its sharpness and purity, the future has been brought into connection with a certain moral ideal. The need that has always prompted construction of the future was that the present seemed imperfect in one respect or another. Therefore no mere simple result of present conditions was expected from future law, but rather an ideal and desired result. Thought was directed not to what *will be* by the force of natural causes, but to what *ought to be,* in correspondence with the moral law. According to the essence of the problem, construction of the future was also an evaluation of the present, and this evaluation was carried out not from the point of view of causal historical succession, but from the point of view of moral "oughtness" [*nravstvennye dolzhenstvovanie*]. An event or phenomenon might have been historically inevitable, but nonetheless declared morally unfit by natural law in virtue of its moral ideal. In this way the question of natural law, clearly and distinctly formulated, possesses a completely special and autonomous sense, sharply distinguishing it from the purely historical question of the development of law. Here the task is not at all to give a theory of the formation of law, *explaining* the natural development of legal institutes, but to establish moral demands, *prescribing* ideal paths of development. The goal is not the explanation but the evaluation of things, an evaluation done independently of how these things developed in the past and how they might develop in the future.

The method, like the question, of natural law has a special and autonomous character. Intended to give criteria for the evaluation of history, it cannot also take its starting principles from history. To the question of what ought to be, knowledge of what has been and what is cannot give an answer. Here it is necessary to turn to the a priori indications of moral consciousness, which in its essence, independent of any experience, contains grounds for the evaluation of any material from experience.[41]

Such is the significance of the natural-law problem. For the historical outlook, remaining faithful to its principles, a threefold approach to this problem is possible. It can bypass the problem, as outside the bounds of its competency; reject it completely as illegitimate; or, finally, replace it with some other problem, similar to it in form, but different in substance.

The first solution is, from our point of view, the only correct one. The moral problem is insoluble in the terms of historicism and inaccessible to the positivist method. Within its own limits, historicism cannot say anything for or against this problem, the affirmation or negation of which requires special philosophical and in particular epistemological demonstration: the data of history have here a highly relative significance. The only argument the historical mode of thought brings against the autonomy of the moral problem is the empirical observation about the historical changeability of moral concepts. The conclusion is that all morality is the product of history, wholly dependent on temporary and local conditions. On this basis it is considered possible to dissolve the moral ideal, entirely and without remainder, into all the empirical elements determining it, and to reduce the very concept of "ought" to some aspect of natural necessity. But here arises the same mistake as in attempting to explain human consciousness by material conditions or to pass it off as a certain property of matter. Imperceptibly for superficial thinking, a logical leap is taken for a natural development of concepts, among which there is in fact an unbridgeable gap.

The second solution, consisting in the rejection of natural law, already in itself exceeds the sphere of competence of historicism. In its most consistent form this rejection includes not only the method but also the very problem of natural law, since it is a problem of moral evaluation, passing from "what is" to "what ought to be" [*dolzhenstvuiushchee*]. We find such a total rejection of the natural-law problem in the views of the old historical school of jurists. Savigny thought that the point of view he advanced, historical inevitability and necessity, excluded the very possibility of evaluation and critique of law: if all law is formed by the action of inevitable historical forces, then it would seem that any attempt to critique the historical process is no more justified than an attempt to critique the elemental processes of nature. Do we critique a storm or bad weather? In Spinoza's words, natural phenomena can be found inconvenient or unpleasant, but there is no place for critiquing them. Such was the point of view of the original historical school, which wanted to abandon all conscious evaluation and critique of law. To philosophers who wanted to outline the future, it suggested the role of simple observers of the historical process. If everything in history comes about on its own and at the appropriate time, then for man it remains only to fathom the results of historical development and to chronicle what happens with inevitable and fatal force, beyond his will and, perhaps, against his wish.

Such was Savigny's view. But its best refutation and the best confirmation of the ineradicability of moral evaluation is that Savigny himself made his historical point of view into a category of evaluation and the basis for conclusions about "what ought to be." He declared the necessary and natural development of law to be *exclusively rational,* and any attempt to depart from it an evasion of the lawmaker from his vocation. Unaware of it himself, he reintroduced the same concept he rejected. He reintroduced it under the cover of the historical view, to the detriment of its true significance, but in any event the rejected category reappeared, testifying to its ineradicability.

Discussing Savigny's outlook now, we can easily see its mistake. Comparing the formation of legal norms and positions, and generally all historical processes, with processes of nature, he forgot that if law is formed naturally [*zakonomerno*], it is also formed through people and by means of their will. As an agent of the historical process, man automatically asks about the path he is to follow, and if his decision is itself connected to certain historical conditions, nonetheless it is made consciously, with a critique of other views and a choice of one's own point of view. It is said that man must follow history and its indications, but what does it mean to follow history? It would still be possible if, in every given moment, in every epoch, history gave us the finished and ready results of its development; then it would be up to us only to read these results, like the last page of a finished book, and to act on their basis. But it does not happen like that. History is not a gently unraveling scroll of events, it is not a book that can be read from one conclusion to the next. It is first of all a struggle; as Hegel expressed it in his time, it is the severe and hard work of the spirit upon itself, a dialectical process proceeding from contradiction to contradiction. In every epoch it presents to us a mixture of old and new, moribund and newly born, bad and good. Man, set among these contradictions and within this living struggle, is automatically called to take account of the process unfolding before him, to evaluate the various historical currents, and to take a stand with one side or another. In other words, he is automatically called to conscious evaluation of "what is" and to ideal constructions. He cannot remove from himself this idea that the future depends on his effort [*sodeistvie*] as well, and the less likely the desired result seems to him, the more energetically he is prepared to invest his thought and will into its realization.

This natural striving of man is perhaps nowhere as clear as in the sphere that interested Savigny, that is, law. Legislation, summoned to regulate life, itself depends on life's needs, but they must first be reflected in it, passing through the prism of legislative creativity. Here there is clearly an enormous role for conscious thought and real insight. This is why it is so understandable that practitioners and theorists want to come to the help of legislative creativity and take part in the rewarding work of creating new forms. This is why there is so much lance-breaking and why passions run so high when talk turns to these new forms. Let historians say that such forms will be the necessary result of inevitable causes: our thought will never give up the conviction that among these causes our will also possesses significance.

This conviction is so natural, authoritative, and invincible that even within the historical school it had to find recognition. With this I pass to the third solution, which consists in the attempt of historicism to settle in its own way the problem arising here. I have already noted that in this case what really happens is a certain substitution: in place of one problem another is raised, essentially different from the first. The natural-law problem, as explained above, is a moral problem. Here the question is not about what will be, by force of historical necessity, but about what ought to be, in conformity with the moral norm. This is why the problem remains insoluble for historicism, which is concerned only with natural correlation between cause and effect. If, however, historicism does pose the question of future forms of law, then, to remain consistent, it must remove from its deliberations any trace of moral qualification. This is indeed what usually happens, which is at least consistent. Much less consistent are those historians who think that they can, on their own ground, solve the moral problem itself and thus raise the question not only about future law, but also about law that ought to be. Juridical literature of the recent past presents examples of both types. Neukamp poses the question of future law, trying to remove any trace of the moral problem from it; Merkel makes an attempt at solving the moral problem itself in terms of historicism. I will focus initially on the second approach, which strikes us as the less consistent, in order to then pass to the first, which also must be recognized as utterly inadequate.

Merkel so little shuns the terms of moral philosophy that we find in him even the usual concept of "the highest criteria for evaluation of law" (*die obersten Wertmaße für die Beurteilung des Rechts*). But he thinks that these criteria, found within the limits of the possible development of present conditions, must be derived from examination of reality: from this we conclude precisely which of the possible directions of development is to be supported. Our idea of "what ought to be" is thus a consequence of our consideration of "what is."

It would seem that there is no need to analyze in detail this strange combination of concepts, the illegitimacy of which is immediately striking. A science about "what is" cannot give any criteria for evaluation. It would violate its objective character were it to take up judgment and evaluation. If in its conclusions it uses the concepts of normative development and normative type — Merkel considers these concepts in particular to be support for conclusions about "what ought to be" — this is not in the least connected with such usage in moral conclusions: it has in view here only generalizations from observations it has made, without any indication of their evaluation. Therefore science can apply the concept of normative development to things that are indifferent to or even incompatible with morality. And only when this concept crosses over into the sphere of moral judgments does it find support in our moral consciousness. From this, and only from this, can we conclude which of the possible directions of development is to be supported. A science of "what is" says nothing on this account: it impassionately investigates good and evil as phenomena equally natural, equally determined by certain causes.

Violating the strict principles of objective science, Merkel does damage to the character of morality as well. For him moral judgments do not bear the halo of absolute "ought," but only the simple sign of relative morality. They do not stand against "what is," as authoritative and absolute imperatives, but are included among the other elements of empirical reality, and are just as relative and conditional. But this means removing from morality its essential quality. For the positive-historical point of view, which rejects any other method of knowledge, nothing else remains: it can recognize the moral problem only having destroyed its essence.[42]

Much more consistent is Neukamp's view. He assiduously avoids any proximity to natural law, and if he nonetheless raises the question of the future, he does so in terms of strict science. He does not know the principles of evaluation, only the laws of development. From laws of the development of law in the past, indications for the future should derive. Neukamp clearly sees that the history of law, as it is ordinarily understood and worked out, gives no precise indications of this type. He therefore considers it necessary to create a special "history of the development of law" (*Entwicklungsgeschichte des Rechts*), which will discover the laws of legal development and serve as the basis for conclusions about the future. The more remote this projected science is, the easier it is to talk about, remaining as it has thus far a dream. But if the project itself is discussed, it turns out to be no more than an unsuccessful dream to create something between history and sociology. It is possible to present history in the form of a "science of natural laws" only if one is completely ignorant of contemporary theory of historical knowledge. Now that Windelband and Rickert have brilliantly solved the task of demarcating history and natural science, to speak about this [history as natural science] means repeating a clearly exposed error. It is just as little possible to speak about the capacity of history, in no matter how perfected a form, to predict the future. In this last respect even positivist historians have raised doubts about Neukamp's project: I refer to the example of M. M. Kovalevskii.

But leaving aside the unrealizability of the dream, can we say that even if it were realized, Neukamp's project would replace the problem of natural law, that is, the problem of ideal law? Is not one concept being substituted here for another, a substitution that goes against the essence of the matter? Precisely because of Neukamp's caution, trying as he does not to exceed the limits of historicism, we can clearly see that such a substitution does in fact take place.

Speaking about future law, he has in mind what will be by natural laws. Here he overlooks that this future is not always better: that which ensues from present conditions can sometimes turn out to be a sad triumph of force and injustice. But when our consciousness looks to the future, it expects not just any forms whatsoever, but the ideal and best ones. Sometimes it can clearly see that these expectations have no basis in reality; it then turns away from the future, and from the present as well, and waits for its hopes, in the words of Plato, to be realized if not here, then in some other country. Clearly the question of the moral ideal has nothing in common with the question of a historically necessary result. What Neukamp offers is completely inadequate.

Incidentally, this is obvious from his own arguments. He himself recognizes that even the perfected history of law about which he dreams would be capable of giving us not absolute certainty, but only a legitimate expectation [*die berechtigte Erwartung*] (p. 75). Were this expectation not to come true, we would feel that our legal sense had been violated (p. 60).[43] But what would this last possibility mean: that our expectation was not sound, or that the development of law took a course not indicated by natural laws? It would seem that in history everything happens by natural laws. How is it possible to oppose legitimate expectations to it? Neukamp, until this point true to historicism, pays here a weak tribute to the moral point of view, although he himself is unaware of it. Under the name of "a legitimate expectation, which can fail to come true only at the expense of our sense of law," he introduces a shadow of the moral ideal, but no more than a shadow, for even more decisively than Merkel he destroys in it the living force of moral striving.

Neukamp's arguments reveal still another weak side of historicism, as it takes on tasks beyond its strengths. Seeking to determine the fate of the future development of law, history can rely exclusively on the examples of the past and on present conditions. From this it is possible to derive nothing except the most hypothetical conjectures, or, as Neukamp expresses it, "legitimate expectations." To affirm one's moral ideal on these conjectures would mean to deprive it of real scope and firmness. It often happens that the more precise historians are just those who turn out to be incapable of crossing intellectually the border that separates the present from the future. Sticking to the present and past, thought of the future loses its wings and boldness of flight. Meanwhile, the peculiarity of progressive development is precisely that the future realizes not the possibility that appeared practically feasible and to follow from present conditions, but the one that seems new and unheard of, the one that frightened people wise in experience and competent in practical affairs when it began to float in the vague visions and bold schemes of utopians and dreamers. The creativity of life is broader than limited human experience, and therefore it constantly happens that utopian theory is more farsighted than sober practice.

When moral philosophy poses this same problem of future law, it does not proceed by taking examples from the past, nor does it undertake prediction. Its source is the demands of moral consciousness. Reflecting on the future from this point of view, we say not that we know it, but rather that we demand it; we want to bring our thoughts and hopes to the indefinite prospects of the future. The natural necessity that stands in contradiction to the moral ideal is simply negated here. The task consists in establishing an absolute precept for moral aspirations. Immediate practical success has no bearing on the force of this precept: *fais ce que dois, advienne que pourra.*[44]

In examining the possible approaches of historicism to the natural-law problem, we have until now spoken of history proper; but the matter is not in the least improved by attempting to entrust a task beyond history to that continuation of and supplement to history known as sociology. Contemporary theory of knowledge has powerfully shaken the hopes placed earlier on this science, and in particular it has completely undermined the credit of sociology as a science capable of foreseeing the social future. Not at all denying the importance of sociological generalizations and their well-known benefit in practice, we must, however, repeat here the conclusion we reached about history, since it is the foundation of sociology. Incapable of predicting the future, nor can sociology discuss it from the moral point of view. As a science of cause and effect, it is deprived of the possibility of establishing demands and norms: the question of "what ought to be" exceeds its sphere. Remaining true to itself as objective theory, it tells us, for example, that in one case it is probable to expect "the victory of egalitarian freedom over the monopolistic and arbitrary regime," while in the other, "a change in the political system favoring the ruling classes and limiting the sovereignty of the masses," but it cannot say in what relation these results stand to our moral ideals. Both results, from the point of view of objective science, are equally necessary or, to adopt an old term of the positivists that has now gone out of usage, both will correspond to "the general consensus of the social organism."[45] And if we stay within the limits of this view, any "consensus," any concrete form of its manifestation, is equally legitimate, to the extent all are equally necessary and natural in given conditions. The moral question is simply removed here, and if the sociologist were to give preference to one form over another, he would in so doing deviate from the path of historical relativism and admit into his deliberations a scale of evaluation. Here is it possible to speak only of forms that are more or less complex, more or less viable, but of nothing further; and no such categories bear relation to ethics. More viable or fit is not at all the same as better or ethically valuable. To recall an example from natural science, by Huxley:[46] in certain conditions of development, lichens can everywhere turn out to be the most fit for life. All this has been repeated many times, and hardly requires more detailed explanation.[47]

The one-sidedness of sociology, indifferent to the moral question, was well shown by the Russian sociological school in its time. But instead of recognizing this one-sidedness as necessary and legitimate, Russian sociologists of the so-called subjective school tried to correct it by supplementing sociology itself. They recognized, speaking in the words of their authoritative representative, Professor Kareev,[48] that "objective study alone of social phenomena and forms, without subjective evaluation of them or an ideal conception of how society ought to be, cannot give complete sociological understanding." They therefore demanded that juridical, political, and economic phenomena be studied in connection with their significance for individual persons. This demand, to the extent it includes the goal of defending the problem of moral evaluation from the objectivism of science, favorably distinguishes the subjective sociologists from those objectivists who not only remove the ethical element from their own sphere, but also reject it entirely. The baseless "replacement of ethicism with historicism" always found resolute opponents among the subjective sociologists.[49] During the recent dominance of positivism they pointed with great keenness to the whole illegitimacy of the eradication of the moral problem, and in this consists their indisputable service. But their mistake, as criticism has now made clear beyond doubt, was that instead of strict delimitation of the ethical element from the scientific, they permitted their compounding. From this came the unsuccessful concept of *subjective* sociology and the idea of the "subjective method," surprising in its philosophical untenability. It is understandable that as a whole this construction had to evoke protests from both the side of positive science and the side of moral philosophy, for the correct correlation of these two spheres is their complete delimitation. Morality shows its distinctiveness precisely in that it judges independently of the necessity disclosed by science; it has its own necessity. On the other hand, science must be indifferent to what follows from its results; it searches for laws, discovers the causes of phenomena, and besides this knows nothing. This delimitation needs to be drawn with utter precision in order to bring to consciousness the fact that moral evaluation does not at all broaden "sociological understanding." It should rather be said that in making a moral evaluation, we depart from sociological knowledge, since the point of such an evaluation consists in asserting its significance despite the causal link of events and their natural course.

The direct result of the imprecision of concepts permitted by the subjectivists was an incorrect formulation of the moral problem. Having been reduced to the premises of positivism, it [the problem as posed] could not be developed in all its fullness. The subjectivists did not so much formulate the problem as sense it, and still less did they solve it. This is why today's champions of the idea of natural law should seek support not in Russian sociology — as Professor Kareev suggests — but in the more profound sources of philosophical idealism. As an integral development within a whole system of philosophical concepts, this idea cannot at all find proper support in a direction that is completely deprived, by its philosophical gaps, of prospects for further development, and that is becoming entirely relegated to history.

IV.

We have examined the possible approaches of historicism to the natural-law problem and have come to the conclusion that this problem remains incommensurate with it. In trying to either modify or replace the problem, in the end historicism succeeds only in destroying it. Sociology does not help in the least here, and when it attempts to broaden its scope by introducing the ethical element, it only undermines its own foundations. The very essence of morality turns out to be beyond the reach of the historical method, which cannot approach it without violating its own competence and exceeding its own limits.

This by no means excludes the possibility of historical inquiry into the development of morality. On the contrary, here a rewarding field for research is opened up, highly interesting and completely accessible to historical analysis. Thus, for example, it is hardly possible to deny the importance of works that endeavor to establish the successive link among different forms of moral consciousness and to show how and to what extent their development depends on changing historical conditions. When studies of this type are then generalized into sociological conclusions, it is a wholly legitimate continuation of properly defined work. In these generalizations there is, however, one danger, which we must now explain. Constituting one of the exaggerations of historicism, this danger presents a great risk to correct understanding of the moral problem; still less can we pass it by in silence since it offers a new perspective on the idea of natural law.

I have in mind those conclusions of historicism that were especially reinforced by the influence in it of positivist sociology. Historians often speak of the sociological method as the greatest addition to their methodology, and to the extent this notion calls for a deepening of historical analysis, it is impossible not to agree that positivism brought in this respect its own share of good. Together with related currents of thought, it solidly confirmed in historians the desire to study every separate phenomenon of social life in connection with its whole milieu, in the general context of the historical process. Who would now deny the importance of this approach, so happily applied in the various branches of historical science? But together with this important indication, positivism not rarely imparted to its adherents its own mistaken conclusions, in which there was already nothing scientific. It combined certain healthy scientific tendencies with its own peculiar "positive philosophy," which, according to B. N. Chicherin's just remark, had nothing in common with positive science.[50] To distinguish the fruitful aims in this combination from false conclusions and principles, philosophical analysis was required, but this was the very thing that was missing in the epoch of initial enthusiasm for positivism, when philosophy was held in the greatest contempt. This explains the prevalence (completely incomprehensible to our generation) among our predecessors of the system of positivism, with all its superficial assertions. We will pause here briefly on these assertions, since they relate to our theme.

Application of the positivist-sociological method to the study of morality and law meant that they began to be treated as social and historical phenomena, in relation to the entire whole of social life and in the process of their successive change under the influence of changes in this whole. In its precise conception, the conclusions obtained by this method rely on the supposition of a certain unity of social life, with which individual phenomena are brought into connection. It is in light of this unity that every phenomenon finds its sociological explanation and becomes more understandable as a social fact.

Accepting within these limits the sociological explanation of morality and law, we must insist, however, that conclusions not be drawn from it in the absence of adequate foundations. From where does it follow, in fact, that sociological explanation exhausts the very essence of things or — to express it with a less responsible phrase, as it would appear to the positivists — that this explanation illuminates its object from all sides? Meanwhile, we encounter precisely such a conclusion among the positivists. From the circumstance that law and morality can be treated as historical and social phenomena, they inferred the surprising result that the very essence of such phenomena consists in this. More precisely, they came to the conclusion that the moral sphere is entirely a product of the historical process and social upbringing. An example of such an inference, well known to jurists, was given by Jhering in his work *Zweck im Recht*. Not himself belonging to the sociological school, but close to it in spirit, he attempted to show that all moral claims can be explained by social development alone, apart from any initial disposition.[51] This is also the usual line of reasoning taken by sociologists-positivists. As Kistiakovskii successfully describes their method, consistent evolutionists "first show how *no* morality *ever* existed; then they trace how, on the ground of this primordial state that is deprived of any trace of what we call morality, the germs of moral relations and notions gradually appear and finally develop with time into a whole system of moral views."[52] The causes of this development are considered to be the conditions of social life, its practical needs and ends.

The basic mistake of this view, which has added so powerful an impulse to the idea of social evolution, has long been indicated by philosophers who remained free of positivist prejudices. It was long ago explained how it is scarcely possible, by the path of evolution, to account for the development of everything from nothing and to forget that the development of something becomes incomprehensible unless we admit the existence of "a substratum already containing elements, if only in potential, of what will later emerge."[53] Skipping over this difficulty and taking morality as a historical product, the positivist-historical view with inescapable consistency endowed morality with the traits of utter relativeness and conditionality. A practical device for practical aims, arising and changing in accordance with these aims, adapting to the times and environment, to the whole of social life: here is the notion positivists have of morality, clarifying more precisely just what is to be understood by their assertion that it is an exclusively historical and social phenomenon.

Thus does fully legitimate sociological analysis turn into a highly pretentious construction, claiming to explain "the ultimate foundations of law and
society." Instead of adhering to the modest limits corresponding to its nature,
sociologism takes here a certain universal position, excluding any other point
of view. Considering its account to be final, it does not permit any other: it is
the only legitimate path, and moreover an exhaustive one, to the study of
morality and law. In this respect the sociological method had to evoke objections and be subject to necessary limitations.

First of all it is necessary to note that the exclusiveness of sociology, seem-
ingly bound to displace all other research methods, is purely imaginary. Historians and sociologists who came from Comte's school too often erred on the
side of shallow dogmatism in applying their concepts, as was especially telling
in the case at hand. The basic categories of sociology, beginning with the very
object of sociological investigation, require careful philosophical critique and
verification. What is necessary here is detailed theoretical, epistemological,
and methodological inquiry, which philosophical analysis is only now beginning to successfully carry out; yet the positivists of the old school had not the
slightest idea of its necessity. This explains why their sociology was a crude
epistemological mistake from its very first step. The mistake consists in the
naive-realist assertion of the objective character of the facts and relations
under examination. The social whole, like any reality subject to our knowledge, seemed to them to be a firm entity existing independently of us, determined in its characteristics already before our cognition of it. The connections
found within this whole seemed like the result of objective correlations and
manifestations of independent social factors. The concept of harmony or,
what is the same, solidarity or consensus, was used to explain these correlations. To the old sociologists it appeared, as it still appears, that these are
perfectly clear categories, requiring no epistemological analysis. The usual
mistake of dogmatic thinking was repeated here: to explain the phenomena in
question, they resorted to certain notions, apparently simple and understandable, but that on closer examination themselves turned out to be complex and
in need of explanation. In this respect the concept of solidarity, to the extent it
stands for something real, is not far from the concepts of national spirit or
historical tradition, with the help of which earlier historians liked to explain
various facts of national life.

In the very founder of positive sociology we find, with regard to the concept
of solidarity, formulations that are not in any way capable of serving as a
precise designation of a strictly defined object of science. Thus Comte speaks
of "an obvious spontaneous harmony which must always strive to prevail
between the whole of a social system and its parts"; he speaks of individual

phenomena "coming into contact with each other and striving to reach a state of harmony."[54] From these definitions it follows that solidarity among social phenomena is not a law necessarily determining them but only a certain "striving" or "tendency." Observing social phenomena, we in fact do see among them certain traits of accord or solidarity; thus, for example, ideas and customs, on the one hand, and political institutions, on the other, are always, at any given time and place, in solidarity to a certain extent. But just as invariably do we observe infractions of this solidarity, cases of disharmony, discord, struggle. This so little escapes Comte's view that he accepted even the possibility of special epochs of movement to which crises and struggle are inherent.[55] But do these crises really not originate in preceding epochs of order and apparent harmony? Are sharp demarcations possible here?

Analyzing further the concept of solidarity, we must come to the conclusion that it is neither a social law nor an objective state of social phenomena, as positivists think. From the point of view of epistemological criticism, it is nothing more than a subjective category, a construction of our thought. To take things in a state of harmony and rest or else in a state of progress and movement refers only to particular methods of inquiry, particular cognitive approaches. In examining social phenomena from the side of their accord, we consciously remove contradictory elements, which are not important for *this point of view.* Thus, for example, in dwelling on the harmony of economic forms, political institutions, and moral ideas in a certain epoch, we intentionally ignore the fact that political institutions can lag behind economic forms, but that moral ideas, in bold presentiment of the future, can go significantly further than economic conditions require. And this disparity is not an exception but a constant fact of social life, just as necessary as the equilibrium observed of social phenomena. From this it would follow that the "consensus" or solidarity of social life is only a certain subjective category, and that for it to become a real scientific achievement, it would need to be given a much more exact determination. It would be necessary to subject it first to epistemological and methodological analysis, and to transfer the whole question from the ground of naive realism to the ground of epistemological criticism.

I have touched upon this point only to say how mistaken the positivist idea is that so-called sociological consideration of phenomena is the only truly scientific one. As soon as we come to the conviction — and the whole contemporary epistemological movement is leading us to it — that sociological inquiry is only a certain point of view, a certain mode of scientific abstraction, we must admit that such inquiry does not in the least exclude other possible points of view. In concrete reality, social life presents not an abstract harmony at all, but a motley combination of various phenomena, which can be studied quite apart from this harmony. There is no logical basis for rejecting the legitimacy of isolated study of various social elements, although Comte considered it irrational and fruitless, illustrating his thought by the example of political economy. Isolated study of certain properties of objects and their causal correlations constitutes the usual method of the exact sciences, and reference to political economy only serves as direct refutation of the point Comte wanted to prove. There is just as little basis to assert that sociological inquiry possesses the advantage of greater depth, or that it leads to the ultimate foundations of social phenomena. On the contrary, it should much rather be said that in some of the most important questions it remains at the threshold of the problem, to the resolution of which it cannot proceed without abandoning its own ground. It is precisely this that needs to be said about the moral problem. Sociological examination takes only the external variability of moral phenomena, in dependence on the general course of social life. But this variability hardly determines the essence of morality. To understand this essence, we must leave the ground of sociology and turn to other methods of study. As soon as we are convinced that the exclusive character of sociological research is pure fantasy, nothing will prevent us from recognizing other approaches as well, not in the least supplanted by the sociological method or any less important.

From this, the formula we are contrasting to the positive-sociological direction becomes understandable: morality (like law) can and must be studied not only as a historical or social phenomenon, but also as an inner-psychic individual experience, as a norm or principle of personhood. Together with sociological inquiry, individual-psychological and normative-ethical inquiry must be recognized; morality must be understood not only from the side of its historical mutability, but also as a phenomenon and law of an individual person's life, as an inner absolute value. All these are terms and concepts completely inaccessible to sociology: to pass to them, sociology needs to be abandoned. It is not surprising if, to jurists and historians trained in positivism, the study of law and morality as individual phenomena simply seems to be sterile dialectics: to appreciate this type of inquiry, one needs to be familiar with philosophy and to renounce the prejudices of the old sociological school.

Of course, psychological and ethical study of morality and law, strictly delimiting itself from sociological study, seeks to neither compete with nor replace the latter: they simply have different paths and tasks of investigation. This is why it is a plain misunderstanding to reproach our view for being "unsociological": to insist on sociologism here is as little appropriate as in mathematics, for example. It is necessary to abandon once and for all this thought that sociology is some kind of science of sciences, without which it is impossible to take a step: it is simply one possible research method, with a strictly defined sphere of application.[56]

Defending the study of law outside the sphere of sociology, we do not wish to suggest that such an approach remained entirely foreign to positivists. In this respect an exception should be made in particular for jurists, who could not have failed to know the side of their subject that constitutes the special task of juridical inquiry, a side so unclear for many historians. In so-called juridical dogmatics, methodologically quite independent of history and sociology, jurists had a famous example of normative inquiry and always defended their special formal point of view on legal norms as having nothing in common with sociological explanation of the content of these norms. The one-sidedness of the sociological understanding of law did not prevent Jhering from giving in Part III of his *The Spirit of Roman Law* a brilliant model of the treatment of the technical side of jurisprudence [*iuridicheskaia tekhnika*], which presents the sum total of independent logical means for working out legal doctrine.[57]

In this connection it is possible to find in the Russian literature some highly valuable observations by Professor Muromtsev, who, despite his adherence to the positive-sociological direction, remained true to the principle of normative inquiry, thanks to his juridical training.[58] Proceeding from a perfectly precise demarcation between juridical principle and juridical law, of which the first "indicates 'what ought to be' according to the opinion of people and the second 'what is' according to the nature of man, society, and the world," Professor Muromtsev wrote: "the confusion of the two points of view, dogmatic and scientific-historical, is the result of a wrongly directed desire to apply to our science the demands of a higher scientific method. ... Earlier jurisprudence, no matter how imperfect, remained for us the solid basis of dogmatics, not tolerating any careless use of it. The reform that jurisprudence requires consists not in disclaiming past ends, which always were and will be its ultimate ends, but in supplementing these ends, for the sake of achieving them more successfully, with new ends and corresponding means. Everything that relates to the construction of the 'science' of civil law, in its strict sense, should be created first of all *not from inside dogmatics, but outside it, although also alongside it.*"[59] From this it is evident that the distinguished scholar presented perfectly clearly the relation of the new approaches of sociological research to the old ones. It must be said, however, that Professor Muromtsev's own "desire to apply to jurisprudence the demands of a higher scientific method" led to certain mistaken results, which stood in contradiction to the abstract-normative essence of jurisprudence. Thus, in various places of his more recent work, *The Definition and Basic Divisions of Law*

(1879), the desire comes through to eliminate the idea of law as an abstract object and to turn the hypothetical [*myslimyi*] juridical relation into a factual one "corresponding to concrete reality."[60] This is reflected, for example, in theories about the succession and restoration of rights, behind which Professor Muromtsev declined to recognize any real meaning.[61]

Meanwhile, a clear understanding of the normative side of law insists on just the opposite view, that law is an abstract, hypothetical relation that far from corresponds to concrete reality, which does not cover or exhaust that hypothetical relation and can, in cases of the infraction of law, stand in contradiction to it. Concrete life introduces many changes, additions, and corrections into the abstract demands of law which, as Jellinek has recently explained,[62] bear relation not to concrete existence, but to abstract "ought" [dolzhenstvovanie]. The example of this scholar, who is respected by our positivists as well, should have finally convinced them that isolated study of the normative side of law is a completely legitimate method, possessing full rights to existence, together with historical-sociological study.

It could be objected, referring to the very examples I have cited, that jurists have always understood this very well. But the excerpt made above from Professor Muromtsev testifies to the danger felt in the epoch of positivist domination about the illegitimate introduction of new research methods into the special sphere of jurisprudence. Professor Muromtsev protested against this, explaining that the new methods were to supplement, not displace, old ones. Incidentally, the conclusions many jurists drew from Professor Sergeevich's book *The Task and Method of the Sciences of Public Law* (1871) also attest that there were grounds for this warning.[63] The fate of this book is so instructive for the question we are considering that we cannot fail to say a few words about it.

In its time this book, belonging to the pen of a recognized and highly authoritative writer, enjoyed enormous popularity. As recently as twenty years ago every jurist considered it his duty to read and master it, as a type of *vade mecum* [handbook] required by anyone who wanted to have a clear idea of the tasks of science. In university courses the branches of methodology were expounded according to this book; from it was learned how to construct the science of law on new positivist foundations, which were supposed to completely succeed the old formal jurisprudence and the philosophy of law. Here was a whole program, composed in the spirit of Comte and Mill. It was offered to public lawyers in particular, but met a sympathetic reception among criminal and civil lawyers as well. But if we ask ourselves now, where are the results of this program, has juridical science actually followed this path, has it been reworked on new principles, we must answer these questions negatively. In essence, the program did not go any further; everything was confined to the first outlines of courses and to good wishes. Still less did the program of positivist methodology find application in the sphere Professor Sergeevich proposed, the sphere of public law. Bluntschli's[64] and Mohl's[65] old school of the science of public law, presenting a varied amalgam of juridical and political elements with historical and philosophical ones, had in fact become obsolete and was abandoned by everyone; Professor Sergeevich was perfectly right in his criticism of it. But the new science of public law went along a path not at all foreseen in the 1870s: it assimilated the so-called juridical direction of Laband[66] and Jellinek, which is still another brilliant demonstration of how fruitful isolated study of a subject from a particular side can be, no matter what the positivists say. Despite the strong opposition of Gierke[67] and Stoerk,[68] despite the attempt to condemn this direction as "civilist" and inapplicable to public law, it can now be considered ascendant. Thus, notwithstanding the expectations of the positivists, recent years in jurisprudence have been marked by a new triumph of the normative-formalist method, while the project for reworking the science of public law in the spirit of Comte and Mill has remained only at the project stage. Is it necessary to add that in other juridical disciplines, having behind them a clearer past, the normative method has been maintained in full force? The program of positivism, which for nearly twenty years constituted its own type of catechism among us, is now totally forgotten by jurists. It is not even considered necessary to critique it, but simply to disregard it. Dust already needs to be shaken from Sergeevich's book, testifying to its rare use. The last Mohicans of positivism vainly try in incidental articles to recall the forgotten claims of Comte. They no longer hold sway in the philosophical sphere, where the living work of thought proceeds in another direction and on other foundations.

Returning to the question of the formulation of normative inquiry, I must add that if positivism did not prevent certain jurists from recognizing its legitimacy within jurisprudence, then in any event it did hinder the normative principle from being carried out with full consistency. Application of the normative principle cannot be limited in any way by the sphere of positive, actual law. If the sociological approach to law as a social phenomenon must necessarily bring it into connection with other sides of social life, then, on the other hand, the normative approach, philosophically formulated, must trace its lineage to the depths of human consciousness, from which all norms draw their force. The technical side of jurisprudence, so masterfully characterized by Jhering, may be adequate for practical needs; but philosophical elaboration of the idea of law must take us further, to the side of the moral problem in all its scope and depth. Only here can the idea of natural law find support.

Thus we again come to our formula that law must be understood not only as a fact of social life, but also as a norm and principle of personhood. It is in precisely this sense that it was taken by the past philosophy of law, from which has been preserved many valuable results for our time as well, and it is in this sense that it will always be studied by those who want to penetrate its inner essence and reach its final grounds. This is why we cannot fail to welcome today's revival of interest in this inner essence of law, independent of the temporary conditions of its social development and of the determinations of positive law. In the Russian literature we must in particular mention the interesting attempt of Professor Petrażycki to free the philosophical elaboration of law from mesmerization by positive law and routine matters [*prakticheskii oborot*], "which narrow and distort the theoretical horizon." We have no doubt whatsoever that the work of this respected scholar will leave a visible trace, and that his "psychological theory of law" will have an honorable place in the literature. But for its completion this psychological theory, as criticism has already indicated,[69] needs to advance to an ethical one. As long as we remain within the limits of psychological observations, we cannot pass from the sphere of "what is": the matter is limited in such a case to establishing the constitutive features of legal consciousness, which must of necessity be taken here in all its diverse manifestations, no matter how accidental. To determine its regulative principles — and without this no philosophy of law is conceivable — a transition to ethics is required, to a theory of "what ought to be." Professor Petrażycki has still not taken this step, but this [hesitancy] is possible only in the first part of his work, dedicated to explication of preliminary concepts. According to the author's plan, a second part is to follow — legal policy [politika prava], and here the necessity of the ethical element speaks for itself: for policy it is first of all necessary to clarify the question of the goal or end of law and to define it from the point of view of "what ought to be." This will only correspond to the ardent support that the ideas of ethical idealism and natural law find in Petrażycki. But without this, the whole project risks remaining within the usual bounds of empirical generalizations and repeating the basic mistake of positivism in relation to the moral problem. Thus the psychological theory must necessarily advance to an ethical theory.

I would say that there are three progressive stages in the development of the normative principle:

1. Formal-positive dogmatics, not going beyond the sphere of work on existing law. Its culmination is the so-called philosophy of positive law, recently advanced in particular by Merkel and Bergbohm[70] and having the goal of adducing on the ground of historical positive law every definition in the philosophy of law. This point of view fully concurs with positivism, to the

extent the latter makes a concession toward isolated study of particular phenomena; but it does not go to the depths of individual legal consciousness and remains at the surface of normative definitions, not reaching their living core.

2. Empirical analysis of the idea of law, as an inner-psychic individual experience. Professor Petrażycki's theory serves as a brilliant model of such analysis. It achieves a necessary broadening of the theoretical field of vision, but is no more than a path and step, remaining on which we still cannot proceed from empirical phenomena to ideal principles.

3. Ethical theory of law, the classic examples of which are given to us in the systems of the great German idealists and which places the philosophy of law within a whole philosophical Weltanschauung; that is, it brings the philosophy of law into a natural system of concepts. Only here is the necessary culmination of the normative understanding of law accomplished. This third stage logically flows from the very concept of law, as a normative demand. Philosophical analysis of this concept must go to the foundations of this demand, and thus to moral foundations, since every norm, every "you ought," gives rise to the question of the moral basis of this "oughtness" [dolzhenstvovanie].

It follows for us to now characterize the basic features of this philosophical outlook. Within a short article an exhaustive development of this theory is out of the question: we have in mind only a necessary outline of its foundations, without which an account of the essence of the natural-law problem cannot be undertaken.[71]

V.

We already established above the formula for the philosophical study of law: such study takes law not as a historical and social phenomenon — this point of view is fully appropriate, but insufficient — but as a phenomenon and law of an individual person's life, as an inner absolute value.

Having posed the question on the ground of ethics, we have thereby justified the view being defended as both individualism and absolutism. For individualism is the starting point of all moral claims, while absolutism is their true form, a form that at the same time characterizes their very essence.

Individualism is so much a part of ethics that these two concepts can be taken for synonyms. As the sphere of freedom, ethics first of all supposes the self-determination of the person. The first and basic definition of ethics is the definition of conscious duty, and such duty can have meaning only in relation to the person, as the one source of conscious decisions. Moral determinations acquire their meaning, their reality, only as the individual experiences of a person. If these determinations relate to the interests of the whole and lead to the organized cooperation of many for the achievement of common goals, these goals are but again the conscious ones of individual persons. The self-determining person is that point, that focus, in which social goals and demands are refracted and acquire their moral character. It is the ground on which is raised the supreme good of the moral world, "the kingdom of persons as ends," in Kant's expression. It is the moral basis of civil society [*obshche-stvennost'*]. Outside of social unions the person cannot manifest all the fullness or the whole content of moral ends, but outside the autonomous person there is no morality at all. Precisely this is the difference between ethical association among people and the social life of animals: combining individual strengths to acquire common goals and self-sacrifice for others are met with in the animal world, but only in the human world does devotion to common goals take the character of conscious duty, and does sacrifice for others become an ethical deed. The person is the border between the kingdom of necessity and the kingdom of freedom, and it is in the moral calling of personhood that man first discovers his infinite tasks and his participation in the world of freedom.

Against individualism, as the principle of morality, it cannot be objected that the person becomes moral only with the help of social upbringing, that only the social milieu gives the moral law its concrete content and the means for its realization. In no way does ethical individualism have in mind denying the necessity of the social milieu for the manifestation of the moral law. On the contrary, as soon as we have formulated the ethical norm of personhood as the law of *universal* "ought," and this is in fact the basic formula of morality, we have thereby already supposed the existence of not one but a number of persons and have put the categorical imperative in a certain connection with the rest of the world. The categorical imperative is directed to the individual person, but it places on the person demands that derive from the idea of a higher objective order. Individualism hardly strives to exhaust all the possible consequences of the moral law; it seeks only to indicate the unconditional basis of moral "oughtness," without which there is not and cannot be any morality. But it does not in the least claim that morality has its beginning and end in the subjective consciousness of persons or that it is merely an internal individual deed. It denies neither the significance of common enterprises nor the importance of social measures that, expressing moral aspirations, create for the moral development of persons a corresponding moral atmosphere and thus strengthen the cause of moral progress. But ethical individualism does indicate the direction and goal of this progress: the development of the social sphere has as its ultimate task the elevation of the moral dignity and moral self-consciousness of persons. This defines the normal relation of society to its members.

Views that insist on the social essence of morality confuse the *conditions* of moral development with its *basis,* the means with the end. From this reproach not even Hegel's profound system is free, seeing as it does in society not only the milieu for man's moral formation, but also an autonomous moral organism, in relation to which persons are only passing phenomena. Meanwhile just the opposite should be said, that not society but the person is the basis and the end. The so-called social organism does not have an independent existence: it exists only in persons, the only realities through which the spirit of association develops. The social organism is no more than an abstraction, by which is understood the sum total of individual persons.[72] This is why, although only life shared in common, and the resulting community of feelings and experiences, give content and reinforcement to the moral consciousness of persons, these experiences and feelings acquire a moral character for each member of the community only when they pass through his personal consciousness: there is no other consciousness in which they could take on the significance of autonomous responsibilities.

Consciousness of this bond of the moral idea with the individualistic principle constitutes the driving force behind the flowering of individualistic theories that we are now unquestionably experiencing. I am not referring here to the partial recognition of the idea of the person found among some historians and sociologists. Attempts to indicate the "role of personality in history," or to explain that with the growth of society personality also grows, have a significance completely different from ethical individualism.[73] When we read, for example, in Simmel or Durkheim about the progressive growth of personality, we know that in essence this conceals a sociological view of its dependence on the growth of society.[74] We know that for Durkheim, who applies the method of the positive sciences to the study of morality, the person remains no more than an organ of society, and that for Simmel it is the point of intersection of different social influences. For both these views, as for any sociological understanding, the person can have no other content or significance except that which it has as part of the social whole. The problem is framed in such a way that the person is to be examined in connection with the whole, and any acknowledgment of its role in the formation of this whole must be made only from this same point of view. No matter how we change the terms and formulas, this role will nonetheless amount to the significance of a transmission point for the general movement — accelerating or delaying this movement, but in unconditional dependence on the environmental capacity for acceleration or delay. In short, no matter what historians and sociologists say about the significance of the person, within the sociological view it must remain locked in the chain of historical necessity. The question about the moral significance and moral vocation of the person, as a free center of ethical decisions, is consciously removed here. This is why it seems incomprehensible to us when, on the ground of this view, the idea is advanced of the inalienable rights of man and citizen, that is, of the absolute moral value of the person. Where the person is taken as a link in a general movement, its position is determined entirely by the present conditions of the environment.

But such a sociological definition of the person is not the only possible one. Besides this, the person can be defined from the side of ethics and metaphysics. The revival of individualism about which we have remarked tends toward this. Especially significant, in my view, is the current that has become so evident in the native land of sociology, in France, since the time of Renouvier.[75] This subtle and penetrating thinker firmly related his defense of individualism to the refutation of the "chimera of the unconditional significance of causality" ("la chimère du principe de causalité poussée à l'absolu"). In doing so he posed the problem on the ground of ethics, as a phenomenon of moral freedom. In this sense the person is wrested, as it were, from history, from the natural course of events, and proclaimed to be a free and absolute center of independent decisions. Among the ardent proponents of individualism who have followed Renouvier, I would name in particular Henri Michel[76] and Beudant,[77] who bear the closest relationship to politics and law.[78] For them as well, personhood has a special moral character, inexpressible in terms of positive sociology. Among us in Russia, the defense of individualism has been taken up by B. N. Chicherin in his recent works, and the new idealist current, being affirmed now as predominant, is also leading in this direction. The individualistic idea of our days represents only part of a general reaction against the universal pretense of historicism and positivism. All this marks a general revival of metaphysics and moral philosophy, which in various respects is everywhere declaring its independence. Correctly understood, this philosophy does not at all remove historicism and sociologism, but only allots them their proper place, the place of a legitimate method, but not the only one, of examining social phenomena.

We have said that normative-ethical inquiry takes the moral principle as an inner absolute value. It consciously contrasts itself with the historical view, and in full opposition to the relative character of moral phenomena that this view asserts, it speaks of their absolute basis. Our preceding observations enable us to clarify in what sense this absolutism should be understood. Those who speak about it do not in the least think of denying the obvious variability of moral views, which vary with time according to changes in the social environment. The concept of the absolute value of moral "oughtness" has a totally different meaning. It is an absolutism not of fact but of idea, not of appearance but of essence, not of concrete content but of abstract form. The absolutism of the moral law relates to the form of universal "ought," in which it can alone be conceived. The content of moral laws might change, but behind them this form always remains — not conditional pieces of advice but unconditional prescriptions, the form of categorical imperatives. Coming from the depths of moral consciousness, this form appears in it as a constant striving for the realization of the moral ideal. Its degrees of realization can differ, but one and the same tendency is always present in them — to find a content for the absolute moral law, to show in a finite act the force of an infinite impulse. In changing moral views, no matter how diverse, we will always find a reflection of this infinite aim, a striving for this absolute form.

This quality of unconditional moral "oughtness" also distinguishes the ground of the moral law that is to be recognized in the concept of personhood. Unconditionally connected with the idea of morality as its necessary supposition, "ought" defines the true end of this concept as well. But in itself, "ought" gives no concrete indications; these flow from the diverse historical conditions in which the person is placed.

In refutation of the unconditional character of the moral law, it is often stated that it is clarified only gradually in the consciousness of humanity, as the fruit of a more mature culture. But on this basis the unconditional character of scientific truth could also be denied. It slips from view here that the discovery or recognition of a law does not create its meaning, but only formulates it. As Kistiakovskii correctly remarks, evolutionists take the process by which certain principles are gradually clarified and brought to consciousness as the actual development of these principles. "In different societies a particular moral prescription can only at a certain moment be discovered, formulated one way or another, and then adopted. But its very meaning does not at all depend on its adoption. The fact that some Ashanti or Zulu, that children or idiots, do not know anything about this affects it as a moral prescription as little as the fact that animals know nothing about it or that no one could have known about it when our solar system was still a chaotic mass of atoms."[79]

But, to repeat, the absolutism of the moral law, as affirmed by moral philosophy, relates to its form and basis, not to its content. From this derives the essential peculiarity of the moral law, that it is not a formula determined once and for all, but first of all a critique and a problem, "eternal searching and unrest," as Hegel expressed it. In moral consciousness infinite striving is given, the unconditional form is given, but the content of this form must be sought, and therefore moral life presents itself as constant creativity. Here everyone must seek and find for himself, perhaps even fulfilling the same task others have already solved.

This character of constant searching and creativity relates not only to individual decisions, but also to social ideals. And here the critical and formal character of moral "oughtness" comes out first of all. It is only from this that we can understand the real nature of the link between the moral law and its content. As the law of unconditional "ought," the categorical imperative is the form of and call to searching. This form must be fulfilled, and the call must lead to a definite result. But this absolute form can never be filled by an adequate content, and the moral call can never be satisfied by an achieved result. The profoundly important significance of Kant's formulation of the moral problem consists in pointing to this basic fact of moral life.

In accordance with the purely formal character of the supreme moral criterion, Kant had to reject the possibility of an absolute moral content that could pretend to eternal recognition. The idea of a personal or social ideal, unchanging in its determinations, was thus undermined at its roots. The eternal remains only a demand relative to the assent of reason with itself and to the faithfulness of man to his rational-moral nature. Expressed in today's language, the formal moral principle is the recognition of the idea of eternal development and improvement. This is why we have noted that the notion of the variability, or development, of moral ideals not only belongs to the historical view, but is also a basic conclusion of moral philosophy. The formal principle of morality equally eliminates both ethical conservatism and the ethical utopia of earthly perfection. It condemns attempts to set an absolute and fixed content for the moral ideal, as well as the notion of the possibility of a universal harmony of interests and forces achievable by the actual realization of this ideal. It equally condemns both excessive hopes and persistent doubts. Faith in the possibility of finding a social ideal with absolute, perfect content impels some to place exaggerated expectations in a better future, and others — finding in this expected future certain shortcomings — to subject it to complete denial. But both approaches are founded on the false notion that the absolute moral idea can be embodied in some concrete ideal. Between this absolute idea and the highest achieved stage of its realization there will always be a disparity, but this must lead not to an utter denial of the achieved stage or to doubts in the possibility of progress, but to improvement of the present and to a search for the higher. Least of all can this denial and doubt, directed to the higher stages of development, be justified from the point of view of the lower stages, for which the higher must remain the goal. Among skeptics and people of a practical bent an obvious sophism occurs here: instead of critiquing their own reality in the interests of improving it, they critique the inevitable imperfections of an unfamiliar and higher reality, in order to remain at the present stage, which is in essence still further from the ideal. This form of skeptical conservatism meets with absolute condemnation from the point of view of ethical idealism. Skeptical denial of progressive aspirations, under the pretext that they will not in any event remove every misfortune, is a consequence of that eudaemonistic direction that puts the tranquillity of social life higher than moral progress and that prefers peaceful sleep to the active unrest of the spirit. But anyone who thinks through the moral problem from beginning to end cannot waver in choosing between a quiet life and a worthy one: the moral law indicates only one path to its realization, the path of eternal searching and striving.

But sometimes anxiety about the future does penetrate the frame of mind of outstanding and even eminent thinkers, who dream in such cases about acquiring powerful conservative methods.[80] It is not easy to be reconciled with the thought that the whole to which we belong might be threatened with the danger of decay or collapse. But it is not within our power to avert an inevitable process of development or annihilation, and even if such a means could be found, it would have to be renounced from the moral point of view. For in no way is it possible to show that the moral question can be resolved for society and even for all of humanity other than as it is resolved for the individual human person. And for the individual person it is resolved such that a worthy and morally valued existence must be preferred to a long and peaceful one. For ethical idealism there can be no other solution. Life, from this point of view, belongs to man not in order to simply live, but to live in a worthy way, to fulfill one's moral calling.

All these formulations convince us that the idea of natural law with changing content is the direct result of the basic concepts of ethical idealism. As the expression of infinite strivings, the moral idea is not satisfied with any given content, with any achieved result, but constantly aspires to the higher and greater. This does not in the least exclude a positive relation to particular concrete goals and aims. The moral idea demands that our aspirations be directed to the highest possible concrete goal; until further prospects emerge, achieving this goal is the only possible path to the realization of the moral law in life. By its nature critical and formal, the moral principle does not at all exclude the possibility of its own combination with temporary concrete goals. It excludes only one thing: declaring some concrete goal to be eternal and final. Any given moral ideal admits "the proviso of the possibility of a higher goal, to which we will need to turn, if it is revealed by a higher view."[81]

From this it follows that in the moral idea, critical aspirations always predominate over positive indications. And in fact the most sublime ideal constructions have quite often been strong in their critical spirit and weak in their positive plans. But the significance of these constructions is not to be diminished in pointing to the predominance in them of the critical element. On the contrary, it would be much more correct to stress the creative force of this critique — *die schaffende Lust der Zerstörung.*[82] It is often said that critique is inappropriate if it is not accompanied by a clearly defined practical goal and a detailed plan for the future. But is it possible to pose these two tasks on the same plane? The practical realization of moral aspirations in social life is a task of the greatest complexity, the fulfillment of which is connected with the collective process of history. The individual person can declare here its own moral demands, but it can neither plan all the details of their realization, nor substitute its individual thought for the combined action of the masses. Moral demands, directed to the future, rest on criticism of the present, already clear in its deficiencies and imperfections, but the anticipated future can never be clear in its concrete features. The vagueness of practical details does not, however, weaken the force of moral demands and critical aspirations. Where the issue is "what ought to be," judgments resulting therefrom speak with a self-legitimate independence, without relation to the conditions of their realization.

We pointed above to the possibility of combining the formal moral principle with concrete goals. But while we remain on the ground of unconditional moral definitions, we are deprived of the possibility of concentrating on concrete aims. This says nothing against the importance of abstract definitions. On the contrary, we would like to emphasize their enormous significance, which so often slips from the attention not only of practitioners but also of theorists engaged in working out the special fields of social science. Only from this can special work and practical activity receive a philosophically substantiated theoretical direction, only from this is it possible to draw a proper understanding of the moral task. Abstract analysis of the idea of "what ought to be" does not, in Windelband's just remark, give advice for settling the questions of the day, but it makes up for that by recalling what is important at the end of days, as at their beginning. For those who would like to be convinced of how fruitful such analysis can be, we recommend, if nothing else, Windelband's article, which we have just quoted, "Vom Princip der Moral" (in his collection, *Präludien*), or else Stammler's well-known chapter, "Vom socialien Ideal" (in his study, *Wirtschaft und Recht*).[83]

The task of ideal constructions is not, however, in the least restricted to this type of analysis, despite its profoundly important significance. Abstract moral philosophy indicates only general goals and basic principles; it gives only a general direction to the moral will. But the essence of the moral will appears not only in the loftiness of its ideals, but also in the need to act. The moral law cannot remain just an abstract norm: it must find its realization in the external world. Here a new side of the moral problem emerges, a side that brings it into connection with the world of actual relations; and since the realization of the moral law in any given set of conditions depends not only on our will and the strength of our moral aspirations, but also on the available means, the idea of moral "oughtness" must be supplemented by study of causal correlations. As Sigwart rightly observes, in its immediate application ethics passes directly to pedagogy and public policy [*politika*], which aim to determine the expedient use of available resources in given conditions.[84]

It is especially important to note that, in this combination of absolute moral principles and the world of actual relations the principle of ethical individualism must be supplemented with the concept of social development. The foundation and goal of morality is personhood, but the development of the person takes place in social conditions. This is why the moral law cannot remain indifferent to these conditions, but must demand that they meet its ends. Society, by its very essence, is not a limitation of personhood, but a broadening and deepening of it. But for society to correspond to its essence, it must be organized toward that end, and in this consists the great task of social progress.

Understanding the significance of social progress for personhood is the service of modern moral philosophy. In this, an enormous step forward was made by Hegel's philosophy. But here it was easy to fall into exaggeration and to take the means for the end. This is indeed what happened with Hegel, who saw in the development of society an autonomous process, reflecting the manifestation of absolute spirit. Meanwhile the correct correlation is to see social organization and progress as only a means to the development of persons. As B. N. Chicherin notes, objecting to Hegel, "the true expression of spirit is not formal and dead institutions, but the living person, endowed with consciousness and will. ... In exactly this consists the essence of spirit, that rational and free persons are its instruments. They constitute the very purpose of association [*soiuzy*]."[85]

The task of objective ethics, which examines the conditions of the realization of the moral law, is contained in the combination of the moral principle with the circumstances of social development. Here we encounter the problem of natural law in its practical formulation. Raising the question of the organization of society necessarily takes us into the sphere of public policy and law, and this is the sphere of natural-law constructions. Natural law takes its starting points, its highest principles, from moral philosophy, and thus the first line of defining it follows the abstract demands of the moral law. But this is only the first line: further it is necessary to study concrete conditions and to construct the ideal that most closely matches them. This is already a question not of ends, but of means. To the assistance of ethics must come all the sciences that study the causal correlations of social life: political economy, sociology, jurisprudence, and history all must be taken into attention and enlisted in solving the complex question of social progress. But it is not to be forgotten that the significance of these sciences in this case is purely auxiliary: they must serve as an arsenal of means for the ends indicated by ethics. Primacy belongs to moral "oughtness": causal correlations are pertinent only in relation to this higher and primary principle. To construct a system of ethics in the reverse order, beginning from conditions and causes and then passing to principles and ends — as, incidentally, positivism insisted — means putting the question on completely false ground: here there is danger of total distortion of the moral problem. Instead of achieving a broad formulation based on principle, it risks getting bogged down in the narrow sphere of present experience and in everyday considerations of practical life.

But most of all, there is danger here of losing the absolute foundation of natural law that is revealed to us in the moral idea of personhood. As an ideal, created in view of the imperfections of the existing order, natural law can serve the most diverse aspirations; but it has long been closely associated with individualism as its most legitimate form of expression, and in this form, on this ground, it has received its broad development. The fact of the matter is that the idea of natural law carries a protest not only against positive law, but also always against the power [vlast'] that issues positive laws. As a limit to this power it was possible to point to a higher moral law, to the will of God, as was often done in the Middle Ages, but even more often have the claims of individual persons been brought forward as a counterbalance to power. This is the meaning theories of natural law have in modern times, as the first formulations of the idea of the inalienable rights of the person. Seen from this point of view, natural law is the expression of the autonomous, absolute significance of the person, a significance that must belong to it in any political system. In this respect natural law is more than a demand for better legislation: it represents the protest of the person against state absolutism, reminding us of the unconditional moral basis that is the only proper foundation of society and the state.[86]

All normal correlations of civil society [obshchestvennost'] must be deduced and established on this basis, and in this empirical social science can render an enormous service. The moral idea does not draw its best inspirations or boldest perspectives from such science, but it can draw from it a notion of the practical means for the realization of its ends. The time has passed when philosophers proposed ideal projects, in the form of nice flights of fantasy or whimsical dreams cut off from reality. The scientific spirit permeates everywhere, and natural law, if it is to be revived as a living idea and not as an antiquated product of times long since passed, must not only rest on deep philosophical analysis, but enter into union with science. It must advance fully armed with all the facts of human knowledge, in order to courageously struggle with social evil and clear the way for moral progress.

Speaking about this desirable formulation of natural law, I cannot fail to mention here that steps in this direction are already being taken. It is sufficient to name Stammler and especially Petrażycki, to whom belongs the service, little valued in our literature, of giving the doctrine of natural law the character of a solid discipline relying on a broad scientific basis. It is possible to take issue with much in his idea of legal policy; it is possible to reproach it for not being worked out in its philosophical foundations. But it can be denied neither fecundity of conception nor boldness of perspective.

But recognizing the significance of these undertakings and their correspondence with the demands of the times, we must never forget that their success depends all the same on clarity of starting principles, which can be given only by philosophy. Only in the union of science and philosophy is it possible to resolve the problem that leads inevitably to the more general questions of a worldview.

Here we have come close to the most cherished and precious conviction of contemporary moral philosophy. We have said that the principles of moral "oughtness" and of causal necessity must be brought together and connected, and for anyone familiar with philosophy this assertion might already indicate our own approach to the question arising here. Kant's philosophy, the first to distinguish with complete clarity between "is" and "ought" [*bytie i dolzhenstvovanie*], also fixed an inescapable and hopeless dualism between these spheres. The moral idea proved to be an exalted but inaccessible goal of our aspirations. The task of our time, as of Kant's immediate followers, is to understand the connection between these two spheres and their ultimate harmony. This task takes us beyond the limits of both positive science and moral philosophy: here we enter the realm of metaphysics. In a higher metaphysical synthesis, in the supposition of an ultimate objective end, the principles of "is" and "ought" are combined in a higher unity. Causal necessity, the natural course of events, can contradict and oppose the moral law, but only within the bounds of limited experience. Final triumph belongs to a higher harmony.

From this the moral task, and the idea of natural law in particular, receive their supreme confirmation. The strength of moral endeavors and the firmness of hopes rest on a foundation that cannot be shaken by temporary disappointments and momentary failures. No matter what these failures and disappointments may be, it is in service to a higher good and in consciousness of the moral law that we find the true path to liberation from the illusory force of fleeting events and to joyous recognition of absolute principles.

Notes

[Novgorodtsev attached the following note to the title of his essay.] In the present year, 1902, three articles have appeared in Russian relating to this question [of the revival of natural law]: one hostile to the school of natural law, by M. M. Kovalevskii, "Sotsiologiia i sravnitel'naia istoriia prava," *Vestnik vospitaniia,* no. 2 (February) (printed earlier in French in 1900); one sympathetic, by V. M. Hessen, "Vozrozhdenie estestvennogo prava," *Pravo,* nos. 10 and 11; and another conciliatory, by N. I. Kareev, "Estestvennoe pravo i sub'ektivnaia sotsiologiia (po povodu odnoi novoi knigi)," *Russkoe bogatstvo,* no. 10 (April). I have taken these articles into account in writing the present essay, in which I would like to rework and develop my earlier views on the subject.

1. Immanuel Kant, *Metaphysical Elements of Justice: Part I of the Metaphysics of Morals,* trans. John Ladd, 2d edition (Indianapolis, Hackett Publishing Co., 1999), p. 162. Novgorodtsev's Russian version is faithful to the German, with one important exception: the phrase I have enclosed in brackets ("the ultimate purpose of law") actually occurs in the next paragraph of Kant's text; relocating it here, Novgorodtsev rewrote the first line of the passage, which he nonetheless presents as a direct quotation. Kant is writing about perpetual peace: "We must . . . act as though perpetual peace were a reality, which perhaps it is not, by working for its establishment and for the kind of constitution that seems best adapted for bringing it about (perhaps republicanism in every state). . . . Even if the realization of this goal were always to remain just a pious wish. . . ." It is clear that "this goal" refers to perpetual peace or abolishing war (Ladd's translation is in fact, "this goal of abolishing war," although that is not strictly the German). The next paragraph begins: "It can be said that the establishment of a universal and enduring peace is not just a part, but rather constitutes the whole, of the ultimate purpose of justice and Law [*Rechtslehre*] within the bounds of pure reason. . . . A state of peace is the only condition under which the security of Mine and Yours is guaranteed by laws, that is, when people live together under a constitution." It is likely that Novgorodtsev wished to avoid direct (but only direct) reference, in view of the censors, to Kant's ideas on constitutionalism. For a recent edition of the German text, see *Metaphysische Anfangsgründe der Rechtslehre,* ed. Bernd Ludwig (Hamburg, 1986). Ed.

2. I am referring to L. I. Petrażycki's remarks in his article "Vvedenie v nauku politiki prava" ["Introduction to the Science of Legal Policy"], *Kievskie universitetskie izvestiia* (August and October 1896), and to my own remarks in my book *Istoricheskaia shkola iuristov: Ee proiskhozhdenie i sud'ba (The Historical School of Jurists: Its Genesis and Fate,* Moscow, September 1896). Petrażycki earlier expressed himself in the same spirit in his German works (beginning in 1893). [Leon I. Petrażycki (1867–1931), eminent Polish

legal scholar, professor and dean of the law faculty at St. Petersburg University, prominent member of the Kadet party. He developed a sociopsychological theory of law against legal positivism, and argued that his idea for a new "science of legal policy," which refers to social reform through law and legal reform through social science, was a type of "revival of natural law." The two books Petrażycki published in Germany are *Fruchtverteilung beim Wechsel des Nutzungsberichtigten: Drei zivilrechtlige Abhandlungen* (1892) and *Die Lehre von Einkommen vom Standpunkt des gemeinen zivilrechts unter Berücksichtigung des Entwurfs eines bürgerlichen Gesetzbuches für das Deutsche Reich,* 2 vols. (1893–1895). On Leon Petrażycki, see Andrzej Walicki, *Legal Philosophies of Russian Liberalism* (Oxford: Oxford University Press, 1987), pp. 213–290 (on the connection between legal policy and natural law, see p. 228).]

3. Albert V. Dicey (1835–1922), English jurist and legal positivist, widely regarded as the foremost theorist of constitutional law in nineteenth- and twentieth-century Britain. Novgorodtsev associated him with the command theory of law (John Austin), according to which the state is the only source of law (see Walicki, *Legal Philosophies,* p. 313). However, Dicey combined his positivist approach with a highly influential defense of the idea of the rule of law by appealing to the historical traditions of the English people (historical jurisprudence). Ed.

4. A. V. Dicey, *Lectures Introductory to the Study of the Law of the Constitution* (London, 1885), p. 14. There was a Russian translation: A Daisi, *Osnovy gosudarstvennogo prava Anglii* (Moscow, 1895). Ed.

5. Alexandru Dimitrie Xenopol (1847–1920), Romanian historian, author of *Les principes fondamentaux de l'histoire* (1899). Ed.

6. *Die Grenzen der naturwissenschaftlichen Begriffsbildung: Eine logische Einleitung in die historischen Wissenschaften* (Tübingen, 1896–1902). Ed.

7. Karl Lamprecht (1856–1915), German historian whose attempt to introduce culture, society, and economics into historical writing (*Kulturgeschichte*), and to generalize from historical detail and description, provoked a bitter controversy in the 1890s with "neo-Rankian" historians defending Leopold von Ranke's (1795–1886) classical conception of historicism with its primacy on politics. Ed.

8. I cannot fail to mention here Lask's book, which has also recently appeared (Dr. Emil Lask, *Fichtes Idealismus und die Geschichte.* Tübingen und Leipzig, 1902). It is important in its considerations about the methodological connection between the concepts of society and history. See pp. 240 ff. [Emil Lask (1875–1915), German philosopher and legal theorist associated with the southwest German or Baden school of neo-Kantianism.]

9. Counting from 1893, when the first declaration of this type, by Petrażycki, appeared in the German literature. The similar statements of Ofner, Menger, and Neukamp, cited below, are from 1894 and 1895. [These jurists are identified below.]

10. The new code, the *Bügerliches Gesetzbuch,* was promulgated in 1896, approved with minor changes by the Federal Council and German parliament, and went into effect on 1 January 1900. A similar effort was undertaken during this period to draft a new civil code for the Russian Empire. To this end, a Civil Code Editing Commission was established in St. Petersburg in 1882. It issued a five-volume draft code between 1899 and 1903, before the commission was disbanded in January 1906. Little of the code was

enacted prior to 1917. On the Editing Commission and draft code, see William G. Wagner, *Marriage, Property, and Law in Late Imperial Russia* (Oxford: Oxford University Press, 1994), pp. 149–169, 316–328. Ed.

11. Anton Menger (1841–1906), Austrian jurist, professor of civil procedure (Vienna), best known for his juridical conception of socialism. He was a consultant on the German Civil Code, urging that civil procedure be revised to better protect the poor. For the Russian reception of his views, see Walicki, *Legal Philosophies,* pp. 370–374, 423. Ed.

12. Anton Menger, *Über die sozialen Aufgaben der Rechtswissenschaft: Inaugurationsrede gehalten am 24 Oktober 1895 bei Übernahme des Rektorats der Wiener Universität,* 2d edition (Vienna and Leipzig, 1905), p. 19. Editor's citation and translation.

13. Bernhard Windscheid (1817–1892), German jurist and main figure in the "Pandectist school," which sought to logically and systematically derive the foundations of civil law in Germany not from the fragmented national sources, but from the *Digest* (or *Pandects*) of Justinian's *Corpus juris civilis.* This approach was characteristic of constructivist or conceptual jurisprudence (*Begriffsjurisprudenz*), which concentrated on dogmatic, immanent analysis and exegesis of legal statutes and texts. Windscheid's work heavily influenced the first draft of the German Civil Code. Ed.

14. Julius Ofner (1845–1924), Austrian jurist, prominent deputy to the Reichsrat, the Austrian parliament. Ed.

15. Ofner, *Studien sozialer Jurisprudenz* (Vienna, 1894), pp. 1–29, esp. 5, 21.

16. Ernst Neukamp (1852–1919), German legal theorist and judge, known for his evolutionary approach to the history of law, which he thought could be supported through comparative study of law. He was also a specialist in industrial and labor law. Ed.

17. Rudolph von Jhering (1818–1892), German legal historian and philosopher who developed legal positivism in a teleological or utilitarian direction by arguing that law is purposive, that it is an instrument through which people realize their will and interests. Author of *Der Zweck im Recht* (Leipzig, 1877–1883). Ed.

18. Adolph Merkel (1836–1896), German jurist, disciple of von Jhering, professor successively at Prague, Vienna, and Strasbourg, elected in 1893 to fill von Jhering's place as corresponding member of the Berlin Academy of Sciences. He sought to rigorously base legal positivism on empirical-inductive foundations, and applied his theory to criminal law and the study of crime and punishment in social life. Ed.

19. Eduard Hölder (1847–1911), German jurist and specialist on Roman law. His most influential works include *Institutionen des römischen Rechts* (1877) and *Natürliche und juristische Personen* (1905). Ed.

20. Friedrich Karl von Savigny (1779–1861), eminent German jurist, professor (Berlin), and main representative of the historical school of jurisprudence, which maintained that law has its origins in the historical and national life of a people, in custom and tradition, not in pure reason or human nature abstracted from a specific historical and cultural context. The historical approach Savigny established thus resisted universalistic ideas of natural law. Ed.

21. Neukamp, *Einleitung in eine Entwicklungsgeschichte des Rechts* (Berlin, 1895), pp. 61 ff.

22. Ibid., p. xiv.

23. *Vestnik prava,* journal of the Juridical Society at St. Petersburg University. Ed.

24. *Vestnik prava,* January 1899.

25. Novgorodtsev is likely referring here to Leon Petrażycki (who was a Pole, not a Russian), whose two works published in Germany did attract the attention of jurists there, and who outlined the new "science of legal policy" to which Novgorodtsev refers in the above paragraph and in note 2. See Walicki, *Legal Philosophies of Russian Liberalism,* pp. 217–218, 220–221. Ed.

26. "Vozrozhdenie estestvennogo prava," *Pravo,* nos. 10–11. The article has also come out as a separate brochure [1902]. [Vladimir M. Hessen (1868–1920), prominent Russian jurist and legal theorist, vice-chairman of the St. Petersburg Juridical Society, one of the founders of *Pravo,* and later a leading member of the Kadet party.]

27. François Gény (1861–1959), major French jurist and theorist of a sociological or social conception of law, according to which immanent analysis of written law is inadequate and must be supplemented with free scientific research into social realities. His concern for social reform and justice led him to significant work in the theory of natural law; this connection is similar to that which Petrażycki drew between his own science of legal policy and the revival of natural law. Ed.

28. Gény formulates his approach to natural law on pages 473–491. It is interesting that in him as well we find the same consciousness of the "social mission" of law.

29. Celestin Louis Tanon (b. 1839), French jurist, president of the Court of Cassation of France. In addition to *L'évolution du droit et la conscience sociale* (cited below), he wrote on the legal history of the early church in France. Ed.

30. Maurice Charles Emmanuel Deslandres (b. 1862), French legal theorist, author of works on French constitutional law. Both Tanon and Deslandres are associated with the development of a historical/social direction in legal idealism. Ed.

31. Tanon's study is entitled *L'évolution du droit et la conscience sociale* (Paris, 1900). Critiquing the one-sidedness of the historical school, the author maintains that the study of law should be based on principles, although he also strives to place this study on the ground of historical data. In this respect he takes a position similar to Neukamp, with whom he sympathizes (p. 41). Deslandres's critique, "La crise de la science politique," *Revue du droit public et de la science politique* (1900), is directed against sociology and one-sided juridical methodology, in the name of the vital and pressing need for policy to clarify the way to the future. Pointing to "the radical insufficiency of the sociological method," he in essence formulates the problem of natural law, saying: "political science cannot limit itself to description of the past and present, it cannot be only explanatory and descriptive, it must evaluate the present, it must also turn toward the future and invent" [translated from the French, which Novgorodtsev quotes] (p. 276). It is the same demand jurists have been repeating constantly in recent times.

32. Raymond Saleilles (1855–1912), professor of law at the University of Paris, representative of analytical positivism in law, but with concessions to equity and practical needs that took him in the direction of François Gény and the revival of natural law. Specialist on German civil law and author of critical studies of the German Civil Code. Ed.

33. Saleilles's article is entitled "École historique et droit naturel d'après quelques ouvrages récents," and the new journal is called *Revue trimestrielle de droit civil.* Judging

by the introductory article by [Adhemar] Esmein ("La jurisprudence et la doctrine"), the journal calls for a broadening of perspectives and adoption of new methods, in the interests of furthering the study of civil law.

34. Oscar Bülow, *Heitere und ernste Betrachtungen über die Rechtswissenschaft* (the first anonymous edition, also from 1901, is *Briefe eines Unbekannten über die Rechtswissenschaft*); see especially the fourth and fifth letters.

35. L. von Savigny, "Das Naturrechtsproblem und die Methode seiner Lösung," *Schmollers Jahrbuch für Gesetzgebung, Verwaltung und Volkswirtschaft,* 1901 (vol. XXV, no. 2), pp. 25 ff. [The author should not be confused with Friedrich Karl von Savigny.]

36. I am speaking of Stammler's recent work, *Die Lehre von dem richtigen Rechte* (Berlin, 1902). On the method of application of the principles of normative law to explanation of existing law, see pp. 201 ff.

37. "The law that nature teaches all animals." Ed.

38. Ulpian (c. 170–228), Roman philosophical jurist. His definition of justice is also famous: "the constant wish to give each his due." His doctrines are preserved in the Justinian Code, the *Corpus juris civilis*. Ed.

39. As Saleilles's article shows, this formula is beginning to take hold in France — "le droit naturel à contenu variable."

40. The reproach against natural law, quoted above in this paragraph, can be found in M. M. Kovalevskii's article [referred to in the head note for this chapter]. If it is in just this sense that the distinguished scholar understands the need for sociology "to enter into open battle" with the revived doctrine of natural law, then this battle would be quite understandable if only it were not belated, in view of the absence in our time of epigones not only of Ulpian but even of Hugo Grotius. With regard to the actual foundations of today's natural-law doctrine, Professor Kovalevskii's article does not in the least touch upon them, except for fleeting mention of Kant's categorical imperative and some remarks about the connection of natural law to metaphysics. But it is no longer possible, as it was twenty years ago, to condemn a theory merely by pronouncing the word "metaphysics." Since that time, philosophical development has made certain successes, even in Russia, so that the old manner of using words instead of arguments in relation to metaphysics no longer satisfies anyone. [Maksim Kovalevskii (1851–1916), major Russian social and legal historian, sociologist, professor (Moscow, 1880–1887), founder and president of the International Institute of Sociology, member of the State Duma and State Council. His wide-ranging comparative historical research and sociological analysis were entirely positivist in conception and methodology; "he manifested a conscious distaste for every metaphysics." See Alexander Vucinich, *Social Thought in Tsarist Russia: The Quest for a General Science of Society, 1861–1917* (University of Chicago Press, 1976), pp. 153–172. Hugo Grotius (1583–1645), Dutch jurist and diplomat famous for his contributions to international law and just war theory. He proceeded on the foundations of natural law, which he secularized to some extent by returning to the Stoics, bypassing the Scholastics. With regard to Novgorodtsev's argument, the relevant point is Grotius's view that "Natural law is so immutable that it cannot be changed by God himself."]

41. Here, I am compelled to repeat as concisely as possible certain basic positions of moral philosophy. I had opportunity to provide a more detailed exposition of these

principles in my book *Kant i Gegel' v ikh ucheniiakh o prave i gosudarstve* (*Kant and Hegel in Their Theories of Law and the State*, Moscow, 1901), especially in the chapter on Kant.

42. I have given a more detailed exposition of Merkel's views in my book *Istoricheskaia shkola iuristov* (Moscow, 1896).

43. "We feel a violation of this 'expectation' as an infringement of our legal sense." Ernst Neukamp, *Entwicklungsgeschichte des Rechts* (Berlin, 1895). Page references are Novgorodtsev's. Ed.

44. "Do what you must, come what may." Ed.

45. "Consensus" is one of Auguste Comte's main concepts. See Lappo-Danilevskii's essay (Chapter 10) in this volume. Ed.

46. Thomas Henry Huxley (1825–1895), British biologist and leading exponent of Darwin's theory of evolution. Ed.

47. Instead of the many references, I will point here to Rickert's recent observations: *Die Grenzen der naturwissenschaftlichen Begriffsbildung: Eine logische Einleitung in die historischen Wissenschaften* (Tübingen und Leipzig, 1902), pp. 616 ff.

48. Nikolai I. Kareev (1850–1931), Russian sociologist, social historian, and philosopher of history. As a professor (Warsaw and St. Petersburg), he was the most prominent academic representative of subjective sociology. He thought "scientific objectivism" and "ethical subjectivism" should be combined in social inquiry. See Alexander Vucinich, *Social Thought in Tsarist Russia*, pp. 50–54. Ed.

49. It is in this sense that Professor Kareev in his last article (on natural law) showed with full clarify all the inadequacy of M. M. Kovalevskii's attempt to replace the natural-law problem with the historical point of view and to explain the indifference of German jurists to their most important task — promoting the development of new forms of law — by the fact that they "have insufficiently studied the history of law" (see Kareev, *Russkoe bogatstvo*, April 1902, pp. 13–14, quoted here).

50. This was one of Chicherin's main conclusions in his book *Polozhitel'naia filosofiia i edinstvo nauki* (*Positive Philosophy and the Unity of Science*, Moscow, 1892). Ed.

51. In the Russian literature this view was recently formulated by Professor Iu. S. Gambarov in the preface to his edited work, *Sbornik po obshchestvenno-iuridicheskim naukam* (St. Petersburg, 1899).

52. Bogdan A. Kistiakovskii, "Kategorii neobkhodimosti i spravedlivosti pri issledovanii sotsial'nykh iavlenii," *Zhizn'* (May–June 1900), reprinted in his *Sotsial'nye nauki i pravo: Ocherki po metodologii sotsial'nykh nauk i obshchei teorii prava* (Moscow, 1916), pp. 120–188 (here, p. 180). Ed.

53. I refer, for example, to Sigwart, who in 1886 wrote apropos of Jhering's *Zweck im Recht*: "If it is said that nature has implanted naked egoism in man and that history alone produces morality, then the result is a disparity between nature and history that history itself threatens to make inexplicable." *Vorfragen der Ethik* (Freiburg, 1886), p. 44 [translated from the German, which Novgorodtsev quotes]. Reference can also be made to Rudolf Eucken, who gave an interesting analysis of the idea of development in his work *Geschichte und Kritik der Grundbegriffe der Gegenwart* (Leipzig, 1878); see the heading "Entwicklung." In Russian see Kistiakovskii's valuable observations in his extremely rich article, "Kategorii neobkhodimosti i spravedlivosti," *Zhizn'* (June 1900), p. 142. [Chris-

toph Sigwart (1830–1904), German philosopher and logician, professor (Tübingen). He maintained that logic is normative rather than descriptive; like ethics, it is concerned with "ought." Rudolf Christoph Eucken (1846–1926), German philosopher of life, professor (Jena), Nobel Prize in literature (1908). His philosophy of life is a critique of naturalism and defense of spiritual autonomy.]

54. See Lappo-Danilevskii's essay (Chapter 10) in this volume. Ed.

55. Related to this is Comte's well-known distinction between statics and dynamics. The inconsistency of this distinction is well indicated in Professor Vipper's article "Neskol'ko zamechanii o teorii istoricheskogo poznaniia," *Voprosy filosofii i psikhologii* 11: 3, kn. 53 (1900), pp. 450–480. This article, from which Comte is quoted above, represents an interesting attempt to show the profound importance of moving from positivism to epistemological criticism in the sphere of exact historical science. Positivism is thus recognized as untenable not only by contemporary philosophy, but also by contemporary science. In just this sense, that is, as a critique by a representative of empirical science, Professor Vernadskii's article "O nauchnom mirovozzrenii," *Voprosy filosofii i psikhologii* 13: 5, kn. 65 (1902), might also be very instructive, based as it is on a subtle and deep understanding of the nature of science and its relation to religion and philosophy. [Robert Iu. Vipper (1859–1954), Russian historian, professor of world history at Moscow University. He was especially interested in historical theory and method. Vladimir I. Vernadskii (1863–1945), distinguished Russian geologist (see the editor's introduction).]

56. In Professor Kareev's article (on natural law) I find the following characteristic passage: "the thought, taken by Hessen to be 'absolutely true,' that 'law is a psychological, inner-human phenomenon' is already too unsociological, when in fact this [Hessen's definition] can be said only of legal consciousness [*pravosoznanie*], to which sphere natural law does indeed relate, but it cannot at all be said of the legal order [*pravoporiadok*], which, together with the state, is already a sociological phenomenon, existing outside of individual consciousness, in social life itself." In this there is already partial acknowledgment of our view (in regard to "legal consciousness, to which sphere natural law does indeed relate"); furthermore, where the sociological approach [*sotsiologichnost'*] is demanded (in the notion of the legal order and the state), it slips from view that on the ground of sociological nominalism (which we accept) it cannot be said of any phenomenon: "existing outside of individual consciousness, in social life itself."

57. Jhering, *Der Geist der römischen Rechts auf den verschiedenen Stufen seiner Entwicklung*, 3 vols. (1852–1865). Ed.

58. Sergei A. Muromtsev (1850–1910), professor of Roman law at Moscow University (1877–1884), chairman of the Moscow Juridical Society and editor of its journal, *Iuridicheskii vestnik* (*Juridical Messenger*); member of the Central Committee of the Kadet party and president of the First State Duma (1906). See Alexander Vucinich, *Social Thought in Tsarist Russia*, pp. 140–143. Ed.

59. Muromtsev, *Ocherki obshschei teorii grazhdanskogo prava* (Moscow, 1877), pp. 83 ff.

60. Muromtsev, *Opredelenie i osnovnoe razdelenie prava* (Moscow, 1879), §§ 19, 25, 40.

61. At the time, philosophical criticism had already made this point: I refer to B. N. Chicherin's observations.

62. Georg Jellinek (1851–1911), major German legal and political theorist. His legal philosophy, as developed in *Die sozialethische Bedeutung von Recht, Unrecht und Strafe* (Vienna, 1878), is an uneasy combination of positivism with a conception of law as an "ethical minimum," a definition that for Jellinek is largely psychological. In his theory of the state, Jellinek wished to combine state sovereignty with international law through the idea of the "self-limitation" of the state. For the Russian reception of his views, see Walicki, *Legal Philosophies*, pp. 201, 314–315, 368–370. Ed.

63. Sergeevich, *Zadacha i metoda gosudarstvennykh nauk* (Moscow, 1871). [Vasilii I. Sergeevich (1835–1911), one of the main Russian representatives of positivistic jurisprudence and the sociology of law, together with Muromtsev and Nikolai M. Korkunov (1853–1904).]

64. Johann Caspar Bluntschli (1808–1881), Swiss-German jurist, political theorist, liberal editor, and publicist, trained by Savigny at Berlin. He treated the state as a "moral-spiritual personality" and was active in efforts to promote peace through codification of international law. Ed.

65. Robert von Mohl (1799–1875), German jurist, professor (Tübingen and Heidelberg), and political figure. He helped develop the idea of the *Rechtsstaat* in a liberal direction. Ed.

66. Paul Laband (1838–1918), German jurist, legal and political philosopher, professor (Königsberg and Strasbourg). He attempted to found public law as a purely juridical discipline, aside from political and sociological factors, by applying the methods of conceptual jurisprudence (*Begriffsjurisprudenz*) to it. As Novgorodtsev indicates, this approach became the representative one in public law in imperial Germany, with certain detrimental effects on the development of a sense of public policy. Ed.

67. Otto von Gierke (1841–1921), eminent German legal historian and theorist. Within the historical school of jurisprudence, he defended the study of Germanic legal history against the Roman (which was cultivated by Savigny), in the "Germanist-Romanist controversy." Gierke's well-known theory of corporate personality opposes individual rights (*Individualrecht*) as characteristic of Roman law and foreign to the Germanic respect for *Sozialrecht*, based on the corporate groups constituting society. Ed.

68. I have in mind certain articles of these writers [Gierke and Stoerk] that are dedicated to the critique of the new direction in public law. For all the necessary details, see Stoerk, *Zur Methodik des öffentlichen Rechts: Separatabdruck aus Grünhuts Zeitschrift* (Vienna, 1885). Deslandres's recent critique (in *Revue du droit public*, May–June 1900) is significant only in that it shows the impossibility of remaining limited to the juridical method alone. [Felix Stoerk (1851–1908), German jurist, editor of *Archiv für öffentliches Recht*, founded 1886.]

69. Novgorodtsev is likely referring to E. N. Trubetskoi, "Filosofiia prava L. I. Petrazhitskogo," *Voprosy filosofii i psikhologii* 12: 2, kn. 57 (1901), pp. 9–33; and to B. N. Chicherin, "Psikhologicheskaia teoriia prava," *Voprosy filosofii i psikhologii* 11: 5, kn. 55 (1900), pp. 365–384. Ed.

70. Karl Bergbohm (1849–1927), German legal theorist. His "philosophy of positive law" rigidly excluded any consideration of legal ideals (what ought to be) from the scientific study of law. He argued that law is always positive law, thus rejecting traditional natural-law theory. Ed.

71. In this concluding section I develop and extend the conclusions I reached in my work *Kant i Gegel' v ikh ucheniiakh o prave i gosudarstve.*

72. I cannot fail to mention here the fine clarifications given in B. N. Chicherin's work *Filosofiia prava,* in particular Book IV.

73. For this reason, "personality" is the more appropriate term for *lichnost'* in the sociological theories to which Novgorodtsev is referring. Ed.

74. I have in mind here Simmel's work *Über soziale Differenzierung* (Leipzig, 1890) and Durkheim's work *De la division du travail social* (Paris, 1893). [Émile Durkheim (1858–1917), French sociologist and philosopher, who worked to establish sociology as a positive, autonomous science that would approach society as an irreducible, sui generis phenomenon, and that would derive a social ethics as a guide to public policy.]

75. Charles Bernard Renouvier (1815–1903), French philosopher whose "neo-criticism" was Kantian in inspiration and the basis for his philosophy of personalism, which insisted on the absolute value of the human person. In his social philosophy Renouvier thus opposed any conception of the state or nation as a subsistent entity existing above and beyond its constituent members. Ed.

76. Henri Michel (1857–1904), French political theorist, professor (Paris). His liberalism upheld the rights of the individual against the claims of state and society. His concern was moral rather than strictly political, as is evident in his defense of freedom of conscience, in which he was influenced by Renouvier. Both Renouvier and Michel promoted a progressive program of social legislation in the interests of individual self-realization, in a way that readily compares to the "right to a dignified existence" championed by Vladimir Solov'ëv and Novgorodtsev. Ed.

77. Charles Beudant (1829–1895), French political theorist. Like Renouvier and Michel, he was concerned to defend individual rights against state intervention. His book, cited below by Novgorodtsev, is credited with a major role in the French revival of natural law. Ed.

78. Renouvier's work, which is immediately relevant to our subject, is entitled *La science de la morale* (1869). For details, see Henri Michel, *L'idée de l'état* (Paris, 1896), pp. 595–622. Beudant's book is *Le droit individuel et l'état,* 2d edition (Paris, 1891).

79. Kistiakovskii, "Kategorii neobkhodimosti i spravedlivosti pri issledovanii sotsial'nykh iavlenii," *Zhizn'* (June 1900), pp. 144–145. [Reprinted in his *Sotsial'nye nauki i pravo: ocherki po metodologii sotsial'nykh nauk i obshchei teorii prava* (Moscow, 1916), p. 183.]

80. Possibly Novgorodtsev has in mind Konstantin P. Pobedonostsev, who exercised a powerful conservative influence on Alexander III and Nicholas II. Ed.

81. See Paul Natorp, *Sozialpädagogik* (Stuttgart, 1899), p. 44. [Novgorodtsev's quotation is a paraphrase.] [Paul Natorp (1854–1924), eminent German neo-Kantian philosopher, professor (Marburg). After Hermann Cohen, he was the principal figure in the Marburg school of neo-Kantianism.]

82. "The creative urge of destruction," a paraphrase of the famous conclusion to Mikhail Bakunin's article, *Die Reaktion in Deutschland* (1842), which puts forward a radical, left-wing interpretation of the Hegelian dialectic. The concluding sentence reads, "Die Lust der Zerstörung ist auch eine schaffende Lust." See Andrzej Walicki, *A*

History of Russian Thought from the Enlightenment to Marxism, trans. Hilda Andrews-Rusiecka (Stanford, Calif.: Stanford University Press, 1979), p. 120. Ed.

83. Wilhelm Windelband, *Präludien: Aufsätze und Reden zur Einleitung in die Philosophie* (Freiburg and Tübingen, 1884). Rudolf Stammler, *Wirtschaft und Recht nach der materialistischen Geschichtsauffassung* (Halle, 1896). Ed.

84. Christoph Sigwart, *Logik,* vol. II (Freiburg, 1893), p. 746.

85. *Filosofiia prava* (Moscow, 1900), p. 225.

86. See my article "Pravo estestvennoe," in *Slovar' Brokgauza i Efrona,* vol. XXIV (St. Petersburg, 1898), p. 887. A vigorous and brilliant formulation of this principle, as the basis of natural law, can be found in P. B. Struve's essay "V chem zhe istinnyi natsionalizm?" See his collection of articles, *Na raznye temy* (St. Petersburg, 1902). [On Struve's essay "What Is True Nationalism," see the editor's introduction.]

9

The "Russian Sociological School" and the Category of Possibility in the Solution of Social-Ethical Problems

B. A. KISTIAKOVSKII

I.

Explorations in the labyrinth of questions that come up on the path toward knowledge of the social world have not only failed to decline in recent times, but have even increased.[1] Having arisen with particular force at the beginning of the 1890s, for a while these explorations seemed to find a solution in the strict application to social phenomena of the same research methods that had already long confirmed their exclusive dominance in relation to natural phenomena. Many even rushed to declare the incontrovertibility of the unity they professed in the world order, a unity they saw in the material essence lying at the basis of the world, as well as in the causal conditionality of everything happening in it, that is, in necessity in its natural-scientific sense.

Deeper penetration into these foundations of the natural-scientific understanding of the world soon led, however, to recognition of its inadequacy as an all-encompassing system. Particularly in relation to the social world, the root contradiction between the spontaneous course of social events and our conscious aspirations became too obvious. No one now doubts that the deepest epistemological contradiction arises between recognition of social phenomena as spontaneously occurring and causally conditioned, that is, as necessary, and the human demand for active participation in the social process, especially where this participation ought to be the result of a rational and conscious choice of action in the name of a self-imposed ideal or a self-professed duty. The natural-scientific point of view does not resolve, but rather removes this epistemological contradiction as something foreign to its nature.

Some opponents of the new movement in the social sciences rushed to see, in the recognition of this basic contradiction between social life and social activity, only a retreat from the one-sidedness and extremes of the original [natural-scientific] point of view. They thought that the new movement, introducing only partial corrections and particular limits to the original claims, would be satisfied by a system composed mechanically of heterogeneous elements, in the same way the Russian sociological school, having retreated from the extremes of scientific positivism, merely replaced them with its own unscientific concoctions. But what was taken for only a retreat from one-sidedness and extremes was in fact a deepening of the basic direction of the whole movement, and reexamination of some of the original claims turned out to be a reexamination of all the foundations of knowledge.

In order to correctly understand our new movement in social science, it must be kept constantly in mind that its most characteristic feature is the aspiration to universalism. The failure that befell the attempt to base sociological universalism on natural-scientific principles did not influence the basic tendency of the overall movement, since universalism is significant for it mainly as a formal principle. In precisely this sense does universalism need to be recognized as the basis of the new sociological *Weltanschauung,* regardless of its material content. This universalism has not given in to the idea of contenting itself with some kind of dualistic or halfway approach, or with simple eclecticism. Therefore, when the dogmas of the natural-scientific understanding of the world proved to be inapplicable to certain dimensions of the social world, these dogmas were subjected not to mere partial corrections, but to fundamental analysis and critique. The question thus came down to a radical reexamination of all the foundations of scientific thought and knowledge, for only bold and unrelenting criticism can produce a new universal Weltanschauung.

Such a critique, aimed at restructuring the entire scientific edifice, does not consist, of course, in doubting any of the factual results obtained by modern natural science. On the contrary, the whole factual side of natural science must remain inviolable. The critic directs his work only against a certain natural-scientific type of thinking, for which facts and their description are everything, while the elements introduced by human thought for working out and explaining these facts are nothing. This type of thinking is extremely congenial to natural science and meshes very easily with it, for it satisfies all the needs of the naturalist. Therefore, nothing can be said against it as long as it remains only a servant of the natural sciences. But when, in the second quarter of the last century, under the influence of the external successes of natural science, this type of thinking was made the basis of the whole philosophical system of positivism, then soon thereafter not only all its poverty, but also its enormous harm to the further development of science, had to be revealed. Anyone who restricts himself only to this form of thought cuts himself off from the path to knowledge of the social world as a whole or, more correctly, of the peculiarities that distinguish it from the natural world. Such an investigator must reject the highest values of human life — duty and the moral ideal — for there is no place for them, or for other higher products of the human spirit, in the sphere of natural-scientific facts. Therefore, in struggling against this type of thinking, the scientific significance of the elements introduced by human thought into all knowledge needs to be advanced and emphasized first of all. It is thus necessary to begin with an analysis and evaluation of the most general concepts, which, because of their epistemological properties, were assigned by Kant into a special group, called the categories.

Since the time of Copernicus and Galileo, scientific investigation of nature has consisted in the establishment of causal correlations between phenomena. The exclusive application of this principle for classifying the factual material obtained by experience constitutes the main distinction between modern and medieval science. In medieval scholastic science, the coherence and unity of the world order were established on the basis of two competing principles. One traces its beginning from Plato and consists in subordinating the particular to the general; the other was first established by Aristotle and defines the ends in the world order. True, together with these principles, the aspiration (arising first with Democritus and then maintained by Epicurus and the Epicureans) toward causal explanation of phenomena never died. But this was a very weak and uncharacteristic direction for medieval thought. It receded into the background behind the first two principles, the same way that the principles of purposiveness and subordination of the particular to the general (i.e., logical consistency, which amounts to the principle of identity) have moved aside in modern natural science, even though without strict application of the latter, scientific thought in general is impossible.

Contemporary natural science, fully recognizing the formal requirement of logical consistency, directs all its attention to the discovery of the real causal correlations among phenomena. Since these correlations have significance for science only to the extent they are unconditionally necessary, that is, everywhere and always in effect, we can say that science examines phenomena from the point of view of the category of necessity, or by applying the category of necessity to them. The category of necessity is thus the central principle that runs through and unites the whole natural-scientific understanding of the world today.

But if such is the universally recognized and undisputed role of the category of necessity in natural science, in the social sciences this category has far from such a solid and undisputed significance. Here the category of necessity is making its way only gradually and very slowly. The reason for this is that social phenomena, capturing the most vital interests of man, evoke more diverse responses from researchers. Therefore study of social phenomena naturally brings out the desire to employ various different points of view. Far from all attempts in this direction have equal scientific value and significance, despite their temporary success and popularity. It is especially characteristic that sociologists today often repeat mistakes that already played a sad role in the history of natural science, but that have passed into complete oblivion, for their influence appeared two centuries ago in a period when the basic principles of modern natural science were only just being worked out. Therefore, analysis of the various methods of approaching social phenomena is extraordinarily important at the present time.

II.

Let us turn first to the most widespread and common attempts to fill in the "gap in understanding" in relation to political and social phenomena — to newspaper and journalistic coverage. Journals and newspapers are ordinarily first to discuss any new phenomenon of political or social life. Occupied primarily with current events, diligently following and precisely recording them, only rarely does [the press] try to explain their origins or causes. This is fully understandable, since the press takes an event as a given, and recognizes that it must be treated first of all as an accomplished fact. All the attention of the press is directed, therefore, to publicizing present circumstances, in order to establish what is new about them, and to draw conclusions about their further development, that is, about the possible future. Thus, in contrast to the relatively indifferent approach to what was and has irrevocably passed, the question of the possible future absorbs the efforts of contemporary journalism and constitutes the main inner meaning of all its activity. . . .

No matter what happens in the political world, the organs of the press all strive to be the first to discuss every possibility arising from such events. . . .

In a word, no matter how heterogeneous the countries, the peoples, the persons exercising influence, the conditions, and the preceding circumstances and events, the European press decides one and the same question: what is possible and what is impossible in the future. This is the question representatives of the European press raise in the face of the whole infinitely diverse and varied mass of utterly heterogeneous political and social events. They permit themselves such a uniform approach to such disparate phenomena not, of course, because they believe, following John Stuart Mill, in the "uniformity of the world order,"[2] which they somehow thought could be seen in the fact that common to all these phenomena and events was the inherent possibility of one or another development, but because, despite the diversity of these events and phenomena, they constantly and invariably apply to them one and the same point of view. In precisely the same way that naturalists, despite the difference among mechanical, physical, chemical, physiological, and psychic phenomena, invariably examine them from the point of view of the necessary causal correlations among them, so representatives of the contemporary press unflinchingly apply to phenomena of the political and social world the point of view of their possible future development. If our juxtaposition of natural science and the contemporary press might evoke a certain objection in view of the very great inequality between these two types of thought and the cultural forces connected with them, still it is fully justified by our conclusion that while modern natural science applies the category of necessity to the phenomena it investigates, the press applies the category of possibility. These two categories are as unequal as science and the press themselves. In evaluating them, it is necessary to recognize that there is the same, if not greater, distance between the first two as between the second two.

Of course, the interests of the press, as expressed in the concentration of all its attention on establishing and indicating one or another possibility, are completely explained by its very nature. . . . Only correlations among phenomena taken in isolation and consistent over time, correlations constantly recurring and everywhere in effect — and therefore appearing as a particular instantiation of a general rule, which itself defines this correlation and consistency — can be defined as necessary. Meanwhile the press would deviate from its task were it to be occupied with correlations among phenomena taken in isolation, and with the general rules defining these correlations. It would be removed from questions of the day and immersed in general theoretical problems uncharacteristic of it; that is, it would appropriate the tasks of science. It is clear that the press would then cease to be the press, for its very purpose is to be entirely absorbed in current events, in all their complexity, diversity, and individuality. . . . It possesses none of the means or data to definitively state that a certain combination or concurrence of circumstances, or a particular consequence, must necessarily ensue. Therefore it falls to the press to constantly ascertain and discuss only the *possibility* of one or another combination or consequence of current events. Here the primary role of the concept of possibility is explained by the fact that it is the most general and unifying concept for expressing the subjective as well as the objective side of expectation or partial confidence.

Our analysis of the essence of the press suggests one method of theoretically approaching political and social phenomena. This method is carried out in the press with remarkable integrity [*tsel'nost'*], unity, and consistency, because in this the press does not yield to science. Therefore, an understanding of the theoretical significance of the press can also serve as a formal clarification of how science must approach its material. We are concerned here, of course, only with the science that deals with the same sphere of facts and events as the press, that is, with the science of political and social phenomena. This science is sociology, the science of society. From everything said above, there is no doubt that sociology, in contrast to the press, must not take individual political and social events immediately from life, in their concrete fullness and integrity, but must rather subject them to a thoroughgoing and careful reworking. This reworking, or distance from immediate perception, entails first of all a change in point of view. There is no place in sociology for adopting the position, taken from practical life, of uncertainty in the future, as expressed in the admission of many possibilities. The sphere of sociology is the sphere of the absolutely certain in social phenomena, and therefore its point of view consists not in determining various possibilities, but in establishing what is necessary.

Representatives of the Russian sociological school apparently think otherwise. To analysis of the formal principles lying at the basis of their views we shall now turn.

III.

Let us see first of all how the most talented representative of Russian sociology, N. K. Mikhailovskii, formulates the view of Russia's future development that was held by the leading elements of his generation, whose spokesman he was. "Skeptically disposed in relation to the principle of freedom," he says, "we were prepared to seek no rights for ourselves; not just privileges, of this nothing was even said, but even the most elementary paragraphs of what used to be called natural right. We all completely agreed to live, in the juridical sense, on locusts and wild honey and to personally endure every adversity. ... And all this on behalf of one *possibility,* into which we put all our soul; the *possibility,* namely, of a direct transition to a better, higher order, bypassing the middle stage of European development, the stage of the bourgeois state. We believed that Russia *could* lay for herself a new historical path, distinct from the European path. It was not important that it be some kind of national path, only that it be a good path, and good for us meant the path of conscious, practical adjustment of the national physiognomy to the interests of the people. It was supposed that certain elements of the available orders, strong either in their power or in their numbers, would take on themselves the initiative of laying this path. It was a *possibility*. And in our eyes it remains a theoretical *possibility*. But it diminishes, it can be said, with every day."[3] In another place the same writer "welcomes from his soul the enthusiastic words of Iakovlev,"[4] which begin with the declaration: "the emancipation of the peasants with land made Russia in the social sense a *tabula rasa,* on which the *possibility* is still open to write one or another future. This *possibility* to begin from the beginning and to plant the seed of future development places a broad task on the representatives of intellectual life in Russia: guided by the experience of other countries, to avoid their mistakes, the correction of which now constitutes the concern of all progressive figures there."[5] . . . Mikhailovskii time and again and in every way repeats this idea of the possibility for Russia to avoid a certain path of development. . . . True, with the years his certainty in this possibility has much weakened, and now he even reproaches his opponents for not taking this into account. "Did the work belonging to the direction that appeared in the 1890s, that is, to our Marxism, really consist," he asks, "only in criticism of a '*theoretical possibility?*' If so, the representatives of this direction ought to have noticed that even we ourselves, long before their criticism, pointed to the 'ruthless cutting back' of this theoretical *possibility,* as well as to the fact that 'our program accordingly became more complex, adhering to the same goal, but working out new means.' "[6]

[. . .] [Mikhailovskii discerns two possible political programs for Russia, European bourgeois or Russian communal, which correspond to his theoretical views on Russia's possible courses of development. Kistiakovskii quotes him at length.]

These passages all indicate that Mikhailovskii unflinchingly examined the process of Russia's development from the point of view of one or another possibility arising on its path. His constant application of the category of possibility to such an important sociological question is all the more striking in that the passages selected by us span almost thirty years. The reader will naturally wish to explain these views by the publicistic character of Mikhailovskii's work. As a journalist, Mikhailovskii could be satisfied with the point of view that is always brought to bear in the press. This supposition finds particular support in the fact that what Mikhailovskii examines so consistently from the point of view of the category of possibility was always the property of journalistic literature. But, first, the press, despite the widest application of the category of possibility, always makes use of it in relation to individual consequences of individual phenomena, while Mikhailovskii examines the whole process of the development of a people from this point of view. And, second, the question of the development of Russia, to which Mikhailovskii applies the category of possibility, is far from the only question he examines from this point of view.

Mikhailovskii discusses not only future phenomena, but also past events that have become objects of historical investigation, from the point of view of the possibility or impossibility of one or another path of development. . . . [Kistiakovskii reviews Mikhailovskii's consideration of the possibility of the development of the third estate under Catherine II. He also indicates that "V. V."[7] had similar views on this question. Kistiakovskii then seizes upon a reference by Mikhailovskii to the *possibility and necessity* of the emancipation of the Russian peasants, and continues his exposition as follows.]

The last passage is highly characteristic of Mikhailovskii. He is not satisfied by historical necessity on its own, but requires further substantiation of it in the possibility preceding it. By contrast, possibility has for him a completely independent significance; it is given in itself. This makes clear Mikhailovskii's preference for the category of possibility. He directs all his energy, as a sociologist, to study of the processes and phenomena in which he supposes a combination of various possibilities. . . . We will see below that an entire philosophical system is expressed in the priority Mikhailovskii assigns to the category of possibility over the category of necessity. There was already once an attempt, in working out the theoretical foundations of modern natural science, to make the category of possibility the center of a whole scientific edifice. Representatives of the Russian sociological school, striving for a more stable basis for sociology, only repeat old mistakes and, themselves not knowing it, support the weakest metaphysical doctrines. This will be explained more precisely below; here we need only indicate that all "possibilities" in the past have, in truth, already been buried there, and not a trace remains of them. Once historical research has precisely ascertained every sequence of facts in the past, then science no longer has any concern whatsoever with what might have been. Its only task consists in researching the causes that made these facts necessary. Meanwhile Mikhailovskii invests all his efforts into studying any past possibility. In his literary activity Mikhailovskii does not, in general, like to venture into the depths of history; it is thus very remarkable that, in relation to the most important events in Russian history of the past century, he does not consider it necessary to employ a more fruitful point of view than exploring various possibilities. This significant fact ought to serve as an important index in evaluating the scientific merits of Mikhailovskii's sociological works and theories.

All the passages we have thus far quoted from Mikhailovskii's works have related to the real process of development in Russia, on which his point of view has been so striking. Much more important, however, is that this same approach, consisting in discussion of one or another possibility, dominates his theoretical views in general, and his solutions to sociological and ethical questions in particular. . . .

IV.

[. . .] [This section is a critique of Mikhailovskii's theory of knowledge, in particular his subjective method in sociology. First, Kistiakovskii argues that Mikhailovskii's concepts of the socially "desirable" and "undesirable," subjective preferences that cannot but help shape the sociologist's own research, are particular cases of the broader category of possibility. From this he turns to another problem, as follows.]

Mikhailovskii's theory of knowledge is not exhausted by his solution to the methodological question. An extremely important question remains unsettled — what, ultimately, is truth [*istina*]?[8] A passage from one of Mikhailovskii's critical articles, reprinted instead of a preface to the first volume of his works, is often cited in clarification of his view on this basic problem of the theory of knowledge.[9] There he says that he "cannot fail to be enraptured by the striking inner beauty" of the word "truth" [*pravda*]. This passage possesses, however, a purely lyrical character. Therefore, for elucidation of Mikhailovskii's theoretical approach to the question of truth [istina], his "Letters on Truth and Untruth" [*pravda i nepravda*] [1878] are much more instructive. From the outset he says that "the force that once bound together the concepts of truth [istina] and justice [*spravedlivost'*] in one word, 'pravda,' now threatens, it seems, to dissipate."[10] He then directs all his arguments against the "efforts," "attempts," and the "ill-fated desire" to split pravda into two halves.[11] In his opinion, not only science, but also art speaks to the "whole ill-fated desire to split Pravda into two, to the wild, absurd desire, logically justified by nothing, but stubbornly filtering into all spheres of thought and shrouding contemporary humanity from all sides in a thick mist."[12] Declaring that he imagines this desire to be some kind of fairy-tale struggle between two "ferocious beasts," one embodying truth [istina], the other justice, he considers it necessary to turn to the young generation with the exhortation: "do not participate in this shameful fight. With heavy blows it will tell upon you and those close to you and upon all that is dear to you. This fight is not only terrible, not only disgraceful. In itself, it is *simply impossible*. In the darkness — let it be damned — these fantastic, contorted semblances of truth and justice *can* struggle."[13] Thus, this time as well Mikhailovskii settles the question before him by citing impossibility. In his words: "everywhere where there is place for both halves of one Pravda, that is, in all matters that touch man as a social animal, truth alone is not enough—justice is also needed. We *can* understand justice narrowly, shallowly, even basely, but by its very nature we *cannot* repudiate it, and this forgotten, artificially suppressed half of Pravda guides us, without our knowledge, even against our will."[14] Thus, in the end Mikhailovskii opposes the very real and, by his own recognition, extraordinarily persistent efforts to split pravda into two only to his own personal belief in the impossibility of doing so, because, according to his conviction, the unity of pravda is inviolable, as expressed even in the very word, "pravda." Blinded by his faith, he seeks support even in Lange and thinks he has found, in a passage he quotes from the *History of Materialism,*[15] confirmation that not only he but also Lange speak "of the *impossibility* of splitting pravda into two without doing damage to both halves."[16]

This reference to the authority of Lange only indicates how poorly Mikhailovskii understood and understands him. The entire structure of thought behind neo-Kantianism, one of the founders of which was Lange, remained completely foreign to Mikhailovskii. This scientific-philosophic current undoubtedly directs all its efforts to achieving an integral understanding of the world through uniting every side of "pravda." But this aspiration grew not in counterbalance to any theoretical attempts to divide pravda into parts, but thanks to an understanding of the deepest practical contradictions among different *pravdy* [truths], in comparison to which the unity of pravda in one word is mere trivia. By contrast, this verbal unity is everything for Mikhailovskii. He finishes where the problems only begin for neo-Kantianism, and therefore he cannot even understand the neo-Kantians, let alone think that he agrees with them. If he understood them, their aspirations and efforts toward the unification of pravda would seem to him a completely vain expenditure of energy, since he, not noticing life's contradictions, supposes in advance that "pravda" is one and that there exist only unfortunate theoretical attempts to divide "pravda," but that ultimately this is impossible since it contradicts human nature.

[. . .] [The remainder of this section is devoted to brief consideration of Nikolai Kareev's "subjectivism" and Eduard von Hartmann's theory of categories (*Kategorienlehre,* 1896), and to further terminological clarifications.]

V.

Directly related to the question of the subjective method is the question of the ideal. Mikhailovskii constructs his theory of the ideal by relying exclusively on his same category; here as well the subjective sense of possibility and impossibility must obviously have preponderance, since the ideal is created by man and is in any case a phenomenon of the inner world. In order to explain the essence of the ideal, Mikhailovskii introduces a distinction between idols and ideals, his understanding of which strongly speaks to Feuerbach's influence. But he is wholly original and not subject to anyone's influence in thinking that the formal distinction between them is that attainment of the first is impossible, while realization of the second is fully possible. In his words: "gods are products of the idealization of various phenomena of nature in general and human nature in particular, but they are not at all ideals, not beacons on life's path. They are idols, objects of worship, terror, adoration, in the presence of which one is firmly conscious of the *impossibility* of being equal to them, of achieving their greatnesses and strengths. The ideal, on the contrary, is something practically obligatory for us: we desire and sense the *possibility* of achieving this or that state."[17] Mikhailovskii develops this idea in far more detail. In his opinion, an idol "is precisely what man would like to be, but by his own recognition *cannot* be. And the very acts that man *cannot* accomplish are ascribed to it: thus we appeal to it primarily in cases where ordinary human strengths and abilities are not enough to obtain a certain result. The ideals of humanity, although they are more or less interwoven with idolatry in one or another form, have a completely opposite character. The *possibility* of acquiring some combination of things through our own human means constitutes their necessary condition."[18]

Having thus formally defined the significance of the ideal through application of the category of possibility, Mikhailovskii strives to give his definition in terms of content as well. The category of possibility, of course, again has decisive significance. "The only common denominator," he asserts, "to which all processes *can* legitimately be reduced is man, that is, a being with certain limits, possessing a definite sum of strengths and abilities, evaluating things under the weight of its own conditions. The normal fulfillment of these limits, that is, the even development of all the strengths and capabilities given to man by nature, is our only *possible* ultimate ideal."[19] Mikhailovskii thus defends his ideal of the well-rounded, developed personality, which lies at the basis of his theory of the struggle for individuality [*individual'nost'*], as the *only possible* one.

In another place, explicating the views of Kavelin,[20] the first thinker to substantiate the theory of personality in Russian literature, and agreeing with his basic positions, Mikhailovskii nonetheless considers it necessary to introduce certain corrections into Kavelin's terminology. He strives more precisely than Kavelin to delimit and fix the concepts of "personality" [*lichnost'*] and "man" [*chelovek*] and in connection with this gives his formulations of the development of the personality principle [*lichnoe nachalo*].[21] As is to be expected, the category of possibility again plays the main role in his formulations. "Casting off one natural yoke after another," he says, "the personality principle *can* take a dual tendency. It *can* 'make itself the absolute measure of everything' and recognize no limits, whether old or new, spontaneous or conscious. This will be a purely egoistic principle, which can arise only with a narrow sphere of interests and a one-sided conception of tasks, 'with one-sided historical determinants,' as Kavelin puts it.[22] This tendency is too egoistic to doubt that it is the personality principle. But at the same time it is too one-sided to recognize it as being [universally] human. But the development of the personality principle *can* take another direction. A human being *can* break out of the natural fetters imposed on him by, for example, family origin, but he *can* also submit to the consciously chosen limits of, for example, comradeship. Depending on the greater or lesser latitude of conditions in which a human being finds himself, his development of distinctive qualities is, more or less, a tendency toward the [universally] human."[23] The simultaneous and harmonious development of the principles of personality and humanity [*chelovechnost*'], so desirable for Mikhailovskii, was possible (according to him) only in Russia and, moreover, only since the time of Peter the Great. "In Russia," he writes, "personality and man *could* actually enter the arena of history together, almost without hindrance, precisely because personality hardly existed until Peter and, consequently, could not have any 'historical [national] determinants.' In fact, 'all Peter's private life and public work constitute the first phase of the realization in Russian history of the personality principle,'[24] not in the sense of the tendency that it partially took under him, and that it especially took after him in Europe, but rather in the sense of humanity. Here is the general formula sought for Peter's activity."[25]

The historical facts, however, far from confirm the path of ideal development that Mikhailovski outlined for the personality principle in Russia. As is well known, Peter the Great, simultaneously with activity that promoted the development of the personality, did not refrain from directly contrary measures when he, for example, intensified the enserfment of peasants and even extended serfdom to hitherto free peoples. Mikhailovskii's formula for the development of the personality principle, like the majority of his sociological formulas, specifies a certain possibility, but any specification of one possibility contains the assumption of all remaining possibilities, the number of which can sometimes be infinitely great. Therefore, if what Mikhailovskii supposed as possible did not in reality occur, he always has in reserve the justification that various circumstances might have made impossible what was at first possible. In his words, "a collision of circumstances more often than not forced Peter — *because of the impossibility* of creating new restraints on the exclusive reign of the personality principle, on the absolute measurement of everything by this one principle — to leave the old restraints in full force, and even to tighten them."[26]

Thus, the category of possibility and impossibility fully turns out in this case to be what indeed it is, a crude instrument for justifying and explaining anything at all. Appearing by its very nature as the embodiment of relativism, this category is very convenient for those who reject everything absolute even in the moral world, because on the one hand it provides the broadest scope in the choice of paths, while on the other hand it gives the right to cite the hopelessness of the situation, if the path chosen does not lead to the desired goal. We had to note here this characteristic of Mikhailovskii's favorite category, even if it is a fact — one that speaks to the extreme relativism lying at the basis of the category, a relativism verging on complete moral unscrupulousness — that belongs to what has long since passed into Russian history. For the time being we will defer actual evaluation of Mikhailovskii's views and particularly the influence of his point of view on the foundations of moral convictions.

VI.

[. . .] [This section considers Mikhailovskii's idea of the role of personality in the social-historical process. Kistiakovskii argues that for Mikhailovskii, causal relations among social phenomena are not necessary but relative, since otherwise there would be no place for possibility. Mikhailovskii sees the social process itself as either the realization or nonrealization of possibilities. This conception gives broad scope for personality to act in history according to its idea of "desirability," which is only a more subjective version of the primary category of possibility.]

VII.

[. . .] [Kistiakovskii presents the basic approach of the Russian sociologists (Mikhailovskii and Vorontsov) to the Russian intelligentsia: the ideals of the intelligentsia could and had to serve not the interests of the bourgeoisie or any other privileged class, but rather the good of the people (*narod*). He concludes as follows.]

. . . It is well known that these questions played an enormous role in the social development of Russia in the last decades of the nineteenth century. The generation of the Russian intelligentsia belonging to the 1870s, the most characteristic years of this era, has every right to take pride in its formulation and resolution of these questions about the social tasks of the Russian intelligentsia and its relation to the people, about the significance of the people, its economic interests, and certain features of its social-ethical Weltanschauung for the future of Russia. This era, in truth, is one of the most glorious periods in the history of the Russian intelligentsia. It is understandable that the Russian sociologists, belonging to this generation, not only were imbued with the views of their time, but also strived to give them a more solid sociological substantiation. The reader already knows that this sociological substantiation consisted in the fact that the Russian sociologists demonstrated the "theoretical possibility" of the realization of the ideals of the Russian intelligentsia, although they recognized that "with every year" this possibility was being "ruthlessly cut back." They further believed that even if the Russian intelligentsia did obtain full freedom of action, then "perhaps" the Russian bourgeoisie would "not devour the Russian people," and, consequently, "perhaps" the ideals of the Russian intelligentsia would be realized. In the opposite case, "the people will surely be devoured," and the ideals of the Russian intelligentsia will "surely" suffer collapse.

Only timidly did the idea sometimes occur to the Russian sociologists that substantiating an ideal required demonstrating that it belonged to the sphere of "what ought to be" [*dolzhenstvuiushchee byt'*]; instead, with them this "ought" [*dolzhenstvovanie*] was deprived of indisputability, because it always relied on possibility. Meanwhile, the whole originality of the Russian sociological school resides precisely in showing such possibility, since the content of the school's ideals, as well as its understanding of the meaning of the social process, were entirely given to it by the social movement of the 1870s and by Russian life. The Russian sociologists were not leaders of the intelligentsia in the social movement, but followers. Somehow it can hardly even be believed that such a grandiose movement of practical virtue, which had such heroic manifestations in life, received so sorry an expression in sociological theories. We have no grounds, however, to deny this, since we already know that it was not by chance that the Russian sociologists demonstrated only the possibility of the ideals of the Russian intelligentsia; rather, they constructed their whole sociological system on the category of possibility.

VIII.

[. . .] [This section examines the uses of "possibility" and "impossibility" by the populist sociologists (again, Mikhailovskii and Vorontsov) in their debate with the Marxists over the question of the capitalist development of Russia.]

IX.

[. . .] [Kistiakovskii further considers various concepts of "impossibility" in Mikhailovskii. The first case Kistiakovskii takes up is the "impossibility" of an exclusively objective method in the social sciences. From this he turns to a second case, as follows.]

Another occasion for Mikhailovskii to use the concept of impossibility is his solution to the question of truth [*istina*] and justice. As we already know, in his opinion it is impossible to split pravda (made up of istina and justice) into two, without doing damage to both halves. Mikhailovskii directs his demonstrations of this impossibility against theoretical efforts to make such a split. . . . Consequently, Mikhailovskii could not have had absolute impossibility in mind here, for otherwise theoretical attempts to divide pravda would not make any sense. More careful consideration of this question inevitably leads to the conclusion that it is a misunderstanding to speak not only of the absolute impossibility of disjoining istina and justice, but of any impossibility of doing so. We indicated above that the unification of istina and justice in one integral Weltanschauung is the basic problem of philosophy as well as of any moral life, for the nonconcurrence of istina and justice in theory as in practical life leads to the most tragic conflicts. Mikhailovskii looked at this basic problem and evaded its solution: here the concept of impossibility served as a cover for evasion of his direct responsibility. A mass of refutations can, however, always be advanced against such an indictment of Mikhailovskii. Indeed, in the preface to his collected works (the significance of which I described above as more lyrical than theoretical), Mikhailovskii declares that working out a point of view "from which pravda-istina and pravda-justice would go hand in hand, one supplementing the other," is "the highest task that can be posed to the human mind, and no effort spent on it would be wasted. To fearlessly face reality and its reflection — pravda-istina, objective pravda — and at the same time protect pravda-justice, subjective pravda, is the task of my whole life." Thus, at this point Mikhailovskii no longer argues for the impossibility of dividing a united pravda into its constituent parts — istina and justice — but on the contrary points, as a higher task, to the unification of both parts of pravda into one great whole. Consequently, we again have a clear contradiction between Mikhailovskii's different statements.

Only in one thing does he remain true to himself, in the fact that in both cases he proceeds from the verbal unity of "pravda." Of course, only Mikhailovskii himself can resolve this contradiction and remove it from his system of thought. For the reader it is not resolvable and therefore we can only explain its origin by historical-biographical causes, since Mikhailovskii's contradictory views date from various times and belong to different historical epochs. The lines quoted above from the preface to his works were written in 1889, twelve years after his "Letters on Truth and Untruth" and already toward the end of his literary work. Apparently, Mikhailovskii rushed at the beginning of his activity to anticipate as a premise and starting point that which ought to have been the result of his research and the culmination of his whole social-philosophical system; only much later, toward the end of his work, did he finally recognize and grasp that precisely the unification of both sides of pravda is a problem and the greatest theoretical task of our time.

Nonetheless, the impossibility of splitting pravda into the separate spheres of istina and justice has a far from episodic significance in Mikhailovskii's social-philosophical system. On the contrary, this impossibility, on the theoretical recognition of which Mikhailovskii so insists, shows the tightest inner connection with a whole set of his views, first of all with his theory of idols and ideals. In this theory, as we already know, the concept of impossibility plays a decisive role. And here as well Mikhailovskii gives the concept of impossibility an incorrect and inappropriate meaning, analysis and critique of which deserve especially serious attention, since the concepts of possibility and impossibility in the question at hand inevitably lead to fatal errors in both moral theory and practical activity. First of all, in no way can it be admitted that the possibility of realization somehow characterizes, if even derivatively, the ideal, and still less is there basis to agree with Mikhailovskii that this possibility is its essential mark. If the question of possibility does play some type of role, then it is only in the selection of ends, and even in this case it has decisive significance in relation more to means than to ends. But the significance of the category of possibility for moral concepts will concern us below; here our specific task is analysis of the concept of impossibility, which Mikhailovskii uses to define what he calls an idol.

There is no doubt that this time Mikhailovskii coined his original terminology and broadly applied the concept of impossibility to sharply contrast religious ideals — which he principally had in mind for his term "idol" — to nonreligious ideals. However, the construction of his concepts (for which he required special use of the terms "idol" and "ideal"), like his whole theory (erected on these very concepts), represents a complete mistake, which only made for stylistically nice comparisons and contrasts. No one, of course, denies the enormous difference between religious ideals and personal and social ones, which makes it legitimate to sharply contrast them. Without doubt, we experience different spiritual states, depending on whether we believe in the immortality of the soul or whether we strive toward an absolutely moral and yet profoundly happy personal life or rather toward the universal, equal happiness of everyone without exception, that is, toward the elimination of social evil. Within us, this difference consists only in the fact that with the first ideal we can be fully satisfied with a contemplative attitude to everything that happens and especially to the phenomena of social life, while with the second a sense of duty imperatively demands from us the most active participation in life and its affairs. Regarding the state of the ideal outside us, it is always postulated as "what ought to be" [dolzhnoe], independently of its content, by our moral consciousness. In this respect there is no difference between religious and nonreligious ideals, for nothing that we reject as "what ought to be" [dolzhenstvuiushchee byt'] is an ideal for us, even if this "not what ought to be" possesses the most elevated content, religious or otherwise. Nonetheless, the enormous difference between religious ideals, on the one hand, and personal and social ideals, on the other, needs to be recognized as well, especially in connection with their external features. The difference is that all personal and social ideals always have some type of real preconditions and living roots in the social or even in the world process, in contrast to religious ideals, which are not only deprived of this, but are even consciously and clearly opposed to everything earthly. Thus, from no matter what side we look at the difference (or even opposition) between religious and nonreligious ideals, this difference is not subject to examination from the point of view of the category of possibility and impossibility, for this category (as we shall be persuaded below) is in general inapplicable to moral questions.

But Mikhailovskii uses the term "idol" not only for religious ideals. He also resorts to this term to designate those nonreligious ideals that he does not recognize as worthy of being called ideals. He considers art for art's sake, science for science, and morality for morality to be such idols. "Art for art," he says, "is not the only idol of this sort for modern humanity. An entire collection of them exists: science for science, justice for justice, wealth for wealth."[27] . . . "Metaphysics, which holds practical work in complete contempt and is not even capable of approaching it," he continues, further developing the same thought, "desires knowledge for knowledge, and seeks truth for truth."[28] But all these are idols, according to Mikhailovskii's conviction, and therefore, apart from the antipathy he feels for them as falsely formulated ends, he is in any event sure that their realization is impossible. . . .

These quotations very clearly reveal the mix of ideas in which Mikhailovskii's theory of idols and ideals intersects with his theory of the indivisibility of "pravda" into its component parts. The impossibility of realizing an idol (not of the first, religious type, but of the second, scientific-moral-artistic type) is completely identical in content with the impossibility of dividing pravda into two. Of course, it is necessary to recognize that here Mikhailovskii's theory of "pravda" must be amended, for if we proceed on the basis of the above enumeration of idols of the scientific-moral-artistic type, then we can no longer speak about two halves of pravda, but must admit a threefold division of it and, consequently, must point to the impossibility of separating istina, justice, and beauty. But we will leave aside this shortcoming in Mikhailovskii's social-philosophical system and only note in passing that it comes from the fact that Mikhailovskii proceeds in his studies not from contemplation of the higher spiritual goods of humanity—from istina, justice, and beauty in themselves—but from analysis of their names, especially of the word "pravda." Here we are concerned only with the formal character of that impossibility that, in the case of idols as of pravda, is completely identical in terms of content. More carefully considering the nature of this impossibility, we come to the conclusion that in both cases Mikhailovskii insisted on absolute impossibility. Only absolute impossibility had a certain theoretical value for him, and he, apparently proceeding from certain of his beliefs, relied precisely on it. But it needs to be recognized that this impossibility makes sense only if it is ascribed ideal significance, since in reality it is not at all an impossibility. Mikhailovskii himself speaks neither of the absolute character of this impossibility, nor of its ideal significance, but both of these characteristics follow from how he uses impossibility.

For example, he does not and cannot deny that there are whole epochs when exclusively one-sided tasks are posed to science and art, tasks he characterizes as idols that man cannot realize. It is clear that there has never been a lack of pure representatives of science and art who pursue only tasks of this type. Despite the fact, for example, that metaphysics, according to Mikhailovskii, is set with impossible goals, philosophers-metaphysicians have never ceased to appear throughout the whole course of human history. True, Mikhailovskii holds that all these people, even the representatives of whole epochs, chase mirages and are engaged in self-deception, since istina alone in social science is not real istina, since beauty alone in art is not real beauty, and since knowledge obtained by metaphysicians for the sake of integral knowledge alone does not give any real or useful knowledge. But these evaluations have meaning only if Mikhailovskii compares bogus conceptions of science, art, and integral knowledge to models of real science, real art, and real integral and complete knowledge. Because, however, science, art, and integral complete knowledge are not something ready-made and finished, but are created together with life, there are no precise models of real science, art, and integral complete knowledge to which the manifestations of these spheres of our spiritual activity could be compared. Instead of ready-made models there always is and must be only confidence in what science, art, and integral complete knowledge ought to be.

We call an ideal that which does not exist in a ready and complete form, but appears only as a task in which we believe and to which we consider it our duty to strive. Mikhailovskii, without doubt, had in mind his ideal of science, art, and integral complete knowledge when he pronounced his verdict on manifestations in these spheres of human creativity that fail to correspond to his ideal; in other words, he spoke about what science, art, and integral complete knowledge ought to be in his opinion. Thus, we come to the conviction that even for Mikhailovskii the criterion of an ideal is necessarily "what ought to be" [dolzhenstvovanie], and not possibility. Therefore, Mikhailovskii would have been far more correct had he directly described as *not what ought to be* [*ne dolzhnye byt'*], rather than as impossible, those manifestations of scientific thought and artistic creativity that did not fit under his ideas of true science and true art. In precisely the same way, in an earlier period of his work, when he criticized attempts to split pravda into two, he should have argued that pravda *ought not to be* divisible, rather than trying to convince us that it is impossible. Then it would have been more natural and normal for him to pass to the demand that istina and justice *ought* to be united in one great whole, designated by pravda, and that science and art *ought* to serve this one integral pravda.

Thus, we have arrived at the conclusion that in all the above cases, the concept of "morally what ought to be" [*nravstvennoe dolzhenstvovanie*] is concealed under the concept of impossibility in Mikhailovskii. He has no right to make this substitution of "what ought to be" with the impossibility of its opposite, since in relation to questions pertaining to the ideal order, the category of possibility and impossibility is completely out of place. This category introduces terrible confusion and leads even to absurd conclusions in view of the fact that, relying on it, one usually ends up arguing for the impossibility of what constantly exists and never ceases to arise. Sensing the extreme precariousness of his epistemological foundation, Mikhailovskii himself passes from impossibility to "what ought to be." "We demand from science," he affirms, expounding his program, "service to us, not to the military, not to industry, not to civilization, not even to truth, but precisely to us laymen." "We say directly: science ought to serve us."[29] In another place he insists on the same idea, arguing that, "the whole edifice of Pravda ought to be constructed on personality."[30] The "layman" and the integral, well-rounded "personality" are for him synonyms. Recognizing, however, the abstractness of these definitions, he considers it necessary to point, in their place, toward a definite social element. In this way he draws the conclusion that science, art, and one integral pravda ought to serve the people, "not in the sense of the nation, but of all laboring people."[31] Unfortunately, these transitions to the idea of "what ought to be" are only isolated glimmers in Mikhailovskii's theories that do not have great theoretical value, since they do not possess independent significance and serve only as an addendum to his favorite ideas of possibility and impossibility. First, in order to rise to the idea of "what ought to be," he relies on possibility and impossibility, then he derives, in the form of a result of the idea of "what ought to be," only the possibility of every particular content of this idea and the impossibility of the contrary. He thus preserves a firm position only at the level of the idea of possibility and impossibility. New confirmations of this position with further quotations are, we hope, superfluous, since [it is clear enough that Mikhailovskii] insists that the well-rounded personality and the working people are the only possible ideals and the only possible criteria of istina.

As a result of careful analysis, we have come to the rather unexpected conclusion that Mikhailovskii, distorting the formal side of moral concepts, very often speaks about something as impossible when, according to the content of the concept, he should rather insist that it is not what ought to be [dolzhno byt'], but ought to be otherwise. . . .

. . . "What ought to be" [dolzhenstvovanie] is of an ethical character; that is, it has the significance of a certain postulate or moral demand. It "must be" [dolzhno byt'] only because I apprehend this "must" [dolzhnoe] as a categorical imperative [so that this "must" is actually "ought"]. Therefore, substitution of this "what ought to be" [dolzhenstvovanie] by the impossibility of the contrary is explained only by a total misunderstanding of the nature of this "what ought to be," which is incompatible with other categories. In contrast to this ethical "what ought to be," [a] second type of "must be" [dolzhno byt'] has the meaning not of "what ought to be," but of natural necessity. . . .

[. . .] [Kistiakovskii concludes his analysis of the different concepts of impossibility in Mikhailovskii. He returns to the meaning of V. P. Vorontsov's statement that the capitalist development of Russia is impossible, considers the concept of possibility in N. I. Kareev's theory of progress, and stresses the importance of attentiveness toward the logical and epistemological significance of words.]

X.

[. . .] [This section opens with an analysis of the epistemological significance of the category itself of possibility, apart from its use by the Russian sociological school. Kistiakovskii begins by returning to the concept of possibility as used in the press.]

... We determined not only that this concept lacks a specific connection to formulations of causal correlations among phenomena, formulations that help modern science work, but that it even stands completely outside them. It relates to the absolutely singular and nonrecurring element in external phenomena in general and in social-political events in particular, an element not subject to research in the sciences that work out the regularity or "lawfulness" [*zakonomernost'*] of phenomena.[32] But if we put aside the theory of knowledge, that is, if we disregard the relation this concept of possibility has to what happens in reality and look only at the place it occupies among our ideas, then we will be convinced that we have the most commonplace concept of factual possibility. Because it is so commonplace, it was especially important to determine its formal-logical significance or its relation to all the other concepts we use in science and in life. Windelband was the first to disclose the fully independent formal-logical significance of this concept and to give a complete analysis of it, and in this is his undoubted service. He established that, together with affirmation and negation, or with the definite solution of a question one way or the other (negative or positive), there is a "special problematical relation" (*das problematische Verhalten*), or state of uncertainty in which the researcher can determine only different possibilities.[33] But since science demands exact and definite answers to its questions, since the absence of such answers characterizes only the preliminary stage of any scientific research, and since our life, on the contrary, is full of uncertainty and every possible supposition, it must be clear to anyone that the concept of factual possibility, occupying a conspicuous place in all of life's calculations, does not have strict scientific significance.

But even that which is only factually possible can be an object of precise scientific research. True, the result of such research is not a simple indication of factual possibility, but a more precise determination of it, which is why it is acquiring a special designation in science. This fully scientific and therefore, it would seem, new concept of possibility also applies to singular phenomena, but only to those that are encountered more or less often and can therefore be examined as recurring. Phenomena of this type are grouped and treated in statistical research, which employs various methods of mathematical calculation.

It is often thought that statistical research, by the very fact that it, like natural science, relies on mathematics and deals with various numerical data, belongs to the natural sciences. ... [This view is incorrect], because in statistics, as a science, we have a special type of scientific research, absolutely distinct from the natural-sciences type. The main difference between these two types of research is that statistical research is directed to a quite different side of phenomena than natural-scientific research, so that their respective results are different in principle, and not just relatively. While natural-scientific research directs its attention to what is common to every type of singular phenomena, statistical research turns its attention to the incidents themselves of singular phenomena. True, statistical research examines singular incidents not in themselves, not as absolutely singular, for if every occurring incident were examined only as singular, it would also need to be recognized as non-recurring and, consequently, studied completely separately in its unique, non-recurring situation and individual peculiarity. Meanwhile, the distinctive trait of statistics, as a science, is precisely that it examines similar singular incidents as recurring. For this it schematizes them, grouping and calculating sometimes very complex and highly individual phenomena according to common characteristics and abstracting from all remaining dissimilar characteristics. In this way, the starting point of statistical research is not so much singular incidents as so-called statistical aggregates, groups, or masses (*Gesamtheit, Gruppe, Masse*) of these incidents. But neither schematization nor formation of statistical aggregates must lead to misunderstanding about the object of statistical research. We must not confuse the schematization that results in statistical aggregates with the type of generalization that leads to the formation of generic concepts and that lies at the basis of all natural science–type thinking. The object of statistical research remains incidents of singular phenomena, although not in themselves but in their aggregates, and also in the numerical correlations calculated by comparison of these aggregates. Statistical research does not, however, subject incidents of singular phenomena to any reworking [of what they are in themselves]; it never loses sight of the singular incidents themselves or treats them as instances of generic concepts, as is done in the natural sciences. In other words, statistical research investigates incidents of deaths, births, illnesses, and so forth, not death, birth, and illness as such.[34]

Thus, statistical research, studying incidents of singular phenomena, acquaints us with these phenomena, as singularly occurring and connected with other singularly occurring phenomena, and also with the environment in which these phenomena take place. For this, such research employs various mathematical methods, beginning with calculation of the aggregates of these incidents and ending with calculation of various correlations among various aggregates, determining in this way the extent to which incidents of a phenomenon of one type match incidents of another type. The main task of the researcher is to obtain not just a result from purely mathematical correlations among numerical data, but rather a real conclusion about how incidents of one phenomenon relate to incidents of another or to the environment in which they occur. Only then will the statistical data give a definite and integral characterization of the singular phenomena being studied. Along with other approaches to studying singular phenomena, such as description and analysis, this type of characterization is fully independent and very valuable, and even possesses an indisputable advantage over all other methods in that it, thanks to relatively simple techniques, acquaints us with masses of singular phenomena taken in aggregate, and with each separately. To the extent, however, that all these methods of statistical calculation determine what already exists, or how it exists, they are not of interest to us here.

For our theme, statistical research interests us only to the extent it studies what is occurring and will occur. For determination of singular incidents that are occurring or will occur, statistics uses, as a method, the mathematical theory of probability. Therefore, first of all the question arises about the relationship of mathematically determined probability to what is occurring in reality, or about the epistemological significance of probability. One of the most visible representatives of philosophical thought in contemporary Germany, Windelband, has resolutely said of this question, "probability is never the property of some expected event, but rather always only the degree of expectation. It is an entirely subjective condition. . . ." "Precisely speaking, the probable does not now and never will exist, only probability as a psychological condition between certainty and uncertainty. The objectively probable is nonsense."[35]

Against this interpretation of probability the entirely correct objection has been expressed that this view can only explain why we have a greater expectation of probable events than of less probable ones. But it hardly explains and even makes incomprehensible why what is calculated on the basis of precise data with the help of probability theory, and therefore is expected by us, is actually realized with just the degree of probability we expect. This objection belongs to [Johannes von] Kries [1853–1928], professor of physiology at Freiburg University. Specially developing the principles of probability theory and researching different cases of their application to what takes place in reality, he came to the conclusion that probability theory gives us fully objective and positive knowledge, which acquaints us, however, not with what necessarily is occurring or will occur, but only with what might occur. Kries thus calls the object that is researched with the help of probability theory the "objectively possible."[36]

But having correctly determined the logical significance of the concept of objective possibility, as well as the correlation between it and probability, Kries gave a completely incorrect explanation of its epistemological premises. [. . .]

Despite all this, to Kries belongs the indisputable service of discovering the importance of researching objective possibility through calculating probability.[37] Only he could not, as a natural scientist, emancipate himself from natural science–type thinking and rushed to connect research of the objectively possible with causal explanation of phenomena. Meanwhile the value of the process of knowledge that determines the objectively possible is precisely that this process is not directed to the establishment of causal connections. Instead of determining causal correlations among phenomena, this path investigates the incidents themselves of singular phenomena. Thus, we have here entirely original research methods, yielding results just as original.

But the significance of applying probability theory to the treatment of statistical material, as well as of using this method to determine the objectively possible in social events, is much greater than might at first be supposed. We begin here with exact science, which even uses mathematical methods, but which, by the nature of the data it treats and the results it obtains, clearly and sharply diverges from the natural sciences. Therefore, in the development of scientific thought — which tends now to extol natural science–type thinking in its exclusive and autocratic supremacy, while also recognizing the equal rights of all other types of scientific and extra-scientific (e.g., metaphysical) thinking and creativity — this new type of scientific knowledge, determining the objectively possible in social and other events, is destined to play a visible role.[38]

We have juxtaposed the concept of objective possibility, by the help of which statistical research on social phenomena is carried out, to factual possibility, which plays so great a role in the daily press and in ordinary life. The similarity between these two concepts of possibility consists only in that they both apply to singular phenomena. In everything else these concepts of possibility are completely different. While determination of objective possibility is the result of applying exact scientific methods to the treatment of factual data obtained and grouped in a certain way, indication of factual possibility in the daily press and in ordinary life does not have scientific significance and is only a certain way of ascertaining the circumstances at hand. Even the character of the singularity is far from the same in both cases, for the concept of objective possibility applies to incidents that, although singular, are examined as recurring, while the factually possible ordinarily designates an absolutely singular (in its individual peculiarity) continuation or effect of a particular event. Nonetheless, the singularity of the phenomena to which these concepts of possibility apply is sufficiently characteristic of them that, from the formal-logical point of view, a theoretical likening of them is quite admissible.

This most characteristic feature of these concepts of possibility also defines their relation to our more special theme. Clearly, these are not the concepts of possibility that rendered such immense services to the Russian sociologists in the solution of their sociological problems in general and their social-ethical problems in particular. There cannot be any doubt of this regarding objective possibility, for this concept is obtained through treating statistical material with the help of probability theory. Regarding factual possibility, we have already refuted the proposition that Mikhailovskii, and consequently the other Russian sociologists, make use of it. This unscientific concept could not, in any event, be a very expedient method for solving the most fundamental questions of sociology and ethics. Nonetheless, it, being so ordinary a concept, repeatedly intruded into the theoretical constructions of the Russian sociologists, and we even think that it had a much greater role than would be warranted by its internal merits.

If we want to find out the deeper reasons and motives that compelled the Russian sociologists to construct their own basic concept of possibility, we will have to condense to two basic problems all the diverse questions they discussed from the point of view of possibility. The first problem is theoretical and the second is practical. The first and basic task the Russian sociologists posed for themselves consisted in solving the question of active human influence, or the influence of personality, on the social process. Or, expressing this task in a more general formula, we must say that the Russian sociologists strove first of all to theoretically reconcile the idea of freedom with necessity. The second task consisted in justifying ethical evaluation of social phenomena, an evaluation we always make well before facing the question about the right to do so. Both of these tasks must be resolved either from the transcendental-normative point of view, or metaphysically; there is no third positive-scientific or empirical solution to them. Because, however, the normative point of view not only was inadequately known to Mikhailovskii and consequently to the Russian sociologists who followed him, but was foreign to the whole spirit of their theoretical constructs, they based their solutions to these two social-ethical problems on metaphysical premises.

Of course, the Russian sociologists would never admit that their concept of possibility, with the help of which they so easily and simply resolved the most difficult social-ethical problems, was filled through and through with a metaphysical spirit. Very probably, even they themselves were not conscious of the extent to which their basic theoretical construction was metaphysical. The concept of factual possibility undoubtedly obliged them in this case. As a result of its extremely frequent use in everyday life, it very naturally masked the true metaphysical sense of their own concept of possibility and concealed this sense from the reader's intellectual view. The affinity of the concept of factual possibility with the concept of metaphysical possibility only confirms the indisputable fact that views taken immediately from life are much closer to the metaphysical framing of questions than are scientific theories.[39]

But having worked out their concept of metaphysical possibility, the Russian sociologists devised nothing new, for this concept was known in metaphysics long before them. At the beginning of this article it was mentioned that already two hundred years ago, at the end of the seventeenth and beginning of the eighteenth century, this same problem of freedom and necessity, and the ethical questions connected with it, called for solution, and that the concept of metaphysical possibility also served then as the basis for their solution. If the problem and its solution were one and the same, the occasion that elicited the solution and the material on which it was based were, however, different. The causal explanation of natural phenomena celebrated its first triumphs then, and the application of this explanation not only to physical but also to physiological phenomena poignantly raised the question of the relationship between body and soul. A whole series of ethical problems depended on the solution to this question, and indeed they even more urgently required it. It was necessary to substantiate free will, to reconcile the existence of evil and suffering with belief in a higher, all-good being, and to demonstrate the final victory of spirit and the good over matter and evil. In his time Leibniz tried to resolve these questions, relying on the concept of metaphysical possibility. It must be admitted, however, that this part of Leibniz's metaphysics is the weakest, not only in his system, but in general among all the metaphysical doctrines of his epoch. Yet the Russian sociologists, overstepping the limits of positive science in the solution of social-ethical problems and turning to metaphysical constructs, revived precisely this, the weakest of metaphysical doctrines. In his *History of Modern Philosophy*, Windelband gave an excellent analysis and evaluation of all the weak sides of this prototype of every theory erected on the concept of metaphysical possibility. Since, in evaluating the significance of the concept of metaphysical possibility and in disclosing the mistaken conclusions to which it leads, we would have to repeat what Windelband has already said, we permit ourselves to quote him.

[. . .] [Kistiakovskii quotes Windelband at length (more than four pages). The first passage considers Leibniz's distinction between eternal or necessary truths and factual or contingent ones. A necessary truth is such that its opposite is logically impossible (i.e., a contradiction), while the opposite of a contingent truth is not logically impossible. In Leibniz's rationalist philosophy, logical principles are also metaphysical ones, and logical necessity is metaphysical necessity. The existing world is contingent because it can be thought of as other than it is without contradiction; it is one of an infinite number of possible worlds. In the second passage Kistiakovskii quotes, Windelband focuses on Leibniz's theodicy, his idea that this world is the best of all possible worlds.[40]]

Familiar with the basic positions of Leibniz's philosophy, we can now see how the Russian sociologists, not having been followers of Leibniz, nonetheless came up with nothing that he could not already have said. Only they left aside the two worlds—the world of man and the cosmic world—the meta-physical essence of which Leibniz wanted to grasp, and turned instead to a third world, the social world. But striving to understand the social world, they created for themselves a system that revived all the weak sides of Leibniz. In their arguments they also proceeded from the idea of impossibility, as, for example, in their theory of knowledge (the impossibility of an exclusively objective method) and in their explanations of real social processes (the impossibility of struggling with certain currents in history). In this, as we have seen, they generally preferred to express everything that is necessary in the form of the impossibility of the opposite, which they considered a higher criterion than necessity, as if following Leibniz in opposition to contemporary natural science and logic. Accordingly, they examined everything that fell outside the sphere of impossibilities as the field of possibilities, where possibility, just because it corresponds to impossibility, turned out to be the basis of everything creative and progressive in the social process. Thus, the social process was for them mainly the aggregate of various possibilities. The social environment, the people, the peasantry seemed to them to be bearers of passive possibilities; personality and the intelligentsia embodied active possibilities. *This distribution of everything occurring in the social world between two spheres—the possible and the impossible—naturally destroyed the question of freedom and necessity: instead of the principle of freedom, the idea of possibility was advanced.*

But precisely in the question of social creativity and progress do we meet the main disagreement in principle between the Russian sociologists and Leibniz. In Leibniz's metaphysical system eternal, necessary truths are put at the basis of the world. It is because the finite world cannot consist of infinite things that an element of suffering, imperfection, and evil is inherent to it. Thus, in this system only the origin of suffering and evil rests on the idea of possibility, but the good itself is an eternal necessary truth. By contrast, for the Russian sociologists precisely everything that is progressive, good, ethical, and ideal has possibility as its source.

The Russian sociologists, we recall, substantiate the ideal and progress on the idea of possibility, and consider desirability and undesirability to be the highest criteria of moral evaluation. In their attempt to prop up ethics by formally relating it to the concepts of possibility and desirability, the Russian sociologists are not only original, but even unique in the whole history of human thought. Until them, the human mind had never come up with the idea of the good as something only possible and desirable, since for this relativism had to be taken to its highest form of development, to a social relativism in which all higher goods of human life are seen only as the results of social relations.

The Russian sociologists take pride in introducing an ethical element into the understanding of social phenomena, and in bringing about recognition that the social process cannot be examined apart from the ideas of the good and of justice that inspire this process. But of what value is an ethical element for which the highest criterion is possibility?

It is understandable that representatives of the new current in sociology have had first of all to break with the examination of social phenomena from the point of view of possibility and impossibility. Instead, they have advanced two principles: necessity and "ought" [dolzhenstvovanie]. These two principles do not contradict each other, since "ought" subsumes necessity and rises above it. In knowing what is necessarily occurring in the social process, we also know the material in relation to which, and the borders within which, we ought to fulfill our duty.

We strive for the realization of our ideals not because they are possible, but because our conscious duty imperatively demands it of us and everyone around us.

Notes

1. This article relates to the same series as my essay "Kategorii neobkhodimosti i spravedlivosti pri issledovanii sotsial'nykh iavlenii" ["The Categories of Necessity and Justice in Studying Social Phenomena"], published more than two years ago in the journal, *Zhizn'* (May and June 1990) [reprinted in his *Sotsial'nye nauki i pravo: Ocherki po metodologii sotsial'nykh nauk i obshchei teorii prava* (Moscow, 1916), pp. 120–188]. As the title itself of the present article indicates, my goal is not to present a complete literary or scientific characterization of the "Russian sociological school." . . . I examine the theory of the Russian sociological school in connection with the very specific question of the category of possibility in application to social phenomena in general and to the solution of social-ethical problems in particular. In view of the fact, however, that possibility occupies the leading position within the structure of the ideas of the Russian sociologists, and that it exerts enormous influence on their solution to the ethical questions that constitute an indelible part of their sociological systems, a fully integral picture of their views emerges from exposition and analysis of the significance the idea of possibility has for the theoretical constructs of the Russian sociologists. . . .

I ask readers to excuse the somewhat unfinished form of the present article, a result of the extreme haste with which I had to prepare it for print. This haste also prevented me from taking into account the literature on the Russian sociological school, especially on Mikhailovskii. I regret in particular that I could not refer to Berdiaev's book on Mikhailovskii or to Struve's preface to it, all the more so in that our starting points are identical and that our paths often meet, even though we adhere to different systems in treating particular questions.

2. See John Stuart Mill, *System of Logic,* trans. Ivanovskii (Moscow, 1900), pp. 244 ff. Not recognizing the categories, Mill strives to substantiate induction, that is, ultimately the entire process of empirical knowledge, on the supposition of a basic uniformity in the order of nature. Thus, instead of formal elements introduced by thought into the process of knowledge, he bases this process on a preconceived notion about how nature itself is structured. Meanwhile, for such a preconceived notion to have absolute certainty, creating a thoroughly stable foundation for the theory of knowledge, it must be a metaphysical truth. Consequently, instead of creating a truly empirical theory of knowledge, free from transcendental elements, Mill erects his theory of knowledge on a transcendent foundation, that is, he returns the formulation and solution of epistemological problems to the pre-Kantian situation. Indeed, Mill's supposition of a basic uniformity in the order of nature is very similar to Leibniz's famous axiom of preestablished harmony. But whereas Leibniz, with the sincerity of a consistent thinker, advanced his axiom in all the fullness of its metaphysical content, Mill insists on the purely empirical character of the premise at the basis of his theory of knowledge. He contended that any inductive conclusion by its very essence necessarily supposes that the order of nature is uniform, but he arrives at this supposition by inductive conclusions. This supposition was the basic premise of his entire system of knowledge and yet its final link. His system is thus not only based on an obvious vicious circle, but its starting and end points are so identical that knowledge itself must be abolished as an unnecessary roundabout way of returning to the point of departure. Only so superficial a thinker as Mill could give so little thought to the foundations of his philosophical constructions.

3. N. K. Mikhailovskii, *Sochineniia,* IV, p. 952. [Italics throughout Kistiakovskii's. Kistiakovskii uses the following edition of Mikhailovskii's works: *Sochineniia N. K. Mikhailovskogo,* six volumes (St. Petersburg, 1896–1897).]

4. For the following passage, Mikhailovskii cites A. V. Iakovlev, "Assotsiatsiia i artel'," [in *Russkie obshchestvennye voprosy,* eds. P. A. Gaideburov and E. I. Konrad (St. Petersburg, 1872)], p. 300. Iakovlev (1835–1888), an activist in the agricultural cooperative movement in Russia, was also the author of *Ocherk narodnogo kredita v zapadnoi Evropii i v Rossii* (St. Petersburg, 1869). On him see Yanni Kotsonis, *Making Peasants Backward: Agricultural Cooperatives and the Agrarian Question in Russia, 1861–1914* (New York: St. Martin's Press, 1999), pp. 13–18. Ed.

5. N. K. Mikhailovskii, *Sochineniia,* I, pp. 654–655.

6. N. K. Mikhailovskii, "Literatura i Zhizn," *Russkoe bogatstvo,* 1901, no. 4, part 2, p. 128.

7. Vasilii P. Vorontsov (1847–1918), a zemstvo physician, was a leading representative of "legal" or nonrevolutionary Russian populism. His highly influential book, *Sud'by kapitalizma v Rossii* (*The Fate of Capitalism in Russia,* St. Petersburg, 1882), argued that capitalism could not become the dominant form of industrial production in Russia. Ed.

8. On the Russian terms for truth, *istina* and *pravda,* see Struve's essay (Chapter 3) in this volume. Note 28. Ed.

9. The passage, "Pravda," is translated by James P. Scanlan in *Russian Philosophy,* ed. James M. Edie, James P. Scanlan, and Mary-Barbara Zeldin, with the collaboration of George L. Kline, vol. II (Knoxville: University of Tennessee Press, 1976), pp. 175–176. Ed.

10. N. K. Mikhailovskii, *Sochineniia*, IV, p. 385.

11. Ibid., pp. 387, 421, 431.

12. Ibid., p. 421.

13. Ibid., p. 385.

14. Ibid., p. 430.

15. Friedrich Albert Lange, *Geschichte des Materialismus und Kritik seiner Bedeutung in der Gegenwart*, 2 vols. (Iserlohn and Leipzig, 1866). Friedrich Albert Lange (1828–1875), German philosopher whose critique of materialism helped revive interest in Kant and thus contributed to the rise of neo-Kantianism. Ed.

16. N. K. Mikhailovskii, *Sochineniia*, IV, p. 388.

17. N. K. Mikhailovskii, *Sochineniia*, IV, p. 51. Italics Kistiakovskii's throughout.

18. Ibid., p. 52; cf. *Sochineniia*, V, p. 534 ff.

19. Ibid., p. 64; cf. *Sochineniia*, IV, p. 460; V, p. 536; VI, p. 492.

20. Konstantin D. Kavelin (1818–1885), Russian historian, philosopher, and leading liberal Westernizer. In his essay "Vzgliad na iuridicheskii byt drevnei Rossii" (A Survey of Juridical Life in Old Russia, 1847), he interpreted Russian history as a process of the gradual emancipation of the individual through the rationalization of social relations and the introduction of legal order. His later works, *The Tasks of Psychology* (1872) and *The Tasks of Ethics* (1885), were also concerned with the defense (from a semi-positivist position) of the autonomous personality. Ed.

21. N. K. Mikhailovskii, *Sochineniia*, I, p. 645. [In the sense used here, "man" represents universal humanity, as opposed to a particular estate or culture. Mikhailovskii's conception, following Kavelin's, suggests Georg Simmel's definition of the eighteenth-century idea of "individuality": "It is man in general, universal man, who occupies the center of interest for this period instead of historically given, particular, and differentiated man. The latter is in principle reduced to the former; in each individual person, man in general lives as his essence." Georg Simmel, *On Individuality and Social Forms: Selected Writings*, ed. Donald N. Levine (Chicago: University of Chicago Press, 1971), p. 219. For Kavelin's views, see Andrzej Walicki, *The Slavophile Controversy: History of a Conservative Utopia in Nineteenth-Century Russian Thought*, trans. Hilda Andrews-Rusiecka (Oxford: Oxford University Press, 1975), pp. 404–412.]

22. In fact, Kavelin's phrase is "exclusively national determinants." See his essay "Vzgliad na iuridicheskii byt drevnei Rossii," in K. D. Kavelin, *Nash umstvennyi stroi: Stat'i po filosofii russkoi istorii i kul'tury*, ed. V. K. Kantor (Moscow: Pravda, 1989), p. 59. Ed.

23. N. K. Mikhailovskii, *Sochineniia*, I, p. 646.

24. K. D. Kavelin, "Vzgliad na iuridicheskii byt drevnei Rossii," p. 59. Quotation marks added. Ed.

25. N. K. Mikhailovskii, *Sochineniia*, I, p. 647.

26. Ibid., p. 648.

27. N. K. Mikhailovskii, *Sochineniia*, V, p. 536.

28. N. K. Mikhailovskii, *Sochineniia*, III, p. 340.

29. Ibid., p. 337.

30. N. K. Mikhailovskii, *Sochineniia*, IV, p. 461.

31. N. K. Mikhailovskii, *Sochineniia*, V, p. 537 ff.; also see *Sochineniia*, IV, p. 462 ff.

32. In his recent work, [Heinrich] Rickert provides a logical construction of the basic science — history — among those of the opposing type [i.e., sciences that do not research *zakonomernost'*], but we cannot touch upon it here, for it would take us too far from our theme. See H. Rickert, *Die Grenzen der naturwissenschaftlichen Begriffsbildung,* 2 Hälfte (Tübingen, 1902).

33. Wilhelm Windelband, "Beiträge zur Lehre vom negativen Urteil," *Strassburger Abhandlungen zur Philosophie: Eduard Zeller, zu seinem siebenzigsten Geburtstage* (Freiburg, Tübingen, 1884), pp. 185 ff. [citation corrected].

34. Because generic-concept thinking, having been specially cultivated by the natural sciences, is not, however, their exclusive province, but on the contrary is the most widespread and common type of thinking, the object of statistical research is often designated in generic concepts. . . . It is clear, however, that singular incidents themselves of phenomena, as well as their aggregates and correlations, but not the phenomena as such, are generalized in these generic concepts.

35. "Das objectiv Wahrscheinlich ist ein Unbegriff." Wilhelm Windelband, *Über die Gewißheit der Erkenntnis* (Berlin, 1873), pp. 24–25 ff. [editor's translation]. Cf. Windelband, *Die Lehren vom Zufall* (Berlin, 1870), pp. 26–52.

36. We made use of the following works of Kries: *Die Prinzipien der Wahrscheinlichkeitsrechnung* (Freiburg, 1886); *Über den Begriff der objectiven Möglichkeit und einige Anwendung desselben* (Leipzig, 1888); "Über den Begriff der Wahrscheinlichkeit und Möglichkeit und ihre Bedeutung im Strafrechte," *Zeitschrift für die gesamte Strafrechtswissenschaft,* Band 9, Berlin, 1889.

37. In the Russian literature, A. A. Chuprov has an excellent article on the history and theory of the question examined here. He sides in general with Kries, but independently develops and extends the point of view Kries indicates. See Chuprov's entry, "Nravstvennaia statistika," in the Brokhaus and Efron *Entsiklopedicheskii slovar',* v. XXI, i (St. Petersburg, 1897), pp. 403–408. [Aleksandr A. Chuprov (1874–1926), liberal Russian economist and statistician who sought to quantity social science. His father, Aleksandr I. Chuprov (1842–1908), was one of the founders of Russian statistics.]

38. In the near future I hope to work out more thoroughly, in a special work in German, the questions raised here.

39. It is interesting that a completely identical direction of thought has arisen among criminologists working out this same question of freedom and necessity for clarification of the special problems of criminal law. Because human behavior is causally conditioned and therefore necessary, it would seem there is no place for any responsibility, including criminal responsibility. In view of this, certain experts have proposed that the *possibility* of acting one way or another be recognized as the theoretical basis of responsibility. Like the Russian sociologists, they insist on the empirical nature of this concept, unaware of its metaphysical foundations.

40. Wilhelm Windelband, *Die Geschichte der neueren Philosophie in ihrem zusammenhange mit der allgemeinen Kultur und den besonderen Wissenschaften,* vol. 1, 2d edition (Leipzig, 1899), pp. 464–466, 495–497.

The Basic Principles of Auguste Comte's Sociological Doctrine

A. S. LAPPO-DANILEVSKII

Introduction

In the course of the first decades of the nineteenth century, enthusiasm for the scientific spirit was perhaps nowhere as strong as in France: there science was enriched by a number of new fields of knowledge and acquired great popularity. At the same time, however, French society during the Restoration began to react against the excesses of individualism and revealed a clear inclination for the establishment of some type of spiritual authority. Such an attitude was felt not only by reactionaries, but also by progressive people, who believed that the time had arrived for the "reorganization"[1] of the social order. They included, for example, the ardent admirer of science and bold precursor of socialism, Saint-Simon;[2] not able to focus his lively mind, he did not, however, create anything whole and finished his versatile literary activity with his famous discourse on the principles of a "new Christianity."[3] Auguste Comte, an associate of Saint-Simon for a time,[4] must be recognized as a much more systematic representative of the new attitude. A profound faith in the all-encompassing significance of science and a strong desire for the moral renewal of society permeate all Comte's philosophy: his *Cours de philosophie positive* vividly reflects the basic currents dominant in French thought since the second half of the eighteenth century, and represents one of the first attempts to construct a logic of the individual sciences. And his *Système de politique positive* resounds with the convinced voice of someone calling people to fulfill their moral duty, of someone proclaiming a "religion of humanity."

Although almost half a century has passed since the appearance of Comte's main works, they still have not lost their interest; not only in the 1840s, when Mill,[5] with his course of logic,[6] did so much to facilitate the spread of Comte's basic views, but in recent decades as well a number of works have appeared that are specifically devoted to exposition or critique of the "positive philosophy. . . ."[7]

In the extensive literature on Comte's positivism, it is impossible, however, not to notice essential gaps. The history of its origins has barely been touched.[8] Only [Georg] Misch, under the influence of Dilthey,[9] has undertaken study of the philosophy of d'Alembert[10] and Turgot[11] in relation to Comte's system; but Misch's detailed study[12] only paves the way for future works, which still have not been done, and without which critique of Comte's "positive philosophy" will always suffer from one-sidedness.[13] Apart from that, it is remarkable that evaluation of Comte has thus far been too little dedicated to examination of his basic thesis about the relative nature of our knowledge; instead, criticism ordinarily turns directly to the so-called law of three stages, which has only secondary and derivative significance in the system of positivism as a whole.[14] True, the "positive" theory of knowledge has now elicited some mention in the literature, but study of the extent to which and how successfully Comte applied it to the construction of sociology nonetheless remains among the tasks of the future: no one, it seems, has yet attempted to carefully discuss the basic principles of the field of knowledge whose solid substantiation Comte considered to be one of his most essential services. Meanwhile it is possible to speak of Comte having founded sociology only if it is demonstrated that he firmly established its principles. Critical inquiry into the main premises of Comte's sociological doctrine might not only facilitate evaluation of Comte as a typical representative of "positive sociology," but also lead to clarification of the general principles that would have to lie at the basis of a minimally satisfactory theory of social science. The desire to contribute, to the best of my ability, to the establishment of such a theory underlies the present work, which is devoted to a short survey of the epistemological and psychological views of Comte, views that are closely related to his sociology, and to critical reconsideration of the premises he in part consciously, in part "spontaneously," admitted into his "social physics."

I. Comte's Epistemological Premises in Relation to His Sociology

The doctrine of the relativity of human knowledge arose long before Comte based his philosophical system on it: it was already dominant in French literature prior to the appearance of the *Cours de philosophie positive,* and it exerted marked influence on its construction. Without clarifying the specific features of the epistemological deliberations of Comte's predecessors and his relation to them, it is impossible, of course, to indicate the distinctive characteristics of his theory of knowledge; yet his epistemology fundamentally influenced his whole system and determined the direction he took in his sociology. Thus, the history of the "positive" doctrine of the relativity of knowledge naturally must serve to introduce an account of Comte's own analogous theory, while characterization of his epistemological premises will make it possible for us to examine their link with "positive" sociology.[15]

1. HISTORY OF THE "POSITIVE" DOCTRINE OF THE RELATIVITY OF KNOWLEDGE

The theory of the relativity of knowledge in ancient times. The revival of Epicureanism in seventeenth and eighteenth-century France; J. O. de La Mettrie. Skepticism and empiricism in eighteenth-century French literature, mainly among the Encyclopedists: d'Alembert, Diderot, Turgot, Barthez, and Helvétius. Heirs of the Encyclopedists: the *idéologues.* Comte, as successor to the Encyclopedists and *idéologues.* Hume and Comte.

Kant and Comte: Comte's contempt for transcendental philosophy.

The theory of the relativity of human knowledge already appears in the speculations of the Sophists and Epicureans, and is clearly enough felt in the views of the Skeptics, who did not doubt that only "phenomena" are experienced by us and who maintained that the very concepts of cause and effect are relative.

Unable to trace here the gradual penetration of the basic ideas of Epicureanism into modern European thought, we note only that this system acquired new force in the seventeenth century, thanks to the works of Gassendi.[16] His students and followers formed "Epicurean circles,"[17] which, judging by the testimony of one of the learned Encyclopedists of the time, enjoyed considerable respect among contemporaries, mainly in France, already by the 1720s.[18] Some later French writers remained under the influence of the same direction. An example is the well-known materialist La Mettrie,[19] who opposed the doctrines of causation and purposiveness in his work, *Le Système d'Epicure*

(1750). "The wings of our genius," La Mettrie wrote, "cannot elevate us to knowledge of causes. The most ignorant of men is as enlightened in this regard as the greatest philosopher. ... In all bodies, as in our own, the first springs are hidden from us, and will likely remain so." We can just as little understand, according to La Mettrie, the purposiveness that many recognize in nature. "Nature no more thought of making the eye to see than water to serve as a mirror for a simple shepherdess. Water happened to be able to reflect images; the shepherdess saw with pleasure there her nice pretty face. ... All arguments about final causes are ... frivolous (*frivoles*)."[20]

An analogous current also gradually arose on the ground of the English empiricism that so influenced the French *Encyclopédie:* not for nothing did the *Encyclopédie* place itself under the patronage of Francis Bacon, John Locke, and Isaac Newton. David Hume also came to enjoy great authority among French thinkers, especially after 1763.[21] But already well before then, in 1743,[22] d'Alembert wrote on behalf of the theory of the relativity of knowledge. Most likely under the influence of the well-known thesis once formulated by Newton (*hypotheses non fingo*),[23] as well as of Hume's theory, d'Alembert, inclined as he was toward skepticism, protested repeatedly against introducing any "metaphysical" premises into science and remained on the ground of naïve realism.[24] "In any science," he wrote, "there are principles, true or appearing as such, which we grasp by a type of instinct, and on which we must rely without resistance; otherwise our thought would rest on nothing and our knowledge would have no certainty. ..."[25] With such a view, discussion of the conditions or forms of our knowledge seemed like idle business to d'Alembert. "To reach the fullness of true knowledge we would have to recognize the cause and purpose of things and phenomena; but we cannot know their essence in the same way we know the active principle in ourselves; it is difficult to even determine whether we grasp their essence in the same way we represent them, or whether we are dealing with phenomena alone. The latter, though, is more likely."[26] Thus, in d'Alembert's opinion, we must renounce knowledge of the internal relation between our soul and objects of the outside world. Further, discussing the question of time and space, the author of the *Eléments de philosophie* comes to the conclusion that in both cases, "we ascribe more reality than we should."[27] The basic concepts of our thought, such as substance or causation, lack any real content; we introduce such "dark" concepts into our word usage only as something like an abbreviated designation for the universal laws that can be expressed in mathematical formulas. In general we do not know things-in-themselves, but only their relation to us. Thus, all that we "see" is nothing other than phenomena, the relations among which can be represented in the form of laws.[28] D'Alembert's skepticism, it is clear, easily led him to the theory of the relativity of our knowledge and even forced him to raise epistemological questions, which he nonetheless left without any solution.[29]. . .

The relative nature of our knowledge was thus a very widespread opinion among French *philosophes* already at the time the *Encyclopédie* was printed (1751–1764), and naturally was passed on to the younger generation. The legends of the *Encyclopédie* had not yet outlived their day when Comte began his activity. Lagrange,[30] so revered by Comte, was a student of d'Alembert; Turgot and Condorcet, a friend of d'Alembert, both influenced Saint-Simon, with whom Comte worked in his youth (1818–1824). Apart from the living legends, Comte was, of course, familiar from primary sources with La Mettrie and the Encyclopedists, not to mention their later followers.[31] Comte was, however, rather contemptuous toward one of the contemporaries of the Encyclopedists, Condillac,[32] in particular to his theory of "transformation," and Holbach gave him nothing new.[33]

Finally, the heirs of the Encyclopedists, the *idéologues,* such as Destutt de Tracy and especially Cabanis,[34] continued to insist, following Helvétius,[35] that our knowledge is of relations alone; occasionally they suggested, like Turgot, that "order and succession" were the only relations accessible to our knowledge.[36] In this the *idéologues* were also joined by the learned celebrities of the time: Ampère and Bichat, as well as Broussais.[37]

Thus, proceeding in his fundamental principles from the views of the Encyclopedists, Comte found in their successors only new combinations of the same pattern of ideas: the theory of the relativity of our knowledge was practically a commonplace in the classic literature of the time.[38]

Hume's skepticism also produced a strong impression on both the Encyclopedists and Comte. In any event, Comte's reading of the works of the "sober-minded" Hume invigorated and reinforced the doctrine he absorbed from the French *philosophes* of the eighteenth and early nineteenth centuries: by Comte's own testimony, acquaintance with Hume's works "had a very useful influence on his initial philosophical education."[39] It cannot be said, however, that Comte assimilated Hume's semi-skepticism: the well-known theory of the Scottish philosopher about "belief" and his teaching about the probability of our empirical evidence did not make its way into the *Cours de philosophie positive;* Hume's fully candid and very clear indications about the epistemological complications into which consistent empiricism falls likewise drew too little attention from Comte. Nonetheless, under the influence of Hume's critique, Comte probably lost once and for all his faith in the possibility of legitimately using the principle of causation in scientific philosophy;

he also limited, perhaps while remembering Hume's categories of "association among ideas," the sphere of "certain" knowledge to that of only relations of resemblance and succession among "phenomena" and their laws.[40]

Thus, Comte not only accepted the theory of the relativity of knowledge without any attempt to substantiate it critically, but formulated it more sharply than his predecessors. And yet it cannot be said that when Comte wrote his *Cours de philosophie positive,* the new theory of Kant remained completely unknown to the French intelligentsia: at the beginning of the nineteenth century, for example, Kant was even proposed as a candidate for foreign membership in the Institut de France and received a good many votes. True, his works were barely accessible to French readers, but besides [Charles de] Villers's poor, eleven-page summary of the "transcendental philosophy" (1801),[41] there was Le Fèvre's French translation of Kinker's exposition of the *Critique of Pure Reason,*[42] as well as a thorough survey of Kant's teaching in Degérando's comparative history of philosophical systems.[43] Thus, not mentioning the works of Madame de Staël,[44] "who pointed only to the general spirit of the philosophy of Kant," in his opposition to the old-fashioned metaphysics, or the works of Cousin,[45] who soon became subject to Schelling's influence, it was possible to know something about the "transcendental philosophy" even from the French literature at the end of the eighteenth and beginning of the nineteenth century. And in fact some of the educated people of the time did grasp it; the leading youth, especially after 1823, also became interested in Kant's philosophy. Nonetheless the majority either did not undertake study of the new ideas, presented as they were in an extremely difficult form, or rejected them as if they "were based on poor knowledge of our intellectual capabilities."[46]

Comte followed the prevailing opinion: like Destutt de Tracy, Laromiguière,[47] and several other philosophers, he was not able to avail himself of the "bright light with which Kant illuminated the demarcation line separating the soul's spontaneous activity from the sensations felt by us." Indeed, although he considered the Königsberg philosopher to be closest among the "metaphysicians" to positivism, and also recognized his merit in that "Kant for the first time attempted to escape from the circle of metaphysical concepts about the absolute by constructing a concept of reality that was at once subjective and objective," even so, Comte himself was hardly well acquainted with the works of the great thinker; later he even declared that he doubted anything could be learned from them. Kant's "illusory" attempt had not led, according to Comte, to the collapse of metaphysics; having touched on his point of view in passing, Comte left it without further attention and limited himself to dogmatic statement of the fact itself of the relativity of knowledge.[48]

2. COMTE'S THEORY OF THE RELATIVE NATURE OF KNOWLEDGE

Elements of transcendental idealism in Comte's teaching; he did not make use of them to substantiate his theory. Causes and characteristics of the relativity of knowledge.
Difficulties evoked by Comte's theory.

Under the influence of the philosophical teachings outlined above, Comte not only came to the conclusion of the relativity of knowledge, but did not hesitate in asserting that this principle of the relativity of our knowledge is the only absolute principle.

In his works Comte time and again tried to explain in what sense he called human knowledge relative, and even somewhat approximated, especially in his *Système de politique positive*, Kant's understanding of it. True, Comte asserted, probably under the influence of the philosophy of Reid[49] and his followers, that "the main principles of our real knowledge are essentially derived from the spontaneous development of human reason" and considered it fruitless to subject them to critical analysis.[50] Even so, in some instances Comte discusses knowledge as if he were under the spell of Kant. In any case positivism, according to Comte, must not be confused with empiricism: if reason is ever passive in experience, it is only at the moment of the first "impression"; the activity of reason is noticeable already with re-presentation [*povtorenie*] or even the most simple impression.[51] Thus, Comte insists "on the continual participation of reason in operations attributed to sensation alone":[52] reason gives form to the matter that is introduced [into our consciousness] by the external world.[53] Therefore, "it could never be conceived that the function through which we alone know any law, external or internal, is itself deprived of its own laws";[54] [on the basis of them?] reason "connects" the separate data of sense perception.[55] No isolated or purely empirical observation can be known for sure; "a real observation is possible only insofar as it is first made and finally interpreted according to some theory."[56] What is more: even the uniform order of nature is as much the result of our reason as of the external world, even though we cannot determine in what measure one or the other factor participates in the formation of such a concept. Be that as it may, "all our real knowledge is necessarily relative, on the one hand as a result of the environment, insofar as it is capable of acting on us, and on the other hand as a result of the organism, insofar as it is susceptible to this action."[57]

In these fragments it is easy to notice certain points of contact with transcendental idealism; nonetheless, Comte cannot, of course, be taken for either an independent representative of it, or a convinced follower of Kant. Indeed, in his fragmentary and at times extremely confused remarks on the theory of knowledge, Comte never focuses on the "unity of apperception" or on the basic principles of cognition. Recognizing a certain degree of "subjectivity" common to the entire human species and supposing that basic principles of cognition exist and that reason forms the data given in experience, he nonetheless could not renounce crude realism. Comte did not, for example, at all clearly distinguish the concept of the thinking subject's relation to the material of its sensible perceptions, on the one hand, from its relation to the environment, on the other. Apparently he sometimes saw the relativity of knowledge not in the constituent features of human consciousness, but in the results of the generalizing activity of thought: knowledge seemed relative to him to the extent it consisted of generalized representations. With such an arbitrary and wavering terminology, Comte naturally could not uphold the transcendental point of view and was in essence ready to reject the a priori nature of knowledge, since he considered it possible to ascribe, at the moment of an initial "impression" experienced by a given subject, empirical origin even to the general concepts governing that experience.[58]

Not having clarified the grounds on account of which our knowledge is relative (which likely led him to understand this relativity in very different senses), Comte could not outline the criteria and limits of knowledge; he restricted himself solely to indicating the causes of the limited nature of our scientific knowledge in particular. Such causes turn out to be: "our constitution [as an organism] and the place occupied by the knowing subject in the evolution of humanity." In fact, Comte considers the "relativity of knowledge" by returning to the idea, already widespread in the seventeenth century and explained especially well by Diderot, that if we had a different organization, our knowledge would change in a corresponding way:[59] if people were blind, astronomy would not exist as a science, while if people had new, different organs, they might well have an understanding of such phenomena as we cannot imagine. It is clear that here Comte has in mind not so much the formal characteristics of knowledge as the completeness of its content, to the extent such content derives from experience, and that therefore he is already using the term "relativity" in a new sense. The same must be said also about the second sort of circumstances giving rise to the "relativity" of our fields of knowledge: the degree of their scientific perfection depends, of course, on what stage humanity has reached in its development, and in this sense every science represents a "great social fact," changing in accordance with the state of civilization at any given time. But in considerations of this sort Comte, apparently, has in mind not our knowledge in general but the state of the various sciences at one time or another.

On the contrary, from the point of view of the constancy of the basic traits of human nature, on which Comte himself insisted, the formal characteristics of knowledge would also, so it seems, have to remain constant. Consequently, the theory of the relativity of knowledge cannot be based on the above considerations, and Comte himself apparently adduces them only in relation to positive science. Thus, it is impossible not to recognize that the doctrine of the relative nature of knowledge is espoused by Comte in the form of dogmatic propositions, relying on which he tried to claim that such relativity existed as a fact.

According to our philosopher, who strived to transform science into philosophy but not philosophy into science, man does not know absolute being, nor the first causes behind essences, nor their final ends, but only phenomena. Man must be satisfied with answers to the question "How?" but not to the questions "Why?" and "For what?" He is not capable of forming "absolute concepts," for he can know neither the internal nature (*nature intime*) of bodies or events nor the actual mode of their origin (since, for example, the causes giving rise to organic life or those spurring its development will always remain hidden from him), nor the purpose of the world. He knows facts only relatively, for he knows only the relations of "resemblance" and "succession" among them. These constant relations of resemblance and succession among phenomena are called laws.[60]

Comte's theory is based, however, on assumptions that are hardly consistent with his positivism: in his arguments about the relativity of knowledge it is easy to uncover premises that cannot be derived from his doctrine.

Indeed, Comte ascribed absolute character to the principle of the relativity of our knowledge, which does not, of course, accord with his basic theory. Further, the epistemological untenability of Comte's construction is also revealed in other respects: removing the principle of causation from his system, he deprived himself of the possibility of using perhaps the main feature distinguishing a genuine law from empirical generalization;[61] and by eliminating the principle of purposiveness he also forsook logical substantiation of a number of basic positions in science, beginning with mechanics and ending with sociology.[62] Finally, Comte expresses his firm conviction that "all phenomena, no matter what type, the most simple and most common facts, have always been regarded as essentially subject to natural laws."[63] True, he suggests that such a principle arose through slow and gradual induction, individual as well as collective; even recognition of "the fundamental universality of the laws of thought" can almost be said to have such an origin. But he does not explain on what basis we transform a generalization, obtained by induction from observed cases, into a "fundamental dogma," applicable to cases that have never been subject to observation by anyone; he is thus compelled by some force of *"irresistible analogie"* to "explain" why we acknowledge laws unknown to us as nonetheless "existing."[64] From such a point of view, the complete certainty of scientific predictions, as if they were obtained exclusively by induction, is essentially unfounded by Comte.[65]

In constructing his philosophy of the sciences, Comte was, of course, very far from solipsism. Like Reid, he considered it possible, for example, to dogmatically posit the objective existence of a certain substrate lying at the basis of real phenomena. There is also the same premise in Comte's theory of the reliability of our knowledge, since this theory rests on the correspondence (*cohérence*) of our ideas with reality.[66] At the same time, in distinguishing two types of existence in this reality, the world of essences from the world of "phenomena," Comte apparently considered it possible to recognize the border separating them from each other, for otherwise no one, including Comte himself, would be able to ask: does he know essences or only phenomena?[67]

Thus, in surveying Comte's points of departure, one cannot fail to notice that he was far from having freed himself of the worldview of the old-fashioned metaphysicians, the very worldview against which he was obliged to struggle in his *Cours de philosophie positive*. Like them he retained a naïve realism, putting it at the basis of his "positive" system, and thus remaining a dogmatist in the formulation of this system.

3. COMTE'S APPLICATION OF THE THEORY OF THE RELATIVITY OF KNOWLEDGE TO THE CONSTRUCTION OF SOCIOLOGY

> Direct application: the relativity of sociological knowledge. Indirect application by means of the systematization of the abstract sciences: sociology as the last link in this system.
> Contradictions in Comte's views.

Comte did not delay in applying the doctrine of the relativity of human knowledge to the construction of his sociology. If every abstract science investigates not essences, but only phenomena, then sociology as an abstract science, in Comte's opinion, must of course occupy itself with the same. Following the example of the other sciences, sociology must convert all social concepts from absolute to relative ones; it studies only laws in the sense indicated above. The establishment of such "natural laws" in sociology is all the more possible in that the development of humanity shows itself in very complex phenomena, where irregularities brought about by any type of individual conditions must naturally be less evident than in the other sciences.[68]

In order to fully apply the general conclusions of his theory to sociology, however, Comte also needed some new premises, which are tightly connected with his attempt to establish a system of abstract sciences.

As a result of the principle of the relativity of knowledge, man cannot, according to Comte, know one single law of the universe to which all phenomena could be traced. With the unity of the positive method, the "doctrines of positivism" are only similar (*homogène*) to each other. Each of them encompasses a group of laws delimited from other such groups by the frailty of human knowledge. Consequently, every science has its own laws, apart from the laws of the sciences standing above it. In such conditions, there arise the special sciences that Comte introduced into his well-known system.[69] Comte's system belongs to the type of so-called reconstructed classifications:[70] in his system, classification in equal measure satisfies the demands of reason and reproduces reality. Thanks to this property, as well as to the greater development of the simplest sciences over the most complex ones, Comte thought it possible to transfer methods and laws from one science to another. Thus, the content (doctrine) of every science, at least in a formal sense, is predetermined by its position in the system. Sociology, as the last link in the system, must be a science that investigates phenomena that are included, if even *implicite,* in the sphere of physiological phenomena, but which also have their own peculiarities. The phenomena observed by the sociologist depend, of course, on other phenomena, the "simplest" and more general ones, and are distinguished by the most complexity. Consequently, the sociologist studies the most concrete and particular phenomena, that is, those observed in the least number of cases. In explaining social phenomena the sociologist must thus use known laws, for example, [those constituting] natural science: they are necessary for social phenomena, but not vice versa.[71] Nonetheless sociology must be recognized as a special science and not a simple extension of physiology: "collective study of the species cannot be treated as a pure deduction from study of the individual, for social conditions, modifying the action of physiological laws, are precisely the most essential considerations in this case."[72]

All the objections that were briefly made against Comte's general theory of the relativity of knowledge are relevant, of course, in evaluating its application to the relativity of sociological knowledge. And here the claim about the "laws" of sociology and their universal significance is just as poorly substantiated as the reliability of sociological predictions. What is more, all this supposes the real existence of the object itself of sociological study, and the reliability of the results of such study.

The grouping of the sciences proposed by Comte and predetermining the task of sociology also poses great difficulties from the point of view of his theory of the relativity of knowledge and has already evoked not a few objections in the literature. On what is founded, for example, Comte's conviction in the spontaneous striving of human reason to the "unity" (*unité*) of the positivist method? And on the basis of what principles can such unity be achieved? Apparently Comte either never posed such questions to himself or consciously ignored them; in any case, not answering them, he dogmatically formulated a position that can hardly be substantiated from a purely "positive" point of view. The same precariousness is also noticeable in Comte's further assertion that his classification of the sciences is of a reconstructed character: at the basis of this claim there again lies a hidden epistemological premise about the correspondence of a logical construction with the reality of the external world. Finally it is clear that Comte, calling phenomena not only simple or complex, but also abstract or concrete, confused the objective point of view with the subjective and so gave an artificial unity to the foundation of his system of sciences.[73]

Despite all this, Comte proceeded, in formulating his sociology, from the premises indicated above; consequently such formulation suffers the same precariousness as his point of departure, from which Comte drew a further conclusion about the content of sociology: it does not differ in essence from the other sciences. Indeed, like the Encyclopedists, Comte dogmatically asserted, for example, that social phenomena are governed by entirely the same laws as are phenomena of inorganic nature;[74] hence his desire, again fully concordant with the dreams of the Encyclopedists and their immediate successors, to construct a "social physics." In fact, however, this social physics, already in the *Cours de philosophie positive,* relied quite often on collective psychology, and in the *Système de politique positive* it finally came to amount to social ethics,[75] in the sphere of which Comte's arbitrary hypotheses, thanks to his "subjective method," were easily transformed into "laws" of sociology or norms of politics.

II. Comte's Psychological Premises in Relation to His Sociology

If at the time Comte composed his *Cours,* psychology had already succeeded in acquiring significance as an autonomous science, he likely would have found it in certain warnings against applying his doctrine of the relativity of knowledge to sociology. But even after the new scientific-psychological movement took root in European thought, psychology did not at once achieve independent significance. In the first third of the nineteenth century, many representatives of French philosophy continued to conflate metaphysics with

368   A. S. Lappo-Danilevskii

psychology, while Comte's learned compatriots were for the most part attracted to "empirical or experimental psychology" and too rarely looked into
the sphere of phenomena proper to psychic life. Comte followed their example; hardly well acquainted with the rudiments of the scientific-psychological
movement, he removed psychology from his system of sciences, but nonetheless used it in constructing his sociology.

1. THE STATE OF PSYCHOLOGICAL KNOWLEDGE IN COMTE'S TIME
AND HIS RELATION TO PSYCHOLOGY

The metaphysical direction in psychology and Comte's aversion toward it. The
physiological direction in psychology: the sensualists and *idéologues* (Destutt de
Tracy and Cabanis, Gall and Broussais). Dominance of the physiological school
owing to the weakness of Maine de Biran's and Jouffroy's attempts to advance
psychology as an autonomous science.

Comte's relation to the materialists, sensualists, and *idéologues*. Comte — follower of the physiological direction in psychology; his recognition of the new
sphere of psychological inquiry into social phenomena.

In French literature at the beginning of the nineteenth century it was still
possible to encounter the old-fashioned view of psychology as a branch of
metaphysics. According to one of Comte's older contemporaries,[76] the basic
task of psychology, understood in the narrow sense, consists in knowing the
human spirit, which is drawing us ever closer to the Supreme Being; man
constitutes one of the great objects of metaphysics. Knowledge of the human
soul is possible, however, only by studying its properties (*facultés*) and sensations. To the metaphysician, man is thus endowed with will and feelings,
which are to be studied from the metaphysical point of view.[77] Even more
recently, in, for example, Cousin's brilliant lectures, it was not difficult to
hear similar pronouncements.[78] Meanwhile, Comte rejected any metaphysics.
Since psychology had not yet managed to finally free itself of metaphysics, the
founder of positivism, himself not having tried to achieve such an autonomization, naturally had to relate negatively to psychology, and so incorporated the
branches of positive knowledge relating to it partly into his biology, partly into
his sociology.

The scientific movement among the French Encyclopedists and "*idéologues*"
of the eighteenth and early nineteenth centuries led to an analogous result.

To a significant extent, eighteenth-century French materialism and sensualism prepared the physiological point of view from which Comte was ready to
examine the phenomena of mental life. Not mentioning Boerhaave's pupil[79] —
La Mettrie with his purely mechanistic understanding of human nature — the

Encyclopedists, with their goal of "studying nature as a whole" and deriving all thought from sensation alone, already paved the way for the formation of the new discipline: physiological psychology.[80] In this connection Condillac's views, as is known, received further development in the school of the *idéologues*. Destutt de Tracy, partly under Buffon's influence,[81] partly owing to his study of the works of Locke and Condillac, directly included ideology, that is, the science of human thought, in the sphere of "zoology." But, dividing ideology into two parts, "physiological" and "rational," Destutt de Tracy did not insist too sharply on the exclusive importance of "physiological" ideology, all the more so in that he himself was intensely occupied with the "rational" type, and in his study of the capacity for movement (*motilité* in the original sense) was even an immediate predecessor of [Maine de] Biran.[82] Only Cabanis, linking the origin of sense perceptions to physiological organization, can be considered a dramatic representative of the approach which concludes that the brain must be recognized as a special organ producing thought (rather than merely directing the functions of thought).[83] Broussais, who carried on Cabanis's work and was a very well known doctor in his time, went even further than Cabanis: for Broussais, sense perception (*sensibilité*) is nothing other than a product of nerve activity, passions are the effect of internal organs, and reason is something like a brain excretion. Finally, in the last period of his work, Broussais, who was generally inclined to the idea of the localization of disease processes in the organism, became a defender of phrenological theory, in which Gall,[84] an opponent of the psychologists and *idéologues,* tried to localize the instincts, affects, moral feelings, and mental "propensities" of a human being in various centers of the brain.[85]

Thus, at the time Comte was composing his *Cours,* the physiological direction in psychology had many influential adherents: it was bound to influence the ardent admirer of positive knowledge all the more in that the opposing direction was still rather weakly represented in French literature at the end of the 1820s. The attempts of Maine de Biran and Jouffroy[86] to demarcate the special sphere of mental phenomena subject to study by psychology did not at the time show much influence on the development of the science. Maine de Biran's theory of the will, which as an autonomous force is directly known by every person as his own "self," was too peculiar and expounded in the form of the most general arguments and in an extremely obscure style, none of which could attract readers with positivist tastes nurtured on the simple and clear works of Condillac, Destutt de Tracy, and their successors. Jouffroy was even less able than Maine de Biran of influencing the positivists. His theory of the "self" as a special essence causing mental phenomena, his diffuse thought and one-sided recognition of nothing except the method of introspection, and finally his contempt for objective facts were all too striking to convince his opponents of the independent significance of psychology.[87]

In such conditions Comte naturally remained under the influence of the old direction and struggled with the new "metaphysical" school in psychology, for from the point of view of the relativity of knowledge, any doctrine of the soul, the will, and even more so of the absolute unity of the "self" seemed to him "metaphysical."[88] Comte did not, however, consider himself at all a materialist: man, in his opinion, depends on the external environment, but is not created by it. In vain do materialists exaggerate the influence of external nature on man, trying to nullify the independence and spontaneity (*spontanéité*) of organic life. The dualism they would wish to remove from their system remains in force. Nor can it be maintained that Comte belonged entirely to the camp of the sensualists: he protested against the theories of Condillac, Helvétius and in general of the eighteenth-century "metaphysicians," reproaching them for not ascribing any significance "in their psychology" to the "predisposition of the internal cerebral organs" and for deriving all mental life from the activity of the external senses.[89]

Finally, the doctrine of the *idéologues* also seemed not fully satisfactory to Comte, since they neglected feeling too much in favor of reason.[90] Nonetheless, Comte proceeded mainly from the views of the most important *idéologues*.[91] Agreeing with Destutt de Tracy that ideology must be a part of zoology, Comte saw, however, that Tracy then retreated from his main position, which is why Comte continued to call him a metaphysician. Only Cabanis, in his well-known work on the relation of physical factors to moral ones, first attempted, in the opinion of our philosopher, to introduce moral phenomena into the sphere of physiology.[92] Broussais also enjoyed great authority in Comte's eyes: his treatise on irritability and insanity (*Traité de l'irritation et de la folie,* 1828) earned Comte's full approval as a book useful most of all for protecting the reader from "psychological infection" or for curing him of its baneful consequences.[93] Finally, Comte rated the works of Gall even more highly than Broussais's treatise, thinking that Gall had once and for all subordinated psychology to the physiological point of view: in his opinion, the mental propensities innate to a person can be studied only insofar as they are manifested in bodily organs. Comte did not, however, accept Gall's theory without reservations: acknowledging the innateness of mental propensities and their distinctness, as well as the principle of localization, Come did not consider Gall's attempt to employ this principle to be successful and objected to his theory of the differentiation of the basic faculties (*facultés*). Agreeing with Spurzheim's view,[94] Comte suggested that in themselves our faculties do not lead to a predetermined type and degree of activity; only various combinations of them and the right circumstances (*l'ensemble des circonstances corre-spondantes*) produce definite results.[95]

Thus, generally submitting to the influence of the physiological direction in psychology, Comte, following the example of its most prominent representatives, saw virtually the fundamental task of psychological research in explaining "from the static point of view" the organic conditions on which so-called mental phenomena depend. "The positive theory of affective and intellectual functions," he wrote in his *Cours*, "is therefore always conceived as consisting in the study ... of the diverse phenomena of the sensibility inherent to the cerebral ganglions ...; this theory is only a simple extension of animal psychology, properly speaking."[96]

Comte, while fully recognizing the importance of this new branch of "animal physiology" as a science of the future, was at the same time extremely disdainful of psychology as a science studying the phenomena of individual consciousness. Nor could it be otherwise. From the point of view of his theory of the relativity of knowledge, Comte could recognize neither the worldview of Cousin or Jouffroy, nor their method of psychological research. Comte forgot, as it were, about the existence of other directions in psychology; polemicizing with Cousin's religious-metaphysical views or with Jouffroy's method of "inner observation," he came to reject psychology itself, to the extent it investigates the phenomena of individual consciousness. Despite the fact that Condorcet, Comte's "spiritual father," had already pointed to introspection as the source of our knowledge about man—insofar as he is a being capable of feeling, reasoning, and acquiring moral concepts—Comte firmly denied the suitability of such a method. To a significant degree under the influence of Gall and Broussais, he suggested that introspection, while it can very likely be applied to weak sensations, since they have different "organs" than thought in the narrow sense, is not suitable for study of the latter. A very broad and important group of mental phenomena is not, according to Comte, accessible to introspection: the mental life of animals and children, as well as pathological cases, for example. No introspection is possible, moreover, of a mental event at the moment of its occurrence in the consciousness of the observer; it is impossible to "look at yourself at the moment you are thinking." Nor does strong agitation, caused by passion, facilitate introspection, yet such cases merit special study. Thus, in Comte's opinion, the method of introspection, producing a mass of contradictory conclusions, possesses no positive significance, and with it collapses any possibility of studying the phenomena of individual consciousness apart from external manifestations.[97]

Nonetheless, it should be noted that Comte himself tried to save his followers from excessive enthusiasm for biology. "With regard to methodology,"

372 A. S. Lappo-Danilevskii

he wrote, "the logical analogy between biology and sociology is too obvious to
need to especially insist here on the irrefutable necessity for sociologists to first
prepare their intellect by a suitably thorough study of biological methods."[98]
The author of the *Cours,* it is clear, thus insisted that biology had more of a
methodological than a phenomenological significance for sociologists. Yet
"the pernicious predominance of biological considerations [in sociological
doctrine], and the irrational disdain for historical notions, have led," in the
opinion of our philosopher, "to a profound underestimation of true social
evolution, and to the supposition of a chimerical *fixité* for dispositions that are
essentially variable."[99] Humanity cannot, for example, be compared to something like a giant polyp, for such a comparison "leads to the conflation of a free
(*volontaire*) and facultative association with an involuntary and inseparable
one." In general, Comte did not think that conclusions deduced from biology
had exclusive significance for sociology, and considered it necessary to employ
induction here.[100] Comte's warnings did not, however, keep him from excessive enthusiasm for the biological point of view. He included study of the
phenomena of individual consciousness in biology, but, perhaps influenced by
the above point of view, he also came to study such phenomena apart from
biology — in sociology.

Together with elucidation of the organic conditions on which psychic phenomena depend, Comte did in fact consider it desirable to investigate the
external manifestations of individual mental life in society. One of the *idéologues,* Destutt de Tracy, already turned attention, although only in passing, to
this task; Cabanis as well supported such a principle in, for example, the study
of the influence of sex on the psychological characteristics of people. Nonetheless Comte reproaches Cabanis, and Gall and Broussais as well, precisely for
restricting all phenomena of mental life to the sphere of physiology.[101] According to his opinion, perhaps formed under Hume's influence, physiological
psychology is to be supplemented with observation of the "actual course of
development of human thought in the history of humanity"; it is clear that
such a task must be examined from a dynamic point of view.[102]

Thus, in Comte's eyes psychology lost its independent significance: it became in part a subdivision of biology, in part a subdivision of sociology.

2. PSYCHIC FACTORS OF SOCIAL LIFE IN COMTE'S SOCIOLOGY

Comte's warnings against enthusiasm for biology and his theory of the distinctness of the sciences did not keep him from an exclusively biological point of view
on individual psychology. Absence of evidence on behalf of such a view. A shift in
Comte's method of psychological observation: analysis of mental phenomena and

introspection. Comte's denial of the will, and yet acknowledgment of it as a factor in social life. The role of "affective faculties" in Comte's sociology; inclinations and feelings. Emotions in social statics, especially the feelings of sympathy, cooperation, and solidarity; their significance in social unions. Emotions in social dynamics: the instinct for improvement, boredom. The role of intellectual faculties in Comte's sociology: isolation of feeling from reason; recognition of intellectualized emotions. Growing influence of intellectual faculties on the progressive development of humanity; psychological formula of progress. Consequences resulting from Comte's rejection of psychology and from his recognition of psychic factors in social life.

Comte did not succeed in suitably applying his point of view to explanation of the phenomena of mental life: apparently he considered it superfluous to demonstrate the legitimacy of his supposition that all psychic phenomena have an exclusively physiological origin. Consequently, this formula was no less dogmatic than the several others we have referred to above.

In many cases insisting too strongly on the distinctness of the spheres of scientific knowledge, by virtue of which he almost had to leap from one to the other, Comte apparently did not consider it necessary to take account of this principle in deriving psychology from biology: he recognizes that physics and chemistry, for example, are particular and independent sciences, but does not agree to recognize the same distinctness between biology and psychology, and yet at the same time distinguishes biology from sociology and even sociology from ethics.[103]

As a result of this flaw, Comte himself gradually passed to study of the psychic factors in social phenomena, which naturally altered his relation to psychology. In fact, depending on how much of his system he had completed, Comte came to increasingly ascribe real significance to his psychological terms: in the *Système de politique positive,* he is already using the "subjective method" to engage in "positive study of intellectual and moral functions" and has posed as his main task not the localization of these functions, but rather "a sufficiently deep appreciation of intellectual and moral existence."[104] From such a point of view Comte easily proceeded to the proper sphere of psychological research, and in fact his theory in its final form produces the impression of a number of phrenological conclusions from psychological observations, rather than physiological explanation of the phenomena of mental life.[105]

Not entering into evaluation of such phenomena from the perspective of individual psychology, we shall turn our attention only to Comte's conclusion about introspection, since it is very important for characterization of his negative view of psychology and for subsequent construction of his sociological doctrine.

Comte resolutely rejects the significance of introspection, and yet also states that by means of introspection it is possible to confirm the laws revealed in social evolution, and he uses it in demonstrating his main "law" of the three stages.[106] Here Comte is likely under the influence of Condorcet. Having established his concept of the "progress of the human mind," Condorcet remarks that such progress is subject to the same general laws observed in the individual development of our capabilities, because progress, the result of the latter, is found simultaneously in a large number of individuals united in society.[107] Comte makes precisely the same argument. He elevates the psychic process of the individual to a general law of sociology. The "general course of the development of the human spirit," he observes, "can be easily ascertained today, in a very tangible if indirect manner, by considering the development of the individual intellect. ... Does not each of us remember, in thinking over his own life history, being ... a theologian in childhood, a metaphysician in youth, and a physicist as an adult?"[108] Such "verification" of the law of the successive change of these worldviews is, in Comte's opinion, accessible to anyone with a modern level of education.[109] Comte recommends that every educated person confirm for himself the truth of this basic "law" through inner observation, which he himself identifies so closely with psychology and against which he protests so strongly in other parts of his *Cours*. Thus, we cannot, with Comte, hold introspection in contempt, even if we do not ascribe it the significance of a special method in psychology, although it does have such significance in psychology today.[110] Experimental psychology could hardly manage without introspection, and Comte himself, of course, used it when he was occupied with phrenology, especially later in compiling his "*tableau cérèbral*" in the *Système de politique positive*.[111]

Be that as it may, Comte, in rejecting individual psychology (on the grounds, incidentally, that it relies on introspection), deprived himself of the possibility of substantiating his sociology.

Comte's superficial observations about self-consciousness — which he defines as the notion, arising in a given subject, of a sense of harmony among the diverse functions of its organism — cannot, of course, be recognized as a satisfactory attempt to explain the very concept of "subject." Comte was also very little concerned to elaborate a theory of the unity and continuity of individual consciousness: only in his work on politics, in deliberating about "the soul as the truly fundamental harmony between the heart and reason," did he suggest that "the unity and continuity of existence in every animal is maintained through the constant vigil kept by the mass of its affective faculties."[112] On such shaky grounds it was hardly possible to construct a solid concept of the subject in the psychological, and consequently in the moral and juridical sense:

and in fact Comte ignores this concept and ends up denying the human person any rights whatsoever.

In the majority of cases, however, Comte's negative relation to psychology did not prevent him from widely using its material in explaining the phenomena of social life.

Like the main representatives of the physiological school, Comte generally disparages the theory of the will; in his *Cours* he came out on behalf of determinism and completely rejected the possibility of man "at will (*à son gré*) altering (*transformer*) his own spiritual nature." But already in the *Système de politique positive* Comte's approach to the theory of the will has apparently changed somewhat. Here he discusses some kind of "energy of the heart," and then defines the will "as the last stage of desire," ensuing once a person has decided that his dominant impulse is advantageous [for achieving a given goal].[113] Since without the will there can be no influence of the individual on the surrounding environment, even if such influence is expressed here only in "secondary" effects, it follows that "the direct and complete objective manifestation of the life" of each of us "is mainly characterized by the will."[114] Thus, rejecting "voluntarism" in his *Cours,* Comte allotted the volitional principle a highly visible role in his *Politique;* but really already in the *Cours* Comte gave the will the significance of almost an independent factor in the phenomena of social life, and only clarified his point of view in the treatise on politics. At the very least he often discusses the will in precisely such a sense in both works. Explaining, for example, the emergence of human speech by the action of purely emotional factors, Comte conceives its development as taking place through the replacement of "involuntary signs" with voluntary ones.[115] Further, in his sociology Comte discusses "voluntary relations" (*relations volontaires*), "cooperatives, arising naturally or by agreement," "the free and deliberate effect of our political combinations on the development of humanity," "the voluntary subordination of our minds to spiritual authority," "voluntary" town unions, "the artificiality and arbitrariness of the social order," and so on, without ever explaining in what sense he is using all these expressions.[116] Finally, in his theory of progress Comte is also prepared to recognize the essential significance of this same factor, as in, for example, "the desire for the better," the importance of which the Scottish school already indicated as a characteristic feature of "the progressive nature of man." Comte, likely influence by the school, claimed that man strives "in all respects to always develop the totality of his physical, moral, and intellectual life, to the extent this is permitted by the set of circumstances in which he then finds himself."[117] In his last work Comte ascribed to the "will" primary significance in the "perfecting of universal harmony."[118]

Comte also adheres to the same psychological terminology in his deliberations on the role of feelings in the phenomena of sociability. Following the
example of Cabanis and Gall, he distinguished "affective faculties" from "intellectual" ones, and in defining their relation to each other was perhaps influenced by Hume, who claimed that "reason is, and ought to be the slave of the
passions";[119] in any event he was in accordance with Gall's theory. In fact
Comte, like Gall, gave affects predominant significance in the psychic life of
man and sharply isolated them from reason. Comte's classification of affects is
done not from a physiological but rather from a psychological point of view.
From their composition he gradually derived individual-social feelings, such
as "pride" and "vanity" — which "are essentially personal by their origin and
end, but they become social by their means of satisfaction"[120] — and under
"social" he included "affection, respect, and love." Although social feelings
(affections sociales) are less intense than personal passions, nonetheless they
are the foundation of society and maintain it despite very powerful individual
inclinations.[121]

In his social statics Comte gives great significance to emotions. They lie at the
basis of social order: stable conviction is grounded in them.[122] The condition
into which revolution has plunged people will end only when "reason becomes
subordinate to the heart," for feeling, less clouded than reason [by revolutionary metaphysics], will promote the restoration of order; only in such a situation
will morality acquire leading significance in our society.[123] Comte's psychological point of view emerges still more clearly than before in his considerations
about the role he gives to basic social "instincts" in the formation of human
associations. Thus, for example, like the most important representatives of the
Scottish school, Comte came to point to sympathy [simpatiia] as a factor in
sociability.[124] Hume, and Smith after him, defined sympathy as a mental state
arising because we, in observing an expression of joy or sorrow in other people,
or in vividly imagining the causes of such states, evoke in ourselves a real feeling
of joy or sorrow.[125] Comte apparently accepts this definition, or at least nowhere proposes his own physiologically based definition, and only in passing
wonders at the spontaneity that irresistibly draws us to take part in the "joy" of
beings resembling us. At the same time the definition of sympathy accepted by
Comte gives us reason to suppose that he used the term "sympathy" mainly in a
psychological sense. Not for nothing did he sometimes call sympathy a "social
feeling" and identify it at one moment with "bienveillance," a term highly
reminiscent of Hume's "benevolence,"[126] and at another moment, most often in
the Système de politique positive, with "love."[127]

Comte distinguishes the "instinct of sympathy," which he obviously con-
flates with highly complex emotions, from "feelings of cooperation and solidarity." By the "feeling of cooperation" Comte apparently means the feeling

that arises within a member of a given undertaking as a result of consciousness of participating in it.[128] Still broader is the "feeling of solidarity": The very term "solidarity" has various meanings in Comte: in some cases he uses it to designate the mutual dependence among parts of a whole; in other cases he means the consciousness of such dependence, which gives rise to a "feeling of solidarity."[129] It is clear that Comte uses both terms in a psychological sense. The intellectualized character of the "feeling of solidarity" serves as a superfluous argument on behalf of our supposition: such a feeling forms under the influence of the concept of the dependence that exists not only among "contemporary individuals and peoples," but also among preceding and following generations.[130] Examples of such a substitution of physiological considerations with psychological ones can also be found in Comte's later deliberations about the family, which is "based" mainly on "affection and gratitude," and about the social union, which requires "a community of certain basic concepts, beliefs, and moral convictions." Finally, the social and state order also presupposes, according to Comte, "a feeling of respect" among subsequent generations for preceding ones, and society's "trust" in governmental power.[131] Thus, in his social statics Comte gradually abandons the physiological ground and passes to the sphere of the study of emotions as psychic factors of sociability, in which he unquestionably showed subtle power of observation and great power of generalization.

Something similar also happened with Comte's social dynamics: and here he relies not so much on a physiological as on a psychological understanding of emotions. He himself noted that "a methodological treatise on political philosophy should undoubtedly first analyze the individual motives that form the proper elements of the progressive force behind the human species, relating them to this fundamental instinct ... that directly drives man to unceasingly improve his given condition in all respects."[132] Further, in studying the secondary factors that promote the acceleration of development, Comte, following the example of [Georges] Leroy, points to "boredom,"[133] and in his treatise on politics also directs attention to the feeling for the continuity of development, by virtue of which people always sense that they are located within the whole formed by their ancestors and descendants.[134]

Comte's sociology shows still another psychological concession in constantly enlisting reason as a psychic factor behind progress. In accordance with Gall's theory of the distinctness of human faculties, Comte liked to treat emotions and reason in isolation; such a point of view led to one of Comte's most substantial errors in his theory of morality, which he often confused with simple feeling, tenderness, etc.[135] Nonetheless he acknowledged the possibility of the formation of intellectualized feelings.[136] In his statics Comte already pointed, for example, to the "feeling of solidarity," but this feeling, as we were obliged to note above, cannot arise without the help of sufficiently complex and abstract concepts. In his social dynamics Comte also allocates an essential role to intellectual faculties in the progressive development of humanity. For example, he explains the later development of language by the replacement of emotions with intellectual factors, thanks to which language becomes a means for communicating not so much feelings as thoughts.[137] In general Comte did not a little for clearer awareness of the growing influence, on the course of the development of humanity, of the intellectual state generally common to everyone having a philosophical Weltanschauung. The vague reference that Comte sometimes makes in such arguments to the necessity of studying "the faculties of man located in the frontal portion of the brain" poorly conceals a different conception. In his consideration of the influence of fetishism on the transition of human societies from hunting and raising livestock to agriculture he, for example, directly ascribes decisive significance to "spiritual" factors, "essencially distinct and independent of material factors," and even by these latter he meant mainly intellectual factors.[138] The same point of view generally comes through in his explanation of the characteristics of the "theological" period in modern times, as well as in his belief about the role the positive philosophy must play in the immediate future.[139] If we recall that in Comte's opinion "feelings are the motive forces of our existence," then his historical construction as well at once takes on a psychological coloring: in all the above arguments Comte in essence assumes the possibility of the influence of a general philosophical worldview on the activity of people, through the formation in them of intellectualized feelings. Gradually improving themselves, people also engender progress in the life activity of human societies; with this the excessive predominance of "affective life" over "intellectual life" progressively diminishes.[140]

Thus, rejecting "psychology" on the grounds that it belongs to "metaphysics," Comte denied himself the possibility of psychologically substantiating his sociological premises; passing over clarification of the foundations of knowledge of social phenomena, he could not base the social sciences on clear concepts of the phenomena of consciousness. Comte's desire to study social phenomena from completely the same point of view as the phenomena of unconscious nature did not find support in his psychology: he directed too little attention, for example, to the theory of the will, [a neglect] which few scholars today would countenance,[141] and thus virtually forsook explanation of the correlation that exists between concepts of the will and those of the "laws" of social phenomena. And yet nonetheless he constantly resorted to many psychological facts and methods in constructing his sociology. Not mentioning the internal contradiction into which Comte thus fell, it should be noted that in scorning psychology he of course used it quite arbitrarily: it needs only to be recalled how he treats volitional processes, how loose is his concept of the "instinct" of sympathy, how difficult it is to grasp the precise sense of his "feeling of solidarity," how he admits into his concept of society a multitude of psychic factors without adequately clarifying their meaning, and finally how he introduces into his definition of the progressive development of humanity a psychological point of view that he quite declined to substantiate in advance. In such conditions Comte could not relate the principles of psychology to those of sociology, thus clearly giving a dogmatic character to his sociological structure, which he was not able to sustain on the heights of truly positive knowledge alone.

III. Comte's Sociological Principles

The features indicated above of Comte's epistemological and psychological views are reflected clearly enough in his sociology: diligently avoiding any type of "metaphysical" premises, he was impelled, however, to admit many of them, surreptitiously or openly, into his "social physics," as a result of which he fell into essential contradictions with his own theory of knowledge. Let us try from precisely such a point of view to look at the most important "principles" of Comte's sociology. There are, it seems, no less than four, namely: (1) the principle of "the conditions of existence"; (2) the principle of the uniformity of human nature; (3) the principle of "consensus," that is, concordance among the elements of any given group of social phenomena; and (4) the principle of evolution.

1. THE PRINCIPLE OF THE CONDITIONS OF EXISTENCE

The concept of the environment among Comte's immediate predecessors: the theory of the physical environment; origins of the theory of the social environment in Helvétius, Turgot, d'Holbach, Saint-Simon, and Robert Owen.

Comte's theory of the environment; he does not distinguish between the concepts of environment and social environment. Substitution of the principle of causation by that of the conditions of existence; Comte's confusion of the logical point of view with the phenomenological. Objections against such a substitution and Comte's contradictions with his own premise. Substitution of the principle of purposiveness with that of "the conditions of existence"; Comte's recognition of the principle of purposiveness in its objective significance, contradicting such a substitution.

[...]

Comte considered it possible to use his "principle" of the environment to banish any teleology from sociological deliberations. "According to the example of physiologists," he tried to replace the principle of purposiveness with his "principle of the conditions of existence," but here he apparently considered it sufficient to demonstrate "the positive transformation of the doctrine of final causes or ends" only with respect to "the most important social dispositions." To the extent it is possible to judge from an extremely obscure suggestion, he thought it possible to derive the history of humanity from these social dispositions, as if they were conditions of human existence, without resorting to any teleological considerations.[142] Apart from the fact that the absolute character of such an assertion remains unproven from the point of view of the relativity of knowledge, Comte's argument can hardly be considered substantiated in many other respects as well: he himself not only often argued from the subjective-teleological point of view (see below), but was ready to assign objective significance to the principle of purposiveness. In his "plan for the reorganization of scientific works," he, for example, already indicated that from the static point of view any society, regardless of its quantitative composition, "can exist only where there is a general goal for the activity of all private efforts."[143] If, in addition, Comte's argument about the environment is extended, then it easily leads to the same understanding of a goal or end in social dynamics as well. But most of all it is to be noted that from Comte's argument it is not clear precisely which social dispositions should, in his opinion, be considered the most important and in what sense; do the same dispositions remain predominant or does primacy belong to different faculties, depending on the circumstances?

In any event, Comte's conclusions are far from fully consistent: first, he states that man's characteristic dispositions not only remain "one and the same," but their coordination "or equilibrium cannot be displaced," such that even in our time part of the direction of human activity is given by affective faculties; then he points to the gradual reduction of "the extreme preponderance of affective over intellectual life," to next recognize that the intellect is acquiring leading significance in human development; and, finally, in the last part of his *Cours*, he ascribes such a leading role to ethics.[144] Thus, the coordination of "dispositions" does not remain constantly one and the same over the course of the entire development of humanity, but Comte does not explain how it can change. It will not do to derive such a change from only the external conditions of existence, if only because "the organism is not the result of the environment, but only presupposes it," as well as because man can influence his own nature and because the source of social changes, as Comte himself recognizes, is not only perturbations in the environment but also "modifications" of it by man's conscious and free action (*action volontaire*). True, Comte dogmatically avoids working out a theory of the will in his psychology, depriving himself of the possibility of at least psychologically clarifying the concept of an end, as the moment orienting any volitional act; nonetheless he makes use of such a concept when needed and even concedes its influence on the "degree" of intensity of "the tendencies (*tendances*) inherent to a given social situation."[145] What is more, the influence of human consciousness on the social environment not only exists, according to Comte, but increases with the development of humanity. Recognition of this type of influence obviously had to lead Comte to the conclusion that consciousness has independent significance in the progressive development of humanity, to the extent humanity is capable of recognizing the goal or end of such development.[146] Consequently, Comte's attempt to reduce "the doctrine of final causes" to "the principle of the environment" in sociology can hardly be recognized as entirely successful: Comte himself apparently suggested that the principle of the environment, as he formulates it, does not in the least exclude the principle of purposiveness, understood even in its objective sense.

2. THE PRINCIPLE OF THE UNIFORMITY OF HUMAN NATURE

The concept of the uniformity of human nature among Comte's immediate predecessors. Absence of precise formulation of this principle in Comte's sociology. Uniformity of human knowledge. Uniformity in the recognition of another animal being. Affinity of affective and intellectual faculties in people. Comte's omissions and mistakes in defining the principle of the uniformity of human nature. Constancy of the uniformity of human nature. Biological premises from which Comte derives this constancy. Absence of a psychic justification of it. The link between the principle of the constancy of the uniformity of human nature and the laws of sociology; Comte's neglect of studying this link.
[...]

3. THE PRINCIPLE OF "CONSENSUS"

The principle of "consensus" among Comte's immediate predecessors.

Comte's attempt to substantiate the principle of "consensus." Its significance in his sociology.

Excessive generality of Comte's formula. His inclusion of the principles of causation and purposiveness in the concept of consensus; application of the concept from the objective-teleological point of view in the "religion of humanity."
[...]

Comte gave the concept of "consensus" [*konsensus*] the broadest significance: any system of elements, even, for example, astronomy, can in his opinion be examined from such a point of view. But there are "immense differences of intensity and variety" within consensus: it "becomes ever more inherent and marked in application to phenomena that are gradually more complex and less general";[147] consequently, concordance is most evident in social phenomena, which are distinguished in their coexistence with one another by "inner affinity."[148] Thus, the effect and influence that different elements of a given social system continuously exert on one another, whereby every element is always more or less directly in contact (*touché*) with the aggregate of all the others, leads to a natural harmony among the coexisting parts of the social system. Such is the solidarity among the sciences, where the state of one now affects the others, or the solidarity between the state of civilization of a given society and its corresponding political system.[149] From this, Comte derives the basic principle of social statics, namely the principle of the concordance of social phenomena (*consensus universel*), on account of which the elements of a given social system are always seen as striving to solidarity with one another.

[. . .]

Comte included in his concept of "consensus" the very same principles of causation and purposiveness that he rejected in his theory of knowledge. In fact, even simple social interaction between two individuals can, if it is of a certain duration, be examined from the point of view of the concordance of its elements; and the concept of interaction between them cannot be constructed without such principles. Comte himself in essence admitted them into his construction. Often repeating that individuals "act" on each other, he obviously conceived the relation between them not in the form of mere succession: any "action" supposes a certain expenditure of force, no matter how we understand its nature, and it goes without saying that every conscious (volitional) action cannot be conceived other than as directed toward a certain end.

[. . .]

Comte's teleological point of view is also evident in his opinion that we must conceive concordance not only as mutual "solidarity among elements of a given social system," but also as "harmony" between parts and the whole. Such a point of view already clearly comes through in Comte's biological arguments. Thus, following Kant but without his consistency, Comte observes that we cannot understand an organism without thinking of its elements as parts of a whole.[150] Consequently, proper study of the elements of a given organism already supposes a certain knowledge of it as a whole: "a living being [must] therefore cease to be defined as a collection of organs, as if they could exist separately"; in biology "the general idea of such a being always precedes an idea of any of its parts."[151] Comte brought the same principle, of course, to sociology: in his opinion it must, more than any other science, logically apply this principle to investigation of social phenomena; with the exception of truly preliminary research, any inquiry into the various elements of a given social system, if it takes them separately, must be considered a completely "irrational and sterile" method here.[152] Thus, the principle of purposiveness, in Comte's opinion, serves first of all as a basic tenet of social statics, to the extent it acquires applicability to the field through the principle of "consensus."

Comte, however, far from always applied his principle with adequate caution, especially in the *Système de politique positive*. In the *Cours* he discusses it first of all as a "concept," with the help of which social phenomena are to be studied; but already here he does not distinguish the principle of consensus from the very fact of its actual existence, and in his later work he ascribes it, as an existing fact, a completely exclusive role. From a truly human point of view, Comte remarks, "a human being, properly speaking, is basically nothing but a pure abstraction; there is nothing more real than humanity, especially in the intellectual and moral sphere."[153] It is not quite clear whether Comte took this claim as only a subjective principle or whether he gave it real significance.[154] In any event, the subjective significance of the principle of consensus faded when Comte began to discuss an objectively existing humanity, calling it a "collective organism." From such a point of view it was easy to treat a human being as a "pure abstraction" and to recognize the "reality" of humanity alone. And in fact Comte deduced from his principle consequences that were in accord with it having either a real or even a moral sense. Thus, the human person, taken in itself, loses any significance for Comte. In the future positive social order, it is first of all subject to obligations but not endowed with rights; it really serves only as a means for achieving the general end of humanity. Ultimately Comte developed his theory by means of considerations that were not scientific but rather "religious" in character. His thinking apparently consisted in the notion that humanity must be understood not only in a methodological but also in a "religious" sense; in the course of his earthly life a human being as a "separately existing" individual strives to serve humanity, but becomes an "organ" of it only after death, when his "objective" existence is transformed into a "subjective" one, that is, when he will exist in the concept of "humanity."[155] Thus, applying his principle of consensus to construction of the "religious" concept of the *Grand Être,* Comte began to speak of the "existence" or "reality" of this principle; from the religious point of view the human person was finally dissolved in the "collective organism," to the extent the latter became a transitional moment in the life of the Grand Être.[156] "The true purpose of our objective existence," Comte writes, "is to pass on to our descendants the progressive heritage that we received from our ancestors, but in an improved form";[157] every human being becomes a simple organ of the Grand Être.[158]

Thus, it cannot be said that Comte adequately substantiated the "principle of consensus" of social phenomena or clarified its meaning in sociology; he uses it too arbitrarily and for ends that lie beyond the scientific horizon.

4. THE PRINCIPLE OF EVOLUTION

The concept of progress among French writers of the eighteenth century and changes in its formulation at the beginning of the nineteenth century. The principle of development in Comte's sociology. Objections against his theory and Comte's own contradictions; his combination of the concept of development with that of progress. The principle of progress in Comte's sociology; the subjective significance he gives it; the historical process from the point of view of intellectual and moral progress. Application of the principle of progress to explanation of the struggle between affects and the intellect, egoism and altruism. The fiction of one people, progressively developing, and of an abstract representation of the historical process. Objective significance of progress in Comte. Objective-psychological significance of the principle of purposiveness, as a condition of the objectification of progress. The immanent goal of progress, as an objective fact: intellectual and moral perfection. The final goal of progress and explanation of the historical process from Comte's point of view.

The principle of moral duty and its relation to the principle of progress as moral perfectibility in Comte's theory. His wavering in defining morality; morality in the sense of "ought." Difficulties with the "positive" formulation of the idea of "what ought to be." New contradictions in Comte with his determination of the relations between the concepts of morality and the *Grand Être*. The final goal of progress as the combination of a moral end with positivism, and consciousness of them as a factor in the further perfectibility of humanity.

Conclusion: Comte's confusion of the diverse meanings of the principle of evolution.

Representatives of eighteenth-century Enlightenment philosophy eagerly discussed the concept of the perfectibility [*sovershenstvovanie*] of humanity and looked at it from the most diverse points of view, but the influence on Comte came mainly through Enlightenment writing in France, where the ardent champions of the idea of progress were Turgot, Condorcet and many of their successors. Turgot's well-known argument already contains the germs of almost all subsequent theory on the progressive development of humanity: he pointed to the cultural legacy passed on by preceding generations to following ones, to the constantly (albeit not without temporary hesitations) growing and accelerating perfectibility of this legacy in humanity as a whole, and to progress in the intellectual life of humanity. The latter is expressed in the succession of three stages, later called theological, metaphysical, and positive; such perfectibility has no determined limit (*perfectibilité indéfinie*).[159] Condorcet only formulated more sharply than his predecessor the basic claims of the same theory: he was the "first" to clearly establish the concept of the continuity of development, to the extent it is evident in the social progress of humanity, taken as a whole, and to give primary significance in it to the progressive development of the mind (*lumières*), which carries with it progress in all other respects. The gradual, but true, progress of humanity is limitless, according to Condorcet, in the sense that it is conceived by us in the form of an infinite process of improvements, the limit of which is unknown to us; the question whether this limit will prove to be higher than any particular specification remains open.[160] After, however, Turgot and Condorcet discussed the perfectibility of humanity, the concept was made more complicated by romanticism and several other cultural moments. At the beginning of the nineteenth century French society began to take an interest in morality and to lose its former facile approach to religion. Moral perfectibility began to be posed together with and even higher than the perfectibility of the mind. Already in the works of the *idéologues,* who loved to talk about the perfectibility of the mind, it is possible to find signs of the new attitude: in 1798 Destutt de Tracy, for example, remarked that the perfectibility of ideology depends on the progress of "physics," and then it is morality's turn. Cabinis expressed analogous views.[161] The *idéologues* did not, however, ascribe independent significance to morality. Saint-Simon looked at it differently. The "new Christians," in his opinion, must recognize the "doctrine of the moral perfectibility of humanity" as most important of all; with time, Saint-Simon even started to conflate morality with "religion," to which he allotted a "leading" role in society.[162]

All these thinkers adhered to naïve realism, as a result of which they examined progress as an objectively existing fact. Understanding of it became deeper after Kant pointed to the principle of purposiveness as a guiding idea in comprehending the historical process, complex in the highest degree and not subject to mechanical explanation. Kant also noted the close link between the notion that history follows a course and the concept of its systematic development and final (and thus rational) goal. Kant's work on the philosophy of history was familiar to early nineteenth-century French literature through three translations.[163]

French thought of the time, however, hardly succeeded in properly assimilating Kant's point of view or in consistently applying it to study of the history of humanity.[164]

The very fact of human progress was clearer to the new generation than before. Thanks to the appearance in Paris of the "savage" found in Aveyron, and to information collected by various explorers (for example, [Louis Antoine de] Bougainville, [James] Cook and [Jean François de Galaup] La

Pérouse) about the tribes in the New World and Oceania, it was now possible
to point to a number of successive states of civilization, "beginning with the
Aveyron savage, followed by the inhabitants of the shores of the Strait of
Magellan, and ending with the Europeans."[165] Further, the French Romantic
school, in establishing the positive significance of the Middle Ages, showed the
existence of uninterrupted progress in Europe's own history; the same opinion
was also held by people with a different outlook.[166] Finally, the rapid development in recent times of positive scientific knowledge, especially in France,
excluded the possibility of doubting the progressive development of society,
which nonetheless remained fairly low in other respects. In such circumstances
it was natural to not only study the life of humanity from the evolutionary
point of view, but to recognize progress as real.

All these waverings in understanding the main goal of humanity's development and in the methods of studying such development also influenced in an
essential way Comte's theory of evolution: having first tried to formulate his
principle of evolution in its subjective sense, independently of the idea of
"perfectibility," he ended up recognizing the objective existence of humanity's
moral perfectibility.

Comte in fact begins his deliberations on evolution by declaring that the
"concept" of development must not to be confused with the term "perfectibility." Social dynamics, in Comte's words, studies nothing but the succession of
social phenomena that comes to light in "the simple spontaneous unfolding
(essor spontané) — gradually fostered by a suitable culture — of our preexisting
fundamental faculties, which constitute the totality of our nature."[167] Such a
slow, gradual, and also continuous movement, occurring by virtue of an invariable law, is called development.[168] Social dynamics observes development
in "the gradually growing and always increasingly evident influence of earlier
human generations on later ones," whereby "each successive state of society is
conceived as the necessary result of the preceding state and as the indispensable motive force behind the next one."[169]

Apart from the fact that Comte, in his definition of development, did not
explain in what sense he understood as objectively existing either the concept
of the time over which development takes place or ideas about the general law
of development, his theory of the influence of one generation on another does
not fully concur with the premises themselves of "positive" philosophy. Judging by Comte's expressions "result" and "motive force," he conceived the
preceding state of society as the cause producing the next one.[170] Moreover, in
maintaining the constancy of such influence, he took the very link between
cause and effect to be a general law. In this case as well, however, Comte did
not explain how preceding generations influence succeeding ones. Be that as it

may, it is clear that Comte tried to base his principle of development on the same principle of causation he so vehemently rejected in the positive philosophy. Furthermore, in the space of a few pages Comte calls the development of humanity a "philosophical conception," but then discusses it as a "fact, not open to doubt,"[171] thus confusing the "conception" he uses to examine reality with assertion of the actual existence of its object. In the case at hand this contradiction did not lead to exceedingly harmful consequences for the theory as a whole, because apparently Comte had not yet included ideas of an end or goal in his concept of development.

Teleology did not delay, however, in revealing itself in Comte's thought, when he began to see the existence of improvement [*uluchshenie*] alongside "development." Development, in Comte's view, entails improvement, if one speaks not about one people, in the life of which there might not be progress, but about humanity as a whole: improvement in it comes to light not only in the conditions of life, but also in human capabilities, where improvement can mainly be called perfectibility.[172] Meanwhile, not considering whether development without a goal makes any sense, Comte combines the concept of development with that of progress, and in particular with perfectibility, thereby himself including purposiveness in his principle of evolution. As a result, Comte began to give the principle of evolution, essentially transformed as it was into the principle of progress, highly diverse meanings, depending on his wavering in understanding purposiveness.

Initially Comte was apparently inclined to use evolutionary teleology only as a subjective, albeit leading, principle. The concept of progress, in his opinion, must not be confused with that of revolution; all progress is nothing other than the development of order, development "that is subject to constant conditions and takes place by certain laws determining its course as well as its limit";[173] consequently, the concept of progress must not to be confused with that of the unlimited perfectibility of humanity.[174] Be that as it may, the concept of progress, according to Comte, includes the concept of its goal: "progress consists of social movement that, by a series of definite stages, makes its way toward a certain goal, which is, however, never attainable."[175] Thus, the author himself of the *Cours* undertakes to explain the development of humanity from the point of view of purposiveness, as a result of which such development is, for the most part, transformed into progress. What is more, Comte does not even entirely reject a multitude of possible orientations of development; at least he indicated more than once that the existing order of things is not the only possible one, and that the definiteness of an orientation grows with the extent of development; otherwise it is difficult to understand, for example, his statement that "the basic faculties of humanity are fully revealed only after a very long period of civilization."[176] The further determination of the orientation had to consist, obviously, in making clear which faculties of human nature were to be seen as the basic ones. And, in fact, Comte indicates that the development of human capabilities can be conceived in different degrees of dependence on each other; only intellectual development can be understood (*peut être concu*) independently of the others, whereas it is always presupposed in studying the remaining evolutionary series.[177] In the same sense, according to Comte, it is possible to "imagine" (*concevoir*) every capability of our nature as "means subordinate to morality," "the fundamental and great end of human life."[178] In using the principle of evolution in its subjective sense, concrete factual reality must not, however, be included in its very construction. Comte indeed entertains fictional construction of the evolution of humanity; adopting Condorcet's idea, he suggests imagining a fictional people successively passing through the basic stages of evolution actually taken by various peoples; in this case it is obvious that the principle of evolution, with the help of which such succession can alone be established, is of a subjective character.[179]

Nonetheless Comte correctly considers it possible to use his principle for supplementary explanation of the actual facts of social life. Thus, for example . . . Comte explains the dual antagonism between passions and reason, between personal interest and social instincts, not only by the innate faculties of man and the natural concordance between the development of altruism and the evolution of sociability [*obshchestvennost'*], but by purely teleological considerations: passions and egoism "must" exist in human nature not only because there is no sharp line between animal and human, but in order to give rise to the struggle making possible further evolution.[180]

The same point of view on purposiveness, as a subjective principle, also comes through in the "abstract" depiction of the historical process that Comte undertook in the last two volumes of his *Cours*. At the beginning of his disquisition, Comte himself calls it an "evaluation." And in fact Comte explains historical facts mechanistically and yet evaluates these same facts from a teleological point of view; many of them he treats as conditions that prepared the advent of the positive era and so fulfilled their "social purpose." Thus, for example, "polytheism had to prepare all future evolution"; monotheism naturally had to characterize the final and least stable form of the theological stage, since it was destined to prepare the collapse of this system; and Catholicism in particular was destined to lay "the elements of positivism," and so on. In general "the entirety of our past has served as preparation for the relativism and altruism" characteristic of positivism.[181] Such constructions reveal, of course, the teleological perspective from which Comte evaluated historical facts, insofar as they not only prepared but "were destined" to prepare positivism.

In these deliberations Comte uses the principle of purposiveness as a subjective point of view suitable for the theory of social evolution, and in particular for depiction of the history of humanity. The last case, however, clearly exposed Comte's new approach to the teleological principle: in it he came to see an independent and the most important objective factor in the "development" of humanity, by virtue of which the principle of progress received new significance.

To clarify Comte's view, it might help to return to his theory of the influence of human consciousness on the social environment. . . . In his treatise on politics Comte directly calls the results of such influence "perfectibility." . . . He also tried to show the role of consciousness in human progress by turning to the concrete history of European thought. The "metaphysical" stage, for example, breaks into two halves, "very distinct from each other," namely: the fourteenth and fifteenth centuries, when "the critical movement remains essentially spontaneous and involuntary (*spontané et involontaire*)," and the sixteenth to eighteenth centuries, in the course of which "disorganization, having become more profound and decisive, takes place henceforth mainly under the growing influence of formally negative philosophy."[182] Something similar happens in the modern era as well, characterized by the gradual establishment of positive philosophy, reorganizing society. From the beginning of the fourteenth century, such reorganization is found only in the form of an "involuntary movement," but now it starts to consciously "move toward an end under the direction of modern political philosophy."[183] In these deliberations Comte, it seems, treats human consciousness not so much as a product of environmental conditions, but as a factor acting independently on the environment; the last fragment indicates even in the name of what it acts: consciousness of the goal toward which evolution strives itself exerts a certain effect on the orientation of evolution. Thus, ascribing objective-psychological significance to the principle of purposiveness, Comte could easily pass to understanding the principle of progress in the same objective sense, especially when he related it to the "perfectibility" of humanity.

And in fact Comte began to discuss the progress of humanity as an objective process, the immanent goal of which turns out to be the "perfection"[184] accessible to human nature proper. Indeed, if the development of humanity is the unfolding in history of its characteristic properties, and the most characteristic properties are our intellectual and moral "faculties," then the immanent goal of evolution must also consist in the greatest degree of the progressive development of such capacities, especially the moral ones; that is, it must consist in their "perfection."[185] How the psychic energy of humanity grows and how our "faculties" are perfected Comte does not, however, at all explain. In any event, it seems Comte saw the objective results of "perfectibility," to the extent they have already revealed themselves in history, as pertaining mainly to man's intellectual capacities.[186] . . . Intellectual development not only can be understood independently of all other types of development, but in fact best represents the aggregate of human perfectibility. This is why the succession of the three basic intellectual stages (theological, metaphysical, and positive) acquires in Comte's eyes the significance not of a simple schema of the history of humanity, but of a "law" precisely representing reality.[187] Thus, Comte sees the objective existence of progress mainly in the fact of our intellectual perfectibility, although that, however, does not at all prevent him from also taking intellectual perfection as an immanent goal. But an immanent teleology of human progress comes out especially clearly only in Comte's reflections on moral perfectibility. "The great problem of human life, the ascendancy (l'ascendant) of altruism over egoism, is susceptible to real solution, toward which all our destinies constantly tend; the gradual realization of this solution, which will never be complete, constitutes the best measure of our continuous progress."[188] This indicates clearly enough the immanent goal of human perfectibility, that is, moral perfection, to the extent, of course, it is accessible to human nature.

Comte, however, did not always remain true to such an understanding of human evolution: he also discussed the "final goal" of an objectively existing progressive development; such development has its own limit, according to the given properties of human nature. Comte takes the "final goal" (but final) of human evolution to be positivism, which not only will unconditionally replace the former worldviews (theological and metaphysical), but will be the culmination of all human perfectibility, to which humanity has always and in ever greater degree strived. In one of his last works, Comte even declared that "my public course of 1847 marked the irrevocable establishment of religious positivism, concentrating our sentiments, thoughts, and actions around Humanity, which has definitely taken the place of God."[189]

With such a view of the goal of perfectibility it was easy to pass to historical "evaluation" of social facts from nothing but a teleological point of view of their relation to this final goal. That, for example, happened with Comte's account of the transition from the theological stage to the metaphysical. True, in an article from 1825 Comte still argued that whereas theology recognizes general causes behind things, metaphysics, as a transitional stage, created the theory of force or abstract properties, after which comes positivism with its theory of the relativity of knowledge. But in the *Cours* the replacement of theology by metaphysics is depicted mainly from the point of view of the final goal of progress: "the political triumph of the metaphysical school had to serve ... as an indispensable preparation for the social establishment of the positivist school," that is, the past phenomenon is "explained" by its purpose and is seen as a means for achieving the objectively given and, moreover, final goal of positivism.[190]

In these considerations, it is clear the principle of progress underwent new modifications: Comte not only began to give it objective meaning, but indicated the general "final" goal of all human perfectibility, attainable in "positivism." It is obvious that the absolute character of such an assertion was not at all in agreement with the theory of the relativity of knowledge, which rejected anything transcendent.

Thus, initially using the principle of evolution only to study the history of humanity from an evolutionary point of view, Comte gradually passed to recognition of the objective existence of human perfectibility. Seeing in such perfectibility an immanent goal, he also related it, however, to the idea of a final goal and so exceeded the limits of "positive" sociology.

Comte's concept of progress underwent, finally, still another essential change, when he delved more deeply into progress, considering it as moral perfectibility. Here Comte entered into a new sphere of inquiry: it was necessary for him to substantiate the principle of moral progress, but he could not derive such substantiation from his sociology: a moral goal began to appear to him not only as something natural, but as something that ought to be [*dolzhnoe*]. From such a point of view Comte came to put the principle of moral duty at the basis of moral perfectibility.

At first, however, Comte tried to deal in his usual way with this new difficulty. Not accepting utilitarianism, he nonetheless proceeded from the claim that man's social inclinations "preexist" in the brain; from this point of view he, apparently following the example of the physiological school, called morality a "natural tendency" and tried to substantiate it through the physiological predominance of the "heart" over reason. This did not prevent him from thinking that the nature of every social union is mainly intellectual and not moral, or from understanding progress in the same spirit.[191] In his sociology, Comte, however, already indicates that, despite the necessary invariability of the various basic dispositions of our nature, the most elevated of them are found in a constant state of relative development, which strives to raise them more and more to the level of being the predominant forces in human existence, even if such an inversion of the initial relation cannot and ought not to be ever fully realized. Further, morality turns out to be, according to Comte,

"the fundamental principle of social life." Discussing, for example, the significance of Catholicism, Comte remarks already in his *Cours* that thanks to
Catholicism, "morality was finally placed with dignity at the head of social
needs, since all other faculties of our nature were now conceived as only more
or less effective means, always subordinate to this great fundamental end of
human life."[192] Thus, only morality is capable of finally uniting humanity;[193]
the development of the latter must present itself to us mainly in the form of
moral perfectibility, which becomes the indicator of human progress.[194]

But in the name of what does morality acquire primary significance in the life
of humanity? On what basis must every theory be subordinate to the moral end,
does "living for others" (*vivre pour autrui*) prove to be the obligatory altruistic
principle of human development and progress, and must perfectibility be first
of all moral and, as such, binding on people? To such questions Comte does not
give direct answers:[195] now he recognizes the simple feeling of love as "the
universal and exclusive principle of morality";[196] now he is prepared to agree
that "the development of moral feeling can be understood only as the result of
the influence on it of the development of the intellect";[197] now he attributes to
the feeling of love or to morality itself the force guiding and controlling our
actions, or "obliging" us to promote universal perfectibility;[198] now he points
to the "imperative precepts" of the heart, regulating our conduct;[199] now,
finally, he is content to discuss duty.[200] The concept of duty is nearly put at the
basis of the whole *Système de politique positive*. Already in the *Cours* Comte
remarks that the fulfillment of duty "can often give no certain reward except an
inevitable inner satisfaction."[201] Since, in view of Comte's own statement, the
last expression cannot be taken in a utilitarian sense, it can only be supposed
that a moral act, in his opinion, must be done in the name of the concept of
moral duty, which is thus given absolute significance.[202]

With such a view, Comte falls into a new difficulty, which he probably did
not foresee when he discussed the "natural" laws of sociology as being essentially identical with physical laws. Denying the unity of apperception in human consciousness, denying indeed the very concept of "subject," Comte
could not ascribe moral freedom to it. Neither in his sociology nor in his ethics
does he suitably pose or answer such a question.[203] Speaking with aversion
about the individualism of "revolutionary metaphysics," which leads to "anar-
chy," Comte, once a student of Saint-Simon and an adherent of his theory,
went further than his teacher and was prepared to reject any autonomous
significance behind the human person: everything belonging to it, beginning
with life and ending with moral goods, comes from and belongs to humanity.
Only by returning to society everything he owes can man lay claim to any
rights; obliged to society for everything, he remains forever indebted to it.[204]

The real dependence, indicated by Comte, of each of us on society does not in itself lead at all, however, to a moral duty to devote one's existence to serving humanity, nor does it explain why man ought to "act so as to be prepared to answer for each of his deeds without any fear." Nonetheless, the grounds on which Comte demands the unconditional fulfillment of such a duty remained without further explanation, and his ethics, deprived of theoretical substantiation, acquired a dogmatic character.[205]

The same waverings are also noticeable in his concept of the Grand Être, with which, according to Comte, ethics is concerned. The closely related concept of "humanity" arose in Comte partly under the influence of Pascal[206] and the enthusiasm many eighteenth- and nineteenth-century thinkers showed for the idea,[207] and partly as a result of the sociological views of Comte himself, who added moral demands to them.[208] Combining the static point of view with the dynamic and turning the "fiction of linear evolution" into reality, Comte came to the conclusion that growing solidarity among elements of a social system, no matter how complex in themselves, leads to the formation of a "collective organism," the elements of which acquire significance only to the extent they are parts of the given whole. The latter acquires a more and more individual character, and consequently greater and greater unity; this is achieved not only by a mechanical process, but also by consciousness of a common goal, which is reached in humanity by successive generations.[209] Since with this, moreover, the scientific predominance of the social point of view over all others and the logical supremacy of generalization over specialization prove to be the main and "ultimate" features (*caractère final*) of the positive philosophy, the whole future of humanity appears to Comte in the form of its striving to achieve such results. Meanwhile they are best realized in that system of scientific knowledge that will have as its center the same relative concept of humanity. Indeed, the "conditions of its existence" must include the mechanical laws of the solar system, the physical and chemical laws acting on our planet and, finally, the biological laws of living organisms. Therefore, Comte concludes, only the concept of humanity can be called a true generalization; having been last from the objective point of view, it becomes first from the subjective-human point of view. The world must be studied not for itself, but for man, or rather for humanity.[210]

Nonetheless Comte ascribes to this concept the significance of an objective goal; the whole becomes in his eyes something valuable in itself, in relation to which, and to it alone, are human acts evaluated and subjected to a certain moral norm. What is more, turning the concept of humanity into the concept of the Grand Être, he makes it the object of religious devotion. Yet the concept of the Grand Être is doubly subjective, in its origins as well as in its goals. For although it is created by people, its makeup includes only such substances and even only such qualities that, according to the positivist priesthood, "are suitable for assimilation," that is, that actually serve humanity and are not a burden to it.[211] Such a selection must obviously take place from the same moral point of view that, as we have seen, was not securely established in its foundations by Comte; consequently, the selection itself could turn out to be not only subjective but also arbitrary. Even so, Comte in essence gives it the objective and absolute significance of the final goal of all human aspirations, intentions, and acts.[212]

In constructing his ethics and "religion of humanity" Comte, it is clear, did not at all avoid a number of premises that went unexplained and could thus be used too arbitrarily. Detailed consideration of them would take us, however, far beyond the limits of Comte's sociology, from which he himself eventually had to separate the special science of ethics. Thinking it possible to proceed in the construction of ethics from physiology, he ended by putting at its basis the pure concept of duty and trying to erect on this even his "religion of humanity," although Comte himself did not reject the "need for eternity, always inherent to our nature."[213]

Because Comte took morality to be positive, despite the transcendent nature of many of his reflections about it, he considered it possible to combine a moral end in general with positivism as the "ultimate" end of human progress.[214] Thanks to the positive philosophy, he wrote, society will understand that successive generations of humanity all contribute to one final end (i.e., the establishment of positivism), the gradual realization of which required from each of them a definite part [in the common work].[215]

Finally, it should be noted that Comte, in recognizing humanity's capacity to be conscious not only of immediate ends but also of an ultimate end, complicated still further the teleology of the historical process by combining the objective significance of the principle of purposiveness with its "ultimate" significance. Indeed, if people can be conscious of the ultimate end of their perfectibility, then it is obvious that consciousness in its own turn becomes a new factor in such perfectibility, as Comte recognized in the passages cited above.[216]

Thus, Comte not only put the principle of purposiveness at the basis of his theory of human progress, but arbitrarily used it in its diverse meanings. It is permissible, of course, to dream about the time when such diversity will give way to a certain unity, but that time has not yet come. In the construction of evolutionary theory, the various meanings of the principle of purposiveness have to be distinguished, not confused. Not having defined the distinctions among them, Comte was in no position to combine them; he constantly confused them and so radically undermined his construction of the evolution of humanity.

5. FINDINGS

General character of Comte's sociological principles; their interrelation and significance in his system.

On the basis of historical and critical evaluation of the principles Comte tried to use in constructing his sociology, it is not difficult to draw some conclusions about their general character, interrelation, and significance in his system.

The sources of these principles can be found in eighteenth-century French literature: Turgot already had the concepts of the cultural environment and the uniformity of human nature, of consensus and progress, dwelling mainly on study of the latter. The same concepts were also discussed by Condorcet, Destutt de Tracy, Cabanis, and Saint-Simon; Comte used principally their works in substantiating his new theory of social science. In his considerations of the social environment he even remained somewhat behind his contemporaries; on the other hand he gave more attention than them to the other principles, in particular to the principle of consensus, to which he assigned primary significance in statics, and to the principle of evolution, which he applied to "abstract" representation of the historical process.

Comte went further, however, than his predecessors in that he related his theory of knowledge to the above concepts and tried to give them the significance of principles of sociology. Comte's theory of "the principle of the conditions of existence" clearly reveals, for example, the desire to remove from sociology the principles of causation and purposiveness; the same disdain for them is not difficult to uncover in Comte's discussions of the other "sociological concepts." Such an approach to basic categories of thought deprived Comte of the possibility of substantiating his sociological principles or of adding the principle of interaction to them, and also caused him to constantly confuse their subjective meaning with the objective. Coming close to repudiating psychology and yet making use of it when the occasion presented itself, Comte could not precisely determine the content of his principles: in his formulation of the principles of the environment and consensus it is impossible not to point out essential flaws, less noticeable in his theory of the uniformity of human nature and of evolution. In his sociological deliberations he constantly used concepts that were not at all explained beforehand or in agreement with his general worldview.

Nor did Comte direct enough attention to the interrelation that should have been established among his principles: he did not even place the principle of the environment in connection with that of the uniformity of human nature, a relation Turgot had already suggested.[217] Comparing such uniformity with the interaction of individuals and with the concordance of social phenomena might have reflected favorably on Comte's considerations of their characteristics and of the properties of social consensus. Finally, it is strange to simultaneously assert, as Comte does, that human nature remains constantly the same in its essential traits and yet is also perfecting itself, without explaining how the principles of the uniformity of human nature and evolution should be related to each other. Only the link between consensus and evolution served as the object of repeated discussion by Comte; but, asserting that the "laws" of consensus reveal themselves in the evolution of humanity, that without order there could not be progress and that the development of order is in fact progress, Comte inadequately explained the theory of their correlation. Neglecting the general relation among all his principles, he was excessively carried away by the idea of the connection between consensus and evolution. This fascination exerted an essential influence on Comte's approach to the construction of sociology.

It is remarkable that in general Comte barely used his principles to discover any laws of sociology. With regard to the influence of the environment on human society or of the uniformity of human nature on the recurrence of certain social phenomena, Comte might well have been able to reach some empirical generalizations of one type or another. But, while calling himself the founder of sociology, the first to have indicated the "natural laws" of social phenomena, Comte did not undertake work of this type, not even to more solidly substantiate his principles or test them through application to explanation of reality. Nor did Comte, while often returning to the idea that social laws are constant, explain in what sense their constancy was to be understood; apparently he did not consider it necessary to distinguish between the constancy of quantitative relations and that of qualitative relations. He forgot that if it is possible to speak of the constancy of a given social relation, or more precisely of its recurrence, then it is only in the qualitative sense.[218] With convenient selection of material, Comte could perhaps point to some examples of this type; but he avoided the very branches and methods of social science that provided the possibility of observing a certain constancy of human nature in the regularity [zakonosoobraznost'] of social phenomena. Without psychology, which Comte rejected, it was impossible, of course, to discern such phenomena. Further, given the negative approach Comte took in his psychology to the theory of the will, presumably it would have been natural to emphasize phenomena, like language, in which will plays a comparatively small role; but Comte turned to language only in his treatise on politics, and then not from the point of view of the regularity of its phenomena.[219] The almost total contempt Comte had for the most important of the social sciences (especially political economy) also deprived him of the possibility of approaching the study of social facts from a point of view that would disclose some regularity in their relations. Finally, Comte, in rejecting the possibility of applying the theory of probability to the study of social facts, failed to use statistics (which in his time had already acquired a scientific character, thanks to Quételet's works[220]) to indicate the means by which it would be possible at least to prepare to ascertain certain laws of social phenomena, if not to actually ascertain them in the proper way.[221] This explains why Comte, who so eagerly discussed the existence of laws of sociology, in fact hardly discovered even one of them: he only in passing touches upon certain laws of social interaction or upon laws of social differentiation and integration, on the subsequent establishment of which sociologists-evolutionists have worked so hard.

Apart from the accidental circumstances that gave rise in Comte to so one-sided an understanding of sociology, there were theoretical considerations that prevented him from noticing the full significance of the shortcoming we have indicated:[222] Comte ignored the theory of probability and the individual social sciences because they, in his opinion, examined certain properties of social facts in too much isolation, artificially separating them from the remaining properties. In view of social consensus, such isolation can, according to him, lead only to false results. Moreover, depending on the extent of his immersion in the study of social dynamics, Comte gradually passed from sociology to philosophy of history:[223] in it he came to search for almost nothing but the sociological "law" of the three stages, although it hardly has the right to pretend to such a title.[224]

IV. Conclusion

"The simplest and truest criterion of the real value of any social doctrine," Comte wrote in his consideration of the timeliness of constructing a social physics, "must be seen in the degree of correspondence between its basic claims and their subsequent development in practice."[225] Obviously Comte recognized that the same demand had to be made of the doctrine itself, before it could be used to evaluate the doctrine's applicability; but, true to habit, he

398   A. S. Lappo-Danilevskii

included his premise in his derivative conclusion about the correspondence between theory and practice. Comte's own doctrine, however, cannot be recognized as concordant in all its basic claims: using in its construction the theory of the relativity of knowledge, formed long before, he gave it a dogmatic character inadmissible after Hume's critique. Comte nonetheless made use of his relativism in all its categoricalness, in the struggle not only with the theological worldview but also with outdated eighteenth-century metaphysics. In working out his own system, he proved unable to maintain his "positive" demands and constantly resorted to assumptions having nothing in common with "positivism."

The same internal contradiction is also felt in Comte's attempt to apply the principles of positive philosophy to social science. In the study of human life, which he wanted to explain without exception by the action of mechanical processes, Comte came up against human consciousness. Trying in vain to construct a biological psychology, he could not, of course, also provide a social "physics." It has already been indicated above how Comte, under the cover of phrenological terms, in essence operated with psychological concepts and how widely, and in particular cases how rather successfully, he used them to explain the phenomena of social life. By this alone, however, "social physics" was turned into a special science, distinct from the physical sciences.

If Comte had consciously used the epistemological and psychological premises that actually ran through his philosophy, he would likely have easily understood the nature of this metamorphosis; but he explained neither the grounds of his hidden assumptions nor in what measure they had to be or could be applied to the construction of sociology. Therefore his properly sociological claims are not at all substantiated, and indeed are not even subject to critical evaluation. And in fact Comte succeeded neither in solidly establishing the significance or system behind his sociological principles nor in precisely formulating the laws of sociology. Gradually becoming absorbed in speculation about the totality of human history and increasingly subordinating science to ethics, more and more he discussed nothing but the "collective organism" as a single and individual fact; but here were revealed just those waverings in his thought that depended on his various understanding of the principles of ethics.

Thus, the example of Comte can serve as a warning to anyone who would wish to set about constructing a science of society without having first explained to himself its foundations. Comte, of course, could not manage without them: arbitrarily using concepts he had not established beforehand, he deprived himself of the possibility of maintaining balance and consistency in the course of his ideas and could not guard the edifice he erected from unsteadiness. As a result, it succumbed to elements not only completely foreign to truly positive knowledge, but contradicting "positivism" itself.

Notes

1. Or "rénovation," as progressive French thinkers often put it. Ed.
2. Claude-Henri de Rouvroy, Comte de Saint-Simon (1760–1825), French social philosopher, founder of French socialism, and major influence on Comte. He thought society should be reorganized along industrial lines and that scientists should be its new spiritual leaders. Ed.
3. His most important work, *Nouveau christianisme* (1825). Ed.
4. Comte was Saint-Simon's secretary for seven years, beginning in August 1817. Ed.
5. John Stuart Mill (1806–1873), English empiricist philosopher, economist, and social reformer, author of the classic liberal treatise, *On Liberty* (1859). He sponsored and supported Comte, but criticized him for not including psychology in his system of sciences (see below), and eventually came to fear that Comte's ideas on social planning amounted to a complete "system of spiritual and temporal despotism." Mill wrote an important study of Comte, *Auguste Comte and Positivism* (London, 1865). Ed.
6. *System of Logic,* 2 vols. (1843), the sixth book of which, on the moral sciences, treats Comte. Ed.
7. The following are the works to which Lappo-Danilevskii refers here (often only by author): F. Allengry, *Essai historique et critique sur la sociologie chez Auguste Comte* (Paris, 1900); E. Caird, *The Social Philosophy and Religion of Comte,* 2d edition (Glasgow, 1893); R. Eucken, "Zur Würdigung Comtes und des Positivismus," in *Philosophische Aufsätze Eduard Zeller gewidmet* (Leipzig, 1887); H. Lietz, *Die Probleme im Begriff der Gesellschaft bei Auguste Comte* (Jena, 1891); H. Gruber, *Der Positivismus* (Freiburg, 1891); L. Lévy-Bruhl, *La philosophie d'Auguste Comte* (Paris, 1900); H. Waentig, *Auguste Comte und seine Bedeutung für die Entwicklung der Sozialwissenschaft* (Leipzig, 1894); and *La philosophie positive,* par Auguste Comte, résumé par Jules Rig (Paris, 1880–1881). In the Russian literature on Comte, Lappo-Danilevskii refers to: B. N. Chicherin, *Polozhitel'naia filosofiia i edinstvo nauki* (Moscow, 1892); V. I. Ger'e, "O. Kont i ego znachenie v istoricheskoi nauke," *Voprosy filosofii i psikhologii* 9: 2–5, kn. 42–45 (1898); V. S. Solov'ëv, "Kont (Auguste Comte)," in *Slovar' Brokgauza i Evfrona,* vol. XVI (St. Petersburg, 1895), pp. 121–136; V. S. Solov'ëv, "Ideia chelovechestva u Avgusta Konta" (1898), reprinted in *Sobranie sochinenii Vladimira Sergeevicha Solov'ëva,* ed. S. M. Solov'ëv and E. L. Radlov, vol. IX, 2d edition (St. Petersburg, 1911–1914), pp. 172–193; S. Smolikovskii, *Uchenie O. Konta ob obshchestve* (Warsaw, 1881); and N. Spiridonov's translation of essays on Comte by Mill, Herbert Spencer, and James Ward (Moscow, 1897), which contains additional Russian bibliography on Comte. Lappo-Danilevskii writes that Chicherin "subjected Comte's system to a very severe critique," and that Solov'ëv and Ger'e "give a broad evaluation of Comte's scientific contributions, primarily in the fields of history and sociology." Ed.
8. This is, of course, no longer the case. See, for example, the relevant essays in F. A.

Hayek, *The Counter-Revolution of Science: Studies on the Abuse of Reason* (Glencoe, Ill.: Free Press, 1952), which nicely complements Lappo-Danilevskii's essay. Ed.

9. Wilhelm Dilthey (1833–1911), German philosopher and historian of ideas, best known for his theory of the *Geisteswissenschaften,* the human or cultural sciences. Misch helped edit his *Gesammelte Schriften* (1913–1936). Ed.

10. Jean Le Rond d'Alembert (1717–1783), French mathematician and rationalist philosopher; with Denis Diderot he edited the *Encyclopédie.* Ed.

11. Anne Robert Jacques Turgot (1727–1781), French economist (physiocrat) and philosopher of history, comptroller general of finance under Louis XVI. His *Tableau philosophique des progrès successifs de l'esprit humain* and "Plan de deux discours sur l'histoire universelle" (both from 1750) advanced the notion that humanity passes through three main stages (the religious, the philosophical or metaphysical, and the scientific) on its path toward perfectibility. This substantially anticipated Comte's interpretation of history (see below). Ed.

12. See note 24 below. Ed.

13. In works devoted to the history of the life and writings of Comte's contemporaries, it is possible to find indications of the historical genesis of "positivism," but they are made only in passing. See, for example, François Picavet, *Les idéologues* (Paris, 1891), and G. Weill, *Un précurseur du socialisme, Saint-Simon et son oeuvre* (Paris, 1894).

14. Although Comte himself begins his *Cours* with an account of the law of the gradual development of human thought, we shall follow neither his example nor that of several of his supporters and opponents. The so-called law of three stages is not the foundation of the positive philosophy, but rather a conclusion to which it arrived in the study of social dynamics and which it uses as proof of the truth of its claims. "The theory of the three phases," in Professor M. I. Karinskii's correct observation, "necessarily presupposes empiricism, it is true, but if consistently applied to the whole history of humanity, it can itself become if not a decisive, then a very strong and compelling argument on behalf of empiricism. Therefore it has happened that the essence of positivism has become identified in the general consciousness not with the view that expresses it most precisely," that is, not with the relative nature of knowledge, but with the law of the three stages. M. Karinskii, "K voprosu o pozitivizme," *Pravoslavnoe obozrenie,* 1875, vol. III, p. 357.

15. For references I have used the second edition of Comte's *Cours de philosophie positive* [Paris, 1864] and the first edition of his *Système de politique positive* [Paris, 1851–1854].

16. Pierre Gassendi (1592–1655), French philosopher and mathematician, advocated Epicurean atomism and a fundamental epistemological skepticism in opposition to Aristotelianism and Cartesianism. Ed.

17. *Encyclopédie, ou dictionnaire raisonné des sciences, des arts et des métiers . . . ,* vol. V (Paris, 1751–1780), p. 785 (see "Epicure"); cf. D. Diderot, *Oeuvres,* ed. J. Assezat et M. Tourneux, vol. XIV (Paris, 1875–1877), pp. 528 ff. Diderot calls them "écoles d'épicuréisme morales."

18. J. G. Walch, *Philosophischer Lexicon* (Leipzig, 1733), "Vorrede der ersten Auflage," p. 6. . . .

19. Julien Offray de La Mettrie (1709–1751), French physician and materialist philosopher, whose best known work is *L'Homme Machine* (1747). Ed.

20. J. O. de La Mettrie, *Oeuvres philosophiques,* vol. 2, 2d edition (Berlin, 1796), pp. 3, 11–12 [editor's translation].

21. Hume was attached to the British embassy in Paris from 1763 to 1766. Ed.

22. In 1743 d'Alembert published his *Traité de dynamique* and was admitted to the Académie des Sciences. Ed.

23. "I do not frame hypotheses." Sir Isaac Newton recommends this principle in the *Principia.* "For whatever is not deduced from the phenomena is to be called an hypothesis; and hypotheses, whether metaphysical or physical, whether of occult qualities or mechanical, have no place in experimental philosophy. In this philosophy particular propositions are inferred from the phenomena, and afterwards rendered general by induction." Sir Isaac Newton's *Mathematical Principles of Natural Philosophy and His System of the World.* Translated into English by Andrew Motte in 1729. The translations revised and supplied with an historical and explanatory appendix by Florian Cjori (Berkeley: University of California Press, 1962), pp. 546–547, 671–676. Ed.

24. G. Misch, "Zur Enstehung des französischen Positivismus," *Archiv für Geschichte der Philosophie,* vol. XIV, 1901, pp. 5, 9, 10, 12, 15.

25. D'Alembert, *Eléments de philosophie,* in *Oeuvres philosophiques et littéraires,* ed. J. F. Bastien, vol. 2 (Paris, 1805), p. 136: "Il est dans chaque science des principes vrais ou supposés, qu'on saisit par une espèce d'instinct, auquel on doit s'abandonner sans résistance; autrement il faudroit admettre dans les principes un progrès à l'infini qui seroit aussi absurde qu'un progrès à l'infini dans les êtres et dans les causes, et qui rendroit tout incertain, faute d'un point fixe, d'òu l'on pût partir." [Obviously the second part of Lappo-Danilevskii's quotation is a paraphrase.]

26. This appears to be a paraphrase of d'Alembert, possibly pp. 137–138. Ed.

27. D'Alembert, p. 402. Ed.

28. G. Misch, pp. 19, 22–23, 29, 31, 35–36.

29. Lappo-Danilevskii outlines the similar views of D. Diderot, A. Turgot, P. Barthez, and C. Helvétius. Ed.

30. Joseph Louis Lagrange (1736–1813), French mathematician and astronomer, influential professor at the *Ecole polytechnique.* He sought to free mechanics of all metaphysical concepts. Ed.

31. Comte's acquaintance with the philosophical views of La Mettrie, d'Alembert, Diderot, and Turgot is not subject to doubt; for Barthez's influence on Comte's epistemological views, see Comte, *Opuscules de philosophie sociale 1819–1828* (Paris, 1883), p. 183; *Cours,* III, 451.

32. Étienne Bonnot de Condillac (1715–1780), in his best known work, *Traité des sensations* (1754), developed Locke's view that all knowledge derives from the senses. According to Condillac, even more complex intellectual operations can be reduced to "transformed sensations." Ed.

33. *Cours,* III, 550. P. d'Holbach, *Système de la nature,* vol. II (Paris, 1820), ch. VII.

34. Antoine Louis Claude Destutt de Tracy (1754–1836) gave the name "ideology" to the analysis of ideas into the sensory elements of which he believed them to be composed (although in practice he was more concerned with studying the human faculties and their operation than with the origin of ideas); he considered his new discipline to be a branch of zoology. Pierre-Jean Georges Cabanis (1757–1808), another leading *idéologue,* was even

402   A. S. Lappo-Danilevskii

more reductive in his crude mechanistic and materialistic approach. The *idéologues* (who also included Condillac and Helvétius) had two main centers, the École Normal and the Institut National (also called the Institut de France), both founded in 1795. So great was the prestige of the Institut that Napoleon became an honorary member in 1797, only to turn in 1803 against its inner core, the "classe des sciences morales et politiques," because of his fear that the *idéologues* had too much hold over public opinion. On the Institut, the *idéologues,* and their relation to positivism, see George Lichtheim, *The Concept of Ideology and Other Essays* (New York: Random House, 1967), pp. 4–11. Ed.

35. Claude-Adrien Helvétius (1715–1771) was one of the Encyclopedists. His chief work, *De l'esprit* (1758), claims that the source of all intellectual activity is physical sensation and that self-interest — the love of pleasure and fear of pain — is the mainspring of human conduct. This crude reductive psychology was the basis of his utilitarian ethics, which strongly influenced Bentham. Ed.

36. F. Picavet, *Les idéologues* (Paris, 1891), pp. 246, 313, 463....

37. André Marie Ampère (1775–1836), physicist and mathematician who made major discoveries in the fields of magnetism and electricity; M. F. X. Bichat (1771–1802), author of *Recherches physiologiques sur la vie et la mort* (1800); F. J. V. Broussais (1772–1838) was the most prominent of the "Paris physicians" (on him, see the text below). Ed.

38. Comte himself gives an outline of the rise of the positive doctrine (*Système de politique positive,* III, 614–618), but there are no indications here to the genesis of his theory of knowledge.

39. *Cours,* III, 553; VI, 259–260. [In fact Comte refers here (*Cours,* VI, 260) to Hume and Adam Smith, "dont l'influence fut très-utile à ma première éducation philosophique."]

40. D. Hume, *Treatise of Human Nature,* ed. T. Green and T. Grose (London, 1882), Part III, sec. 7 ff., sec. 11 ff.; *Enquiry Concerning Human Understanding,* vol. IV in his *Works* (1854), sec. 3 ff. In such circumstances it is strange to call, as V. Solov'ëv does, Comte's teaching "theoretical skepticism": V. Solov'ëv, "Kont (Auguste Comte)," in *Slovar' Brokgauza i Evfrona,* vol. XVI (St. Petersburg, 1895), p. 129 ... Comte speaks only of *similitude* and *succession;* nonetheless, Caird and Watson add the relation of coexistence, so it turns out that for Comte, in the exposition of these scholars, we study the relations of resemblance, coexistence, and succession. See E. Caird, *The Social Philosophy and Religion of Comte,* 2d edition (Glasgow, 1893), p. 19; J. Watson, *Comte, Mill and Spencer* (Glasgow, 1895), p. 25. Chicherin does not include coexistence, but nor does he think that Comte's terminology is successful, since "resemblance serves as the basis for deducing contiguous as well as successive phenomena." B. Chicherin, *Polozhitel'naia filosofiia i edinstvo nauki* (Moscow, 1892), p. 314....

41. "Exposition des principes fondamentaux de la philosophie transcendantale de Kant." Ed.

42. Johannes Kinker, *Essai d'une exposition succincte de la Critique de la raison pure,* trans. J. Le Fèvre (Amsterdam, 1801). Ed.

43. [M. J. Degérando, *Histoire comparée des systèmes de philosophie* (Paris, 1804).] *Critique de la raison pratique,* trans. François Picavet, avec un avant-propos sur "La philosophie de Kant en France, de 1773 à 1814," 2d edition (Paris, 1902)....

44. Madame de Staël (1766–1817), French writer and salonist whose works, especially *De l'Allemagne* (1813), anticipated French romanticism. Ed.

45. Victor Cousin (1792–1867), French philosopher, historian of philosophy, and edu-

cational reformer. He was inspired by the common-sense philosophy of Thomas Reid, which he interpreted to mean eclecticism, or combining the best traditions in philosophy (for him, empiricism in epistemology and spiritualism in religion). In 1840 he became minister of public instruction, director of the École Normale, and a member of the Institut de France. Ed.

46. Madame de Staël, *De l'Allemagne*, t. II (1820), pp. 225–252 (ch. VI); Cousin became acquainted with Schelling's system in 1818. See H. Taine, *Les philosophes classiques du XIX siécle*, 3d edition (Paris, 1868), pp. 130, 131, 144. Cousin's "Leçons sur la philosophie de Kant" appeared in 1842; cf. François Thurot's comments about Kantians in France in 1830 in F. Picavet, *Les idéologues*, p. 467.

47. Pierre Laromiguière (1756–1837), influential professor of philosophy, studied with Condillac and was associated with the *idéologues*. His best known work was *Leçons de philosophie sur les principes de l'intelligence* (1815–1818). One of his more famous students was Victor Cousin. Ed.

48. *Cours*, VI, 619: "L'illustre Kant a noblement mérité une éternelle admiration en tentant le premier d'echapper directement à l'absolu philosophique par sa célébre conception de la double réalité, à la fois objective et subjective, qui indique un si juste sentiment de la philosophie." Cf. *Système de politique positive*, III, 588–589. Emile Littré, *Auguste Comte et la philosophie positive*, 2d edition (Paris, 1864), p. 156. Comte was once prepared, apparently, to take up the study of German philosophy, but on Mill's advice abandoned his intention; in a letter to him Comte remarked: "qu'il y a de longues années que de tels contacts ne peuvent plus avoir pour lui aucune haute utilité philosophique." See L. Lévy-Bruhl, "A. Comte et S. Mill d'aprés leur correspondence," *Revue Philosophique*, 1898, no. 12, p. 629.

49. Thomas Reid (1710–1796), Scottish philosopher, professor of moral philosophy at Glasgow, and the founder of the Scottish commonsense school of philosophy, which was a reaction against the excesses of philosophical skepticism (Hume and Berkeley). Ed.

50. [Comte, *Cours*, VI, 604, editor's translation.] H. Taine, *Les philosophes classiques du XIX siècle*, 3d edition (Paris, 1868), pp. 21–22: Comment nacquit le spiritualisme. Royer-Collard, who reacted sharply against the doctrines of Condillac and Cabanis, could hardly have enjoyed Comte's favor, however. F. Thurot was also, apparently, well acquainted with Reid's philosophy: see F. Picavet, Introduction etc. [presumably "La philosophie de Kant en France, de 1773 à 1814," in his translation of *Critique de la raison pratique* (Paris, 1902)], p. XXXI, and *Les idéologues*, p. 465. In secret circles, too, especially after 1823, Reid's philosophy began to be studied (G. Weill, *Histoire du parti républicain en France*, Paris, 1900, p. 17). Finally, Jouffroy provided (with his foreword) a French translation of the works of Reid [six volumes, 1828]. See Comte, *Cours*, VI, 604–605; *Système de politique positive*, I, 57. Lamennais also recognized the doctrine of common sense, but he proceeded from premises different from those of Comte; see E. Faguet, *Politiques et moralistes du XIX siècle* (Paris, 1898), pp. 89, 98–107. [Pierre Paul Royer-Collard (1763–1845), professor of philosophy and dean at the Sorbonne (1811–1814), introduced Reid's philosophy into France. Théodore Simon Jouffroy (1796–1842), spiritualist philosopher who sought to found a science of psychology on the Scottish commonsense principles. On Lamennais, see S. F. Ol'denburg's essay (Chapter 11) in this volume.]

51. Lappo-Danilevskii paraphrases Comte, *Système de politique positive*, I, 712. Ed.

52. *Système de politique positive,* I, 713, editor's translation.

53. *Système de politique positive,* II, 33. Inset Lappo-Danilevskii's. Ed.

54. *Système de politique positive,* II, 35, editor's translation.

55. Inset Lappo-Danilevskii's.

56. *Cours,* IV, 300, editor's translation.

57. *Cours,* VI, 620–621, editor's translation. Lappo-Danilevskii provides here one unwieldy citation for the above passages. From it I have tried to provide more exact references (notes 51–57). He also cites here Comte, *Opuscules de philosophie sociale 1819–1828* (Paris, 1883), p. 186. Ed.

58. *Cours,* VI, 618, 620–621. Comte, *Discours sur l'ésprit positif* (Paris, 1844), pp. 17, 46; *Système de politique positive,* I, 425–427, 438–441. . . . E. Caird, *The Social Philosophy and Religion of Comte,* pp. 104–105. An opposition of subject to object is also noticeable in Comte's "subjective synthesis," although Comte himself was not far from the concept of the objective significance of the "subjectivity" common to the human race as a whole. See E. Caird, pp. 113, 115 ff.

59. D. Diderot, *Oeuvres,* I ("Lettre sur les aveugles," "Lettre sur les sourds," etc.). *Cours,* VI, 640–641; *Système de politique positive,* I, 422. Comte's deliberations on "nôtre organisation" and "nôtre situation," as causes of the relativity of positive science, are treated in detail in L. Lévy-Bruhl, *La Philosophie d'Auguste Comte* (Paris, 1900), pp. 83–88.

60. Comte, *Opuscules,* p. 191. . . .

61. "Like other people, he admits the study of causes, in every sense in which one physical fact can be the cause of another." John Stuart Mill, *Auguste Comte and Positivism* (London, 1865), p. 57. [Lappo-Danilevskii quotes the N. Spiridonov translation (Moscow, 1897), pp. 61–63.] But our philosopher replaces the concept of causality, or more precisely the principle of causation, even in Kant's sense, with the concept of succession, which raises difficulties.

62. Wilhelm Wundt, *Logik: Eine Untersuchung der Prinzipien der Erkenntniss und der Methoden wissenschaftlicher Forschung,* II (1), 2d edition (Stuttgart, 1893–1895), pp. 302 ff., on teleology in mechanics; on causation and teleology in sociology, see below.

63. *Cours,* IV, 491, editor's translation and citation.

64. *Cours,* IV, 78, 491; V, 73; VI, 624. . . .

65. *Opuscules,* p. 156; *Système de politique positive,* I, 426.

66. *Cours,* I, 68, 79; VI, 624, 654, 663. Comte also refers sometimes to the "cohérence logique" in our thoughts (L. Lévy-Bruhl, pp. 30, 55), but more in the sense of the integral structure of a worldview. In any case, Comte does not explain the relation of one type of "cohérence" to the other.

67. Watson, *Comte, Mill and Spencer: An Outline of Philosophy* (Glasgow, 1895), pp. 21–37, on the contradictions Comte allowed in his theory of the relativity of knowledge. Also see V. Lesevich, *Opyt kriticheskogo issledovaniia osnovo-nachal pozitivnoi filosofii* (St. Petersburg, 1877), pp. 117 ff.

68. *Cours,* IV, 297, 377.

69. *Cours,* I, 43–45; IV, 252; VI, 611.

70. *Cours,* I, 68, 77; *Système de politique positive,* IV, 185.

71. *Cours,* I, 21, 68. *Système de politique positive,* III, 42. . . .

72. *Cours,* I, 74, editor's translation.

73. *Cours,* I, 71, 78, 87. Sometimes Comte even speaks of "existence mathématique"; see *Système de politique positive,* III, 43; IV, 211. For criticism of Comte's position on the concurrence between the degree of simplicity and the degree of similarity of phenomena, and of the application to them of the concept of abstraction, see B. Chicherin, *Polozhitel'naia filosofiia i edinstvo nauki* (Moscow, 1892), pp. 23–24.

74. *Opuscules,* p. 199: "J'entends par physique sociale," Comte wrote in 1825, "la science qui a pour objet propre l'étude des phénomènes sociaux, considérés dans le même esprit que les phénomènes astronomiques, physiques, chimiques et physiologiques, c'est à dire comme assujettis à des lois naturelles invariables"; the same idea is stated many times in the *Cours* and *Système de politique positive* (of the latter see, for example, II, 53).

75. C. A. Helvétius, *De l'Esprit* (1758), Préface: "J'ai cru qu'on devait traiter la morale, comme toutes les autres sciences et faire une morale comme une physique experimentale" (*Oeuvres complètes,* vol. 1, London, 1781, p. LXIX). L. Ducros, *Les encyclopédistes* (Paris, 1900), p. 135. On the same direction in the "Academie des sciences morales et politiques," founded in 1795, see John T. Merz, *A History of European Thought in the Nineteenth Century,* vol. 1 (Edinburgh, 1896), pp. 145–146. F. Picavet, *Les idéologues* (Paris, 1891), p. 455. Saint-Simon, *Science de l'homme* (a collection of his essays), ed. Barthélemy-Prosper Enfantin (Paris, 1858), pp. 249, 257. Comte, *Opuscules,* p. 199; *Cours,* IV, 252.

76. Lappo-Danilevskii is probably referring to François-Pierre Maine de Biran (1766–1824), whose *Essai sur les fondements de la psychologie* (1812) conceives metaphysics as the science of interior phenomena, or as introspective psychology based on an interior sense (*sens intime*), and whose *Journal intime* (entries from 1815 onward) and *Nouveaux Essais d'anthropologie* (1824) are concerned with the life of the spirit and its approach to God. On Maine de Biran, see the text below. Ed.

77. Jean-Etienne-Marie Portalis, *De l'usage et de l'abus de l'esprit philosophique durant le XVIII siécle,* vol. I, 2d edition (Paris, 1827), pp. 79, 82, 86.

78. H. Taine, *Les philosophes classiques du XIX siécle,* 3d edition (Paris, 1868), p. 148.

79. La Mettrie pursued medical studies under Hermann Boerhaave (1668–1738). Ed.

80. D. Diderot, *Oeuvres,* XVI, 464; L. Ducros, *Les encyclopédistes,* pp. 71, 100. D'Holbach, of course, also held similar views; see P. d'Holbach, *Système de la nature,* vol. II, pp. 447, 448.

81. Georges-Louis Leclerc Buffon (1707–1788), French naturalist and author of a monumental 44-volume *Histoire naturelle* (1749–1788). Ed.

82. M. Ferraz, *Histoire de la philosophie pendant la révolution* (Paris, 1889), pp. 32, 35, 62. F. Picavet, *Les idéologues,* pp. 311, 313, 343. [On Maine de Biran, see note 76.]

83. The roots of this theory can be found in the predecessors of Cabanis; see, for example, P. d'Holbach, *Système de la nature,* vol. II, p. 448. P. J. G. Cabanis, *Rapports,* I (Paris, 1824), p. 133. As is well known, Cabanis became attracted to spiritualism not long before his death; see M. Ferraz, pp. 105–111.

84. Franz Joseph Gall (1758–1828), Austrian physician and founder of phrenology. Ed.

85. M. Mignet, *Notice historique sur la vie et les travaux de M. Broussais,* in *Mémoires*

de l'Institut (*Sciences morales et politiques*), vol. IV (Paris, 1884), pp. I–XXXIX. Comte, *Opuscules*, pp. 299, 304; *Système de politique positive*, I, 704–710....

86. On Jouffroy, see note 50 above. Ed.

87. H. Höffding, *Geschichte der neueren Philosophie*, I, pp. 67–72; H. Taine, *Les philosophes classiques du XIX siécle*, 3d edition (Paris, 1868), pp. 49–60 (Taine was one of the first to indicate the similarity between Fichte and Maine de Biran).

88. *Opuscules*, p. 292.

89. *Opuscules*, p. 296; the term "prédisposition" is most likely used here in the sense employed by Gall.

90. *Cours*, III, 542 ff. *Système de politique positive*, I, 73–75.

91. Comte's closeness to the *idéologues* was likely facilitated by his friendly relations with Armand Marrast, a convinced supporter of ideology. On him see F. Picavet, pp. 554–555; cf. G. Weill, *Histoire du parti républicain en France* (Paris, 1900), p. 241.

92. *Opuscules*, pp. 291, 296; *Cours*, III, 533, 541–542.

93. Comte, "Examen du traité de Broussais sur l'irritation" (August 1828), in *Opuscules*, pp. 290–306; *Cours*, III, 539.

94. Johann Gaspar Spurzheim (1776–1832), Austrian physician and co-founder with F. J. Gall of phrenology. Ed.

95. *Opuscules*, pp. 291, 296; *Cours*, III, 533, 555, 563, 570, 573; VI, 253; *Système de politique positive*, I, 729.

96. [*Cours*, III, 534, editor's translation.] *Cours*, I, 30; III, 534, 535, 540.

97. *Opuscules*, pp. 293–295; *Cours*, I, 30–34; III, 538–541; VI, 402–403. Comte makes this argument already in 1819, well before the appearance of Broussais's tract in 1828.

98. *Cours*, IV, 350, editor's translation and citation.

99. *Cours*, IV, 349, editor's translation and citation.

100. *Cours*, I, 74; III, 258–259; IV, 2, 345–346, 349–350; VI, 606, 713.

101. *Opuscules*, pp. 296–297; *Cours*, IV, 345. M. Ferraz, *Histoire de la philosophie pendant la révolution*, pp. 59, 97....

102. *Opuscules*, pp. 294–295; *Cours*, I, 30....

103. *Système de politique positive*, II, 434....

104. *Système de politique positive*, I, 671–672, editor's translation.

105. *Système de politique positive*, I, 669–735....

106. *Système de politique positive*, I, 672....

107. Saint-Simon made an analogous comparison; his views might also, of course, have influenced Comte.

108. *Cours*, I, 11, editor's translation.

109. *Opuscules*, p. 170; *Cours*, I, 11–12, IV, 490. For Comte's curious indications, obtained by him through introspection, about how he reexperienced, at the time of his illness, the "law" of three stages, see *Système de politique positive*, III, 75. Cf. V. I. Ger'e, "O. Kont i ego znachenie v istoricheskoi nauke," *Voprosy filosofii i psikhologii* 9: 2–5, kn. 42–45 (1898).

110. W. Wundt, *Logik*, II (1), pp. 170–171. Hugo Münsterberg, *Über Aufgaben und Methoden der Psychologie*, in *Schriften der Gesellschaft für psychologische Forschung*, vol. 2 (Leipzig, 1891), p. 175. Alfred Binet, *Vvedenie v eksperimental'nuiu psikhologiiu*, trans. E. Maksimova (St. Petersburg, 1895), pp. 22–24.

111. *Cours,* I, 32; *Système de politique positive,* I, 682, 685, 726; IV, 235. John Stuart Mill has also indicated that the phrenologist must use introspection. See his *Auguste Comte and Positivism,* pp. 65–66. [Lappo-Danilevskii cites the Spiridonov translation, pp. 70–71.]

112. ["Mais sa masse affective veille toujours, pour maintenir l'unité et la continuité de chaque existence animale." *Système de politique positive,* I, 690.] *Cours,* III, 545; *Système de politique positive,* I, 690, 691, 726, 728.

113. *Cours,* III, 563–567; *Système de politique positive,* I, 711: "La volonté proprement dite ne constitue que le dernier état du désir, quand la délibération mentale a reconnu la convenance d'une impulsion dominante." [Insets in text are Lappo-Danilevskii's.]

114. *Système de politique positive,* I, 616, 684, 711, 724, 727 (here the possibility of "choice" is supposed); IV, 36–39, 77–79, 166, 237.

115. *Système de politique positive,* II, 217 ff.; cf. L. Lévy-Bruhl, *La philosophie d'Auguste Comte,* pp. 254–261.

116. *Cours,* IV, 252, 420; V, 359. *Système de politique positive,* I, 95, 334, 368, 613, 702; II, 159, 168, 266; IV, 462. In his last work Comte also considers the will; see *Synthèse subjective* (Paris, 1856), pp. 8 ff., 25.

117. *Cours,* IV, 262, editor's translation.

118. Adam Ferguson, *Principles of Moral and Political Science,* vol. 1 (Edinburgh, 1792), pp. 190–339. *Cours,* IV, 262; *Système de politique positive,* IV, 185; *Synthèse subjective,* p. 25.

119. David Hume, *A Treatise of Human Nature,* ed. L. A. Selby-Bigge (Oxford: Oxford University Press, 1951; reprint of 1888–1896 edition), II, iii, 3, p. 415. Ed.

120. *Système de politique positive,* I, 698, editor's translation and citation.

121. *Cours,* III, 558, 562; *Système de politique positive,* I, 670, 681, 687, 698, 710–711, 726. Gall's division of affects into *penchants* and *sentiments* was at first accepted by Comte but later rejected by him; see *Système de politique positive,* I, 680, 683; Rousseau's influence on Comte is doubtful.

122. *Cours,* III, 542; IV, 387, 389, 391, 397; *August Comte conservateur,* pp. 200, 230, 279, 293.

123. *Auguste Comte conservateur,* pp. 220, 229, 230. *Système de politique positive,* III, 68. [Inset Lappo-Danilevskii's.]

124. *Cours,* III, 538, 553; IV, 392, 422.

125. David Hume, *Works,* II (Boston, 1854), 105. Adam Smith, *Theory of Moral Sentiments,* I (London, 1797), 1 ff.

126. David Hume, *Enquiry Concerning the Principles of Morals,* sec. II (1751): *Hume's Philosophical Works,* IV, eds. T. H. Green and T. H. Grose (London, 1874–1875), 237 ff.

127. As is well known, Gall supposed the existence of special organs of the brain for social instincts. Comte sometimes discusses such instincts in the same spirit. He speaks, for example, about the "irrésistible tendance sociale de la nature humaine" and about the "sociabilité essentiellement spontanée de l'espèce humaine en vertu d'un penchant instinctif à la vie commune." Following the opinion of the Scottish philosophers, for example, Adam Ferguson, *Essay on the History of Civil Society,* 7th edition (Edinburgh, 1814), pp. 30–31, he suggests that such an instinct anticipates consciousness in the individual of the benefits of a given social exchange (*Cours,* IV, 384–387). Comte also calls sympathy

an instinct (ibid., 395); for his definition of sympathy, see *Cours,* IV, 392. Nonetheless Comte's regard for the Scottish school (*Cours,* III, 553; IV, 392) and the absence in the *Cours* of any physiological definition of sympathy evoke doubt about the meaning Comte gave it. For examples of the identification of "sympathy" with social feeling, benevolence, and love, see *Cours,* IV, 395; VI, 467; *Système de politique positive,* II, 149, 177, 400. Cf. *A. Comte conservateur,* pp. 39, 82, 91, 112.

128. *Cours,* IV, 420; VI, 481–486.

129. H. Lietz, *Die Probleme im Begriff der Gesellschaft bei Auguste Comte* (Jena, 1891), p. 46.

130. *Cours,* IV, 326–327; V, 315.

131. *Cours,* IV, 328, 419, 433, 481; V, 304; VI, 475. The author also points to an "instinct de soumission" (ibid., IV, 438); cf. H. Lietz, pp. 48–52, 57–58.

132. *Cours,* IV, 262, editor's translation and citation.

133. "Les passions et la haine de l'ennui," as already Helvétius wrote, "communiquent à l'âme son mouvement." Claude-Adrien Helvétius, *Oeuvres,* I (London, 1781), p. 180. . . . G. Leroy, *Lettres philosophiques sur les animaux et sur l'homme* (Paris, 1892), pp. 20, 38, 64–65, 70–71. *Cours,* IV, 449; cf. VI, 570, 716, 717. *Système de politique positive,* I, 696, 686.

134. *Système de politique positive,* II, 263; IV, 24.

135. Comte also observes, however, that "l'ensemble de la nature humaine reste nécessairement indivisible, malgré nos séparations anarchiques." *Système de politique positive,* II, 227, 240, 437. . . .

136. *Cours,* III, 561; IV, 327, 395, 396, 420. *Système de politique positive,* III, 11–12, 68; I, 450; IV, 30, 56, 167. Without any reservation (and surely without foundation), Caird ascribes to Comte the view that altruistic feelings develop in man without the influence of the intellect, although Comte himself granted such influence in his *Cours.* E. Caird, *The Social Philosophy and Religion of Comte,* 2d edition (Glascow, 1893), pp. 160, 162–163.

137. *Cours,* IV, 458–462.

138. *Cours,* V, 62; cf. Paul Barth, *Die Philosophie der Geschichte als Soziologie* (Leipzig, 1897), pp. 41–42.

139. *Cours,* VI, 56–57, 191–192, 723–774.

140. *Cours,* VI, 490; V, 35, 215.

141. W. Wundt, *Logik,* II (1), p. 17. O. Külpe, *Die Lehre vom Willen in der neueren Psychologie,* in *Philosophischen Studien,* Band V, p. 444.

142. *Opuscules,* p. 154; *Cours,* II, 27–28, IV, 353–354. . . .

143. *Opuscules,* p. 81 [paraphrase].

144. *Cours,* IV, 343, 391; V, 304; cf. B. Chicherin, *Polozhitel'naia filosofiia i edinstvo nauki,* pp. 226–227, 238–239.

145. *Cours,* IV, 393; *Système de politique positive,* I, 27, 327, 735; II, 37, 444, 454. . . .

146. *Cours,* VI, 545.

147. *Cours,* IV, 252–253, editor's translation and citation.

148. In the section of his *Cours* dedicated to characterization of "consensus," Comte consistently enough calls it a "principe" or "notion philosophique"; see *Cours,* IV, 234–261, especially 234, 242, 251.

149. *Cours,* IV, 252–253; V, 349; VI, 47, 57.

150. Lévy-Bruhl, who is in general glad to smooth over every contradiction in Comte's doctrine, observes: "Comte ne conteste pas du tout la finalité que Kant appellait interne. ..." (Lévy-Bruhl, *La philosophie d'Auguste Comte,* p. 100). Kant, however, clearly defined the meaning he gave to the principle of internal purposiveness, as Comte did not at all think of doing, having constantly confused the various meanings of the term "purposiveness." I. Kant, *Kritik der Urteilskraft,* § 66, *Sämmtliche Werke,* ed. Gustav Hartenstein, vol. V (Leipzig, 1867–1868), pp. 388–390.

151. *Système de politique positive,* I, 641, editor's translation; *Cours,* IV, 260.

152. *Cours,* IV, 255, 260 [Lappo-Danilevskii encloses much of this sentence in quotation marks, but it is rather a paraphrase]. ...

153. *Cours,* VI, 590, editor's translation.

154. Comte himself espouses such a principle "du *point de vue* humain" and considers it true "sous le *rapport* statique," as well as "sous l'*aspect* dynamique." The expressions italicized by us, as well as the text that follows (especially *Cours,* VI, 592), suggest the extent to which Comte gave his principle only subjective significance, although this did not prevent him from drawing conclusions of another type from it. Nonetheless Comte's position is often given directly objective significance: see, for example, R. Eucken, "Zur Würdigung Comtes und des Positivismus," in *Philosophische Aufsätze Eduard Zeller gewidmet* (Leipzig, 1887); B. Chicherin, *Polozhitel'naia filosofiia i edinstvo nauki,* pp. 203, 234 (who frankly calls Comte's claim "monstrous"); and F. Allengry, *Essai historique et critique sur la sociologie chez Auguste Comte,* p. 267.

155. In the *Système de politique positive,* there is in fact a passage that seems to speak on behalf of another interpretation: "... L'homme proprement dit," Comte writes here, "n'existe que dans le cerveau trop abstrait de nos métaphysiciens. Il n'y a, au fond, de réel que l'humanité. ..." (*Système de politique positive,* I, 334; cf. IV, 31–32). But in other passages of the same tract Comte discusses the human being "comme être distinct," and states that "l'homme proprement dit, considéré dans sa réalité fondamentale ... ne peut être *compris* sans la *connaissance* préalable de l'humanité, dont il dépend nécéssairement" (*Système de politique positive,* II, 60–62, 433; IV, 182–183). Cf. Comte's remarks about "valeur personelle," man's "personalité," and that he represents "une certaine personification du Grand Être," and so on.

156. *Système de politique positive,* II, 164, 168–169, 467; IV, 27–28, 30.

157. *Système de politique positive,* II, 71, editor's translation and citation.

158. *Système de politique positive,* I, 363, 421; II, 71; IV, 34; cf. H. Michel, *Idée de l'Etat* (Paris, 1895), p. 439.

159. Turgot, *Oeuvres* (1808), II, 53, 54, 56, 236, 294–295, 339; on the "law" of the three stages among Turgot's successors, see F. Picavet, *Les idéologues,* 453–455, 459.

160. Condorcet, *Esquisse d'un tableau historique des progrès de l'esprit humain* (1795), pp. 11, 214, 235, 265, 282, 286, 293, 299, 303, 305.

161. D. de Tracy, *Idéologie* (1817), I, 284–302; P. Cabanis, "Lettre sur la perfectibilité," as an appendix to Picavet, *Les idéologues,* pp. 590–596. ...

162. G. Weill, *Un précurseur du socialisme, Saint-Simon et son oeuvre* (Paris, 1894), pp. 181–194.

163. Kant, *Werke,* ed. Hartenstein, IV, 155, 156. Kant's work ("Idee zu einer allge-

meinen Geschichte in weltbürgerlicher Absicht") was issued in two editions in Charles de Viller's translation, and then it was published again in François de Neufchâteau's translation. See François Picavet, "La philosophie de Kant en France, de 1773 à 1814," in his translation of *Critique de la raison pratique* (Paris, 1902), p. XIII. . . .

164. There is not a little in common between the views of Kant and Comte on the evolution of humanity. Besides the subjective significance of the principle of evolution, Kant touches upon many other themes. Thus, for example, speaking against transformism (Kant, *Werke,* ed. Hartenstein, IV, 180) and for a certain constancy in human nature (VII, 395), he supposes the existence in man of "seeds or original tendencies," in the sense of "limitations—otherwise inexplicable—of a self-constituting faculty acting on itself. These limitations we simply cannot explain further or render comprehensible" (IV, 188). [Review of Johann Gottfried Herder's *Ideen zur Philosophie der Geschichte der Menscheit* (Part Two), as translated by Robert E. Anchor in *Kant on History,* ed. Lewis White Beck (New York: Macmillan, 1963), p. 48. Lappo-Danilevskii quotes the German original.] Naturally, given such a condition Kant speaks not of "revolution," but of "evolution" (VII, 401, 407). The process of evolution seems to him to be a struggle (*Zweitracht*) between the animal and properly human traits of our nature, as a result of which man is transformed from an *animal rationabile* into an *animal rationale;* in the scheme [*planomernost'*] of nature such a struggle becomes a means for achieving the goal of human perfectibility (*Perfektionierung des Menschen*) (IV, 146–148, especially clearly in VII, 647). Moreover, man, as a rational being, is capable of perfecting himself according to ends posed by and for himself (IV, 145; VII, 646–647). [From "Idee zu einer allgemeinen Geschichte in weltbürgerlicher Absicht" (*Werke,* IV) and *Anthropologie in pragmatischer Hinsicht* (*Werke,* VII).] Perfectibility consists, however, not in "civilization" alone, which has been acquired to an excess, but in the achievement of moral excellence (IV, 152). Finally, discussing progress as manifesting itself only in humanity as a whole and in the continuity [of the species] (IV, 144, 147; VII, 393, 397, 649), Kant comes to the conclusion that "the ultimate end that man has cause to ascribe to nature, with regard to the human species, can only be culture" (V, 445). [*Kritik der Urteilskraft,* § 83, editor's translation.] All of Kant's above conclusions (not to mention certain others) can be found in Comte's works; we are not suggesting, however, that this is a case of direct borrowing. Comte knew German poorly, was only superficially familiar with Kant's philosophy, and usually referred to him only in discussing the theory of knowledge; the founder of sociology might make use of Kant's thought on the subjective character of the principle of evolution, but he hardly mastered the rest of Kant's views. In any event, Kant's consistent teleology in his *Kritik der Urteilskraft* and short essays on the philosophy of history could not at all accord in spirit with Comte. Nonetheless Comte unwittingly came in many cases to analogous conclusions, which again shows how much his philosophy was, in significant measure, the historical product of the general course of eighteenth- and early nineteenth-century European thought.

165. Henri de Saint-Simon, *Science de l'homme,* éd. Enfantin (Paris, 1858), p. 324.

166. Henri de Saint-Simon, *Science de l'homme,* pp. 287, 362, 432; Comte himself referred often enough to [Joseph] de Maistre; see *Cours,* IV, 28; V, 241; *Système de politique positive,* III, 615.

167. *Cours,* IV, 278, editor's translation and citation.

168. *Cours*, IV, 261 ff.

169. [The first part of this quotation appears to be a paraphrase; the second part is my translation from *Cours*, IV, 263.] Comte, *Opuscules*, p. 166; *Cours*, IV, 282, 287; V, 62.

170. For examples of the identification of the terms "influence" and "cause," see *Cours*, IV, 282, 287; V, 62.

171. *Cours*, IV, 261, 264.

172. *Opuscules*, p. 115; *Cours*, IV, 274–275, 331–334.

173. This appears to be a paraphrase of *Cours*, IV, 274. Ed.

174. *Cours*, IV, 261 ff; *Système de politique positive*, I, 105–106; II, 2, 41, 425.

175. *Cours*, IV, 146: "L'idée rationelle de progrès ... , c'est-à-dire de développement continu, avec tendance inévitable et permanente vers un but déterminé, doit être certainement attribuée ... à l'influence inaperçue de la philosophie positive, seule capable d'ailleurs de dégager irrévocablement cette grande notion de l'état. ..." *Système de politique positive*, II, 38.

176. [This appears to be a paraphrase of *Cours*, IV, 274.] Henri de Saint-Simon, *Science de l'homme*, p. 370. . . . Saint-Simon's thought might have influenced Comte; see *Cours*, III, 218; VI, 623–631. . . . B. Chicherin, *Polozhitel'naia filosofiia i edinstvo nauki*, p. 239, has already pointed out the antinomy in Comte between recognizing only one possible orientation and the possibility of many orientations.

177. *Cours*, IV, 459; V, 339; L. Lévy-Bruhl, pp. 190, 204, 210, 211.

178. *Cours*, IV, 302.

179. Condorcet, *Esquisse d'un tableau historique des progrès de l'esprit humain*, p. 11. It might well be possible to find the roots of this approach in Pascal's well-known comparison between the development of the individual and that of humanity. I will call Condorcet's and Comte's fiction the "fiction of linear evolution."

180. *Cours*, IV, 392–397; V, 215; *Système de politique positive*, I, 92; II, 142. . . . Cf. E. Littré, *Auguste Comte et la philosophie positive*, p. 551; V. I. Ger'e, "O. Kont i ego znachenie v istoricheskoi nauke," *Voprosy filosofii i psikhologii* 9: 2–5, kn. 42–45 (1898).

181. *Cours*, V, 195, 333, 344, 346; *Système de politique positive*, II, 89, 95, 136. . . .

182. *Cours*, V, 362, editor's translation and citation.

183. *Opuscules*, 30, 124, 127; *Cours*, IV, 292, 388, 459–460; V, 362; VI, 40, 545; *Système de politique positive*, I, 40, 53; II, 465; III, 46, 55, 530–534; IV, 6, 185.

184. Comte does not use the term *"perfection,"* but employs the words *"progrès"* and *"perfectionnement"* in the sense of process as well as of goal; to distinguish these concepts, we will call the first "perfectibility" [*sovershenstvovanie*] and the second "perfection" [*sovershenstvo*], not depriving them of the content Comte gave them.

185. *Cours*, IV, 278; *Système de politique positive*, I, 27–28, 106–107, 321, 609, 658; II, 2, 160–169, 174.

186. *Système de politique positive*, II, 129, 465; IV, 7, 21.

187. Exposition of the "law of the three stages" can be found in the works of Comte himself (*Opuscules*, pp. 100–101, 147–149, 182–194; more completely in the *Cours*, IV, 462–520, as well as elsewhere there and in the *Système de politique positive*) and in a number of works indicated in the appendixes to F. Allengry, *Essai historique et critique sur la sociologie chez Auguste Comte* (Paris, 1900) and H. Waentig, *A. Comte und seine Be-*

deutung für die Entwicklung der Sozialwissenschaft (Leipzig, 1894), especially in the following books and essays: E. Faguet, *Politiques et moralistes du XIX siècle* (Paris, 1898); L. Lévy-Bruhl, *La philosophie d'Auguste Comte* (Paris, 1900), pp. 39–55; P. Barth, *Philosophie der Geschichte als Soziologie* (Leipzig, 1897), pp. 36–48; E. Caird, *The Social Philosophy and Religion of A. Comte,* 2d edition (Glasgow, 1893), 1–46; V. Solov'ëv, "Teoriia Ogiusta Konta o trekh fazisakh v umstvennom razvitii chelovechestva," *Pravoslavnoe obozrenie,* no. 11 (November 1874), pp. 589–608; and V. I. Ger'e, "O. Kont i ego znachenie v istoricheskoi nauke," *Voprosy filosofii i psikhologii* 9: 2–5, kn. 42–45 (1898). . . .

188. *Système de politique positive,* II, 172, editor's translation.

189. [*Système de politique positive,* III, 618, editor's translation.] *Opuscules,* pp. 60, 192; *Cours,* I, 15; *Système de politique positive,* I, 330; III, 618. In several cases it is as if Comte personifies evolution; see, for example, *Cours,* IV, 23; V, 207; *Système de politique positive,* I, pp. 3, 8; IV, 232. It is difficult to say whether we are dealing here with simple metaphor or the fantastic transformation of evolution into a special motive principle drawing humanity to positivism. In *Système de politique positive,* it is possible to find passages in which Comte discusses the "providential" work of the *Grand Être* (I, 168–169, 174).

190. *Cours,* IV, 35, editor's translation; cf. *Système de politique positive,* II, 95. P. Janet, "Les origines de la philosophie d'Auguste Comte," *Revue de deux mondes,* August 1887, pp. 626 ff. P. Barth, *Philosophie der Geschichte als Soziologie,* pp. 49–50. . . .

191. *Cours,* V, 293; *Système de politique positive,* I, 5, 12, 15, 17, 20, 97–98, 681, 700; II, 14; IV, 230–245.

192. *Cours,* V, 302, editor's translation; *Cours,* IV, 396; *Système de politique positive,* III, 68; IV, 20.

193. *Opuscules,* p. 23; *Système de politique positive,* I, 22.

194. *Cours,* V, 23; *Système de politique positive,* I, 108.

195. Representatives of the Russian "subjective" school pointed long ago to this essential gap in Comte's social philosophy. See P. Lavrov, "Zadachi positivizma i ikh reshenie," *Sovremennoe obozrenie* (May 1868), pp. 137, 139–140; and N. Mikhailovskii, *Sobranie Sochinenii,* I, 70 [*Sochineniia N. K. Mikhailovskogo,* six volumes (St. Petersburg, 1896–1897)].

196. *Système de politique positive,* I, preface, 4; 94, 96, 352, 356, 417; II, 19, 47, 148; III, 48; IV, 45, 51, 61, 685.

197. [This may be a paraphrase of *Système de politique positive,* I, 405.] *Système de politique positive,* I, 127, 405, 693–694; III, 68; IV, 79. Still later Comte hints at a connection between the will and moral action; *Système de politique positive,* IV, 331. *Synthèse subjective,* p. 25.

198. *Cours,* IV, 396; V, 304. *Système de politique positive,* I, 323; II, 170; IV, 535.

199. *Système de politique positive,* I, 396.

200. *Système de politique positive,* I, 325, 361; II, 59, 103, 120, 123, 169, 466; III, 601; IV, 537. Saint-Simon's formula about the duty to work ("L'homme doit travailler") influenced Comte.

201. *Cours,* VI, 467, editor's translation.

202. *Cours*, VI, 467; *Système de politique positive*, I, 352. . . .

203. Rudolf Eucken, "Zur Würdigung Comtes und des Positivismus," in *Philosophische Aufsätze Eduard Zeller gewidmet* (Leipzig, 1887). "The unity of the person," Eucken writes, "an act done from one's own nature, the force of one's inner convictions against all authority, the demand for external as well as inner freedom, self-directed activity, the life of the Spirit for its own sake — none find any place in Comte. Yet precisely these ideas are the motive forces of modern times. . . . Even his reform proposals show that he took evil to be something merely temporary and external. The depths of the spiritual conflicts of inner life had as little importance for him as the impassioned clash of individuals in the wild struggle for existence and even less for the enjoyment of existence." [Editor's translation from the German, which Lappo-Danilevskii quotes.] Comte himself, however, could not fail to recognize the autonomous significance of the person as a creative force (*Cours*, V, 222, VI, 339, 486), as H. Lietz has already noted in part: *Die Probleme im Begriff der Gesellschaft bei Auguste Comte* (Jena, 1891), pp. 91–92. Gradually Comte increasingly emphasized the "noble" qualities of man. See, for example, *Cours*, VI, 762; *Système de politique positive*, I, 297, 342; II, 63, 67, 73; IV, 24. Also see F. Picavet, *La philosophie de Kant*, p. XXXII.

204. *Système de politique positive*, I, 98, 330, 363; II, 45, 66, 95; IV, 280–290.

205. L. Lévy-Bruhl, *La philosophie d'Auguste Comte*, 375–378. Lévy-Bruhl tries to soften the categorical nature of this type of conclusion: first, Comte, in his opinion, struggled against the metaphysical (i.e., absolute) idea of right worked out by the Revolution, as affirmed by certain of his texts (for example, *Système de politique positive*, I, 361; II, 87); second, equal obligations, falling on everyone, give rise to corresponding rights. Lévy-Bruhl himself cites, however, Comte's remark that "modern philosophy has tended more and more to replace vague and emotional discussion of rights with calm and rigorous determination of respective duties" (*Cours*, VI, 454); and he might have quoted the following text as well: "Each has duties toward everyone else, but no one has any rights, properly speaking. . . . In other words, no one has any rights except that of always doing his duty . . ." (*Système de politique positive*, I, 361; IV, 342). [Editor's translation from the French, which Lappo-Danilevskii quotes.] Neither Comte's basic view of the person, nor the absence of a system of guarantees of private rights, nor the positive restriction of them (e.g., of freedom of opinion) speaks on behalf of Lévy-Bruhl's view. The opposite opinion has already been expressed by R. Eucken, "Zur Würdigung Comtes und des Positivismus," and after him by H. Lietz, *Die Probleme im Begriff der Gesellschaft bei Auguste Comte*, pp. 88, 90, 91, and by H. Michel, *Idée de l'Etat* (Paris, 1895), pp. 439–441.

206. Blaise Pascal (1623–1662), French mathematician, physicist, and Christian philosopher. His chief philosophical works are the *Lettres provinciales* (1656–1657), written in defense of Jansenism against the Jesuits, and *Pensées* (1670), a Christian apologia in aphoristic form. Comte wrote that his own conception of social science fulfilled the "famous suggestion" of Pascal that the whole human race, past, present, and future, constituted a vast and eternal social unit, whose different organs, individual and national, concur in the evolution of humanity (*Cours*, IV, 293). Ed.

207. *Système de politique positive*, IV, 30. Marie Jean Guyau, *La Morale d'Épicure et ses rapports avec les doctrines contemporaines* (Paris, 1878), pp. 270, 277. . . .

208. A concise but clear account can be found in H. Gruber, *Auguste Comte, der*

Begründer des Positivismus (Freiburg in Breisgau, 1889), pp. 101–116. Also see E. Caird, pp. 1–46. . . .

209. *Opuscules,* p. 199; *Cours,* III, 207; IV, 327. *Système de politique positive,* I, 335–337. On the fiction of linear evolution, see above; about its influence on the idea of humanity, see *Système de politique positive,* IV, 30.

210. *Cours,* III, 216; VI, 748, 760; *Système de politique positive,* I, 4, 5, 14–36, 301, 446; II, 53–58. Cf. Lévy-Bruhl, p. 409.

211. *Système de politique positive,* II, 62. . . .

212. *Cours,* VI, 743; *Système de politique positive,* II, 360.

213. *Cours,* VI, 743; *Système de politique positive,* II, 434; III, 48–50; IV, 181, 183, 230–245; for Comte's peculiar concept of religion, which likely came about under the influence of Saint-Simon, see *Système de politique positive,* I, 8.

214. *Cours,* IV, 327, 486.

215. Inset Lappo-Danilevskii's.

216. Also see *Système de politique positive,* II, 117.

217. Comte sometimes made incidental remarks about race as a product of the environment and heredity; see, for example, *Système de politique positive,* II, 449. Yet for some reason he considered it his duty to declare, "J'ai du soigneusement écarter les conditions de climat et de race en fondant la sociologie abstraite" (ibid., I, 436).

218. In his last work Comte, together with "sciences physiques" and "lois physiques," refers in passing to "sciences morales" and "lois morales," but he did not make further use of the idea. *Système de politique positive,* II, 34; IV, 226.

219. At the time linguistics was making some gains; these were facilitated by certain French scholars already in the eighteenth century. See Charles de Brosses, *Traité de la formation mécanique des langues,* 2 vols. (1765); A. Turgot, "Etymologie," in the *Encyclopédie.* G. Leroy directed attention to animal language: *Lettres sur les animaux et sur l'homme* (Paris, 1802), pp. 82 ff. The *idéologues* also liked to discuss language; see, for example, D. de Tracy, *Idéologie,* èd. 1817, I, ch. XVI and others; about the other *idéologues,* including the philologist F. Thurot, see F. Picavet, *Les idéologues,* pp. 457–466, 506–508, etc. On the arguments of Bonald and Ballanche, see E. Faguet, *Politiques et moralistes du XIX siècle* (Paris, 1898), p. 142. Comte recognized the universal basis of language, but treated it mainly as a means of intercourse: *Système de politique positive,* I, 289–291, 720–723; II, 216, 263. It is enough to recall the names of Adam Smith and J. B. Say, Jeremy Bentham and Friedrich Karl von Savigny, to come to the conclusion that the author of the *Cours* could not have been ignorant of the social sciences; on the situation of political science in France at the time, see H. Michel, *L'idée de l'Etat* (Paris, 1895). [L. G. A. de Bonald (1754–1840) and P. S. Ballanche (1776–1847) were French traditionalists. Jean Baptiste Say (1767–1832), French political economist associated with the *idéologues,* generally followed Smith. On Savigny, see Novgorodtsev's essay (Chapter 8) in this volume.]

220. Lampert Adolphe Quételet (1796–1874), Belgian astronomer and mathematician, one of the founders of modern statistics and particularly of its application to social phenomena. His works include *Physique sociale, ou essai sur le développement des facultés de l'homme* (1835, 2d edition 1869), which contains the construction of the "average man" (*homme moyen*), and *Lettres sur la théorie des probabilités* (1846). Ed.

221. Apparently Comte did not reject the theory of probability as an abstract mathematical calculus, but only the applications that, for example, Condorcet, Laplace, and Poisson made from it in the depositions of witnesses and in the decisions of a number of judges and jurors, and that in Comte's time already evoked the criticism of F. Thurot (F. Picavet, *Les idéologues*, p. 464) and now are considered arbitrary (J. Bertrand, *Théorie des probabilities*, Paris, 1889, pp. 319–325). Comte transferred his doubts regarding the legitimacy of the arguments of Condorcet and his successors to the application of the statistical method in general to the social sciences. D'Alembert testifies already in 1802 to the development of statistics in France after the Revolution (John T. Merz, *A History of European Thought in the Nineteenth Century*, vol. 1, pp. 149, 153). . . . [Pierre Simon Laplace (1749–1827), mathematician, physicist, and astronomer. He formulated the nebular hypothesis of the origins of the solar system (1796) and also developed the theory of probability. S. D. Poisson (1781–1840), French mathematician and statistician.]

222. Toward Laplace (chairman of the council of the École polytechnique) and Poisson Comte experienced, it seems, hostile feelings; he despised the "légistes" as closely connected to the Revolution and so forth.

223. At least Comte himself, in his last works, uses this term in application to his "abstract" depiction of the history of humanity, which is what his "social dynamics" amounts to. See, for example, *Système de politique positive*, II, 463; III, 5, 67; IV, 17, 505.

224. *Système de politique positive*, III, 70. Here the author speaks of "four sociological laws," but he confuses his principles with his laws, and psychological laws with sociological ones (ibid., IV, 173–180).

225. *Cours*, IV, 24 [the second part of this quotation is a paraphrase].

I I

Renan as Champion of Freedom of Thought

S. F. OL'DENBURG

The more often dogmatism and intolerance are encountered, especially within the scientific *Weltanschauung,* the more we learn to value the true free-thinking that corresponds to the critical and progressive spirit of science. In the present sketch we would like to remember one of the most prominent champions of such free-thinking. The dogmatism against which Renan[1] struggled cannot be considered entirely obsolete. In order to be free of it, one needs great tolerance and a deep conviction in the "infinite diversity of tasks the universe presents to us."[2] In both respects Renan can serve as an instructive model for our times. The scientific spirit he defended has very little in common with that of outdated positivism: we find in Renan neither the desire to use a one-sided understanding of science to exclude other manifestations of spiritual life, nor a narrow outlook on the future. In this he is, in our view, especially valuable, and therefore it is all the more important to remember him now, as a representative of the true spirit of science, when a new wave of philosophical criticism, defending the legitimate diversity of the tasks and manifestations of the human spirit, is purifying the very idea of science from foreign encroachments.

[...]

The introduction of this "scientific spirit" into that sphere from which it, even in the twentieth century, is so often banned, the sphere of religion, constituted the task of Renan's whole life and took the form of a struggle for the right of every conscientious and honest-minded person to think and believe as he considers right. A full and impartial acquaintance with the works of Renan leads to the undoubted conviction that they have not, and could not have, impaired anyone's sincere beliefs, but have only taught people to recognize and respect the convictions of others as equal in rights to their own.

[. . .]

From . . . Renan's writings we should dwell first on a work of his youth, published forty years after it was written, *L'Avenir de la science*. In this book, where the abundance of thoughts somewhat interferes with the symmetry of exposition, all Renan is contained in embryo, like a plan of everything he would accomplish in life. What is said here he subsequently repeated many times, only less sharply, less emphatically. The whole book is a passionate genuflection to science.

Here he already insists on his favorite idea, that truth is only a compromise among innumerable different opinions.[3] Leaving Catholicism for science, he breaks with the church in moving words. . . . The belief, ardently professed in *The Future of Science,* in free inquiry into all questions and in the impossibility of being sure you possess the absolute final truth, made it inconceivable for Renan to return to the bosom of the church he abandoned, a church that did not include tolerance among the virtues it professed.

The development of the ideas set forth in *The Future of Science* . . . occupies several collections of Renan's articles. . . . In some of them he — touching upon all possible questions of history, history of religion, literature, and ethics — pursues the idea of the necessity of a constant broadening of man's intellectual horizon, of the necessity of delving into and trying to understand as many sides of life as possible, so that narrowness of worldview will not hinder continuous searching for the approximate truth accessible to human understanding. . . .

Another series of articles, mainly included in two collections — *Études d'histoire religieuse* and *Nouvelles études d'histoire religieuse* — is of rather different character: they speak about people of faith and acts of faith, and attest to the profound understanding of religion that always distinguished Renan. Here, before such figures as St. Francis of Assisi, he expresses in ardent, beautiful words his admiration for the faith of "these little ones," who in their simple, artless faith do not think about theoretical, unconditional proofs of that which gives meaning and beauty to their lives.[4] Renan, a man of science who knows that any claim is true only to a certain extent, is moved by this immense faith, this simplicity, that does not know any limits or doubts.

[. . .]

The task to which Renan dedicated his scientific work and his whole life was very difficult, and it cannot be said that even now, more than half a century after his work began, we have gone especially far along the path to recognizing a person's right to construct his own worldview according to his convictions: the desire to level, to bring everything under definite general formulas and dogmas, is still deeply rooted in contemporary man. If heretics are no longer burned at the stake, nonetheless there is no form of persecution, beginning with jail and ending with the contempt and disdain of others, to which someone could not be subjected once he has resolved to follow his own path to faith and truth, as he senses and understands them.

The basic obstacle to eliminating this distressing situation impeding the forward movement of humanity is that, as Renan perceived perfectly correctly, a person is generally inclined to defend stubbornly the exclusiveness of his own truths, which seem to him absolute. They so much possess him that he has left neither feelings for, nor thoughts of, those truths that seem in their own turn absolute to others. In one of his speeches Renan, speaking of Spinoza, who was cursed by his convinced co-religionists for his independent search for truth,[5] tells the story about how even on the day of his death the great thinker conversed with his hosts about the church sermon they had heard that day, praised it, and advised them to follow the behests of their pastor.[6] In these few lines the whole question is boldly posed: narrowness of worldview and intolerance toward freedom of thought on the one hand; breadth of view, respect, and attention toward a faith you do not share, on the other. It often seems to people that giving attention and especially sympathy or understanding to views whose truth they dispute belittles and demeans their own beliefs. Their reasoning is very simple: they possess the truth, that is, that which is completely right, with the exception of everything else not in agreement with it; consequently, everything else, since it is incorrect, does not exist for them. With this they lose even the desire for independent verification of this something else.

But how is such an attitude to be overcome, how are people to be convinced that the "absolute truths" of others can be respected without shaking one's own? Renan's answer is clear — by knowledge, by science. It alone can give man the breadth he needs. True, passing to it is difficult: "Who, after having *really* given himself to science, has not cursed the day he was born to thought, and has not had to mourn over some dear illusion? As for me, I acknowledge that I have had much to mourn; yes, there have been days when I would have wished for the sleep once more of simple people, when I would have been angry at critique and rationalism, if only one could be angry at inevitability. The first feeling of one who is passing from naïve belief to critical examination is regret and almost cursing of that inflexible force that, once it has seized you, forces you to travel with it through all the stages of its inevitable march until the end, where you stop to cry."[7] But it is not the end, Renan says, and precisely these regrets, this agitation of the soul seeking truth, serve as the best proof that this apparent end is only the beginning of something else, something new: the skeptics of the eighteenth century gladly destroyed and did not feel the need for any new faith; they were occupied only with the business of destruction and with consciousness of the living force in them.[8]

The new that is constructed on the ground prepared by science already differs significantly from what came before: first, it is to a large degree personal, and then it is also much broader. It is so broad and free that it is called indifference: "From this stinking source of *indifferentism* flows the absurd and erroneous claim, or rather fantasy, that *freedom of conscience* is to be affirmed and guaranteed for everyone. The path to this pernicious error is prepared by freedom of opinion, complete and unlimited, which to the misfortune of religious and civil society is widespread, with people repeating, extremely impudently, that it even has some benefit for religion itself. *But,* St. Augustine asks, *what death is worse for the soul than freedom of error?* In truth, when every restraint that has kept people on the paths of truth is removed, their nature, inclined to evil, falls into the abyss."[9] Thus does Pope Gregory XVI's encyclical [*Mirari vos*], condemning the passionate search for truth by the ardently believing Lamennais,[10] inveigh against freedom of conscience. The papal words distinctly and clearly state why there must not be this freedom: human nature itself is inclined to evil, *ipsorum natura ad malum inclinata.* But science does not know about this inclination to evil; on the contrary, it sees that at any given time there are people who are considered evil, as there are people who are considered good. It sees that man has always been capable of what he calls improvement; it has seen and sees that he has striven and strives to broaden the horizon of his mind and heart, and that the obstacles that have tried to block him on this path have fallen. It has seen and sees that those who have disavowed generally recognized truths have often remained and still remain, as everyone acknowledges, just as moral as those who have followed these truths, and often even more so.

Thus science cannot accept the usual objections against freedom of conscience: it does not make man indifferent, nor does it make him immoral. It does not impede man's quest for answers to the questions that torment him, but transfers these answers to the personal sphere, depriving them of general, binding significance.

Renan gives us an example of such an attempt in his essay, "Examen de conscience philosophique."[11] "The first duty of the sincere man is to not influence his own opinions, to let reality be reflected in him as in a photographer's darkroom, and to be present as a spectator at the battles inside him, among the ideas at the depths of his consciousness. We must not intervene in this spontaneous work, but must remain passive before the internal changes of our intellectual retina. It is not that the result of this unconscious evolution would be indifferent to us or that it would not entail grave consequences; but we do not have the right to a desire when reason speaks."[12] And thus his reason speaks, using every means, to what science can give him, and before us arises the balanced structure of a whole worldview, where God is in the process of "becoming," gradually taking shape from the interaction of individual consciousnesses into a world consciousness: "The world, at present governed by blind or feeble consciousness, may one day be governed by a more reflective consciousness. Every injustice will then be atoned, every tear dried."[13] It is possible to agree or not agree with this worldview, but one cannot fail to recognize in it all the grounds of a *personal-religious* worldview, hints of which (or constructions close to it) are dispersed among Renan's various works. It is proof, as it were, that tolerance, when combined with the broadest understanding of the thoughts and feelings of others and with an adaptability that is the result of extraordinary breadth, does not make a sincerely thinking person barren in the religious respect.

Reading "Examen de conscience philosophique," we understand that it was not easy play with ideas or theories, with which Renan is reproached by those not knowing or not wishing to know him, that compelled him to write the following lines: "We are dogmatists-critics. We believe in truth, although we would not claim to possess absolute truth. ... We neither impose ourselves on the future, nor accept without verification the heritage of the past." "The critic examines all systems not as a skeptic to find them false, but to find them true in certain regards."[14] These words are an expression, in the language of the nineteenth century, of an idea advanced many centuries earlier by the Buddhist emperor Asoka: "The faiths of others all deserve to be honored. ... For if a man extols his own faith and disparages another because of devotion to his own and because he wants to glorify it, he seriously injures his own faith."[15] The same idea was expressed several hundred years after Asoka by a Jew, a teacher of the law, the Pharisee Gamaliel, who advised the Sanhedrin not to persecute the apostles: "Let these men be and release them. For if this plan or this undertaking is of human origin, it will fail; but if it is of God, you will not be able to overthrow them."[16]

An Indian, a Jew, and a European — all are spokesmen of the same eternal truth: "Believe, as you know, and let another believe, as he knows."

Notes

1. Joseph Ernest Renan (1832–1892), French critic and historian, best known for his *Life of Jesus* (1863). He studied for the priesthood but left the seminary in 1845 because of doubts raised by his philological study of the Bible. He was interested in the evolution of languages and religions as manifestations of the development of human consciousness, which he thought was, however, ultimately the product of natural causes. Renan rejected any supernatural (i.e., theistic) content in religion, but often used religious language in expressing his philosophical views. His own religion was "the progress of reason, that is to say, of science." Ed.

2. Ernest Renan, *Études d'histoire religieuse* (Paris, 1857), p. iv. Ed.

3. Renan, *L'Avenir de la science* (Paris, 1890), p. 433.

4. Renan, *Nouvelles études d'histoire religieuse* (Paris, 1884), pp. 323–351, especially 340–344. Ed.

5. Spinoza was expelled from his synagogue in 1656 for unorthodoxy. S. A. Askol'dov also makes this point in his essay (Chapter 6) in this volume. Ed.

6. *Nouvelles études d'histoire religieuse*, p. 500.

7. *L'Avenir de la science*, p. 92, editor's translation.

8. Ibid., pp. 500–501, 93 ff.

9. These words so clearly and forcefully express an opinion hostile to freedom of conscience that we cite them in their original . . . [Ol'denburg quotes the Latin]. Renan, *Essais de morale et de critique*, 2d edition (Paris, 1860), pp. 160–161, editor's translation.

10. Hugues Félicité Robert de Lamennais (1782–1854), French ecclesiastic and philosopher who defended ultramontanism within the Church while advocating separation of church and state; the latter led to his condemnation by the Vatican in 1832. Ed.

11. Renan, *Feuilles détachées* (Paris, 1924), pp. 401–443.

12. Ibid., pp. 401–402, editor's translation.

13. Ibid., p. 442, editor's translation.

14. *L'Avenir de la science*, pp. 445, 447, editor's translation.

15. Edict XII. [*The Edicts of Asoka*, edited and translated by N. A. Nikam and Richard McKeon (Chicago: University of Chicago Press, 1959), pp. 51–52. Asoka (died 232 B.C.E.), one of the greatest Indian emperors (reigned ?273–232 B.C.E.), was the grandson of Chandragupta Maurya, who founded the Maurya dynasty in 325 B.C.E. Asoka tried to combine tolerance with a policy of making Buddhism the official state religion.]

16. Acts of the Apostles 5:38–39.

On the Question of Moral Creativity

D. E. ZHUKOVSKII

I.

What is morality? "If we keep more clearly in view the standpoint of the 'moral' as we have to take it in the best sense of the word today, it is soon obvious that its concept does not immediately coincide with what apart from it we generally call virtue, conventional life, respectability, and so on. From this point of view a conventionally virtuous man is not ipso facto *moral*, because to be moral needs *reflection*, the specific consciousness of what accords with duty, and action on this preceding consciousness. Duty itself is the law of the will, a law that man nevertheless *freely lays down out of himself, and then he ought to determine himself to this duty for the sake of duty* and its fulfillment, by doing good solely from the conviction he has won that it is the good."[1] According to this definition, the usual concept of "moral" narrows. The ethical or virtuous person, that is, someone acting according to a generally accepted ethical code, can still not be called moral, if his conduct is not preceded by "reflection, the specific consciousness of what accords with duty, and action on this consciousness." This underscores that morality is actual activity. This activity has two sides or, more correctly, two stages. First, it is the activity of "reflection," the result of which is "consciousness of what accords with duty." Second, it is already purely volitional activity: its result will be "action on this consciousness of duty." Thus, morality is *activity*, and this in two ways: reflective and volitional. It requires a certain psychic effort, an expenditure of psychic energy. It is not that I have a code of rules imparted to me from before, borrowed from a given environment or existing in the form of instinct, and that the task of morality consists only in bringing acts under a given code and accepting or rejecting them as suitable or unsuitable. Every individual person must pose the *problem of morality* independently, for himself; he must ask himself what is good and what is bad. Only after this independent reflective activity does the second activity ensue, volitional activity, which will consist in an effort of the will to proceed according to this conviction.

The result of any conscious, and often even unconscious, activity of reason can be expressed in the form of a judgment. And the result of reflective moral activity is expressed as a judgment in which the concepts of good and bad, "ought" and "not-ought" [*dolzhnoe i nedolzhnoe*], form the predicate. In a moral judgment, these concepts are taken in an unconditional sense — not as what might be good or bad for something, that is, useful or harmful, but in the sense of unconditionally good or unconditionally bad.

Do such judgments exist? We call people bad or worthless, upright or blessed, we love or despise people and with our love or hatred ordinarily hasten to ascribe an unconditional sanction in one of the aforementioned forms or similar epithet. Consequently, the fact of unconditional moral evaluation does exist. We are not interested now in whether all people are capable of pronouncing such judgments. We want to state the fact itself, even if it occurred in only a single instance.

A moral judgment is a judgment under the category of good or "*ought.*" It is clear this judgment has something in common with a theoretical judgment and something distinct from it. It is analogous to a theoretical judgment in that it demands universal assent. When I say this person or this act is good, I am making a claim, at least, to an unconditional statement that, in my opinion, all would accept, just as all would accept the statement that the earth revolves around the sun. In other words, I am sure that it is a truth and that, consequently, everyone is obliged to accept it as such. The distinction between this truth and a theoretical truth is first of all that I do not have the same means to convince people of the obviousness of this truth that I have for a theoretical truth. I can be convinced, but I do not know how to convince others. The methods of logic and experience that exist to demonstrate a theoretical truth are closed to me in the given case. Even I myself am unable to understand the method by which I arrived at this judgment. But a moral judgment is also distinguished materially from a theoretical judgment. The categories of good or "*ought*" do not enter into the sphere of the concepts of theoretical reason.

Theoretical judgments amount to either the establishment of a fact or the establishment of a law. The concepts of good and evil, beauty and ugliness, are not scientific concepts. With these concepts science has nothing in common. The activity of reason that leads to judgments with a predicate of good or bad Kant called "practical reason." For us it is now clear why. It is reason, because it gives or claims to give a universally binding judgment, but it is not scientific or theoretical reason, for it does not state a scientific truth, that is, it establishes not a fact or "law of what is, but rather a law of what ought to be."[2] It is reason, and yet not reason. It is the sphere of faith, compelling enough that we not only do not subordinate it to theoretical thought, but often construct a theoretical edifice on it.

Such psychic activity, the result of which will be a judgment of unconditional character that cannot be verified by the methods of logic, we shall call *creativity*. And creativity that leads to moral judgments we shall call *moral creativity*. The concept of creativity indicates an essential element of the moral activity that is connected with the concept of the person as a certain unity. It also indicates that this activity is wholly or partly unconscious, and that only the result of this activity enters clearly into consciousness.

II.

The concept of moral creativity includes the whole formal side of morality, as derived by Kant: "Act so that you could will your maxim to become a universal law."[3] Relating this rule to the part of moral activity that leads to a moral judgment, that is, to moral creativity, we can rephrase it as follows: regard as good what you would want everyone to regard as good; that is, establish the law of the good, or be morally creative.

The content of morality has not been touched upon at all here. Whether it is good to love people or hate them, to be compassionate or cruel, all this has so far remained uncertain. The distinguishing feature of morality consists in a person acting one way and not another solely because he finds he ought to. To Kant it seemed that a formal definition provided the best criterion for recognition of "ought." The fact that a moral judgment is binding not only on the person who states it (in this case it would be only a maxim) but also on everyone (in this case it is a law) impelled Kant to disclose the very content of duty, that is, to establish the moral law.

Proceeding from the fact that man "could not will" theft, deception, murder, or mutual hatred as a universal law, that he "could not will" the absence generally of a certain solidarity among people or the presence of the state characterized by the proverb, "*homo homini lupus est*,"[4] Kant supposed that the content of the moral law could in any given case be easily established from the formula, "act so that you could will your maxim to become a universal law." Undoubtedly the moral law, by the very fact that it is a law, expresses a certain solidarity among people, but neither the extent nor type of this solidarity is fully determined by this formula. It is easy to imagine a society with a custom whereby all misunderstandings are decided by a fistfight, and it is very likely that a good fighter "could will" the exclusive supremacy of such a custom, representing a certain type of solidarity among people. In certain places in Russia a modus vivendi has been established between organized gangs of horse thiefs and the peasants, whereby the horse thiefs steal not from the herd, but only from the farmstead. This custom is its own type of moral law, and any deft horse thief "could will" that horse-stealing be a law and that no punishment follow from it. Nietzsche considered the struggle for existence to be a necessary condition for the perfectibility of man, and from this point of view he took up arms against all that constrains, restricts, or eases this struggle. It is natural that a clever, energetic, and strong man "could will" an unrestricted struggle, since it would give him an advantageous position, but even the man incapable of the struggle could unselfishly will it, knowing he shall perish but regarding it as necessary for man's improvement, as was in fact advocated by the ill and infirm Nietzsche.

From this it is clear that the content of the moral law is not derived from Kant's formula. Hegel already pointed out this mistake. Content is created by a person, in moral creativity. But from what psychic material is it created? If we decline to specify the method by which a moral judgment is obtained, then we must indicate the material on which such a judgment operates, and the subject of activity that exercises this creativity. With its a priori forms, theoretical reason reworks the sensations given to it, and in this way creates experience. What does practical reason or moral creativity do? It has the a priori form of "ought." To what content does it apply this formula? The concepts of good or evil, "ought" or "not-ought," constitute the predicate of a moral judgment. They express an evaluation of an act, its correspondence to, or discrepancy from, a posed goal, that is, its *desirability* or *undesirability*. Thus, the content of "ought" relates psychologically to the sphere of desires and strivings. The predicate of "ought" can relate to its object only indirectly, insofar as this object is desirable. Therefore the only material on which moral creativity can operate consists of desires, strivings, passions, that is, the instinctive side of man. Kant, as is well known, removed from morality any participation by feelings, strivings, or passions. He was right only insofar as he refused to recognize as moral any acts that *originate from* feelings, that is, acts *motivated* by the instinctive side of man. An act engendered by a feeling, passion, or affect, in general by any inclination, is not moral, of course, even if it externally coincides with duty. Only an act originating in consciousness of (i.e., motivated by) duty is moral. Kant's rigorism, refusing to recognize as moral any acts stemming from the feeling of compassion, from the impulse of love or heroism, can lead to confusion. All the beauty of morality disappears. It is well known how Schiller attacked Kant in his epigram[s] "Scruple of Conscience" [and "Decision"]: "Willingly I serve my friends, but, alas, I do it with / Pleasure, / And thus it often vexes me that I am not virtuous." "There is no other recommendation, you must try to despise them, / And with aversion do, then, as duty demands."[5]

Schiller, as an artist, noted this paradoxical nature of Kantian ethics, but he could not indicate its mistake. The mistake is not that morality is connected with duty and only with duty. The issue is how to derive the very content of duty. If it is derived by deduction from some determined form, then there is no creativity, no participation by feeling or passion, by the instinctive side of man in general, that is, precisely all that connects him to life. The moral person must then appear as a dry and stale rigorist, removed from any participation in life.

The conflict between duty and feeling has long been a theme of artistic literature, beginning with Sophocles' Antigone and ending with Ibsen's Brand. With extraordinary consistency, Ibsen poses and resolves this problem, in a way that clearly exposes the untenability of its very formulation. To many, this conflict seemed ineradicable and fatal: on the one hand, strict and unbending duty; on the other, living and adaptable feeling. If the question is resolved on behalf of feeling, then morality is smashed to smithereens. Which feeling is to be preferred? Why love and not hatred? Why chastity and not dissipation? If all feelings are equal, where is morality? If the question is resolved on behalf of duty, to the exclusion of the whole instinctive, sensual side of man, then morality loses all living interest. It will relate only to the constant unchanging striving to be true to the pure idea of duty, a striving, moreover, that does not rule over life but only rejects it. Duty says "love," but hatred seethes in me. How can the naked form of duty compel me to change hatred into love? I cannot throw off my feeling. Duty says "love," but love for some evokes hatred in me for others. How will duty in its naked form help me? Duty, ignoring all surrounding life, ignoring the whole instinctive side of man, strives to turn man into a narrow and inflexible doctrinaire rigorist. Such a concept of duty also contradicts the idea of the autonomy of morality, which demands that man derive the content of duty freely from himself, not by perfunctory and mechanical application of its abstract formula, but by individual and free moral creativity. Nietzsche directed all his passion against duty in precisely its naked form. He did not understand that he was struggling not with duty as such, but only with duty that a person has not acquired through the process of moral creativity. Kant's autonomous concept of duty does not contradict Nietzsche's ethics; on the contrary, Nietzsche supplements and completes Kantian morality.

"Just as duty or obligation defines the general *form* of the moral principle as universal and necessary, so a sympathetic inclination is the psychological motive of moral activity; as a result, these two factors cannot contradict each other, since they relate to different sides of the matter, formal and material. In ethics, as in everything else, form and matter are equally necessary; consequently, the rational principle of morality — as unconditional duty or obligation, that is, as a universal and necessary law for any rational creature — is fully compatible with the empirical principle of morality, as a natural inclination toward sympathy in a living creature."[6] Or, as Kant says, "sensations without concepts are blind, concepts without sensations are empty."[7] Duty and the whole instinctive, sensual side of man are found in just such a relation. Instinct without duty is blind, for it is deprived of any moral value; duty without feeling or passion is empty, for it is deprived of any content. If a person, in developing the content of duty, draws it from his sensual instinctive side, then the conflict between duty and feeling disappears. Its place is taken by the conflict between those inclinations sanctioned by duty and those not so sanctioned. Thus, the content of "ought" cannot be given and fixed, but must be constantly created by every individual person; every person must give his own sanction to "ought." Only then will morality be autonomous, or self-legislated. The concept of creativity includes the concept of the person. Creativity presupposes a subject. In Kant's theoretical reason, the subject evaporates into impersonal personhood, into the "transcendental unity of apperception." It is an impersonal, supra-individual unity. This is understandable, since Kant investigated the capacity for knowledge and sought the justification of knowledge taken as a result, but did not investigate knowledge as a psychic activity. In theoretical reason the person fades into the transcendental, while in practical reason it is affirmed as transcendent. In science, in knowledge, the person as such is not of interest; on the contrary, everything personal is eliminated. From the scientific point of view, I am little interested in the fact that it was Newton who discovered the law of gravity, or in how he discovered it; I am interested only in how it is proved and whether it is true. It is completely different in questions of morality, where I can evaluate the act of a person only by examining his motives.

The very process of moral creativity presents itself approximately in the following form. Wishes, strivings, affects, and passions are present in the soul as the grounds of activity. While moral consciousness is undeveloped, this instinctive side rules over man. At this stage there is properly speaking no personhood, for there is nothing to give a certain unity or order to these passions and inclinations. These inclinations seize and abandon man. But once moral consciousness arises in the soul, the picture changes. Moral consciousness makes a selection among strivings and impulses. It produces its own inner experience. As in the process of intellectual consciousness, in which two distinct spheres, "self" and "not-self," gradually emerge from the whole realm of sensations, so in the process of moral creativity the sensual-instinctive side of man divides into two halves: into one more like me and one less like me, into my real "self" and something else that, although still mine, I do not want to claim as my own. This internal division makes itself clearly felt in the feeling of shame. The feeling of shame indicates that in man a new psychic activity, moral activity, has been created. Solov'ëv is thus profoundly right in his view that the feeling of shame is found at the very basis of moral activity, at its very onset.[8] . . . Kant identified practical reason with the will. But what is the will? Is it not really also desire and striving? Absolutely, but it is a striving sui generis. It is a striving that has been sanctioned by my person, it is a striving that has been appropriated by my moral consciousness. In this way, moral consciousness is precisely what gives unity to the sensual-instinctive side of man and what creates personhood. In essence, the concepts of personhood and creativity are connected with each other. Creativity points to personhood; it cannot be impersonal, it is the individual unconscious psychic activity of synthesis. The person is the subject we necessarily posit under the concept of synthetic activity.

From what has been said, it is clear that if moral activity is to have a place, a concept of "ought" or the good is necessary, as are the sensations and strivings that serve as the material for creativity. The more plentiful and diverse this material, and the wider the range of sensations and inclinations, the richer the moral experience, and the more interesting and fruitful the result. Hence the interest that so-called tragic characters, distinguished by the intensity and richness of their passion and instinct, pose for the moral problem. Precisely in them does moral creativity appear with the greatest force. This makes it understandable how strong emotional shocks can completely alter a person's moral makeup. In these cases moral experience is suddenly expanded by the unfamiliar feelings and emotions, enabling the person to undertake new creative work.

III.

Morality is creativity, activity. At the basis of any human activity is the need or urge for activity. Therefore, at the basis of moral activity must lie the urge for moral creativity. This urge thus compares to urges for muscular activity, to the need for love, and so forth. The use of such teleological terms as need and attraction (teleological because they indicate the state caused by them and the one causing their next state) shows that any psychic causal series breaks off into a regression. A need, like a sensation or feeling, is not explained by other psychic states, but is among the primary data of psychology.

"Gradually, man has become a fantastic animal that has to fulfill one more condition of existence than any other animal: man *has to* believe, to know, from time to time *why* he exists; his race cannot flourish without a periodic trust in life—without faith in *reason in life*."⁹ Thus speaks Nietzsche, not believing in world reason. His lack of belief lets him sense all the more clearly the need for it. In his next aphorism Nietzsche speaks exactly about what we have called the aspiration to moral creativity, referring to it as intellectual conscience. "I keep having the same experience and keep resisting it every time. I do not want to believe it although it is palpable: *the great majority of people lacks an intellectual conscience* ... [and] does not consider it contempt-ible to believe this or that and to live accordingly, without first having given themselves an account of the final and most certain reasons pro and con, and without even troubling themselves about such reasons afterward: the most gifted men and the noblest women still belong to this 'great majority.' But what is goodheartedness, refinement, or genius to me, when the person who has these virtues tolerates slack feelings in his faith and judgments and when he does not account *the desire for certainty* as his inmost craving and deepest distress—as that which separates the higher human beings from the lower. Among some pious people I found a hatred of reason and was well disposed to them for that; for this at least *betrayed* their bad intellectual conscience. But to stand in the midst of this *rerum concordia discors*¹⁰ and of this whole mar-velous uncertainty and rich ambiguity of existence *without questioning*, with-out trembling with the craving and the rapture of such questioning, without at least hating the person who questions, perhaps even finding him faintly amusing—that is what I feel to be *contemptible,* and this is the feeling for which I look first in everybody. Some folly keeps persuading me that every human being has this feeling, simply because he is human. This is my type of injustice."¹¹

The need for certainty (*Gewißheit*) in questions of morality and conduct divides people into higher and lower human beings. Certainty is a type of confidence, but it is possible to be confident not only on logical grounds. In the period of fascination with positivism in which *Die Fröhliche Wissenschaft* was written, Nietzsche did not turn attention to the fact that it is possible to be confident without logical grounds, and that moral confidence is precisely this type of confidence. At the basis of moral creativity lies the need for confidence, for conviction in the possibility of moral evaluation, but not for certainty. It is possible to be convinced that it is good to love people and to follow Christ's commandment, "love thy neighbor as thyself," but this cannot be an object of certain knowledge, since no logical grounds exist or can exist for it. This conviction is the result of our psychic activity, relying on our sympathies, feelings, and strivings, but not on logical axioms and theories. In a word, this conviction is the result of creativity, but not theoretical analysis. The skeptic-positivist Nietzsche concludes his aphorism with the words, "This is *my* type of injustice." What did he want to say by this? His demand that people feel contempt for a detached and indifferent attitude toward the moral question does not itself have the slightest logical foundation. Thus, Nietzsche himself comes to alogism.

Nietzsche bemoans a passive approach to the problem of morality, the absence of "the craving of questioning"; such an approach does not correspond, in his opinion, to the dignity of man and is thus contemptible. According to Nietzsche, *every* human being senses that it is contemptible.

But we can pose the question, is there in every human being an urge to moral creativity, an inner striving to know what is good and what is bad in an absolute sense, a striving to know what one ought to do and what one need not do, to know what one ought to aspire toward and what one need not aspire toward, in a word, a striving to uncover the content of the concept of the absolute good — is all this inherent to every human being or not? Repeating Nietzsche's words, we can ask, has every human being really become a fantastic animal that must know for what and why he exists?

If we wanted to answer this question affirmatively, we would have to exclude from consideration such categories of people as the insane, idiots, savages at a lower stage of development, and children. We are prepared to answer the question negatively, but with certain reservations. The question of the presence or absence in a human being of the urge to moral creativity can be decided only approximately in the majority of cases. This striving can be expressed more or less clearly, it can remain concealed or unknown even to its possessor, it can appear sporadically at various times of life. Taking into account such factors, we can divide people into two categories: those possessing the urge to moral creativity and a desire to solve the moral problem, and those in whom we do not notice this desire, in whom the moral problem has not presented itself to consciousness. We have adopted this division because in philosophy (Aristotle) and in history people have been divided into slaves and freemen. We are making this division now not on the basis of the social fact of slavery, but by proceeding from psychological analysis, and there is no doubt that the mental makeup of a slave has a very definite relation to social slavery. People not obtaining their moral judgments through personal moral creativity but borrowing them from other people, as if a judgment pronounced by others becomes a sanction—these people are slaves. The connection between a slave and a human being without moral creativity becomes clearer if we recall that personhood emerges in moral creativity, so that people deprived of this creativity are also lacking in personhood [*liudy bezlichnye*]. . . . Such people either have no absolute at all, or they make another human being into an absolute, to whose will they are utterly subordinate. . . .

Moral creativity, as an evaluation with the help of ideal concepts of good and evil, entails the desire to realize the principles thus obtained and to construct life on new foundations. Moral activity, as indicated above, consists of two sides or stages: an inner creative one and an external volitional one. . . . Since the material for moral creativity is given by feelings and strivings, such creativity cannot take place outside life. The moral problem is resolved by deeds; thus the refusal of the person to be involved in organizing or actively participating in life is also slavery.

This form of slavery, of heteronomy, even found philosophical expression — and moreover in a slave, Epictetus. This slave consciousness refuses to be involved in organizing life or in broadening it through the introduction of new content or of one's own personal principle. Such consciousness does not strive toward creativity, but produces a closing off of the person, a self-limiting and self-satisfaction not with one's activity but with one's passivity, a satisfaction with given reality. "Do not seek to have events happen as you want them to, but instead want them to happen as they do happen, and your life will go well."[12] Here personhood, as an absolute a priori principle, is removed. It takes the principle of its activity not from itself, but from outside. This is the only consistent derivation of "what ought to be" from "what is," which essentially amounts to the abolition of "ought." The morality of the free person, creative morality, should be expressed in exactly the reverse way: "struggle with everything in the name of your principles, strive not to surrender to events, but to direct and create them. Never say, 'it is so, and thus ought to be,' but rather, 'it ought to be so, and thus what is not so ought to be otherwise.'" In this consists creativity and the affirmation of personhood. "For the slave, his natural, sensuous existence is more precious than personhood, simple life is more precious than the value of life resting on self-consciousness; he regards himself as no higher than a thing among things; for him existence as a thing [*Dingsein*] or thinghood [*Dingheit*] is essential, while consciousness is unessential: precisely in this consists the slave consciousness. What makes the master a master is that he did not fear death and risked his own life. What makes the slave a slave is that he feared death and values his life most of all, entirely submerged in his own physical existence."[13]

With regard to the last words of Hegel[14] it can be said, however, that the slave can accept even death in a purely slavish way, as "what ought to be." The slave's will is paralyzed or undeveloped to such extent that he does not have the strength to struggle with death, so that he can die, too, with resignation and without protesting.

We have already mentioned that the formal criterion of morality, consisting in the presence of the urge to moral creativity, is not capable of specifying the content of morality. The content of morality remains uncertain. In this is the *problem* of morality. The urge to moral creativity is the aspiration to solve this problem. Personal subjective moral creativity is the only path to working out moral content. But if universality and the universally binding, that is, objectivity, are at the essence of morality, *then where and how is moral creativity objectified?*

Because every human being decides this problem autonomously, for himself, then what must take place does in fact take place, namely, moral codes, customs, manners, principles, and views are infinitely diverse, with no single absolute ethics. But in a given country, society, or circle there are nonetheless certain manners, customs, and principles. Every human being experiences the weight of certain traditions, and feels psychically connected with a certain moral code. To break these traditions, he must undertake inner work. These codes and traditions have also been formed by the subjective creative activity of individual people; they themselves are the result of previous creative activity.

If, as we have seen earlier, the act of moral creativity is sustained by feelings, passions, and affects and is thus bound up with historical reality, then the result of moral creativity is also crystallized, as it were, by history. The moral creativity of individual people is preserved in manners and customs, in law and in the state. In this way moral creativity is bound up with the historical process.

IV.

Thus, moral activity is the autonomous introduction of content into the concepts of good and evil. My personhood, my moral creativity, introduces one or another content, and does so with complete conviction. My inner feeling says, "It is good, or it is bad."

While we have so far accented mainly the alogical side of moral activity, this does not yet exhaust morality. Personhood, as the synthesis of all sides of the spirit, has still not achieved its fullest expression or the unity toward which it strives. The content of morality is introduced by the person, and the issue is the justification of this content through specifying its connection to a system of integral and whole knowledge. Here "intellectual conscience" fully comes into its own. "The desire for certainty" impels me to construct a metaphysical system of integral knowledge, in which philosophical and religious creativity is joined with moral creativity. Only the satisfaction of this need actually makes a human being a person in the full sense of the word. Only then does he obtain an answer to the question, Why and for what does he exist?

Because we are not planning to specify the content of morality, we do not need to construct such a system, but we would like to indicate how it could be constructed, from which principles it would proceed. The first starting principle is given by the categorical and absolute concept of "ought." In recognizing one thing as good and another as bad, we have in mind the unconditional and absolute nature of good and evil. We thus place ourselves in a certain relation to the absolute, and the need for a rational justification of the results of moral creativity brings us to the idea of the absolute. Any aspiration is directed to some end. If we state that moral creativity brings us to an unconditional and absolute evaluation of the good, then the end to which this evaluation strives must also be absolute. Moral creativity itself is directed to nothing other than the search for the absolute end, for the absolute meaning of life. Therefore what leads to the absolute end, to God, is good. This is not the good that is commanded by God, although I see God in what my consciousness affirms as good, as beautiful, as true. Not theological morality, but moral theology, as Kant formulated his own theology. Intellectual striving is directed toward revealing the meaning and end contained in the concepts: good, the good. If there is no absolute end, life is deprived of value.

Thus, the first point of departure and support in the rational justification of moral creativity is the concept of an absolute end. Another bearing should be recognized in the concept of the person, as the subject of moral creativity. The person is that absolute principle in which moral content is created. Every system of complete moral philosophy must keep both these principles in view and must find a connection between them. This link can be discovered in the teleological concept of the world process. Moral creativity makes man a participant in the world process.

We have a need to believe in world reason, in "reason in life," to believe that history will reward us, that it will justify our hopes. . . . We can look at a creative-moral deed as an instinctive-purposive deed, purposive in relation to an absolute world end. Leaves of a plant turn toward the light. Yet we cannot suppose the plant has a conscious idea of an end. In just the same way, man might not clearly see in the act of moral creativity the connection between his deed and world reason. But it is a big mistake to think that, in wishing to justify my own moral judgment, in resorting to ethical pathos, I can manage without the idea of the absolute, that I need not place myself in one or another relation to it, that I do not seek a sanction in it. Any morality, we are told, bears a transient and temporary significance. Agreed! But this does not exclude it from also bearing an absolute significance. Any morality strives toward the absolute, wants to be absolute, is guided by the idea of the absolute as by a norm, and therefore itself stands in some relation to it.

Every discrete effort of the person, every step of moral creativity, is an approach to the absolute, a moment in the realization of the moral ideal. But only in the combined work of many, in the collective process of history, is an absolute morality objectified. With such a view the process of history is also the process of the creation of an absolute morality.

Notes

1. Hegel, *Ästhetik,* Einleit. [*Hegel's Introduction to Aesthetics: The Introduction to the Berlin Aesthetics Lectures of the 1820s,* trans. T. M. Knox, with an interpretive essay by Charles Karelis (Oxford: Oxford University Press, 1979), pp. 52–53. The last set of italics is Zhukovskii's.]

2. "Theoretical knowledge may be defined as knowledge of what *is,* practical knowledge as the representation of what *ought to be.*" Immanuel Kant, *Critique of Pure Reason,* trans. Norman Kemp Smith, unabridged edition (New York: St. Martin's, 1965), p. 526. "In practical philosophy we are not concerned with accepting reasons for what *happens,* but with accepting laws of what *ought to happen,* even if it never does happen." Kant, *Groundwork of the Metaphysic of Morals,* trans. H. J. Paton (New York: Harper Torchbooks, 1964), p. 94. Ed.

3. "Act only on that maxim through which you can at the same time will that it should become a universal law." *Groundwork of the Metaphysic of Morals,* trans. H. J. Paton, p. 88. Ed.

4. Man is wolf to man. Ed.

5. "Gerne dien ich den Freunden, doch tu ich es leider mit / Neigung, / Und so wurmt es mir oft, daß ich nicht tugendhaft bin." "Da ist kein anderer Rat, du mußt suchen, sie zu verachten, / Und mit Abscheu alsdann tun, wie die Pflicht dir gebeut." "Gewissenssskrupel" and "Decisum," from Schiller's "Philosophen" (1797). Zhukovskii uses a translation by Vladimir Solov'ëv. Ed.

6. Vladimir Solov'ëv, *Kritika otvlechennykh nachal,* in *Sobranie sochinenii Vladimira Sergeevicha Solov'ëva,* vol. II (St. Petersburg, 1901–1907), p. 66.

7. "Thoughts without content are empty, intuitions without concepts are blind." *Critique of Pure Reason,* p. 93. Ed.

8. Vladimir Solov'ëv, *Opravdanie dobra: Nravstvennaia filosofiia* (*Justification of the Good: Moral Philosophy,* St. Petersburg, 1897, 2d edition 1899), ch. 1, sections 1–2. Ed.

9. Friedrich Nietzsche, *The Gay Science,* Book One, aphorism 1, "The teachers of the purpose of existence," trans. Walter Kaufmann (New York: Vintage Books, 1974), p. 75. Ed.

10. "Discordant concord of things": Horace, *Epistles*, I.12.19. Kaufmann's note. Ed.

11. Nietzsche, *Fröhliche Wissenschaft*, Erstes Buch, pp. 37–38. [*The Gay Science*, Book One, aphorism 2, "The intellectual conscience," pp. 76–77.]

12. *Epictets Handbüchlein der Moral* (Leipzig, Universal-Bibliotek), § 8, p. 15. [*Handbook of Epictetus*, translated with introduction and annotations by Nicholas White (Indianapolis: Hackett, 1983), p. 13.]

13. Kuno Fischer, *Hegels Leben, Werke und Lehre*, in *Geschichte der neuern Philosophie*, vol. VIII, part 1 (Heidelberg, 1901), p. 326, page citation corrected; editor's translation. [Zhukovskii has obviously missed the larger point of Hegel's famous discussion of master–slave relations. See G. W. F. Hegel, *The Phenomenology of Mind*, trans. J. B. Baillie (New York: Harper and Row, 1967), pp. 228–240.]

14. The words are in fact Kuno Fischer's paraphrase of Hegel, *The Phenomenology of Mind*, pp. 232–234. Ed.

Glossary of Names

This glossary includes philosophers and thinkers referred to in more than one essay of the text. Names occurring in only one essay are identified in the notes. The few exceptions to these guidelines are also indicated in the notes.

Richard Avenarius (1843–1896). German positivist philosopher and founder of empiriocriticism, which maintains that philosophy should restrict itself to what is given in pure experience, without any "introjection" of metaphysical concepts. Empiriocriticism, which is also associated with Ernst Mach, acquired a Russian following among certain Bolshevik thinkers, most notably Aleksandr A. Bogdanov (Malinovskii) (1873–1928), but not Lenin, who attacked it as surreptitious idealism in *Materialism and Empiriocriticism: Critical Comments on a Reactionary Philosophy* (1909).

Eduard Bernstein (1850–1932). German Social Democrat and main theorist of Marxist revisionism, which he advanced in a series of articles, "Problems of Socialism," published in *Die neue Zeit* from the end of 1896, and in his book, *Die Voraussetzungen des Sozialismus und die Aufgaben der Sozialdemokratie* (1899), translated as *Evolutionary Socialism* (1909). Some of his ideas, for example, that Marxist theory should be supplemented with neo-Kantianism and that capitalism was not doomed to collapse (rejection of the *Zusammenbruchstheorie*), were anticipated in Russia by Pëtr Struve in particular during his Marxist period.

Boris N. Chicherin (1828–1904). "The greatest theoretician of Russian liberalism" (Viktor Leontovich). As a Hegelian "conservative liberal," he saw the state as the primary agent of progress in Russian history, and looked to "strong government" to promote

the development of an autonomous civil society. His classic works, *On Popular Representation* (1866) and *Property and the State* (1882–1883), argue for the primacy of civil
rights and legal consciousness before political rights and democracy. On the eve of the
twentieth century, he called for the transformation of the Russian autocracy into a constitutional monarchy, thus adding his voice to the emerging Liberation Movement. His last
major work, *Philosophy of Law* (1900), defended a metaphysical conception of the person
as an absolute end-in-itself. This conception, more Kantian than Hegelian, was an important influence on *Problems of Idealism,* as was the general anti-positivist direction of his
legal philosophy.

Auguste Comte (1798–1857).   French philosopher, founder of positivism as a philosophical
system and philosophy of history, and pioneer of the new science of sociology. Comte's work
is often seen as falling into two periods, an "objective" or scientific phase culminating in the
Cours de philosophie positive (1830–1842), and a "subjective" one devoted to the "religion
of humanity," expounded in the *Système de politique positive* (1851–1854). In the first
period, Comte worked out his classification of the sciences and advanced his "law of the
three stages" of the development of human thought and society: the theological, the metaphysical, and the positive. The positive stage recognizes that real knowledge deals only with
phenomena and laws of "relations of succession and resemblance," not with absolute or
final causes. The highest of the sciences is sociology, which consists of two parts: social
statics (which studies social solidarity or "order") and social dynamics (which studies social
progress, or development toward order). Positive sociology, knowledge of humanity as a
whole, can provide a synthesis of the other sciences through its "subjective" method, which
coordinates or unifies them from a "human" or "subjective" point of view, where the subject
is humanity in general and its needs. This Humanity (*le Grand Être*) became the object of an
elaborate religious cult in Comte's second period.

Marie-Jean-Antoine-Nicolas Caritat, Marquis de Condorcet (1743–1794).   French mathematician, Encyclopedist, social philosopher, and reformer. As a deputy to the National
Convention, he drafted the "Girondin constitution" of 1793, for which the Jacobins declared him an enemy of the new republic. He went into hiding, where he worked on his
Sketch for a Historical Picture of the Progress of the Human Mind (1795), published after
his death in prison.

Ludwig Feuerbach (1804–1872).   German materialist philosopher whose most celebrated
work, *Das Wesen des Christentums* (*The Essence of Christianity,* 1841), maintains that the
idea of God is the external projection of man's inner self or essence, the alienation of man
from himself or his self-objectification. Feuerbach's critique of Hegelianism was an important influence on Marx and Engels.

Johann Gottlieb Fichte (1762–1814).   Among the classic German idealist philosophers,
Fichte most deserves the label "subjective idealist." His first major work, *Versuch einer
Kritik aller Offenbarung* (*Toward a Critique of All Revelation,* 1792), advances the divinity
of the moral law as the basis of religion. This paramount respect for duty was preserved as
Fichte expanded his system into a whole metaphysics of ethical idealism, which had a certain
influence on the Russian idealists Bulgakov, Berdiaev, and, by 1904, Frank. In Fichte's system
the doctrine of the self-positing absolute ego can be conceived as the pure autonomy of ethical activity or rational will, for which the world exists as an object of duty. This dialectic of
ego and non-ego constitutes the phenomenology of consciousness in Fichte's *Wissenschafts-
lehre* (theory of science), the focus of his first period. In his second period the focus shifts to

the philosophy of absolute being. The demarcation line between the two periods can be taken as 1800, with the publication of *Die Bestimmung des Menschen* (*The Vocation of Man*), which stipulates that subjective idealism requires faith in an eternal and infinite Will, an ontologically real moral world-order, as the ground of the finite self. Nonetheless Fichte tends to collapse Kant's distinction between the phenomenal and noumenal, thus anticipating the absolute idealism of Hegel. Today he is perhaps best known for his *Addresses to the German Nation* (1808).

Jean-Marie Guyau (1854–1888).   French moral and religious philosopher whose works sought to reconcile positivism and vitalism.

Eduard von Hartmann (1842–1906).   German pessimistic philosopher, generally regarded as a follower of Schopenhauer, whose ideas he developed in a Hegelian direction. His most famous work, *Die Philosophie des Unbewußten* (*Philosophy of the Unconcious*, 1869), claims that the absolute is unconscious, although it is not merely blind Will as Schopenhauer maintained, but purposive Idea. Teleological movement of the world process toward self-consciousness liberates the Idea from its servitude to the Will. Metaphysical pessimism follows from Hartmann's conclusion that the capacity for suffering increases with the evolution of consciousness. Hartmann's philosophy became better known in Russia through Vladimir Solov'ëv, who showed some interest in him in his 1874 master's thesis.

Georg Wilhelm Friedrich Hegel (1770–1831).   The most influential of the classic German idealist philosophers in nineteenth-century Russian thought. The *Phenomonology of Mind* (1807) advances a monistic metaphysics of what has been called "self-enriching alienation," a process through which the Absolute realizes itself in the history of human consciousness. The *Science of Logic* (1812–1816) expounds Hegel's concept of the dialectic, according to which the contradiction between thesis and antithesis is resolved at a higher level of truth (synthesis). His major tract on moral and political philosophy, known as the *Philosophy of Right* (1821), seeks to overcome the putative subjectivism of Kant's ethical individualism in an objective ethics, centered on society and the state. In Russia, Hegelianism formed the main frame of reference during the "remarkable decade" (1838–1848) of the classic debate between the Westernizers and Slavophiles. In the second half of the century, the greatest representative of Russian Hegelianism was Boris Chicherin. In *Problems of Idealism* (and Russian neo-idealism more generally), Hegel is both valued for his efforts to bridge the Kantian dualism between "is" and "ought," and criticized for collapsing it.

Aleksandr Herzen (1812–1870).   Among the most interesting and influential figures in Russian intellectual history. From 1842 until his departure from Russia in 1847 he was one of the main Russian Hegelians and Westernizers; during the first several years of lifelong emigration, he developed the idea of "Russian socialism," based on values he imputed (following the Slavophiles) to the peasantry (see, e.g., "The Russian People and Socialism," 1851). In 1853 he founded the Free Russian Press; its periodical publications, especially *Kolokol* (*The Bell,* 1857–1867), had a major impact on Russian public opinion. The main theme of Herzen's works is the defense of the freedom and dignity of the individual against teleological systems of historical necessity. Most important in this regard are *Dilettantism in Science* (1843), *Letters on the Study of Nature* (1845–1846), and especially *From the Other Shore* (1850). In *Letters from France and Italy* (1847–1851) and other works, he expressed the view that European bourgeois society was a threat to individual development. His memoirs, *My Past and Thoughts,* are a classic of that genre.

Paul-Henri Thiry, Baron d'Holbach (1723–1789).   *Philosophe* and major contributor to the

Encyclopédie, was the foremost exponent of atheistic materialism and the fiercest critic of religion in the Enlightenment.

Immanuel Kant (1724–1804).   A fundamental point of reference for the main contributors to *Problems of Idealism,* who were indebted to both his epistemology (theory of knowledge or experience) and ethics in their defense of the self against positivist reductionism. The system of transcendental idealism advanced in the *Critique of Pure Reason* (1781) brought about a "Copernican revolution" in epistemology by arguing that "the order and regularity in objects, which we call nature," are not intrinsic to them but depend on the transcendental structure of consciousness, including the a priori forms (space and time) of sensibility and the categories of the understanding. The *Critique of Practical Reason* (1788) and Kant's other writings on moral philosophy, such as the *Groundwork of the Metaphysic of Morals* (1785), base ethics on a rigorous notion of duty, formulated as the categorical imperative. The *Critique of Judgment* (1790) is concerned with the nature of aesthetic judgment and purposiveness. Russian idealists tended to emphasize the metaphysical implications of Kant's philosophy, and some criticized him for having introduced too sharp a dualism between the phenomenal and noumenal realms.

Pëtr L. Lavrov (1823–1900).   One of the main theorists of Russian populism and the co-founder, with N. K. Mikhailovskii, of "subjective sociology." Primarily a scholar, he was also a prominent figure in the Russian revolutionary and international socialist movements. In 1860 he defined his philosophical position as "anthropologism," a defense of the individual against what he saw as the objectifying, totalizing systems of absolute idealism. A similar concern shaped his criticism of the one-sided "objectivism" of contemporary positivism, which he sought to correct with the "subjective method." Here he drew on Feuerbach, Kant, and the later Comte. Lavrov applied his "subjectivist" approach to the theory of progress in his very popular *Historical Letters* (1868–1869), which argued that the intellectual and spiritual development of the cultivated privileged minority in Russia was bought by the suffering and toil of the peasant masses, and that this debt ought to be repaid by working for the good of the people. By taking responsibility for introducing their ideals into historical reality, "critically thinking individuals" could become the main agents of progress. They could, in particular, help to steer Russia away from capitalism, which Lavrov and other populist socialists denied was a necessary, unavoidable law of historical development. In general, the contributors to *Problems of Idealism* valued Lavrov's defense of the free individual acting on his or her own moral values, but thought it required a more thoroughgoing idealist substantiation.

Gottfried Wilhelm Leibniz (1646–1716).   German philosopher, mathematician, historian, and diplomat. His *Monadology* (1714) conceives the universe as a hierarchy of independent individual substances (monads), created by the supreme monad, God, and correlated in a preestablished harmony. Monads are simple (without parts), nonextended, and immaterial; they are essentially and spontaneously active, but do not interact. Each monad changes only in terms of its own nature, but each "mirrors" the changes of other monads; the harmonious correlation of the states of each monad with every other is the principle of preestablished harmony. The mind, in its unity and purposeful activity, can be compared to a monad. In his *Theodicy* (1710), Leibniz argues that God has created the best of all possible worlds. Leibniz's influence in Russia began in 1697 with his correspondence and subsequent meetings with Peter the Great, and later found expression in "neo-Leibnizianism" in Russian philosophy (A. A. Kozlov, S. A. Askol'dov, and L. M. Lopatin).

Lev M. Lopatin (1855–1920). Major Russian idealist and personalist philosopher, was professor of philosophy at Moscow University from 1892, chair of the Moscow Psychological Society from 1900 to 1919, and editor of the society's journal *Questions of Philosophy and Psychology*. His *Polozhitel'nye zadachi filosofii* (*The Positive Tasks of Philosophy,* two vols., 1886–1891) was a milestone in the philosophical revolt against positivism and the development of Russian neo-idealism. In this and subsequent works, Lopatin advanced his "system of concrete spiritualism." His idea of the person as an ontologically grounded spiritual entity relates him to Leibniz's monadology, and he is regarded as one of the main representatives of "neo-Leibnizianism" in Russia, following A. A. Kozlov. Another source of his ideas was his longtime friend, the Russian religious philosopher Vladimir Solov'ëv.

Rudolf Hermann Lotze (1817–1881). German idealist philosopher whose main work is the three-volume *Mikrokosmus* (1856–1864). His philosophy, a pluralistic idealism in which the world consists of personal spirits or souls in interaction with God, is a variant of Leibnizian monadology. Lotze based his "teleological idealism" on introspective analysis of the unity of self-consciousness, moral experience, and appreciation of value, all of which convinced him that the world cannot be simply a mechanistic system without purpose, despite the scientific value of the mechanistic interpretation of nature. His metaphysics aspired to the ultimate unity between "the world of values" and "the world of mechanism." In Russia, one of the most influential followers of Lotze was Lev M. Lopatin.

Ernst Mach (1838–1916). Austrian physicist and philosopher, widely regarded as the father of the Vienna circle and the founder of logical positivism. His philosophy of science is strictly empiricist in defining knowledge as the economical description of the phenomena of sense experience. In this he was heavily indebted to George Berkeley and David Hume.

Nikolai K. Mikhailovskii (1842–1904). The most influential thinker in Russian populism. With Pëtr Lavrov he developed the "subjective method" of Russian sociology, but his principle of individuality was distinctive. For him, individuality meant inner wholeness, self-sufficiency, and many-sided, harmonious development, which he saw as incompatible with Western progress and modernization (involving as they do functional specialization and social differentiation), but as fully consistent with Russian communalism. His notion of individuality recalled the Slavophile ideal of "integral personality" more than Lavrov's Westernizing idea of the individual. In "What Is Progress?" (1869), Mikhailovskii argued that the modern division of labor in society was not progressive but regressive from the perspective of individuality, since it entailed fragmentation and alienation and prevented versatility and integrity. His series of articles, "The Struggle for Individuality" (1875–1876), idealized peasant life as primitive but full, and suggested that it was a higher type of development than Western individualism. Marx's *Capital* only reinforced Mikhailovskii in his populist conviction that Russia must do everything possible to avoid capitalist development. Criticism of Mikhailovskii and "subjective sociology" was of developmental importance for Russian Marxism, the evolution "from Marxism to idealism" (Struve, Bulgakov, Berdiaev, and Frank), and for the neo-idealist critique of positivism.

Friedrich Nietzsche (1844–1900). German philosopher, poet, and radical critic of Western bourgeois civilization and Christianity. His major works include *The Birth of Tragedy* (1872), *Untimely Meditations* (1873–1876), *The Gay Science* (1882), *Thus Spoke Zarathustra* (1883–1885), *Beyond Good and Evil* (1886), *Genealogy of Morals* (1887), *The Antichrist* (1895), and *The Will to Power* (1901). In them he explores his main themes: art and the "Dionysian" affirmation of life, the philistinism of contemporary culture, time as "eternal recurrence," the self-creating and self-transcending *Übermensch* (superman) as a higher human type, the transvaluation of all values, Christian slave morality versus aristo-cratic master morality, the will to power as the basic human drive, the denial of objective truth, and the rejection of metaphysical and theistic beliefs. Nietzsche had a major, multi-faceted impact on Russian thought and culture. His Russian reception began in 1892, when the journal *Questions of Philosophy and Psychology* published V. P. Preobrazhenskii's essay, "Friedrich Nietzsche: A Critique of the Morality of Altruism," which in several ways antici-pated the interpretations of Nietzsche in *Problems of Idealism*.

Heinrich Rickert (1863–1936).   German philosopher, student and protégé of Windelband in the southwest German or Baden school of neo-Kantianism. Proceeding from Windelband's theory of values, he further distinguished the methodologies of the natural and cultural sciences. History is a cultural science (*Kulturwissenschaft*) because it is a science of values; the particular, unique event constitutes (or rather is constituted as) the proper object of historical research because of its value-relevance, in fact because it realizes a universal value. One task of the historian is to determine the value criteria that endow cultural facts with meaning.

Alois Riehl (1844–1924).   Austrian neo-Kantian philosopher and theorist of "critical real-ism." He argued that philosophy should have a scientific focus on theory of knowledge and the methodology of the natural sciences; metaphysics is an "opiate of the mind." His own philosophical outlook was a type of realistic monism that saw mental life as a product of natural evolution. Late in his life he turned more to practical philosophy and values.

Friedrich Wilhelm Joseph von Schelling (1775–1854).   German idealist philosopher who is generally regarded as the principal philosopher of romanticism, especially through his *Naturphilosophie* and aesthetics. He held that the world is a living work of art and that in art the mind can become fully aware of itself and realize its infinite nature. In Russia, he inspired the development of philosophical romanticism, represented by the Society of Wis-dom Lovers (founded 1823) and Vladimir F. Odoevskii. In his last period, Schelling ad-vanced a "positive philosophy," based on the philosophy of myth and revelation, against Hegelian rationalism. This had strong influence on the Slavophiles Aleksei Khomiakov and especially Ivan Kireevskii, and through them on Vladimir Solov'ëv. Schelling's ideas on the personhood of God, developed in his *Philosophie der Offenbarung*, may have been a source of the Russian neo-idealist recovery of the absolute value of the human person.

Arthur Schopenhauer (1788–1860).   German post-Kantian pessimist philosopher. In his chief work *Die Welt als Wille und Vorstellung* (*The World as Will and Idea*, 1818), he gave the will a leading place in metaphysics, arguing that will is creative and primary, while idea or intellect is receptive and secondary. Will is not only the inner or noumenal self, it is the inner essence of the world, an irrational blind force without ultimate purpose. Schopen-hauer's pessimistic doctrine of the will helps explain the status he gave to art, since he thought man could escape subjection to the will in detached aesthetic contemplation. The goal of moral activity was also liberation from the will, from egoism, through identification with others, or compassion.

Georg Simmel (1858–1918).   German philosopher and one of the founders of sociology in Germany. His wide interests fall broadly into the philosophy of culture and the philosophy of life. His major work on ethics, *Einleitung in die Moralwissenschaft* (1892), which was studied by Struve, Frank, Bulgakov, and Berdiaev, gives extended treatment (from a gener-ally psychological perspective) to "ought" as a primary datum (*Urtatsache*) of moral experience and feeling. Simmel's *Philosophie des Geldes* (*The Philosophy of Money,* 1900) and *Soziologie* (1908) have also had wide influence.

Vladimir S. Solov'ëv (1853–1900).   Widely regarded as Russia's greatest religious philosopher. His master's thesis, *The Crisis of Western Philosophy: Against the Positivists* (1874), anticipated by about fifteen years the revolt against positivism in Russian thought. His metaphysics and philosophy of history are a profound synthesis of the concepts of all-unity (*vseedinstvo*), Godmanhood (*bogochelovechestvo*), and Sophia (the divine wisdom). In social philosophy his highly syncretic views ranged from advocacy of "free theocracy" to rule-of-law liberalism, which he modernized with his idea of the "right to a dignified existence." His major treatise on ethics, *Opravdanie dobra* (*Justification of the Good,* 1897), argued for the autonomy of ethics (vis-à-vis religion and metaphysics) and thus helped prepare the way for the appearance of *Problems of Idealism.* Among the contributors to the symposium, Solov'ëv had an especially strong influence on Novgorodtsev, Bulgakov, and Sergei and Evgenii Trubetskoi.

Herbert Spencer (1820–1903).   English philosopher who applied evolutionary theory to all branches of knowledge, including the study of society and ethics. He sought to transform Charles Darwin's concept of evolution into an all-embracing philosophical system. As an early proponent of social Darwinism, he favored laissez-faire doctrines.

Rudolf Stammler (1856–1938).   German neo-Kantian legal philosopher. His book *Wirtschaft und Recht nach der materialistischen Geschichtsauffassung* (*Economy and Law in the Materialist Conception of History,* 1896) generated a debate between Pëtr Struve and Sergei Bulgakov over the role of freedom, necessity, and teleology in history. More important was his idea of "natural law with changing content," which helped inspire the contemporary revival of natural law. In his *Die Lehre von dem richtigen Rechte* (1902), translated as *The Theory of Justice* (1925), Stammler developed his concept of the "social ideal," or the final end of law and the state (his own definition of the social ideal was a "community of free-willing persons").

Wilhelm Windelband (1848–1915).   German philosopher and historian of philosophy, leading figure in the southwest German or Baden school of neo-Kantianism. The focus of his work was value theory. In his 1894 Strasbourg rectoral lecture, "Geschichte und Naturwissenschaft," he made his famous distinction between the generalizing procedure of natural science and the individualizing method of history, between the "nomothetic" (universal and law-positing) and "idiographic" (particular) approaches. According to this distinction, historical facts, as singular, nonrecurring events, possess inherent value. Windelband grounded the validity of judgments of value in the ideal necessity (*Sollen*) of a universal normative consciousness, as distinct from the natural necessity (*Müssen*) of the empirical world.

Ludwig Woltmann (1871–1907).   German philosopher, on the fringe of the German Social Democratic party, who influenced Bernstein's interest in a Kantian-inspired ethics. Author of *System des moralischen Bewußtseins mit besonderer Darlegung des Verhältnisses der kritischen Philosophie zu Darwinismus und Sozialismus* (1898).

Wilhelm Wundt (1832–1920).   German philosopher and psychologist, one of the founders of psychology as a modern science. In 1879, in Leipzig, he established the world's first experimental laboratory in psychology, which served as a model for similar institutions in other countries, including Russia. In psychology he valued the introspective method. In philosophy he was an idealist, indebted to Leibniz in particular. His ethics was duty-based and opposed to contemporary utilitarianism, hedonism, and relativism.

Contributor Biographies

Sergei A. Askol'dov (1870–1945) was the son of Russian philosopher Aleksei A. Kozlov. (Askol'dov was a pseudonym; his legal name was Alekseev, i.e., "son of Aleksei," because he was born out of wedlock and could not take his father's surname.) He continued the Russian neo-Leibnizian tradition of "panpsychism" that was founded by Kozlov, but developed it much further in the direction of religious philosophy. After graduating from the Physics-Mathematics Faculty of St. Petersburg University, Askol'dov entered government service as a chemist, hoping to have enough spare time to study philosophy. In 1900 he made his philosophical debut with *Osnovnye problemy teorii poznaniia i ontologii* (*Fundamental Problems of the Theory of Knowledge and Ontology*). Like his father, he turned to an academic career only later in life. In 1914 Moscow University awarded him the *magister* degree for his book *Mysl' i deistvitel'nost'* (*Thought and Reality*), in which he criticizes neo-Kantianism for a misplaced emphasis on "consciousness in general" instead of the concrete living person. He believed that unless consciousness were grounded in substantial reality, ultimately in God, idealism was a "lifeless worldview." Hence his abiding interest in "philosophy and life," the theme of his essay in the present volume. Askol'dov was an active member of the Moscow Psychological Society, the St. Petersburg Religious-Philosophical Society, and the Vladimir Solov'ëv Religious-Philosophical

Society in Moscow. He remained in Russia after the Revolution, initially in Kazan (1918–1920) and then in Petrograd/Leningrad, where he taught chemistry at the Polytechnical Institute until the mid-1920s. In 1921 he founded a secret religious-philosophical society, known after 1926 as the Brotherhood of St. Seraphim of Sarov. In 1928 the group's members were arrested, and Askol'dov was exiled to the northern Urals. In 1935 he was permitted to move to Novgorod, where he taught school mathematics. After Novgorod was occupied by the Nazis in World War Two, Askol'dov fled to Riga, Prague, and Berlin. He died in Potsdam in May 1945, in the Soviet occupation zone, under threat of arrest by Red Army counterintelligence.

Nikolai A. Berdiaev (1874–1948), perhaps the most famous Russian philosopher outside Russia, was a religious thinker, personalist, and existentialist champion of the freedom and creativity of the individual human spirit. He was born near Kiev into a family of landed gentry with a military tradition, and always remained proud of his aristocratic heritage. He entered Kiev University in 1894, but was arrested and expelled in 1898 for Marxist activities; that marked the end of his formal education. In 1900 he was exiled to the northern town of Vologda. There he traveled the path from (critical) Marxism to idealism, guided by Pëtr Struve, who arranged for the publication of (and wrote a foreword to) Berdiaev's first book *Sub"ektivizm i individualizm v obshchestvennoi filosofii: Kriticheskii etiud o N. K. Mikhailovskom* (*Subjectivism and Individualism in Social Philosophy: A Critical Study of N. K. Mikhailovskii*) (1901). There immediately followed a series of articles, including the essay in the present volume, which marked Berdiaev's conversion to idealism. In 1903 he returned to Kiev, spent some time in Germany, and helped organize the Union of Liberation. The following year he moved to St. Petersburg, where he was an editor of the religious-philosophical journals *Novyi put'* (*New Path*) (1903–1904) and *Voprosy zhizni* (*Problems of Life*) (1905), and was otherwise an integral part of the search for a "new religious consciousness." In 1908, having turned to a more traditional form of Christianity, he relocated to Moscow and became a prominent figure in the Vladimir Solov'ëv Religious-Philosophical Society (1905–1918) and in the religious-philosophical publishing house *Put'* (*The Way*) (1910–1919). His culminating work of this period is *Smysl tvorchestva: Opyt opravdaniia cheloveka* (*The Meaning of Creativity: An Essay in the Justification of Man*) (1916), the first comprehensive account of his religious philosophy. In 1917, he welcomed the February Revolution but opposed the Bolsheviks. Even so, during the winter of 1918–1919 he was able to found the Free Academy of Spiritual Culture in Moscow, and in

1920 was elected professor of philosophy at Moscow University. In 1922, however, he and many other Russian intellectuals were expelled from the country. He lived in Berlin until 1924, then in Paris, where he directed the Russian Religious-Philosophical Academy (founded by him in Berlin), edited the religious-philosophical journal *Put'* (1925–1940), and served as editor-in-chief of the YMCA Press, the most important Russian publisher in the emigration. With the appearance of his widely translated book *Novoe srednevekov'e: Razmyshlenie o sud'be Rossii i Evropy* (*The New Middle Ages: Reflections on the Destiny of Russia and Europe*) (1924), his reputation spread throughout Europe and beyond. In his many subsequent books, he explored further his main themes of spiritual freedom and creativity, developed an eschatological philosophy of history, but gave little attention to concrete social and political philosophy, in which he was content with a form of anarchism. He died in Clamart, a suburb of Paris.

Sergei N. Bulgakov (1871–1944), major Russian philosopher and theologian, was born in Livny, Orel province, the son of a provincial priest, from a long line of priests (six generations). At the age of thirteen he entered Orel Theological Seminary, but lost his faith and transferred to a neighboring gymnasium. As a student at Moscow University, he was already interested in Marxism. He graduated from the Faculty of Law in 1894 and began graduate studies, also at Moscow University, in political economy. His first book, *O rynkakh pri kapitalisticheskom proizvodstve* (*On Markets in Capitalist Production*) (1897), made him a nationally prominent "legal Marxist." After two years of study abroad, mostly in Germany, he defended his *magister* dissertation, *Kapitalizm i zemledelie* (*Capitalism and Agriculture,* two vols.) (1900), and was appointed professor of political economy at Kiev Polytechnical Institute (1901). His dissertation research convinced him that Marx's critique of capitalism was flawed. This, together with his interest in neo-Kantianism, brought about his conversion to idealism. At this point (1902–1903) he took an active part in the Russian Liberation Movement: he collaborated on P. B. Struve's journal *Osvobozhdenie* (*Liberation*) and was a founder of the Union of Liberation and a member of its council. In 1904 he was a contributor to the journal *Novyi Put'* (*New Path*) and in 1905 a co-editor (with N. A. Berdiaev) of *Voprosy zhizni* (*Questions of Life*). One of his main concerns was liberation of the Russian church from autocratic state control, which he hoped would lead to the overall religious renewal of society. To that end, he joined the Brotherhood of Christian Struggle (1905) and formed a (short-lived) Union of Christian Politics (1906), which advocated a program of Christian socialism. In 1907 he served as a (nonparty) deputy to the Second State Duma. By then he had moved from Kiev to Moscow and was appointed professor of political economy at the Higher Commerce Institute, directed by P. I. Novgorodtsev. He was a leading figure in the Vladimir Solov'ëv Religious-Philosophical Society (1905–1918) and in the religious-philosophical publishing house *Put'* (1910–1919). In this period he published two important works in social and religious philosophy: *Filosofiia khoziaistva (Philosophy of Economy)* (1912), for which Moscow University awarded him the doctorate, and *Svet nevechernyi (Unfading Light)* (1917). In 1917 he was named professor of political economy at Moscow University. As a prominent lay delegate to the Russian Church Council that opened in August 1917, he played an important role in the restoration of the patriarchate. In June 1918 Bulgakov was ordained a priest. He then moved to the Crimea, where he taught at the University of Simferopol' until 1920. He was deported in December 1922. He settled first in Prague, where he taught church law at the Russian Faculty of Law, organized by Novgorodtsev at Charles University. Bulgakov moved to Paris in 1925, where he became founding dean and professor of dogmatic theology at the Orthodox Theological Institute. In this period he produced a large body of work in dogmatic theology, culminating in the trilogy *O Bogochelovechestve (On the Humanity of God)* (1933–1945). He died in Paris.

Semën L. Frank (1877–1950), prominent twentieth-century Russian religious philosopher, was born in Moscow to Jewish parents. At the age of sixteen he joined a Marxist circle at his gymnasium in Nizhnii Novgorod (his family had recently moved there). He soon returned to Moscow to study law and political economy at Moscow University (1894–1899) but was arrested and expelled for inciting student unrest. He continued his studies in Berlin (1899–1901), concentrating on political economy and philosophy. Within a year of the publication of his first book *Teoriia tsennosti Marksa i ee znachenie (Marx's Theory of Value and Its Significance)* (1900), Frank had abandoned Marxism for an eclectic, transitional philosophical position that combined elements of Nietzsche, Kantianism, and (by 1904) Fichtean idealism. A major influence on him was P. B. Struve; their lifelong collaboration began in 1898. They worked closely together in the Liberation Movement (on its journal *Osvobozhdenie* and in the Union of Liberation). Frank represented Struve at the founding congress of the Constitutional Democratic (Kadet) Party in October 1905, but otherwise did not have a significant role in the party. With Struve he edited the political weekly *Poliarnaia zvezda (Polar Star)* and its sequel *Svoboda i kul'tura (Freedom and Culture)* (December 1905–May 1906). During this period Frank defined his philosophical position as "humanist individualism." From 1907 to 1917 he was an editor and frequent contributor to *Russkaia mysl'* (*Russian Thought*). In his well-known contribution to *Vekhi* (*Landmarks*) (1909), he indicated that his philosophical outlook had shifted to "religious humanism." In 1912 Frank was baptized into the Russian Orthodox Church and became a lecturer in philosophy at St. Petersburg University, where four years later he defended his *magister* dissertation, *Predmet znaniia* (*The Object of Knowledge*) (1915). This was his first major work and the foundation of his mature metaphysical system of "all-unity." His second book, *Dusha cheloveka* (*Man's Soul*) (1917), a treatise on personhood and the metaphysics of human nature, could not be defended for the doctorate because of political circumstances. This did not prevent him from serving as professor of philosophy and dean of the Historical-Philological Faculty at the University of Saratov (1917–1921). He returned to Moscow in 1921, was elected professor of philosophy at the University of Moscow, and was active in Berdiaev's Free Academy of Spiritual Culture. Frank was deported in 1922. For the next fifteen years he lived in Berlin, where he was professor at the Russian Scientific Institute (1923–1933). He fled Nazi Germany in 1937, settling first in Paris, then, for the last five years of his life, in London. In exile Frank characterized himself as a "Christian Platonist" and produced a number of important works, including *Dukhovnye osnovy obshchestva: Vvedenie v sotsial'nuiu filosofiiu* (*The Spiritual Foundations of Society: An Introduction to Social Philosophy*) (1930), *Nepostizhimoe: Ontologicheskoe vvedenie v filosofiiu religii* (*The Unknowable: An Ontological Introduction to the Philosophy of Religion*) (1939), and *Svet vo t'me: Opyt khristianskoi etiki i sotsial'noi filosofii* (*The Light Shineth in Darkness: An Essay in Christian Ethics and Social Philosophy*) (1949).

Bogdan A. Kistiakovskii (1868–1920) came from a prominent Ukrainian family and grew up in the atmosphere of the Ukrainian national movement, in which his father, Aleksandr F. Kistiakovskii, professor of criminal law at Kiev University, was involved. Bogdan Kistiakovskii was committed to the development of Ukrainian culture and national identity. At the same time, he was part of Russian intellectual life, and his works in sociology and legal philosophy deserve to be seen as contributions to both Ukrainian and Russian intellectual history. As a student he belonged to various study groups in Ukrainian history and culture; for such illicit activities he was expelled from Kiev University, and then from Kharkov University. In 1891 he enrolled in the Law Faculty of Dorpat (Tartu) University, where he promptly joined a Marxist circle. In 1892 he was arrested for distributing subversive literature

in Volhynia and imprisoned for several months from late 1893 to early
1894. In 1895 he went to Germany to pursue graduate studies, first with
Georg Simmel in Berlin and then with Wilhelm Windelband in Strasbourg,
where he defended his doctoral dissertation, *Gesellschaft und Einzelwesen*
(*Society and the Individual*), published in 1899. The book established his
reputation as a neo-Kantian social and legal philosopher and marked his
break with Marxism. Henceforth Kistiakovskii divided his time between
Russia and Germany. He was active in the Russian Liberation Movement,
helping P. B. Struve to edit the journal *Osvobozhdenie* (*Liberation*), attend-
ing the Schaffhausen conference, which planned the Union of Liberation,
and working in the Kiev branch of the Union of Liberation. In Germany he
collaborated with Max Weber, who commended Kistiakovskii's essay in
Problems of Idealism. In Russia, beginning in 1906, Kistiakovskii taught
at the Moscow Higher Commerce Institute, Moscow University, and the
Demidov Lycée in Iaroslavl. In 1912 he became editor of the revived *Iuridicheskii vestnik* (*Juridical Messenger*), the prestigious journal of the Moscow Juridical Society. He is perhaps best known for his essay "In Defense of
Law: The Intelligentsia and Legal Consciousness," which appeared in *Vekhi*
(*Landmarks*) (1909). His magnum opus is *Sotsial'nye nauki i pravo* (*The
Social Sciences and Law*) (1916), for which Kharkov University awarded
him a second doctorate. After the February Revolution Kistiakovskii was
appointed to the chair in law at Kiev University. In 1919 he was elected to
the Ukrainian Academy of Sciences. He died in Ekaterinodar.

Aleksandr S. Lappo-Danilevskii (1863–1919), Russian historian and philosopher of history, was born into an aristocratic family in Ekaterinoslav province, Ukraine. In 1886 he graduated from the Historical-Philological Faculty
at St. Petersburg University. After the defense of his *magister* dissertation,
*Organizatsiia priamogo oblozheniia v Moskovskom gosudarstve so vremen
Smuty do epokhi preobrazovanii* (*Organization of Direct Taxation in the
Muscovite State from the Time of Troubles to the Reform Era*) (1890), he
was appointed *privat-docent* in Russian history at St. Petersburg University.
A year later he became professor of history at the Historical-Philological
Institute in St. Petersburg. In 1905 the Academy of Sciences elected him to
full membership. His main areas of research were Muscovy, eighteenth-
century Russia, economic and legal history, intellectual history, theory of
history and the social sciences, and the identification and analysis of historical sources. His most important work is *Metodologiia istorii* (*Methodology
of History,* two vols.) (1910–1913). Lappo-Danilevskii's conception of Russian history was essentially liberal and owed much to the "state school" of

Russian historiography: he believed in historical progress and thought that its measure was the emancipation of the individual, the growth of personal autonomy, and the institutionalization of the rule of law. In 1917 the Provisional Government appointed him to the committee charged with preparing the electoral law for the Constituent Assembly. He died two years later.

Pavel I. Novgorodtsev (1866–1924), editor of the Russian edition of *Problems of Idealism,* was a jurist and arguably the most significant legal and social philosopher of twentieth-century Russia. He founded and headed the Russian neo-idealist school of the philosophy of law, which promoted the revival of natural law and a human rights–based understanding of the rule-of-law state. Novgorodtsev, the son of a Russian merchant, came from Bakhmut, a small town in the Ekaterinoslav province of Ukraine. After graduating from Moscow University's Faculty of Law in 1888, he pursued graduate training there in the history of the philosophy of law. He studied in Berlin and Paris for several years, and in 1897 was awarded the *magister* degree for his first book, *Istoricheskaia shkola iuristov: Ee proiskhozhdenie i sud'ba* (*The Historical School of Jurists: Its Genesis and Fate*) (published in 1896). For his next book, *Kant i Gegel' v ikh ucheniiakh o prave i gosudarstve* (*Kant and Hegel in Their Theories of Law and the State*) (1901), he received the doctorate from St. Petersburg University. In 1903, he was appointed associate professor, and in 1904 full professor, at Moscow University, in the history and philosophy of law. By this time he had a prominent role in liberal politics. From 1901 to 1905 he helped organize and lead the Liberation Movement, serving on the Council of the Union of Liberation. He also served on the bureau of the Academic Union, formed in early 1905 as the corporate voice of the Russian professoriate in the Liberation Movement. He was an influential member of the Constitutional Democratic (Kadet) Party from its beginning in 1905. In 1906 his native province of Ekaterinoslav elected him to the First State Duma. By signing the Vyborg Appeal (1906), Novgorodtsev forfeited membership in future Dumas, as well as his professorship at Moscow University, although he continued to teach there as a lecturer. In 1911, he resigned (along with 100 of his colleagues) from Moscow University in protest over government violation of university autonomy. From 1906 to 1918, he was professor and director of the Moscow Higher Commerce Institute, which he organized along broad educational lines and made into one of the most popular "polytechnics" in Russia. After the February Revolution he was reinstated in his professorship at Moscow University. In May 1917 he was elected to the Central Committee of the Kadet Party, and by January 1918 was its acting chairman. He led Kadet efforts, such as the formation of the National Center in May 1918, to coordinate effective resistance against the Bolsheviks. Novgorodtsev left Moscow at the end of 1918 for Ukraine and southern Russia, and in 1919 headed the Ekaterinodar Kadet Party office. After the defeat of Gen. Anton Denikin, he went to Berlin, where he helped edit the Kadet émigré newspaper *Rul'* (1920). Finally settling in Prague, in May 1922 he founded the Russian Faculty of Law at Charles University. He died in Prague in April 1924. His other works include *Krizis sovremennogo pravosoznaniia* (*The Crisis in Modern Legal Consciousness*) (1909) and *Ob obshchestvennom ideale* (*On the Social Ideal*) (1917).

Sergei F. Ol'denburg (1863–1934), Russian Orientalist and Indologist, was born into a family that descended from the Mecklenburg nobility of Germany, and that moved to Russia and became part of the service nobility under Peter the Great. After graduating from the Oriental Languages Faculty of St. Petersburg University in 1885, Ol'denburg spent three years in Western Europe pursuing graduate research. With the completion of his dissertation *Buddiiskie legendy* (*Buddhist Legends*) (1894), he became professor of Indian language and literature at St. Petersburg University. He soon achieved an international reputation as a scholar and was elected to the Russian Academy of Sciences in 1900. He became its permanent secretary in 1904, and held that position until 1929. A liberal by conviction, he assisted P. B. Struve in going abroad to set up the journal *Osvobozhdenie* (*Liberation*), but otherwise seems not to have played a major role in the Liberation Movement. In 1906 he was elected to the State Council by the Academy of Sciences. In May 1917 he became a member of the Central Committee of the Constitutional Democratic (Kadet) Party, and served on the Council of the League of Russian Culture, organized by Struve at that time to preserve Russian national culture. In the Provisional Government Ol'denburg was minister of education from July to August. After the Bolsheviks came to power, his overriding concern was to maintain the autonomy and integrity of the Academy of Sciences. For ten years, he was remarkably successful in that effort. He was removed from his post as permanent secretary in 1929, when the Academy was finally brought under Communist control. Even then, Ol'denburg was not purged but was permitted to serve as director of the Academy's Institute of Oriental Studies from 1930 until his death in 1934.

Pëtr B. Struve (1870–1944) conceived and planned *Problems of Idealism* before Novgorodtsev assumed most of the editorial responsibility in late

1901. Struve, whose grandfather was a famous astronomer and whose father was a provincial governor, was an outstanding scholar and thinker of encyclopedic breadth in fields such as economics, law, history, and philosophy. Together with Berdiaev, Bulgakov, and Frank, he is well known for his dramatic intellectual evolution from Marxism to idealism. In the 1890s he was a leading Russian Marxist. His first book, *Kriticheskie zametki k voprosu ob ekonomicheskom razvitii Rossii* (*Critical Notes on the Question of Russia's Economic Development*) (1894), was a Marxist critique of Russian populism, but in it Struve already suggests that Marxism needed to be supplemented by neo-Kantianism. In 1898 he wrote the manifesto of the Russian Social Democratic Labor Party for its first congress. A year later his essay *Die Marxische Theorie der sozialen Entwicklung* was in some respects more "revisionist" than Eduard Bernstein's theses. By 1901 Struve had completed his evolution toward neo-idealism in philosophy and liberalism in politics, as traced in his collection of articles from 1893 to 1901, *Na raznye temy* (*On Various Themes*) (1902). He went abroad, and in July 1902 began publishing his famous émigré journal *Osvobozhdenie* (*Liberation*), which was smuggled back into Russia and was the most important organ of the Liberation Movement. After his return to Russia in late October 1905, he was elected to the Central Committee of the Constitutional Democratic (Kadet) Party at its second congress (January 1906). In 1907 he served as a deputy in the Second State Duma. After its dissolution, he turned to editing the influential liberal journal *Russkaia mysl'* (*Russian Thought*), and to teaching at the St. Petersburg Polytechnical Institute. His 1908 article "Great Russia" signaled an increasingly nationalistic and imperialistic position. In 1911 he published *Patriotica,* a collection of his essays from 1905 to 1910. His views on the nationality question, particularly on Ukraine, led to his resignation from the Kadet Central Committee in 1915. His two-volume work *Khoziaistvo i tsena* (*Economy and Price*) (1913–1916) earned him the *magister* degree from Moscow University and the doctorate from Kiev University. In 1917 he was elected to the Academy of Sciences. In the Provisional Government he briefly held a position in the Foreign Ministry. In 1918 he organized and contributed to *Iz glubiny* (*Out of the Depths*), a volume of essays on the Russian Revolution. During the Civil War he was active in the White movement, and in 1920 he became foreign minister in Gen. P. N. Wrangel's government in the Crimea. In European emigration he devoted himself to editorial work, scholarship, and Russian émigré politics. He died in Paris.

Evgenii N. Trubetskoi (1863–1920), jurist and major Russian religious philosopher, was a disciple of Vladimir Solov'ëv. He and his brother Sergei were princes and came from one of the most distinguished aristocratic families in Russia. After graduating from the Faculty of Law at Moscow University in 1885, Trubetskoi taught at the Demidov Juridical Lycée in Iaroslavl. His *magister* and doctoral dissertations were critical studies in the intellectual history of theocracy in medieval Europe, two volumes under the general title, "The Religious-Social Ideal of Western Christianity in the Fifth and Eleventh Centuries": the first was on St. Augustine (1892), the second on Gregory VII (1897). His university appointments were in the history and philosophy of law, first at Kiev (1892–1905) and then at Moscow (1906–1918), where he in effect succeeded his brother. He had a prominent role in the Moscow Psychological Society, the Vladimir Solov'ëv Religious-Philosophical Society, and the religious-philosophical publishing house *Put'*. He was deeply influenced by Solov'ëv, to whom he devoted a fundamental two-volume work, *Mirosozertsanie Vl. S. Solov'ëv* (*Vl. S. Solov'ëv's Weltanschauung*) (1913). In politics, Trubetskoi belonged to both the Union of Liberation and the Union of Zemstvo Constitutionalists. With P. I. Novgorodtsev, he was a central figure in the Academic Union. He was a founding member of the Constitutional Democratic (Kadet) Party, but resigned from it in January 1906. Later that year he joined the Party of Peaceful Renewal, which shared with the right Kadets and left Octobrists a political program of moderate liberalism. This program was advanced in the newspaper that Trubetskoi and his younger brother Grigorii published from March 1906 to August 1910, *Moskovskii ezhenedel'nik* (*The Moscow Weekly*). Trubetskoi served in the State Council from February 1907 to August 1908. During the Great War he wrote a number of essays in which he developed a liberal conception of Russian national identity. In 1917, he was lay co-chair of the Russian Church Council, and with S. N. Bulgakov was influential in the restoration of the patriarchate. He rejoined the Kadets at the party's seventh congress in March 1917, and contributed to the White movement, mostly by lecturing and writing. He died of typhus in Novorossiisk in January 1920. His other works include *Metafizicheskie predpolozheniia poznaniia: Opyt preodoleniia Kanta i kantiantstva* (*The Metaphysical Premises of Knowledge: An Essay in Transcending Kant and Kantianism*) (1917) and *Smysl zhizni* (*The Meaning of Life*) (1918).

Sergei N. Trubetskoi (1862–1905), major Russian idealist philosopher and historian of philosophy, was the scion of one of Russia's great aristocratic families. He was close, both personally and intellectually, to Vladimir Solov'ëv, whose ideas he developed in a liberal direction. His own conception of an ontological, "concrete idealism" had great influence on the development of Russian philosophy during this period. In broadest terms, he aspired toward a universalistic, philosophical theism. Trubetskoi graduated in 1885 from the Historical-Philological Faculty of Moscow University, where he then devoted himself to graduate work in philosophy. His *magister* dissertation, *Metafizika v drevnei Gretsii* (*Metaphysics in Ancient Greece*) (1890), established his reputation as a major historian of philosophy and earned him appointment as associate professor at Moscow University. Ten years later he defended his doctoral dissertation, *Uchenie o logose v ego istorii* (*The Doctrine of the Logos in Its History*), and was made full professor. He was deputy chair (1901–1905) of the Moscow Psychological Society and co-editor (1900–1905) of its journal, *Voprosy filosofii i psikhologii* (*Questions of Philosophy and Psychology*). He published several major essays in the journal, including "O prirode chelovecheskogo soznaniia" ("On the Nature of Human Consciousness") (1889–1891), "Osnovaniia idealizma" ("The Foundations of Idealism") (1896), and "Vera v bessmertie" ("Belief in Immortality") (1902–1904). Trubetskoi, the philosopher, was also a public figure who emerged as a national symbol of rule-of-law liberalism and moderate constitutionalism. In June 1905 he presented, as head of a national zemstvo delegation, a petition to Nicholas II that urged the tsar to summon a representative assembly. Among Trubetskoi's most abiding concerns were separation of church and state and freedom of conscience. He was also a forceful advocate of university autonomy, convinced that the university should be administered by professors, not bureaucrats, and that students should have the right to academic association. The culmination of his struggle for the university came on 27 August 1905, when Nicholas II, apparently influenced by a memorandum he had asked Trubetskoi to prepare, granted autonomy to the universities. Within a week Trubetskoi was elected rector of Moscow University. He died twenty-seven days later, on 29 September 1905. His funeral procession drew a crowd of many thousands.

Dmitrii E. Zhukovskii (1868–1943), wealthy landowner and veteran zemstvo constitutionalist, financed both the journal *Osvobozhdenie* (*Liberation*) and *Problems of Idealism*. He began studies in the natural sciences at St. Petersburg University, but was arrested and expelled in connection with the student disturbances of 1887. He went abroad, and obtained a doctorate in zoology from Heidelberg University, where he also attended Kuno Fischer's lectures in the history of philosophy. His political evolution passed from

Tolstoianism to socialism and finally conservative liberalism. He was close to Struve, became a leading figure in the Russian Liberation Movement, and organized the Schaffhausen conference. He had philosophical interests and was a publisher of philosophical works. His last known position was that of assistant in the Faculty of Botany at the Crimean Pedagogical Institute in Simferopol'. He was arrested in the 1930s and may have perished in the camps.

Index

This index does not include notes when their content is clear from the corresponding point in the text, authors cited only as part of bibliographical references, or works of present-day scholarship (except for scholars named in the text).

Biblical References

RUSSIAN LITERATURE AND THOUGHT

Strolls with Pushkin
Abram Tertz (Andrei Sinyavsky)

Untimely Thoughts: Essays on Revolution, Culture, and the Bolsheviks, 1917–1918
Maxim Gorky

Abram Tertz and the Poetics of Crime
Catharine Theimer Nepomnyashchy

Dostoevsky and Soloviev: The Art of Integral Vision
Marina Kostalevsky

Toward Another Shore: Russian Thinkers Between Necessity and Chance
Aileen M. Kelly

Liberty, Equality, and the Market: Essays by B. N. Chicherin
Edited and translated by G. M. Hamburg

Pushkin's Historical Imagination
Svetlana Evdokimova

Rereading Russian Poetry
Edited by Stephanie Sandler

View from the Other Shore: Essays on Herzen, Chekhov, and Bakhtin
Aileen M. Kelly

See No Evil: Literary Cover-Ups and Discoveries of the Soviet Camp Experience
Dariusz Tolczyk

Philosophy of Economy
Sergei Bulgakov
Translated by Catherine Evtuhov

The Little Tragedies
Alexander Pushkin
Translated, with Critical Essays, by Nancy K. Anderson

A Voice from the Chorus
Abram Tertz (Andrei Sinyavsky)

1920 Diary
Isaac Babel

Earthly Signs
Marina Tsvetaeva

Problems of Idealism: Essays in Russian Social Philosophy
Translated, edited, and introduced by Randall A. Poole